D1560646

The 8086 and 80286 Microprocessors

Hardware, Software, and Interfacing

The 8086 and 80286 Microprocessors

Hardware, Software, and Interfacing

AVTAR SINGH
San Jose State University
San Jose, CA

WALTER A. TRIEBEL
Intel Corporation

PRENTICE HALL
Englewood Cliffs, NJ 07632

Library of Congress Cataloging-in-Publication Data

Avtar Singh
    The 8086 and 80286 microprocessors : architecture, software, and
interfacing / Avtar Singh, Walter A. Triebel.
        p.   cm.
    Includes bibliographical references.
    ISBN 0-13-245325-8
    1. Intel 8086 (Microprocessor) 2. Intel 80286 (Microprocessor)
I. Triebel, Walter A.   II. Title.   III. Title: The Eight thousand
eighty-six and eighty thousand two hundred eighty-six
mircoprocessors.
QA76.8.I292A98 1990
004.165--dc20
                                                        89-16126
                                                          CIP
                                                          r89

Editorial/production supervision: Gretchen Chenenko
Cover design: Photo Plus Art
Manufacturing buyer: David Dickey

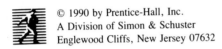 © 1990 by Prentice-Hall, Inc.
A Division of Simon & Schuster
Englewood Cliffs, New Jersey 07632

Printed in the United States of America
10 9 8 7 6 5 4 3 2 1

ISBN 0-13-245325-8

Prentice-Hall International (UK) Limited, *London*
Prentice-Hall of Australia Pty. Limited, *Sydney*
Prentice-Hall Canada Inc., *Toronto*
Prentice-Hall Hispanoamericans, S.A., *Mexico*
Prentice-Hall of India Private Limited, *New Delhi*
Prentice-Hall of Japan, Inc., *Tokyo*
Simon & Schuster Asia Pte. Ltd., *Singapore*
Editora Prentice-Hall do Brasil, Ltda., *Rio de Janeiro*

Contents

8   INTERRUPT INTERFACE OF THE 8086 MICROPROCESSOR   320

9   THE HARDWARE OF THE SDK-86 MICROCOMPUTER   355

10 SOFTWARE ARCHITECTURE OF THE 80286 MICROPROCESSOR   383

11 HARDWARE ARCHITECTURE OF THE 80286 MICROPROCESSOR   431

SUGGESTED LABORATORY ASSIGNMENTS   487

Preface

Today Intel's 8086 family is the most widely used 16-bit microprocessor architecture in microcomputer-based products. The original 8086 microprocessor, which was introduced in 1978, was soon followed by an 8-bit bus version, the 8088. The 8088 was the microprocessor employed in the popular IBM PC and IBM PCXT. Intel introduced the 80286 microprocessor in 1982. The 80286 offered the systems designer an enhanced software architecture, new hardware features, and higher performance operation. It is the microprocessor used in the design of IBM's advanced architecture personal computer, the IBM PCAT. The 8088, 8086, and 80286 are used in a number of other personal computers as well as in a wide variety of electronic equipment.

Individuals involved in the design of personal computers and other types of microcomputer-based equipment need a systems-level understanding of the 8086 and 80286 microcomputer systems. That is, they require a thorough knowledge of both its software and hardware architectures. This book provides such a study of the architecture, software, and interfacing techniques used in the design of 8086- and 80286-based microcomputers. This material is developed in Chapter 2, "The 8086 Microprocessor"; Chapter 3, "8086 Microprocessor Programming 1"; Chapter 4, "Microprocessor Programming 2"; Chapter 6, "Memory Interface of the 8086 Microprocessor"; Chapter 7, "Input/Output Interface of the 8086 Microprocessor"; Chapter 8, "Interrupt Interface of the 8086 Microprocessor"; Chapter 10, "Software Architecture of the 80286 Microprocessor"; and Chapter 11, "Hardware Architecture of the 80286 Microprocessor."

In Chapters 2 through 4, we first develop a thorough understanding of the internal architecture of the 8086 microprocessor and show how it executes instructions. This includes material on its pipelined instruction prefetch and types of bus cycles. Next we present in detail software issues such as data types, addressing modes, the instruction set, and the analysis and writing of assembly language programs. A large number of practical applications are illustrated in example problems.

Chapters 6 through 8 cover the hardware of the 8086-based microcomputer system. Here the hardware architectural features of the microcomputer are introduced and circuit design techniques for the memory, input/output, and interrupt interfaces are explored. Extensive coverage of bus cycle timing, address maps, bus demultiplexing techniques, program memory (ROM, PROM, and EPROM), data memory (SRAM and DRAM), memory interface circuits, input/output interface circuits, and interrupt interface circuits is included. A wide variety of material on large-scale (LSI) peripheral controllers is provided in this section. Examples are the 8255A (parallel peripheral interface), 8251 (universal synchronous/asynchronous receiver/transmitter), 8253 (interval timer), 8237A (direct memory access controller), 8259 (interrupt controller), and 8279 (keyboard/display controller).

Finally, the 80286 microprocessor is presented in Chapters 10 and 11. These chapters focus on the differences between the 80286's software and hardware architecture and that of the 8086. For instance, Chapter 10 begins with an overview of the 80286's real-addressed mode software model and extended instruction set and then continues with a detailed study of its protected-address mode architecture and operation. This material on protected mode includes topics such as memory management, virtual memory, virtual-to-physical address translation, and the system control instruction set. The 80286's protection model is examined, and the concepts of task switching and multitasking are presented.

Chapter 11 is a thorough study of the hardware of the 80286 microprocessor and its interfaces. It includes information such as pin layout, signal interfaces, signal functions, clock requirements, address maps, bus cycles, interfaces for memory, input/output, and interrupts. Included in this material is coverage of the 82C284 clock generator and 82288 bus controller ICs.

Two additional chapters are included that introduce Intel's 8086 Microcomputer System Design Kit (SDK-86). The SDK-86 is an educational microcomputer system that can be used to execute and debug programs written for the 8086 microprocessor. Chapter 5 introduces the SDK-86 microcomputer and the commands that can be issued to the microcomputer from its keypad. Examples are used to show how programs are entered, verified, executed, and debugged on the SDK-86.

Chapter 9, a study of the hardware of the microcomputer in the SDK-86, illustrates a practical application of the material on interfacing techniques studied in Chapters 6, 7, and 8. The architecture and circuit design of the 8086-based microcomputer is described in detail. Some elementary troubleshooting and diagnostic techniques are also introduced.

Nine laboratory exercises are included after Chapter 11. They can be run on the SDK-86 to explore the software architecture of the 8086; load and observe the operation of instructions; and load, run, and debug programs. A number of the hardware features of the SDK-86 microcomputer and I/O interfacing techniques are also explored in the assignments.

The 8086 and 80286 Microprocessors was written for use as a textbook in the electrical engineering and electronics technology curricula offered at universities and colleges and its use requires a prior knowledge of basic digital electronics. Because the book includes a large amount of practical information, it is also a valuable reference for practicing engineers and technicians. An instructor's solution manual and transparencies are available from Prentice Hall.

Avtar Singh
Walter A. Triebel

Chapter 1

Introduction to Microprocessors and Microcomputers

1.1 INTRODUCTION

The most recent advances in computer system technology have been closely related to the development of high-performance 16-bit microprocessors and their microcomputer systems. Today, the 16-bit microprocessor market is quite mature. Several complete 16-bit microprocessor families are available. They include support products such as very large-scale integrated (VLSI) peripheral devices, development systems, emulators, and high-level software languages. These higher-performance microprocessors have become widely used in the design of new electronic equipment and computers. This book presents a detailed study of one of the most popular 16-bit microprocessors, Intel Corporation's 8086, and a thorough introduction to the 80286 microprocessor.

In this chapter we begin our study of microprocessors and microcomputers. The following topics are discussed.

1. The digital computer
2. Mainframe computers, minicomputers, and microcomputers
3. Hardware elements of the digital computer system
4. General architecture of a microcomputer system
5. Evolution of the microprocessor architecture

1.2 THE DIGITAL COMPUTER

As a starting point, let us consider what a *computer* is, what it can do, and how it does it. A computer is a digital electronic data processing system. Data are input to the computer in one form, processed within the computer, and the information that results is either output or stored for later use. Figure 1.1 shows a modern computer system.

Computers cannot think about how to process the data that were input. Instead, the user must tell the computer exactly what to do. The procedure by which a computer is told how to work is called *programming* and the person who writes programs for a computer is known as a *programmer*. The result of the programmer's work is a set of instructions for the computer to follow. This is the computer's *program*. When the computer is operating, the instructions of the program guide it step by step through the task that is to be performed.

For example, a large department store can use a computer to take care of bookkeeping for its customer charge accounts. In this application, data about items purchased by the customers, such as price and department, are entered into the computer by an operator. These data are stored in the computer under the customer's account number. On the next billing date, the data are processed and a tabular record of each customer's account is output by the computer. These statements are mailed to the customers as a bill.

In a computer, the program controls the operation of a large amount of electronic circuitry. It is this circuitry that actually does the processing of data. Electronic computers first became available in the 1940s. These early computers were built with vac-

Figure 1.1 Modern large-scale computer (Courtesy of International Business Machines Corp.).

uum-tube electronic circuits. In the 1950s, a second generation of computers was built. During this period, transistor electronic circuitry, instead of tubes, was used to produce more compact and more reliable computer systems. When the *integrated circuit* (IC) came into the electronic market during the 1960s, a third generation of computers appeared. With ICs, industry could manufacture more complex, higher-speed, and very reliable computers.

Today, the computer industry is continuing to be revolutionized by the advances made in integrated-circuit technology. It is now possible to manufacture *very large-scale integrated circuits* (VLSI) that can form a computer with a just small group of ICs. In fact, in some cases, a single IC can be used. These new technologies are rapidly advancing the computer marketplace by permitting simpler and more cost-effective designs.

1.3 MAINFRAME COMPUTERS, MINICOMPUTERS, AND MICROCOMPUTERS

For many years the computer manufacturers' aim was to develop large and more powerful computer systems. These are what we call *large-scale* or *mainframe computers*. Mainframes are always *general-purpose computers*. That is, they are designed with the ability to run a large number of different types of programs. For this reason, they can solve a wide variety of problems.

For instance, one user can apply the computer in an assortment of scientific applications where the primary function of the computer is to solve complex mathematical problems. A second user can apply the same basic computer system to perform business tasks such as accounting and inventory control. The only difference between the computer systems used in these two applications could be their programs. In fact, today many companies use a single general-purpose computer to resolve both their scientific and business needs.

Figure 1.1 is an example of a mainframe computer manufactured by International Business Machines Corporation (IBM). Because of their high cost, mainframes find use only in central computing facilities of large businesses and institutions.

The many advances that have taken place in the field of electronics over the past two decades have led to rapid advances in computer system technology. For instance, the introduction of *small-scale integrated* (SSI) *circuits*, followed by *medium-scale integrated* (MSI) *circuits, large-scale integrated* (LSI) *circuits,* and *very large-scale integrated* (VLSI) *circuits* has led the way in expanding the capacity and performance of large mainframe computers. But at the same time, these advances have also permitted the introduction of smaller, lower-performance, and lower-cost computer systems.

As computer use grew, it was recognized that the powerful computing capability of a mainframe was not needed by many customers. Instead, they desired easier access to a machine with smaller capacity. It was to satisfy this requirement that the *minicomputer* was developed. Minicomputers, such as that shown in Fig. 1.2, are also digital computers and are capable of performing the same basic operations as the earlier, larger systems. However, they are designed to provide a smaller functional capability. The

Figure 1.2 Minicomputer system
(Courtesy of Digital Equipment Corp.).

processor section of this type of computer is typically manufactured using SSI and MSI
electronic circuitry.

Minicomputers have found wide use as general-purpose computers, but their lower
cost also allows their use in dedicated applications. A computer used in a dedicated
application represents what is known as a *special-purpose computer*. By "special-
purpose computer" we mean a system that has been tailored to meet the needs of a
specific application. Examples are process control computers for industrial facilities,
data processing systems for retail stores, and medical analysis systems for patient care.
Figure 1.3 shows a minicomputer-based retail store data processing system.

The newest development in the computer industry is the *microcomputer*. Today,
the microcomputer represents the most important step in the evolution of the computer
world. It is a computer that has been designed to provide reduced size and capability
from that of a minicomputer, with a much lower cost.

The heart of the microcomputer system is the *microprocessor*. A microprocessor
is a general-purpose processor built into a single IC. It is an example of a VLSI device.
Through the use of VLSI circuitry in the microcomputer have come the benefits of

Figure 1.3 Retail store data processing
system (Courtesy of Hugin·Sweda, Inc.).

smaller size, lighter weight, lower cost, reduced power requirements, and higher reliability.

The low cost of microprocessors, which can be as low as $1, has opened the use of computer electronics to a much broader range of products. Figures 1.4 and 1.5 show some typical systems in which a microcomputer is used as a special-purpose computer.

Microcomputers are also finding wide use as general-purpose computers. Figure

Figure 1.4 Calculator (Courtesy of Texas Instruments, Inc.).

Figure 1.5 Electronic toy (Courtesy of Texas Instruments, Inc.)

Sec. 1.3   Mainframe Computers, Minicomputers, and Microcomputers   **5**

Figure 1.6 Personal computer (Courtesy of International Business Machines Corp.).

1.6 is an example of a personal computer system. In fact, microcomputer systems designed for the high-performance end of the microcomputer market are rivaling the performance of minicomputers and at a much lower cost to the user.

1.4 HARDWARE ELEMENTS OF THE DIGITAL COMPUTER SYSTEM

The hardware of a digital computer system is divided into four functional sections. The block diagram of Fig. 1.7 shows the four basic units of a simplified computer: the *input unit, central processing unit, memory unit,* and *output unit.* Each section has a special function in terms of overall computer operation.

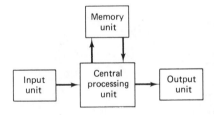

Figure 1.7 Block diagram of a digital computer (Walter A. Triebel, *Integrated Digital Electronics,* © 1979. Adapted by permission of Prentice-Hall, Inc., Englewood Cliffs, N.J.).

The *central processing unit* (CPU) is the heart of the computer system. It is responsible for performing all arithmetic operations and logic decisions initiated by the program. In addition to arithmetic and logic functions, the CPU controls overall system operation.

On the other hand, the input and output units are the means by which the CPU communicates with the outside world. The *input unit* is used to input information and commands to the CPU for processing. For instance, a CRT terminal can be used by the programmer to input a new program.

After processing, the information that results must be output. This output of data from the system is performed under control of the *output unit.* Examples of ways of outputting information are as printed pages produced by a high-speed printer or displayed on the screen of a video display terminal.

The *memory unit* of the computer is used to store information such as numbers, names, and addresses. By "store," we mean that memory has the ability to hold this information for processing or for outputting at a later time. The programs that define how the computer is to process data also reside in memory.

In computer systems, memory is divided into two different sections, known as *primary storage* and *secondary storage*. They are also sometimes called *internal memory* and *external memory*, respectively. *External memory* is used for long-term storage of information that is not in use. For instance, it holds programs, files of data, and files of information. In most computers, this part of memory employs storage on magnetic media such as magnetic tapes, magnetic disks, and magnetic drums. This is because they have the ability to store large amounts of data.

Internal memory is a smaller segment of memory used for temporary storage of programs, data, and information. For instance, when a program is to be executed, its instructions are first brought from external memory into internal memory together with the files of data and information that it will affect. After this, the program is executed and its files updated while they are held in internal memory. When the processing defined by the program is complete, the updated files are returned to external memory. Here the program and files are retained for use at a later time.

The internal memory of a computer system uses electronic memory devices instead of storage on a magnetic media memory. In most modern computer systems, semiconductor *read-only memory* (ROM) and *random access read/write memory* (RAM) are in use. These devices make internal memory much faster-operating than external memory.

Neither semiconductor memory nor magnetic media memory alone can satisfy the requirements of most general-purpose computer systems. Because of this fact, both types are normally present in the system. For instance, in a personal computer system, working storage is typically provided with RAM, while long-term storage is provided with floppy disk memory. On the other hand, in special-purpose computer systems, such as a video game, semiconductor memory is used. That is, the program that determines how the game is played is stored in ROM, and data storage, such as for graphic patterns, is in RAM.

1.5 GENERAL ARCHITECTURE OF A MICROCOMPUTER SYSTEM

Now that we have introduced the *general architecture* of a digital computer, let us look at how a microcomputer fits this model. Looking at Fig. 1.8, we find that the architecture of the microcomputer is essentially the same as that of the digital computer in Fig. 1.7. It has the same functional elements: input unit, output unit, memory unit and, in place of the CPU, a *microprocessor unit* (MPU). Moreover, each element serves the same basic function relative to overall system operation.

The difference between minicomputers, mainframe computers, and microcomputers does not lie in the fundamental blocks used to build the computer; instead, it relates

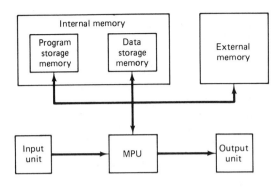

Figure 1.8 General microcomputer system architecture.

to the capacity and performance of the electronics used to implement their blocks and the resulting overall system capacity and performance. As indicated earlier, microcomputers are typically designed with smaller capacity and lower performance than either minicomputers or mainframes.

Unlike the mainframe and minicomputer, a microcomputer can be implemented with a small group of components. Again the heart of the computer system is the MPU (CPU) and it performs all arithmetic, logic, and control operations. However, in a microcomputer the MPU is implemented with a single microprocessor chip instead of a large assortment of SSI and MSI logic functions such as in older minicomputers and mainframes. Notice that correct use of the term "microprocessor" restricts its use to the central processing unit in a microcomputer system.

Notice that we have partitioned the memory unit into an internal memory section for storage of active data and instructions and an external memory section for long-term storage. As in minicomputers, the long-germ storage medium in a microcomputer is frequently a floppy disk. However, hard disk drives are used when storage requirements are higher than those provided by floppy disks.

Internal memory of the microcomputer is further subdivided into *program storage memory* and *data storage memory*. Typically, internal memory is implemented with both ROM and RAM ICs. Data, whether they are to be interpreted as numbers, characters, or instructions, can be stored in either ROM or RAM. But in most microcomputer systems, instructions of the program and data such as lookup table are stored in ROM. This is because this type of information does not normally change. By using ROM, its storage is made *nonvolatile*. That is, if power is lost, the information is retained.

On the other hand, the numerical and character data that are to be processed by the microprocessor change frequently. These data must be stored in a type of memory from which they can be read by the microprocessor, modified through processing, and written back for storage. For this reason, they are stored in RAM instead of ROM.

Depending on the application, the input and output sections can be implemented with something as simple as a few switches for inputs and a few light-emitting diodes (LEDs) for outputs. In other applications, for example in a personal computer, the input/output (I/O) devices can be more sophisticated, such as video display terminals and printers, just like those employed in minicomputer systems.

Up to this point, we have been discussing what is known as a *multichip micro-*

computer system, that is, a system implemented with a microprocessor and an assortment of support circuits, such as ROMs, RAMs, and I/O peripherals. This architecture makes for a very flexible system design. Its ROM, RAM, and I/O capacity can be easily expanded by just adding more devices. This is the circuit configuration used in most larger microcomputer systems. An example is the personal computer system shown in Fig. 1.9(a).

Devices are now being made that include all the functional blocks of a microcomputer in a single IC. This is called a *single-chip microcomputer.* Unlike the multichip microcomputer, single-chip microcomputers are limited in capacity and not as easy to expand. For example, a microcomputer device can have 8K bytes of ROM, 256 bytes of RAM, and 32 lines for use as inputs or outputs. Because of this limited capability, single-chip microcomputers find wide use in special-purpose computer applications. A block diagram of a calculator implemented with a single-chip microcomputer is shown in Fig. 1.9(b)

1.6 EVOLUTION OF THE MICROPROCESSOR ARCHITECTURE

The principal way in which microprocessors and microcomputers are categorized is in terms of the number of binary bits in the data they process, that is, their word length. Four standard data widths have evolved for microprocessors and microcomputers over time, *4-bit, 8-bit, 16-bit,* and *32-bit.*

Figure 1.10 illustrates the evolution of Intel's microprocessors since their introduction in 1972. The first microprocessor, the *4004,* was designed to process data arranged as 4-bit words. This organization is also referred to as a *nibble* of data.

The 4004 implemented a very low performance microcomputer by today's standards. This low performance and limited system capability restricted its use to simpler, special-purpose applications, such as in calculators and electronic toys.

In 1974 second-generation microprocessors became available. These devices, such as the *8008, 8080,* and *8085* identified in Fig. 1.10, were 8-bit microprocessors; that is, they were all designed to process 8-bit (1-byte-wide) data instead of 4-bit data.

These newer 8-bit microprocessors were characterized by higher-performance operation, larger system capabilities, and greater ease of programming. They were able to provide the system requirements for many applications that could not be satisfied by the earlier 4-bit microprocessors. These extended capabilities led to widespread acceptance of multichip 8-bit microcomputers for special-purpose system designs. Examples of these dedicated applications are electronic instruments, cash registers, and printers.

The plans for development of third-generation 16-bit microprocessors were announced by many leading semiconductor manufacturers in the mid 1970s. Looking at Fig. 1.10 we see that Intel's first 16-bit microprocessor, the *8086,* became available in 1979; its 8-bit bus version, the *8088,* was available in 1980. This was the birth of Intel's 8086 family architecture. Other family members, such as the *80286, 80186,* and *80188,* were introduced in the years that followed.

These 16-bit microprocessors provide high performance and have the ability to satisfy a broad scope of special-purpose and general-purpose microcomputer applications. They all have the ability to handle 8-bit, 16-bit, and special-purpose data types,

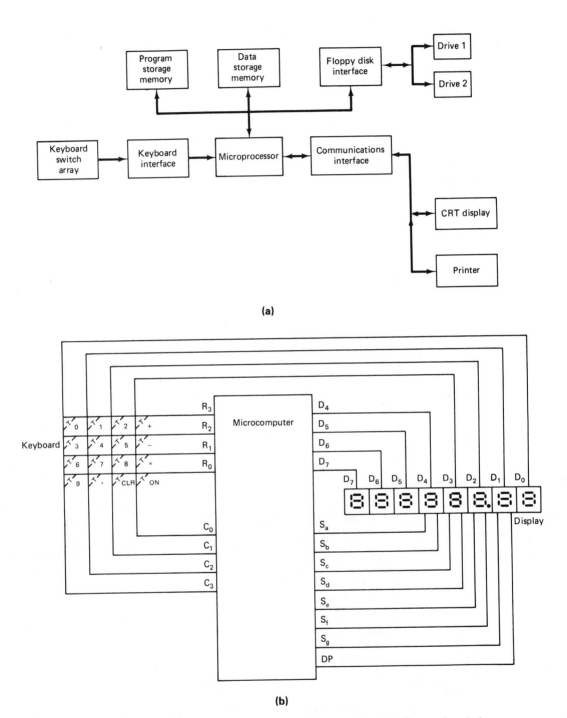

Figure 1.9 (a) Block diagram of a personal computer; (b) block diagram of a calculator.

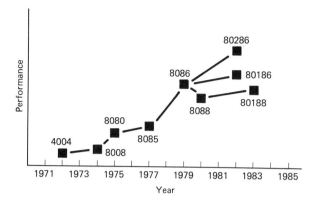

Figure 1.10 Evolution of the Intel microprocessor architecture.

and their powerful instruction sets are more in line with those provided by minicomputers instead of an 8-bit microcomputer.

This evolution of microprocessors was made possible by advances in semiconductor process technology. During this period, semiconductor device geometries were decreased from about 5 microns in the early 1970s to submicron today. This has permitted integration of one order of magnitude more transistors into the same size chip and at the same time has led to higher operating speeds. In Fig. 1.11 we see that the 4004 contained about 10,000 transistors. Transistor density was increased to about 30,000 with the development of the 8086 in 1979, and with the introduction of the 80286, device transistor count was increased to approximately 140,000.

Microprocessors can be classified according to the type of application for which they have been designed. In Fig. 1.12 we have placed Intel microprocessors in two application-oriented categories: *embedded microcontrollers* and *reprogrammable microprocessors*. Initially devices such as the 8080 were most widely used as *special-purpose microcomputers*. These special-purpose microcomputers were used in embedded control applications, that is, an application in which the microcomputer performs a dedicated control function.

Embedded control applications are further divided into those that primarily involve *event control* and those that require *data control*. An example of an embedded control

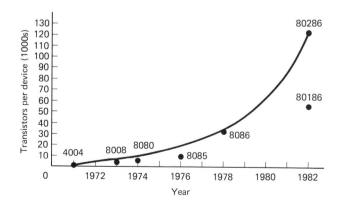

Figure 1.11 Device complexity.

Sec. 1.6   Evolution of the Microprocessor Architecture

11

application that is primarily event control is a microcomputer used for industrial process control. Here the program of the microprocessor is used to initiate a timed sequence of events. An application that focuses more on data control is a hard disk controller interface. In this case, a block of data that is to be processed, for example a data base, must be quickly transferred from external memory to internal memory.

The spectrum of embedded control applications requires a wide variety of system features and performance levels. Devices developed specifically for the needs of this marketplace have stressed low cost and high integration. In Fig. 1.12 we see that the earlier multichip 8080 solutions were initially replaced by the highly integrated 8-bit, single-chip microcomputer devices such as the 8048 and 8051. These devices were tailored to work best as event controllers. For instance, the 8051 offers one-order-of-magnitude-higher performance than the 8080, a more powerful instruction set, and special on-chip functions such as ROM, RAM, an interval/event timer, a universal asynchronous receiver/transmitter (UART), and programmable parallel I/O ports. Today these types of devices are called *microcontrollers*.

Later, devices such as the 80186 and 80188 were designed to better meet the needs of data-control applications. They are also highly integrated but have additional features, such as string instructions and direct memory access channels, which better handle the movement of data.

The category of reprogrammable microprocessors represents the class of applications in which a microprocessor is used to implement a *general-purpose microcomputer*. Unlike a special-purpose microcomputer, a general-purpose microcomputer is intended to run a wide variety of applications; that is, while it is in use it can be easily reprogrammed to run a different application. Two examples of reprogrammable microcomputers are the personal computer and the minicomputer. In Fig. 1.12 we see that the 8086, 8088, and 80286 are the Intel microprocessors in this category.

Architectural compatibility is a critical need of processors developed for use in reprogrammable applications. As shown in Fig. 1.13, the 80286 provides a super set of the 8086/8088 architecture. Actually the 80286 can operate in either of two modes—the *real-address mode* or *protected-address mode*. When in the real mode, the 80286 operates like a high-performance 8086/8088. It can be used to execute the base instruction set, which is object code compatible with the 8086/8088. For this reason, operating systems and programs written for the 8086 and 8088 can be run on the 80286 without modification. However, a number of new instructions have been added in the instruction set of the 80286 to enhance performance and functionality. We say that object code is *upward compatible* within the 8086 architecture. This means that 8086/8088 code will run on the 80286, but the reverse is not true if any of the new instructions are in use.

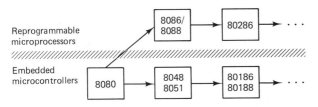
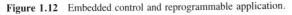

Figure 1.12 Embedded control and reprogrammable application.

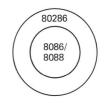

Figure 1.13 Code and system-level compatibility.

A microprocessor such as the 80286 that is designed for implementing general-purpose microcomputers must offer more advanced system features than a microcontroller. For example, it needs to support and manage a large memory subsystem. The 80286 is capable of managing a 1G-byte (Gigabyte) address space. Moreover, a reprogrammable microcomputer, such as a personal computer, normally runs an operating system. The architecture of the 80286 has been enhanced with on-chip support for operating system functions such as memory management, protection, and multitasking. These new features become active only when the 80286 is operated in the protected mode.

Reprogrammable microcomputers, such as those based on the 8086 family, require a wide variety of I/O resources. Figure 1.14 (page 14) shows the kinds of interfaces that are frequently implemented in a personal computer or minicomputer system. A large family of VLSI peripheral ICs are needed to support a reprogrammable microprocessor such as the 8086 or 80286; for example, floppy disk controllers, hard disk controllers, local-area-network controllers, and communication controllers. For this reason, the 8086, 8088, and 80286 are designed to implement a multichip microcomputer system. In this way, a system can be easily configured with the appropriate set of I/O interfaces.

ASSIGNMENT

Section 1.2

1. What tells a computer what to do, where to get data, how to process data, and where to put the results when done?
2. What is the name given to a sequence of instructions that is used to guide a computer through a task?
3. What type of electronic devices are revolutionizing the computer industry today?

Section 1.3

4. Name the three classes of computers.
5. What are the main similarities and differences between minicomputers and microcomputers?
6. What is meant by "general-purpose computer"?
7. What is meant by "special-purpose computer"?
8. What is the heart of the microcomputer system?

Section 1.4

9. What are the four building blocks of a digital computer system?
10. What is the heart of the digital computer called?
11. What is the function of the input unit?
12. What is the function of the output unit?
13. What is the purpose of memory in a computer system?

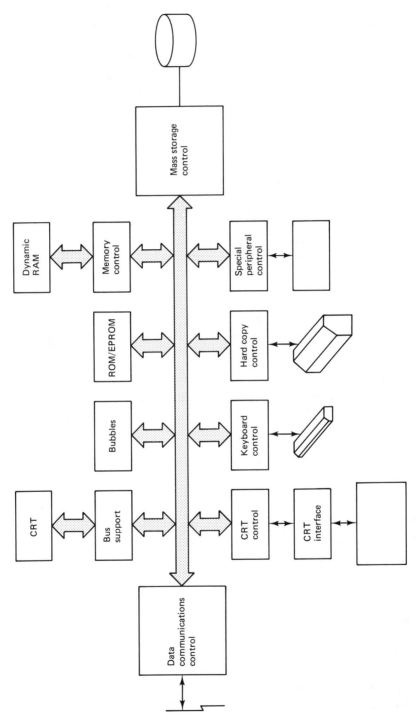

Figure 1.14 Peripheral support for the MPU.

14. What is the difference between primary and secondary storage?
15. What does ROM stand for?
16. What does RAM stand for?

Section 1.5

17. What does MPU stand for?
18. Give two examples of devices used to implement external memory in a microcomputer system.
19. Into what two sections is the internal memory of a microcomputer partitioned?
20. Which part of the internal memory is normally implemented with RAM ICs?
21. Is ROM volatile or nonvolatile?
22. What is meant by the phrase ''volatile memory''?
23. What is the difference between a multichip microcomputer and a single-chip microcomputer?

Section 1.6

24. What are the standard data word lengths for which microprocessors have been developed?
25. When was the first 4-bit microprocessor introduced by Intel Corporation? Eight-bit microprocessor? Sixteen-bit microprocessor?
26. Name five members of the 8086 family architecture.
27. Approximately how many transistors are used to implement the 8088 microprocessor? The 80286 microprocessor?
28. What is an embedded microcontroller?
29. Name the two types of embedded microcontrollers.
30. Name three 16-bit microprocessors intended for use in reprogrammable microcomputer applications.
31. Give the names for the 80286's two modes of operation.
32. What is meant by upward software compatibility relative to 8086 architecture microprocessors?
33. List three advanced architectural features provided by the 80286 microprocessor.
34. Give three types of VLSI peripheral support devices needed in a reprogrammable microcomputer system.

Chapter 2 ——————————————

The 8086
Microprocessor ————————

2.1 INTRODUCTION ——————————————————

In Chapter 1 some general aspects of microprocessors and microcomputers were introduced. With the present chapter we begin our study of Intel's 8086 microprocessor. In this chapter, the general architectural aspects of the 8086 are covered. The next five chapters are devoted to other aspects such as instruction set, programming, memory interface, I/O interface, and interrupt handling. Specifically, this chapter deals with

1. The 8086 microprocessor
2. Minimum- and maximum-mode systems and interfaces
3. Electrical characteristics
4. Internal architecture of the 8086 microprocessor
5. The 8284 clock generator and 8086 bus cycle
6. Instruction execution in the 8086 system

2.2 THE 8086 MICROPROCESSOR ——————————————

The 8086, first announced in 1978, was the first 16-bit microprocessor introduced by Intel Corporation. It has been followed by a steady stream of family components such as the 8088 microprocessor, the 8087 numeric coprocessor, and the 8089 I/O processor.

The 8086 is manufactured using *high-performance metal-oxide-semiconductor* (HMOS) *technology* and the circuitry on its chip is equivalent to approximately 29,000 transistors. It is enclosed in a 40-pin package as shown in Fig. 2.1. Many of its pins have multiple functions. For example, in the pin layout we see that address lines A_0 through A_{15} and data bus lines D_0 through D_{15} are multiplexed. For this reason, these leads are labeled AD_0 through AD_{15}.

The 8086 is a true 16-bit microprocessor with 16-bit internal and external data paths. It has the ability to address up to 1M byte of memory via a 20-bit-wide address bus. Moreover, it can address up to 64K of byte-wide I/O ports or 32K of word-wide ports.

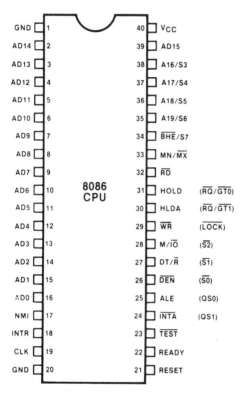

Figure 2.1 Pin layout of the 8086 microprocessor (Courtesy of Intel Corp.).

2.3 MINIMUM-MODE AND MAXIMUM-MODE SYSTEMS

The 8086 microprocessor can be configured to work in either of two modes. These modes are known as the *minimum system mode* and the *maximum system mode*. The minimum system mode is selected by applying logic 1 to the MN/MX input lead. Minimum 8086 systems are typically smaller and contain a single microprocessor. Changing MN/MX to logic 0 selects the maximum mode of operation. This configures the 8086 system for use with multiple processors. This mode-selection feature lets the 8086 better meet the needs of a wide variety of system requirements.

Depending on the mode of operation selected, the assignments for a number of the pins on the 8086's package are changed. As shown in Fig. 2.1, the pin functions specified in parentheses are those that pertain to a maximum-mode system.

The signals that are common to both modes of operation, those unique to minimum mode, and those unique to maximum mode are listed in Fig. 2.2(a), (b), and (c), respectively. Here we find the name, function, and type for each signal. For example, the signal $\overline{RD}$ is in the common group. It functions as a read control output and is used to signal memory or I/O devices when the 8086's system bus is set up for input of data. Moreover, notice that the signals hold request (HOLD) and hold acknowledge

Common Signals		
Name	Function	Type
AD15–AD0	Address/Data Bus	Bidirectional, 3-State
A19/S6– A16/S3	Address/Status	Output, 3-State
$\overline{BHE}$/S7	Bus High Enable/ Status	Output, 3-State
MN/$\overline{MX}$	Minimum/Maximum Mode Control	Input
$\overline{RD}$	Read Control	Output, 3-State
$\overline{TEST}$	Wait On Test Control	Input
READY	Wait State Control	Input
RESET	System Reset	Input
NMI	Non-Maskable Interrupt Request	Input
INTR	Interrupt Request	Input
CLK	System Clock	Input
V$_{CC}$	+5V	Input
GND	Ground	

(a)

Minimum Mode Signals (MN/$\overline{MX}$ = V$_{CC}$)		
Name	Function	Type
HOLD	Hold Request	Input
HLDA	Hold Acknowledge	Output
$\overline{WR}$	Write Control	Output, 3-State
M/$\overline{IO}$	Memory/IO Control	Output, 3-State
DT/$\overline{R}$	Data Transmit/ Receive	Output, 3-State
$\overline{DEN}$	Data Enable	Output, 3-State
ALE	Address Latch Enable	Output
$\overline{INTA}$	Interrupt Acknowledge	Output

(b)

Figure 2.2 (a) Signals common to both minimum and maximum modes (Courtesy of Intel Corp.); (b) unique minimum-mode signals (Courtesy of Intel Corp.); (c) unique maximum-mode signals (Courtesy of Intel Corp.).

Maximum Mode Signals (MN/$\overline{\text{MX}}$ = GND)		
Name	Function	Type
$\overline{\text{RQ}}$/$\overline{\text{GT1, 0}}$	Request/Grant Bus Access Control	Bidirectional
$\overline{\text{LOCK}}$	Bus Priority Lock Control	Output, 3-State
$\overline{\text{S2}}$-$\overline{\text{S0}}$	Bus Cycle Status	Output, 3-State
QS1, QS0	Instruction Queue Status	Output

(c)

Figure 2.2(c)

(HLDA) are produced only in the minimum-mode system. If the 8086 is set up for maximum mode, they are replaced by the request/grant bus access control lines $\overline{\text{RQ}}$/$\overline{\text{GT}}_0$ and $\overline{\text{RQ}}$/$\overline{\text{GT}}_1$.

2.4 MINIMUM-SYSTEM-MODE INTERFACE

When the minimum system mode of operation is selected, the 8086 itself provides all the control signals needed to implement the memory and I/O interfaces. Figure 2.3 shows a block diagram of a minimum-mode configuration of the 8086. The minimum-mode signals can be divided into the following basic groups: address/data bus, status, control, interrupt, and DMA. For simplicity in the diagram, multiplexed signal lines are shown to be independent.

Address/Data Bus

Let us first look at the address/data bus. In an 8086-based system these lines serve two functions. As an *address bus,* they are used to carry address information to the memory and I/O ports. The address bus is 20 bits long and consists of signal lines A_0 through A_{19}. Of these, A_{19} represents the most significant bit (MSB) and A_0 the least significant bit (LSB). A 20-bit address gives the 8086 a 1M-byte memory address space. Moreover, it has an independent I/O address space which is 64K bytes in length.

The sixteen *data bus* lines D_0 through D_{15} are actually multiplexed with address lines A_0 through A_{15}, respectively. By "multiplexed" we mean that the bus works as an address bus during one period of time and as a data bus during another period. D_{15} is the MSB and D_0 the LSB. When acting as a data bus, they carry read/write data for memory, input/output data for I/O devices, and interrupt-type codes from an interrupt controller.

Status Signals

The four most significant address lines, A_{19} through A_{16} are also multiplexed, but in this case with status signals S_6 through S_3. These status bits are output on the bus at the same time that data are transferred over the other bus lines. Bits S_4 and S_3 together

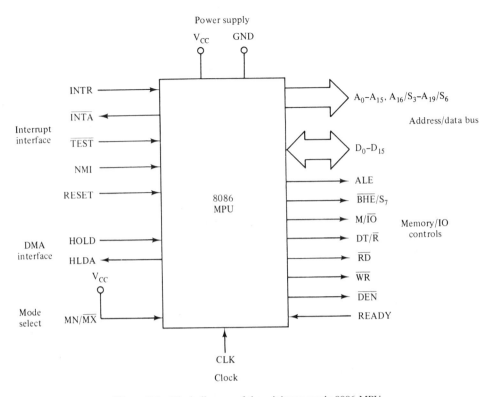

Figure 2.3 Block diagram of the minimum-mode 8086 MPU.

form a 2-bit binary code that identifies which of the 8086's internal segment registers was used to generate the physical address that was output on the address bus during the current bus cycle. These four codes and the register they represent are shown in Fig. 2.4. Notice that the code $S_4S_3 = 00$ identifies a register known as the *extra segment register* as the source of the segment address.

Status line S_5 reflects the status of another internal characteristic of the 8086. It is the logic level of the internal interrupt enable flag. The last status bit S_6 is always at the 0 logic level.

S_4	S_3	Segment register
0	0	Extra
0	1	Stack
1	0	Code/none
1	1	Data

Figure 2.4 Memory segment status codes.

Control Signals

The *control signals* are provided to support the 8086's memory and I/O interfaces. They control functions such as when the bus is to carry a valid address, in which direction data are to be transferred over the bus, when valid write data are on the bus, and when to put read data on the system bus. For example, *address latch enable* (ALE) is a pulse to logic 1 that signals external circuitry when a valid address word is on the bus. This address must be latched in external circuitry on the 1-to-0 edge of the pulse at ALE.

Another control signal that is produced during the bus cycle is $\overline{BHE}$ *(bank high enable)*. Logic 0 on this line is used as a memory enable signal for the most significant byte half of the data bus, D_8 through D_{15}. This line also serves a second function, which is as the S_7 status line.

Using the M/$\overline{IO}$ *(memory/IO)* and DT/$\overline{R}$ *(data transmit/receive)* lines, the 8086 signals which type of bus cycle is in progress and in which direction data are to be transferred over the bus. The logic level of M/$\overline{IO}$ tells external circuitry whether a memory or I/O transfer is taking place over the bus. Logic 1 at this output signals a memory operation, and logic 0 an I/O operation. The direction of data transfer over the bus is signaled by the logic level output at DT/$\overline{R}$. When this line is logic 1 during the data transfer part of a bus cycle, the bus is in the transmit mode. Therefore, data are either written into memory or output to an I/O device. On the other hand, logic 0 at DT/$\overline{R}$ signals that the bus is in the receive mode. This corresponds to reading data from memory or input of data from an input port.

The signals *read* ($\overline{RD}$) and *write* ($\overline{WR}$), respectively, indicate that a read bus cycle or a write bus cycle is in progress. The 8086 switches $\overline{WR}$ to logic 0 to signal external devices that valid write or output data are on the bus. On the other hand, $\overline{RD}$ indicates that the 8086 is performing a read of data off the bus. During read operations, one other control signal is also supplied. This is $\overline{DEN}$ *(data enable),* and it signals external devices when they should put data on the bus.

There is one other control signal that is involved with the memory and I/O interface. This is the READY signal. It can be used to insert wait states into the bus cycle such that it is extended by a number of clock periods. This signal is provided by way of an external clock generator device and can be supplied by the memory or I/O subsystem to signal the 8086 when they are ready to permit the data transfer to be completed.

Interrupt Signals

The key interrupt interface signals are *interrupt request* (INTR) and *interrupt acknowledge* (INTA). INTR is an input to the 8086 that can be used by an external device to signal that it needs to be serviced. This input is sampled during the final clock period of each *instruction acquisition cycle*. Logic 1 at INTR represents an active interrupt request. When an interrupt request has been recognized by the 8086, it indicates this fact to external circuits with pulses to logic 0 at the $\overline{INTA}$ output.

The $\overline{TEST}$ input is also related to the external interrupt interface. Execution of a

WAIT instruction causes the 8086 to check the logic level at the $\overline{\text{TEST}}$ input. If logic 1 is found, the MPU suspends operation and goes into what is known as the *idle state*. The 8086 no longer executes instructions; instead, it repeatedly checks the logic level of the $\overline{\text{TEST}}$ input waiting for its transition back to logic 0. As $\overline{\text{TEST}}$ switches to 0, execution resumes with the next instruction in the program. This feature can be used to synchronize the operation of the 8086 to an event in external hardware.

There are two more inputs in the interrupt interface: the *nonmaskable interrupt* (NMI) and *reset* (RESET). On the 0-to-1 transition of NMI, control is passed to a nonmaskable interrupt service routine. The RESET input is used to provide a hardware reset for the 8086. Switching RESET to logic 0 initializes the internal registers of the 8086 and initiates a reset service routine.

DMA Interface Signals

The *direct memory access* (DMA) interface of the 8086 minimum-mode system consists of the HOLD and HLDA signals. When an external device wants to take control of the system bus, it signals this fact to the 8086 by switching HOLD to the 1 logic level. At the completion of the current bus cycle, the 8086 enters the hold state. When in the hold state, signal lines AD_0 through AD_{15}, A_{16}/S_3 through A_{19}/S_6, $\overline{\text{BHE}}$, $M/\overline{\text{IO}}$, $DT/\overline{R}$, $\overline{\text{RD}}$, $\overline{\text{WR}}$, $\overline{\text{DEN}}$, and INTR are all in the high-Z state. The 8086 signals external devices that it is in this state by switching its HLDA output to the 1 logic level.

2.5 MAXIMUM-SYSTEM-MODE INTERFACE

When the 8086 is set for the maximum-mode configuration, it produces signals for implementing a *multiprocessor/coprocessor system environment*. By "multiprocessor environment" we mean that more than one microprocessor exists in the system and that each processor is executing its own program. Usually in this type of system environment, there are some system resources that are common to all processors. They are called *global resources*. There are also other resources that are assigned to specific processors. These dedicated resources are known as *local* or *private resources*.

Coprocessor also means that there is a second processor in the system. However, in this case, the two processors do not access the bus at the same time. One passes control of the system bus to the other and then may suspend its operation. In the maximum-mode 8086 system, facilities are provided for implementing allocation of global resources and passing bus control to other microcomputers or coprocessors.

8288 Bus Controller—Bus Commands and Control Signals

Looking at the maximum-mode block diagram in Fig. 2.5, we see that the 8086 does not directly provide all the signals that are required to control the memory, I/O, and interrupt interfaces. Specifically, the $\overline{\text{WR}}$, $M/\overline{\text{IO}}$, $DT/\overline{R}$, $\overline{\text{DEN}}$, ALE, and $\overline{\text{INTA}}$ signals are no longer produced by the 8086. Instead, it outputs three status signals $\overline{S_0}$, $\overline{S_1}$, and

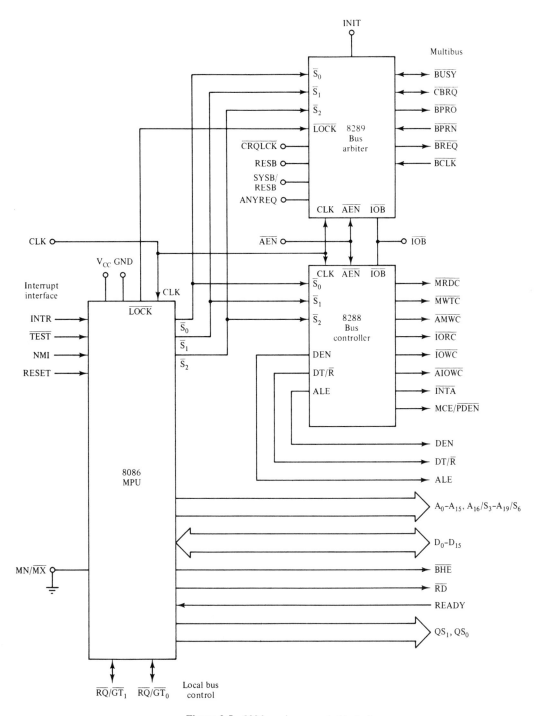

Figure 2.5 8086 maximum-mode block diagram.

Sec. 2.5   Maximum-System-Mode Interface   **23**

$\overline{S}_2$ prior to the initiation of each bus cycle. This 3-bit *bus status code* identifies which type of bus cycle is to follow. $\overline{S}_2\overline{S}_1\overline{S}_0$ are input to the external *bus controller* device, the 8288, which decodes them to identify the type of MPU bus cycle. The block diagram and pin layout of the 8288 are shown in Figs. 2.6(a) and (b), respectively. In response, the bus controller generates the appropriately timed command and control signals.

Figure 2.7 shows the relationship between the bus status codes and the types of bus cycles. Also shown are the output signals that are generated to tell external circuitry which type of bus cycle is taking place. These output signals are: *memory read command* ($\overline{MRDC}$), *memory write command* ($\overline{MWTC}$), *advanced memory write command* ($\overline{AMWC}$), *I/O read command* ($\overline{IORC}$), *I/O write command* ($\overline{IOWC}$), *advanced I/O write command* ($\overline{AIOWC}$), and *interrupt acknowledge command* ($\overline{INTA}$).

The 8288 produces one or two of these seven command signals for each bus cycle. For instance, when the 8086 outputs the code $\overline{S}_2\overline{S}_1\overline{S}_0$ equals 001, it indicates that an I/O read cycle is to be performed. In turn, the 8288 makes its $\overline{IORC}$ output switch to

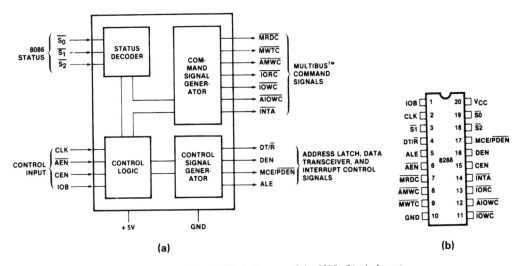

Figure 2.6 (a) Block diagram of the 8288; (b) pin layout.

Status Inputs			CPU Cycle	8288 Command
$\overline{S2}$	$\overline{S1}$	$\overline{S0}$		
0	0	0	Interrupt Acknowledge	$\overline{INTA}$
0	0	1	Read I/O Port	$\overline{IORC}$
0	1	0	Write I/O Port	$\overline{IOWC}, \overline{AIOWC}$
0	1	1	Halt	None
1	0	0	Instruction Fetch	$\overline{MRDC}$
1	0	1	Read Memory	$\overline{MRDC}$
1	1	0	Write Memory	$\overline{MWTC}, \overline{AMWC}$
1	1	1	Passive	None

Figure 2.7 Bus status codes (Courtesy of Intel Corp.).

The 8086 Microprocessor   Chap. 2

logic 0. On the other hand, if the code 111 is output by the 8086, it is signaling that no bus activity is to take place.

The control outputs produced by the 8288 are DEN, DT/$\overline{R}$, and ALE. These three signals provide the same functions as those described for the minimum system mode. This set of bus commands and control signals is compatible with the *Multibus,* an industry standard for interfacing microprocessor systems.

The 8289 Bus Arbiter—Bus Arbitration and Lock Signals

Looking at Fig. 2.5, we see that an 8289 *bus arbiter* has also been added in the maximum-mode system. It is this device that permits multiple processors to reside on the system bus. It does this by implementing the *Multibus arbitration protocol* in an 8086-based system. Figures 2.8(a) and (b) show a block diagram and pin layout of the 8289, respectively.

Addition of the 8288 bus controller and 8289 bus arbiter frees a number of the 8086's pins for use to produce control signals that are needed to support multiple processors. *Bus priority lock* ($\overline{LOCK}$) is one of these signals. It is input to the bus arbiter together with status signals $\overline{S}_0$ through $\overline{S}_2$. The outputs of the 8289 are bus arbitration signals: *bus busy* ($\overline{BUSY}$), *common bus request* ($\overline{CBRQ}$), *bus priority out* ($\overline{BPRO}$), *bus priority in* ($\overline{BPRN}$), *bus request* ($\overline{BREQ}$), and *bus clock* ($\overline{BCLK}$). They correspond to the *bus exchange* signals of the Multibus and are used to lock other processors off the system bus during the execution of an instruction by the 8086. In this way the processor can be assured of uninterrupted access to *common system resources* such as *global memory.*

Queue Status Signals

Two new signals that are produced by the 8086 in the maximum-mode system are queue status outputs QS_0 and QS_1. Together they form a 2-bit *queue status code,* QS_1QS_0. This code tells the external circuitry what type of information was removed from the

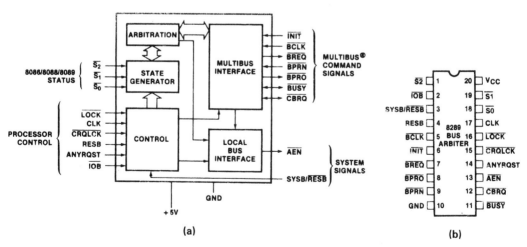

(a)   **(b)**

Figure 2.8 (a) Block diagram of the 8289; (b) pin layout.

queue during the previous clock cycle. Figure 2.9 shows the four different queue statuses. Notice that $QS_1QS_0 = 01$ indicates that the first byte of an instruction was taken off the queue. As shown, the next byte of the instruction that is fetched is identified by the code 11. Whenever the queue is reset due to a transfer of control, the reinitialization code 10 is output.

QS1	QS0	Queue Status
0 (low)	0	No Operation. During the last clock cycle, nothing was taken from the queue.
0	1	First Byte. The byte taken from the queue was the first byte of the instruction.
1 (high)	0	Queue Empty. The queue has been reinitialized as a result of the execution of a transfer instruction.
1	1	Subsequent Byte. The byte taken from the queue was a subsequent byte of the instruction.

Figure 2.9 Queue status codes (Courtesy of Intel Corp.).

Local Bus Control Signals—Request/Grant Signals

In a maximum-mode configuration, the minimum-mode HOLD, $\overline{\text{HLDA}}$ interface is also changed. These two signals are replaced by *request/grant lines* $\overline{\text{RQ/GT}}_0$ and $\overline{\text{RQ/GT}}_1$, respectively. They provide a prioritized bus access mechanism for accessing the *local bus*.

2.6 ELECTRICAL CHARACTERISTICS

In the preceding sections, the pin layout and minimum- and maximum-mode interface signals of the 8086 microprocessor were introduced. Here we will first look at the 8086's power supply ratings and then its input and output electrical characteristics.

A power supply voltage must be applied to the 8086 in order for its circuitry to operate. Looking at Fig. 2.1 we find that power is applied between pin 40 (V_{cc}) and pins 1 and 20, which are grounds (GND). Pins 1 and 20 should be connected electrically. The nominal value of V_{cc} is specified as $+5$ V dc with a tolerance of $\pm$ 10%. This means that the 8086 will operate correctly as long as the difference in voltage between V_{cc} and GND is greater than 4.5 V dc and less than 5.5 V dc. At room temperature (25°C), the 8086 will draw a maximum of 340 mA from the supply.

Let us now look at the dc I/O characteristics of the 8086, that is, its input and output logic levels. These ratings tell the minimum and maximum voltages for the 0 and 1 logic states for which the circuit will operate correctly. Different values are specified for the inputs and outputs.

The I/O voltage specifications for the 8086 are shown in Fig. 2.10. Notice that the minimum logic 1 (high-level) voltage at an output (V_{OH}) is 2.4 V. This voltage is specified for a test condition that identifies the amount of current being sourced by the output (I_{OH}) as -400 μA. All 8086s must be tested during manufacturing to assure that under this test condition the voltages at all outputs will remain above the value of V_{OHmin}.

Input voltage levels are specified in a similar way. Except here the ratings identify the range of voltage that will be correctly identified as a logic 0 or logic 1 at all inputs. For instance, voltages in the range $V_{ILmin} = -0.5$ V to $V_{ILmax} = +0.8$ V represents a valid logic 0 (lower-level) at an input of the 8086.

Symbol	Meaning	Minimum	Maximum	Test condition
V_{IL}	Input low voltage	-0.5 V	$+0.8$ V	
V_{IH}	Input high voltage	$+2.0$ V	$V_{cc} + 0.5$ V	
V_{OL}	Output low voltage		$+0.45$ V	$I_{OL} = 2.5$ mA
V_{OH}	Output high voltage	$+2.4$ V		$I_{OH} = -400$ uA

Figure 2.10 I/O voltage levels.

2.7 INTERNAL ARCHITECTURE OF THE 8086

The internal architecture of a microprocessor describes its functional components and their interaction. Figure 2.11 shows a block diagram of the internal architecture of the 8086 microprocessor.

Internal Blocks of the 8086

Within the 8086 microprocessor, the internal functions are divided between two separate processing units. They are the *bus interface unit* (BIU) and the *execution unit* (EU). In general, the BIU is responsible for performing all bus operations, such as instruction fetching, reading and writing operands for memory, and inputting or outputting of data for peripherals. On the other hand, the EU is responsible for executing instructions.

Both units operate asynchronously to give the 8086 an overlapping instruction fetch and instruction execution mechanism. In essence, this parallel processing of the BIU and EU eliminates the time needed to fetch many of the instructions. This results in efficient use of the system bus and significantly improved system performance.

Bus Interface Unit

The bus interface unit is the 8086's interface to the outside world. It provides a full 16-bit bidirectional data bus and 20-bit address bus. The bus interface unit is responsible for performing all external bus operations. Specifically, it has the following functions: *instruction fetch, instruction queueing, operand fetch and storage, address relocation,* and *bus control*. To implement these functions, the BIU contains the *segment registers, internal communication registers, instruction pointer, instruction object code queue, address summer,* and *bus control logic*. These components are identified in Fig. 2.11.

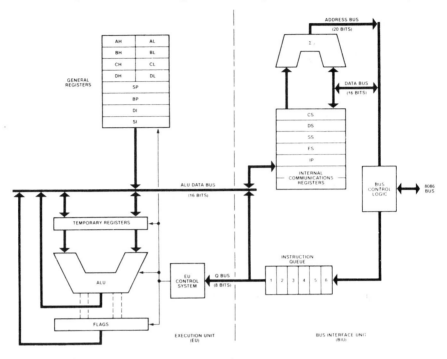

Figure 2.11 Internal architecture of the 8086 (Courtesy of Intel Corp.).

The BIU uses a mechanism known as an *instruction stream queue* to implement a *pipeline architecture*. This queue permits prefetch of up to six bytes of instruction code. Whenever the queue of the BIU is not full, that is, it has room for at least two more bytes, and at the same time, the EU is not requesting it to read or write operands from memory, the BIU is free to look ahead in the program by prefetching the next sequential instruction. These prefetched instructions are held in its *first in, first out (FIFO) queue*. With its 16-bit data bus, the BIU fetches two instruction bytes in a single memory cycle. After a byte is loaded at the input end of the queue, it automatically shifts up through the FIFO to the empty location nearest the output. The EU accesses the queue from the output end. It reads one instruction byte after the other from the output of the queue.

If the queue is full and the EU is not requesting access to operands in memory, the BIU does not perform any bus cycles. These intervals of no bus activity, which may occur between bus cycles, are known as *idle states*. Moreover, if the BIU is already in the process of fetching an instruction when the EU requests it to read or write operands from memory or I/O, the BIU first completes the instruction fetch bus cycle before initiating the operand read/write cycle.

The BIU also contains a dedicated adder which is used to generate the 20-bit *physical address* that is output on the address bus. This address is formed by adding an appended 16-bit segment address and a 16-bit offset address. For example, the physical address of the next instruction to be fetched is formed by combining the current contents of the code segment (CS) register and the current contents of the instruction pointer (IP) register.

The BIU is also responsible for generating bus control signals such as those for memory read or write and I/O read or write. These signals are needed for control of the circuits in the memory and I/O subsystems.

Execution Unit

The execution unit is responsible for *decoding* and *executing* all instructions. Notice in Fig. 2.11 that it consists of an *ALU, status and control flags, eight general-purpose registers, temporary registers,* and *queue control logic.*

The EU extracts instructions from the top of the queue in the BIU, decodes them, generates operand addresses if necessary, passes them to the BIU and requests it to perform the read or write bus cycles to memory or I/O, and performs the operation specified by the instruction on the operands. During execution of the instruction, the EU tests the status and control flags and updates them based on the results of executing the instruction. If the queue is empty, the EU waits for the next instruction byte to be fetched and shifted to the top of the queue.

When the EU executes a branch or jump instruction, it transfers control to a location corresponding to another set of sequential instructions. Whenever this happens, the BIU automatically resets the queue and then begins to fetch instructions from this new location to refill the queue.

2.8 INTERNAL REGISTERS OF THE 8086

The 8086 has four groups of user-accessible internal registers. They are the *instruction pointer, four data registers, four pointer and index registers,* and *four segment registers.* They represent a total of thirteen 16-bit registers. In addition to these registers, there is another 16-bit register called the *status register,* with nine of its bits implemented for *status* and *control flags.*

Instruction Pointer

The *instruction pointer* (IP) is a 16-bit register within the 8086 that identifies the location of the next instruction to be executed in the current code segment. It is similar to a program counter (PC); however, IP contains an offset pointer instead of the physical address of the next instruction. This is because the 8086 contains 16-bit registers and memory, but requires a 20-bit address. The offset must be combined with the contents of another register, in this case the code segment register (CS), to generate the physical address of the instruction. This register is physically located in the BIU.

Every time an instruction word is fetched from memory, the BIU updates the value in IP such that it points to the next sequential instruction word in memory.

Data Registers

As shown in Fig. 2.11, there are four general-purpose data registers that are located within the EU of the 8086. During program execution, they are used for temporary storage of frequently used intermediate results. The advantage of storing these data in internal registers instead of memory is that they can be accessed much faster.

The *data registers* are shown in more detail in Fig. 2.12(a). Here we see that the four data registers are referred to as the *accumulator register* (A), the *base register* (B), the *count register* (C), and the *data register* (D). Each register can be accessed either as a 16-bit word or as two 8-bit bytes. References to a register as a word are identified by an X after the register letter. For instance, the accumulator is referenced as AX. In a similar way, the other three registers are referred to as BX, CX, and DX.

On the other hand, when referencing one of these registers on a byte-wide basis, its high byte and low byte are identified by following the register name with the letter H or L, respectively. For the A register, the most significant byte is referred to as AH and the least significant byte as AL. The other byte-wide register pairs are BH and BL, CH and CL, and DH and DL.

Any of the general-purpose data registers can be used for arithmetic or logic operations such as add or AND. However, for some operations, such as those performed by string instructions, specific registers are used. In the case of a string instruction, register C is used to store a count representing the number of bytes to be moved. This is the reason it is given the name "count register."

Another example of dedicated use of data registers is that all I/O operations require the data that are to be input or output to be in the A register, while register DX holds the address of the I/O port. Figure 2.12(b) summarizes the dedicated functions of the data registers.

Pointer and Index Registers

There are four other general-purpose registers shown in Fig. 2.12, two *pointer registers* and two *index registers*. They are used to store offset addresses of memory locations relative to the segment registers. The values held in these registers can be loaded or

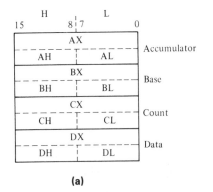

Register	Operations
AX	Word multiply, word divide, word I/O
AL	Byte multiply, byte divide, byte I/O, translate, decimal arithmetic
AH	Byte multiply, byte divide
BX	Translate
CX	String operations, loops
CL	Variable shift and rotate
DX	Word multiply, word divide, indirect I/O

(a)   (b)

Figure 2.12 (a) General purpose data registers (Courtesy of Intel Corp.); (b) dedicated register functions (Courtesy of Intel Corp.).

modified through software. This is done prior to executing the instruction that references the register for address offset. In this way, the instruction simply specifies which register contains the offset address.

Figure 2.13 shows that the two pointer registers are the *stack pointer* (SP) and *base pointer* (BP). The stack pointer permits easy access to locations in the stack segment of memory. The value in SP represents the offset of the next stack location which can be accessed relative to the current address in the stack segment (SS) register; that is, it always points to the top of the stack. BP also represents an offset from the SS register. However, it is used to access data within the stack segment.

The index registers are used to hold offset addresses for instructions that access data stored in the data segment of memory. For this reason, they are always referenced to the value in the data segment (DS) register. The *source index* (SI) register is used to store an offset address for a source operand and the *destination index* (DI) register is used for storage of an offset that identifies the location of a destination operand. For example, a string instruction that requires an offset to the location of a source or destination operand would use these registers.

Segment Registers

As we indicated earlier, the physical address of the 8086 is 20 bits wide, but its registers and memory locations which contain logical addresses are just 16 bits wide. This gives a 1M-byte address space. However, the address space is segmented into 64K-byte segments and just four segments can be active at a time. It is for selection of the four active segments that the 16-bit *segment registers* are provided within the BIU of the 8086.

These four registers are the *code segment* (CS) *register,* the *data segment* (DS) *register,* the *stack segment* (SS) *register,* and the *extra segment* (ES) *register.* These registers are shown in Fig. 2.14. They are loaded with 16-bit addresses that identify which segments of memory are active. For example, the value in CS identifies the starting address of the 64K-byte segment known as the code segment. By ''starting address,'' we mean the lowest-addressed byte in the active code segment. The values held in these registers are frequently referred to as the current segment register values, for instance, the current code segment address.

Code segments of memory contain instructions of the program. The contents of CS identify the starting location of the current code segment in memory. To access the

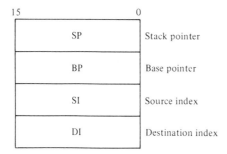

Figure 2.13 Pointer and index registers (Courtesy of Intel Corp.).

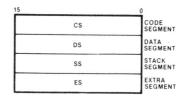

Figure 2.14 Segment registers (Courtesy of Intel Corp.).

storage location of an instruction in the active code segment, the 8086 must generate its 20-bit physical address. To do this, it combines the contents of the instruction pointer (IP) register with the value in CS to produce the physical address that will be output on the address bus.

The active code segment can be changed by simply executing an instruction that loads a new value into the CS register. For this reason, we can use any 64K-byte segment of memory for storage of code.

The contents of the data segment (DS) register identify the starting location of the current data segment in memory. This is a second active 64K segment that provides a read/write memory space in which data can be stored. Operands for most instructions are fetched from this segment. However, a prefix may be included with the instruction to obtain operands from any of the other segments. Values in the source index (SI) register or destination index (DI) register are combined with the value in DS to form the 20-bit physical address of the source or destination operand in the data segment.

The stack segment (SS) register contains a logical address that identifies the starting location of the current stack segment in memory. It is the 64K segment to which the values of the instruction pointer (IP), status flags, and other registers are pushed whenever a hardware interrupt, software interrupt, or subroutine call occurs. After the service routine or subroutine is complete, the original system status is restored from the stack by executing pop instructions and the return instruction. The next location to which a word is to be pushed or from which a word is to be popped is identified by combining the current value in SS with the stack pointer (SP).

The last segment register identifies the fourth active 64K-byte memory area. This area is called the *extra segment* (ES). The extra segment is usually used for data storage. For instance, the string instructions use the value in ES with the contents of DI as an offset to specify the destination address.

Flag Register

The *flag register* is a 16-bit register within the EU. However, as shown in Fig. 2.15, just nine of its bits are implemented. Six of these bits represent status flags. They are the *carry flag* (CF), the *parity flag* (PF), the *auxiliary carry flag* (AF), the *zero flag* (ZF), the *sign flag* (SF), and the *overflow flag* (OF).

The *status flags* indicate conditions that are produced as the result of executing an arithmetic or logic instruction. That is, specific flag bits are reset (logic 0) or set (logic 1) at the completion of execution of the instruction.

Let us first summarize the operation of these status flags.

1. The *carry flag* (CF): CF is set if there is a carryout or a borrowin for the most significant bit of the result during the execution of an arithmetic instruction. Otherwise, CF is reset.

2. The *parity flag* (PF): PF is set if the result produced by the instruction has even parity, that is, if it contains an even number of bits at the 1 logic level. If parity is odd, PF is reset.

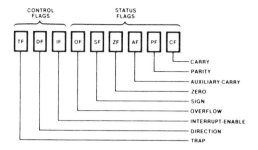

Figure 2.15   Status and control flags (Courtesy of Intel Corp.).

3. The *auxiliary carry flag* (AF): AF is set if there is a carryout from the low nibble into the high nibble or a borrow in from the high nibble into the low nibble of the lower byte in a 16-bit word. Otherwise, AF is reset.

4. The *zero flag* (ZF): ZF is set if the result of an arithmetic or logic operation is zero. Otherwise, ZF is reset.

5. The *sign flag* (SF): The MSB of the result is copied into SF. Thus SF is set if the result is a negative number or reset if it is positive.

6. The *overflow flag* (OF): When OF is set, it indicates that the signed result is out of range. If the result is not out of range, OF remains reset.

For example, at the completion of execution of a byte addition instruction, the carry flag (CF) could be set to indicate that the sum of the operands caused a carryout condition. The auxiliary carry flag (AF) could also be set due to the execution of the instruction. This depends on whether or not a carryout occurred from the least significant nibble to the most significant nibble when the byte operands are added. The sign flag (SF) is also affected and it will reflect the logic level of the MSB of the result.

The 8086 provides instructions within its instruction set which are able to use these flags to alter the sequence in which the program is executed. For instance, ZF equal to logic 1 could be tested as the condition that would initiate a jump to another part of the program.

The other three implemented flag bits are *control flags*. They are the *direction flag* (DF), the *interrupt enable flag* (IF), and the *trap flag* (TF). These three flags control functions of the 8086 as follows:

1. The *trap flag* (TF): If TF is set, the 8086 goes into the single-step mode. When in the single-step mode, it executes one instruction at a time. This type of operation is very useful for debugging programs.

2. The *interrupt flag* (IF): For the 8086 to recognize maskable interrupt requests at its INT input, the IF flag must be set. When IF is reset, requests at INT are ignored and the maskable interrupt interface is disabled.

3. The *direction flag* (DF): The logic level of DF determines the direction in which string operations will occur. When it is set, the string instruction automatically decrements the address. Therefore, the string data transfers proceed from high address to low address. On the other hand, resetting DF causes the string address

to be incremented. In this way, transfers proceed from low address to high address.

Bits CF, DF, IF, and TF of the flag register can be modified at any point in the program through user software. That is, special instructions are provided in the instruction set of the 8086 such that they can be set or cleared. For instance, at the beginning of an interrupt service routine, IF could be reset. This locks out the occurrence of another maskable interrupt. At the end of the service routine, it is set to enable the maskable interrupt interface.

2.9 SYSTEM CLOCK

The time base for synchronization of the internal and external operations of the 8086 microprocessor is provided by the CLK input signal. At present, the 8086 is available in three different speeds. The standard part operates at 5 MHz, the 8086-2 operates at 8 MHz, and the 8086-1 can be run at 10 MHz. CLK is externally generated by the 8284 clock generator and driver IC. Figure 2.16 is a block diagram of this device.

The normal way in which this clock chip is used is to connect a 15-MHz crystal between its X_1 and X_2 inputs. This circuit connection is shown in Fig. 2.17. Notice that a series capacitor C_L is also required. Its typical value when used with the 15-MHz crystal is 12pF. The *fundamental crystal frequency* is divided by 3 within the 8284 to give a 5-MHz clock signal. This signal is buffered and output at CLK. CLK can be directly connected to CLK of the 8086.

The waveform of CLK is shown in Fig. 2.18. Here we see that the signal is at

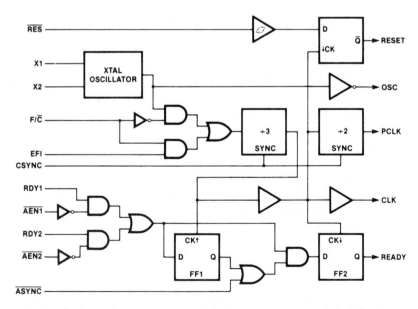

Figure 2.16 Block diagram of the 8284 clock generator (Courtesy of Intel Corp.).

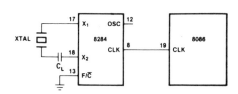

Figure 2.17 Connecting the 8284 to the 8086 (Courtesy of Intel Corp.).

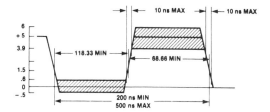

Figure 2.18 CLK voltage and timing characteristics (Courtesy of Intel Corp.).

MOS-compatible voltage levels and not TTL levels. Its minimum and maximum low logic levels are $V_{Lmin} = -0.5$ V and $V_{Lmax} = 0.6$ V, respectively. Moreover, the minimum and maximum high logic levels are $V_{Hmin} = 3.9$ V and $V_{Hmax} = V_{CC} + 1$ V, respectively. The *period* of the 5-MHz clock signal is 200 ns, and the maximum *rise* and *fall times* of its edges equal 10 ns.

In Fig. 2.16 we see that there are two more clock outputs on the 8284. They are *peripheral clock* (PCLK) and *oscillator clock* (OSC). These signals are provided to drive peripheral ICs. The clock signal output at PCLK is always half the frequency of CLK. That is, it is 2.5 MHz. Also, it is at TTL-compatible levels rather than MOS levels. On the other hand, the OSC output is at the fundamental clock frequency, which is three times that of CLK. These relationships are illustrated in Fig. 2.19.

The 8284 can also be driven from an external clock source. The external clock signal is applied to the *external frequency input* (EFI). Input F/C̄ is provided for clock source selection. When it is strapped to the 0 logic level, the crystal between X_1 and X_2 is used. On the other hand, applying logic 1 to F/C̄ selects EFI as the source of the clock. The *clock sync* (CSYNC) input can be used for external synchronization in systems that employ multiple clocks.

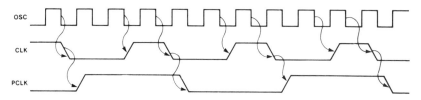

Figure 2.19 Relationship between CLK and PCLK (Courtesy of Intel Corp.).

2.10 BUS CYCLE

The *bus cycle* of the 8086 is used to access memory, I/O devices, or the interrupt controller. As shown in Fig. 2.20(a), it corresponds to a sequence of events that starts with an address being output on the system bus followed by a read or write data transfer. During these operations a series of control signals are also produced by the 8086 to control the direction and timing of the bus.

The bus cycle of the 8086 processor consists of at least four clock periods. These

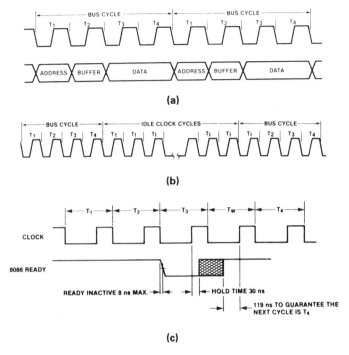

Figure 2.20 (a) Bus cycle clock periods (Courtesy of Intel Corp.); (b) bus cycle with idle states (Courtesy of Intel Corp.); (c) bus cycle with wait states (Courtesy of Intel Corp.).

four time states are called T_1, T_2, T_3, and T_4. During T_1, the BIU puts an address on the bus. For a write memory cycle, data are put on the bus during period T_2 and maintained through T_3, and T_4. When a read cycle is to be performed, the bus is first put in the high-Z state during T_2 and then the data to be read must be put on the bus during T_3 and T_4. These four clock states give a *bus cycle duration* of 125 ns $\times$ 4 = 500 ns in an 8-MHz 8086 system.

If no bus cycles are required, the BIU performs what are known as *idle states*. During these states no bus activity takes place. Each idle state is one clock period long and any number of them can be inserted between bus cycles. Figure 2.20(b) shows two bus cycles separated by idle states. Idle states are also performed if the queue is full and the EU does not require the BIU to read or write operands from memory.

Wait states can also be inserted into a bus cycle. This is done in response to a request by an event in external hardware instead of an internal event such as a full queue. In fact, the READY input of the 8086 is provided specifically for this purpose. Figure 2.20(c) shows that logic 0 at this input indicates that the current bus cycle should not be completed. As long as READY is held at the 0 level, wait states are inserted between periods T_3 and T_4 of the current bus cycle, and in the case of a write cycle, data that were on the bus during T_3 are maintained. The bus cycle is not completed until the external hardware returns READY back to the 1 logic level. This extends the duration of the bus cycle, thereby permitting the use of slower memory devices in the system.

During normal system operation, the 8086 fetches instructions one after the other from program memory and executes them. After an instruction is fetched it must be decoded within the 8086 and if necessary its operands read from either data memory or from internal registers. The operation specified in the instruction is performed on the operands and the results written back to either an internal register or a location in data memory. The 8086 is now ready to execute the next instruction.

Figure 2.21 shows in detail the overlapping of instruction fetch and execution by the 8086. Notice that as the EU is executing the previously fetched first instruction, the BIU fetches the second sequential instruction over the system bus. After this, a third instruction is fetched and put in the queue. During the third period, the second instruction is available at the output of the queue. It is extracted from the queue by the EU and executed. At the same time, the BIU uses the bus to write the result of the first instruction into memory. In the next period, a fourth instruction is fetched by the BIU and put into its queue. During the fifth period, an operand required by the third instruction is read over the bus. Finally, the third instruction is executed and a fifth instruction fetched. Notice that during this interval of time four new instructions were fetched and loaded into the queue and three instructions were executed.

An assembly language program and its equivalent 8086 machine code are shown

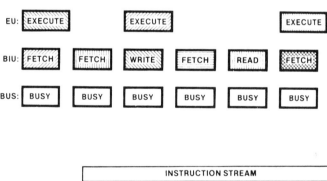

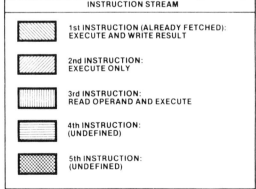

Figure 2.21   Overlapping instruction fetch and execution (Courtesy of Intel Corp.).

in Fig. 2.22(a). This program is a loop that executes repeatedly. Notice that the instructions are coded using one, two, three, or four bytes. For example, the instruction MOV AX,F802 is represented with the three bytes $B8_{16}$, 02_{16}, and $F8_{16}$. On the other hand, PUSH AX takes up just one byte, which is 50_{16}.

The program is stored in the code segment of memory as consecutive bytes as shown in Fig. 2.22(b). Notice that it takes 16 byte addresses to hold the complete program.

Remember that the queue status and bus status are output signals of the maximum-mode 8086. QS_1QS_0 identifies the instruction queue status initiated by the EU during the previous clock period. Moreover, the code at $\overline{S_2}\overline{S_1}\overline{S_0}$ tells an external 8288 bus controller which type of bus cycle is currently in progress.

Also remember that the interaction between the BIU and EU is by way of the queue for prefetched instruction opcodes and immediate operands. On the other hand, bus cycles must be requested of the BIU by the EU for accessing data operands in memory.

Figure 2.22(c) shows in detail the relationships between signals, bus activity, and internal queue status that are important to understand the instruction execution sequence of the 8086. This diagram includes the clock periods (CLK), bus status codes ($\overline{S_2}\overline{S_1}\overline{S_0}$), types of bus cycle (BIU activity), contents of the queue (QUEUE), queue status codes (QS_1QS_0), and instruction execution cycle (EU instruction execution).

Let us now trace the operation of the 8086 step by step through the execution of an instruction from the program in Fig. 2.22(a). In this example we will assume that

ASSEMBLY LANGUAGE	MACHINE CODE
MOV AX, 0F802H	B802F8
PUSH AX	50
MOV CX, BX	8BCB
MOV DX, CX	8BD1
ADD AX, [SI]	0304
ADD SI, 8086H	81C68680
JMP $ −14	EBF0

(a)

B8
02
F8
50
8B
CB
8B
D1
03
04
81
C6
86
80
EB
F0

(b)

Figure 2.22 (a) Example program (Courtesy of Intel Corp.); (b) code storage in memory (Courtesy of Intel Corp.); (c) execution sequence (Courtesy of Intel Corp.).

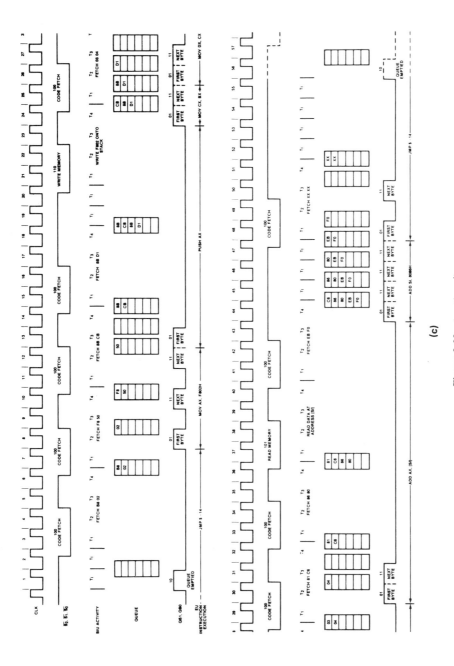

Figure 2.22 (continued)

(c)

39

the jump instruction JMP -14 has already been read out of the queue by the EU. Therefore, during clock periods 1 through 7 the EU is performing this operation. At clock period 1 in Fig. 2.22(c), we see that the queue has been initialized and contains no valid opcodes. Therefore, during this period, queue status $QS_1QS_0 = 10$ is output. This indicates that the queue is empty. Moreover, the bus is idle (TI) for clock periods 1 and 2.

The next four clock periods, 3 through 6, represent a code fetch bus cycle. Notice that the bus activity identifies the four clock periods T_1 through T_4 of a read bus cycle. During this bus cycle, $B802_{16}$ is fetched from program storage memory and loaded into the queue. The code fetch status code $\bar{S}_2S_1S_0 = 100$ is output by the 8086 during periods T_1 and T_2 of the bus cycle.

The next four clock periods, 7 through 10, represent another read bus cycle. This cycle corresponds to the fetch of $F850_{16}$ and its placement in the queue. But at the same time, the EU reads the first two bytes of the MOV instruction from the queue. The first byte, which is $B8_{16}$, is accompanied by the first byte queue status code, $QS_1QS_0 = 01$, and the second byte, 02_{16}, is accompanied by the $QS_1QS_0 = 11$ status code. Remember that this is a three-byte instruction and the last byte, which is $F8_{16}$, was just fetched into the queue. At the end of this second instruction fetch bus cycle, we find that just two bytes, $F8_{16}$ and 50_{16}, remain in the queue. They represent the last byte of the MOV instruction and the complete PUSH instruction.

During clock periods 11 through 14, another code fetch bus cycle takes place. Moreover, during the first half of the bus cycle, the EU removes the third byte of the MOV instruction from the queue. This completes execution of the MOV AX,0F802H instruction. Execution of the remaining instructions proceeds in a similar way.

ASSIGNMENT

Section 2.2

1. Name the technology used to fabricate the 8086 microprocessor.
2. What is the transistor count of the 8086?
3. Which pin is used as the NMI input?
4. Which pin provides the $\overline{BHE}$, and S_7 output signals?
5. How much memory can the 8086 directly address?
6. How large is the I/O address space of the 8086?

Section 2.3

7. How is minimum or maximum mode of operation selected?
8. Describe the difference between the minimum-mode 8086 system and maximum-mode 8086 system.
9. What output function is performed by pin 29 when in the minimum mode? Maximum mode?
10. What type signal is $M/\overline{IO}$?

Section 2.4

11. What are the word lengths of the 8086's address bus and data bus?

12. Does the 8086 have a multiplexed address/data bus or independent address and data buses?

13. What mnemonic is used to identify the least significant bit of the address bus? The most significant bit of the data bus?

14. What does status code $S_4S_3 = 01$ mean in terms of the memory segment being accessed?

15. Which output is used to signal external circuitry that a byte of data is available on the upper half of the data bus?

16. What does the logic level on $\overline{M/IO}$, signal to external circuitry?

17. Which output is used to signal external circuitry that valid data is on the bus during a write cycle?

18. What signal does a minimum-mode 8086 respond with when it acknowledges an active interrupt request?

19. Which signals implement the DMA interface?

20. List the signals that go to the high-Z state in response to a DMA request.

Section 2.5

21. Identify the signal lines of the 8086 that are different for the minimum-mode and maximum-mode interfaces.

22. What status outputs of the 8086 are input to the 8288?

23. What maximum-mode control signals are generated by the 8288?

24. What function is served by the 8289 in a maximum-mode 8086 microcomputer system?

25. What status code is output by the 8086 to the 8288 if a memory read bus cycle is taking place?

26. What command output becomes active if the status inputs of the 8288 are 100_2?

27. If the 8086 executes a jump instruction, what queue status code would be output?

28. Which pins provide signals for local bus control in a maximum-mode 8086 system?

Section 2.6

29. What is the range of power supply voltage over which the 8086 is guaranteed to work correctly?

30. What is the maximum value of voltage that could be output as a valid logic 0 at bit D_0 of the data bus? Assume that the output is sinking 2.5 mA.

31. What is the minimum value of voltage that would represent a valid logic 1 at the INTR input?

Section 2.7

32. Name the two internal processing units of the 8086.

33. How large is the instruction stream queue?

34. List three functions performed by the BIU.

35. Describe the function performed by the EU.

Section 2.8

36. Make a list of the general-purpose data registers of the 8086 and specify their lengths.

37. What dedicated word-wide operations are assigned to the data registers?

38. What is the difference between an instruction pointer and a program counter?

39. Identify the pointer and index registers of the 8086. In what way are they different from the data registers?

40. What segment registers are provided in the 8086? State the function of each segment register.

41. What is the difference between the functions of status and control flags? Make a list of the status and control flags provided in the 8086. Describe the function of each.

42. If a borrow occurs during the execution of a word subtraction instruction, what is the state of CF at completion of the operation?

43. To what value must IF be set to enable the maskable interrupt interface?

Section 2.9

44. What speed 8086s are available today?

45. What frequency crystal must be connected between the X_1 and X_2 inputs of the clock generator if an 8086-2 is to run at full speed?

46. What clock outputs are produced by the 8284? What would be their frequencies if a 30 MHz crystal is used?

47. What are the logic levels of the clock waveforms applied to the 8086?

Section 2.10

48. How many clock states are in an 8086 bus cycle that has no wait states? How are these states denoted?

49. What is the duration of the bus cycle for an 8086-1 that is running at full speed and with no wait states?

50. What is an idle state?

51. What is a wait state?

52. If an 8086 running at 10 MHz performs bus cycles with two wait states, what is the duration of the bus cycle?

Section 2.11

53. Explain why and how the execution time of the current instruction can get affected by the previous instruction.

Chapter 3

8086 Microprocessor Programming 1

3.1 INTRODUCTION

Chapter 2 was devoted to the general architectural aspects of the 8086 microprocessor. In this chapter we introduce a large part of its instruction set. These instructions provide the ability to write simple straight-line programs. Chapter 4 covers the rest of the instruction set and some more sophisticated programming concepts. The following topics are presented in this chapter.

1. Software model of the 8086 microprocessor
2. Software—the microcomputer program
3. The 8086 addressing modes
4. The 8086 instruction set
5. Data transfer instructions
6. Arithmetic instructions
7. Logic instructions
8. Shift instructions
9. Rotate instructions

3.2 SOFTWARE MODEL OF THE 8086 MICROPROCESSOR

The purpose of developing a *software model* is to aid the programmer in understanding the operation of the microcomputer system from a software point of view. To be able to program a microprocessor, one does not need to know all of its hardware features.

For instance, we do not necessarily need to know the function of the signals at its various pins, their electrical connections, or their switching characteristics. Moreover, the function, interconnection, and operation of the internal circuits of the microprocessor also need not normally be considered.

What is important to the programmer is to know the various registers within the device and to understand their purpose, functions, and operating capabilities and limitations. Furthermore, it is essential to know how external memory is organized and how it is addressed to obtain instructions and data.

The software architecture of the 8086 is illustrated with the model in Fig. 3.1. Looking at the model, we see that it includes the 13 internal registers and flags of the 8086 and 1M byte of external memory. Our concern here is with what can be done with this architecture and how to do it through software. For this purpose, let us review briefly the elements of the model. Moreover, this time we concentrate on their relationship to software.

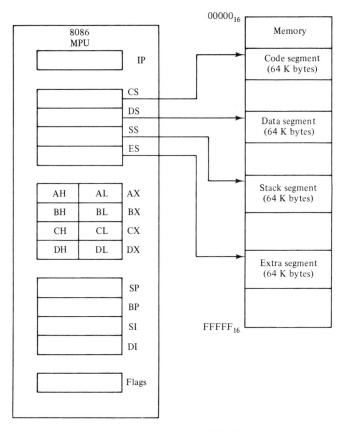

Figure 3.1 Software model of the 8086 microprocessor.

Memory Structure and the Segment Registers

As shown in Fig. 3.1, the 8086 microprocessor supports 1M byte of external memory. This memory space is organized as bytes over the address range 00000_{16} to $FFFFF_{16}$. From an addressing point of view, even- or odd-addressed bytes of data can be independently accessed. Information in the form of 16-bit words can also be stored and accessed. For words of data, the most significant byte is stored at the higher byte address and the least significant byte at the lower byte address.

Notice in Fig. 3.1 that just four 64K-byte segments of memory are active at a time. These segments are called the *code segment, stack segment, data segment,* and *extra segment.* Instructions and data operands in these segments are referenced with the help of the 16-bit segment registers CS, SS, DS, and ES that are located within the microprocessor. Each of these registers contains a 16-bit base address that is used in the generation of the physical memory address that points to the start of the corresponding segment in memory. For example, the code segment register (CS) points to the lowest-addressed location in the current code segment. It is this segment of memory that contains instructions of the program.

The offset of the next instruction that is to be fetched from the current code segment is identified by instruction pointer IP. That is, the contents of CS and IP are combined to form the 20-bit address of the next instruction. After the instruction is fetched, IP is incremented such that it points to the next sequential instruction.

The data segment register (DS) points to the segment of memory in which data to be processed are typically stored. The locations of this segment can be accessed by instructions for use as source or destination operands.

The programmer has the ability to change the values in the segment registers under software control. For example, a new data segment can be established by simply changing the value in DS. This can be done by executing just one or two instructions.

The Data Registers

The data registers consist of four 16-bit registers called AX, BX, CX, and DX. Each of these registers is addressable as a whole for 16-bit operations or as two 8-bit registers to handle byte operations. For instance, the register AX is a 16-bit register for word operations. But for byte operations, it is considered as two separate 8-bit registers, AH for the high byte and AL for the low byte. In a similar way, word registers BX, CX, and DX are also addressable as byte-wide register pairs BH,BL, CH,CL and DH,DL.

The registers in this group are known as the *accumulator register* (AX or AH,AL), *base register* (BX or BH,BL), *count register* (CX or CH,CL) and the *data register* (DX or DH,DL). These names imply special functions that are performed by each register.

Each of the four data registers can be used as the source or destination of an operand during an arithmetic, logic, shift, or rotate operation. The use of the accumulator register is also assumed by some instructions. For example, it is either the source or destination register for data during all I/O-mapped input and output operations. Furthermore, multiplication and division arithmetic operations, translate-table operations, and string operations also always use part or whole of the AX register.

During the execution of instructions using what is called the *based addressing mode,* base register BX is used as a pointer to an operand in the current data segment. Thus it contains a memory offset address, not a source or destination operand.

The count register gets its name from the fact that it is used as a counter by some instructions. For instance, its lower byte, CL, contains the count of the number of bits by which the contents of the operand must be rotated or shifted by multiple-bit rotate or shift instructions. It is also used as a counter by string and loop instructions.

The data register, DX, is used in all multiplication and division operations. It must also contain an input/output port address for some types of input/output operations.

Pointer and Index Registers

The next group of four registers consists of two pointer and two index registers. The two pointer registers are the *stack pointer* (SP) and *base pointer* (BP). The contents of the stack pointer are used as an offset from the current value of SS during the execution of instructions that involve the stack segment in external memory. It identifies the location of the top of the stack in the current stack segment. The value in SP is automatically incremented or decremented, respectively, whenever a POP or a PUSH instruction is executed.

The base pointer also contains an offset address into the current stack segment. This offset address is employed when using the based addressing mode and is commonly used by instructions in a subroutine that reference parameters that were passed by way of the stack.

The *source index register* (SI) and the *destination index register* (DI) are used to hold offset addresses for use in indexed addressing of operands in memory. In instructions that use the indexed type of addressing, the source index is generally with reference to the current data segment, and the destination index is with reference to the current extra segment.

The index registers can also be used as source or destination registers in arithmetic and logical operations. Unlike the data registers, these registers must always be used for 16-bit information and cannot be accessed as two separate bytes.

Flags

The 8086 microprocessor also contains nine 1-bit flags. These flags, identified in Chapter 2, are CF, PF, AF, ZF, SF, TF, IF, DF, and OF. The states of most of these flags reflect the result of the instruction just executed. Specifically, these are the carry, auxiliary carry, zero, sign, parity, and overflow flags. These flag bits can be tested under software control to determine the sequence in which the program should be executed.

The rest of the flags control operating features of the 8086. For instance, the logic level of DF determines whether the contents of the count register are to be incremented or decremented during string operations. Similarly, the flags IF and TF are used to enable/disable interrupts and the single-step mode of operation, respectively. The instruction set of the 8086 includes instructions for saving, loading, and manipulating these flags.

Data Types

Data are stored in the memory of the 8086 microcomputer in one of three fundamental data formats: the byte (8 bits), word (16 bits), or double word (32 bits). As shown in Fig. 3.2, these basic formats represent data elements that span one, two, or four consecutive bytes of memory, respectively.

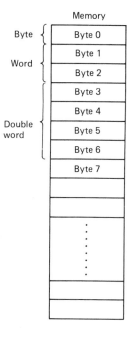

Figure 3.2 Byte, word, and double-word data organization.

The 8086 microprocessor can directly process data expressed in a number of different data types. Let us begin with the *integer data type*. The 8086 can process data as either *unsigned* or *signed* integer numbers; each type of integer can be either byte-wide or word-wide. Figure 3.3(a) represents an *unsigned byte integer*. This data type can be

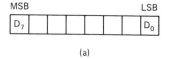

(a)

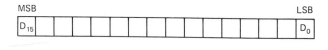

(b)

Figure 3.3 (a) Unsigned byte integer; (b) unsigned word integer.

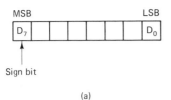

(a)

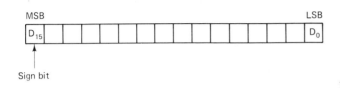

(b)

Figure 3.4 (a) Signed byte integer; (b) signed word integer.

used to represent decimal numbers in the range 0 through 255. The *unsigned word integer* is shown in Fig. 3.3(b). It can be used to represent decimal numbers in the range 0 through 65,535.

The *signed byte integer* and *signed word integer* of Figs. 3.4(a) and (b) are similar to the unsigned integer data types just introduced; however, here the most significant

Decimal	BCD
0	0000
1	0001
2	0010
3	0011
4	0100
5	0101
6	0110
7	0111
8	1000
9	1001

(a)

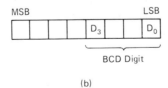

(b)

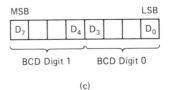

(c)

Figure 3.5 (a) BCD numbers; (b) unpacked BCD byte; (c) packed BCD digits.

bit is a sign bit. A 0 in the MSB position identifies a positive number. For this reason, signed integers can represent decimal numbers in the ranges $+127$ to -128 and $+32767$ to -32768, respectively. For example $+3$ is expressed as 00000011 (03_{16}). On the other hand, the 8086 represents negative numbers in 2's-complement notation. Therefore, -3 is coded as 11111101 (FD_{16}).

The 8086 can also process data that is coded as *BCD numbers*. Figure 3.5(a) lists the BCD values for decimal numbers 0 through 9. BCD data can be stored in either unpacked or packed form. For instance, the *unpacked BCD byte* in Fig. 3.5(b) shows that a single BCD digit is stored in the four least significant bits, and the upper four

b_7		0	0	0	0	1	1	1	1
b_6		0	0	1	1	0	0	1	1
b_5		0	1	0	1	0	1	0	1
$b_4\,b_3\,b_2\,b_1$ $\diagdown$ $\frac{H_1}{H_0}$		0	1	2	3	4	5	6	7
0 0 0 0	0	NUL	DLE	SP	0	@	P	'	p
0 0 0 1	1	SOH	DC1	!	1	A	Q	a	q
0 0 1 0	2	STX	DC2	''	2	B	R	b	r
0 0 1 1	3	ETX	DC3	#	3	C	S	c	s
0 1 0 0	4	EOT	DC4	$	4	D	T	d	t
0 1 0 1	5	ENQ	NAK	%	5	E	U	e	u
0 1 1 0	6	ACK	SYN	&	6	F	V	f	v
0 1 1 1	7	BEL	ETB	'	7	G	W	g	w
1 0 0 0	8	BS	CAN	(	8	H	X	h	x
1 0 0 1	9	HT	EM	)	9	I	Y	i	y
1 0 1 0	A	LF	SUB	*	:	J	Z	j	z
1 0 1 1	B	$\vee$	ESC	+	;	K	[	k	}
1 1 0 0	C	FF	FS	,	<	L	\	l	|
1 1 0 1	D	CR	GS	–	=	M	]	m	{
1 1 1 0	E	SO	RS	.	>	N	$\wedge$	n	~
1 1 1 1	F	SI	US	/	?	O	-	o	DEL

(a)

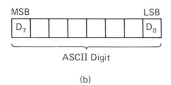

(b)

Figure 3.6 (a) ASCII table; (b) ASCII number.

bits are set to 0. Figure 3.5(c) shows a byte with packed BCD digits. Here we find two BCD numbers stored in a byte. The upper four bits represent the most significant digit of a two-digit BCD number.

Information expressed in *ASCII (American Standard Code for Information Interchange)* can also be directly processed by the 8086 microprocessor. Figure 3.6(a) shows how numbers, letters, and control characters are coded in ASCII. For instance, the number 5 is coded as

$$H_1 H_0 = 00110101 = 35H$$

As shown in Fig. 3.6(b), ASCII numbers are stored one number per byte.

3.3 SOFTWARE—THE MICROCOMPUTER PROGRAM

In Section 3.2, we described the software model of the 8086 microprocessor and the software functions of the internal registers. This leads us to the topic of *software*. Software is a general name used to refer to a variety of programs that can be run by a microcomputer. Examples are *languages, operating systems, application programs,* and *diagnostics.*

The native language of the 8086 microprocessor is *machine language.* Programs must always be coded in this machine language before they can be executed by the 8086. The 8086 microprocessor understands and performs operations for many instructions. When expressed in machine code, an instruction is encoded using 0s and 1s. A single machine instruction takes up one or more bytes of code.

Even though the 8086 understands only machine code, it is almost impossible to write programs directly in machine language. For this reason, programs are normally written in other languages, such as *8086 assembler* or a high-level language such as *C.*

In 8086 assembly language each of the *instructions* that can be performed by the 8086 microprocessor is described with alphanumeric symbols instead of with 0s and 1s. In a program, each instruction is represented by one *assembly language statement.* This statement must specify which operation is to be performed and what data operands are to be processed. For this reason, an instruction can be divided into two parts: its *opcode* and its *operands.* The opcode is the part of the instruction that identifies the operation that is to be performed. For example, typical operations are add, subtract, and move. Each opcode is assigned a unique letter combination called a *mnemonic.* The mnemonics for the just-mentioned operations are ADD, SUB, and MOV. Operands identify the data that are to be processed as the microprocessor carries out the operation specified by the opcode.

An example of an instruction written in 8086 assembly language is

ADD   AX, BX

This instruction says, "Add the contents of BX and AX together and put the sum in AX." AX is called the *destination operand* because it is the place where the result ends up; BX is called the *source operand.*

Another example of an assembly language statement is

```
START:    MOV   AX,BX     ; COPY BX INTO AX
```

This statement begins with the word START:. It is an address identifier for the instruction MOV AX,BX. This type of identifier is called a *label* or *tag*. The instruction is followed by ;COPY BX INTO AX. This part of the statement is called a *comment*. Thus a general format for an assembly language statement is

```
LABEL    INSTRUCTION    COMMENT
```

Programs written in assembly language are referred to as *source code*. An example of a short 8086 assembly language program is shown in Fig. 3.7(a). The assembly language statements are located on the left. Frequently, comments describing the statements are included on the right. This type of documentation makes it easier for a program to be read and debugged.

Assembly language programs cannot be directly run on the 8086. They must still be converted to an equivalent machine language program for execution by the 8086. This conversion is automatically done by running the program through what is called an *assembler*. The machine language output produced by the assembler is called *object code*.

Figure 3.7(b) is the *listing* produced by assembling the assembly language source code in Fig. 3.7(a). Reading from left to right, this listing contains addresses of memory locations, the machine language instructions, the original assembly language statements, and comments. For example, the line

```
0013   8A 24          NXTPT:    MOV   AH,[SI]     ;Move a byte
```

shows that the assembly language instruction MOV AH,[SI] is encoded as 8A24 in machine language and that this 2-byte instruction is loaded into memory starting at address 0013_{16} and ending at address 0014_{16}. Note that for simplicity the machine language instructions are expressed in hexadecimal notation, not in binary.

Use of assembly language makes it easier to write a program. But notice that there is still a one-to-one relationship between assembly and machine language instructions.

High-level languages make writing programs even easier. In a language such as BASIC, high-level commands such as FOR, NEXT, and GO are provided. These commands no longer correspond to single machine language statements; in fact, they implement functions that may require many assembly language statements. Again, the statements must be converted to machine code before they can be run on the 8086. The program that converts high-level language statements to machine code instructions is called a *compiler*.

Some languages—for instance, BASIC—are not always compiled. Instead, *interpretive* versions of the language are available. When a program written in an interpretive form of BASIC is executed, each line of the program is interpreted just before it is

```
TITLE    BLOCK-MOVE PROGRAM

         PAGE    ,132

COMMENT *This program moves a block of specified number of bytes
         from one place to another place*

;Define constants used in this program

         N          =        16          ;Bytes to be moved
         BLK1ADDR=            100H        ;Source block offset address
         BLK2ADDR=            120H        ;Destination block offset addr
         DATASEGADDR=         1020H       ;Data segment start address


STACK_SEG        SEGMENT         STACK 'STACK'
                 DB              64 DUP(?)
STACK_SEG        ENDS


CODE_SEG         SEGMENT         'CODE'
BLOCK            PROC            FAR
         ASSUME  CS:CODE_SEG,SS:STACK_SEG

;To return to DEBUG program put return address on the stack

         PUSH    DS
         MOV     AX, 0
         PUSH    AX

;Set up the data segment address

         MOV     AX, DATASEGADDR
         MOV     DS, AX

;Set up the source and destination offset adresses

         MOV     SI, BLK1ADDR
         MOV     DI, BLK2ADDR

;Set up the count of bytes to be moved

         MOV     CX, N

                        (a)
```

Figure 3.7 (a) An example of an assembly language program; (b) assembled version of the example program.

;Copy source block to destination block

```
NXTPT:  MOV     AH, [SI]                ;Move a byte
        MOV     [DI], AH
        INC     SI                      ;Update pointers
        INC     DI
        DEC     CX                      ;Update byte counter
        JNZ     NXTPT                   ;Repeat for next byte
        RET                             ;Return to DEBUG program
BLOCK           ENDP
CODE_SEG        ENDS
        END     BLOCK                   ;End of program
```

(a)

```
                        TITLE    BLOCK-MOVE PROGRAM

                        PAGE     ,132

                        COMMENT  *This program moves a block of specified number of bytes
                                 from one place to another place*

                        ;Define constants used in this program

= 0010                          N         =       16              ;Bytes to be moved
= 0100                          BLK1ADDR=         100H            ;Source block offset address
= 0120                          BLK2ADDR=         120H            ;Destination block offset addr
= 1020                          DATASEGADDR=      1020H           ;Data segment start address

0000                    STACK_SEG        SEGMENT          STACK 'STACK'
0000      40 [                           DB               64 DUP(?)
            ??
                ]

0040                    STACK_SEG        ENDS

0000                    CODE_SEG         SEGMENT          'CODE'
0000                    BLOCK            PROC             FAR
                                 ASSUME  CS:CODE_SEG,SS:STACK_SEG
```

(b)

Figure 3.7   *(continued)*

Sec. 3.3   Software—The Microcomputer Program

```
                                    ;To return to DEBUG program put return address on the stack

0000  1E                                    PUSH    DS
0001  B8 0000                               MOV     AX, 0
0004  50                                    PUSH    AX

                                    ;Set up the data segment address

0005  B8 1020                               MOV     AX, DATASEGADDR
0008  8E D8                                 MOV     DS, AX

                                    ;Set up the source and destination offset adresses

000A  BE 0100                               MOV     SI, BLK1ADDR
000D  BF 0120                               MOV     DI, BLK2ADDR

                                    ;Set up the count of bytes to be moved

0010  B9 0010                               MOV     CX, N

                                    ;Copy source block to destination block

0013  8A 24                        NXTPT:   MOV     AH, [SI]        ;Move a byte
0015  88 25                                 MOV     [DI], AH
0017  46                                    INC     SI              ;Update pointers
0018  47                                    INC     DI
0019  49                                    DEC     CX              ;Update byte counter
001A  75 F7                                 JNZ     NXTPT           ;Repeat for next byte
```

(b)

The IBM Personal Computer MACRO Assembler 06-11-89   PAGE   1-2
BLOCK-MOVE PROGRAM

```
001C  CB                                    RET                     ;Return to DEBUG program
001D                                BLOCK   ENDP
001D                                CODE_SEG ENDS
                                            END     BLOCK           ;End of program
```

(c)

Figure 3.7 *(continued)*

Segments and groups:

N a m e	Size	align	combine	class
CODE_SEG	001D	PARA	NONE	'CODE'
STACK_SEG.	0040	PARA	STACK	'STACK'

Symbols:

N a m e	Type	Value	Attr	
BLK1ADDR	Number	0100		
BLK2ADDR	Number	0120		
BLOCK.	F PROC	0000	CODE_SEG	Length =001D
DATASEGADDR.	Number	1020		
N.	Number	0010		
NXTPT.	L NEAR	0013	CODE_SEG	

Warning	Severe
Errors	Errors
0	0

(c)

Figure 3.7 *(continued)*

executed and at that moment replaced with the corresponding machine language routine. It is this machine code routine that is executed by the microprocessor.

You may be asking why is it important to know how to program the 8086 in its assembly language if it is so much easier to write programs with a high-level language. Let us now answer this question.

We have just pointed out that if a program is written in a high-level language it must be compiled into machine code before it can be run on the 8086. The general way in which compilers must be designed usually results in inefficient machine code. That is, the quality of the machine code that is produced for the program depends on the quality of the compiler program in use. What is found is that a compiled machine code implementation of a program that was written in a high-level language results in many more machine language instructions than an assembled version of an equivalent hand-written assembly language program. This leads us to the two key benefits derived from writing programs in assembly language: first, the machine code program that is produced will take up less memory space than the compiled version of the program; second, it will execute faster.

Now we know the benefits attained by writing programs in assembly language, but we still do not know when these benefits are important. To be important, they must outweigh the additional effort that must be put into writing the program in assembly language instead of in a high-level language. One of the major uses of assembly language programming is in *real-time applications*. By *real time* we mean that the task required by the application must be completed before any other input to the program can occur that will alter its operation.

The *device service routine* that controls the operation of the floppy disk drive of a personal computer is a good example of the kind of program that is usually written in assembly language. This is because it is a segment of the program that must closely control hardware of the microcomputer in real time. In this case, a program that is written in a high-level language probably could not respond quickly enough to control the hardware, and even if it could, operations performed with the disk subsystem would be much slower. Some other examples of hardware-related operations typically performed by routines written in assembler are communication routines such as those that drive the display and printer and the I/O routine that scans the keyboard.

Assembly language is important not only for controlling hardware devices of the microcomputer system, but also for performing purely software operations. For instance, applications frequently require the microcomputer to search through a large table of data in memory looking for a special string of characters—for instance, a person's name. This type of operation can be easily performed by writing a program in a high-level language; however, for large tables of data the search will take very long. By implementing the search routine through assembly language, the performance of the search operation is greatly improved. Other examples of software operations that may require implemention with high-performance routines derived from assembly language are *code translations,* such as from ASCII to EBCDIC; *table sort* or *search routines,* such as a bubble sort; and *mathematical routines,* such as those for floating-point arithmetic.

Not all parts of an application require real-time performance. For this reason, it is a common practice for programs to contain routines developed through a high-level language as well as routines developed with assembly language. That is, assembler is used to code those parts of the application that must perform real-time operations; high-level language is used to write those parts that are not time critical. The machine-code obtained by assembling or compiling the two types of program segments are linked to form the final application program.

3.4 THE 8086 ADDRESSING MODES

When the 8086 executes an instruction, it performs the specified function on data. These data are called its *operands* and may be part of the instruction, reside in one of the internal registers of the 8086, stored at an address in memory, or held at an I/O port. To access these different types of operands, the 8086 is provided with various *addressing modes.* Here are the modes available on the 8086: *register addressing, immediate addressing, direct addressing, register indirect addressing, based addressing, indexed addressing, based indexed addressing, string addressing,* and *port addressing.*

Of these nine modes, all but register addressing and immediate addressing make reference to an operand stored in memory. Therefore, they require the BIU to initiate a read or write bus cycle to the memory subsystem. Thus the addressing modes provide different ways of computing the address of the operand that is output on the address bus during the bus cycle. Let us now consider in detail each of these addressing modes.

Register Addressing Mode

With the register addressing mode, the operand to be accessed is specified as residing in an internal register of the 8086. An example of an instruction that uses this addressing mode is

MOV AX, BX

This stands for move the contents of BX, the *source operand,* to AX, the *destination operand*. Both the source and destination operands have been specified as the contents of internal registers of the 8086.

Let us now look at the effect of executing the register addressing mode MOV instruction. In Fig. 3.8(a) we see the state of the 8086 just prior to fetching the instruc-

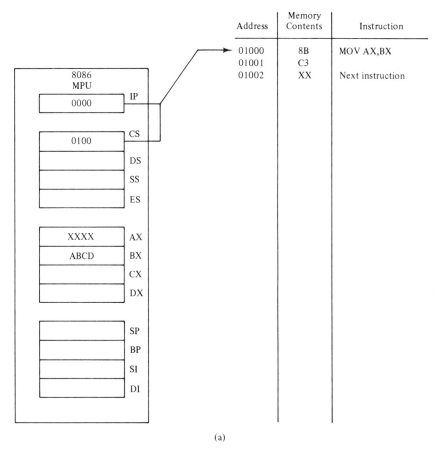

(a)

Figure 3.8 (a) Register addressing mode instruction before execution; (b) after execution.

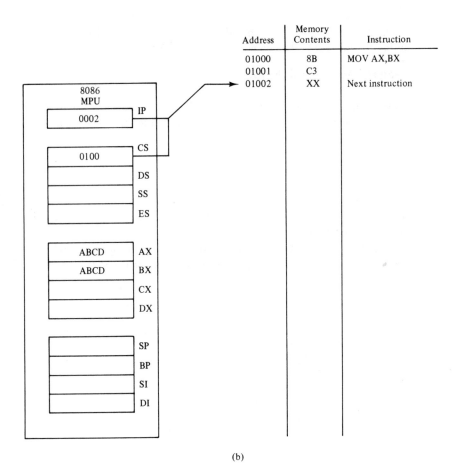

Address	Memory Contents	Instruction
01000	8B	MOV AX,BX
01001	C3	
01002	XX	Next instruction

(b)

Figure 3.8 *(continued)*

tion. Notice that IP and CS point to the MOV AX,BX instruction at address 01000_{16}. Prior to execution of this instruction, the contents of BX are $ABCD_{16}$ and the contents of AX represent a don't-care state. As shown in Fig. 3.8(b), the result of executing the instruction is that $ABCD_{16}$ is copied into AX.

Immediate Addressing Mode

If a source operand is part of the instruction instead of the contents of a register or memory location, it represents what is called an *immediate operand* and is accessed using the immediate addressing mode. Typically, immediate operands represent constant data.

Immediate operands can be either a byte or word of data. In the instruction

MOV AL, 15

the source operand 15_{16} is an example of a byte-wide immediate source operand. The destination operand, which is the contents of AL, uses register addressing. Thus this instruction employs both the immediate and register addressing modes.

Figure 3.9(a) and (b) illustrate fetch and execution of this instruction. Here we find that the immediate operand 15_{16} is stored in program storage memory in the byte location immediately following the opcode of the instruction. This value is also fetched into the instruction queue in the BIU. When the EU performs the MOV operation, the source operand is fetched from the instruction queue; therefore, no external memory bus cycle is initiated. The result of executing this instruction is that the immediate operand is loaded into the lower byte part (AL) of the accumulator register.

Direct Addressing Mode

Direct addressing differs from immediate addressing in that the locations following the instruction opcode hold an *effective memory address* (EA) instead of data. This effective address is a 16-bit offset of the storage location of the operand from the current value

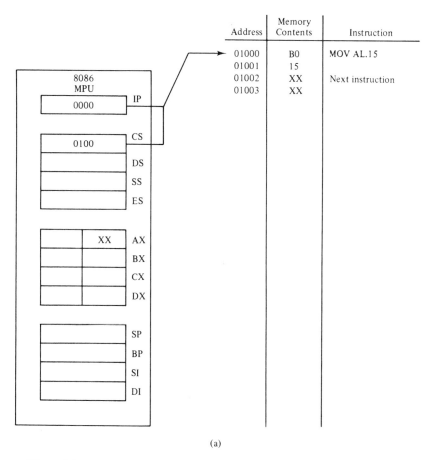

(a)

Figure 3.9 (a) Immediate addressing mode instruction before execution; (b) after execution.

Sec. 3.4   The 8086 Addressing Modes

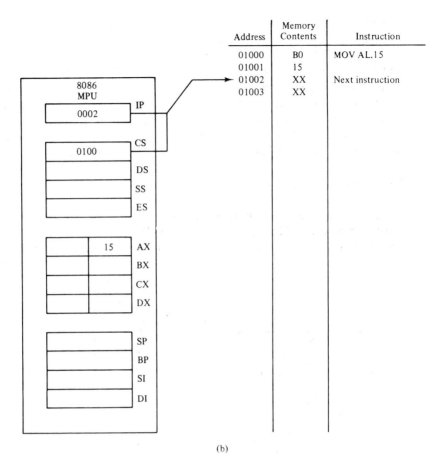

Address	Memory Contents	Instruction
01000	B0	MOV AL,15
01001	15	
01002	XX	Next instruction
01003	XX	

8086 MPU

IP 0002

CS 0100

DS

SS

ES

	15	AX
		BX
		CX
		DX

SP

BP

SI

DI

(b)

Figure 3.9 *(continued)*

in the data segment (DS) register. EA is combined with the contents of DS in the BIU to produce the *physical address* of the operand.

An example of an instruction that uses direct addressing for its source operand is

MOV CX, [BETA]

This stands for "move the contents of the memory location which is offset by BETA from the current value in DS into internal register CX."

In Fig. 3.10(a) we find that the value of the offset is stored in the two byte locations that follow the instruction. It is also known as the *displacement*. Notice that the value assigned to constant BETA is 1234_{16}.

Another way of writing the instruction is

MOV CX, [1234]

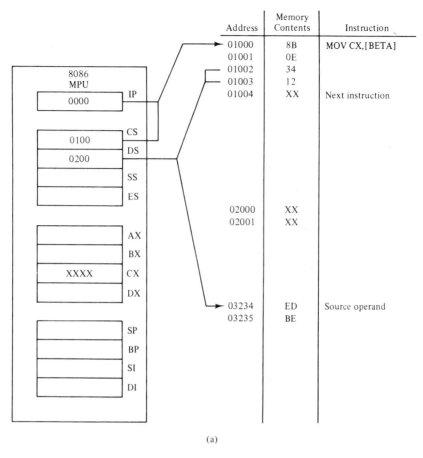

Address	Memory Contents	Instruction
01000	8B	MOV CX,[BETA]
01001	0E	
01002	34	
01003	12	
01004	XX	Next instruction
02000	XX	
02001	XX	
03234	ED	Source operand
03235	BE	

8086
MPU

0000	IP
0100	CS
0200	DS
	SS
	ES
	AX
	BX
XXXX	CX
	DX
	SP
	BP
	SI
	DI

(a)

Figure 3.10 (a) Direct addressing mode instruction before execution; (b) after execution.

As the instruction is executed, the BIU combines 1234_{16} with 0200_{16} to obtain the physical address of the source operand. This gives

$$PA = 02000_{16} + 1234_{16}$$

$$= 03234_{16}$$

Then it initiates an external memory bus cycle to read the word of data starting at this address. This value is $BEED_{16}$. The execution unit causes this value to be loaded in the CX register. This result is illustrated in Fig. 3.10(b).

Register Indirect Addressing Mode

Register indirect addressing is similar to direct addressing in that an effective address is combined with the contents of DS to obtain a physical address. However, it differs in the way the offset is specified. This time EA resides in either a pointer register or an

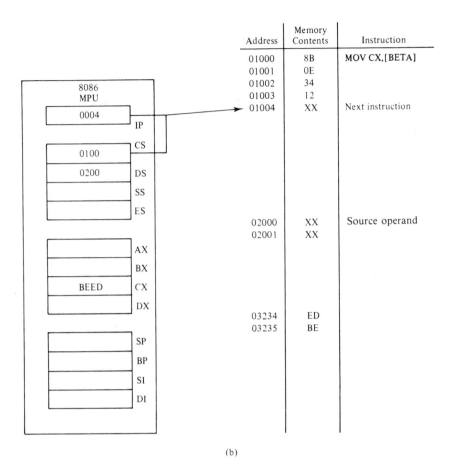

Address	Memory Contents	Instruction
01000	8B	MOV CX,[BETA]
01001	0E	
01002	34	
01003	12	
01004	XX	Next instruction
02000	XX	Source operand
02001	XX	
03234	ED	
03235	BE	

8086 MPU

0004   IP

CS   0100

0200   DS

SS

ES

AX

BX

BEED   CX

DX

SP

BP

SI

DI

(b)

Figure 3.10 *(continued)*

index register within the 8086. The pointer register can be either base register BX or base pointer register BP, and the index register can be source index register SI, or destination index register DI.

An example of an instruction that uses register indirect addressing is

MOV AX, [SI]

This instruction moves the contents of the memory location offset by the value of EA in SI from the current value in DS to the AX register.

For instance, as shown in Fig. 3.11(a) and (b), if SI contains 1234_{16} and DS contains 0200_{16}, the result produced by executing the instruction is that the contents of memory location

$$PA = 02000_{16} + 1234_{16}$$

$$= 03234_{16}$$

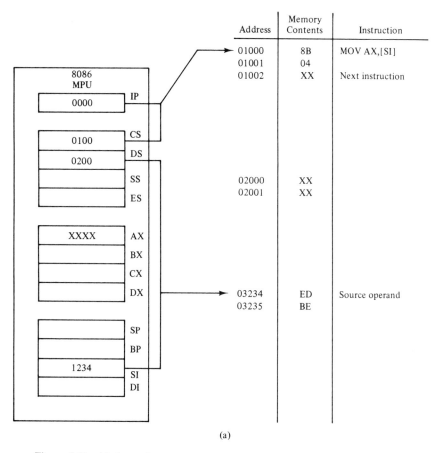

Address	Memory Contents	Instruction
01000	8B	MOV AX,[SI]
01001	04	
01002	XX	Next instruction
02000	XX	
02001	XX	
03234	ED	Source operand
03235	BE	

8086
MPU

0000	IP
0100	CS
0200	DS
	SS
	ES
XXXX	AX
	BX
	CX
	DX
	SP
	BP
1234	SI
	DI

(a)

Figure 3.11 (a) Instruction using register indirect addressing before execution; (b) after execution.

are moved to the AX register. Notice in Fig. 3.11(b) that this value is $BEED_{16}$. In this example, the value 1234_{16} that was found in the SI register must be loaded with another instruction prior to the MOV instruction.

Notice that the result produced by executing this instruction and the example for the direct addressing mode are the same. However, they differ in the way in which the physical address was generated. The direct addressing method lends itself to applications where the value of EA is a constant. On the other hand, register indirect addressing can be used when the value of EA is calculated and stored for example in SI by a previous instruction. That is, EA is a variable.

Based Addressing Mode

In the based addressing mode, the physical address of the operand is obtained by adding a direct or indirect displacement to the contents of either base register BX or base pointer register BP and the current value in DS and SS, respectively. A MOV instruc-

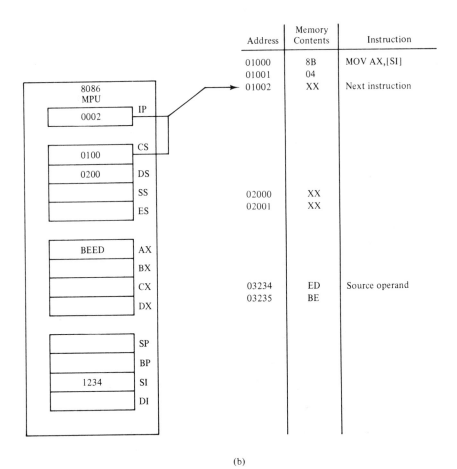

Address	Memory Contents	Instruction
01000	8B	MOV AX,[SI]
01001	04	
01002	XX	Next instruction
02000	XX	
02001	XX	
03234	ED	Source operand
03235	BE	

8086 MPU

0002	IP
0100	CS
0200	DS
	SS
	ES
BEED	AX
	BX
	CX
	DX
	SP
	BP
1234	SI
	DI

(b)

Figure 3.11 *(continued)*

tion that uses based addressing to specify the location of its destination operand is as follows:

$$\text{MOV } [BX].BETA, AL$$

This instruction uses base register BX and direct displacement BETA to derive the EA of the destination operand. The based addressing mode is implemented by specifying the base register in brackets followed by a period and the direct displacement. The source operand in this example is located in byte accumulator AL.

As shown in Fig. 3.12(a) and (b), the fetch and execution of this instruction causes the BIU to calculate the physical address of the destination operand from the contents of DS, BX, and the direct displacement. The result is

$$PA = 02000_{16} + 1000_{16} + 1234_{16}$$

$$= 04234_{16}$$

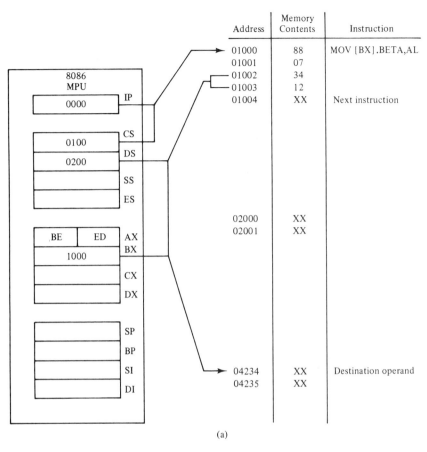

Address	Memory Contents	Instruction
01000	88	MOV [BX].BETA,AL
01001	07	
01002	34	
01003	12	
01004	XX	Next instruction
02000	XX	
02001	XX	
04234	XX	Destination operand
04235	XX	

(a)

Figure 3.12 (a) Instruction using direct base pointer addressing before execution; (b) after execution.

Then upon request of the EU it initiates a write bus cycle such that the source operand, AL, is written into the storage location at 04234_{16}. The result is that ED_{16} is copied into the destination memory location.

If BP is used instead of BX, the calculation of the physical address is performed using the contents of the stack segment (SS) register instead of DS. This permits access to data in the stack segment of memory.

Indexed Addressing Mode

Indexed addressing works identically to the based addressing we just described; however, it uses the contents of one of the index registers, instead of BX or BP, in the generation of the physical address. Here is an example.

```
MOV AL, ARRAY[SI]
```

The source operand has been specified using direct indexed addressing. Notice that the

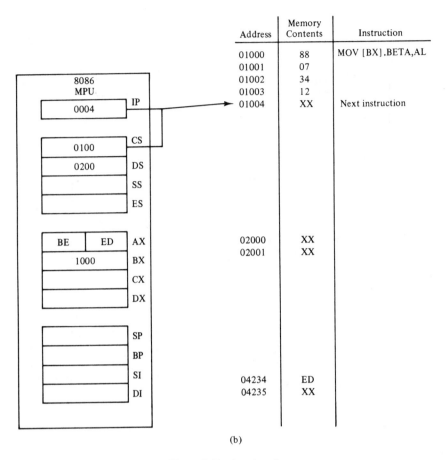

Address	Memory Contents	Instruction
01000	88	MOV [BX].BETA,AL
01001	07	
01002	34	
01003	12	
01004	XX	Next instruction
02000	XX	
02001	XX	
04234	ED	
04235	XX	

8086 MPU

	IP
0004	

	CS
0100	
0200	DS
	SS
	ES

BE	ED	AX
1000		BX
		CX
		DX

	SP
	BP
	SI
	DI

(b)

Figure 3.12 *(continued)*

notation this time is such that ARRAY, which is a direct displacement, prefixes the selected index register, SI. Just like for the base register in based addressing, the index register is enclosed in brackets.

The effective address is calculated as

$$EA = (SI) + ARRAY$$

and the physical address is obtained by combining the contents of DS with EA.

The example in Fig. 3.13(a) and (b) shows the result of executing the MOV instruction. First the physical address of the source operand is calculated from DS, SI, and the direct displacement.

$$PA = 02000_{16} + 2000_{16} + 1234_{16}$$

$$= 05234_{16}$$

Then the byte of data stored at this location, which is BE_{16}, is read into lower byte AL of the accumulator register.

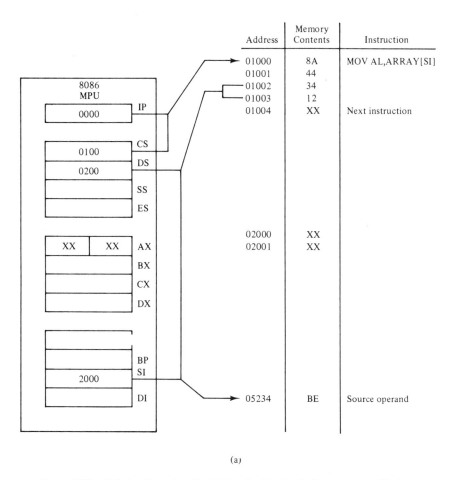

Address	Memory Contents	Instruction
01000	8A	MOV AL,ARRAY[SI]
01001	44	
01002	34	
01003	12	
01004	XX	Next instruction
02000	XX	
02001	XX	
05234	BE	Source operand

(a)

Figure 3.13 (a) Instruction using direct indexed addressing before execution; (b) after execution.

Based Indexed Addressing Mode

Combining the based addressing mode and the indexed addressing mode together results in a new, more powerful mode known as based indexed addressing. Let us consider an example of a MOV instruction using this type of addressing.

$$MOV \ AH, \ [BX].BETA[SI]$$

Notice that the source operand is accessed using based indexed addressing mode. Therefore, the effective address of the source operand is obtained as

$$EA = (BX) + BETA + (SI)$$

and the physical address of the operand from the current DS and the calculated EA.

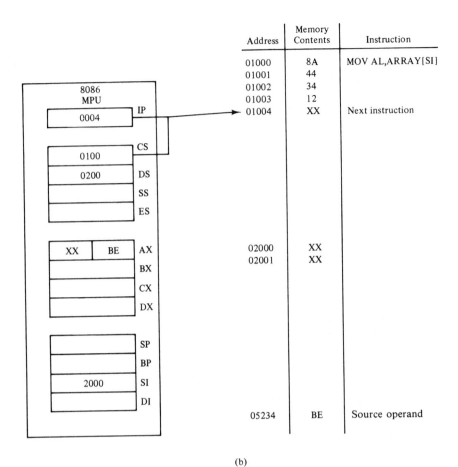

Address	Memory Contents	Instruction
01000	8A	MOV AL,ARRAY[SI]
01001	44	
01002	34	
01003	12	
01004	XX	Next instruction
02000	XX	
02001	XX	
05234	BE	Source operand

(b)

Figure 3.13 *(continued)*

An example of executing this instruction is illustrated in Fig. 3.14(a) and (b). The address of the source operand is calculated as

$$PA = 02000_{16} + 1000_{16} + 1234_{16} + 2000_{16}$$

$$= 6234_{16}$$

Execution of the instruction causes the value stored at this location to be written into AH.

String Addressing Mode

The string instructions of the 8086's instruction set automatically use the source and destination index registers to specify the effective addresses of the source and destination operands, respectively. The move string instruction

MOVS

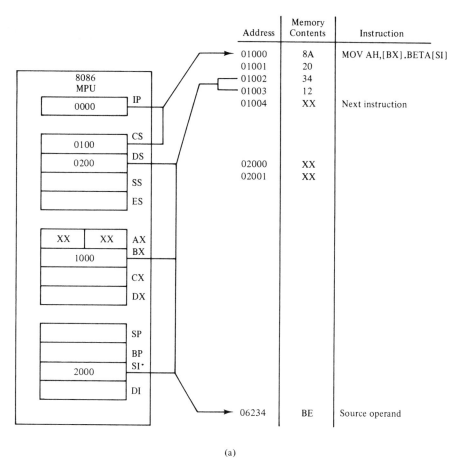

Address	Memory Contents	Instruction
01000	8A	MOV AH,[BX].BETA[SI]
01001	20	
01002	34	
01003	12	
01004	XX	Next instruction
02000	XX	
02001	XX	
06234	BE	Source operand

(a)

Figure 3.14 (a) Instruction using based indexed addressing before execution; (b) after execution.

is an example. Notice that neither SI nor DI appears in the string instruction, but both are used during its execution.

Port Addressing Mode

Port addressing is used in conjunction with the IN and OUT instructions to access input and output ports. Any of the memory addressing modes can be used for the port address for memory-mapped ports. For ports in the I/O address space, only the direct addressing mode and an indirect addressing mode using DX are available. For example, direct addressing of an input port is used in the instruction

IN AL, 15

This stands for "input the data from the byte wide input port at address 15_{16} of the I/O address space to register AL."

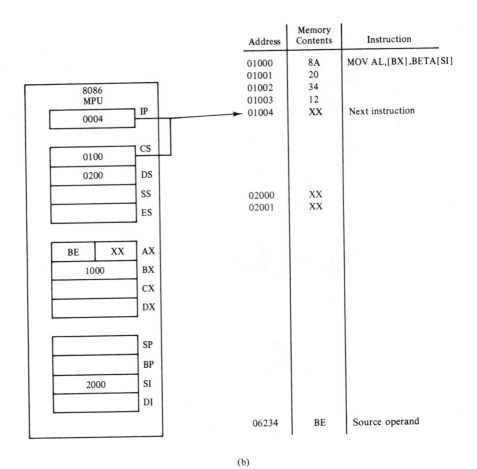

Address	Memory Contents	Instruction
01000	8A	MOV AL,[BX].BETA[SI]
01001	20	
01002	34	
01003	12	
01004	XX	Next instruction
02000	XX	
02001	XX	
06234	BE	Source operand

(b)

Figure 3.14 *(continued)*

Next, let us consider another example. Using indirect port addressing for the source operand in an IN instruction, we get

IN AL, DX

It means "input the data from the byte-wide input port whose address is specified by the contents of register DX." For instance, if (DX) equals 1234_{16}, the contents of the port at this I/O address are loaded into AL.

3.5 INSTRUCTION SET

Having introduced a software model and the various addressing modes of the 8086 microprocessor, we will now continue with its *instruction set*.

The 8086 microprocessor provides a powerful instruction set containing 117 basic instructions. The wide range of operands and addressing modes permitted for use with these instructions further expand the instruction set into many more instructions executable at the machine code level. For instance, the basic MOV instruction expands into 28 different machine-level instructions.

For the purpose of discussion, the instruction set will be divided into a number of groups of functionally related instructions. In this chapter we consider the data transfer instructions, arithmetic instructions, logic instructions, shift instructions, and rotate instructions. Advanced instructions such as those for program and processor control are described in Chapter 4.

3.6 DATA TRANSFER INSTRUCTIONS

The 8086 microprocessor has a group of *data transfer instructions* that are provided to move data either between its internal registers or between an internal register and a storage location in memory. This group includes the *move byte or word* (MOV) instruction, *exchange byte or word* (XCHG) instruction, *translate byte* (XLAT) instruction, *load effective address* (LEA) instruction, *load data segment* (LDS) instruction, and *load extra segment* (LES) instruction. These instructions are discussed in this section.

The MOV Instruction

The MOV instruction of Fig. 3.15(a) is used to transfer a byte or a word of data from a source operand to a destination operand. These operands can be internal registers of the 8086 and storage locations in memory. Figure 3.15(b) shows the valid source and destination operand variations. This large choice of operands results in many different MOV instructions. Looking at this list of operands, we see that data can be moved between registers, between a register and a segment register, between a register or segment register and memory, or between a memory location and the accumulator.

Notice that the MOV instruction cannot transfer data directly between a source and a destination that both reside in external memory. Instead, the data must first be moved from memory into an internal register, such as to the accumulator (AX), with one move instruction and then moved to the new location in memory with a second move instruction.

All transfers between data registers and memory can involve either a byte or word of data. The fact that the instruction corresponds to byte or word data is designated by the way in which its operands are specified. For instance, AL or AH would be used to specify a byte operand, and AX a word operand. On the other hand, data moved between one of the registers and a segment register or between a segment register and a memory location must always be word-wide.

In Fig. 3.15(a) we also find additional important information. For instance, flag bits within the 8086 are not modified by execution of a MOV instruction.

An example of a segment register to general-purpose register MOV instruction shown in Fig. 3.15(c) is

MOV DX, CS

Mnemonic	Meaning	Format	Operation	Flags Affected
MOV	Move	MOV D,S	(S) → (D)	None

(a)

Destination	Source
Memory	Accumulator
Accumulator	Memory
Register	Register
Register	Memory
Memory	Register
Register	Immediate
Memory	Immediate
Seg-reg	Reg16
Seg-reg	Mem16
Reg16	Seg-reg
Mem16	Seg-reg

(b)

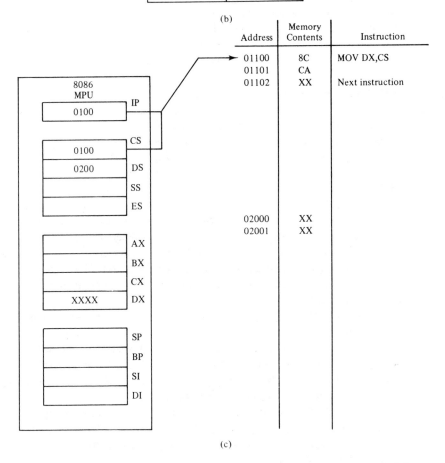

(c)

Figure 3.15 (a) MOV data transfer instructions; (b) allowed operands; (c) MOV DX, CS instruction before execution; (d) after execution.

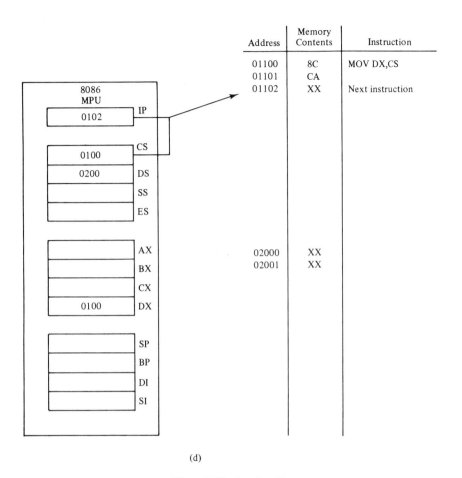

Address	Memory Contents	Instruction
01100	8C	MOV DX,CS
01101	CA	
01102	XX	Next instruction
02000	XX	
02001	XX	

8086
MPU

0102	IP
0100	CS
0200	DS
	SS
	ES

	AX
	BX
	CX
0100	DX

	SP
	BP
	DI
	SI

(d)

Figure 3.15 *(continued)*

In this instruction, the code segment register is the source operand and the data register is the destination. It stands for "move the contents of CS into DX." That is,

$$(CS) \rightarrow (DX)$$

For example, if the contents of CS are 0100_{16}, execution of the instruction MOV DX,CS as shown in Fig. 3.15(d) makes

$$(DX) = (CS) = 0100_{16}$$

In all memory reference MOV instructions, the machine code for the instruction includes an offset address relative to the contents of the data segment register. An example of this type of instruction is

```
MOV [SUM],AX
```

In this instruction, the memory location identified by the variable SUM is specified using direct addressing. That is, the value of the offset is included in the two byte locations that follow its opcode in program memory.

Let us assume that the contents of DS equals 0200_{16} and that SUM corresponds to a displacement of 1212_{16}; then this instruction means "move the contents of accumulator AX to the memory location offset by 1212_{16} from the starting location of the current data segment." The physical address of this location is obtained as

$$PA = 02000_{16} + 1212_{16} = 03212_{16}$$

Thus the effect of the instruction is

$$(AL) \rightarrow (\text{Memory location } 03212_{16})$$

$$(AH) \rightarrow (\text{Memory location } 03213_{16})$$

EXAMPLE 3.1

If the DS register contains 1234_{16}, what is the effect of executing the instruction

MOV CX, [ABCD]

SOLUTION Execution of this instruction has the following results.

$$((DS)0_{16} + ABCD_{16}) \rightarrow (CL)$$

$$((DS)0_{16} + ABCD_{16} + 1_{16}) \rightarrow (CH)$$

In other words, CL is loaded with the contents of memory location

$$12340_{16} + ABCD_{16} = 1CF0D_{16}$$

and CH is loaded with the contents of memory location

$$12340_{16} + ABCD_{16} + 1_{16} = 1CF0E_{16}$$

In Example 3.1, source operand $ABCD_{16}$ has been considered to be the direct address of a memory location. The question is why $ABCD_{16}$ does not represent immediate data that are to be loaded into CX. The answer to this question is given by how the 8086's assembler codes instructions. An immediate mode transfer with operand $ABCD_{16}$ is specified without brackets around ABCD. Therefore, the instruction would have to have been written as

MOV CX, ABCD

to represent an immediate data operand. The result produced by this instruction is

$$ABCD_{16} \rightarrow (CX)$$

The XCHG Instruction

In our study of the move instruction, we found that it could be used to copy the contents of a register or memory location into a register or contents of a memory location to a register. In all cases, the original contents of the source location are preserved and the original contents of the destination are destroyed. In some applications, it is required to interchange the contents of two registers. For instance, we might want to exchange the data in the AX and BX registers.

This could be done using multiple move instructions and storage of the data in a temporary register such as DX. However, to perform the exchange function more efficiently, a special instruction has been provided in the instruction set of the 8086. This is the exchange (XCHG) instruction. The format of the XCHG instruction and its allowed operands are shown in Fig. 3.16(a) and (b). Here we see that it can be used to swap data between two general-purpose registers or between a general-purpose register and a storage location in memory. In particular, it allows for the exchange of words of data between two of the general-purpose registers, including the pointers and index registers, and the accumulator (AX); exchange of a byte or word of data between two of the general-purpose registers.

Let us consider an example of an exchange between two internal registers. Here is a typical instruction.

$$\text{XCHG AX, DX}$$

Its execution by the 8086 swaps the contents of AX with that of DX. That is,

$$(\text{AX original}) \rightarrow (\text{DX})$$

$$(\text{DX original}) \rightarrow (\text{AX})$$

or

$$(\text{AX}) \longleftrightarrow (\text{DX})$$

EXAMPLE 3.2

For the data shown in Fig. 3.16(c), what is the result of executing the instruction

$$\text{XCHG [SUM], BX?}$$

SOLUTION Execution of this instruction performs the function

$$((\text{DS})0 + \text{SUM}) \longleftrightarrow (\text{BX})$$

In Fig. 3.16(c) we see that $(\text{DS}) = 0200_{16}$ and the direct address $\text{SUM} = 1234_{16}$. Therefore, the physical address is

$$\text{PA} = 02000_{16} + 1234_{16} = 03234_{16}$$

Notice that this location contains FF_{16} and the address that follows contains 00_{16}. Moreover, note that BL contains AA_{16} and and BH contains 11_{16}.

Execution of the instruction performs the following 16-bit swap.

$$(03234_{16}) \longleftrightarrow (\text{BL})$$

$$(03235_{16}) \longleftrightarrow (\text{BH})$$

As shown in Fig. 3.16(d), we get

$$(\text{BX}) = 00\text{FF}_{16}$$

$$(\text{SUM}) = 11\text{AA}_{16}$$

The XLAT Instruction

The translate (XLAT) instruction has been provided in the instruction set of the 8086 to simplify implementation of the lookup-table operation. This instruction is described in Fig. 3.17. When using XLAT, the contents of register BX represent the offset of the starting address of the *lookup table* from the beginning of the current data segment. Also the contents of AL represent the offset of the element to be accessed from the beginning of the lookup table. This 8-bit element address permits a table with up to 256 elements. The values in both of these registers must be initialized prior to execution of the XLAT instruction.

Execution of XLAT replaces the contents of AL by the contents of the accessed lookup-table location. The physical address of this element in the table is derived as

$$PA = (\text{DS})0 + (\text{BX}) + (\text{AL})$$

An example of the use of this instruction would be for software *code conversions:* for instance, an ASCII-to-EBCDIC conversion. This requires an EBCDIC table in memory. The individual EBCDIC codes are located in the table at element displacements (AL) equal to their equivalent ASCII character value. That is, the EBCDIC code $\text{B}1_{16}$ for letter A would be positioned at displacement 41_{16}, which equals ASCII A, from the start of the table. The start of this ASCII-to-EBCDIC table in the current data segment is identified by the contents of BX.

As an illustration of XLAT, let us assume that the contents of DS = 0300_{16}, BX = 0100_{16}, and AL = 0D_{16}. 0D_{16} represents the ASCII character CR (carriage return). Execution of XLAT replaces the contents of AL by the contents of the memory location given by

$$PA = (\text{DS})0 + (\text{BX}) + 0(\text{AL})$$

$$= 03000_{16} + 0100_{16} + 0\text{D}_{16}$$

$$= 0310\text{D}_{16}$$

Thus the execution can be described by

$$(0310\text{D}_{16}) \rightarrow (\text{AL})$$

Assuming that this memory location contains EBCDIC CR(52_{16}), this value is placed in AL.

$$(\text{AL}) = 52_{16}$$

Mnemonic	Meaning	Format	Operation	Flags Affected
XCHG	Exchange	XCHG D,S	(D) ↔ (S)	None

(a)

Destination	Source
Accumulator	Reg16
Memory	Register
Register	Register

(b)

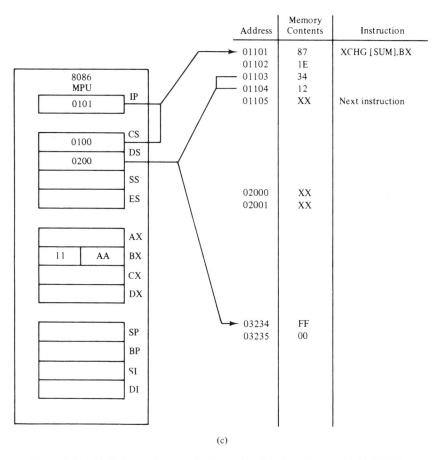

(c)

Figure 3.16 (a) Exchange data transfer instruction; (b) allowed operands; (c) XCHG [SUM], BX instruction before execution; (d) after execution.

Sec. 3.6   Data Transfer Instructions

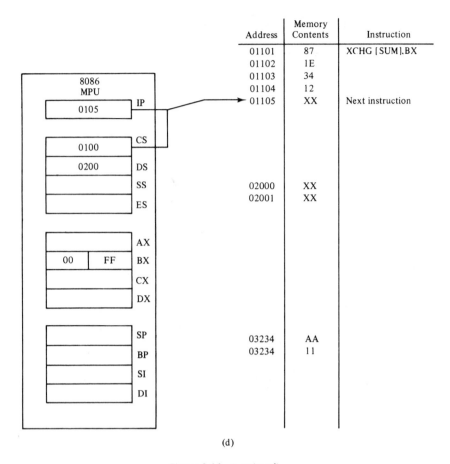

Address	Memory Contents	Instruction
01101	87	XCHG [SUM],BX
01102	1E	
01103	34	
01104	12	
01105	XX	Next instruction
02000	XX	
02001	XX	
03234	AA	
03234	11	

8086 MPU

IP 0105

CS 0100

DS 0200

SS

ES

AX

BX 00 FF

CX

DX

SP

BP

SI

DI

(d)

Figure 3.16 *(continued)*

Mnemonic	Meaning	Format	Operation	Flags Affected
XLAT	Translate	XLAT	$((AL) + (BX) + (DS)0) \rightarrow (AL)$	None

Figure 3.17 Translate data transfer instruction.

The LEA, LDS, and LES Instructions

Another type of data transfer operation that is important is to load a segment or general-purpose register with an address directly from memory. Special instructions are provided in the instruction set of the 8086 to give a programmer this capability. These instructions are described in Fig. 3.18(a). They are load register with effective address (LEA), load register and data segment register (LDS), and load register and extra segment register (LES).

Mnemonic	Meaning	Format	Operation	Flags Affected
LEA	Load effective address	LEA Reg 16,EA	EA → (Reg 16)	None
LDS	Load register and DS	LDS Reg16,Mem32	(Mem32) → (Reg16) (Mem32+2) → (DS)	None
LES	Load register and ES	LES Reg16,Mem32	(Mem32) → (Reg16) (Mem32+2) → (ES)	None

(a)

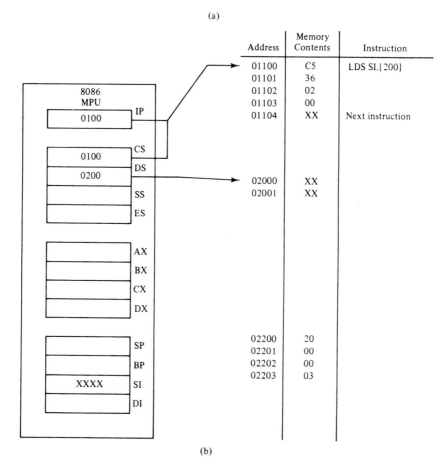

(b)

Figure 3.18 (a) LEA, LDS, and LES data transfer instructions; (b) LDS SI, [200] instruction before execution; (c) after execution.

Looking at Fig. 3.18(a), we see that these instructions provide the ability to manipulate memory addresses by loading a specific register with either a 16-bit offset address or a 16-bit offset address together with a 16-bit segment address into either DS or ES.

The LEA instruction is used to load a specified register with a 16-bit offset address. An example of this instruction is

        LEA SI, INPUT

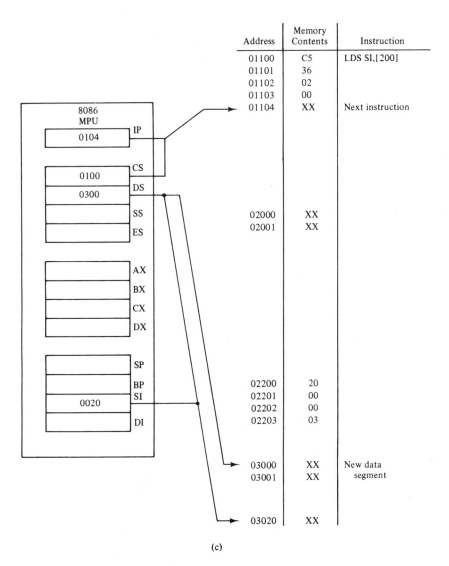

Address	Memory Contents	Instruction
01100	C5	LDS SI,[200]
01101	36	
01102	02	
01103	00	
01104	XX	Next instruction
02000	XX	
02001	XX	
02200	20	
02201	00	
02202	00	
02203	03	
03000	XX	New data
03001	XX	segment
03020	XX	

8086 MPU

IP 0104

CS 0100

DS 0300

SS

ES

AX

BX

CX

DX

SP

BP

SI 0020

DI

(c)

Figure 3.18 *(continued)*

When executed, it loads the SI register with an offset address value. The value of this offset is represented by the value of constant INPUT. INPUT is stored following the instruction opcode in program memory. This value is prefetched by the BIU; therefore, the instruction does not require any external bus cycles during its execution.

The other two instructions, LDS and LES, are similar to LEA except that they load the specified register as well as either the DS or the ES segment register.

EXAMPLE 3.3

Assuming that the 8086 is set up as shown in Fig. 3.18(b), what is the result of executing the instruction

$$\text{LDS} \quad \text{SI, [200]}$$

SOLUTION Execution of the instruction loads the SI register from the word location in memory whose offset address with respect to the current data segment is 200_{16}. Figure 3.18(b) shows that the contents of DS are 0200_{16}. This gives a physical address of

$$PA = 02000_{16} + 0200_{16} = 02200_{16}$$

It is the contents of this location and the one that follows that are loaded into SI. Therefore, in Fig. 3.18(c), we find that SI contains 0020_{16}. The next two bytes, that is, the contents of addresses 2202_{16} and 2203_{16}, are loaded into the DS register. As shown, this defines a new data segment starting at address 03000_{16}.

3.7 ARITHMETIC INSTRUCTIONS

The instruction set of the 8086 microprocessor contains an extensive complement of *arithmetic instructions*. They include instructions for the *addition, subtraction, multiplication,* and *division* operations. Moreover, these operations can be performed on numbers expressed in a variety of numeric data formats. They include: *unsigned or signed binary bytes or words, unpacked or packed decimal bytes,* or *ASCII numbers.* By ''packed decimal,'' we mean that two BCD digits are packed into a byte register or memory location. Unpacked decimal numbers are stored one BCD digit per byte. These decimal numbers are always unsigned. Moreover, ASCII numbers are expressed in ASCII code and stored one number per byte.

The status that results from the execution of an arithmetic instruction is recorded in the flags of the 8086. The flags that are affected by the arithmetic instructions are: carry flag (CF), auxiliary flag (AF), sign flag (SF), zero flag (ZF), parity flag (PF), and overflow flag (OF). Each of these flags was discussed in Chapter 2.

We will divide the arithmetic instructions into the subgroups shown in Fig. 3.19.

Addition Instructions—ADD, ADC, INC, AAA, and DAA

The form of each of the instructions in the *addition group* is shown in Fig. 3.20(a) and their allowed operand variations, for all but the INC instruction, are shown in Fig. 3.20(b). Let us begin by looking more closely at the *add* (ADD) instruction. Notice in Fig. 3.20(b) that it can be used to add an immediate operand to the contents of the accumulator, the contents of another register, or the contents of a storage location in memory. It also allows us to add the contents of two registers or the contents of a register and a memory location.

In general, the result of executing the instruction is expressed as

$$(S) + (D) \rightarrow (D)$$

Addition	
ADD	Add byte or word
ADC	Add byte or word with carry
INC	Increment byte or word by 1
AAA	ASCII adjust for addition
DAA	Decimal adjust for addition
Subtraction	
SUB	Subtract byte or word
SBB	Subtract byte or word with borrow
DEC	Decrement byte or word by 1
NEG	Negate byte or word
AAS	ASCII adjust for subtraction
DAS	Decimal adjust for subtraction
Multiplication	
MUL	Multiply byte or word unsigned
IMUL	Integer multiply byte or word
AAM	ASCII adjust for multiply
Division	
DIV	Divide byte or word unsigned
IDIV	Integer divide byte or word
AAD	ASCII adjust for division
CBW	Convert byte to word
CWD	Convert word to doubleword

Figure 3.19 Arithmetic instructions (Courtesy of Intel Corp.).

Mnemonic	Meaning	Format	Operation	Flags Affected
ADD	Addition	ADD D, S	$(S) + (D) \rightarrow (D)$ Carry $\rightarrow (CF)$	OF, SF, ZF, AF, PF, CF
ADC	Add with carry	ADC D, S	$(S) + (D) + (CF) \rightarrow (D)$ Carry $\rightarrow (CF)$	OF, SF, ZF, AF, PF, CF
INC	Increment by 1	INC D	$(D) + 1 \rightarrow (D)$	OF, SF, ZF, AF, PF
AAA	ASCII adjust for addition	AAA		AF, CF OF, SF, ZF, PF undefined
DAA	Decimal adjust for addition	DAA		SF, ZF, AF, PF, CF, OF, undefined

(a)

Destination	Source
Register	Register
Register	Memory
Memory	Register
Register	Immediate
Memory	Immediate
Accumulator	Immediate

(b)

Destination
Reg16
Reg8
Memory

(c)

Figure 3.20 (a) Addition arithmetic instructions; (b) allowed operands for ADD and ADC; (c) allowed operands for INC.

That is, the contents of the source operand are added to those of the destination operand and the sum that results is put into the location of the destination operand.

EXAMPLE 3.4

Assume that the AX and BX registers contain 1100_{16} and $0ABC_{16}$, respectively. What are the results of executing the instruction ADD AX,BX?

SOLUTION   Execution of the ADD instruction causes the contents of source operand BX to be added to the contents of destination register AX. This gives

$$(BX) + (AX) = 0ABC_{16} + 1100_{16} = 1BBC_{16}$$

This sum ends up in destination register AX.

$$(AX) = 1BBC_{16}$$

Execution of this instruction is illustrated in Fig. 3.21(a) and (b).

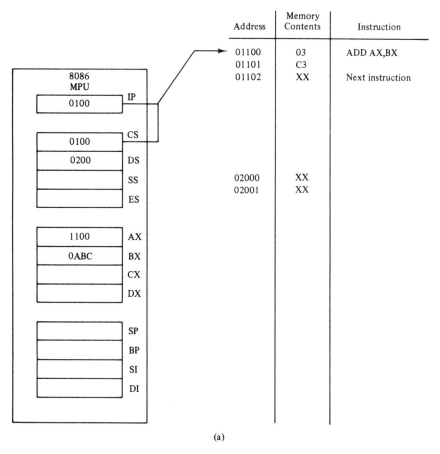

(a)

Figure 3.21   (a) ADD instruction before execution; (b) after execution.

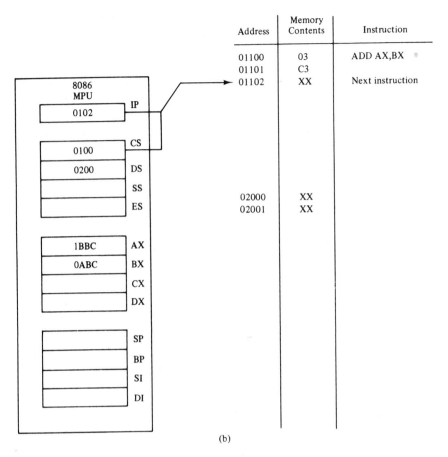

Address	Memory Contents	Instruction
01100	03	ADD AX,BX
01101	C3	
01102	XX	Next instruction
02000	XX	
02001	XX	

(b)

Figure 3.21 *(continued)*

The instruction *add with carry* (ADC) works similar to ADD. But in this case, the content of the carry flag is also added; that is,

$$(S) + (D) + (CF) \rightarrow (D)$$

The valid operand combinations are the same as those for the ADD instruction.

Another instruction that can be considered as part of the addition subgroup of arithmetic instructions is the *increment* (INC) instruction. As shown in Fig. 3.20(c), its operands can be the contents of a 16-bit internal register, an 8-bit internal register, or a storage location in memory. Execution of the INC instruction adds 1 to the specified operand. An example of an instruction that increments the high byte of AX is

```
INC AH
```

Looking at Fig. 3.20(a), we see that execution of any one of these three instructions affects all six of the flags mentioned earlier.

EXAMPLE 3.5

The original contents of AX, BL, memory location SUM, and carry flag (CF) are 1234_{16}, AB_{16}, $00CD_{16}$, and 0_{16}, respectively. Describe the results of executing the following sequence of instruction.

$$\text{ADD} \quad \text{AX, [SUM]}$$

$$\text{ADC} \quad \text{BL, 05}$$

$$\text{INC} \quad \text{[SUM]}$$

SOLUTION   By executing the first instruction, we add the word in the accumulator to the contents of the memory location identified as SUM. The result is placed in the accumulator. That is,

$$(AX) \leftarrow (AX) + (SUM)$$

$$= 1234_{16} + 00CD_{16} = 1301_{16}$$

The carry flag remains reset.

The second instruction adds the lower byte of the base register (BL), immediate operand 5_{16}, and the carry flag, which is 0_{16}. This gives

$$(BL) \leftarrow (BL) + IOP + (CF)$$

$$= AB_{16} + 5_{16} + 0_{16} = B0_{16}$$

Again CF stays reset.

The last instruction increments the contents of memory location SUM by 1. That is,

$$(SUM) \leftarrow (SUM) + 1_{16}$$

$$= 00CD_{16} + 1_{16} = 00CE_{16}$$

These results are summarized in Fig. 3.22.

Instruction	(AX)	(BL)	(SUM)	(CF)
Initial state	1234	AB	00CD	0
ADD AX,[SUM]	1301	AB	00CD	0
ADC BL,05	1301	B0	00CD	0
INC [SUM]	1301	B0	00CE	0

Figure 3.22   Results due to execution of arithmetic instruction.

The addition instructions we just covered can also be used directly to add numbers expressed in ASCII code. This eliminates the need for doing a code conversion on ASCII form data prior to processing it with addition operations. Whenever the 8086 does an addition on ASCII format data, an adjustment must be performed on the result to convert it to a decimal number. It is specifically for this purpose that the *ASCII adjust for addition* (AAA) instruction is provided in the instruction set of 8086. The AAA instruction should be executed immediately after the instruction that adds ASCII data.

Assuming that AL contains the result produced by adding two ASCII-coded numbers, execution of the AAA instruction causes the contents of AL to be replaced by its equivalent decimal value. If the sum is greater than 9, AL contains the LSDs, and AH is incremented by 1. Otherwise, AL contains the sum and AH is unchanged. Both the AF and CF flags can get affected. Since AAA can only adjust data that are in AL, the destination register for ADD instructions that process ASCII numbers should be AL.

EXAMPLE 3.6

What is the result of executing the following instruction sequence?

ADD AL, BL

AAA

Assume that AL contains 32_{16}, which is the ASCII code for number 2, BL contains 34_{16}, which is the ASCII code for number 4, and AH has been cleared.

SOLUTION   Executing the ADD instruction gives

$$(AL) \leftarrow (AL) + (BL)$$

$$= 32_{16} + 34_{16} = 66_{16}$$

Next the result is adjusted to give its equivalent decimal number. This is done by execution of the AAA instruction. The equivalent of adding 2 and 4 is decimal 6 with no carry. Therefore, the result after the AAA instruction is

$$(AL) = 06_{16}$$

$$(AH) = 00_{16}$$

and both AF and CF remain cleared.

The instruction set of the 8086 includes another instruction, called *decimal adjust for addition* (DAA). This instruction is used to perform an adjust operation similar to that performed by AAA but for the addition of packed BCD numbers instead of ASCII numbers. Information about this instruction is also provided in Fig. 3.20. Similar to AAA, DAA performs an adjustment on the value in AL. A typical instruction sequence is

ADD AL, BL

DAA

Remember that contents of AL and BL must be packed BCD numbers. That is, two BCD digits packed into a byte. The adjusted result in AL is again a packed BCD byte.

Subtraction Instructions—SUB, SBB, DEC, AAS, DAS, and NEG

The instruction set of the 8086 includes an extensive group of instructions provided for implementing subtraction. As shown in Fig. 3.23(a), the subtraction subgroup is similar to the addition subgroup. It includes instructions for subtracting a source and destination operand, decrementing an operand, and for adjusting subtractions of ASCII and BCD data. An additional instruction in this subgroup is negate.

The *subtract* (SUB) instruction is used to subtract the value of a source operand from a destination operand. The result of this operation in general is given as

$$(D) \leftarrow (D) - (S)$$

As shown in Fig. 3.23(b), it can employ the identical operand combinations as the ADD instruction.

The *subtract with borrow* (SBB) instruction is similar to SUB; however, it also subtracts the content of the carry flag from the destination. That is,

$$(D) \leftarrow (D) - (S) - (CF)$$

Mnemonic	Meaning	Format	Operation	Flags affected
SUB	Subtract	SUB D,S	$(D) - (S) \rightarrow (D)$ Borrow $\rightarrow$ (CF)	OF, SF, ZF, AF, PF, CF
SBB	Subtract with borrow	SBB D,S	$(D) - (S) - (CF) \rightarrow (D)$	OF, SF, ZF, AF, PF, CF
DEC	Decrement by 1	DEC D	$(D) - 1 \rightarrow (D)$	OF, SF, ZF, AF, PF
NEG	Negate	NEG D	$0 - (D) \rightarrow (D)$ $1 \rightarrow (CF)$	OF, SF, ZF, AF, PF, CF
DAS	Decimal adjust for subtraction	DAS		SF, ZF, AF, PF, CF OF undefined
AAS	ASCII adjust for subtraction	AAS		AF, CF OF, SF, ZF, PF undefined

(a)

Destination	Source
Register	Register
Register	Memory
Memory	Register
Accumulator	Immediate
Register	Immediate
Memory	Immediate

(b)

Destination
Reg16
Reg8
Memory

(c)

Destination
Register
Memory

(d)

Figure 3.23 (a) Subtraction arithmetic instructions; (b) allowed operands for SUB and SBB; (c) allowed operands for DEC; (d) allowed operands for NEG.

EXAMPLE 3.7

Assume that the contents of registers BX and CX are 1234_{16} and 0123_{16}, respectively, and the carry flag is 0. What will be the result of executing the instruction

$$\text{SBB BX, CX?}$$

SOLUTION Since the instruction implements the operation,

$$(BX) - (CX) - (CF) \rightarrow (BX)$$

we get

$$(BX) = 1234_{16} - 0123_{16} - 0_{16}$$

$$= 1111_{16}$$

Just as the INC instruction could be used to add 1 to an operand, the *decrement* (DEC) instruction can be used to subtract 1 from its operand. The allowed operands are shown in Fig. 3.23(c).

In Fig. 3.23 (d) we see that the *negate* (NEG) instruction can operate on operands in a register or a storage location in memory. Execution of this instruction causes the value of its operand to be replaced by its negative. The way this is actually done is through subtraction. That is, the contents of the specified operand are subtracted from 0 using 2's-complement arithmetic and the result is returned to the operand location.

EXAMPLE 3.8

Assuming that register BX contains $3A_{16}$, what is the result of executing the following instruction?

$$\text{NEG BX}$$

SOLUTION Executing the NEG instruction causes the following 2's-complement subtraction.

$$00_{16} - (BX) = 0000_{16} + 2\text{'s complement of } 3A_{16}$$

$$= 0000_{16} + FFC6_{16}$$

$$= FFC6_{16}$$

This value is returned to BX.

$$(BX) = FFC6_{16}$$

In our study of the addition instruction subgroup, we found that the 8086 was capable of directly adding ASCII and BCD numbers. The SUB and SBB instructions can also subtract numbers represented in these formats. Just as for addition, the results that are obtained must be adjusted to produce their corresponding decimal numbers. In the case of ASCII subtraction, we use the *ASCII adjust for subtraction* (AAS) instruction, and for packed BCD subtraction we use the *decimal adjust for subtract* (DAS) instruction.

An example of an instruction sequence for direct ASCII subtraction is

SUB AL, BL

AAS

ASCII numbers must be loaded into AL and BL before the execution of the subtract instruction. Notice that the destination of the subtraction should be AL. After execution of AAS, AL contains the difference of the two numbers and AH is unchanged if no borrow takes place or is decremented by 1 if a borrow occurs.

Multiplication and Division Instructions—MUL, DIV, IMUL, IDIV, AAM, AAD, CBW, and CWD

The 8086 has instructions to support multiplication and division of binary and BCD numbers. Two basic types of multiplication and division instructions, those for the processing of unsigned numbers and signed numbers, are available. To do these operations on unsigned numbers, the instructions are MUL and DIV. On the other hand, to multiply or divide signed numbers, the instructions are IMUL and IDIV.

Figure 3.24(a) describes these instructions. Notice in Fig. 3.24(b) that only a byte-wide or word-wide operand is specified in a multiplication instruction. It is the source operand. As shown in Fig. 3.24(a), the other operand, which is the destination, is assumed already to be in AL for 8-bit multiplications or in AX for 16-bit multiplications.

The result of executing a MUL or IMUL instruction on byte data can be represented as

$$(AX) \leftarrow (AL) \times (\text{8-bit operand})$$

That is, the resulting 16-bit product is produced in the AX register. On the other hand, for multiplications of data words, the 32-bit result is given by

$$(DX,AX) \leftarrow (AX) \times (\text{16-bit operand})$$

where AX contains the 16 LSBs and DX the 16 MSBs.

For the division operation, again just the source operand is specified. The other operand is either the contents of AX for 16-bit dividends or the contents of both DX and AX for 32-bit dividends. The result of a DIV or IDIV instruction for an 8-bit divisor is represented by

$$(AH),(AL) \leftarrow (AX)/(\text{8-bit operand})$$

where (AH) is the remainder and (AL) the quotient. For 16-bit divisions, we get

$$(DX),(AX) \leftarrow (DX,AX)/(\text{16-bit operand})$$

Here AX contains the quotient and DX contains the remainder.

Mnemonic	Meaning	Format	Operation	Flags Affected
MUL	Multiply (unsigned)	MUL S	$(AL) \cdot (S8) \rightarrow (AX)$ $(AX) \cdot (S16) \rightarrow (DX),(AX)$	OF, CF SF, ZF, AF, PF undefined
DIV	Division (unsigned)	DIV S	(1) $Q((AX)/(S8)) \rightarrow (AL)$ $R((AX)/(S8)) \rightarrow (AH)$ (2) $Q((DX,AX)/(S16)) \rightarrow (AX)$ $R((DX,AX)/(S16)) \rightarrow (DX)$ If Q is FF_{16} in case (1) or $FFFF_{16}$ in case (2), then type 0 interrupt occurs	OF, SF, ZF, AF, PF, CF undefined
IMUL	Integer multiply (signed)	IMUL S	$(AL) \cdot (S8) \rightarrow (AX)$ $(AX) \cdot (S16) \rightarrow (DX),(AX)$	OF, CF SF, ZF, AF, PF undefined
IDIV	Integer divide (signed)	IDIV S	(1) $Q((AX)/(S8)) \rightarrow (AX)$ $R((AX)/(S8)) \rightarrow (AH)$ (2) $Q((DX,AX)/(S16)) \rightarrow (AX)$ $R((DX,AX)/(S16)) \rightarrow (DX)$ If Q is positive and exceeds $7FFF_{16}$ or if Q is negative and becomes less than 8001_{16}, then type 0 interrupt occurs	OF, SF, ZF, AF, PF, CF undefined
AAM	Adjust AL for multiplication	AAM	$Q((AL)/10) \rightarrow AH$ $R((AL)/10) \rightarrow AL$	SF, ZF, PF OF, AF, CF undefined
AAD	Adjust AX for division	AAD	$(AH) \cdot 10 + AL \rightarrow AL$ $00 \rightarrow AH$	SF, ZF, PF OF, AF, CF undefined
CBW	Convert byte to word	CBW	(MSB of AL) $\rightarrow$ (All bits of AH)	None
CWD	Convert word to double word	CWD	(MSB of AX) $\rightarrow$ (All bits of DX)	None

(a)

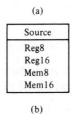

(b)

Figure 3.24 (a) Multiplication and division arithmetic instructions; (b) allowed operands.

EXAMPLE 3.9

If the contents of AL equal -1_{10} and the contents of CL are -2_{10}, what will be the result produced in AX by executing the instructions

MUL CL

and

IMUL CL

SOLUTION The first instruction multiplies the contents of AL and CL as unsigned numbers.

$$-1_{10} = 11111111_2 = FF_{16}$$

$$-2_{10} = 11111110_2 = FE_{16}$$

Thus, executing the MUL instruction, we get

$$(AX) = (11111111_2) \times (11111110_2) = 1111110100000010_2$$
$$= FD02_{16}$$

The second instruction multiplies the same two numbers as signed numbers and gives

$$(AX) = (-1_{16}) \times (-2_{16})$$
$$= 2_{16}$$

As shown in Fig. 3.24(a), adjust instructions for BCD multiplication and division are also provided. They are *adjust AX for multiply* (AAM) and *adjust AX for divide* (AAD). The multiplication performed just before execution of the AAM instruction is assumed to have been performed on two unpacked BCD numbers with the product produced in AL. The AAD instruction assumes that AH and AL contain unpacked BCD numbers.

The division instructions can also be used to divide an 8-bit dividend in AL by an 8-bit divisor. However, to do this, the sign of the dividend must first be extended to fill the AX register. That is, AH is filled with zeros if the number in AL is positive or with ones if it is negative. This conversion is automatically done by executing the *convert byte to word* (CBW) instruction.

In a similar way, the 32-bit by 16-bit division instructions can be used to divide a 16-bit dividend in AX by a 16-bit divisor. In this case, the sign bit of AX must be extended by 16 bits into the DX register. This can be done by another instruction, which is known as *convert word to double word* (CWD). These two sign-extension instructions are also shown in Fig. 3.24(a).

Notice that the CBW and CWD instructions are provided to handle operations where the result or intermediate results of an operation cannot be held in the correct word length for use in other arithmetic operations. Using these instructions, we can extend a byte or word of data to its equivalent word or double word.

EXAMPLE 3.10

What is the result of executing the following sequence of instructions?

```
MOV   AL, A1

CBW

CWD
```

SOLUTION The first instruction loads AL with $A1_{16}$. This gives

$$(AL) = A1_{16} = 10100001_2$$

Executing the second instruction extends the most significant bit of AL, which is 1, into all bits of AH. The result is

$$(AH) = 11111111_2 = FF_{16}$$

$$(AX) = 1111111110100001_2 = FFA1_{16}$$

This completes conversion of the byte in AL to a word in AX.

The last instruction loads each bit of DX with the most significant bit of AX. This bit is also 1. Therefore, we get

$$(DX) = 1111111111111111_2 = FFFF_{16}$$

Now the word in AX has been extended to the double word

$$(AX) = FFA1_{16}$$

$$(DX) = FFFF_{16}$$

3.8 LOGIC INSTRUCTIONS

The 8086 has instructions for performing the logic operations *AND, OR, exclusive-OR, and NOT*. As shown in Fig. 3.25(a), the AND, OR, and XOR instructions perform their respective logic operations bit by bit on the specified source and destination operands,

Mnemonic	Meaning	Format	Operation	Flags Affected
AND	Logical AND	AND D,S	$(S) \cdot (D) \rightarrow (D)$	OF, SF, ZF, PF, CF AF undefined
OR	Logical Inclusive-OR	OR D,S	$(S) + (D) \rightarrow (D)$	OF, SF, ZF, PF, CF AF undefined
XOR	Logical Exclusive-OR	XOR D,S	$(S) \oplus (D) \rightarrow (D)$	OF, SF, ZF, PF, CF AF undefined
NOT	Logical NOT	NOT D	$(\bar{D}) \rightarrow (D)$	None

(a)

Destination	Source
Register	Register
Register	Memory
Memory	Register
Register	Immediate
Memory	Immediate
Accumulator	Immediate

(b)

Destination
Register
Memory

(c)

Figure 3.25 (a) Logic instructions; (b) allowed operands for AND, OR, and XOR; (c) allowed operands for NOT.

the result being represented by the final contents of the destination operand. Figure 3.25(b) shows the allowed operand combinations for the AND, OR, and XOR instructions.

For example, the instruction

$$\text{AND} \quad \text{AX, BX}$$

causes the contents of BX to be ANDed with the contents of AX. The result is reflected by the new contents of AX. If AX contains 1234_{16} and BX contains $00F_{16}$, the result produced by the instruction is

$$1234_{16} \bullet 000F_{16} = 0001001000110100_2 \bullet 0000000000001111_2$$

$$= 0000000000000100_{16}$$

$$= 0004_{16}$$

This result is stored in the destination operand.

$$(AX) = 0004_{16}$$

In this way we see that the AND instruction was used to mask off the 12 most significant bits of the destination operand.

The NOT logic instruction differs from AND, OR, and exclusive-OR instructions in that it operates on a single operand. Looking at Fig. 3.25(c), which shows the allowed operands of the NOT instruction, we see that this operand can be either the contents of an internal register or a location in memory.

EXAMPLE 3.11

Describe the result of executing the following sequence of instructions.

$$\text{MOV} \quad \text{AL, 01010101B}$$

$$\text{AND} \quad \text{AL, 00011111B}$$

$$\text{OR} \quad \text{AL, 11000000B}$$

$$\text{XOR} \quad \text{AL, 00001111B}$$

$$\text{NOT} \quad \text{AL}$$

SOLUTION The first instruction moves the immediate operand 01010101_2 into the AL register. This loads the data that are to be manipulated with the logic instructions. The next instruction performs a bit-by-bit AND operation of the contents of AL with immediate operand 00011111_2. This gives

$$01010101_2 \bullet 00011111_2 = 00010101_2$$

This result is produced in destination register AL. Note that this operation has masked off the three most significant bits of AL.

Sec. 3.8   Logic Instructions   **93**

The next instruction performs a bit-by-bit logical OR of the present contents of AL with immediate operand CO_{16}. This gives

$$00010101_2 + 11000000_2 = 11010101_2$$

$$(AL) = 11010101$$

This operation is equivalent to setting the two most significant bits of AL.

The fourth instruction is an exclusive-OR operation of the contents of AL with immediate operand 00001111_2. We get

$$11010101_2 \oplus 00001111_2 = 11011010_2$$

$$(AL) = 11011010$$

Note that this operation complements the logic state of those bits in AL that are ones in the immediate operand.

The last instruction, NOT AL, inverts each bit of AL. Therefore, the final contents of AL become

$$(AL) = \overline{11011010}_2 = 00100101_2$$

These results are summarized in Fig. 3.26.

Instruction	(AL)
MOV AL,01010101B	01010101
AND AL,00011111B	00010101
OR AL,11000000B	11010101
XOR AL,00001111B	11011010
NOT AL	00100101

Figure 3.26 Results of example program using logic instructions.

3.9 SHIFT INSTRUCTIONS

The four *shift instructions* of the 8086 can perform two basic types of shift operations. They are called the *logical shift* and the *arithmetic shift*. Moreover, each of these operations can be performed to the right or to the left. The shift instructions are *shift logical left* (SHL), *shift arithmetic left* (SAL), *shift logical right* (SHR), and *shift arithmetic right* (SAR).

The logical shift instructions, SHL and SHR, are described in Fig. 3.27(a). Notice in Fig. 3.27(b) that the destination operand, the data whose bits are to be shifted, can be either the contents of an internal register or a storage location in memory. Moreover, the source operand can be specified in two ways. If it is assigned the value 1, a 1-bit shift will take place. For instance, as illustrated in Fig. 3.28(a), executing

SHL AX, 1

Mnemonic	Meaning	Format	Operation	Flags Affected
SAL/SHL	Shift arithmetic left/shift logical left	SAL/SHL D,Count	Shift the (D) left by the number of bit positions equal to Count and fill the vacated bits positions on the right with zeros	CF, PF, SF, ZF, OF AF undefined OF undefined if count $\neq 1$
SHR	Shift logical right	SHR D,Count	Shift the (D) right by the number of bit positions equal to Count and fill the vacated bit positions on the left with zeros	CF, PF, SF, ZF, OF AF undefined OF undefined if count $\neq 1$
SAR	Shift arithmetic right	SAR D,Count	Shift the (D) right by the number of bit positions equal to Count and fill the vacated bit positions on the left with the original most significant bit	OF, SF, ZF, PF, CF AF undefined

(a)

Destination	Count
Register	1
Register	CL
Memory	1
Memory	CL

(b)

Figure 3.27 (a) Shift instructions; (b) allowed operands.

causes the 16-bit contents of the AX register to be shifted one bit position to the left. Here we see that the vacated LSB location is filled with 0 and the bit shifted out of the MSB is saved in CF.

On the other hand, if the source operand is specified as CL instead of 1, the count in this register represents the number of bit positions the operand is to be shifted. This permits the count to be defined under software control and allows a range of shifts from 1 to 256 bits.

An example of an instruction specified in this way is

SHR AX, CL

Assuming that CL contains the value 02_{16}, the logical shift right that occurs is shown in Fig. 3.28(b). Notice that the two MSBs have been filled with 0s and the last bit shifted out at the LSB, which is 0, is maintained in the carry flag.

In an arithmetic shift to the left, SAL operation, the vacated bits at the right of the operand are filled with 0s, whereas in an arithmetic shift to the right, SAR operation, the vacated bits at the left are filled with the value of the original MSB of the operand. Thus in an arithmetic shift to the right, the original sign of the number is extended. This operation is equivalent to division by 2 as long as the bit shifted out of the LSB is a 0.

Sec. 3.9   Shift Instructions

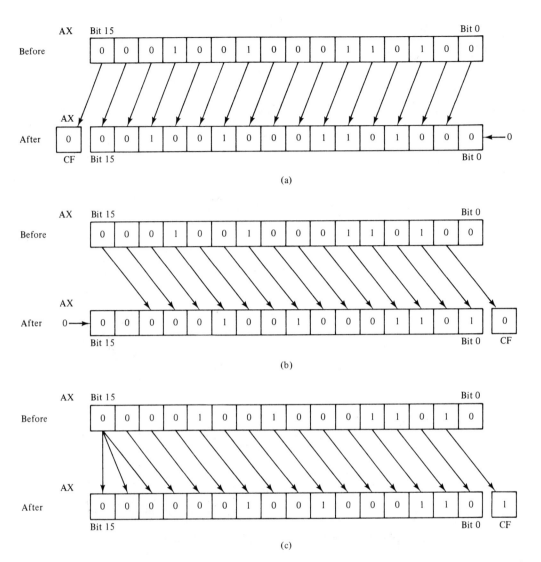

Figure 3.28 (a) Results of executing SHL AX,1; (b) results of executing SHR AX,CL; (c) results of executing SAR AX,CL.

EXAMPLE 3.12

Assume that CL contains 02_{16} and AX contains $091A_{16}$. Determine the new contents of AX and the carry flag after the instruction

```
SAR AX, CL
```

is executed.

SOLUTION Figure 3.28(c) shows the effect of executing the instruction. Here we see that since CL contains 02_{16}, a shift right by two bit locations takes place and the original sign bit, which is logic 0, is extended to the two vacated bit positions. Moreover, the last bit shifted out from the LSB location is placed in CF. This makes CF 1. Therefore, the results produced by execution of the instruction are

$$(AX) = 0246_{16}$$

and

$$(CF) = 1_2$$

EXAMPLE 3.13

Write a program to implement the following expression using shift instructions to perform the arithmetic.

$$3(AX) + 7(BX) \rightarrow (DX)$$

SOLUTION Shifting left by one bit position causes a multiplication by 2. To perform multiplication by an odd number, we can use a shift instruction to multiply to the nearest multiple of 2 and then add or subtract the appropriate value to get the desired result.

The algorithm for performing the arithmetic operations in the expression starts by shifting (AX) left by one bit. This gives 2 times (AX). Then adding the original (AX) gives multiplication by 3. Next, the contents of BX are shifted left by 3 bits to give 8 times its value and subtracting the original (BX) once gives multiplication by 7. Expressing this with instructions, we get

```
MOV  SI,AX   ;Copy (AX) into SI

SAL  SI,1    ;2(AX)

ADD  SI,AX   ;3(AX)

MOV  DX,BX   ;Copy (BX) into DX

MOV  CL,3    ;Load shift count

SAL  DX,CL   ;8(BX)

SUB  DX,BX   ;7(BX)

ADD  DX,SI   ;Result
```

It is important to note that we have assumed that to obtain any of the intermediate results and the final result, overflow does not occur. For instance, if 8(BX) cannot be accommodated in the 16 bits of BX, an overflow condition would occur and the result produced by executing the program may be incorrect.

3.10 ROTATE INSTRUCTIONS ━━━━━━━━━━━━━━━━━━━━━━━━━━━━━━

Another group of instructions, known as the *rotate instructions,* is similar to the shift instructions we just introduced. This group, as shown in Fig. 3.29(a), includes the *rotate left* (ROL), *rotate right* (ROR), *rotate left through carry* (RCL) and *rotate right through carry* (RCR) instructions.

As shown in Fig. 3.29(b), the rotate instructions are similar to the shift instructions in several ways. They have the ability to shift the contents of either an internal register or storage location in memory. Also, the shift that takes place can be from 1 to 256 bit positions to the left or to the right. Moreover, in the case of a multibit shift, the number of bit positions to be shifted is again specified by the contents of CL. Their difference from the shift instructions lies in the fact that the bits moved out at either the MSB or LSB end are not lost; instead, they are reloaded at the other end.

As an example, let us look at the operation of the ROL instruction. Execution of ROL causes the contents of the selected operand to be rotated left the specified number of bit positions. Each bit shifted out at the MSB end is reloaded at the LSB end. Moreover, the contents of CF reflects the state of the last bit that was shifted out. For instance, the instruction

ROL AX, 1

Mnemonic	Meaning	Format	Operation	Flags Affected
ROL	Rotate left	ROL D,Count	Rotate the (D) left by the number of bit positions equal to Count. Each bit shifted out from the leftmost bit goes back into the rightmost bit position.	CF OF undefined if count ≠ 1
ROR	Rotate right	ROR D,Count	Rotate the (D) right by the number of bit positions equal to Count. Each bit shifted out from the rightmost bit goes into the leftmost bit position.	CF OF undefined if count ≠ 1
RCL	Rotate left through carry	RCL D,Count	Same as ROL except carry is attached to (D) for rotation.	CF OF undefined if count ≠ 1
RCR	Rotate right through carry	RCR D,Count	Same as ROR except carry is attached to (D) for rotation.	CF OF undefined if count ≠ 1

(a)

Destination	Count
Register	1
Register	CL
Memory	1
Memory	CL

(b)

Figure 3.29 (a) Rotate instructions; (b) allowed operands.

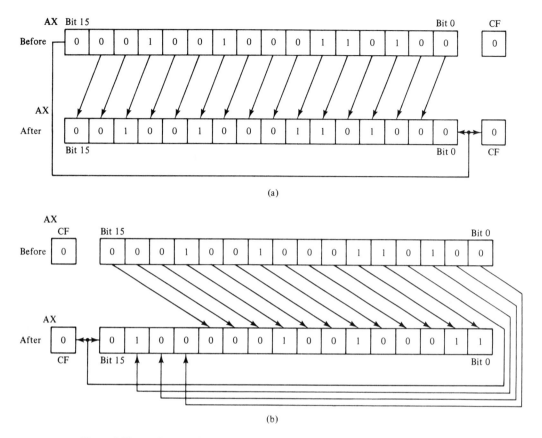

Figure 3.30 (a) Results of executing ROL AX,1; (b) results of executing ROR AX,CL.

causes a 1-bit rotate to the left. Figure 3.30(a) shows the result produced by executing this instruction. Notice that the original value of bit 15 is 0. This value has been rotated into both CF and bit 0 of AX. All other bits have been rotated one bit position to the left.

The ROR instruction operates the same way as ROL except that it causes data to be rotated to the right instead to the left. For example, execution of

ROR AX, CL

causes the contents of AX to be rotated right by the number of bit positions specified in CL. The result for CL equal to 4 is illustrated in Fig. 3.30(b).

The other two rotate instructions, RCL and RCR, differ from ROL and ROR in that the bits are rotated through the carry flag. Figure 3.31 illustrates the rotation that takes place due to execution of the RCL instruction. Notice that the bit returned to bit 0 is the prior contents of CF and not bit 15. The bit shifted out of bit 15 goes into the carry flag. Thus the bits rotate through carry.

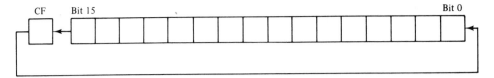

CF   Bit 15   Bit 0

Figure 3.31 Rotation caused by execution of the RCL instruction.

EXAMPLE 3.14

What is the result in BX and CF after execution of the following instruction?

$$RCR \ \ BX, CL$$

Assume that prior to execution of the instruction $(CL) = 04_{16}$, $(BX) = 1234_{16}$, and $(CF) = 0_2$.

SOLUTION The original contents of BX are

$$(BX) = 0001001000110100_2 = 1234_{16}$$

Execution of the RCR instruction causes a 4-bit rotate right through carry to take place on the data in BX. Therefore, the original content of bit 3, which is 0, resides in carry; $CF = 0_2$ and 1000_2 has been reloaded from bit 15. The resulting contents of BX are

$$(BX) = 1000000100100011_2 = 8123_{16}$$

ASSIGNMENT

Section 3.2

1. What is the purpose of a software model for a microprocessor?
2. What must an assembly language programmer know about the registers within the 8086 microprocessor?
3. Which of the 8086's internal registers are used for memory segmentation?
4. What is the function of the instruction pointer register?
5. How is the word value of a data register labeled?
6. How are the upper and lower bytes of a data register denoted?
7. What kind of information is stored in the pointer and index registers?
8. For which segment register are the contents of the pointer registers used as an offset?
9. For which segment register are the contents of the index registers used as an offset?
10. What is the difference between SI and DI?
11. Categorize each flag bit of the 8086 as either a control flag or a flag that monitors the status due to execution of an instruction.
12. How are the status flags used by software?
13. Can the state of the flags be modified through software?

14. List five data types directly processed by the 8086.
15. Express each of signed decimal integers that follow as either a byte or word hexadecimal number (use 2's-complement notation for negative numbers).
    (a) $+127$
    (b) -10
    (c) -128
    (d) $+500$
16. How would the integer in problem 10(d) be stored in memory starting at address $0A000_{16}$?
17. How would the decimal number -1000 be expressed for processing by the 8086?
18. Express the decimal numbers that follow as unpacked and packed BCD bytes.
    (a) 29
    (b) 88
19. How would the BCD number in problem 15 (a) be stored in memory starting at address $0B000_{16}$? Assume that the least significant digit is stored at the lower address.
20. What is the statement that follows that is coded in ASCII as

    1001110

    1000101

    1011000

    1010100

    0100000

    1001001

21. How would the decimal number 1234 be coded in ASCII and stored in memory starting at address $0C000_{16}$? Assume that the least significant digit is stored at the lower addressed memory location.

Section 3.3

22. What is the native language of the 8086?
23. How does machine language differ from assembly language?
24. What does *opcode* stand for?
25. What is an *operand?* Give two types.
26. In the assembly language statement

    START: ADD AX, BX   ; Add BX to AX

    what is the label?
27. What is the function of an assembler?
28. What is *object code?*
29. Give two benefits derived from writing programs in assembly language instead of a high-level language.

Section 3.4

30. Make a list of the addressing modes available on the 8086.

31. Identify the addressing modes used for the source and the destination operands in the instructions that follow.
- **(a)** MOV AL, BL
- **(b)** MOV AX, 0FF
- **(c)** MOV [DI], AX
- **(d)** MOV DI, [SI]
- **(e)** MOV [BX] + XYZ, CX
- **(f)** MOV [DI] + XYZ, AH
- **(g)** MOV [BX] [DI] + XYZ, AL

32. Compute the physical address for the specified operand in each of the following instructions from the problem 31. The register contents and variables are as follows: CS = $0A00_{16}$, DC = $0B00_{16}$, SI = 0100_{16}, DI = 0200_{16}, BX = 0300_{16}, and XYZ = 0400_{16}.
- **(a)** Destination operand of the instruction in (c)
- **(b)** Source operand of the instruction in (d)
- **(c)** Destination operand of the instruction in (e)
- **(d)** Destination operand of the instruction in (f)
- **(e)** Destination operand of the instruction in (g)

Section 3.5

33. List five groups of instructions.

Section 3.6

34. Explain what operation is performed by each of the instructions that follows.
- **(a)** MOV   AX, 0110
- **(b)** MOV   DI, AX
- **(c)** MOV   BL, AL
- **(d)** MOV   [0100], AX
- **(e)** MOV   [BX+DI], AX
- **(f)** MOV   [DI] + 4, AX
- **(g)** MOV   [BX] [DI] + 4, AX

35. Assume that registers AX, BX, and DI are all initialized to 0000_{16} and that all data storage memory has been cleared. Determine the location and value of the destination operand as instructions a through g from problem 34 are executed as a sequence.

36. Write an instruction sequence that will initialize the ES register with the immediate value 1010_{16}.

37. Write an instruction that will save the contents of the the ES register in memory at address DS:1000H.

38. Why will the instruction MOV CL,AX result in an error when it is assembled?

39. Describe the operation performed by each of the instructions that follows.
- **(a)** XCHG   AX, BX
- **(b)** XCHG   BX, DI
- **(c)** XCHG   DATA, AX
- **(d)** XCHG   [BX+DI], AX

40. If register BX contains the value 0100_{16}, register DI contains 0010_{16}, and register DS contains 1075_{16}, what physical memory location is swapped when the instruction in problem 9(d) is executed?

41. Assume that AL $= 0010_{16}$, BX $= 0100_{16}$, and DS $= 1000_{16}$, what happens if the XLAT instruction is executed?

42. Write a single instruction that will load AX from address 0200_{16} and DS from address 0202_{16}.

43. Two code-conversion tables starting with offsets TABL1 and TABL2 in the current data segment are to be accessed. Write a routine that initializes the needed registers and then replaces the contents of memory locations MEM1 and MEM2 (offsets in the data segment) by the equivalent converted codes from the code-conversion tables.

Section 3.7

44. What operation is performed by each of the following instructions?
   (a) ADD   AX, 00FF
   (b) ADC   SI, AX
   (c) INC   BYTE PTR [0100]
   (d) SUB   DL, BL
   (e) SBB   DL, [0200]
   (f) DEC   BYTE PTR [DI + BX]
   (g) NEG   BYTE PTR [DI] + 0010
   (h) MUL   DX
   (i) IMUL   BYTE PTR [BX + SI]
   (j) DIV   BYTE PTR [SI] + 0030
   (k) IDIV   BYTE PTR [BX] [SI] + 0030

45. Assume that the state of 8086's registers and memory is as follows just prior to the execution of each instruction in problem 44.

$$AX = 0010H$$
$$BX = 0020H$$
$$CX = 0030H$$
$$DX = 0040H$$
$$SI = 0100H$$
$$DI = 0200H$$
$$CF = 1H$$
$$DS{:}100 = 10H$$
$$DS{:}101 = 00H$$
$$DS{:}120 = FFH$$
$$DS{:}121 = FFH$$
$$DS{:}130 = 08H$$
$$DS{:}131 = 00H$$
$$DS{:}150 = 02H$$
$$DS{:}151 = 00H$$
$$DS{:}200 = 30H$$
$$DS{:}201 = 00H$$
$$DS{:}210 = 40H$$
$$DS{:}211 = 00H$$
$$DS{:}220 = 30H$$
$$DS{:}221 = 00H$$

What is the result produced in the destination operand by executing instructions a through k?

46. Write an instruction that will add the immediate value $111F_{16}$ and the carry flag to the contents of the data register.

47. Write an instruction that will subtract the word contents of the storage location pointed to by the base register and the carry flag from the accumulator.

48. Two word-wide unsigned integers are stored at the memory addresses $0A00_{16}$ and $0A02_{16}$, respectively. Write an instruction sequence that computes and stores their sum, difference, product, and quotient. Store these results at consecutive memory locations starting at address $0A10_{16}$ in memory. To obtain the difference, subtract the integer at $0A02_{16}$ from the integer at $0A00_{16}$. For the division, divide the integer at $0A00_{16}$ by the integer at $0A02_{16}$. Use register indirect relative addressing mode to store the various results.

49. Assuming that $(AX) = 0123_{16}$ and $(BL) = 10_{16}$, what will be the new contents of AX after executing the instruction DIV BL?

50. What instruction is used to adjust the result of an addition that processed packed BCD numbers?

51. Which instruction is provided in the instruction set of the 8086 to adjust the result of a subtraction that involved ASCII coded numbers?

52. If AL contains $A0_{16}$, what happens when the instruction CBW is executed?

53. If the value in AX is $7FFF_{16}$, what happens when the instruction CWD is executed?

54. Two byte-sized BCD integers are stored at the symbolic addresses NUM1 and NUM2, respectively. Write an instruction sequence to generate their difference and store it at NUM3. The difference is to be formed by subtracting the value at NUM1 from that at NUM2.

Section 3.8

55. Describe the operation performed by each of the following instructions.
   (a) AND   BYTE PTR[0300], 0F
   (b) AND   DX, [SI]
   (c) OR   [BX+DI], AX
   (d) OR   BYTE PTR [BX] [DI] +10, F0
   (e) XOR   AX, [SI+BX]
   (f) NOT   BYTE PTR [0300]
   (g) NOT   WORD PTR [BX+DI]

56. Assume that the state of 8086's registers and memory is as follows just prior to execution of each instruction in problem 55.

$$AX = 5555H$$
$$BX = 0010H$$
$$CX = 0010H$$
$$DX = AAAAH$$
$$SI = 0100H$$
$$DI = 0200H$$
$$DS:100 = 0FH$$
$$DS:101 = F0H$$
$$DS:110 = 00H$$
$$DS:111 = FFH$$
$$DS:200 = 30H$$
$$DS:201 = 00H$$

DS:210 = AAH
DS:211 = AAH
DS:220 = 55H
DS:221 = 55H
DS:300 = AAH
DS:301 = 55H

What is the result produced in the destination operand by executing instructions a through g?

57. Write an instruction that when executed will mask off all but bit 7 of the the contents of the data register.

58. Write an instruction that will mask off all but bit 7 of the word of data stored at address DS:0100.

59. Specify the relation between the old and new contents of AX after executing the following instructions.

NOT AX

ADD AX, 1

60. Write an instruction sequence that generates a byte-sized integer in the memory location identified by label RESULT. The value of the byte integer is to be calculated as follows:

$$RESULT = AL \cdot NUM1 + \overline{(NUM2 \cdot AL + BL)}$$

Assume that all parameters are byte sized.

Section 3.9

61. Explain what operation is performed by each of the instructions that follow.
 (a) SHL   DX, CL
 (b) SHL   BYTE PTR [0400], CL
 (c) SHR   BYTE PTR [DI], 1
 (d) SHR   BYTE PTR [DI + BX], CL
 (e) SAR   WORD PTR [BX+DI], 1
 (f) SAR   WORD PTR [BX] [DI] + 10, CL

62. Assume that the state of 8086's registers and memory is as follows just prior to execution of each instruction in problem 61.

AX = 0000H
BX = 0010H
CX = 0105H
DX = 1111H
SI = 0100H
DI = 0200H
CF = 0
DS:100 = 0FH
DS:200 = 22H
DS:201 = 44H
DS:210 = 55H
DS:211 = AAH

$$DS:220 = AAH$$
$$DS:221 = 55H$$
$$DS:400 = AAH$$
$$DS:401 = 55H$$

What is the result produced in the destination operand by executing instructions a through f?

63. Write an instruction that shifts the contents of the count register left by one bit position.

64. Write an instruction sequence that when executed shifts left by eight bit positions the contents of the word-wide memory location pointed to by the address in the destination index register.

65. Identify the condition under which the contents of AX would remain unchanged after executing any of the instructions that follow.

MOV CL, 4

SHL AX, CL

SHR AX, CL

66. Implement the following operation using shift and arithmetic instructions.

$$7(AX) - 5(BX) - (BX)/8 \rightarrow (AX)$$

Assume that all parameters are word sized.

Section 3.10

67. Describe what happens as each of the instructions that follow is executed by the 8086.
   (a) ROL   DX, CL
   (b) RCL   BYTE PTR [0400] , CL
   (c) ROR   BYTE PTR [DI] , 1
   (d) ROR   BYTE PTR [DI + BX] , CL
   (e) RCR   WORD PTR [BX + DI] , 1
   (f) RCR   WORD PTR [BX] [DI] + 10 , CL

68. Assume that the state of 8086's registers and memory is as follows just prior to execution of each of the instructions in problem 67.

$$AX = 0000H$$
$$BX = 0010H$$
$$CX = 0105H$$
$$DX = 1111H$$
$$SI = 0100H$$
$$DI = 0200H$$
$$CF = 1$$
$$DS:100 = 0FH$$
$$DS:200 = 22H$$
$$DS:201 = 44H$$
$$DS:210 = 55H$$
$$DS:211 = AAH$$
$$DS:220 = AAH$$
$$DS:221 = 55H$$

$$DS:400 = AAH$$
$$DS:401 = 55H$$

What is the result produced in the destination operand by executing instructions a through f?

69. Write an instruction sequence that when executed rotates left through carry by one bit position the contents of the word-wide memory location pointed to by the address in the base register.

70. Write a program that saves the content of bit 5 in AL in BX as a word.

Chapter 4

8086 Microprocessor Programming 2

4.1 INTRODUCTION

In Chapter 3 we discussed many of the instructions that can be executed by the 8086 microprocessor. Furthermore, we used these instructions to write simple programs. In this chapter we introduce the rest of the instruction set and at the same time cover some more complicated programming techniques. The following topics are discussed in this chapter.

1. Flag control instructions
2. Compare instruction
3. Jump instructions
4. Subroutines and subroutine handling instructions
5. Loop instructions
6. String instructions

4.2 FLAG CONTROL INSTRUCTIONS

The 8086 microprocessor has a set of flags which either monitor the status of executing instructions or control options available in its operation. These flags were described in detail in Chapter 2. The instruction set includes a group of instructions which when executed directly affect the setting of the flags. These instructions, shown in Fig. 4.1(a), are: *load AH from flags* (LAHF), *store AH into flags* (SAHF), *clear carry* (CLC), *set*

Mnemonic	Meaning	Operation	Flags Affected
LAHF	Load AH from flags	(AH) ← (Flags)	None
SAHF	Store AH into flags	(Flags) ← (AH)	SF, ZF, AF, PF, CF
CLC	Clear carry flag	(CF) ← 0	CF
STC	Set carry flag	(CF) ← 1	CF
CMC	Complement carry flag	(CF) ← ($\overline{CF}$)	CF
CLI	Clear interrupt flag	(IF) ← 0	IF
STI	Set interrupt flag	(IF) ← 1	IF

(a)

```
LAHF

MOV      MEM1, AH

MOV      AH, MEM2

SAHF
```

(b)

Figure 4.1   (a) Flag control instructions; (b) program for example 4.1.

carry (STC), *complement carry* (CMC), *clear interrupt* (CLI), and *set interrupt* (STI). A few more instructions exist that can directly affect the flags; however, we will not cover them until later in the chapter when we introduce the subroutine and string instructions.

Looking at Fig. 4.1(a), we see that the first two instructions, LAHF and SAHF, can be used either to read the flags or to change them, respectively. Notice that the data transfer that takes place is always between the AH register and the flag register. For instance, we may want to start an operation with certain flags set or rest. Assume that we want to preset all flags to logic 1. To do this, we can first load AH with FF_{16} and then execute the SAHF instruction.

EXAMPLE 4.1

Write an instruction sequence to save the current contents of the 8086's flags in memory location MEM1 and then reload the flags with the contents of memory location MEM2.

SOLUTION   To save the current flags, we must first load them into the AH register and then move them to the location MEM1. The instructions that do this are

```
LAHF


MOV      [MEM1] , AH
```

Similarly, to load the flags with the contents of MEM2, we must first copy the contents of MEM2 into AH and then store the contents of AH into the flags. The instructions for this are

```
MOV     AH, [MEM2]

SAHF
```

The entire instruction sequence is shown in Fig. 4.1(b).

The next three instructions, CLC, STC, and CMC, are used to manipulate the carry flag. They permit CF to be cleared, set, or complemented to its inverse logic level, respectively. For example, if CF is 1 when a CMC instruction is executed, it becomes 0.

The last two instructions are used to manipulate the interrupt flag. Executing the clear interrupt (CLI) instruction sets IF to logic 0 and disables the interrupt interface. On the other hand, executing the STI instruction sets IF to 1 and the microprocessor starts accepting interrupts from that point on.

EXAMPLE 4.2

Of the three carry flag instructions CLC, STC, and CMC only one is really an independent instruction. That is, the operation that it provides cannot be performed by a series of the other two instructions. Determine which one of the carry instructions is the independent instruction.

SOLUTION   Let us begin with the CLC instruction. The clear carry operation can be performed by an STC instruction followed by a CMC instruction. Therefore, CLC is not an independent instruction. Moreover, the operation of the set carry (STC) instruction is equivalent to the operation performed by a CLC instruction followed by a CMC instruction. Thus STC is also not an independent instruction. On the other hand, the operation performed by the last instruction, complement carry (CMC), cannot be expressed in terms of the CLC and STC instructions. Therefore, it is the independent instruction.

4.3 COMPARE INSTRUCTION

There is an instruction included in the instruction set of the 8086 which can be used to compare two 8-bit or 16-bit numbers. It is the *compare* (CMP) instruction of Fig. 4.2(a). Figure 4.2(b) shows that the operands can reside in a storage location in memory, register within the MPU, or as part of the instruction. For instance a byte-wide number in a register such as BL can be compared to second byte-wide number that is supplied as immediate data.

The result of the comparison is reflected by changes in six of the status flags of the 8086. Notice in Fig. 4.2(a) that it affects the overflow flag, sign flag, zero flag, auxiliary carry flag, parity flag, and carry flag. The logic state of these flags can be

Mnemonic	Meaning	Format	Operation	Flags Affected
CMP	Compare	CMP D,S	(D) − (S) is used in setting or resetting the flags	CF, AF, OF, PF, SF, ZF

(a)

Destination	Source
Register	Register
Register	Memory
Memory	Register
Register	Immediate
Memory	Immediate
Accumulator	Immediate

(b)

Figure 4.2 (a) Compare instruction; (b) allowed operands.

referenced by instructions in order to make a decision whether or not to alter the sequence in which the program executes.

The process of comparison performed by the CMP instruction is basically a subtraction operation. The source operand is subtracted from the destination operand. However, the result of this subtraction is not saved. Instead, based on the result the appropriate flags are set or reset.

For example, let us assume that the destination operand equals $10011001_2 = -103_{10}$ and that the source operand equals $00011011_2 = +27_{10}$. Subtracting the source from the destination, we get

$$10011001_2 = -103_{10}$$
$$-00011011_2 = -(+27_{10})$$
$$\overline{01111110_2 = +126_{10}}$$

In the process of obtaining this result, we set the status that follows.

1. Borrow is needed from bit 4 to bit 3; therefore, the auxiliary carry flag AF is at logic 1.
2. There is no borrow to bit 7. Thus carry flag CF is reset.
3. Even through a borrow to bit 7 is not needed, there is a borrow from bit 7 to bit 6. This is an overflow condition and the OF flag is set.
4. There is an even number of 1s; therefore, this makes parity flag PF equal to 1.
5. Bit 7 is 0 and therefore sign flag SF is at logic 0.
6. The result that is produced is not 0, which makes zero flag ZF logic 0.

Notice that the result produced by the subtraction of the two 8-bit numbers is not correct. This condition was indicated by setting the overflow flag.

EXAMPLE 4.3

Describe what happens to the status flags as the sequence of instructions that follow is executed.

```
MOV   AX, 1234

MOV   BX, ABCD

CMP   AX, BX
```

Assume that flags ZF, SF, CF, AF, OF, and PF are all initially reset.

SOLUTION   The first instruction loads AX with 1234_{16}. No status flags are affected by the execution of a MOV instruction. The second instruction puts $ABCD_{16}$ into the BX register. Again status is not affected. Thus, after execution of these two move instructions, the contents of AX and BX are

$$(AX) = 1234_{16} = 0001001000110100_2$$

and

$$(BX) = ABCD_{16} = 1010101111001101_2$$

The third instruction is a 16-bit comparison with AX representing the destination and BX the source. Therefore, the contents of BX are subtracted from that of AX.

$$(AX) - (BX) = 0001001000110100_2 - 1010101111001101_2$$

$$= 0110011001100111_2$$

The flags are either set or rest based on the result of this subtraction. Notice that the result is nonzero and positive. This makes ZF and SF equal to 0. Moreover, the carry, auxiliary carry, and no overflow conditions occur. Therefore, CF and AF are at logic 1 while OF is at logic 0.

Finally, the result has odd parity; therefore, PF is set to 0. These results are summarized in Fig. 4.3.

Instruction	ZF	SF	CF	AF	OF	PF
Initial state	0	0	0	0	0	0
MOV AX,1234	0	0	0	0	0	0
MOV BX,ABCD	0	0	0	0	0	0
CMP AX,BX	0	0	1	1	0	0

Figure 4.3   Effect on flags of executing instructions.

The purpose of a *jump* instruction is to alter the execution path of instructions in the program. In the 8086 microprocessor, the code segment register and instruction pointer keep track of the next instruction to be executed. Thus a jump instruction involves altering the contents of these registers. In this way, execution continues at an address other than that of the next sequential instruction. That is, a jump occurs to another part of the program. Typically, program execution is not intended to return to the next sequential instruction after the jump instruction. Therefore, no return linkage is saved when the jump takes place.

The Unconditional and Conditional Jump

The 8086 microprocessor allows two different types of jumps. They are the *unconditional jump* and the *conditional jump*. In an unconditional jump, no status requirements are imposed for the jump to occur. That is, as the instruction is executed, the jump always takes place to change the execution sequence.

This concept is illustrated in Fig. 4.4(a). Notice that when the instruction JMP AA in part I is executed, program control is passed to a point in part III identified by the label AA. Execution resumes with the instruction corresponding to AA. In this way, the instructions in part II of the program have been bypassed. That is, they have been jumped over.

On the other hand, for a conditional jump instruction, status conditions that exist at the moment the jump instruction is executed decide whether or not the jump will occur. If this condition or conditions are met, the jump takes place; otherwise, execution continues with the next sequential instruction of the program. The conditions that can be referenced by a conditional jump instruction are status flags such as carry (CF), parity (PF), and overflow (OF).

Looking at Fig. 4.4(b), we see that execution of the conditional jump instruction in part I causes a test to be initiated. If the conditions of the test are not met, the NO path is taken and execution continues with the next sequential instruction. This corresponds to the first instruction in part II. However, if the result of the conditional test is YES, a jump is initiated to the segment of the program identified as part III and the instructions in part II are bypassed.

Unconditional Jump Instruction

The unconditional jump instruction of the 8086 is shown in Fig. 4.5(a) together with its valid operand combinations in Fig. 4.5(b). There are two basic kinds of unconditional jumps. The first, called an *intrasegment jump,* is limited to addresses within the current code segment. This type of jump is achieved by just modifying the value in IP. The other kind of jump, the *intersegment jump,* permits jumps from one code segment to another. Implementation of this type of jump requires modification of the contents of both CS and IP.

Jump instructions specified with a *Short-label, Near-label, Memptr16,* or

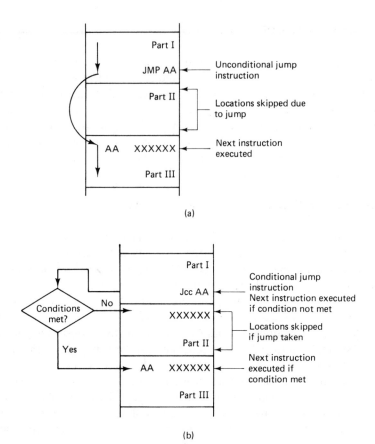

Figure 4.4 (a) Unconditional jump program sequence; (b) conditional jump program sequence.

Regptr16 operand represent intrasegment jumps. The Short-label and Near-label operands specify the jump relative to the address of the jump instruction itself. For example, in a Short-label jump instruction an 8-bit number is coded as an immediate operand to specify the *signed displacement* of the next instruction to be executed from the location of the jump instruction. When the jump instruction is executed, IP is reloaded with a new value equal to the updated value in IP, which is (IP) + 2, plus the signed displacement. The new value of IP and current value in CS give the address of the next instruction to be fetched and executed. With an 8-bit displacement, the Short-label operand can only be used to initiate a jump in the range − 126 to + 129 bytes from the location of the jump instruction.

On the other hand, Near-label operands specify a new value of IP with a 16-bit displacement. The value of the displacement is automatically added to the IP upon execution of the instruction. In this way, program control is passed to the location identified by the new CS:IP. An example is the instruction

JMP LABEL

Mnemonic	Meaning	Format	Operation	Flags Affected
JMP	Unconditional jump	JMP Operand	Jump is initiated to the address specified by Operand	None

(a)

Operand
Short-label
Near-label
Far-label
Memptr16
Regptr16
Memptr32

(b)

Figure 4.5 (a) Unconditional jump instruction; (b) allowed operands.

This means to jump to the point in the program corresponding to the tag LABEL. The programmer does not have to worry about counting the number of bytes from the jump instruction to the location to which control is to be passed. The fact that it is coded as a Short- or Near-label displacement is determined by the Assembler.

The jump to address can also be specified indirectly by the contents of a memory location or the contents of a register. These two types correspond to the Memptr16 and Regptr16 operands, respectively. Just as for the Near-label operand, they both permit a jump to any address in the current code segment.

For example,

```
JMP BX
```

uses the contents of register BX for the displacement. That is, the value in BX is copied into IP. Then the physical address of the next instruction is obtained by using the current contents of CS and this new value in IP.

To specify an operand to be used as a pointer, the various addressing modes available with the 8086 can be used. For instance,

```
JMP WORD PTR [BX]
```

uses the contents of BX as the address of the memory location that contains the offset address. This offset is loaded into IP, where it is used together with the current contents of CS to compute the ''jump to'' address.

The intersegment unconditional jump instructions correspond to the *Far-label* and *Memptr32 operands* that are shown in Fig. 4.5(b). Far-label uses a 32-bit immediate operand to specify the jump to address. The first 16 bits of this 32-bit pointer are loaded into IP and are an offset address relative to the contents of the code segment register.

The next 16 bits are loaded into the CS register and define the new 64K-byte code segment.

An indirect way to specify the offset and code segment address for an intersegment jump is by using the Memptr32 operand. This time four consecutive memory bytes starting at the specified address contain the offset address and the new code segment address, respectively. Just like the Memptr16 operand, and Memptr32 operand may be specified using any one of the various addressing modes of the 8086.

An example is the instruction

```
JMP DWORD PTR[DI]
```

It uses the contents of DS and DI to calculate the address of the memory location that contains the first word of the pointer that identifies the location to which the jump will take place. The two-word pointer starting at this address is read into IP and CS to pass control to the new point in the program.

Conditional Jump Instruction

The second type of jump instructions are those that perform conditional jump operations. Figure 4.6(a) shows a general form of this instruction and Fig. 4.6(b) is a list of each of the conditional jump instructions in the 8086's instruction set. Notice that each of these instructions tests for the presence or absence of certain conditions.

For instance, the *jump-on-carry* (JC) instruction makes a test to determine if carry flag (CF) is set. Depending on the result of the test, the jump to the location specified by its operand either takes place or does not. If CF equals 0, the test fails and execution continues with the instruction at the address following the JC instruction. On the other hand, if CF is set to 1, the test condition is satisfied and the jump is performed.

Notice that for some of the instructions in Fig. 4.6(b) two different mnemonics can be used. This feature can be used to improve program readability. That is, for each occurrence of the instruction in the program, it can be identified with the mnemonic that best describes its function.

For instance, the instruction *jump on parity* (JP)/*jump on parity even* (JPE) can be used to test parity flag PF for logic 1. Since PF is set to 1 if the result from a computation has even parity, this instruction can initiate a jump based on the occurrence of even parity. The reverse instruction JNP/JNPE is also provided. It can be used to initiate a jump based on the occurrence of a result with odd parity instead of even parity.

In a similar manner, the instructions *jump if equal* (JE) and *jump if zero* (JZ) have the same function. Either notation can be used in a program to determine if the result of a computation was 0.

All other conditional jump instructions work in a similar way except that they test different conditions to decide whether or not the jump is to take place. The status condition for each instruction is shown in Fig. 4.6(b). Examples of these conditions are that the contents of CX are 0, an overflow has occurred, or the result is negative.

To distinguish between comparisons of signed and unsigned numbers by jump instructions, two different names, which seem to be the same, have been devised. They are above and below for comparison of unsigned numbers and less and greater for

Mnemonic	Meaning	Format	Operation	Flags Affected
Jcc	Conditional jump	Jcc Operand	If the specific condition cc is true, the jump to the address specified by the Operand is initiated; otherwise, the next instruction is executed	None

(a)

Mnemonic	Meaning	Condition
JA	above	CF = 0 and ZF = 0
JAE	above or equal	CF = 0
JB	below	CF = 1
JBE	below or equal	CF = 1 or ZF = 1
JC	carry	CF = 1
JCXZ	CX register is zero	(CF or ZF) = 0
JE	equal	ZF = 1
JG	greater	ZF = 0 and SF = OF
JGE	greater or equal	SF = OF
JL	less	(SF xor OF) = 1
JLE	less or equal	((SF xor OF) or ZF) = 1
JNA	not above	CF = 1 or ZF = 1
JNAE	not above nor equal	CF = 1
JNB	not below	CF = 0
JNBE	not below nor equal	CF = 0 and ZF = 0
JNC	not carry	CF = 0
JNE	not equal	ZF = 0
JNG	not greater	((SF xor OF) or ZF) = 1
JNGE	not greater nor equal	(SF xor OF) = 1
JNL	not less	SF = OF
JNLE	not less nor equal	ZF = 0 and SF = OF
JNO	not overflow	OF = 0
JNP	not parity	PF = 0
JNS	not sign	SF = 0
JNZ	not zero	ZF = 0
JO	overflow	OF = 1
JP	parity	PF = 1
JPE	parity even	PF = 1
JPO	parity odd	PF = 0
JS	sign	SF = 1
JZ	zero	ZF = 1

(b)

Figure 4.6 (a) Conditional jump instruction; (b) types of conditional jump instructions.

comparison of signed numbers. For instance, the number $ABCD_{16}$ is above the number 1234_{16} if considered as an unsigned number. On the other hand, if they are considered as signed numbers, $ABCD_{16}$ is negative and 1234_{16} is positive. Therefore, $ABCD_{16}$ is less than 1234_{16}.

EXAMPLE 4.4

Write a program to move a block of N bytes of data starting at offset address BLK1ADDR to another block starting at offset address BLK2ADDR. Assume that both blocks are in the same data segment, whose starting point is defined by the data segment address DATASEGADDR.

SOLUTION   The steps to be implemented to solve this problem are outlined in the flow-chart in Fig. 4.7(a). It has four basic operations. The first operation is initialization. Initialization involves establishing the initial address of the data segment. This is done by loading the DS register with the value DATASEGADDR. Furthermore, source index register SI and destination index register DI are initialized with addresses BLK1ADDR and BLK2ADDR, respectively. In this way, they point to the beginning of the source block and the beginning of the destination block, respectively. To keep track of the count, register CX is initialized with N, the number of points to be moved. This leads us to the following assembly language statements.

```
MOV     AX, DATASEGADDR

MOV     DS, AX

MOV     SI, BLK1ADDR

MOV     DI, BLK2ADDR

MOV     CX, N
```

Notice that DS cannot be directly loaded by immediate data with a MOV instruction. Therefore, the segment address was first loaded into AX and then moved to DS. SI, DI, and CX can be loaded directly with immediate data.

The next operation that must be performed is the actual movement of data from the source block of memory to the destination block. The offset addresses are already loaded into SI and DI; therefore, move instructions that employ indirect addressing can be used to accomplish the data transfer operation. Remember that the 8086 does not allow direct memory-to-memory moves. For this reason, AX will be used as an intermediate storage location for data. The source byte is moved into AX with one instruction and then another instruction is needed to move it from AX to the destination location. Thus the data move is accomplished by the following instructions.

```
NXTPT:  MOV     AH, [SI]

        MOV     [DI], AH
```

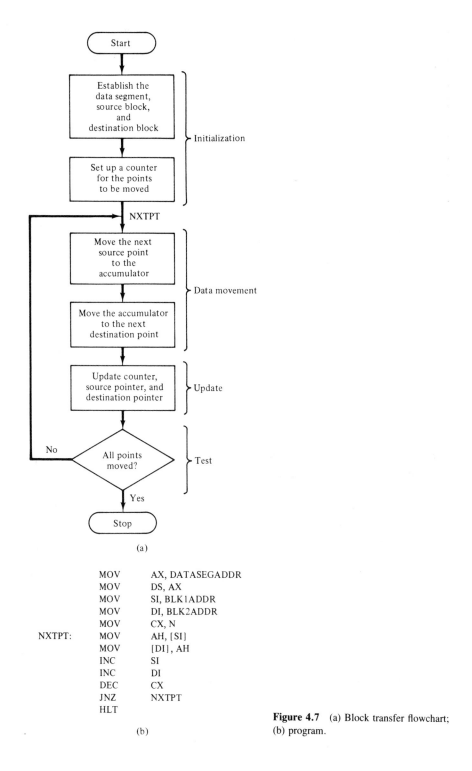

Figure 4.7 (a) Block transfer flowchart; (b) program.

Notice that for a byte move only the higher eight bits of AX are used. Therefore, the operand is specified as AH instead of AX.

The next operation is to update the pointers in SI and DI so that they are ready for the next byte move. Also, the counter must be decremented so that it corresponds to the number of bytes that remain to be moved. These updates can be done by the following sequence of instructions.

```
INC   SI

INC   DI

DEC   CX
```

The test operation involves determining whether or not all the data points have been moved. The contents of CX represents this condition. When its value is not 0, there still are points to be moved; whereas a value of 0 indicates that the block move is complete. This 0 condition is reflected by 1 in ZF. The instruction needed to perform this test is

```
JNZ NXTPT
```

Here NXTPT is a label that corresponds to the first instruction in the data move operation. The last instruction in the program can be a *halt* (HLT) instruction to indicate the end of the block move operation. The entire program is shown in Fig. 4.7(b).

4.5 SUBROUTINES AND SUBROUTINE-HANDLING INSTRUCTIONS

A *subroutine* is a special segment of program that can be called for execution from any point in a program. Figure 4.8(a) illustrates the concept of a subroutine. Here we see a program structure where one part of the program is called the *main program*. In addition to this, we find a smaller segment attached to the main program, known as a subroutine. The subroutine is written to provide a function that must be performed at various points in the main program. Instead of including this piece of code in the main program each time the function is needed, it is put into the program just once as a subroutine.

Wherever the function must be performed, a single instruction is inserted into the main body of the program to "call" the subroutine. Remember that the physical address CS:IP identifies the next instruction to be executed. Thus, to branch to a subroutine that starts elsewhere in memory, the value in either IP or CS and IP must be modified. After executing the subroutine, we want to return control to the instruction that follows the one that called the subroutine. In this way, program execution resumes in the main program at the point where it left off due to the subroutine call. A return instruction must be included at the end of the subroutine to initiate the *return sequence* to the main program environment.

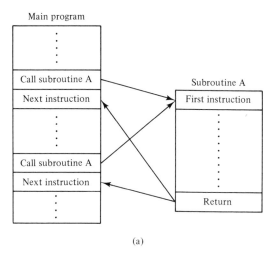

Main program

Call subroutine A
Next instruction

Call subroutine A
Next instruction

Subroutine A

First instruction

Return

(a)

Mnemonic	Meaning	Format	Operation	Flags Affected
CALL	Subroutine call	CALL operand	Execution continues from the address of the subroutine specified by the operand. Information required to return back to the main program such as IP and CS are saved on the stack.	None

(b)

Operand
Near-proc
Far-proc
Memptr16
Regptr16
Memptr32

(c)

Figure 4.8 (a) Subroutine concept; (b) subroutine call instruction; (c) allowed operands.

The instructions provided to transfer control from the main program to a subroutine and return control back to the main program are called *subroutine-handling instructions*. Let us now examine the instructions provided for this purpose.

CALL and RET Instructions

There are two basic instructions in the instruction set of the 8086 for subroutine handling. They are the *call* (CALL) and *return* (RET) instructions. Together they provide the mechanism for calling a subroutine into operation and returning control back to the main program at its completion. We will first discuss these two instructions and later introduce other instructions that can be used in conjunction with subroutines.

Just like the JMP instruction, CALL allows implementation of two types of operations, the *intrasegment call* and the *intersegment call*. The CALL instruction is shown in Fig. 4.8(b) and its allowed operand variations are shown in Fig. 4.8(c).

It is the operand that initiates either an intersegment or an intrasegment call. The operands Near-proc, Memptr16, and Regptr16 all specify intrasegment calls to a subroutine. In all three cases, execution of the instruction causes the contents of IP to be saved on the stack. Then the stack pointer (SP) is decremented by 2. The saved values of IP is the address of the instruction that follows the CALL instruction. After saving this return address, a new 16-bit value, which corresponds to the storage location of the first instruction in the subroutine, is loaded into IP.

The different types of intrasegment operands represent different ways of specifying this new value of IP. In a Near-proc operand, the displacement of the first instruction of the subroutine in the current code segment is supplied directly by the instruction. An example is

CALL NEARPROC

Here the label NEARPROC identifies the 16-bit displacement that gets added to IP. This displacement is coded as an immediate operand following the opcode for the call instruction. With a 16-bit displacement, the subroutine can reside anywhere in the current code segment.

The Memptr16 and Regptr16 operands provide indirect subroutine addressing by specifying a memory location or an internal register, respectively, as the source of a new value for IP. The value specified is the actual offset that is to be loaded into IP. An example of a Regptr16 operand is

CALL BX

When this instruction is executed, the contents of BX are loaded into IP and execution continues with the subroutine starting at a physical address derived from CS and the new value of IP.

By using one of the various addressing modes of the 8086, an internal register can be used as pointer to an operand that resides in memory. This represents a Memptr16 type of operand. In this case, the value of the physical address of the offset is obtained from the current contents of the data segment register DS and the address or addresses held in the specified registers. For instance, the instruction

CALL WORD PTR [BX]

has its subroutine offset address at the memory location whose physical address is derived from the contents of DS and BX. The value stored at this memory location is loaded into IP. Again the current contents of CS and the new value in IP point to the first instruction of the subroutine.

Notice that in both intrasegment call examples the subroutine was located within the same code segment as the call instruction. The other type of CALL instruction, the intersegment call, permits the subroutine to reside in another code segment. It corresponds to the Far-proc and Memptr32 operands. These operands specify both a new offset address for IP and a new segment address for CS. In both cases, execution of the call instruction causes the contents of the CS and IP registers to be saved on the stack and then new values are loaded into IP and CS. The saved values of CS and IP permit return to the main program from a different code segment.

Far-proc represents a 32-bit immediate operand that is stored in the four bytes that follow the opcode of the call instruction in program memory. These two words are loaded directly from code segment memory into IP and CS with execution of the CALL instruction. An example is the instruction

CALL FARPROC

On the other hand, when the operand is Memptr32, the pointer for the subroutine is stored as four consecutive bytes in data memory. The location of the first byte of the pointer can be specified indirectly by one of the 8086's registers. An example is

CALL DWORD PTR [DI]

Here the physical address of the first byte of the 4-byte pointer in memory is derived from the contents of DS and DI.

Every subroutine must end by executing an instruction that returns control to the main program. This is the return (RET) instruction. It is described in Fig. 4.9(a) and (b). Notice that its execution causes the value of IP or both the values of IP and CS that were saved on the stack to be returned back to their corresponding registers. In general, an intrasegment return results from an intrasegment call and an intersegment return results from an intersegment call. In this way, program control is returned to the instruction that follows the call instruction in program memory.

Mnemonic	Meaning	Format	Operation	Flags Affected
RET	Return	RET or RET Operand	Return to the main program by restoring IP (and CS for fat-proc). If Operand is present, it is added to the contents of SP.	None

(a)

(b)

Figure 4.9   (a) Return instruction; (b) allowed operands.

There is an additional option with the return instruction. It is that a 2-byte code following the return instruction can be included. This code gets added to the stack pointer after restoring the return address either into IP (intrasegment return) or IP and CS (intersegment return). The purpose of this stack pointer displacement is to provide a simple means by which the *parameters* that were saved on the stack before the call to the subroutine was initiated, can be discarded. For instance, the instruction

RET 2

when executed adds 2 to SP. This discards one word parameter as part of the return sequence.

PUSH and POP Instructions

After the context switch to a subroutine, we find that it is usually necessary to save the contents of certain registers or some other main program parameters. These values are saved by pushing them onto the stack. Typically, these data correspond to registers and memory locations that are used by the subroutine. In this way, their original contents are kept intact in the stack segment of memory during the execution of the subroutine. Before a return to the main program takes place, the saved registers and main program parameters are restored. This is done by popping the saved values from the stack back into their original locations. Thus a typical structure of a subroutine is that shown in Fig. 4.10.

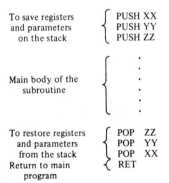

To save registers and parameters on the stack
{ PUSH XX
PUSH YY
PUSH ZZ }

Main body of the subroutine

To restore registers and parameters from the stack
Return to main program
{ POP ZZ
POP YY
POP XX
RET }

Figure 4.10 Structure of a subroutine.

The instruction that is used to save parameters on the stack is the *push* (PUSH) instruction and that used to retrieve them back is the *pop* (POP) instruction. Notice in Fig. 4.11(a) and (b) that the standard PUSH and POP instructions can be written with a general-purpose register, a segment register (excluding CS), or a storage location in memory as their operand.

Execution of a PUSH instruction causes the data corresponding to the operand to be pushed onto the top of the stack. For instance, if the instruction is

PUSH AX

Mnemonic	Meaning	Format	Operation	Flags Affected
PUSH	Push word onto stack	PUSH S	$((SP)) \leftarrow (S)$	None
POP	Pop word off stack	POP D	$(D) \leftarrow ((SP))$	None

(a)

Operand (S or D)
Register Seg-reg (CS illegal) Memory

(b)

Figure 4.11 (a) Push and pop instructions; (b) allowed operands.

the result is as follows:

$$((SP) - 1) \leftarrow (AH)$$

$$((SP) - 2) \leftarrow (AL)$$

$$(SP) \leftarrow (SP) - 2$$

This shows that the two bytes of AX are saved in the stack part of memory and the stack pointer is decremented by 2 such that it points to the new top of the stack.

On the other hand, if the instruction is

POP AX

its execution results in

$$(AL) \leftarrow ((SP))$$

$$(AH) \leftarrow ((SP) + 1)$$

$$(SP) \leftarrow (SP) + 2$$

In this manner, the saved contents of AX are restored back into the register.

At times, we also want to save the contents of the flag register and if saved we will later have to restore them. These operations can be accomplished with *push flags* (PUSHF) and *pop flags* (POPF) instructions, respectively. These instructions are shown in Fig. 4.12. Notice that PUSHF saves the contents of the flag register on the top of the

Mnemonic	Meaning	Operation	Flags Affected
PUSHF	Push flags onto stack	$((SP)) \leftarrow (Flags)$	None
POPF	Pop flags from stack	$(Flags) \leftarrow ((SP))$	OF, DF, IF, TF, SF, ZF, AF, PF, CF

Figure 4.12 Push flags and pop flags instructions.

stack. On the other hand, POPF returns the flags from the top of the stack to the flag register.

EXAMPLE 4.5

Write a procedure named SUM that adds two numbers, 5_{10} and 31_{16}, together and places their sum in DX. Assume that this procedure is to be called from another procedure in the same code segment and that at the time it is to be called, DX contains the value $ABCD_{16}$ and this value must be saved at entry of the procedure and restored at its completion.

SOLUTION The beginning of the procedure can be defined with the pseudo-op statement

SUM PROC NEAR

At entry of the procedure, we must save the value currently held in DX. This is done by pushing its contents to the stack with the instruction

PUSH DX

Now we load DX with the value 5_{10} using the instruction

MOV DX, 5

and add 31_{16} to it with the instruction

ADD DX, 31

This completes the addition operation, but before we return to the main part of the program, the original contents of DX that were saved on the stack are restored with the pop instruction

POP DX

Then a return instruction is used to pass control back to the main program.

RET

The procedure must be terminated with the end procedure pseudo-op statement that follows.

SUM ENDP

The complete instruction sequence is shown in Fig. 4.13.

```
        SUM   PROC   NEAR
              PUSH   DX
              MOV    DX,5
              ADD    DX,31
              POP    DX
              RET
        SUM   ENDP
```

Figure 4.13 Program for example 4.5

4.6 LOOP INSTRUCTIONS

The 8086 microprocessor has three instructions specifically designed for implementing *loop operations*. These instructions can be used in place of certain conditional jump instructions and give the programmer a simpler way of writing loop sequences. The loop instructions are listed in Fig. 4.14.

The first instruction, *loop* (LOOP), works with respect to the contents of the CX register. CX must be preloaded with a count representing the number of times the loop is to be repeated. Whenever LOOP is executed, the contents of CX are first decremented by 1 and then checked to determine if they are equal to 0. If they are equal to 0, the loop is complete and the instruction following LOOP is executed; otherwise, control is returned to the instruction at the label specified in the loop instruction. In this way, we see that LOOP is a single instruction that functions the same as a decrement CX instruction followed by a JNZ instruction.

For example, the LOOP instruction sequence shown in Fig. 4.15(a) will cause the part of the program from the label NEXT through the instruction LOOP to be repeated a number of times equal to the value of count stored in CX. For example, if CX contains $000A_{16}$, the sequence of instructions included in the loop is executed 10 times.

The other two instructions in Fig. 4.14 operate in a similar way except that they

Mnemonic	Meaning	Format	Operation
LOOP	Loop	LOOP Short-label	$(CX) \leftarrow (CX) - 1$ Jump is initiated to location defined by short-label if $(CX) \neq 0$; otherwise, execute next sequential instruction
LOOPE/LOOPZ	Loop while equal/ loop while zero	LOOPE/LOOPZ Short-label	$(CX) \leftarrow (CX) - 1$ Jump to location defined by short-label if $(CX) \neq 0$ and $(ZF) = 1$; otherwise, execute next sequential instruction
LOOPNE/ LOOPNZ	Loop while not equal/ loop while not zero	LOOPNE/LOOPNZ Short-label	$(CX) \leftarrow (CX) - 1$ Jump to location defined by short-label if $(CX) \neq 0$ and $(ZF) = 0$; otherwise, execute next sequential instruction

Figure 4.14 Loop instructions.

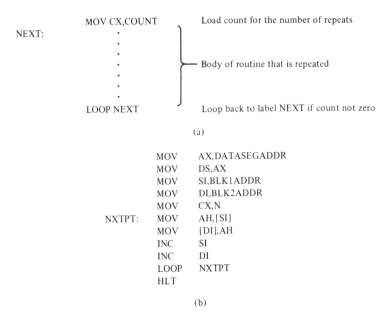

```
                  MOV CX,COUNT          Load count for the number of repeats
        NEXT:         .
                      .
                      .                ┐
                      .                ├─ Body of routine that is repeated
                      .                ┘
                      .
        LOOP NEXT                       Loop back to label NEXT if count not zero
```

(a)

```
              MOV    AX,DATASEGADDR
              MOV    DS,AX
              MOV    SI,BLK1ADDR
              MOV    DI,BLK2ADDR
              MOV    CX,N
    NXTPT:    MOV    AH,[SI]
              MOV    [DI],AH
              INC    SI
              INC    DI
              LOOP   NXTPT
              HLT
```

(b)

Figure 4.15 (a) Typical loop routine structure; (b) block move program employing the LOOP instruction.

check for two conditions. For instance, the instruction *loop while equal* (LOOPE)/*loop while zero* (LOOPZ) checks the contents of both CX and the ZF flag. Each time the loop instruction is executed, CX decrements by 1 without affecting the flags, its contents are checked for 0, and the state of ZF that results from execution of the previous instruction is tested for 1. If CX is not equal to 0 and ZF equals 1, a jump is initiated to the location specified with the Short-label operand and the loop continues. If either CX or ZF is 0, the loop is complete and the instruction following the loop instruction is executed.

Instruction *loop while not equal* (LOOPNE)/*loop while not zero* (LOOPNZ) works in a similar way to the LOOPE/LOOPZ instruction. The difference is that it checks ZF and CX looking for ZF equal to 0 together with CX not equal to 0. If these conditions are met, the jump back to the location specified with the Short-label operand is performed and the loop continues.

Figure 4.15(b) shows a practical implementation of a loop. Here we find the block move program that was developed in example 4.4 rewritten using the LOOP instruction. Comparing this program with the one in Fig. 4.7(b), we see that the instruction LOOP NXTPT has replaced both the DEC and JNZ instructions.

EXAMPLE 4.6

Given the following sequence of instructions:

```
              MOV   AX, 0

              MOV   DS, AX
```

```
                MOV   AL,05

                MOV   DI,A000

                MOV   CX,0F

       AGAIN:   INC   DI

                CMP   [DI],AL

                LOOPNE  AGAIN

       NEXT:
```

Explain what happens as they are executed.

SOLUTION The first four instructions are for initializing internal registers. Data segment register DS is cleared; accumulator register AL is loaded with the 05_{16}; destination index register DI is loaded with $A000_{16}$; and count register CX is loaded with $000F_{16}$ (15_{10}). After initialization, a data segment is set up at address 00000_{16} and DI points to the memory location at offset $A000_{16}$ in this data segment. Moreover, AL contains the data 5_{10} and the CX register contains the loop count 15_{10}.

The part of the program that starts at the label AGAIN and ends with the LOOPNE instruction is a software loop. The first instruction in the loop increments DI by one. Therefore, the first time through the loop DI contains $A001_{16}$. The next instruction compares the contents of this memory location with the contents of AL, which is 5_{10}. If the data held at $A001_{16}$ is 5_{10}, the zero flag is set; otherwise, it is left at logic 0. The LOOPNE instruction then decrements CX (making it E_{16}) and then checks for CX = 0 or ZF = 1. If neither of these two conditions are satisfied, program control is returned to the instruction with the label AGAIN. This causes the comparison to be repeated for the examination of the contents of the next byte in memory. On the other hand, if either condition is satisfied, the loop is terminated and execution continues with the instruction identified by the label NEXT. In this way, we see that the loop is repeated until either a number 5_{16} is found or all locations in the address range $A001_{16}$ through $A00F_{16}$ have been tested and found to not contain 5_{16}.

4.7 STRING INSTRUCTIONS

The 8086 microprocessor is equipped with special instructions to handle *string operations*. By "string" we mean a series of data words (or bytes) that reside in consecutive memory locations. The string instructions of the 8086 permit a programmer to implement operations such as to move data from one block of memory to a block elsewhere in memory. A second type of operation that is easily performed is to scan a string of data elements stored in memory looking for a specific value. Other examples are to compare the elements of two strings together in order to determine whether they are the same or different, and to initialize a set of consecutive memory locations. Complex operations such as these typically require several nonstring instructions to be implemented.

There are five basic string instructions in the instruction set of the 8086. These instructions, as listed in Fig. 4.16, are *move byte* or *word string* (MOVS, MOVSB/MOVSW), *compare strings* (CMPS), *scan string* (SCAS), *load string* (LODS), and *store string* (STOS). They are called the *basic string instructions* because each defines an operation for one element of a string. Thus these operations must be repeated to handle a string of more than one element. Let us first look at the basic operations performed by these instructions.

Mnemonic	Meaning	Format	Operation	Flags Affected
MOVS	Move string	MOVS Operand	$((ES)0 + (DI)) \leftarrow ((DS)0 + (SI))$ $(SI) \leftarrow (SI) \pm 1$ or 2 $(DI) \leftarrow (DI) \pm 1$ or 2	None
MOVSB	Move string byte	MOVSB	$((ES)0 + (DI)) \leftarrow ((DS)0 + (SI))$ $(SI) \leftarrow (SI) \pm 1$ $(DI) \leftarrow (DI) \pm 1$	None
MOVSW	Move string word	MOVSW	$((ES)0 + (DI)) \leftarrow ((DS)0 + (SI))$ $((ES)0 + (DI) + 1) \leftarrow ((DS)0 + (SI) + 1)$ $(SI) \leftarrow (SI) \pm 2$ $(DI) \leftarrow (DI) \pm 2$	None
CMPS	Compare string	CMPS Operand	Set flags as per $((DS)0 + (SI)) - ((ES)0 + (DI))$ $(SI) \leftarrow (SI) \pm 1$ or 2 $(DI) \leftarrow (DI) \pm 1$ or 2	CF, PF, AF, ZF, SF, OF
SCAS	Scan string	SCAS Operand	Set flags as per $(AL$ or $AX) - ((ES)0 + (DI))$ $(DI) \leftarrow (DI) \pm 1$ or 2	CF, PF, AF, ZF, SF, OF
LODS	Load string	LODS Operand	$(AL$ or $AX) \leftarrow ((DS)0 + (SI))$ $(SI) \leftarrow (SI) \pm 1$ or 2	None
STOS	Store string	STOS Operand	$((ES)0 + (DI)) \leftarrow (AL$ or $AX) \pm 1$ or 2 $(DI) \leftarrow (DI) \pm 1$ or 2	None

Figure 4.16 Basic string instructions.

Move String—MOVS, MOVSB/MOVSW

The instructions MOVS, MOVSB, and MOVSW all perform the same basic operation. An element of the string specified by the source index (SI) register with respect to the current data segment (DS) register is moved to the location specified by the destination index (DI) register with respect to the current extra segment (ES) register. The move can be performed on a byte or a word of data. After the move is complete, the contents of both SI and DI are automatically incremented or decremented by 1 for a byte move and by 2 for a word move. Remember the fact that the address pointers in SI and DI increment or decrement depends on how the direction flag DF is set.

The instruction MOVS requires that an operand be specified, whereas MOVSB and MOVSW have no operands. This operand is simply either WORD or BYTE. For example, one way of writing a MOVS instruction is

MOVS BYTE

This instruction could also be written simply as

MOVSB

An example of a program that uses MOVSB is shown in Fig. 4.17. This program is a modified version of the block move program of Fig. 4.15(b). Notice that the two MOV instructions that performed the data transfer and INC instructions that update the pointer have been replaced with one move string byte instruction. We have also made DS equal to ES.

```
        MOV     AX,DATASEGADDR
        MOV     DS,AX
        MOV     ES,AX
        MOV     SI,BLK1ADDR
        MOV     DI,BLK2ADDR
        MOV     CX,N
        CDF
NXTPT:  MOVSB
        LOOP    NXTPT
        HLT
```

Figure 4.17 Block move program using the move string instruction.

Compare Strings and Scan Strings—CMPS and SCAS

The CMPS instruction can be used to compare two elements in the same or different strings. It subtracts the destination operand from the source operand and adjusts flags CF, PF, AF, ZF, SF, and OF accordingly. The result of subtraction is not saved; therefore, the operation does not affect the operands in any way.

An example of a compare strings instruction for bytes of data is

CMPS BYTE

Again, the source element is pointed to by the address in SI with respect to the current value in DS and the destination element is specified by the contents of DI relative to the contents of ES. When executed, the operands are compared, the flags are adjusted, and both SI and DI are updated such that they point to the next elements in their respective strings.

The scan string (SCAS) instruction is similar to CMPS; however, it compares the byte or word element of the destination string at the physical address derived from DI and ES to the contents of AL or AX, respectively. The flags are adjusted based on this result and DI incremented or decremented.

A program using the SCAS instruction that implements the string scan operation described in example 4.6 is shown in Fig. 4.18. Again, we have made DS equal to ES.

```
            MOV       AX,0
            MOV       DS,AX
            MOV       ES,AX
            MOV       AL,05
            MOV       DI,A000
            MOV       CX,0F
            CDF
AGAIN:      SCASB
            LOOPNE    AGAIN
NEXT:
```

Figure 4.18 Block scan operation using the SCAS instruction.

Load and Store Strings—LODS and STOS

The last two instructions in Fig. 4.16, load string (LODS) and store string (STOS), are specifically provided to move string elements between the accumulator and memory. LODS loads either a byte or a word from a string in memory into AL or AX, respectively. The address in SI is used relative to DS to determine the address of the memory location of the string element. For instance, the instruction

LODS WORD

indicates that the word string element at the physical address derived from DS and SI is to be loaded into AX. Then the index in SI is automatically incremented by 2.

On the other hand, STOS stores a byte from AL or a word from AX into a string location in memory. This time the contents of ES and DI are used to form the address of the storage location in memory. For example, the program in Fig. 4.19 will load the block of memory locations from $0A000_{16}$ through $0A00F_{16}$ with number 5.

```
            MOV       AX,0
            MOV       DS,AX
            MOV       ES,AX
            MOV       AL,05
            MOV       DI,A000
            MOV       CX,0F
            CDF
AGAIN:      STOSB
            LOOPNE    AGAIN
NEXT:
```

Figure 4.19 Clearing a block of memory with a STOS operation.

Repeat String—REP

In most applications, the basic string operations must be repeated in order to process arrays of data. This is done by inserting a repeat prefix before the instruction that is to be repeated. The *repeat prefixes* of the 8086 are shown in Fig. 4.20.

The first prefix, REP, causes the basic string operation to be repeated until the contents of register CX become equal to zero. Each time the instruction is executed, it causes CX to be tested for 0. If CX is found not to be 0, it is decremented by 1 and the basic string operation is repeated. On the other hand, if it is 0, the repeat string

Prefix	Used with:	Meaning
REP	MOVS STOS	Repeat while not end of string $CX \neq 0$
REPE/REPZ	CMPS SCAS	Repeat while not end of string and strings are equal $CX \neq 0$ and $ZF = 1$
REPNE/REPNZ	CMPS SCAS	Repeat while not end of string and strings are not equal $CX \neq 0$ and $ZF = 0$

Figure 4.20 Prefixes for use with the basic string operations.

operation is done and the next instruction in the program is executed. The repeat count must be loaded into CX prior to executing the repeat string instruction. Figure 4.21 is the memory load routine of Fig. 4.19 modified by using the REP prefix.

```
          MOV       AX,0
          MOV       DS,AX
          MOV       ES,AX
          MOV       AL,05
          MOV       DI,A000
          MOV       CX,0F
          CDF
          REPSTOSB
NEXT:
```

Figure 4.21 Clearing a block of memory repeating STOS.

EXAMPLE 4.7

Describe what happens as the following sequence of instructions is executed.

```
          MOV       AX, DATA__SEGMENT

          MOV       DS, AX

          MOV       AX, EXTRA__SEGMENT

          MOV       ES, AX

          MOV       CX, 20

          MOV       SI, MASTER

          MOV       DI, COPY

          REPMOVSB
```

SOLUTION The first two instructions initialize DS with the value DATA__SEGMENT. It is followed by two instructions that load ES with the value EXTRA__SEGMENT. Then the number of repeats, 0020_{16}, is loaded into CX. The next two instructions load SI and DI with beginning offset addresses MASTER and COPY for the source and destination strings. Now we are ready to perform the string operation. Execution of REPMOVSB moves a block of 32 consecutive bytes from the block of memory locations starting at offset address MASTER with respect to the current data segment (DS) to a block of locations starting at offset address COPY with respect to the current extra segment (ES).

The prefixes REPE and REPZ stand for the same function. They are meant for use with the CMPS and SCAS instructions. With REPE/REPZ, the basic compare or scan operation can be repeated as long as both the contents of CX are not equal to 0 and the zero flag is 1. The first condition CX not equal to 0 indicates that the end of the string has not yet been reached and the second condition ZF = 1 indicates that the elements that were compared are equal.

The last prefix, REPNE/REPNZ, works similarly to REPE/REPZ except that now the operation is repeated as long as CX is not equal to 0 and ZF is 0. That is, the comparison or scanning is to be performed as long as the string elements are unequal and the end of the string is not yet found.

Autoindexing for String Instructions

Earlier we pointed out that during the execution of a string instruction the address indices in SI and DI are either automatically incremented or decremented. Moreover, we indicated that the decision to increment or decrement is made based on the setting of the direction flag DF. The 8086 provides two instructions, clear direction flag (CLD) and set direction flag (STD), to permit selection between *autoincrement* and *autodecrement mode* of operation. These instructions are shown in Fig. 4.22. When CLD is executed, DF is set to 0. This selects autoincrement mode and each time a string operation is performed SI and/or DI are incremented by 1 if byte data are processed and by two if word data are processed.

Mnemonic	Meaning	Format	Operation	Flags Affected
CLD	Clear DF	CLD	(DF) ← 0	DF
STD	Set DF	STD	(DF) ← 1	DF

Figure 4.22 Instructions for autoincrementing and autodecrementing in string instructions.

EXAMPLE 4.8

Describe what happens as the following sequence of instructions is executed.

```
CLD

MOV   AX, DATA__SEGMENT

MOV   DS, AX

MOV   AX, EXTRA__SEGMENT

MOV   ES, AX
```

```
                    MOV    CX, 20

                    MOV    SI, OFFSET MASTER

                    MOV    DI, OFFSET COPY

                    REPECMPS
```

SOLUTION   The first instruction clears the direction flag and selects autoincrement mode of operation for string addressing. The next two instructions initialize DS with the value DATA_SEGMENT. It is followed by two instructions that load ES with the value EXTRA_SEGMENT. Then the number of repeats, 20_{16}, is loaded into CX. The next two instructions load SI and DI with beginning offset addresses MASTER and COPY for the source and destination strings. Now we are ready to perform the string operation. Execution of REPECMPS compares a block of 32 consecutive bytes from the block of memory locations starting at offset address MASTER with respect to the current data segment (DS) to a block of locations starting at offset address COPY with respect to the current extra segment (ES).

EXAMPLE 4.9

Given a string of 100 EBCDIC characters that are stored starting at offset address EBCDIC_CHAR. Convert them to their equivalent string of ASCII characters and store them at offset address ASCII_CHAR. The translation may be done using an EBCDIC-to-ASCII conversion table that starts at offset memory address EBCDIC_TO_ASCII.

SOLUTION   The problem to be programmed is illustrated in Fig. 4.23(a). Here we have assumed that the various data elements—the 100 given EBCDIC characters, the conversion table for EBCDIC to ASCII, and the generated ASCII characters—all reside in the same data segment. This data segment starts at the address DATA_SEGMENT. With respect to this data segment, the offset addresses EBCDIC_CHAR, ASCII_CHAR, and EBCDIC_TO_ASCII are as shown in the diagram. Moreover we are assuming that the string of 100 EBCDIC characters and the EBCDIC-to-ASCII table already exist at the correct locations in memory.

   Our solution to the problem is flowcharted in Fig. 4.23(b). We will use the string, translate, and loop instructions to implement the solution. Moreover, we will also use autoincrement mode for the string operations.

   The initialization involves setting up the data segment (DS) register to address the area in memory that stores the 100 given EBCDIC characters and conversion table. The same memory area will also be used to store the converted ASCII characters; therefore, we will make the extra segment, which is needed by the string instructions, overlap the data segment by loading both DS and ES with the same address. This is the value assigned to variable DATA_SEGMENT. Then SI and DI must be loaded with addresses that point to the first characters in the EBCDIC string and the ASCII string, respectively. These addresses are equal to EBCDIC_CHAR

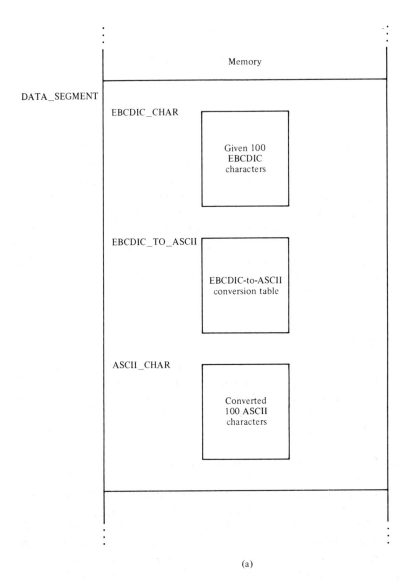

Memory

DATA_SEGMENT

EBCDIC_CHAR

Given 100
EBCDIC
characters

EBCDIC_TO_ASCII

EBCDIC-to-ASCII
conversion table

ASCII_CHAR

Converted
100 ASCII
characters

(a)

Figure 4.23 (a) EBCDIC-to-ASCII conversion; (b) flowchart; (c) program.

and ASCII_CHAR, respectively. The code translation is made using a conversion table and the XLAT instruction. XLAT requires that BX hold a pointer to the beginning of the conversion table. Therefore, BX must be loaded with the address corresponding to EBCDIC_TO_ASCII. To keep track of the number of characters that are converted, CX will be loaded with 100_{10} equal to 64_{16}. Finally, the autoincrement feature is invoked by resetting the direction flag DF. This leads to the following initialization code.

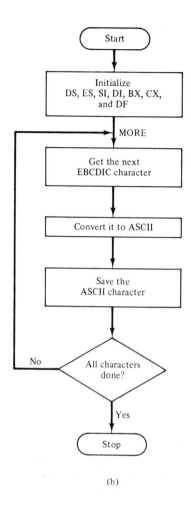

(b)

```
            MOV       AX, DATA_SEGMENT
            MOV       DS, AX
            MOV       ES, AX
            MOV       SI, EBCDIC_CHAR
            MOV       DI, ASCII_CHAR
            MOV       BX, EBCDIC_TO_ASCII
            MOV       CX, 064
            CLD
    MORE:   LODS      BYTE
            XLAT
            STOS      BYTE
            LOOP      MORE
            HLT
```

(c)   **Figure 4.23**   *(continued)*

```
MOV     AX, DATA__SEGMENT

MOV     DS, AX

MOV     ES, AX

MOV     SI, EBCDIC__CHAR

MOV     DI, ASCII__CHAR

MOV     BX, EBCDIC__TO__ASCII

MOV     CX, 64

CLD
```

Next, an EBCDIC character can be loaded, translated to its corresponding AS-CII character, and stored in the memory area reserved for storage of ASCII characters. This gives us the instructions

```
MORE:   LODS    BYTE

        XLAT

        STOS    BYTE
```

Execution of the LODS instruction loads the first element of the EBCDIC string into AL. Notice that use of autoincrementing prepares SI to handle the next conversion. Next, the XLAT instruction uses the EBCDIC character code in AL as an offset to address the equivalent ASCII character in the table at EBCDIC__TO__ASCII. This ASCII character is transferred to AL. The translation is now complete; however, the resulting character must be stored in the table defined by the address ASCII__CHAR. This is done with the STOS instruction. During the execution of this instruction, DI is automatically incremented so that it points to the next storage location in the ASCII string.

To repeat the process starting from label MORE, we can use a loop instruction that will decrement CX and jump to MORE as long as the contents of CX are not 0. This assures that translation is repeated for each of the 100 characters in the EBCDIC string. To do this, the instruction is

```
                LOOP  MORE
```

To end the program, the halt (HLT) instruction can be executed. The entire program is repeated in Fig. 4.23(c).

Section 4.2

1. Explain what happens when the instruction sequence

> LAHF
>
> MOV   [BX+DI],AH

is executed.

2. What operation is performed by the instruction sequence that follows?

> MOV   AH,[BX+SI]
>
> SAHF

3. Which instruction should be executed to assure that the carry flag is in the set state? The reset state?

4. Which instruction when executed disables the interrupt interface?

5. Write an instruction sequence to configure the 8086 as follows: interrupts not accepted; save the original contents of flags SF, ZF, AF, PF, and CF at the address $A000_{16}$; and then clear CF.

Section 4.3

6. Describe the difference in operation and the effect on status flags due to the execution of the subtract words and compare words instructions.

7. Describe the operation performed by each of the instructions that follow.
   (a) CMP   [0100],AL
   (b) CMP   AX,[SI]
   (c) CMP   WORD PTR [DI],1234

8. What is the state of the 8086's flags after executing the instructions in problem 7 (a) through (c)? Assume the following initial state exists before executing the instructions.

> AX = 8001H
>
> SI = 0200H
>
> DI = 0300H
>
> DS:100 = F0H
>
> DS:200 = F0H
>
> DS:201 = 01H

$$DS:300 = 34H$$

$$DS:301 = 12H$$

9. What happens to the ZF and CF status flags as the following sequence of instructions is executed? Assume that they are both initially cleared.

$$MOV \quad BX, 1111$$

$$MOV \quad AX, BBBB$$

$$CMP \quad BX, AX$$

Section 4.4

10. What is the key difference between the unconditional jump instruction and conditional jump instruction?

11. Which registers have their contents changed during a intrasegment jump? Intersegment jump?

12. How large is a Short-label displacement? Near-label displacement? Memptr16 operand?

13. Is a Far-label used to initiate an intrasegment jump or an intersegment jump?

14. Identify the type of jump, the type of operand, and operation performed by each of the instructions that follows.
    (a) JMP   10
    (b) JMP   1000
    (c) JMP   WORD PTR   [SI]

15. If the state of the 8086 is as follows after executing each instruction in problem 14, to what address is program control passed?

$$CS = 0175H$$

$$IP = 0300H$$

$$SI = 0100H$$

$$DS:100 = 00H$$

$$DS:101 = 10H$$

16. Which flags are tested by the various conditional jump instructions?

17. What flag condition is tested for by the instruction JNS?

18. What flag conditions are tested for by the instruction JA?

19. Identify the type of jump, the type of operand, and operation performed by each of the instructions that follows.
    (a) JNC   10
    (b) JNP   PARITY_ERROR
    (c) JO   DWORD PTR [BX]

20. What value must be loaded into BX such that execution of the instruction JMP BX transfers control to the memory location offset from the beginning of the current code segment by 256_{10}?

21. The program that follows implements what is known as a *delay loop*.

```
          MOV   CX, 1000

DLY:      DEC   CX

          JNZ   DLY

NXT:      - - -   - - -
```

(a) How many times does the JNZ DLY instruction get executed?
(b) Change the program so that JNZ DLY is executed just 17 times.
(c) Change the program so that JNZ DLY is executed 2^{32} times.

22. Given a number N in the range $0 < N \le 5$, write a program that computes its factorial and saves the result in memory location FACT.

23. Write a program that compares the elements of two arrays, A(I) and B(I). Each array contains 100 16-bit signed numbers. The comparison is to be done by comparing the corresponding elements of the two arrays until either two elements are found to be unequal or all elements of the arrays have been compared and found to be equal. Assume that the arrays start at addresses $A000_{16}$ and $B000_{16}$, respectively. If the two arrays are found to be unequal, save the address of the first unequal element of A(I) in memory location FOUND; otherwise, write all 0s into this location.

24. Given an array A(I) of 100 16-bit signed numbers that are stored in memory starting at address $A000_{16}$, write a program to generate two arrays from the given array such that one P(J) consists of all the positive numbers and the other N(K) contains all the negative numbers. Store the array of positive numbers in memory starting at address $B000_{16}$ and the array of negative numbers starting at address $C000_{16}$.

25. Given a 16-bit binary number in DX, write a program that converts it to its equivalent BCD number in DX. If the result is bigger than 16 bits, place all 1s in DX.

26. Given an array A(I) with 100 16-bit signed integer numbers, write a program to generate a new array B(I) as follows:

$$B(I) = A(I), \quad \text{for I} = 1, 2, 99, \text{ and } 100$$

and

$$B(I) = \text{median value of A}(I - 2), A(I - 1), A(I), A(I + 1),$$
$$\text{and A}(I + 2), \quad \text{for all other Is}$$

Section 4.5

27. Describe the difference between a jump and call instruction.

28. Why are intersegment and intrasegment call instructions provided in the 8086?

29. What is saved on the stack when a call instruction with a Memptr16 operand is executed? A Memptr32 operand?

30. Identify the type of call, the type of operand, and operation performed by each of the instructions that follows.

(a) CALL   1000
(b) CALL   WORD PTR [0100]
(c) CALL   DWORD PTR [BX+SI]

31. If the state of the 8086 is as follows after executing each instruction in problem 30, to what address is program control passed?

$$CS = 1075H$$

$$IP = 0300H$$

$$BX = 0100H$$

$$SI = 0100H$$

$$DS:100 = 00H$$

$$DS:101 = 10H$$

$$DS:200 = 00H$$

$$DS:201 = 01H$$

$$DS:202 = 00H$$

$$DS:203 = 10H$$

32. What function is performed by the RET instruction?

33. Describe the operation performed by each of the instructions that follow.
   (a) PUSH   DS
   (b) PUSH   [SI]
   (c) POP   DI
   (d) POP   [BX+DI]
   (e) POPF

34. At what addresses will the bytes of the immediate operand in problem 33 (a) be stored after the instruction is executed?

35. Write a subroutine that converts a given 16-bit BCD number to its equivalent binary number. The BCD number is to be passed to a subroutine through register DX and the routine returns the equivalent binary number in DX.

36. When is it required to include PUSHF and POPF instructions in a subroutine?

37. Given an array A(I) of 100 16-bit signed integer numbers, write a subroutine to generate a new array B(I) such that

$$B(I) = A(I), \quad \text{for I} = 1 \text{ and } 100$$

and

$$B(I) = \frac{1}{4}[A(I - 1) - 5A(I) + 9A(I + 1)], \quad \text{for all other Is}$$

The values of A(I − 1), A(I), and A(I + 1) are to be passed to the subroutine in registers AX, BX, and CX and the subroutine returns the result B(I) in register AX.

38. Write a segment of main program and show its subroutine structure to perform the following operations. The program is to check continuously the three most significant bits in register DX and, depending on their setting, execute one of three subroutines: SUBA, SUBB, or SUBC. The subroutines are selected as follows:

(a) If bit 15 of DX is set, initiate SUBA.

(b) If bit 14 of DX is set and bit 15 is not set, initiate SUBB.

(c) If bit 13 of DX is set and bits 14 and 15 are not set, initiate SUBC.

If the subroutine is executed, the corresponding bits of DX are to be cleared and then control returned to the main program. After returning from the subroutine, the main program is repeated.

Section 4.6

39. Which flags are tested by the various conditional loop instructions?

40. What two conditions can terminate the operation performed by the instruction LOOPNE?

41. How large a jump can be employed in a loop instruction?

42. What is the maximum number of repeats that can be implemented with a loop instruction?

43. Using loop instructions, implement the program is problem 22.

44. Using loop instructions, implement the program in problem 23.

Section 4.7

45. What determines whether the SI and DI registers increment or decrement during a string operation?

46. Which segment register is used to form the destination address for a string instruction?

47. Write equivalent string instruction sequences for each of the following:

(a) MOV AX, [SI]   **(c)** MOV AL, [DI]
    MOV [DI], AX   CMP AL, [SI]
    INC SI   DEC SI
    INC DI   DEC DI

(b) MOV AX, [SI]
    INC SI
    INC SI

48. Use string instructions to implement the program in problem 23.

49. Write a program to convert a table of 100 ASCII characters that are stored starting at offset address ASCII_CHAR into their equivalent table of EBCDIC characters and store them at offset address EBCDIC_CHAR. The translation is to be done using an ASCII-to-EBCDIC conversion table starting at offset address ASCII_TO_EBCDIC. Assume that all three tables are located in different segments of memory.

Chapter 5

Using the SDK-86 Microcomputer for Program Development

5.1 INTRODUCTION

In previous chapters we considered the 8086 microprocessor's instruction set and writing of assembly language programs. This chapter describes the SDK-86 microcomputer, which is an instrument that can be used to verify whether a program written for a specific application accurately implements its intended function. The topics discussed are as follows:

1. The microcomputer development system
2. Converting source programs to machine code
3. The monitor program
4. Monitor commands
5. Loading and executing a machine code program
6. Debugging a program

5.2 THE MICROCOMPUTER DEVELOPMENT SYSTEM

A *development system* is an instrument that is used to develop programs and hardware for a microprocessor-based system. Typically, the system is designed to permit development work to be done for only specific microprocessors, for instance, devices produced by a specific manufacturer. It can be a sophisticated system such as Intel's PC-hosted 8086 emulator, which is shown in Fig. 5.1. This kind of system gives the

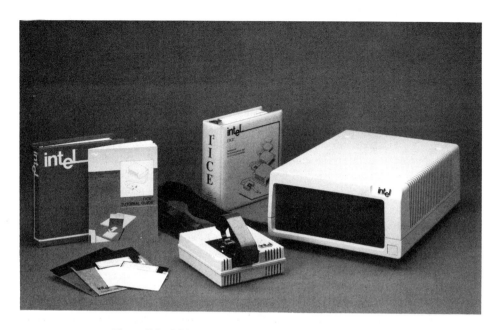

Figure 5.1 PC hosted 8086 emulator (Courtesy of Intel Corp.).

microcomputer designer important capabilities, such as the ability to develop programs in either assembly language or a variety of high-level languages, powerful tools for efficient debugging of programs, facilities for connection to external hardware for circuit debugging, and the ability to integrate the user's software and hardware for testing and debugging. Use of this type of instrumentation system is essential for major microcomputer development projects. Its use results in much saved time and higher-quality hardware and software.

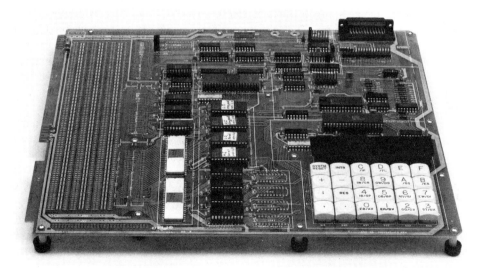

Figure 5.2 Intel's system design kit for the 8086 (SDK-86) (Courtesy of Intel Corp.).

On the other hand, inexpensive systems such as Intel's *System Design Kit 86 (SDK-86)* are also available. The SDK-86, which is shown in Fig. 5.2, can also be considered a development system. However, compared with an 8086 emulator, it offers only a limited set of capabilities to the designer. Even with its limited capabilities, the SDK-86 serves as an effective vehicle for learning the basics of microcomputer program development. This is the development system we describe in this chapter.

The SDK-86 can be used to execute and debug small programs. The programs are entered into the microcomputer using a hexadecimal keypad; therefore, assembly language instructions need to be first converted to machine code and then entered.

Keys are also provided on the SDK-86 to enter program development commands, such as display a register's contents, modify a byte or a word in memory, or start executing the program. Command execution is done with the help of an EPROM-based monitor program on the SDK-86. This program is called the *keypad monitor*. Although the SDK-86 provides another monitor, which is intended for use together with a terminal, we will limit our discussion to the keypad monitor.

5.3 CONVERTING SOURCE PROGRAMS TO MACHINE CODE

To convert an assembly language program to machine code, we must convert each assembly language instruction to its equivalent machine code instruction. In general, for an instruction, the machine code specifies such things as what operation is to be performed, what operand or operands are to be used, whether the operation is performed on byte or word data, whether the operation involves operands that are located in registers or a register and a storage location in memory, and if one of the operands is in memory, how its address is to be generated. All of this information is encoded into the bits of the machine code instruction.

The machine code instructions of the 8086 vary in the number of bytes used to encode them. Some instructions can be encoded with just 1 byte, others in 2 bytes, and many require more. The maximum number of bytes that an instruction might take is six. *Single-byte instructions* generally specify a simpler operation with a register or a flag bit. For instance, complement carry (CMC) is an example of a single-byte instruction. It is specified by the machine code byte 11110101, which equals $F5_{16}$.

$$CMC = 11110101_2 = F5_{16}.$$

The machine codes for instructions can be obtained by following the formats that are used in encoding the instructions of the 8086 microprocessor. Most of the *multibyte instructions* of the 8086 use the *general instruction format* shown in Fig. 5.3. Exceptions to this format will be considered separately late. For now, let us describe the functions of the various bits and fields (groups of bits) in each byte of this format.

Looking at Fig. 5.3, we see that byte 1 contains three kinds of information: the *operation code (opcode)*, the *register direction bit* (D), and the *data size bit* (W). Let us summarize the function of each of these pieces of information.

1. *Opcode field* (6 bits): specifies the operation, such as add, subtract, or move, that is to be performed.

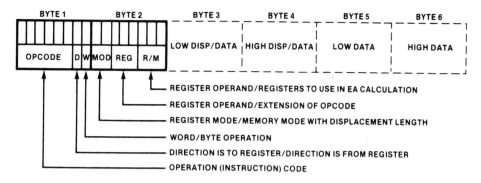

Figure 5.3 General instruction format (Courtesy of Intel Corp.).

2. *Register direction bit* (D bit): specifies whether the register operand that is specified in byte 2 is the source or the destination operand. A logic 1 at this bit position indicates that the register operand is a destination operand, and a logic 0 indicates that it is a source operand.

3. *Data size bit* (W bit): specifies whether the operation will be performed on 8-bit or 16-bit data. Logic 0 selects 8 bits and 1 selects 16 bits.

For instance, if a 16-bit value is to be added to register AX, the six most significant bits specify the add register operation. This opcode is 000000_2. The next bit, D, will be at logic 1 to specify that a register, AX in this case, holds the destination operand. Finally, the least significant bit, W, will be logic 1 to specify a 16-bit data operation.

The second byte in Fig. 5.3 has three fields: the *mode (MOD) field,* the *register (REG) field,* and the *register/memory (R/M) field*. These fields are used to specify which register is used for the first operand and where the second operand is stored. The second operand can be in either a register or a memory location.

The 3-bit REG field is used to identify the register for the first operand. This is the operand that was defined as the source or destination by the D bit in byte 1. The encoding for each of the 8086's registers is shown in Fig. 5.4. Here we find that the 16-bit register AX and the 8-bit register AL are specified by the same binary code. Notice that the decision as to whether to use AX or AL is made based on the setting of the operation-size (W) bit in byte 1.

For instance, in our earlier example, we said that the first operand, which is the destination operand, is register AX. For this case, the REG field is set to 000.

REG	W = 0	W = 1
000	AL	AX
001	CL	CX
010	DL	DX
011	BL	BX
100	AH	SP
101	CH	BP
110	DH	SI
111	BH	DI

Figure 5.4 Register (REG) field encoding (Courtesy of Intel Corp.).

CODE	EXPLANATION
00	Memory Mode, no displacement follows*
01	Memory Mode, 8-bit displacement follows
10	Memory Mode, 16-bit displacement follows
11	Register Mode (no displacement)

*Except when R/M = 110, then 16-bit displacement follows

(a)

MOD = 11			EFFECTIVE ADDRESS CALCULATION			
R/M	W = 0	W = 1	R/M	MOD = 00	MOD = 01	MOD = 10
000	AL	AX	000	(BX) + (SI)	(BX) + (SI) + D8	(BX) + (SI) + D16
001	CL	CX	001	(BX) + (DI)	(BX) + (DI) + D8	(BX) + (DI) + D16
010	DL	DX	010	(BP) + (SI)	(BP) + (SI) + D8	(BP) + (SI) + D16
011	BL	BX	011	(BP) + (DI)	(BP) + (DI) + D8	(BP) + (DI) + D16
100	AH	SP	100	(SI)	(SI) + D8	(SI) + D16
101	CH	BP	101	(DI)	(DI) + D8	(DI) + D16
110	DH	SI	110	DIRECT ADDRESS	(BP) + D8	(BP) + D16
111	BH	DI	111	(BX)	(BX) + D8	(BX) + D16

(b)

Figure 5.5 (a) Mode (MOD) field encoding; (b) register/memory (R/M) field encoding (Courtesy of Intel Corp.).

The 2-bit MOD field and 3-bit R/M field together specify the second operand. Encoding for these two fields is shown in Fig. 5.5(a) and (b), respectively. MOD indicates whether the operand is in a register or memory. Notice that in the case of a second operand that is in a register, the MOD field is always 11. The R/M field together with the W bit from byte 1 selects the register.

For example, if the second operand, the source operand, in our earlier addition example is to be in BX, the MOD and R/M fields will be made MOD = 11 and R/M = 011, respectively.

EXAMPLE 5.1

The instruction

    MOV BL, AL

stands for move the byte contents from source register AL to destination register BL. Using the general format in Fig. 5.3, show how to encode the instruction in machine code. Assume that the 6-bit opcode for the move operation is 100010.

SOLUTION In byte 1 the first six bits specify the move operation and thus must be 100010.

$$\text{OPCODE} = 100010_2$$

The next bit, which is D, indicates whether the register that is specified by the REG part of byte 2 is a source or a destination operand. Let us say that we will encode AL in the REG field of byte 2; therefore, D is set equal to 0 for source operand.

$$D = 0$$

The last bit (W) in byte 1 must specify a byte operation. For this reason, it is also set to 0.

$$W = 0$$

This leads to

$$\text{BYTE 1} = 10001000_2 = 88_{16}$$

In byte 2 the source operand, which is specified by the REG field, is AL. The corresponding code from Fig. 5.4 is

$$\text{REG} = 000$$

Since the second operand is also a register, the MOD field is made 11. The R/M field specifies that the destination register is BL and the code from Fig. 5.5(b) is 011. This gives

$$\text{MOD} = 11$$

$$\text{R/M} = 011$$

Therefore, byte 2 is

$$\text{BYTE 2} = 11000011_2 = C3_{16}$$

The entire hexadecimal code for the instruction is

$$\text{MOV} \quad \text{BL,AL} = 88C3H$$

On the other hand, for a second operand that is located in memory, there are a number of different ways in which its location can be specified. That is, any of the addressing modes supported by the 8086 microprocessor can be used to generate its address. The addressing mode is also selected with the MOD and R/M fields.

Notice that the addressing mode for an operand in memory is indicated by one of the other three values (00, 01, and 10) in the MOD field and an appropriate R/M code. The different ways in which the operand's address can be generated are shown in the effective address calculation part of the table in Fig. 5.5(b). These different address calculation expressions correspond to the addressing modes that we introduced in Chapter 3. For instance, if the base index register contains the memory address, this fact is encoded into the instruction by making MOD = 00 and R/M = 111.

EXAMPLE 5.2

The instruction

ADD   AX, [SI]

stands for add the 16-bit contents of the memory location indirectly specified by SI to AX. Encode the instruction in machine code. The opcode for add is 000000_2.

SOLUTION   To specify a 16-bit add operation with a register as the destination, the first byte of machine code will be

$$\text{BYTE 1} = 00000011_2 = 03_{16}$$

The REG field bits in byte 2 are 000 is specify AX as the destination register. The other operand is in memory and its address is specified by the contents of SI with no displacement. From Fig. 5.5(a) and (b), we find that for indirect addressing using SI with no displacement, MOD equals 00 and R/M equals 100.

$$\text{MOD} = 00$$

$$\text{R/M} = 100$$

This gives

$$\text{BYTE 2} = 00000100_2 = 04_{16}$$

Thus the machine code for the instruction is

$$\text{ADD   AX,[SI]} = 0304\text{H}$$

Some of the addressing modes of the 8086 need either data or an address displacement to be coded into the instruction. These types of information are encoded using additional bytes. For instance, looking at Fig. 5.3, we see that byte 3 is needed in the encoding of an instruction if it uses a byte-size address displacement, and both byte 3 and byte 4 are needed if the instruction uses a word-size displacement.

The size of the displacement is encoded into the MOD field. For example, if the effective address is to be generated by the expression

$$(\text{BX}) + \text{D8}$$

MOD is set to 01 to specify memory mode with an 8-bit displacement and R/M is set to 111 to select BX.

Bytes 3 and 4 are also used to encode byte-wide immediate operands, word-wide immediate operands, and direct addresses. For example, in an instruction where direct addressing is used to specify the location of an operand in memory, the MOD field must be 00 and the R/M field 110. The actual value of the operand's address is coded into the bytes that follow.

If both a 16-bit displacement and an immediate operand are used in the same instruction, the displacement is encoded into bytes 3 and 4 and the immediate operand into bytes 5 and 6.

EXAMPLE 5.3

What is the machine code for the following instruction?

$$XOR \quad CL, \; [1234H]$$

This instruction stands for exclusive-OR the byte of data at memory address 1234_{16} with the byte contents of CL. The opcode for exclusive-OR is 001100_2.

SOLUTION Using the XOR opcode 001100_2, 1 for destination operand, and 0 for byte data, we get

$$BYTE \; 1 = 00110010_2 = 32_{16}$$

The REG field has to specify CL, which makes it equal to 001. In this case a direct address has been specified for operand 2. This requires that MOD = 00 and R/M = 110. Thus

$$BYTE \; 2 = 00001110_2 = 0E_{16}$$

To specify the address 1234_{16}, we must use bytes 3 and 4. The least significant byte of the address is encoded first, followed by the most significant byte. This gives

$$BYTE \; 3 = 34_{16}$$

and

$$BYTE \; 4 = 12_{16}$$

The entire machine code form of the instruction is

$$XOR \quad CL,[1234H] = 320E3412H$$

EXAMPLE 5.4

The instruction

$$ADD \quad [BX].DISP[SI],AX$$

means add the word contents of AX to the contents of the memory location specified by based indexed addressing mode. The opcode for the add operation is 000000_2 and assume that DISP equals 1234_{16}.

SOLUTION The add opcode, which is 000000_2, a 0 for source operand, and a 1 for word data gives

$$BYTE \; 1 = 00000001_2 = 01_{16}$$

The REG field in byte 2 is 000 to specify AX as the source register. Since there is a displacement and it needs 16 bits for encoding, the MOD field obtained from Fig. 5.5(a) is 10. The R/M field, also obtained from Fig. 5.5(b), for an effective address generated by SI and BX is 000. This gives the second byte as

$$\text{BYTE } 2 = 10000000_2 = 80_{16}$$

The displacement 1234_{16} is encoded in the next two bytes with the least significant byte first. Therefore, the machine code that results is

$$\text{ADD} \quad [\text{BX}].\text{DISP}[\text{SI}],\text{AX} = 01803412\text{H}$$

As we indicated earlier, the general format in Fig. 5.3 cannot be used to encode all of the instructions that can be executed by the 8086. There are minor modifications that must be made to this general format to encode a few instructions. In some instructions one or more additional single-bit fields need to be added. These 1-bit fields and their functions are shown in Fig. 5.6.

Field	Value	Function
S	0 1	No sign extension Sign extend 8-bit immediate data to 16 bits if W=1
V	0 1	Shift/rotate count is one Shift/rotate count is specified in CL register
Z	0 1	Repeat/loop while zero flag is clear Repeat/loop while zero flag is set

Figure 5.6 Additional 1-bit fields and their functions (Courtesy of Intel Corp.).

For instance, the general format of the repeat (REP) instruction is

$$\text{REP} = 1111001\text{Z}$$

Here bit Z is made 1 or 0 depending on whether the repeat operation is to be done when the zero flag is set or when it is reset. Similarly, the other two bits, S and V, are used to encode sign extension for arithmetic instructions and to specify the source of the count for shift or rotate instructions, respectively.

The formats for all of the instructions in the 8086's instruction set are shown in Fig. 5.7. This is the information that can be used to encode any 8086 program.

EXAMPLE 5.5

The instruction

        MOV   [BP].DISP[DI],0ABCDH

stands for move the immediate data word $ABCD_{16}$ into the memory location specified by based indexed addressing mode. Express the instruction in machine code. Let DISP equal 1234_{16}.

SOLUTION   Since this instruction does not involve one of the registers as an operand, it does not follow the general format that we have been using. From Fig. 5.7 we find that the format of byte 1 in an immediate data-to-memory move is

$$1100011W$$

In our case, we are moving word-size data; therefore, W equals 1. This gives

$$\text{BYTE } 1 = 11000111_2 = C7_{16}$$

Again from Fig. 5.7, we find that byte 2 has the form

$$\text{BYTE } 2 = \text{MOD } 000 \text{ R/M}$$

For a memory operand using a 16-bit displacement, Fig. 5.5(a) shows that MOD equals 10 and for based indexed addressing using BP and DI with a 16-bit displacement, Fig. 5.5(b) shows that R/M equals 011. This gives

$$\text{BYTE } 2 = 10000011_2 = 83_{16}$$

Bytes 3 and 4 encode the displacement with its low byte first. Thus for a displacement of 1234_{16}, we get

$$\text{BYTE } 3 = 34_{16}$$

and

$$\text{BYTE } 4 = 12_{16}$$

Finally, bytes 5 and 6 encode the immediate data, also with the least significant byte first. For data word $ABCD_{16}$, we get

$$\text{BYTE } 5 = CD_{16}$$

and

$$\text{BYTE } 6 = AB_{16}$$

The entire instruction in machine code is

$$\text{MOV } [\text{BP}].\text{DISP}[\text{DI}], 0\text{ABCDH} = \text{C7833412CDABH}$$

Instructions that involve a segment register need a 2-bit field, to encode which register is to be affected. This field is called the *SR field*. The four segment registers ES, CS, SS, and DS are encoded according to the table in Fig. 5.8.

EXAMPLE 5.6

The instruction

```
MOV   [BP].DISP[DI],DS
```

stands for move the contents of the data segment register to the memory location specified by based indexed addressing mode. Express the instruction in machine code. Let DISP equal 1234_{16}.

SOLUTION From Fig. 5.7 we see that this instruction is encoded as

$$10001100 \text{ MOD } 0 \text{ SR R/M DISP}$$

Sec. 5.3   Converting Source Programs to Machine Code

153

The MOD and R/M fields are the same as in example 5.5. That is,

$$MOD = 10$$

$$R/M = 011$$

Moreover, the value of DISP is given as 1234_{16}. Finally, from Fig. 5.8 we find that for DS the SR field is

$$SR = 11$$

Therefore, the instruction is coded as

$$1000110010011011001101000001001 0_2 = 8C9B3412_{16}$$

Encoding a Complete 8086 Program

To encode a complete assembly language program in machine code, we must individually encode each of its instructions. This can be done by using the instruction formats shown in Fig. 5.7 and the information in the tables of Figs. 5.4, 5.5, 5.6, and 5.8. We first identify the general machine code format for the instruction in Fig. 5.7. After determining the format, the bit fields can be evaluated using the tables of Figs. 5.4,

DATA TRANSFER

MOV = Move:

	7 6 5 4 3 2 1 0	7 6 5 4 3 2 1 0	7 6 5 4 3 2 1 0	7 6 5 4 3 2 1 0	7 6 5 4 3 2 1 0	7 6 5 4 3 2 1 0
Register/memory to/from register	1 0 0 0 1 0 d w	mod reg r/m	(DISP-LO)	(DISP-HI)		
Immediate to register/memory	1 1 0 0 0 1 1 w	mod 0 0 0 r/m	(DISP-LO)	(DISP-HI)	data	data if w = 1
Immediate to register	1 0 1 1 w reg	data	data if w = 1			
Memory to accumulator	1 0 1 0 0 0 0 w	addr-lo	addr-hi			
Accumulator to memory	1 0 1 0 0 0 1 w	addr-lo	addr-hi			
Register/memory to segment register	1 0 0 0 1 1 1 0	mod 0 SR r/m	(DISP-LO)	(DISP-HI)		
Segment register to register/memory	1 0 0 0 1 1 0 0	mod 0 SR r/m	(DISP-LO)	(DISP-HI)		

PUSH = Push:

Register/memory	1 1 1 1 1 1 1 1	mod 1 1 0 r/m	(DISP-LO)	(DISP-HI)
Register	0 1 0 1 0 reg			
Segment register	0 0 0 reg 1 1 0			

POP = Pop:

Register/memory	1 0 0 0 1 1 1 1	mod 0 0 0 r/m	(DISP-LO)	(DISP-HI)
Register	0 1 0 1 1 reg			
Segment register	0 0 0 reg 1 1 1			

Figure 5.7 8086 instruction encoding tables (Courtesy of Intel Corp.).

DATA TRANSFER (Cont'd.)

XCHG = Exchange:

7 6 5 4 3 2 1 0	7 6 5 4 3 2 1 0	7 6 5 4 3 2 1 0	7 6 5 4 3 2 1 0	7 6 5 4 3 2 1 0	7 6 5 4 3 2 1 0

Register/memory with register

1 0 0 0 0 1 1 w	mod reg r/m	(DISP-LO)	(DISP-HI)

Register with accumulator

1 0 0 1 0 reg

IN = Input from:

Fixed port

1 1 1 0 0 1 0 w	DATA-8

Variable port

1 1 1 0 1 1 0 w

OUT = Output to:

Fixed port

1 1 1 0 0 1 1 w	DATA-8

Variable port

1 1 1 0 1 1 1 w

XLAT = Translate byte to AL

1 1 0 1 0 1 1 1

LEA = Load EA to register

1 0 0 0 1 1 0 1	mod reg r/m	(DISP-LO)	(DISP-HI)

LDS = Load pointer to DS

1 1 0 0 0 1 0 1	mod reg r/m	(DISP-LO)	(DISP-HI)

LES = Load pointer to ES

1 1 0 0 0 1 0 0	mod reg r/m	(DISP-LO)	(DISP-HI)

LAHF = Load AH with flags

1 0 0 1 1 1 1 1

SAHF = Store AH into flags

1 0 0 1 1 1 1 0

PUSHF = Push flags

1 0 0 1 1 1 0 0

POPF = Pop flags

1 0 0 1 1 1 0 1

ARITHMETIC

ADD = Add:

Reg/memory with register to either

0 0 0 0 0 0 d w	mod reg r/m	(DISP-LO)	(DISP-HI)

Immediate to register/memory

1 0 0 0 0 0 s w	mod 0 0 0 r/m	(DISP-LO)	(DISP-HI)	data	data if s: w=01

Immediate to accumulator

0 0 0 0 0 1 0 w	data	data if w=1

ADC = Add with carry:

Reg/memory with register to either

0 0 0 1 0 0 d w	mod reg r/m	(DISP-LO)	(DISP-HI)

Immediate to register/memory

1 0 0 0 0 0 s w	mod 0 1 0 r/m	(DISP-LO)	(DISP-HI)	data	data if s: w=01

Immediate to accumulator

0 0 0 1 0 1 0 w	data	data if w=1

INC = Increment:

Register/memory

1 1 1 1 1 1 1 w	mod 0 0 0 r/m	(DISP-LO)	(DISP-HI)

Register

0 1 0 0 0 reg

AAA = ASCII adjust for add

0 0 1 1 0 1 1 1

DAA = Decimal adjust for add

0 0 1 0 0 1 1 1

Figure 5.7   *(continued)*

ARITHMETIC (Cont'd.)

	7 6 5 4 3 2 1 0	7 6 5 4 3 2 1 0	7 6 5 4 3 2 1 0	7 6 5 4 3 2 1 0	7 6 5 4 3 2 1 0	7 6 5 4 3 2 1 0

SUB = Subtract:

Reg/memory and register to either	0 0 1 0 1 0 d w	mod reg r/m	(DISP-LO)	(DISP-HI)		
Immediate from register/memory	1 0 0 0 0 0 s w	mod 1 0 1 r/m	(DISP-LO)	(DISP-HI)	data	data if s: w=01
Immediate from accumulator	0 0 1 0 1 1 0 w	data	data if w=1			

SBB = Subtract with borrow:

Reg/memory and register to either	0 0 0 1 1 0 d w	mod reg r/m	(DISP-LO)	(DISP-HI)		
Immediate from register/memory	1 0 0 0 0 0 s w	mod 0 1 1 r/m	(DISP-LO)	(DISP-HI)	data	data if s: w=01
Immediate from accumulator	0 0 0 1 1 1 0 w	data	data if w=1			

DEC Decrement:

Register/memory	1 1 1 1 1 1 1 w	mod 0 0 1 r/m	(DISP-LO)	(DISP-HI)		
Register	0 1 0 0 1 reg					
NEG Change sign	1 1 1 1 0 1 1 w	mod 0 1 1 r/m	(DISP-LO)	(DISP-HI)		

CMP = Compare:

Register/memory and register	0 0 1 1 1 0 d w	mod reg r/m	(DISP-LO)	(DISP-HI)		
Immediate with register/memory	1 0 0 0 0 0 s w	mod 1 1 1 r/m	(DISP-LO)	(DISP-HI)	data	data if s: w=1
Immediate with accumulator	0 0 1 1 1 1 0 w	data				
AAS ASCII adjust for subtract	0 0 1 1 1 1 1 1					
DAS Decimal adjust for subtract	0 0 1 0 1 1 1 1					
MUL Multiply (unsigned)	1 1 1 1 0 1 1 w	mod 1 0 0 r/m	(DISP-LO)	(DISP-HI)		
IMUL Integer multiply (signed)	1 1 1 1 0 1 1 w	mod 1 0 1 r/m	(DISP-LO)	(DISP-HI)		
AAM ASCII adjust for multiply	1 1 0 1 0 1 0 0	0 0 0 0 1 0 1 0	(DISP-LO)	(DISP-HI)		
DIV Divide (unsigned)	1 1 1 1 0 1 1 w	mod 1 1 0 r/m	(DISP-LO)	(DISP-HI)		
IDIV Integer divide (signed)	1 1 1 1 0 1 1 w	mod 1 1 1 r/m	(DISP-LO)	(DISP-HI)		
AAD ASCII adjust for divide	1 1 0 1 0 1 0 1	0 0 0 0 1 0 1 0	(DISP-LO)	(DISP-HI)		
CBW Convert byte to word	1 0 0 1 1 0 0 0					
CWD Convert word to double word	1 0 0 1 1 0 0 1					

LOGIC

NOT Invert	1 1 1 1 0 1 1 w	mod 0 1 0 r/m	(DISP-LO)	(DISP-HI)		
SHL/SAL Shift logical/arithmetic left	1 1 0 1 0 0 v w	mod 1 0 0 r/m	(DISP-LO)	(DISP-HI)		
SHR Shift logical right	1 1 0 1 0 0 v w	mod 1 0 1 r/m	(DISP-LO)	(DISP-HI)		
SAR Shift arithmetic right	1 1 0 1 0 0 v w	mod 1 1 1 r/m	(DISP-LO)	(DISP-HI)		
ROL Rotate left	1 1 0 1 0 0 v w	mod 0 0 0 r/m	(DISP-LO)	(DISP-HI)		

Figure 5.7 *(continued)*

LOGIC (Cont'd.)

	7 6 5 4 3 2 1 0	7 6 5 4 3 2 1 0	7 6 5 4 3 2 1 0	7 6 5 4 3 2 1 0	7 6 5 4 3 2 1 0	7 6 5 4 3 2 1 0
ROR Rotate right	1 1 0 1 0 0 v w	mod 0 0 1 r/m	(DISP-LO)	(DISP-HI)		
RCL Rotate through carry flag left	1 1 0 1 0 0 v w	mod 0 1 0 r/m	(DISP-LO)	(DISP-HI)		
RCR Rotate through carry right	1 1 0 1 0 0 v w	mod 0 1 1 r/m	(DISP-LO)	(DISP-HI)		

AND = And:

	7 6 5 4 3 2 1 0	7 6 5 4 3 2 1 0	7 6 5 4 3 2 1 0	7 6 5 4 3 2 1 0	7 6 5 4 3 2 1 0	7 6 5 4 3 2 1 0
Reg/memory with register to either	0 0 1 0 0 0 d w	mod reg r/m	(DISP-LO)	(DISP-HI)		
Immediate to register/memory	1 0 0 0 0 0 0 w	mod 1 0 0 r/m	(DISP-LO)	(DISP-HI)	data	data if w=1
Immediate to accumulator	0 0 1 0 0 1 0 w	data	data if w=1			

TEST = And function to flags no result:

	7 6 5 4 3 2 1 0	7 6 5 4 3 2 1 0	7 6 5 4 3 2 1 0	7 6 5 4 3 2 1 0	7 6 5 4 3 2 1 0	7 6 5 4 3 2 1 0
Register/memory and register	0 0 0 1 0 0 d w	mod reg r/m	(DISP-LO)	(DISP-HI)		
Immediate data and register/memory	1 1 1 1 0 1 1 w	mod 0 0 0 r/m	(DISP-LO)	(DISP-HI)	data	data if w=1
Immediate data and accumulator	1 0 1 0 1 0 0 w	data				

OR = Or:

	7 6 5 4 3 2 1 0	7 6 5 4 3 2 1 0	7 6 5 4 3 2 1 0	7 6 5 4 3 2 1 0	7 6 5 4 3 2 1 0	7 6 5 4 3 2 1 0
Reg/memory and register to either	0 0 0 0 1 0 d w	mod reg r/m	(DISP-LO)	(DISP-HI)		
Immediate to register/memory	1 0 0 0 0 0 0 w	mod 0 0 1 r/m	(DISP-LO)	(DISP-HI)	data	data if w=1
Immediate to accumulator	0 0 0 0 1 1 0 w	data	data if w=1			

XOR = Exclusive or:

	7 6 5 4 3 2 1 0	7 6 5 4 3 2 1 0	7 6 5 4 3 2 1 0	7 6 5 4 3 2 1 0	7 6 5 4 3 2 1 0	7 6 5 4 3 2 1 0
Reg/memory and register to either	0 0 1 1 0 0 d w	mod reg r/m	(DISP-LO)	(DISP-HI)		
Immediate to register/memory	0 0 1 1 0 1 0 w	data	(DISP-LO)	(DISP-HI)	data	data if w=1
Immediate to accumulator	0 0 1 1 0 1 0 w	data	data if w=1			

STRING MANIPULATION

	7 6 5 4 3 2 1 0
REP = Repeat	1 1 1 1 0 0 1 z
MOVS = Move byte/word	1 0 1 0 0 1 0 w
CMPS = Compare byte/word	1 0 1 0 0 1 1 w
SCAS = Scan byte/word	1 0 1 0 1 1 1 w
LODS = Load byte/wd to AL/AX	1 0 1 0 1 1 0 w
STDS = Stor byte/wd from AL/A	1 0 1 0 1 0 1 w

Figure 5.7 *(continued)*

CONTROL TRANSFER

CALL = Call:

	7 6 5 4 3 2 1 0	7 6 5 4 3 2 1 0	7 6 5 4 3 2 1 0	7 6 5 4 3 2 1 0	7 6 5 4 3 2 1 0	7 6 5 4 3 2 1 0
Direct within segment	1 1 1 0 1 0 0 0	IP-INC-LO	IP-INC-HI			
Indirect within segment	1 1 1 1 1 1 1 1	mod 0 1 0 r/m	(DISP-LO)	(DISP-HI)		
Direct intersegment	1 0 0 1 1 0 1 0	IP-lo	IP-hi			
		CS-lo	CS-hi			
Indirect intersegment	1 1 1 1 1 1 1 1	mod 0 1 1 r/m	(DISP-LO)	(DISP-HI)		

JMP = Unconditional Jump:

Direct within segment	1 1 1 0 1 0 0 1	IP-INC-LO	IP-INC-HI	
Direct within segment-short	1 1 1 0 1 0 1 1	IP-INC8		
Indirect within segment	1 1 1 1 1 1 1 1	mod 1 0 0 r/m	(DISP-LO)	(DISP-HI)
Direct intersegment	1 1 1 0 1 0 1 0	IP-lo	IP-hi	
		CS-lo	CS-hi	
Indirect intersegment	1 1 1 1 1 1 1 1	mod 1 0 1 r/m	(DISP-LO)	(DISP-HI)

RET = Return from CALL:

Within segment	1 1 0 0 0 0 1 1		
Within seg adding immed to SP	1 1 0 0 0 0 1 0	data-lo	data-hi
Intersegment	1 1 0 0 1 0 1 1		
Intersegment adding immediate to SP	1 1 0 0 1 0 1 0	data-lo	data-hi
JE/JZ = Jump on equal/zero	0 1 1 1 0 1 0 0	IP-INC8	
JL/JNGE = Jump on less/not greater or equal	0 1 1 1 1 1 0 0	IP-INC8	
JLE/JNG = Jump on less or equal/not greater	0 1 1 1 1 1 1 0	IP-INC8	
JB/JNAE = Jump on below/not above or equal	0 1 1 1 0 0 1 0	IP-INC8	
JBE/JNA = Jump on below or equal/not above	0 1 1 1 0 1 1 0	IP-INC8	
JP/JPE = Jump on parity/parity even	0 1 1 1 1 0 1 0	IP-INC8	
JO = Jump on overflow	0 1 1 1 0 0 0 0	IP-INC8	
JS = Jump on sign	0 1 1 1 1 0 0 0	IP-INC8	
JNE/JNZ = Jump on not equal/not zer0	0 1 1 1 0 1 0 1	IP-INC8	
JNL/JGE = Jump on not less/greater or equal	0 1 1 1 1 1 0 1	IP-INC8	
JNLE/JG = Jump on not less or equal/greater	0 1 1 1 1 1 1 1	IP-INC8	
JNB/JAE = Jump on not below/above or equal	0 1 1 1 0 0 1 1	IP-INC8	
JNBE/JA = Jump on not below or equal/above	0 1 1 1 0 1 1 1	IP-INC8	
JNP/JPO = Jump on not par/par odd	0 1 1 1 1 0 1 1	IP-INC8	
JNO = Jump on not overflow	0 1 1 1 0 0 0 1	IP-INC8	

Figure 5.7 *(continued)*

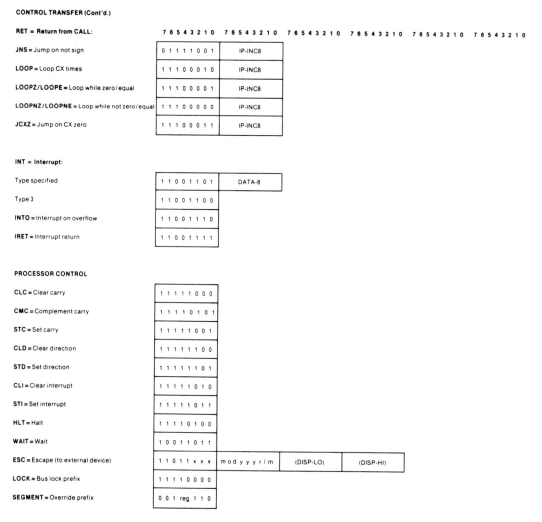

CONTROL TRANSFER (Cont'd.)

RET = Return from CALL:

	7 6 5 4 3 2 1 0	7 6 5 4 3 2 1 0	7 6 5 4 3 2 1 0	7 6 5 4 3 2 1 0	7 6 5 4 3 2 1 0	7 6 5 4 3 2 1 0

JNS = Jump on not sign — 0 1 1 1 1 0 0 1 | IP-INC8

LOOP = Loop CX times — 1 1 1 0 0 0 1 0 | IP-INC8

LOOPZ/LOOPE = Loop while zero/equal — 1 1 1 0 0 0 0 1 | IP-INC8

LOOPNZ/LOOPNE = Loop while not zero/equal — 1 1 1 0 0 0 0 0 | IP-INC8

JCXZ = Jump on CX zero — 1 1 1 0 0 0 1 1 | IP-INC8

INT = Interrupt:

Type specified — 1 1 0 0 1 1 0 1 | DATA-8

Type 3 — 1 1 0 0 1 1 0 0

INTO = Interrupt on overflow — 1 1 0 0 1 1 1 0

IRET = Interrupt return — 1 1 0 0 1 1 1 1

PROCESSOR CONTROL

CLC = Clear carry — 1 1 1 1 1 0 0 0

CMC = Complement carry — 1 1 1 1 0 1 0 1

STC = Set carry — 1 1 1 1 1 0 0 1

CLD = Clear direction — 1 1 1 1 1 1 0 0

STD = Set direction — 1 1 1 1 1 1 0 1

CLI = Clear interrupt — 1 1 1 1 1 0 1 0

STI = Set interrupt — 1 1 1 1 1 0 1 1

HLT = Halt — 1 1 1 1 0 1 0 0

WAIT = Wait — 1 0 0 1 1 0 1 1

ESC = Escape (to external device) — 1 1 0 1 1 x x x | m o d y y y r / m | (DISP-LO) | (DISP-HI)

LOCK = Bus lock prefix — 1 1 1 1 0 0 0 0

SEGMENT = Override prefix — 0 0 1 reg 1 1 0

Figure 5.7 *(continued)*

5.5, 5.6, and 5.8. Finally, the binary-coded instruction can be expressed in hexadecimal form.

In order to have the SDK-86 microcomputer execute a program, we must first store the machine code of the program in the code segment of memory. The bytes of

Register	SR
ES	00
CS	01
SS	10
DS	11

Figure 5.8 Segment register codes.

machine code are stored in sequentially addressed locations in memory. The first byte of the program is stored at the lowest-value address and it is followed by the other bytes in the order in which they are encoded. That is, the address is incremented by one after storing each byte of machine code in memory.

EXAMPLE 5.7

Encode the "block move" program shown in Fig. 5.9(a) and show how it would be stored in memory starting at address 200_{16}.

SOLUTION To encode this program to its equivalent machine code, we will use the instruction set table in Fig. 5.7. The first instruction

$$\text{MOV} \quad \text{AX, 0020H}$$

is a move immediate data to register instruction. In Fig. 5.7, we find that it has the form

$$1011 \text{ W REG DATA DATA IF W} = 1$$

Since the move is to register AX, Fig. 5.4 shows that the W bit is 1 and REG is 000. The immediate data 0020H follow this byte, with the least significant byte coded first. This gives the machine code for the instruction as

$$1011100000010000000000000_2 = \text{B82000}_{16}$$

The second instruction

$$\text{MOV} \quad \text{DS, AX}$$

represents a move register to segment register operation. This instruction has the general format

$$10001110 \quad \text{MOD 0 SR R/M}$$

From Fig. 5.5(a) and (b), we find that for this instruction MOD = 11 and R/M is 000 for AX. Furthermore, from Fig. 5.8, we find that SR = 11 for the data segment. This results in the code

$$1000111011011000_2 = \text{8ED8}_{16}$$

for the second instruction.

The next three instructions have the same format as the first instruction. In the third instruction, REG is 110 for SI and the data are encoded as 0100H. This gives

$$10111110000000000000000001_2 = \text{BE0001}_{16}$$

The fourth instruction has REG coded as 111 (DI) and the data as 0120H. This results in

$$10111111001000000000000001_2 = \text{BF2001}_{16}$$

```
            MOV AX,020H          ;LOAD AX REGISTER
            MOV DS,AX            ;LOAD DATA SEGMENT ADDRESS
            MOV SI,0100H         ;LOAD SOURCE BLOCK POINTER
            MOV DI,0120H         ;LOAD DESTINATION BLOCK POINTER
            MOV CX,010H          ;LOAD REPEAT COUNTER
NXTPT:      MOV AH,[SI]          ;MOVE SOURCE BLOCK ELEMENT TO AX
            MOV [DI],AH          ;MOVE ELEMENT FROM AX TO DESTINATION BLOCK
            INC SI               ;INCREMENT SOURCE BLOCK POINTER
            INC DI               ;INCREMENT DESTINATION BLOCK POINTER
            DEC CX               ;DECREMENT REPEAT COUNTER
            JNZ NXTPT            ;JUMP TO NXTPT IF CX NOT EQUAL TO ZERO
            HLT                  ;HALT
```

(a)

Instruction	Type of Instruction	Machine Code
MOV AX,020H	Move immediate data to register	$10111000001000000000000_2 = B82000_{16}$
MOV DS,AX	Move register to segment register	$1000111011011000_2 = 8ED8_{16}$
MOV SI,0100H	Move immediate data to register	$1011111000000000000000001_2 = BE0001_{16}$
MOV DI,0120H	Move immediate data to register	$1011111100100000000000001_2 = BF2001_{16}$
MOV CX,010H	Move immediate data to register	$10111001000100000000000_2 = B91000_{16}$
MOV AH,[SI]	Move memory data to register	$1000101000100100_2 = 8A24_{16}$
MOV [DI],AH	Move register data to memory	$1000100000100101_2 = 8825_{16}$
INC SI	Increment register	$01000110_2 = 46_{16}$
INC DI	Increment register	$01000111_2 = 47_{16}$
DEC CX	Decrement register	$01001001_2 = 49_{16}$
JNZ NXTPT	Jump on not equal to zero	$0111010111111000_2 = 75F7_{16}$
HLT	Halt	$11110100_2 = F4_{16}$

(b)

Figure 5.9 (a) Block move program; (b) machine coding of the block move program; (c) storing the machine code in memory.

In the fifth instruction REG is 001 for CX, with 10_{16} as the data. This gives

$$10111001000100000000000_2 = B91000_{16}$$

The sixth instruction changes. It is a move of byte data from memory to a register. From Fig. 5.7 we find that its general format is

$$100010\ D\ W\quad MOD\ REG\ R/M$$

Since AH is the destination and the instruction operates on bytes of data, the D and

Memory address	Contents	Instruction
200H	B8H	MOV AX,020H
201H	20H	
202H	00H	
203H	8EH	MOV DS,AX
204H	D8H	
205H	BEH	MOV SI,0100H
206H	00H	
207H	01H	
208H	BFH	MOV DI,0120H
209H	20H	
20AH	01H	
20BH	B9H	MOV CX,010H
20CH	10H	
20DH	00H	
20EH	8AH	MOV AH,[SI]
20FH	24H	
210H	88H	MOV [DI],AH
211H	25H	
212H	46H	INC SI
213H	47H	INC DI
214H	49H	DEC CX
215H	75H	JNZ $-9
216H	F7H	
217H	F4H	HLT

(c)

Figure 5.9 *(continued)*

W bits are 1 and 0, respectively, and the REG field is 100. The contents of SI are used as a pointer to the source operand; therefore, MOD is 00 and R/M is 100. This gives

$$1000101000100100_2 = 8A24_{16}$$

The last MOV instruction has the same form. However, in this case, AH is the destination and DI is the address pointer. This makes D equal 0 and R/M equal 101. Therefore, we get

$$1000100000100101_2 = 8825_{16}$$

The next two instructions increment a register and have the general form

01000 REG

For the first one, register SI is incremented. Therefore, REG equals 110. This results in

$$01000110_2 = 46_{16}$$

In the second, DI (REG = 111) is incremented and this gives

$$01000111_2 = 47_{16}$$

The two INC instructions are followed by a DEC instruction. Its general form is

$$01001 \text{ REG}$$

To decrement CX (REG = 001), we get

$$01001001_2 = 49_{16}$$

The next instruction is a jump to the location NXTPT. Its form is

$$01110101 \text{ IP-INC8}$$

We will not yet complete this instruction because it will be easier to determine the number of bytes to be jumped after the data have been coded for storage in memory. The final instruction is HLT and it is coded as

$$11110100_2 = F4_{16}$$

The entire machine code program is shown in Fig. 5.9(b)

As shown in Fig. 5.9(c), our encoded program will be stored in memory starting from memory address 200H. The choice of program beginning address establishes the address for the NXTPT label. Notice that the MOV AH,[SI] instruction, which has this label, starts at address $20E_{16}$. This is nine bytes back from the JNZ instruction. Therefore, the displacement (IP-INC8) in the JNZ instruction is -9 and it is encoded as

$$0111010111110001_2 = 75F7_{16}$$

5.4 THE SDK-86 MICROCOMPUTER AND ITS MONITOR PROGRAM

Now that we know how to convert an assembly language program to machine code and how this machine code is to be stored in memory, we are ready to enter the program into the memory of the SDK-86 microcomputer, execute it, examine the results that it produces, and if necessary debug any error. It is the keypad monitor program that permits us to initiate these types of operations from the keypad of the SDK-86 microcomputer.

The keypad monitor is the program that implements the *user interface* to the SDK-86 microcomputer. It is a simple monitor that provides for program entry, execution, and display of information. The monitor program consists of a number of subroutines that are written to perform the various operations that are to be performed by the microcomputer. For instance, the monitor must read inputs from the keypad, analyze the input key sequences, initiate the appropriate operations, and display the required information. The monitor is stored in EPROM on the microcomputer's printed circuit board.

Initially, the microcomputer is reset. When in this state, it repeatedly scans the keypad looking for user entries. The user can issue *commands* to the microcomputer from the keypad. When a command entry sequence is complete, the key entry and decoding part of the monitor causes control to be passed to the subroutine that performs the operation specified by the command. At the completion of the operation, the results are displayed by the display driver part of the monitor and keypad scanning is resumed. The microcomputer remains in this state until new entries are made from the keypad.

The keys of the keypad are shown in Fig. 5.10. This keypad is the input unit of the microcomputer and permits the user to enter data such as the machine code of a program and commands such as "single-step execute the program." Notice that the keys are arranged into two separate sections called the *function keys* and the *hexadecimal keys*.

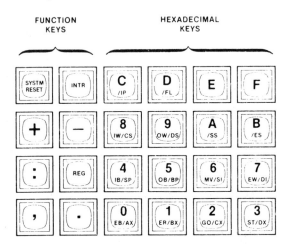

Figure 5.10 Keypad of the SDK-86 microcomputer (Courtesy of Intel Corp.).

Each key in the group of function keys has a single function. These functions are summarized in Fig. 5.11. For example, the key labeled "SYSTM RESET," when depressed, initiates a hardware reset of the microcomputer. Typically, this is the first thing done when the microcomputer is powered on. On the other hand, keys such as "," and "." have different types of functions. They are used to separate the elements in a command and to terminate entry of a command, respectively.

The keys in the hexadecimal key section have multiple functions. First, they serve as the keys for entry of hexadecimal numbers 0 through F. However, as shown in Fig. 5.12, most of these keys also have a command function and a register function. For instance, the 0 key serves two other functions: the EB label stands for the *"examine byte" monitor command* and its AX label stands for *"accumulator register."* The monitor has the ability to determine which of these three functions is to be performed by the sequence in which the keypad entries have been made.

An example of the key sequence needed to load the AX register with the data word $00FF_{16}$ is

$$ER \quad AX \quad 0 \quad 0 \quad F \quad F$$

The output device in the SDK-86 microcomputer is the display. It gives visual feedback to the user of the microcomputer. As shown in Fig. 5.13, the eight digits of the display are organized into two four-digit groups: the *address field* on the left and the *data field* on the right. When keying in entries to the microcomputer, address information, register identifiers, and messages are always displayed in the address field.

Function Key	Operation
SYSTM RESET	The **SYSTM RESET** key allows you to terminate any present activity and to return your SDK-86 to an initialized state. When pressed, the 8086 sign-on message appears in the display and the monitor is ready for command entry.
INTR	The **INTR** (interrupt) key is used to generate an immediate, non-maskable type 2 interrupt (NMI). The NMI interrupt vector is initialized on power up or system reset to point to a routine within the monitor which causes all of the 8086's registers to be saved. Control is returned to the monitor for subsequent command entry.
+	The **+** (plus) key allows you to add two hexadecimal values. This function simplifies relative addressing by allowing you to readily calculate an address location relative to a base address.
−	The **−** (minus) key allows you to subtract one hexadecimal value from another.
:	The **:** (colon) key is used to separate an address to be entered into two parts; a segment value and an offset value.
REG	The **REG** (register) key allows you to use the contents of any of the 8086's registers as an address or data entry.
,	The **,** (comma) key is used to separate keypad entries and to increment the address field to the next consecutive memory location.
.	The **.** (period) key is the command terminator. When pressed, the current command is executed. Note that when using the Go command, the 8086 begins program execution at the address specified when the key is pressed.

Figure 5.11 Uses of the function keys (Courtesy of Intel Corp.).

Figure 5.14 shows what is displayed in the address field to identify each of the 8086's internal registers.

The data field is used to display the contents of registers or memory locations

Hexadecimal Key	Command		Register	
	Acronym	Name	Acronym	Name
0 EB/AX	EB	Examine Byte	AX	Accumulator
1 ER/BX	ER	Examine Register	BX	Base
2 GO/CX	GO	Go	CX	Count
3 ST/DX	ST	(Single) Step	DX	Data
4 IB/SP	IB	Input Byte	SP	Stack Pointer
5 OB/BP	OB	Output Byte	BP	Base Pointer
6 MV/SI	MV	Move	SI	Source Index
7 EW/DI	EW	Examine Word	DI	Destination Index
8 IW/CS	IW	Input Word	CS	Code Segment
9 OW/DS	OW	Output Word	DS	Data Segment
A /SS	none	N/A	SS	Stack Segment
B /ES	none	N/A	ES	Extra Segment
C /IP	none	N/A	IP	Instruction Pointer
D /FL	none	N/A	FL	Flag
E	none	N/A	none	N/A
F	none	N/A	none	N/A

Figure 5.12 Uses of the hexadecimal keys (Courtesy of Intel Corp.).

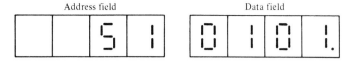

Figure 5.13 Display of the SDK-86 microcomputer.

Register Name	Keypad Acronym	Display Abbreviation
Accumulator	AX	A
Base	BX	b
Count	CX	C
Data	DX	d
Stack Pointer	SP	SP
Base Pointer	BP	bP
Source Index	SI	SI
Destination Index	DI	dI
Code Segment	CS	CS
Data Segment	DS	dS
Stack Segment	SS	SS
Extra Segment	ES	ES
Instruction Pointer	IP	IP
Flag	FL	FL

Figure 5.14 Display abbreviations for the 8086's registers (Courtesy of Intel Corp.).

when they are examined. Moreover, it echos back hexadecimal data as they are entered from the keypad. The seven-segment display format for numbers 0 through F, shown in Fig. 5.15 (page 168), is used to display the hexadecimal data.

5.5 THE KEYPAD MONITOR COMMANDS

In section 5.4 we introduced the SDK-86 microcomputer, its monitor program, keypad, and display. Here we will discuss the actual commands that can be issued to the microcomputer through the monitor.

There are three basic types of information that are typically entered in order to initiate a command: a *command keyword,* and *address or a register name,* and *data.* The entire *command set* of the SDK-86 microcomputer is shown in Fig. 5.16. This table gives the name for each command, briefly describes its function, and illustrates its *syntax.* By syntax, we mean the order in which key entries must be made to initiate the command.

Let us now look at the syntax for one of the commands in more detail. Notice that the syntax for the *"examine byte"* command is

EB<addr>, [[<data>],]*.

Here the command keyword is EB and it is entered into the microcomputer by depressing the EB key of the keypad. When the monitor recognizes that this key has been

Hexadecimal Value	Display Format
0	*0*
1	*1*
2	*2*
3	*3*
4	*4*
5	*5*
6	*6*
7	*7*
8	*8*
9	*9*
A	*A*
B	*b*
C	*C*
D	*d*
E	*E*
F	*F*

Figure 5.15 Display format for hexadecimal numbers (Courtesy of Intel Corp.).

depressed, it considers up to the next four entries from the hexadecimal part of the keypad as the address of the byte location in memory that is to be accessed. This part of the command is identified as <addr> in the syntax diagram and the value of the address is a compulsory entry. The comma that follows the address is used to separate terms in the command. In this case it indicates to the monitor that the complete address has been entered. The element that follows the address in the syntax diagram is enclosed in square brackets. Anything that is enclosed in this type of brackets is optional and may or may not be entered as part of the command. The notation [<data>] represents hexadecimal data. When data are entered, they replace the current contents of the memory location that is being accessed. The data value is also terminated with a comma. The period at the end of the command terminates the command.

Actually, multiple sequential bytes of data can be entered with this command. This is indicated by an outer set of brackets to enclose the inner set and an *. The values are entered separated by commas. In this way, execution of the command causes the contents of consecutive bytes of memory to be modified.

Command	Function/Syntax
Examine Byte	Displays/modifies memory byte locations [EB] \<addr\>⊡ [[\<data\>]⊡]*⊡
Examine Word	Displays/modifies memory word locations [EW] \<addr\>⊡ [[\<data\>]⊡]*⊡
Examine Register	Displays/modifies 8086 register contents [ER] \<reg key\>[[\<data\>]⊡]*[⊡]
Input Byte	Displays data byte at input port [IB] \<port addr\>⊡ [⊡]*⊡
Input Word	Displays data word at input port [IW] \<port addr\>⊡ [⊡]*⊡
Output Byte	Outputs data byte to output port [OB] \<port addr\>⊡ \<data\>[⊡ \<data\>]*⊡
Output Word	Outputs data word to output port [OW] \<port addr\>⊡ \<data\>[⊡ \<data\>]*⊡
Go	Transfers control from monitor to user program [GO] [\<addr\>][⊡ \<breakpoint addr\>]⊡
Move	Moves block of data within memory [MV] \<start addr\>⊡ \<end addr\>⊡ \<destination addr\>⊡
Step	Executes single user program instruction [ST] [\<start addr\>]⊡ [[\<start addr\>]⊡]*⊡

Figure 5.16 Monitor commands (Courtesy of Intel Corp.).

For the purpose of discussion, we will divide the monitor commands in Fig. 5.16 into four groups. We will call them the *examine/enter commands,* the *input/output commands,* the *program execution control commands,* and the *block move command.*

Examine/Enter Commands

The three commands in Fig. 5.16 that we will consider as the examine/enter commands are *"examine byte" (EB),* *"examine word" (EW),* and *"examine register" (ER).* These commands are provided to give the programmer the ability to display or modify the contents of a storage location in memory or a register within the 8086. This capability is essential for debugging a program. For instance, the contents of a specific memory location or register can be examined prior to and after the execution of an instruction. In this way, we can determine if the instruction performed the required operation. Other uses of these commands are for initialization of registers or memory, and for loading of programs into memory.

The syntax we described in the last section is that of the EB and EW commands. For this reason, let us look at a few examples of how the commands can be used. A first example is the command

EB 25,

It is issued by first depressing the "EB" key and then the "2" key, "5" key, and "," key in that sequence. Entering this command causes the contents of memory address 25_{16} to be displayed. Let us assume that this location contains FF_{16}. Then 25 is displayed in the address field of the display and FF in the data field.

Let us now look at a couple of examples of commands that can be used to modify the contents of memory. For example, in order to change the byte contents at address 25_{16} to EF_{16}, we can use the command

EB 25, EF.

Notice that we have included both an address and data element in the command.

If the contents of sequential memory locations are to be modified, the "," key can be depressed after the data entry instead of the "." key. This causes the next address to be displayed and it will be modified by the data that are entered following the comma. For instance, to load the three bytes of memory starting at address 25_{16} with the value $0A_{16}$, $0B_{16}$, and $0C_{16}$, we issue the command

EB 25, 0A, 0B, 0C.

In each of the examples we have considered up to this point, the address that was entered with the command was used relative to the current contents of the code segment register to form the address of the location that is to be accessed in memory. It is also possible to access a location relative to one of the other segment registers. This is done by depressing the REG key followed by the key for the segment register and the colon key before entering the value of the address. For instance, the key sequence

EB REG DS: 25, EF.

changes the contents of address 25_{16} relative to the current contents of the data segment register to EF_{16}.

EXAMPLE 5.8

Write a command sequence that will display the contents of the first three byte locations in the current data segment.

SOLUTION We will use the EB command but must modify the segment register by following it with the REG key and DS key. Moreover, since we want to look at the first three locations in the segment, the address for the first byte is 0_{16} and to examine the next two bytes we simply depress the "," key twice more. This gives

$$EB \; REG \; DS:0, \; , \; , \; .$$

The "examine word" command is similar to EB except that now a word of memory is displayed or modified. For instance, the command

$$EW \; 25,$$

displays the contents of addresses 25_{16} and 26_{16} relative to the current code segment. The byte from address 25_{16} is displayed in the two least significant digits of the data field and the byte from address 26_{16} is displayed in the two most significant digits.

The last of the examine/enter commands, "examine register," is used to display or modify the contents of one of the 8086's internal registers. Looking at Fig. 5.16, we see that its syntax differs from that of the EB and EW commands. Instead of entering an address, the key corresponding to the register that is to be accessed is depressed. For example, to examine the contents of the accumulator register, the command is

$$ER \; AX,$$

The contents of the register is always displayed as a word. For instance, in the case of AX, the high byte, AH, is displayed in the two most significant digits of the data field and the low byte, AL, is displayed in the two least significant digits.

The contents of a register can also be changed with this command. For instance, to change the contents of the code segment register to $A00_{16}$, the command is

$$ER \; CS \; A00.$$

Notice that "." is entered at the end of the command to terminate it.

The contents of any number or all of the internal registers can be displayed or modified with just one "examine register" command. This is done by using a comma after the register or data entry instead of a period. The registers are accessed in the order shown in Fig. 5.14. For example, the sequence

$$ER \; CS, \; , \; , \; .$$

displays the contents of registers CS, DS, SS, and ES in that order.

EXAMPLE 5.9

Write a command sequence that will initialize AX, BX, CX, and DX to the values $A000_{16}$, $B000_{16}$, $000C_{16}$, and $B000_{16}$, respectively.

SOLUTION The ER command must be issued to modify the contents of registers. Looking at the table of Fig. 5.14, we find that these registers can be accessed sequentially starting with AX. Therefore, they can be modified with the command sequence

```
ER AX A000, B000, C, B000.
```

EXAMPLE 5.10

Write a sequence of commands that will create a data segment at address 700_{16} and initialize the first eight storage locations in the data segment to the values 1, 3, 5, 7, 9, B, D, and F, respectively.

SOLUTION First we will initialize the DS register to 70_{16} to create a data segment starting at address 700_{16}. This is done with the command

```
ER DS 70.
```

Now the memory locations can be initialized with the command sequence

```
ER REG DS: 0, 1, 3, 5, 7, 9, B, D, F.
```

Entries that use incorrect syntax or that attempt to modify a part of the memory implemented using PROMs are identified with an *error message (-Err)* in the display.

I/O Commands

There are six byte-wide I/O ports on the SDK-86 microcomputer. Figure 5.17(a) shows that these ports are produced by two parallel I/O devices called P_1 and P_2. Device P_1 implements the three byte-wide I/O ports labeled P_{1A}, P_{1B}, and P_{1C}. As shown in Fig. 5.17(a) and (b), these ports are located at addresses $FFF9_{16}$, $FFFB_{16}$, and $FFFD_{16}$, respectively, of the I/O address space.

Parallel I/O ports P_1 and P_2 can be individually configured under software control to operate as either input ports or output ports. This is done by writing appropriate value control bytes into their control registers. The addresses of the control registers for ports P_1 and P_2 are given in Fig. 5.17(c). Here we see that the control register for P_2 is located at I/O address $FFFE_{16}$ and that for P_1 is at I/O address $FFFF_{16}$. The value loaded into the control register for P_2 determines the operation of I/O ports P_{2A}, P_{2B}, and P_{2C}. At system reset, this register is automatically initialized with $9B_{16}$ by the monitor's reset software routine. This sets all three of these byte-wide ports for input mode of operation. To reconfigure all of them as output ports, Fig. 5.17(c) says that we must write 80_{16} into P_2's control register.

Figure 5.18 shows that the I/O ports of the SDK-86 microcomputer can be accessed through software as word-wide ports instead of byte-wide ports. In this case, the I/O address used in the instruction must be that of the lower addressed port. For example, if ports P_{1A} and P_{2A} are to be read as a word-wide input port, the address of the word-wide port is $FFF8_{16}$. In this example, P_1 supplies the most significant byte of the data word and P_2 the least significant byte. Moreover, as shown in Fig. 5.17(c), the

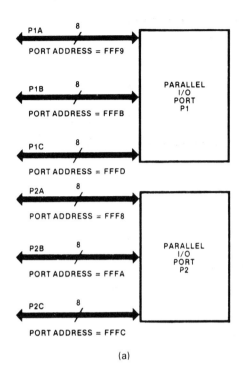

(a)

Port	Address
P2A	FFF8
P1A	FFF9
P2B	FFFA
P1B	FFFB
P2C	FFFC
P1C	FFFD

(b)

Port Number	Port Address	Data Byte or Word	
		Input	Output
P2	FFFEH	9BH	80H
P1	FFFFH	9BH	80H
P2/P1	FFFEH	9B9BH	8080H

(c)

Figure 5.17 (a) Byte-wide parallel I/O ports; (b) byte-wide I/O port address map; (c) control register addresses (Courtesy of Intel Corp.).

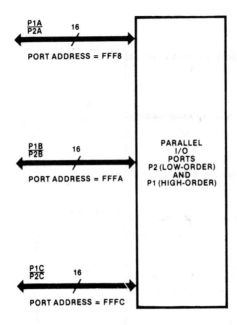

P1A
P2A   16

PORT ADDRESS = FFF8

P1B
P2B   16

PORT ADDRESS = FFFA

PARALLEL
I/O
PORTS
P2 (LOW-ORDER)
AND
P1 (HIGH-ORDER)

P1C
P2C   16

PORT ADDRESS = FFFC

Figure 5.18 Word-wide parallel I/O ports
(Courtesy of Intel Corp.).

control ports of P_1 and P_2 can be written together by outputting a control word to address $FFFE_{16}$.

Looking at the table in Fig. 5.16, we see that the command used to output a byte of data is called *"output byte."* The syntax for this command shows that it is initiated by depressing the OB key on the keypad. This entry must be followed by the address of the I/O port and the value of data to be output. For instance, if we want to set the ports on P_2 for output mode of operation, 80_{16} must be output to the control register at address $FFFE_{16}$. This is done with the command

OB FFFE, 80.

Once this parallel port is initialized for output mode of operation, data can be output to P_{2A}, P_{2B}, and P_{2C} with additional output byte commands. As an example, let us write commands to clear all three of these ports.

OB FFF8, 00.
OB FFFA, 00.
OB FFFC, 00.

EXAMPLE 5.11

Write an output command that will load output port P_{2A} with AA_{16}.

SOLUTION   This operation can be done with an OB command to address $FFF8_{16}$. Therefore, we get

OB FFF8, AA.

It is also possible to output the contents of a register to a port with the OB command. An example would be to output the least significant byte in DX to output port P_{2B}. The command to do this is

OB FFFA, REG DX.

To output a word of data, we use the *"output word" (OW)* command. This command is similar to the OB command; however, now 16 bits of data (four hexadecimal digits) are output to a 16-bit output port. Remember that to use this command on the SDK-86 microcomputer, both parallel I/O ports must be set to the output mode. Assuming that this is the case, the command needed to output the word $AAAA_{16}$ to the word-wide output port consisting of P_{1A} and P_{2A} is

OW FFF8, AAAA.

Similarly, to load this same word-wide port from the DX register, the command is

OW FFF8, REG DX.

The input commands *"input byte" (IB)* and *"input word" (IW)* permit the user of the SDK-86 microcomputer to examine the logic levels applied to input ports. From the table of Fig. 5.16, we see that the form of the input commands are similar to that of their corresponding output commands. However, in this case, no data are entered as part of the command. For instance, to input the data at P_{2B}, the command that must be issued is

IB FFFA,

Moreover, to read the contents of ports P_{1B} and P_{2B} as a word, the command is

IW FFFA,

Remember that before using either of these two commands the ports that are to be accessed must first be set to operate as input ports.

EXAMPLE 5.12

Assume that port P_{2A} is configured for input mode of operation. Write an input command that will repeatedly input the byte contents from P_{2A}.

SOLUTION P_{2A} is a byte-wide input port; therefore, we will use the IB command with the address for P_{2A}, which is $FFF8_{16}$. We can examine the port repeatedly by depressing the "," key. This gives the command sequence

IB FFF8, , , , , ,

Program Execution Control Commands

The SDK-86 microcomputer's monitor has two commands that can be used to control the execution of a program: the *"go" (GO) command* and the *"step" (ST) command*. Let us begin with the GO command. This command gives the programmer the ability to execute a segment of program. The table in Fig. 5.16 shows that the general form of the GO command has two address elements. The first address, <addr>, is the *starting address* of the program segment that is to be executed, that is, the address of the instruction at which execution is to begin. The second address, <breakpoint addr>, is the address of the end of the program segment, that is, the address of the instruction at which execution is to stop. The *breakpoint address* that is specified must correspond to the first byte of an instruction.

An example of the GO command is

GO 10:0, A.

This command loads the code segment register with 10_{16}, thereby creating a code segment that starts at address 100_{16}. The offset that follows the value for CS is 0_{16}; therefore, the starting address is simply 100_{16}. On the other hand, the breakpoint address offset is A_{16}. This sets the breakpoint at address $10A_{16}$. As "." is entered, program execution begins at 100_{16} and proceeds through the 10 bytes of machine code up to address $10A_{16}$. When the breakpoint address is reached, program execution is terminated and control is returned to the monitor.

If CS was already loaded with 10_{16}, the same results could have been obtained by issuing the command

GO 0, A.

Sometimes we just want to execute a program without using a breakpoint. This can also be done with the GO command. For instance, to execute a program that starts at 100_{16}, we can issue the GO command without a breakpoint address. This gives

GO 10:0.

or in the case of a program where CS is already initialized with 10_{16}.

GO.

When the program is being executed, execution can be terminated at any time by depressing the *interrupt request (INTR)* key.

The GO command is typically used to execute programs that are already debugged or to aid in the process of debugging programs in the latter stages of debugging. For example, if the earlier part of a program is already operating correctly, a GO command can be issued to execute this group of instructions and then stop execution at a point in the program where additional debugging is to begin.

The other program execution control command is "step" (ST). This command provides the programmer with the ability to execute one instruction at a time. This mode of operation is also known as single-stepping the program and is very useful during early phases of program debugging. This is because debugging operations such as examining the contents of registers or memory can be performed both before and after the execution of each instruction to determine if the correct operation was performed.

The general form of the command is shown in Fig. 5.16. Notice that a starting address is specified as part of the command. For instance, the command

$$\text{ST } 10:0.$$

causes the instruction at address 100_{16} to be executed. Now the debug operations can be performed. If the code segment register already contains 10_{16}, the command can be issued as

$$\text{ST } .$$

If we want to single-step through several instructions, the step command can be terminated with a comma instead of a period. In this case, depressing the "," key will cause the single-step operation to be performed. Therefore, in order to single-step through five instructions that start at address 100_{16}, the command that must be issued is

$$\text{ST } 10:0, \quad , \quad , \quad , \quad .$$

There are some restrictions on the use of the step command. They are

1. Interrupt instructions should not be single stepped.
2. Instructions that change the stack segment (SS) or stack pointer (SP) registers should not be single stepped.
3. MOV or POP instructions that change the contents of a segment register should not be single stepped.

Block Move Command

The last command available in the SDK-86's keypad monitor is the *"move" (MV) command*. This command permits the user to move a block of data from one part of memory to another part. For instance, using this command, a 256-byte program that resides in memory from address 100_{16} to $1FF_{16}$ can be moved to the address range 200_{16} through $2FF_{16}$ with a single MV command.

Looking at the general form of the command in Fig. 5.16, we find that it is initiated by depressing the MV key. After this, we must key in three addresses. The first two addresses are the *starting address* and *ending address* of the source block of data, that is, the block of data that is to be moved. The third address is the *destination starting address,* that is, the starting address of the memory to which the block is to be moved. The first address may be specified relative to a segment register; however, the second address must assume the same segment register as the first address. The third address can be specified using a segment and an offset value. The move command for our earlier example can be written as

$$MV \ 10:0, \ FF, \ 20:0.$$

The source block of memory can correspond to either ROM or RAM memory, but the destination block must always be in RAM. Notice that we can copy code from ROM into RAM. This means that the whole monitor program is available to the user, and segments of it can be copied into the *user's application program*. This capability is very useful for application program development.

5.6 LOADING AND EXECUTING A PROGRAM

After a machine code program has been prepared, it must be entered into the memory of the SDK-86 microcomputer. We found in Section 5.5 that the monitor program has commands that can be used to modify memory. They are the commands which are used to enter the program into the microcomputer's memory. For instance, the program can be entered byte by byte with a series of examine byte (EB) commands. Programs can also be entered word by word by using the examine word (EW) command.

EXAMPLE 5.13

Show the sequence of keypad entries needed to enter the machine code program of Fig. 5.9(c) into the memory of an SDK-86 microcomputer. The program is to be loaded into memory starting at address 200_{16}.

SOLUTION We will use the EB command to enter the program byte by byte. The first command must set up the starting address, enter the first byte of code, and increment the address for the next byte to be entered. This command is

$$EB \ 20:0, \ B8,$$

The rest of the bytes are entered one after the other each followed by a comma. This gives the following entries.

$$20, \ 00, \ 8E, \ D8, \ BE, \ 00, \ 01, \ BF, \ 20, \ 01, \ B9, \ 10,$$

$$00, \ 8A, \ 24, \ 88, \ 25, \ 46, \ 47, \ 49, \ 75, \ F7, \ F4.$$

EXAMPLE 5.14

Show a key sequence that can be used to examine the program entered in Example 5.13 to assure that it has been entered correctly.

SOLUTION The examine byte command can also be used to verify the entry of a program. In this case, the first command sets up the starting address and displays the first byte to show whether it has been loaded correctly. This command is

$$EB\ 20:0,$$

The rest of the bytes can be examined one after the other by simply repeatedly depressing the comma key.

Once the program has been entered into the microcomputer's memory, it is ready to be executed. The SDK-86's monitor allows us to execute the entire program with one GO command or to execute the program in several segments of instructions by using breakpoints in the GO command. On the other hand, by using the ST command, the program can be stepped through by executing one instruction at a time.

EXAMPLE 5.15

What command must be issued to initiate execution of the program that was entered in example 5.13? What will happen when the last instruction of the program is executed?

SOLUTION The GO command will be issued to initiate execution of the complete program. This command is

$$GO\ 20:0.$$

When the last instruction is reached, program execution stops. This happens because the last instruction is the "halt" instruction.

EXAMPLE 5.16

Show the sequence of key entries needed to single step through the program of example 5.13.

SOLUTION The first step command must set up the starting address and cause execution of the first instruction.

$$ST\ 20:0,$$

The rest of the instructions can be executed one after the other by repeatedly depressing the comma key.

5.7 DEBUGGING A PROGRAM

In Section 5.6 we showed how to load a program into the memory of the SDK-86 microcomputer and how to execute it. However, we did not determine if the program when executed performed the operation for which it was written. It is common to have errors in programs, and even a single error can render the program useless. For instance, if the address to which a "call" instruction passes control is wrong, the program may get hung up. Errors in a program are also referred to as bugs and the process of removing them is called *debugging*.

The two types of errors that can be made by a programmer are the *syntax error* and the *execution error*. A syntax error is an error caused by not following the rules for coding or entering an instruction. These types of errors are typically identified by the microcomputer and signaled to the user with an error message. For this reason, they are usually easy to find and correct.

For example, if the first EB command in Example 5.13 was entered as

EB FE00, B8,

an error condition exists. This is because an attempt was made to modify a part of the address space already implemented as read-only memory. The address entered as part of an EB command that is to modify memory must always correspond to a storage location in data memory. This incorrect entry is signaled by the warning "-Err" in the display.

An execution error is an error in the logic behind the development of the program. That is, the program is correctly coded and entered, but still it does not perform the operation for which it was planned. This type of error can be identified by entering the program into the microcomputer and executing it. Even when an execution error problem has been identified, it is usually not easy to find the exact cause of the problem.

Our ability to debug execution errors in a program is aided by the commands of the monitor program. For instance, the ST command allows us to step through the program by executing just one instruction at a time. In this way, we can use the register examine and memory examine commands to determine the state of the microcomputer prior to execution of the instruction and after its execution. This information will tell us whether the instruction has performed the operation planned for it. If an error is found, its cause can be determined and corrected.

To illustrate the process of debugging a program, let us once again consider the program in Fig. 5.9(a). Its machine code is given in Fig. 5.9(c) and we showed how to enter the program into the memory of the SDK-86 microcomputer in Example 5.13. The program resides in memory starting at address 200_{16}. This program implements a block data transfer operation. The block of data to be moved starts at memory address 300_{16} and is 10_{16} bytes in length. It is to be moved to another block location starting at address 320_{16}.

Before executing the program, let us issue commands to initialize the block of memory locations from address 300_{16} through $30F_{16}$ to FF_{16}. This is done with the command sequence

EB 30:0, FF, FF, FF, FF, FF, FF, FF, FF,

FF, FF, FF, FF, FF, FF, FF, FF, .

Moreover, the bytes in the block starting at 320_{16} can be initialized to 00_{16}. To do this, we issue the command sequence

```
EB 32:0, 0, 0, 0, 0, 0, 0, 0, 0, 0, 0, 0, 0, 0, 0, 0, 0, .
```

The first two instructions of the program in Fig. 5.9(a) are

MOV   AX, 020H

and

MOV   DS, AX

These two instructions when executed load the data segment register and define a data segment starting at address 200_{16}. Let us show how to execute these instructions and then determine if they perform the correct function. The two instructions are executed with the command

ST   20:0, , .

This command sequence establishes the code segment starting at 200_{16} by executing the first two instructions.

To determine if these two instructions performed the correct operation, we need to look at the contents of the DS register. This is done with the "examine register" command

ER DS.

When this command is issued to the microcomputer, DS will be displayed in the address field and 0020 in the data field.

Now we are ready to execute the next three instructions, which are used to load the SI, DI, and CX registers with 100_{16}, 120_{16}, and 10_{16}, respectively. Again the ST command can be used to execute the instructions. This gives

ST , , , .

and their operation is checked by examining the registers with the commands

ER SI.
ER DI.
ER CX.

The next two instructions copy the contents of memory location 300_{16} into the storage location at address 320_{16}. Let us first check the contents of the destination address with the command

EB 32:0,

This should show that the original contents of this location are 00_{16}. After terminating the EB command with a ".", the instructions are executed with the command

$$ST \ , \ , \ .$$

and the contents of address 320_{16} are checked once again with the command

$$EB \ 320:0.$$

This time, FF should be displayed, showing that the first element of the source block was correctly moved to the location of the first element of the destination block. Therefore, both address 300_{16} and address 320_{16} now contain the same data.

The next two instructions are used to increment SI and DI, respectively. To execute them we issue the command

$$ST \ , \ , \ .$$

and to verify their operation, we issue the commands

$$ER \ SI.$$

"." should be entered only after the displayed contents of SI are noted.

$$ER \ DI.$$

The new values found in SI and DI should be 101_{16} and 121_{16}, respectively.

The next instruction decrements the block count in CX. It is executed and the contents of CX are displayed with the command sequence

$$ST,$$

$$ER \ CX$$

The contents of CX should now be $000F_{16}$.

The jump instruction transfers control to the instruction 8 bytes back. It is executed with the command

$$ST,$$

As the result of executing this instruction, the address field of the display should read E. This corresponds to the location of the instruction

$$MOV \ AH, \ [SI]$$

Control has been returned to the part of the program that performs the move operation.

The move operation performed by this part of the program was already checked; however, we must still determine if it runs to completion when the count in CX decrements to zero. Therefore, we will execute the complete loop with a GO command. This command is

GO 20:E, 15.

where 15 specifies the breakpoint address 215H (the address of the jump instruction). Correct operation can by verified by determining if CX has been decremented. This is done with the command

ER CX.

Now we are at address 215H. To execute the instruction at this location, we can use the step command

ST,

Now the previous three commands can be repeated until the complete block is moved and CX equals 0_{16}. At which point a ST command should step the program control to the HLT instruction.

The overall operation of the program can be verified by examining the contents of the destination block with the command sequence

EB 32:0, , , , , , , , , , , , , , , , .

FF_{16} should be displayed as the data held in each storage location.

The entire debugging command sequence and the corresponding information displayed are shown in Fig. 5.19, pages 184–185.

ASSIGNMENT

Section 5.3

1. Encode the following instruction using the information in Figs. 5.3, 5.4, and 5.5.

ADD AX, DX

The opcode for ADD is 000000_2.

2. Encode the following instructions using the information in Figs. 5.3, 5.4, and 5.5.
   (a) MOV [DI], DX
   (b) MOV WORD PTR [1234H], 01234H
   (c) MOV [BX].[SI], BX
   (d) MOV DL, DISP[BX] where DISP = 10_{16}

3. Encode the instructions that follow using the tables in Figs. 5.6, 5.7, and 5.8.
   (a) PUSH DS
   (b) ROL BL, CL
   (c) XCHG CX, AX

Command sequence	Display	
	Address field	Data field
EB 30:0,FF	0	FF.
,FF	1	FF.
,FF	2	FF.
.	.	.
.	.	.
.	.	.
,FF	F	FF.
.	—	
EB 32:0,0	0	00.
,0	1	00.
,0	2	00.
.	.	.
.	.	.
.	.	.
,0	F	00.
.	—	
ST 20:0,	3.	8E
,	5.	bE
.	—	
ER DS	dS	0020.
.	—	
ST,	8.	bF
,	b.	b9
,	E.	8A
.	—	
ER SI	SI	0100.
.	—	
ER DI	dI	0120.
.	—	
ER CX	C	0010.
.	—	
EB 32:0,	0.	00.
.	—	
ST,	10.	88
,	12.	46
,	13.	47
EB 32:0,	0	FF.
.	—	
ST,	14.	49
,	15.	75
.	—	

Figure 5.19 Example command and display sequences.

Command sequence	Display	
	Address field	Data field
ER SI .	SI —	0101.
ER DI .	dl —	0121.
ST, .	E. —	8A
ER CX	C	000F.
ST, .	10. —	88
GO 20:E, 15 .	— —	br
ER CX .	C —	000E.
ST, .	E. —	8A
GO 20:E,15 .	— —	br
ER CX	C . . .	000d. . . .
GO 20:E,15 .	— —	br
ER CX .	C —	0000.
ST, .	17. —	F4
EB 32:0,	0	00.
,	1	00.
, . . .	2 . . .	00. . . .
, .	F —	00.

Figure 5.19 *(continued)*

Section 5.4

4. Describe the difference between the function keys and the hexadecimal keys.
5. Draw a simple flowchart that overviews how the SDK-86 monitor goes through the sequence of accepting entry of a command and initiating execution for it.

Section 5.5

6. Write a command sequence that will load the first 16 locations of the current data segment with FF_{16}.
7. Write a series of commands that will configure the memory segments of the SDK-86 microcomputer as follows: code segment starts at 100_{16}, data segment starts at 200_{16}, extra segment starts at 300_{16}, and the stack segment starts at 400_{16}.
8. Write commands that will first configure all P_1 ports as inputs and all P_2 ports as outputs and then display the byte contents of input port P_{1B} and output AB_{16} to output port P_{2B}.
9. The CS register contents are 20_{16}. A program segment starting at address 250_{16} and ending at $2FF_{16}$ is to be executed. Write the appropriate command or commands to do this.
10. Write a "move" (MV) command that will fill memory locations 300_{16} to $3FF_{16}$ with the number contained in location 300_{16}.

Section 5.6

11. Describe the operation of the command

$$GO \quad CS: 10, 2A.$$

Assume that CS contains 25_{16}.

Section 5.7

12. What is a syntax error?
13. How does an execution error differ from a syntax error?
14. Change the debugging command sequence shown in Fig. 5.19 so that GO commands are used instead of the ST commands. Also indicate what is displayed on the SDK-86 as these commands are executed.

Chapter 6 _____

Memory Interface of the 8086 Microprocessor ____

6.1 INTRODUCTION _____

Up to this point in the book, we have introduced the 8086 microprocessor, its signal leads, and internal architecture. Moreover, from a software point of view, we have covered its instruction set and how to write programs in assembly language. Now we will begin to examine the hardware interfaces of the 8086. This chapter is devoted to its memory interface and external memory subsystems. For this purpose, we have included the following topics in the chapter.

1. Memory interface block diagram
2. Hardware organization of the memory address space
3. Memory bus status codes
4. Memory control signals
5. Read and write bus cycles
6. The stack, stack segment register, and stack pointer
7. Demultiplexing the address/data bus
8. Program storage memory—ROM, PROM, and EPROM
9. Data storage memory—SRAM and DRAM
10. 4K-byte program storage memory, 2K-byte data storage memory circuit

In either the minimum- or maximum-mode-system configuration, the 8086 microprocessor can address up to 1M bytes of memory. However, the interface to the memory subsystem is different for each of these two modes of operation. The circuit diagram in Fig. 6.1 is that of the minimum-system memory interface. Here we find that it consists of the *multiplexed address/data bus lines* AD_0 through AD_{15} together with *additional address lines* A_{16} through A_{19} and *bank high enable* (BHE). Notice that *memory control signals* ALE, $\overline{RD}$, $\overline{WR}$, M/IO, DT/R, and $\overline{DEN}$ are produced by the 8086.

The maximum-mode memory interface is shown in Fig. 6.2. This circuit configuration includes an 8288 bus controller device. Notice that bus *status signals* $\overline{S}_0$ through $\overline{S}_2$ are input to this device. It decodes this 3-bit code to identify the type of bus cycle that is to be initiated. In turn, it generates *read/write signals* $\overline{MRDC}$, $\overline{MWTC}$, and $\overline{AMWC}$ as well as *control signals* ALE, DT/R, and $\overline{DEN}$. In this way we see that in the maximum-mode system the bus controller instead of the 8086 generates most of the timing and control signals for the memory interface.

Address Space and Data Organization

Looking at Figs. 6.1 and 6.2, we find that the 8086 has a 20-bit address bus. This bus consists of address lines AD_0 through AD_{15} and A_{16} through A_{19}. Of these, AD_0 is the LSB of the address and A_{19} the MSB. With this 20-bit *physical address,* it can directly address up to 1,048,576 bytes (1M byte) of memory. As shown in the memory map of Fig. 6.3, these byte storage locations are assigned to consecutive addresses over the range from 00000_{16} to $FFFFF_{16}$.

In this way we see that the memory subsystem in an 8086 microcomputer system is actually organized as 8-bit bytes, not as 16-bit words. However, any two consecutive

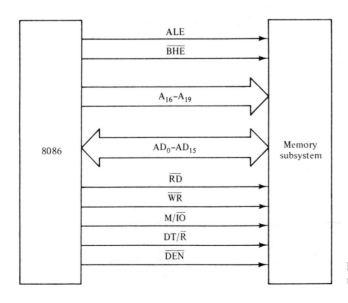

Figure 6.1 Minimum 8086 system memory interface.

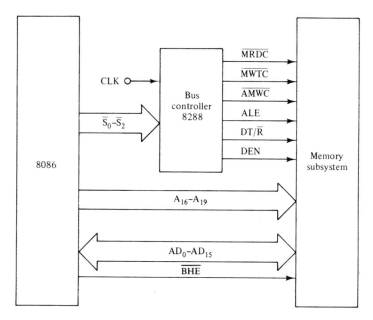

Figure 6.2 Maximum 8086 system memory interface.

Figure 6.3 Address space of the 8086.

bytes can be accessed as a word. The lower-addressed byte is the least significant byte of the word and the higher-addressed byte is its most significant byte.

Figure 6.4(a) demonstrates the storage of a word. Notice that the storage location at the lower address, 00724_{16}, contains the value $00000010_2 = 02_{16}$. Moreover, the

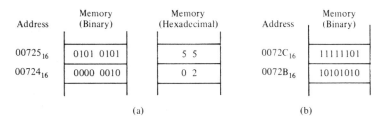

Figure 6.4 (a) Storage of a word at an even-address boundary (Courtesy of Intel Corp.); (b) example word storage (Courtesy of Intel Corp.).

contents of the next-higher-addressed storage location 00725_{16} are $01010101_2 = 55_{16}$. These two bytes represent the word $0101010100000010_2 = 5502_{16}$.

To permit efficient use of memory, words of data can be stored at even- or odd-address boundaries. The LSB A_0 of the address determines the type of *word boundary*. If this bit is 0, the word is said to be held at an *even-address boundary*. That is, a word at an even-address boundary corresponds to two consecutive bytes with the least significant byte located at an even address.

For example, the word in Fig. 6.4(a) has its least significant byte at address 00724_{16}. Therefore, it is stored at an even-address boundary.

EXAMPLE 6.1

What is the data word shown in Fig. 6.4(b)? Express the result in hexadecimal form. Is it stored at an even- or an odd-address boundary?

SOLUTION The most significant byte of the word is stored at address $0072C_{16}$ and equals

$$11111101_2 = FD_{16}$$

Its least significant byte is stored at address $0072B_{16}$ and is

$$10101010_2 = AA_{16}$$

Together these two bytes give the word

$$1111110110101010_2 = FDAA_{16}$$

Expressing the address of the least significant byte in binary form gives

$$0072B_{16} = 00000000011100101011_2$$

Since bit A_o is logic 1, the word is stored at an odd-address boundary in memory.

All data bytes and words at even-address boundaries can be accessed by the 8086 in one bus cycle. With the 5-MHz 8086, this takes 800 ns. On the other hand, accesses of words at odd-address boundaries require two bus cycles instead of one. This takes 1.6 μs when the 8086 is operating at a 5-MHz clock rate.

Data can be accessed either as bytes or words and can be stored at even- or odd-address boundaries. However, instructions are always accessed as words. For this reason they should always be stored at even-address boundaries. This minimizes the number of bus cycles needed to fetch them for execution; thereby maximizing performance.

The *double word* is another data form that can be processed in an 8086 system. A double word corresponds to two consecutive words of data stored in memory. An example of double-word data is a pointer that is used to address data or code outside the current segment. The word of the pointer that is stored at the higher address is the segment base address and the word at the lower address is the offset value.

An example showing storage of a pointer in memory is given in Fig. 6.5(a). Here we find that the higher-addressed word, which represents the segment address, is stored starting at even-address boundary 00006_{16}. The most significant byte of this word is at

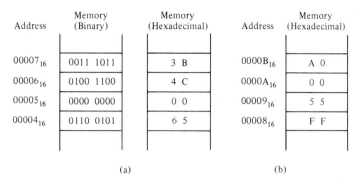

Address	Memory (Binary)	Memory (Hexadecimal)	Address	Memory (Hexadecimal)
00007_{16}	0011 1011	3 B	$0000B_{16}$	A 0
00006_{16}	0100 1100	4 C	$0000A_{16}$	0 0
00005_{16}	0000 0000	0 0	00009_{16}	5 5
00004_{16}	0110 0101	6 5	00008_{16}	F F

(a)   (b)

Figure 6.5 (a) Storage of a double-word pointer (Courtesy of Intel Corp.); (b) another double-word pointer (Courtesy of Intel Corp.).

address 00007_{16} and equals $00111011_2 = 3B_{16}$. Its least significant byte is at address 00006_{16} and equals $01001100_2 = 4C_{16}$. Combining these two values, we get the segment base address, which equals $0011101101001100_2 = 3B4C_{16}$.

The offset part of the pointer is the lower-addressed word. Its least significant byte is stored at address 00004_{16}. This location contains $01100101_2 = 65_{16}$. The most significant byte is at address 00005_{16}, which contains $00000000_2 = 00_{16}$. The resulting offset is $0000000001100101_2 = 0065_{16}$.

EXAMPLE 6.2

How should the pointer with segment base address equal to $A000_{16}$ and offset address $55FF_{16}$ be stored at an even-address boundary starting at 00008_{16}?

SOLUTION   Storage of the two-word pointer requires four consecutive byte locations in memory starting at address 00008_{16}. The least significant byte of the offset is stored at address 00008_{16}. This value is shown as $11111111_2 = FF_{16}$ in Fig. 6.5(b). The most significant byte of the offset, which is 55_{16}, is stored at address 00009_{16}. These two bytes are followed by the least significant byte of the segment base address, 00_{16}, at address $0000A_{16}$ and its most significant byte, $A0_{16}$, at address $0000B_{16}$.

The 1M-byte address space of the 8086 is actually organized into *64K-byte segments*. These segments represent independently addressable units of memory consisting of 64K consecutive byte storage locations. Each segment is assigned a base address that identifies its lowest-addressed byte storage location.

Only four of these 64K-byte segments are active at a time. The segments that are active, as shown in Fig. 6.6(a), are identified by the values held in the four internal address segment registers: CS (code segment), SS (stack segment), DS (data segment), and ES (extra segment). This gives a logical address space of 256K bytes of active memory. Of this, 64K bytes are allocated for code (program) storage, 64K bytes for a stack, and 128K bytes for data storage.

Figure 6.6(b) illustrates the segmentation of system memory. In this diagram we have identified 64K-byte segments with lcttcrs such as A, B, and C. The data segment (DS) register presently contains the value B. Therefore, the 64K-byte segment of mem-

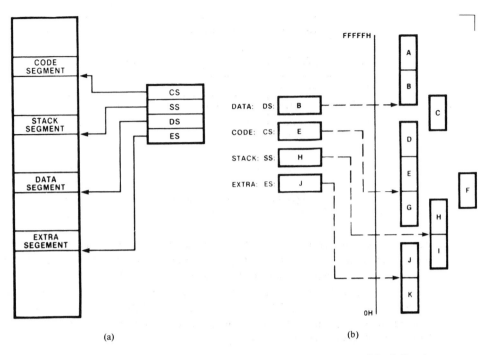

(a)   (b)

Figure 6.6 (a) Active nonoverlapping memory segments (Courtesy of Intel Corp.);
(b) active overlapping memory segments (Courtesy of Intel Corp.).

ory labeled B acts as the data storage segment. Segment E is selected for the current code segment. It is this part of memory from which the 8086 fetches instructions of the program. The stack segment (SS) register contains H, thereby selecting the 64K-byte segment labeled as H for use as a stack. Finally, the extra segment register ES is loaded with J such that segment J of memory can function as a second data storage segment.

The values in the internal segment registers can be modified through software. Therefore, for a program to gain access to another part of memory it just has to change the value of the appropriate register or registers. For instance, a new 128K-byte data space can be brought in by simply changing the values in DS and ES. This can be done with the load data segment (LDS) instruction and load extra segment (LES) instruction, respectively.

There is one restriction on the value that can be assigned to a segment as a base address: that is that it must reside on a 16-byte address boundary. Valid examples are 00000_{16}, 00010_{16}, and 00020_{16}. Other than this restriction, segments can be *contiguous, adjacent, disjointed,* or even *overlapping.* For example, in Fig. 6.6(b), segments A and B are contiguous, whereas segments B and C are overlapping.

Dedicated Memory Locations

Any part of the 1M-byte address space of the 8086 can be implemented with either ROM or RAM. However, some address locations have dedicated functions. These locations should not be used as general memory space for data or program storage.

Figure 6.7 shows the *reserved* and *general use (open) parts* of the 8086's *address space*. Notice that storage locations from address 00000_{16} to $0007F_{16}$ are dedicated. These 128 bytes of memory are reserved for storage of pointers to interrupt service routines. As indicated earlier, each pointer requires four bytes of memory. Two bytes hold the 16-bit segment address and the other two hold the 16-bit offset.

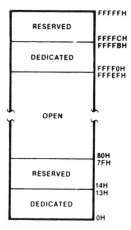

Figure 6.7 Dedicated and general use of memory (Courtesy of Intel Corp.).

At the high end of the memory address space is another pointer area. It is located from address $FFFFC_{16}$ through $FFFFF_{16}$. These four memory locations are reserved for use with future products. Moreover, Intel Corporation has identified the 12 storage locations from address $FFFF0_{16}$ through $FFFFB_{16}$ as dedicated for functions such as hardware reset.

Generating a Memory Address

The addresses that occur in the program of the 8086 are 16 bits in length. This is because all registers and memory locations are 16 bits in length. However, the physical address that is placed on the address bus during a memory cycle is 20 bits. The generation of the physical address involves combining a 16-bit offset value that is located in either an index register or pointer register and a 16-bit base value that is located in a segment register. Together the base value and offset represent the *logical address*.

The source of the offset address depends on which type of memory reference is taking place. It can be the base pointer (BP) register, base (BX) register, source index (SI) register, destination index (DI) register, or instruction pointer (IP). On the other hand, the base value always resides in one of the segment registers: CS, DS, SS, or ES.

For instance, when an instruction acquisition takes place, the source of the base address is always the code segment (CS) register and the source of the offset is always the instruction pointer (IP).

Moreover, if the value of a variable is being written to memory during the execution of an instruction, typically, the base segment address will be in the data segment (DS) register and the offset will be in the destination index (DI) register. Segment override prefixes can be used to change the segment from which the variable is accessed.

Another example is the stack address that is needed when pushing words onto the stack. This address is formed from the contents of the stack segment (SS) register and stack pointer (SP).

Remember that the base segment address represents the starting location of the 64K-byte segment in memory: that is, the lowest-addressed byte in the segment. The offset identifies the distance in bytes that the storage location of interest resides from this starting address. Therefore, the lowest-addressed byte in a segment has an offset of 0000_{16} and the highest-addressed byte has an offset of $FFFF_{16}$.

Figure 6.8 shows how a segment address and offset value are combined to give a physical address. What happens is that the value in the segment register is shifted left by 4 bits with its LSBs being filled with 0s. Then the offset value is added to the 16 LSBs of the shifted segment address. The result of this addition is the 20-bit physical address.

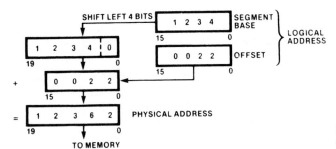

Figure 6.8 Generating a physical address (Courtesy of Intel Corp.).

The example in Fig. 6.8 represents a base segment address of 1234_{16} and an offset address of 0022_{16}. First let us express the base address in binary form. This gives

$$1234_{16} = 0001001000110100_2$$

Shifting left four times and filling with 0s results in

$$00010010001101000000_2 = 12340_{16}$$

The offset in binary form is

$$0022_{16} = 0000000000100010_2$$

Adding the shifted address and offset, we get

$$00010010001101000000_2 + 0000000000100010_2 = 00010010001101100010_2$$

$$= 12362_{16}$$

The bus interface unit does this address calculation each time a memory access is initiated.

EXAMPLE 6.3

What would be the offset required to map to address location $002C3_{16}$ if the segment base address is $002A_{16}$?

SOLUTION   The offset value can be obtained by shifting the segment base address left 4 bits and then subtracting it from the physical address. Shifting left gives

$$002A0_{16}$$

Now subtracting, we get the value of the offset.

$$002C3_{16} - 002A0_{16} = 0023_{16}$$

Actually, many different logical addresses can be mapped to the same physical address location in memory. This is done by simply changing the values of the base address in the segment register and its corresponding offset. The diagram in Fig. 6.9 demonstrates this idea. Notice that base $002B_{16}$ with offset 0013_{16} maps to physical address $002C3_{16}$ in memory. However, if the segment base address is changed to $002C_{16}$ with a new offset of 0003_{16}, the physical address is still $002C3_{16}$.

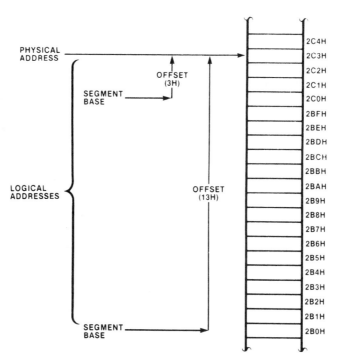

Figure 6.9 Relationship between logical segment address and offset and physical memory address (Courtesy of Intel Corp.).

EXAMPLE 6.4

Show the sequence of instructions that are needed to initialize the code segment to address 00000_{16} and the stack, data, and extra segments such that they are all at address 10000_{16}.

SOLUTION Since memory addresses are formed by the 16-bit contents of a segment register augmented by four zeros in the least significant bit locations, we must load CS with 0000_{16} and SS, DS, and ES with 1000_{16}. CS is loaded with the instruction sequence

```
MOV   AX, 0

MOV   CS, AX
```

Then the other three registers are loaded by the instructions

```
MOV   AX, 1000

MOV   SS, AX

MOV   DS, AX

MOV   EX, AX
```

6.3 HARDWARE ORGANIZATION OF THE MEMORY ADDRESS SPACE

From a hardware point of view, the memory address space of the 8086 is implemented as two independent 512K-byte banks. They are called the *low (even) bank* and the *high (odd) bank*. Data bytes associated with an even address (00000_{16}, 00002_{16}, etc.) reside in the low bank and those with odd addresses (00001_{16}, 00003_{16}, etc.) reside in the high bank.

Looking at the circuit diagram in Fig. 6.10, we see that address bits A_1 through A_{19} select the storage location that is to be accessed. Therefore, they are applied to both banks in parallel. A_0 and bank high enable ($\overline{BHE}$) are used as bank select signals. Logic

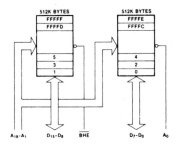

Figure 6.10 High and low memory banks (Courtesy of Intel Corp.).

0 at A_0 identifies an even-addressed byte of data and causes the low bank of memory to be enabled. On the other hand, $\overline{BHE}$ equal to 0 enables the high bank of access of an odd-addressed byte of data. Each of the memory banks provides half of the 8086's 16-bit data bus. Notice that the lower bank transfers bytes of data over data lines D_0 through D_7, while data transfers for the high bank use D_8 through D_{15}.

Figure 6.11(a) shows that when a byte memory operation is performed to address X, which is an even address, a storage location in the low bank is accessed. Therefore, A_0 is set to logic 0 to enable the low bank of memory and $\overline{BHE}$ to logic 1 to disable the high bank. As shown in the circuit diagram, data are transferred to or from the lower bank over data bus lines D_0 through D_7. D_7 carries the MSB of the byte and D_0 the LSB.

On the other hand, to access a byte of data at an odd address such as X + 1 in Fig. 6.11(b), A_0 is set to logic 1 and $\overline{BHE}$ to logic 0. This enables the high bank of memory and disables the low bank. Data are transferred between the 8086 and the high bank over bus lines D_8 through D_{15}. Here D_{15} represents the MSB and D_8 the LSB.

Whenever an even-addressed word of data is accessed, both the high and low banks are accessed at the same time. Figure 6.11(c) illustrates how a word at even address X is accessed. Notice that both A_0 and $\overline{BHE}$ equal 0; therefore, both banks are enabled. In this case, a byte of data is transferred from or to both the low and high banks at the same time. This 16-bit word is transferred over the complete data bus D_0 through D_{15}. The bytes of an even-addressed word are said to be aligned and can be transferred with a memory operation that takes just one bus cycle.

A word at an odd-addressed boundary is different. It is said to be unaligned. That is, the least significant byte is at the lower address location in the high memory bank. This is demonstrated in Fig. 6.11(d). Here we see that the odd byte of the word is located at address X + 1 and the even byte at address X + 2.

Two bus cycles are required to access this word. During the first bus cycle, the odd byte of the word, which is located at address X + 1 in the high bank, is accessed. This is accompanied by select signals $A_0 = 1$ and $\overline{BHE} = 0$ and a data transfer over D_8 through D_{15}.

Next the 8086 automatically increments the address such that $A_0 = 0$. This represents the next address in memory which is even. Then a second memory bus cycle is initiated. During this second cycle, the even byte located at X + 2 in the low bank is accessed. The data transfer takes place over bus lines D_0 through D_7. This transfer is accompanied by $A_0 = 0$ and $\overline{BHE} = 1$.

6.4 MEMORY BUS STATUS CODES

Whenever a memory bus cycle is in progress, an address bus status code S_3S_4 is output on the multiplexed address lines A_{16} and A_{17}. This 2-bit code is output at the same time the data are carried over the other bus lines.

Bits S_3 and S_4 together form a 2-bit binary code that identifies which one of the four segment registers was used to generate the physical address that was output during the address period in the bus cycle. The four *address bus status codes* are listed in Fig.

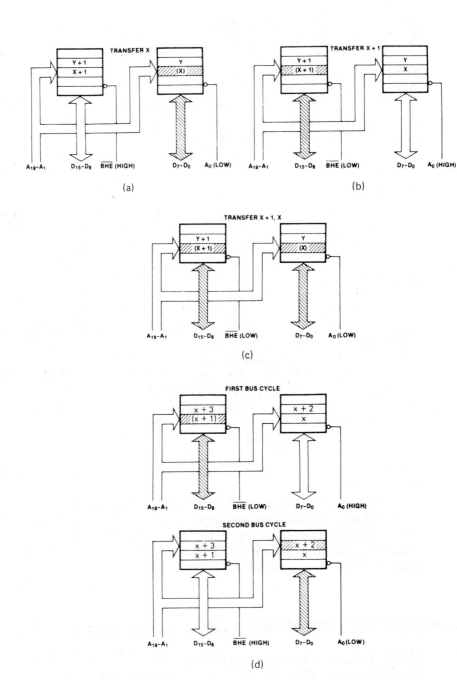

Figure 6.11 (a) Even-addressed byte transfer (Courtesy of Intel Corp.); (b) odd-addressed byte transfer (Courtesy of Intel Corp.); (c) even-addressed word transfer (Courtesy of Intel Corp.); (d) odd-addressed word transfer (Courtesy of Intel Corp.).

6.12. Here we find that code $S_3S_4 = 00$ identifies the extra segment register, 10 identifies the stack segment register, 01 identifies the code segment register, and 11 identifies the data segment register.

S_3	S_4	Address Status
0	0	Alternate (relative to the ES segment)
1	0	Stack (relative to the SS segment)
0	1	Code/None (relative to the CS segment or a default of zero)
1	1	Data (relative to the DS segment)

Figure 6.12 Address bus status code (Courtesy of Intel Corp.).

These status codes are output in both the minimum and the maximum system modes. They can be decoded with external circuitry to enable separate 1M-byte address spaces of ES, SS, CS, and DS. In this way, the memory address reach of the 8086 can be expanded to 4M bytes.

6.5 MEMORY CONTROL SIGNALS

Earlier in the chapter we saw that similar control signals are produced in the maximum- and minimum-mode systems. Moreover, we found that in the minimum-system mode, the 8086 produces all the control signals. But in the maximum-system mode, they are produced by the 8288 bus controller. Here we will look more closely at each of these signals and their function.

Minimum-System Memory Control Signals

In the 8086 microcomputer system of Fig. 6.1, which is configured for the minimum-system mode of operation, we found that the control signals provided to support the interface to the memory subsystem are: ALE, $\overline{\text{BHE}}$, M/$\overline{\text{IO}}$, DT/$\overline{\text{R}}$, $\overline{\text{RD}}$, $\overline{\text{WR}}$, and $\overline{\text{DEN}}$. These control signals are required to tell the memory subsystem when the bus is carrying a valid address, in which direction data are to be transferred over the bus, when valid write data are on the bus, and when to put read data on the bus.

For example, *address latch enable* (ALE) signals external circuitry that a valid address is on the bus. It is a pulse to the 1 logic level and is used to latch the address in external circuitry. Another important control signal involved in the memory interface is bank high enable ($\overline{\text{BHE}}$). Logic 0 is output on this line during the address part of the bus cycle whenever the high-bank part of the memory subsystem must be enabled.

The *memory/input-output* (M/$\overline{\text{IO}}$) and *data transmit/receive* (DT/$\overline{\text{R}}$) lines signal external circuitry whether a memory or I/O bus cycle is in progress and whether the 8086 will transmit or receive data over the bus. During all memory bus cycles, M/$\overline{\text{IO}}$ is held at the 1 logic level. Moreover, when the 8086 switches DT/$\overline{\text{R}}$ to logic 1 during the data transfer part of the bus cycle, the bus is in the transmit mode and data are written into memory. On the other hand, it sets DT/$\overline{\text{R}}$ to logic 0 to signal that the bus is in the receive mode. This corresponds to reading of memory.

The signals *read* ($\overline{\text{RD}}$) and *write* ($\overline{\text{WR}}$), respectively, identify that a read or write bus cycle is in progress. The 8086 switches $\overline{\text{WR}}$ to logic 0 to signal memory that a write cycle is taking place over the bus. On the other hand, $\overline{\text{RD}}$ is switched to logic 0 whenever a read cycle is in progress. During all memory operations, the 8086 produces one other control signal. It is *data enable* (DEN). Logic 0 at this output is used to enable the data bus.

Maximum-System Memory Control Signals

When the 8086 is configured to work in the maximum mode, it does not directly provide all the control signals to support the memory interface. Instead, an external *bus controller*, the 8288, provides memory commands and control signals that are compatible with the *Multibus*. Figure 6.2 shows an 8086 connected in this way.

Specifically, the $\overline{\text{WR}}$, M/$\overline{\text{IO}}$, DT/$\overline{\text{R}}$, $\overline{\text{DEN}}$, ALE, and $\overline{\text{INTA}}$ signal lines on the 8086 are changed. They are replaced with *multiprocessor lock* signal ($\overline{\text{LOCK}}$), a *bus status code* ($\overline{S}_2$ through $\overline{S}_0$), and a *queue status code* (QS_1QS_0). The 8086 still does produce signals $\overline{\text{BHE}}$ and $\overline{\text{RD}}$. Moreover, these two signals provide the same functions as they did in minimum system mode.

The 3-bit bus status code $\overline{S}_2\overline{S}_1\overline{S}_0$ is output prior to the initiation of each bus cycle. It identifies which type of bus cycle is to follow. This code is input to the 8288 bus controller. Here it is decoded to identify which type of bus cycle command signals must be generated.

Figure 6.13 shows the relationship between the bus status codes and the types of 8086 bus cycle produced. Also shown in this chart are the names of the corresponding command signals that are generated at the outputs of the 8288. For instance, the input code $\overline{S}_2\overline{S}_1\overline{S}_0$ equal 100 indicates that an instruction fetch cycle is to take place. This memory read makes the $\overline{\text{MRDC}}$ command output switch to logic 0.

Another bus command that is provided for the memory subsystem is $\overline{S}_2\overline{S}_1\overline{S}_0$ equal to 110. This represents a memory write cycle and it causes both the *memory write*

Status Inputs			CPU Cycle	8288 Command
$\overline{S}_2$	$\overline{S}_1$	$\overline{S}_0$		
0	0	0	Interrupt acknowledge	$\overline{\text{INTA}}$
0	0	1	Read I/O port	$\overline{\text{IORC}}$
0	1	0	Write I/O port	$\overline{\text{IOWC}}$, $\overline{\text{AIOWC}}$
0	1	1	Halt	None
1	0	0	Instruction fetch	$\overline{\text{MRDC}}$
1	0	1	Read memory	$\overline{\text{MRDC}}$
1	1	0	Write memory	$\overline{\text{MWTC}}$, $\overline{\text{AMWC}}$
1	1	1	Passive	None

Figure 6.13 Memory bus cycle status codes (Courtesy of Intel Corp.).

command ($\overline{\text{MWTC}}$) and *advanced memory write command* ($\overline{\text{AMWC}}$) outputs to switch to the 0 logic level.

The control outputs produced by the 8288 are DEN, DT/$\overline{\text{R}}$, and ALE. These signals provide the same functions as those produced by the corresponding pins on the 8086 in the minimum system mode.

The other two status signals, QS_0 and QS_1, form an instruction queue code. This code tells external circuitry what type of information was removed from the queue during the previous clock cycle. Figure 6.14 shows the four different queue statuses. Notice that $QS_1 QS_0 = 01$ indicates that the first byte of an instruction was taken from the queue. The next byte of the instruction that is fetched is identified by queue status code 11. Whenever the queue is reset, for instance due to a transfer of control, the reinitialization code 10 is output. Moreover, if no queue operation occured, status code 00 is output.

QS_1	QS_0	Queue Status
0 (low)	0	No Operation. During the last clock cycle, nothing was taken from the queue.
0	1	First Byte. The byte taken from the queue was the first byte of the instruction.
1 (high)	0	Queue Empty. The queue has been reinitialized as a result of the execution of a transfer instruction.
1	1	Subsequent Byte. The byte taken from the queue was a subsequent byte of the instruction.

Figure 6.14 Queue status code (Courtesy of Intel Corp.).

The last signal is bus priority lock ($\overline{\text{LOCK}}$). This signal is to be used as an input to the 8289 bus arbiter together with bus status code $\overline{S}_0$ through $\overline{S}_2$, and CLK. They are used to lock other processors off the system bus during access to common resources. In this way the processor can be assured of uninterrupted access to common system resources such as *global memory*.

The *bus arbitration* signals produced by the 8289 are: *bus clock* ($\overline{\text{BCLK}}$), *bus request* ($\overline{\text{BREQ}}$), *bus priority in* ($\overline{\text{BPRN}}$), *bus priority out* ($\overline{\text{BPRO}}$), and *I/O busy* ($\overline{\text{BUSY}}$). These are the bus exchange signals of the Multibus. It is this bus arbiter that permits multiple processors to reside on the system bus by implementing the Multibus arbitration protocol in the 8086 microcomputer system.

6.6 READ AND WRITE BUS CYCLES

In the preceding section we introduced the status and control signals associated with the memory interface. Here we continue by studying the sequence in which they occur during the read and write bus cycles of memory.

Read Cycle

The memory interface signals of a minimum-mode 8086 system are shown in Fig. 6.15. Here their occurrence is illustrated relative to the four *time states* T_1, T_2, T_3, and T_4 of the 8086's bus cycle. Let us trace through the events that occur as data or instructions are read from memory.

The *read bus cycle* begins with state T_1. During this period, the 8086 outputs the 20-bit address of the memory location to be accessed on its multiplexed address/data bus AD_0 through AD_{15} and A_{16} through A_{19}. $\overline{BHE}$ is also output during this time. Notice that a pulse is also produced at ALE. The trailing edge of this pulse should be used to latch the address and $\overline{BHE}$ in external circuitry.

Also we see that at the start of T_1, signals M/IO and DT/$\overline{R}$ are set to the 1 and 0 logic levels, respectively. This indicates to circuitry in the memory subsystem that a memory cycle is in progress and that the 8086 is going to receive data from the bus. Notice that both of these signals are maintained at these logic levels throughout all four periods of the bus cycle.

Beginning with state T_2, status bits S_3 through S_6 are output on the upper four bus lines A_{16} through A_{19}. Remember that bits S_3 and S_4 identify to external circuitry which segment register was used to generate the address just output. This status information is maintained through periods T_3 and T_4. The rest of the address/data bus lines, AD_0 through AD_{15}, are put in the high-Z state during T_2.

Late in period T_2, $\overline{RD}$ is switched to logic 0. This indicates to the memory subsystem that a read cycle is in progress. $\overline{DEN}$ is switched to logic 0 to enable the external circuitry such as data buffers.

As shown in the waveforms, input data are read by the 8086 during T_3, after

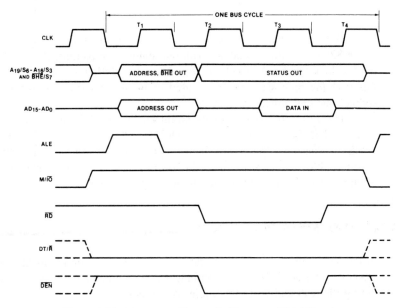

Figure 6.15 Memory read bus cycle (Courtesy of Intel Corp.).

which, as shown in T_4, the 8086 returns $\overline{RD}$ and $\overline{DEN}$ to the 1 logic level. The read cycle is now complete.

Write Cycle

The *write bus cycle* timing, shown in Fig. 6.16, is similar to that given for a read cycle in Fig. 6.15. Looking at the write cycle waveforms, we find that during T_1 the address and $\overline{BHE}$ are output and latched with the ALE pulse. This is identical to the read cycle. Moreover, M/IO is set to logic 1 to indicate that a memory cycle is in progress. However, this time DT/$\overline{R}$ is also switched to logic 1. This signals external circuits that the 8086 is going to transfer data over the bus.

As T_2 starts, the 8086 switches $\overline{WR}$ to logic 0. This tells the memory subsystem that a write operation is to follow over the bus. The 8086 puts the data on the bus late in T_2 and maintains the data valid through T_4. The write of data into memory should be initiated as $\overline{WR}$ returns from 0 to 1 early in T_4. This completes the write cycle.

Wait States in the Memory Bus Cycle

Wait states can be inserted to lengthen the memory bus cycles of the 8086. This is done with the *ready input* signal. Upon request from an event in hardware, for instance slow memory, the READY input is switched to logic 0. This signals the 8086 that the current bus cycle should not be completed. Instead, it is extended by inserting wait states with duration t_w equal 125 ns (for 8-MHz clock operation) between periods T_3 and T_4. The data that were on the bus during T_3 are maintained throughout the wait-state period. In this way, the bus cycle is not completed until READY is returned back to logic 1.

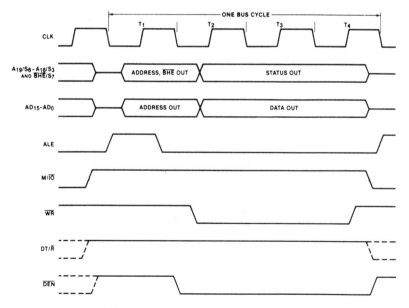

Figure 6.16 Memory write bus cycle (Courtesy of Intel Corp.).

In the 8086 microcomputer system, the READY input of the 8086 is supplied by the READY output of the 8284 clock generator circuit.

EXAMPLE 6.5

What is the duration of the bus cycle in the 8086-based microcomputer if the clock is 8 MHz and two wait states are inserted through wait state logic?

SOLUTION The duration of the bus cycle in an 8 MHz system is given in general by the expression

$$t_{cyc} = 500 \text{ ns} + N (125 \text{ ns})$$

In this expression N stands for the number of wait states. For a bus cycle with two wait states, we get

$$t_{cyc} = 500 \text{ ns} + 2(125 \text{ ns}) = 500 \text{ ns} + 250 \text{ ns}$$
$$= 750 \text{ ns}$$

6.7 THE STACK, STACK SEGMENT REGISTER, AND STACK POINTER

During interrupt and subroutine call types of operations, the contents of specific internal registers of the 8086 are pushed to a section of memory known as the *stack*. Here they are maintained temporarily. At the completion of the service routine or subroutine, these values are popped off the stack and put back into the same internal registers where they originally resided.

For instance, when an interrupt occurs, the 8086 automatically pushes the current flags, the value in CS, and the value in IP to the stack. As part of the service routine for the interrupt, the contents of other registers can be pushed onto the stack by executing PUSH instructions. An example is the instruction PUSH SI. It causes the contents of the source index register to be pushed onto the stack.

At the end of the service routine, POP instructions can be included to pop values from the stack back into their corresponding internal registers. For example, POP SI causes the value at the top of the stack to be popped back into the source index register.

As indicated earlier, stack is implemented in the memory of the 8086 microcomputer system. It is 64K bytes long and is organized as 32K words. The lowest addressed byte in the current stack is pointed to by the address in the stack segment (SS) register.

Any number of stacks may exist in an 8086 microcomputer system. A new stack can be brought in by simply changing the value in the SS register through software. For instance, executing the instruction MOV SS,DX loads a new value from DX into SS. Even though many stacks can exist, only one can be active at a time.

Another register, the stack pointer (SP) contains an offset from the value in SS. The address obtained from the contents of SS and SP is the physical address of the last storage location in the stack to which data were pushed. This is known as the *top of the stack*. The value in the stack pointer starts at $FFFF_{16}$ upon initialization of the 8086.

Combining this value with the current value in SS gives the highest-addressed location in the stack: that is, the *bottom of the stack*.

Since the data transfers to and from stack are always 16-bit words, it is important to configure the system such that all stack locations are at even word boundaries. This minimizes the number of memory cycles required to push or pop data for the stack and minimizes the amount of time required to perform a switch in program context.

The 8086 pushes data and addresses to the stack one word at a time. Each time a register value is to be pushed onto the top of the stack, the value in the stack pointer is first decremented by 2 and then the contents of the register are written into memory. In this way, we see that the stack grows down in memory from the bottom of the stack, which corresponds to the physical address derived from SS and SP, toward the end of the stack, which corresponds to the physical address obtained from SS and offset 0000_{16}.

When a value is popped from the top of the stack, the reverse of this sequence occurs. The physical address defined by SS and SP always points to the location of the last value pushed onto the stack. Its contents are first popped off the stack and put into the specified register within the 8086; then SP is incremented by 2. The top of the stack now corresponds to the previous value pushed onto the stack.

An example that shows how the contents of a register are pushed onto the stack is shown in Fig. 6.17(a). Here we find the state of the stack prior to execution of the PUSH instruction. Notice that the stack segment register contains 105_{16}. As indicated, the bottom of the stack resides at the physical address derived from SS with offset $FFFF_{16}$. This gives the bottom of stack address A_{BOS}

$$A_{BOS} = 1050_{16} + FFFF_{16}$$

$$= 1104F_{16}$$

Furthermore, the stack pointer, which represents the offset from the bottom of the stack

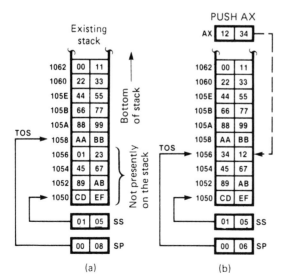

Figure 6.17 Pushing the contents of a register to the stack (Courtesy of Intel Corp.).

to the top of the stack, equals 0008_{16}. Therefore, the current top of the stack is at physical address A_{TOS} equals

$$A_{TOS} = 1050_{16} + 0008_{16}$$

$$= 1058_{16}$$

Addresses with higher values than that of the top of stack, 1058_{16}, contain valid stack data. Those with lower addresses do not yet contain valid stack data. Notice that the last value pushed to the stack in Fig. 6.17(a) was $BBAA_{16}$.

Figure 6.17(b) demonstrates what happens when the PUSH AX instruction is executed. Here we see that AX contains the value 1234_{16}. Notice that execution of the PUSH instruction causes the stack pointer to be decremented by 2 but does not affect the contents of the stack segment register. Therefore, the next location to be accessed in the stack corresponds to address 1056_{16}. It is to this location that the value in AX is pushed. Notice that the most significant byte of AX, which equals 12_{16} now resides in the least significant byte of the word in stack and the least significant byte 34_{16} is held in the most significant byte.

Now let us look at an example in which stack data are popped back into the register from which they were pushed. Figure 6.18 illustrates this operation. In Fig. 6.18(a), the stack is shown to be in the state that resulted due to our prior PUSH AX example. That is, SP equals 0006_{16}, SS equals 105_{16}, the address of the top of the stack equals 1056_{16}, and the word at the top of the stack equals 1234_{16}.

Looking at Fig. 6.18(b), we see what happens when the instructions POP AX and POP BX are executed in that order. Here we see that execution of the first instruction causes the 8086 to read the value 1234_{16} from the top of the stack and put it into the AX register as 1234_{16}. Next, SP is incremented to give 0008_{16} and another read cycle

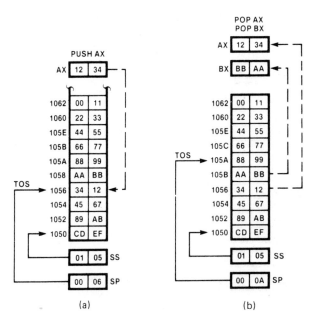

Figure 6.18   Popping the contents of a register from the stack (Courtesy of Intel Corp.).

is initiated from the stack. This second read corresponds to the POP BX instruction and it causes the value $BBAA_{16}$ to be loaded into the BX register. SP is incremented once more and now equals $000A_{16}$. Therefore, the new top of stack is at address $105A_{16}$.

From Fig. 6.18(b) we see that the values read out of 1056_{16} and 1058_{16} still remain at these addresses. But now they reside at locations that are considered to be above the top of the stack. Therefore, they no longer represent valid stack data.

6.8 DEMULTIPLEXING THE ADDRESS/DATA BUS

In an 8086 microcomputer system, memory, I/O devices, and the interrupt interface share use of the multiplexed address/data bus lines. In all three cases, a stable address is required and it must be available at the same time that data are to be transferred over the bus. For this reason, the address and data signals must be separated using external demultiplexing circuits to give a system bus. This *demultiplexed system bus* consists of the 20 address lines A_0 through A_{19}, 16 data bus lines D_0 through D_{15}, and memory control signals $\overline{BHE}$, $M/\overline{IO}$, $\overline{WR}$, and $\overline{RD}$.

Several different techniques can be used to demultiplex the system bus. One approach is shown in Fig. 6.19. Here the microprocessor's bus is demultiplexed into a system bus just once at the MPU and then distributed to all other system elements. This is known as *local demultiplexing* and has the advantage of requiring minimal circuitry.

During bus cycles, a 20-bit address is output by the 8086 on AD_0 through A_{19} during period T_1 of the bus cycle. This address is accompanied by a pulse on the ALE (address latch enable) line. In this circuit, ALE tells external circuitry that a stable address is available and it should be latched.

In the circuit of Fig. 6.19 we have used three 8282 noninverting latches to demultiplex the address. These devices are octal latches. The ALE output of the 8086 is applied to the strobe (STB) input of all three latches. When pulsed at STB, the address applied to the DI_0 through DI_7 inputs of the 8282s is latched into their internal flip-flops. This happens on the 1-to-0 edge of ALE. Even though the address is latched, it is not yet available at address outputs A_0 through A_{19}. This is because the outputs of the octal latches are not yet enabled. To do this, we must switch the output enable ($\overline{OE}$) input on the 8282s to the 0 logic level. In many applications, $\overline{OE}$ can be fixed at the 0 logic level. This permanently enables the outputs of the 8282s and the address is made available at A_0 through A_{19} as soon as it is latched. Notice that signal $\overline{BHE}$ is latched together with the address. In this way, the address is latched and maintained stable throughout the bus cycle.

This circuit configuration also increases the drive capability at the system bus. The outputs of the 8282 are rated to drive up to 32 mA. However, a propagation delay of 30 ns is introduced as signals pass through it.

The data bus D_0 through D_{15} can be directly formed from the AD_0 through AD_{15} lines or buffered with bidirectional bus transceivers to increase drive capability. It is usually necessary to do this buffering because a large number of memory and peripheral devices are attached to the bus.

Two 8286 8-bit bidirectional transceiver devices can be used for this purpose. They are connected as shown in Fig. 6.19. Data can be passed in either direction be-

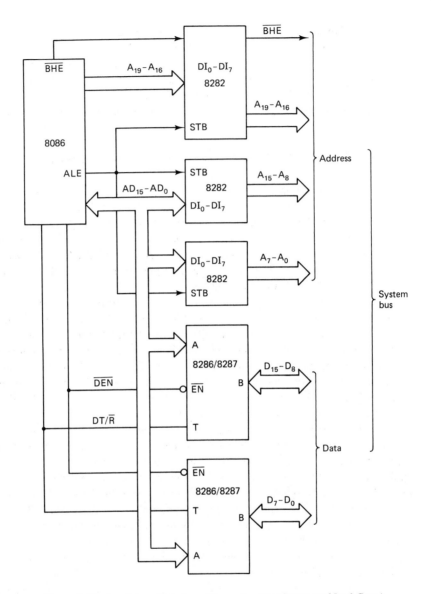

Figure 6.19 Local demultiplexing of the system bus (Courtesy of Intel Corp.).

tween its A and B terminals. The direction of data transfer is determined by the logic level applied at the transfer (T) input. When T is logic 1, data are passed from A to B. This corresponds to the direction required for data transfers during write bus cycles. Changing the logic level of T to 0 causes data to be passed from B to A such as needed for read cycles. Moreover, logic 0 is needed at the $\overline{\text{EN}}$ input of the 8286 to enable the input and output drive circuitry selected by T. The bus side of the 8286 is able to drive up to 32 mA with propagation delays through the device equal to 30 ns.

From the circuit in Fig. 6.19, we see that the 8086 controls the direction and timing of data transfers through the 8286s with signals DT/$\overline{\text{R}}$ at the T input and $\overline{\text{DEN}}$ at its $\overline{\text{EN}}$ input. When DT/$\overline{\text{R}}$ is set to logic 1, the 8286s are set to pass data from MPU to memory. This sets the bus for a write operation. Switching DT/$\overline{\text{R}}$ to logic 0 changes the direction of data transfer through the 8286s such that the MPU can read data out of memory. DEN is switched to logic 0 whenever a data transfer is to take place over the bus and enables the output buffers of the 8286.

A second approach is shown in Fig. 6.20. This configuration is known as *remote demultiplexing*. In this case, the microprocessor's local bus signals are distributed to each part of the system and then demultiplexed by circuits provided in the memory or I/O sections.

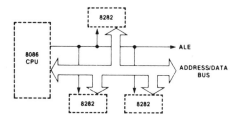

Figure 6.20 Remote demultiplexing of the system bus (Courtesy of Intel Corp.).

6.9 PROGRAM STORAGE MEMORY— ROM, PROM, AND EPROM

Read-only memory (ROM) is one type of semiconductor memory device. It is most widely used in microcomputer systems for storage of the program that determines overall system operation. The information stored within a ROM integrated circuit is permanent—or *nonvolatile*. This means that when the power supply of the device is turned off, the stored information is not lost.

ROM, PROM, and EPROM

For some ROM devices, information (the microcomputer program) must be built in during manufacturing and for others the data must be electrically entered. The process of entering data into a ROM is called *programming*. As the name ROM implies, once entered into the device this information can be read only. Three types of ROM devices exist. They are known as the *mask-programmable read-only memory* (ROM), the *one-time programmable read-only memory* (PROM), and the *erasable programmable read-only memory* (EPROM).

Let us continue by looking more closely into the first type of device, the mask programmable read-only memory. This device has its data pattern programmed as part of the manufacturing process. This is known as *mask programming*. Once the device is programmed, its contents can never be changed. Because of this and the cost for making the programming masks, ROMs are used mainly in high-volume applications where the data will not change frequently.

The other two types of read-only memories, the PROM and EPROM, differ from the ROM in that the data contents are electrically entered by the user. Programming is usually done with equipment called an *EPROM programmer*. Both the PROM and EPROM are programmed in the same way. Once a PROM is programmed, its contents cannot be changed. This is the reason they are sometimes called one-time programmable EPROMs. On the other hand, the contents of an EPROM can be erased by exposing it to ultraviolet light. In this way, the device can be used over and over again simply by erasing and reprogramming. PROMs and EPROMs are most often used during the design of a product and for early production, when the code of the microcomputer may need to be changed frequently.

Block Diagram of a ROM

A block diagram of a typical ROM is shown in Fig. 6.21. Here we see that the device has three sets of signal lines: the address inputs, data outputs, and control inputs. This block diagram is valid for a ROM, PROM, or EPROM. Let us now look at the function of each of these sets of signal lines.

The address bus is used to input the signals that select between the data storage locations within the ROM device. In Fig. 6.21 we find that this bus consists of 11 address lines, A_0 through A_{10}. The bits in the address are arranged such that A_{10} is the MSB and A_0 is the LSB. With an 11-bit address, the memory device has $2^{11} = 2048$ unique data storage locations. The individual storage locations correspond to addresses over the range $00000000000_2 = 000_{16}$ through $11111111111_2 = 7FF_{16}$.

Each bit of data is stored inside a ROM, PROM, or EPROM as either a binary 0 or binary 1. Actually, 8 bits of data are stored at every address. Therefore the total storage capacity of the device we are describing is $2048 \times 8 = 16,384$ bits; that is, the device we are describing is really a 16K-bit ROM. By applying the address of a storage location to the address inputs of the ROM, the byte of data held at the addressed location is read out onto the data lines. In the block diagram of Fig. 6.21, we see that the data bus consists of eight lines labeled D_0 through D_7.

The control bus represents the control signals that are required to enable or disable the ROM, PROM, or EPROM device. In the block diagram of Fig. 6.21, two control leads, output enable ($\overline{OE}$) and chip enable ($\overline{CE}$), are identified. For example, logic 0 at

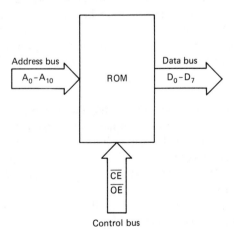

Address bus — $A_0 - A_{10}$ — ROM — Data bus — $D_0 - D_7$

$\overline{CE}$
$\overline{OE}$

Control bus

Figure 6.21 Block diagram of a ROM.

$\overline{\text{OE}}$ enables the three state outputs, D_0 through D_7, of the device. If $\overline{\text{OE}}$ is switched to the 1 logic level, these outputs are disabled (put in the high-Z state). Moreover, $\overline{\text{CE}}$ must be at logic 0 for the device to be active. Logic 1 at $\overline{\text{CE}}$ puts the device in a low-power standby mode. When in this state, the data outputs are in the high-Z state independent of the logic level of $\overline{\text{OE}}$.

Read Operation

For a microprocessor to read a byte of data from the device, it must apply a binary address to inputs A_0 through A_{10}. This address gets decoded inside the device to select the storage location of the byte of data that is to be read. Then the microprocessor must switch $\overline{\text{CE}}$ and $\overline{\text{OE}}$ to logic 0 to enable the device and outputs. Now the byte of data is available at D_0 through D_7 and the microprocessor can read the data over its data bus.

From our description of the read operation, it appears that after the inputs of the ROM are set up the output appears immediately; however, in practice this is not true. A short delay exists between address inputs and data outputs. This leads us to three important timing properties defined for the read cycle of a ROM. They are called *access time* (t_{ACC}), *chip enable time* (t_{CE}), and *chip deselect time* (t_{DF}).

Access time tells us how long it takes to access data stored in a ROM. Here we assume that both $\overline{\text{CE}}$ and $\overline{\text{OE}}$ are at their active 0 levels, and then an address is applied to the inputs of the ROM. In this case, the delay t_{ACC} occurs before the data stored at the addressed location are stable at the outputs. The microprocessor must wait at least this long before reading the data; otherwise, invalid results may be obtained.

Chip enable time is similar to access time. In fact, for most EPROMs they are equal in value. They differ in how the device is set up initially. This time the address is applied and $\overline{\text{OE}}$ is switched to 0, then the read operation is initiated by making $\overline{\text{CE}}$ active. Therefore, t_{CE} represents the chip enable to output delay instead of the address to output delay.

Chip deselect time is the opposite of access or chip enable time. It represents the amount of time the device takes for the data outputs to return to the high-Z state after $\overline{\text{OE}}$ becomes inactive—that is, the recovery time of the outputs.

Standard EPROM ICs

A large number of standard EPROM ICs are available today. Figure 6.22 lists the part numbers, bit densities, and byte capacities of the seven most popular devices. They range in size from the 2716, which is a 16K-bit density (2K × 8) device, to the 27010, which is a 1M-byte (128K × 8) device. Higher-density devices, such as the 27256 through 27010, are most popular for new system designs. In fact, some of the older devices, such as the 2716 and 2732, have already been discontinued by many manufacturers. Let us now look at some of these EPROMs in more detail.

The 27256 is an EPROM IC manufactured with the NMOS technology. Looking at Fig. 6.22, we find that it is a 256KB device and its storage array is organized as 32K × 8 bits. Figure 6.23 shows the pin layout of the 27256. Here we see that it has 15 address inputs, labeled A_0 through A_{14}, eight data outputs, identified as 0_0 through 0_7, and control signals $\overline{\text{CE}}$ and $\overline{\text{OE}}$.

Figure 6.22 Standard EPROM devices.

EPROM	Density (bits)	Capacity (bytes)
2716	16K	2K X 8
2732	32K	4K X 8
2764	64K	8K X 8
27128	128K	16K X 8
27256	256K	32K X 8
27512	512K	64K X 8
27010	1M	128K X 8

Figure 6.23 Pin layouts of standard EPROMs (Courtesy of Intel Corp.).

Right side pin assignments:

2716	2732A	2764A / 27C64	27128A	27512
		V_{CC}	V_{CC}	V_{CC}
		$\overline{PGM}$	$\overline{PGM}$	A_{14}
	V_{CC}	N.C.	A_{13}	A_{13}
V_{CC}	A_8	A_8	A_8	A_8
A_8	A_9	A_9	A_9	A_9
A_9	A_{11}	A_{11}	A_{11}	A_{11}
$V_{PP}/\overline{OE}$	$\overline{OE}/V_{PP}$	$\overline{OE}$	$\overline{OE}$	$\overline{OE}/V_{PP}$
A_{10}	A_{10}	A_{10}	A_{10}	A_{10}
$\overline{CE}$	$\overline{CE}$	$\overline{CE}$	$\overline{CE}$	$\overline{CE}$
O_7	O_7	O_7	O_7	O_7
O_6	O_6	O_6	O_6	O_6
O_5	O_5	O_5	O_5	O_5
O_4	O_4	O_4	O_4	O_4
O_3	O_3	O_3	O_3	O_3

Left side pin assignments:

27512	27128A	2764A / 27C64	2732A	2716
A_{15}	V_{PP}	V_{PP}		
A_{12}	A_{12}	A_{12}		
A_7	A_7	A_7	A_7	A_7
A_6	A_6	A_6	A_6	A_6
A_5	A_5	A_5	A_5	A_5
A_4	A_4	A_4	A_4	A_4
A_3	A_3	A_3	A_3	A_3
A_2	A_2	A_2	A_2	A_2
A_1	A_1	A_1	A_1	A_1
A_0	A_0	A_0	A_0	A_0
O_0	O_0	O_0	O_0	O_0
O_1	O_1	O_1	O_1	O_1
O_2	O_2	O_2	O_2	O_2
Gnd	Gnd	Gnd	Gnd	Gnd

27256 DIP pin layout:

Pin	Signal		Pin	Signal
1	V_{PP}		28	V_{CC}
2	A_{12}		27	A_{14}
3	A_7		26	A_{13}
4	A_6		25	A_8
5	A_5		24	A_9
6	A_4		23	A_{11}
7	A_3		22	$\overline{OE}$
8	A_2		21	A_{10}
9	A_1		20	$\overline{CE}$
10	A_0		19	O_7
11	O_0		18	O_6
12	O_1		17	O_5
13	O_2		16	O_4
14	GND		15	O_3

The 27256 is available in four access-time speed selections. In Fig. 6.24 we find that the speed of an EPROM is denoted by a dash and number at the end of the generic part number. For example, the standard 27256 is a 250 ns access-time device. On the other hand, the 27256-1 is faster; it has an access time of 170 ns.

Part number	Access time
27256-3	300 ns
27256	250 ns
27256-2	200 ns
27256-1	170 ns

Figure 6.24 Speed selections for the 27256.

In an erased 27256, all storage cells hold logic 1. The device is put into the programming mode by switching on the V_{PP} power supply. Once in this mode, the address of the storage location that is to be programmed is applied to the address inputs, and the data that is to be loaded into this location is supplied to the data leads. Now the $\overline{CE}$, input is pulsed to load the data. Actually, a complex series of program and verify

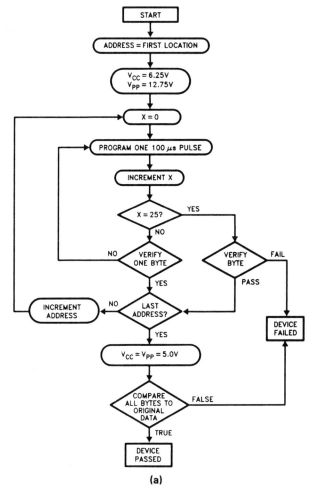

Figure 6.25(a) Quick-Pulse Programming™ algorithm flowchart (Courtesy of Intel Corp.).

(a)

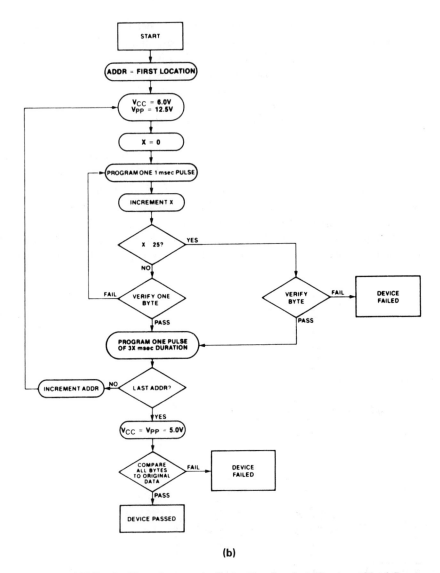

Figure 6.25(b) Intelligent Programming™ algorithm flowchart (Courtesy of Intel Corp.).

operations are performed to program each storage location in an EPROM. The two programming sequences in wide use today are the *Quick-Pulse Programming Algorithm*™ and the *Intelligent Programming Algorithm*™. Flowcharts for these programming algorithms are given in Figs 6.25 (a) and (b), respectively.

Figure 6.23 also shows the pin layouts for the 2716 through 27512 EPROM devices. In this diagram, we find that the 27256 and 27512 are both in a 28-pin package. A comparison of the pin configuration of the 27512 with that of the 27256 shows that the only differences between the two pinouts are that pin 1 on the 27512 becomes the new address input A_{15}, and V_{PP}, which was at pin 1 on the 27256, becomes a second function performed by pin 22 on the 27512.

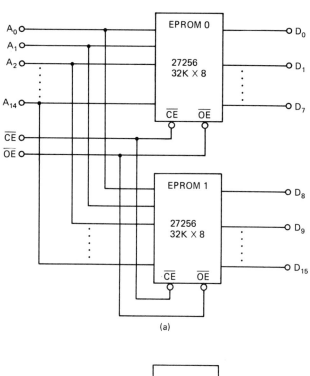

(a)

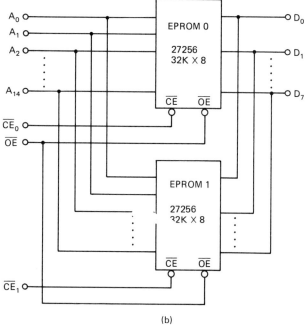

(b)

Figure 6.26 (a) Expanding word length; (b) expanding word capacity.

Expanding ROM Word Length and Word Capacity

In many applications, the microcomputer system requirements for ROM are greater than what is available in a single device. There are two basic reasons for expanding ROM capacity: first, the byte-wide length is not large enough; second, the total storage capacity is not enough bytes. Both of these expansion needs can be satisfied by interconnecting a number of ICs.

For example, the 8086 microprocessor has a 16-bit data bus. Therefore, its program memory subsystem needs to be implemented with two 27256 EPROMs connected as shown in Fig. 6.26(a) on page 215. Notice that the individual address inputs, chip enable lines, and output enable lines on the two devices are connected in parallel. On the other hand, the eight data outputs of the two devices are each used to supply eight lines of the 16-bit data bus. This device configuration has a total storage capacity equal to 32K 16-bit words.

Figure 6.26(b) shows how two 27256s can be interconnected to expand the number of bytes of storage. Here the individual address inputs, data outputs, and output enable lines of the two devices are connected in parallel. However, the CE inputs of the individual devices remain independent and can be supplied by different outputs of an address decoder circuit. In this way, only one of the two devices will be enabled at a time. This configuration results in a total storage capacity of 64K bytes.

6.10 DATA STORAGE MEMORY—SRAM AND DRAM

The memory section of a microcomputer system is normally formed from both read-only memories (ROM) and *random access read/write memories* (RAM). Earlier we pointed out that the ROM is used to store permanent information such as the microcomputer's program. RAM is different from ROM in two important ways. First, we are able both to save data by writing it into RAM and to read it back for additional processing. Because of its versatile read and write features, RAM finds wide use where data changes frequently. For this reason, it is normally used to store data such as numerical and character data. The second difference is that RAM is volatile; that is, if power is removed from RAM all data are lost.

Static and Dynamic RAMs

There are two types of RAMs in general use today, the *static RAM* (SRAM) and *dynamic RAM* (DRAM). For static RAMs, data, once entered, remains valid as long as the power supply is not turned off. On the other hand, to retain data in a DRAM, it is not sufficient just to maintain the power supply. For this type of device, we must both keep the power supply turned on and periodically restore the data in each storage location by addressing them. This added requirement is necessary because the storage elements in a DRAM are capacitive nodes. If the storage nodes are not recharged at regular intervals of time, data would be lost. This recharging process is known as refreshing the DRAM.

Block Diagram of a Static RAM

A block diagram of a typical static RAM IC is shown in Fig. 6.27. By comparing this diagram with the one shown for a ROM in Fig. 6.21, we see that they are similar in many ways. For example, they both have address lines, data lines, and control lines. The data lines of the RAM, however, act as both inputs and outputs. For this reason, they are identified as a *bidirectional bus*.

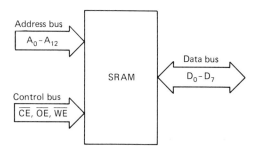

Figure 6.27 Block diagram of a static RAM.

A variety of static RAM ICs are currently available. They differ both in density and organization. The most commonly used densities in new circuit designs are the 64K-bit and 256K-bit devices. The structure of the data bus determines the organization of the RAMs storage array. In Fig. 6.27, an 8-bit data bus is shown. This type of organization is known as a *byte-wide* RAM. Devices are also manufactured with by 1 and by 4 data I/O organizations. At the 64K-bit density, this results in three standard device organizations: $64K \times 1$, $16K \times 4$, and $8K \times 8$.

The address bus on the RAM in Fig. 6.27 consists of the lines labeled A_0 through A_{12}. This 13-bit address is what is needed to select between the 8K individual storage locations in an $8K \times 8$-bit RAM IC. The $16K \times 4$ and $64K \times 1$ devices have a 14-bit and 16-bit address bus, respectively.

To either read or write data from the RAM, the device must first be chip enabled. Just like for a ROM, this is done by switching the $\overline{CE}$ input of the RAM to logic 0. Earlier we indicated that data lines D_0 through D_7 in Fig. 6.27 are bidirectional. This means that they will act as inputs when writing data into the RAM or as outputs when reading data from the RAM. The setting of the *write enable* ($\overline{WE}$) control input determines how the data lines operate. During all write operations to a storage location within the RAM, the $\overline{WE}$ input must be switched to the active 0 logic level. This configures the data lines as inputs. On the other hand, if data are to be read from a storage location, $\overline{WE}$ is left at the 1 logic level.

To read data from the RAM, output enable ($\overline{OE}$) must also be active. Logic 0 at this input enables the device's three-state outputs. Three-state data bus lines allow for the parallel busing needed to expand data memory by interconnecting multiple devices. For example, in Fig. 6.28 we see how four $8K \times 8$-bit RAMs are interconnected to form a $16K \times 16$-bit memory circuit. Here $\overline{CE}_0$ enables the bank 0 RAMs and $\overline{CE}_1$ the bank 1 RAMs.

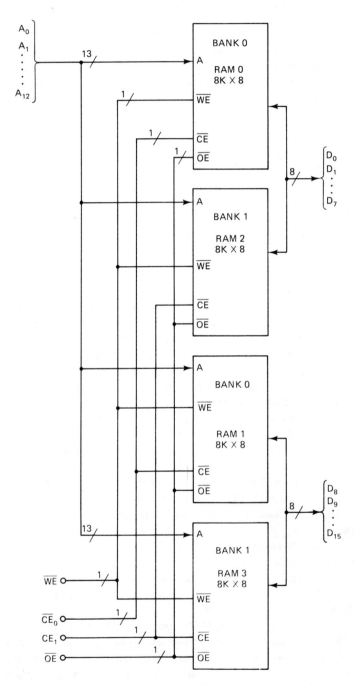

Figure 6.28 16K × 16-bit SRAM circuit.

Memory Interface of the 8086 Microprocessor   Chap. 6

Standard Static RAM ICs

Figure 6.29 is a list of a number of standard static RAM ICs. Here we find their part numbers, densities, and organizations. For example, the 4361, 4363, and 4364 are all 64K-bit density devices; however, they are each organized differently. The 4361 is a 64K × 1-bit device, the 4363 is a 16K × 4-bit device, and the 4364 is an 8K × 8-bit device.

SRAM	Density (bits)	Organization
4361	64K	64K × 1
4363	64K	16K × 4
4364	64K	8K × 8
43254	256K	64K × 4
43256A	256K	32K × 8

Figure 6.29 Standard SRAM devices.

The pin layouts of the 4364 and 43256A ICs are given in Figs. 6.30(a) and (b), respectively. Looking at the 4364 we see that it is almost identical to the block diagram

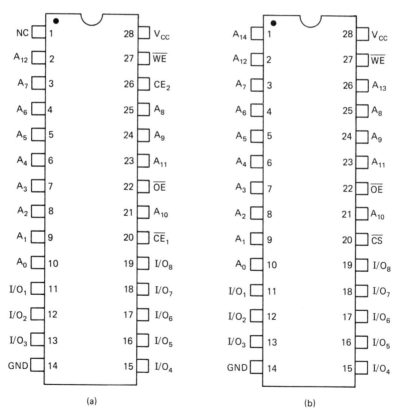

(a)

(b)

Figure 6.30 (a) 4364 pin layout (Courtesy of NEC Electronics, Inc.); (b) 43256A pin layout (Courtesy of NEC Electronics, Inc.).

shown in Fig. 6.27. The one difference is that it has two chip enable lines instead of one. They are labeled $\overline{CE_1}$ and CE_2. Notice that one is activated by logic 0 and the other by logic 1.

As shown in Fig. 6.31, the 4364 is available in four speeds. For example, the minimum read cycle and write cycle times for the 4364-10 is 100 ns.

Part number	Read/write cycle time
4364-10	100 ns
4364-12	120 ns
4364-15	150 ns
4364-20	200 ns

Figure 6.31 Speed selections for the 4364.

The waveforms for a typical write cycle are illustrated in Fig. 6.32. Let us now trace the events that take place during the write cycle. Here we see that all critical timing is referenced to the point at which the address becomes valid. Notice that the minimum duration of the write cycle is identified as t_{WC}. This is the 100 ns *writes cycle time* of the 4364-10. The address must remain stable for this complete interval of time.

Next $\overline{CE_1}$ and CE_2 become active and must remain active until the end of the write cycle. The durations of these pulses are identified as $\overline{CE_1}$ *to end of write* (t_{CW1}) time and CE_2 *to end of write* (t_{CW2}) time. As shown in the waveforms, we are assuming here that they begin at any time after the occurrence of the address but before the

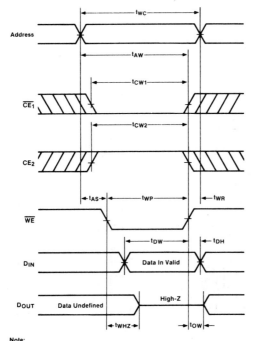

Note:
[1] A write occurs during the overlap of a low $\overline{CE_1}$ and a high CE_2 and a low $\overline{WE}$.
[2] $\overline{CE_1}$ or $\overline{WE}$ (or CE_2) must be high (low) during any address transition.
[3] If $\overline{OE}$ is high the I/O pins remain in a high impedance state.

Figure 6.32 Write-cycle timing diagram.

leading edge of $\overline{WE}$. The minimum value for both of these times is 80 ns. On the other hand, $\overline{WE}$ is shown to not occur until the interval t_{AS} elapses. This is the *address set-up time* and represents the minimum amount of time the address inputs must be stable before $\overline{WE}$ can be switched to logic 0. For the 4364, however, this parameter is equal to 0 ns. The width of the write enable pulse is identified as t_{WP} and its minimum value equals 60 ns.

Data applied to the D_{IN} data inputs are written into the device synchronous with the trailing edge of $\overline{WE}$. Notice that the data must be valid for an interval equal to t_{DW} before this edge. This interval, which is called *data valid to end of write*, has a minimum value of 40 ns for the 4364-10. Moreover, it is shown to remain valid for an interval of time equal to t_{DH} after this edge. This *data hold time*, however, just like address set-up time, equals 0 ns for the 4364. Finally, a short recovery period takes place after $\overline{WE}$ returns to logic 1 before the write cycle is complete. This interval is identified as t_{WR} in the waveforms, and its minimum value equals 5 ns.

The read cycle of a static RAM, such as the 4364, is similar to that of a ROM. Waveforms of a read operation are given in Fig. 6.33.

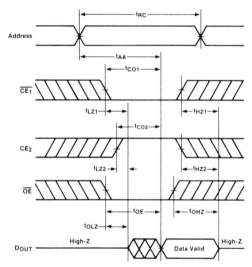

Note:
[1] $\overline{WE}$ is a high for a read cycle.
[2] The address inputs are valid prior to or coincident with the $\overline{CE}_1$ transition low and the CE_2 transition high.

Figure 6.33 Read-cycle timing diagram.

DRAM	Density (bits)	Organization
2164B	64K	64K × 1
21256	256K	256K × 1
21464	256K	64K × 4
421000	1M	1M × 1
424256	1M	256K × 4

Figure 6.34 Standard DRAM devices.

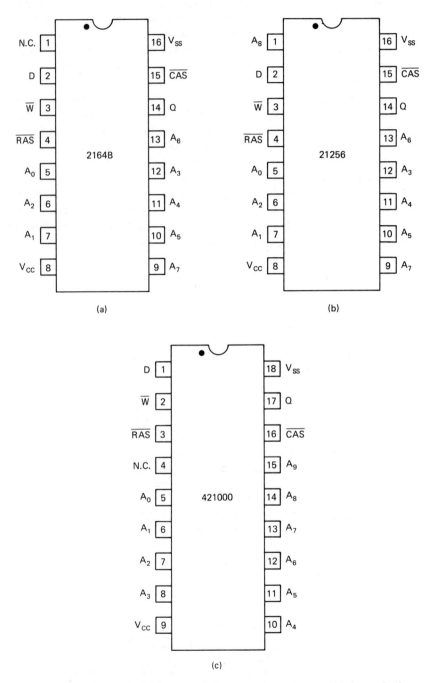

Figure 6.35 (a) 2164B pin layout (Courtesy of Intel Corp.); (b) 21256 pin layout (Intel Corp.); (c) 421000 pin layout (NEC Electronics, Inc.).

Standard Dynamic RAM ICs

Dynamic RAMs are available in higher densities than static RAMs. Currently, the most widely used DRAMs are the 64K-bit, 256K-bit, and 1M-bit devices. Figure 6.34 (page 221) is a list of a number of popular DRAM ICs. Here we find the 2164B, which is organized as 64K × 1 bit, the 21256, which is organized as 256K × 1 bit, the 21464, which is organized as 64K × 4 bits, the 421000, which is organized as 1M × 1 bit, and the 424256, which is organized as 256K × 4 bits. Pin layouts for the 2164B, 21256, and 421000 are shown on page 222 in Figs. 6.35 (a), (b), and (c), respectively.

Some other benefits of using DRAMs over SRAMs are that they cost less, consume less power, and their 16- and 18-pin packages take up less space. For these reasons, DRAMs are normally used in applications that require a large amount of memory. For example, most systems that support at least 1M byte of data memory are designed using DRAMs.

The 2164B is one of the older NMOS DRAM devices. A block diagram of the device is shown in Fig. 6.36. Looking at the block diagram we find that it has eight address inputs, A_0 through A_7, a data input and data output marked D and Q, respectively, and three control inputs, *row address strobe* ($\overline{RAS}$), *column address strobe* ($\overline{CAS}$), and *read/write* ($\overline{W}$).

The storage array within the 2164B is capable of storing 65,536 (64K) individual bits of data. To address this many storage locations, we need a 16-bit address; however, this device's package has just 16 pins. For this reason, the 16-bit address is divided into two separate parts: an 8-bit *row address* and an 8-bit *column address*. These two parts are time-multiplexed into the device over a single set of address lines, A_0 through A_7. First the row address is applied to A_0 through A_7. Then $\overline{RAS}$ is pulsed to logic 0 to latch it into the device. Next, the column address is applied and $\overline{CAS}$ strobed to logic 0. This 16-bit address selects which one of the 64K storage locations is to be accessed.

Data are either written into or read from the addressed storage location in the DRAMs. Write data are applied to the D input and read data are output at Q. The logic levels of control signals $\overline{W}$, $\overline{RAS}$, and $\overline{CAS}$ tell the DRAM whether a read or write data transfer is taking place and control the three-state outputs. For example, during a write operation, the logic level at D is latched into the addressed storage location at the falling edge of either $\overline{CAS}$ or $\overline{W}$. If $\overline{W}$ is switched to logic 0 before $\overline{CAS}$, an early write cycle is performed. During this type of write cycle, the outputs are maintained in the high-Z

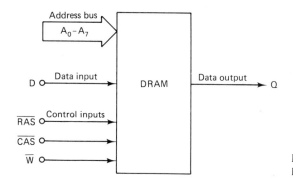

Figure 6.36 Block diagram of the 2164B DRAM.

state throughout the complete bus cycle. The fact that the output is put in the high-Z state during the write operation allows the D input and Q output of the DRAM to be tied together. The Q output is also in the high-Z state whenever $\overline{CAS}$ is logic 1. This is the connection and mode of operation normally used when attaching DRAMs to the bidirectional data bus of a microprocessor. Figure 6.37 shows how sixteen 2164B devices are connected to make a 64K × 16-bit DRAM array.

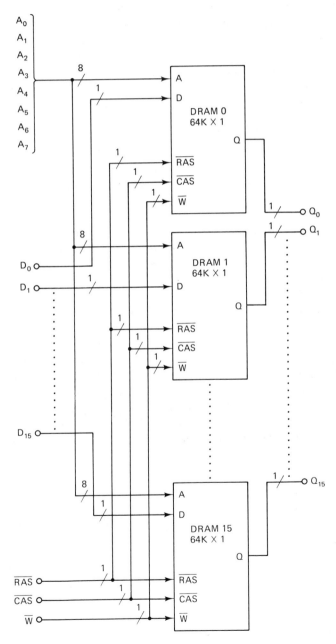

Figure 6.37 64K × 16-bit DRAM array.

Memory Interface of the 8086 Microprocessor   Chap. 6

The 2164B also has the ability to perform what are called *page mode* accesses. If RAS is left at logic 0 after the row address is latched inside the device, the address is maintained within the device. Then data cells along the selected row can be accessed by simply supplying successive column addresses. This permits faster access of memory by eliminating the time needed to set up and strobe additional row addresses.

Earlier we pointed out that the key difference between the DRAM and SRAM is that the storage cells in the DRAM need to be periodically refreshed; otherwise, they lose their data. To maintain the integrity of the data in a DRAM, each of the rows of the storage array must typically be refreshed every 2 ms. All of the storage cells in an array are refreshed by simply cycling through the row addresses. As long as $\overline{CAS}$ is held at logic 1 during the refresh cycle, no data are output.

External circuitry is required to perform the address multiplexing, $\overline{RAS}/\overline{CAS}$ generation, and refresh operations for a DRAM subsystem. *DRAM refresh controller* ICs are available to permit easy implementation of these functions. An example of such a device is the 8208 DRAM refresh controller.

6.11 4K-BYTE PROGRAM STORAGE MEMORY, 2K-BYTE DATA STORAGE MEMORY CIRCUIT

In section 6.8 we showed how the 8086's multiplexed bus is demultiplexed to give a system bus consisting of an independent 20-bit address bus and 16-bit data bus. In sections 6.9 and 6.10 we introduced program and data storage memory and the ROM and RAM devices that are used to construct it. Here we will look at how EPROM and RAM devices are connected to the system bus to implement program and data storage memory subsystems, respectively.

Program Storage Memory

The program storage memory part of a microcomputer is used to store fixed information such as instructions of the program or tables of data. Typically, it is read only, and for this reason is implemented with ROM, PROM, or EPROM devices. EPROM devices, such as the 2716, 2764, and 27256, are organized with a byte-wide output; therefore, a minimum of two devices are required to supply the 16-bit data bus of the 8086.

Figure 6.38 shows how two 2716s are connected to the demultiplexed system bus of a minimum-mode 8086-based microcomputer. These devices supply 4K bytes (2K words) of program storage memory. To select one of the 2K of word storage locations, 11 bits of address are applied to address inputs A_0 through A_{10} of the EPROMs. Assuming that bits A_1 through A_{11} of the 8086's address bus supply these inputs, the address range corresponding to program memory is from

$$A_{11} A_{10} \ldots A_1 A_0 = 00000000000_2 = 00000_{16}$$

to

$$A_{11} A_{10} \ldots A_1 BHE = 11111111111_2 = 00FFF_{16}$$

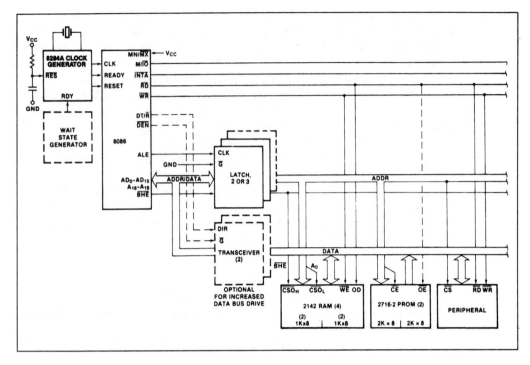

Figure 6.38 Minimum-mode system memory interface.

Data outputs D_0 through D_7 of the two EPROMs are applied to data bus lines D_0 through D_{15}, repectively, of the 8086's system data bus. Data held at the addressed storage location are enabled onto the data bus by the control signal $\overline{RD}$ (read), which is applied to the $\overline{OE}$ (output enable) inputs of the EPROMs.

In most applications, the capacity of program storage memory is expanded by attaching several EPROM devices to the system bus. In this case, additional high-order bits of the 8086's address are decoded to produce chip select signals. For instance, two address bits, A_{13} and A_{12}, can be decoded to provide four chip select signals. Each of these chip selects is applied to the $\overline{CE}$ (chip enable) input of both EPROMs in a bank. When an address is on the bus, just one of the outputs of the decoder becomes active and enables the corresponding EPROMs for operation. By using eight 2716s, the program storage memory is increased to 16K bytes.

Now that we have explained how EPROMs are attached to the 8086's system bus, let us trace through the operation of the circuit for a bus cycle in which a word of code is fetched from program storage memory. During an instruction acquisition bus cycle, the instruction fetch sequence of the 8086 causes the instruction to be read from memory word by word. The values in CS and IP are combined within the 8086 to give the address of a storage location in the address range of the program storage memory. This address is output on A_0 through A_{19} and latched into the address latches synchronously with the signal ALE. Bits A_1 through A_{11} of the system address bus are applied to the address inputs of the 2716s. This part of the address selects the word of code to be output. When the 8086 switches $\overline{RD}$ to logic 0, the outputs of the 2716s are enabled and the word of data at the addressed storage location is output onto system data bus lines D_0 through D_{15}. Early in the read bus cycle, the 8086 switches DT/$\overline{R}$ to logic 0 to signal the bus transceivers that data are to be input to the microprocessor, and later in the bus cycle $\overline{DEN}$ is switched to logic 0 to enable the transceiver for operation. Now the word of data is passed from the system data bus onto the multiplexed address data bus from which it is read by the MPU.

The circuit in Fig. 6.39 shows a similar program storage memory implementation for a maximum-mode 8086 microcomputer system.

Data Storage Memory

Information that frequently changes is stored in the data storage part of the microcomputer's memory subsystem. Examples of information typically stored in data storage memory are application programs and data bases. This part of the memory subsystem is normally implemented with random access read/write memory (RAM). If the amount of memory required in the microcomputer is small, for instance, less than 64K bytes, the memory subsystem will usually be designed with static RAMs. On the other hand, systems that require a larger amount of data storage memory normally use dynamic RAMs. This is because most DRAMs are organized as 64K $\times$ 1 bit, 256K $\times$ 1 bit, or 1M $\times$ 1 bit. Moreover, DRAMs require refresh support circuits. This additional circuitry is not warranted if storage requirements are small.

A 2K-byte random access read/write memory is also implemented in the minimum-mode 8086-based microcomputer circuit of Fig. 6.38. This part of the memory subsystem is implemented with four 2142 static RAM ICs. Each 2142 contains 1K, 4-bit storage locations; therefore, they each supply storage for just 4 bits of the word. The storage location to be accessed is selected by a 10-bit address, which is applied to all RAMs in parallel over address lines A_1 through A_{10}. Data are read from or written into the selected storage location over data bus lines D_0 through D_{15}. Of course, through software, the 8086 can read data from memory either as bytes, words, or double words. The logic level of $\overline{WR}$ (write), which is applied to the write enable ($\overline{WE}$) input of all RAMs in parallel, signals whether a read or write bus cycle is in progress. Moreover, $\overline{RD}$ is applied to the $\overline{OD}$ (output disable) input of both RAMs in parallel. When a write cycle is in progress, $\overline{RD}$ is at logic 1 and disables the outputs of the RAMs. Now the data lines act as inputs.

Just as for program storage memory, data storage memory can be expanded by simply attaching additional banks of static RAMs to the system bus. Once again, high-order address bits can be decoded to produce chip select signals. Each chip select output is applied to the chip enable input of all RAMs in a bank and, when active, it enables that bank of RAMs for operation.

Let us assume that the value of a word-wide data operand is to be updated in memory. In this case, the 8086 must perform a write bus cycle to the address of the operand's storage location. First, the address of the operand is formed and output on the multiplexed address/data bus. When the address is stable, a pulse at ALE is used to latch it into the address latches. Bits A_1 through A_{10} of the system address bus are applied to the address inputs of 2142s. This part of the address selects the storage location into which the word of data is to be written. Since a word of data is being

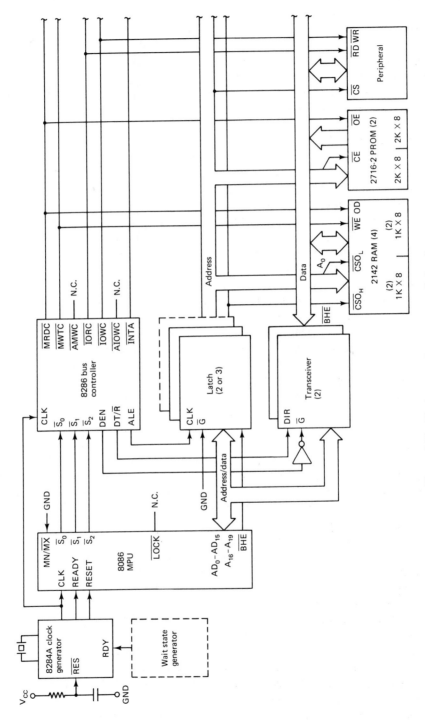

Figure 6.39 Maximum-mode system memory interface.

228

written to memory, both BHE and A_0 are at the 0 logic level. Therefore, both the high bank and low bank RAMs are enabled for operation. Next the 8086 switches DT/$\overline{R}$ to logic 1 to signal the transceivers that data are to be output to memory. Later in the bus cycle. $\overline{DEN}$ is switched to logic 0 to enable the data bus transceivers for operation. Now the word of data is output on the multiplexed address/data bus and passed through the transceivers to the system data bus and data inputs of the RAMs. Finally, the word of data is written into the addressed storage location synchronously with the occurrence of the $\overline{WR}$ control signal.

Figure 6.39 shows a maximum-mode 8086-based microcomputer system that implements a similar data storage memory.

ASSIGNMENT

Section 6.2

1. Which device products the ALE control signal in a minimum-mode 8086 microcomputer system? Maximum-mode system?
2. How large is the 8086's maximum-mode address space?
3. Is the address space of the 8086 organized as bytes or words?
4. Show how the word of data $AA55_{16}$ is stored in memory starting at address 01000_{16}.
5. Show how the double word 12345678_{16} will be stored in memory starting at address $0A001_{16}$.
6. How many bus cycles are required to access the word of data in problem 4? The double word of data in problem 5?
7. If CS contains $A000_{16}$, what is the address range of the current code segment?
8. The data segment is to be located from address $B0000_{16}$ to $BFFFF_{16}$. What value must be loaded into DS?
9. If the segment registers of the 8086 are loaded as follows: CS = $A000_{16}$, DS = ES = $B000_{16}$, and SS = $C000_{16}$, how much memory can be currently accessed?
10. Which range of memory can be used to store instructions of the program?
11. What part of the address range is dedicated to interrupts supported on the 8086?
12. Write a sequence of instructions that will initialize CS, DS, SS, and ES so that their corresponding segments of memory start at $A0000_{16}$, $B0000_{16}$, $C0000_{16}$, $D0000_{16}$, respectively.

Section 6.3

13. In which bank of memory are odd-addressed bytes of data stored? What bank select signal is used to enable this bank of memory?
14. Over which data bus lines are even-addressed bytes of data transferred and which bank select signal is active?
15. List the memory control signals together with their active logic levels that occur when a word of data is written to memory address $A0000_{16}$.
16. List the memory control signals together with their active logic levels that occur when a byte of data is written to memory address $B0003_{16}$. Over which data lines is the byte of data transferred?

Section 6.4

17. In a maximum-mode 8086 microcomputer, what code is output on S_3S_4 when an instruction-fetch bus cycle is in progress?
18. What is the value of S_3S_4 if the operand of a pop instruction is being read from memory? The microcomputer employs the 8086 in the maximum mode.

Section 6.5

19. What memory bus status code is output when a word of instruction code is fetched from memory? Which memory control output(s) is produced by the 8288?
20. What memory bus status code is output when a destination operand is written to memory? Which memory control output(s) is (are) produced by the 8288?
21. When the instruction PUSH AX is executed, what address bus status code and memory bus cycle code are output by the 8086 in a maximum-mode microcomputer system? Which command signals are output by the 8288?

Section 6.6

22. How many clock states are in an 8086 bus cycle that has no wait states? What would be the duration of this bus cycle if the 8086 is operating at 10 MHz?
23. What does T_1 stand for? What happens in this part of the bus cycle?
24. Describe the bus activity that takes place as the 8086 writes a word of data into memory address $B0010_{16}$.
25. What is an idle state?
26. What is a wait state? Which input is used to initiate a wait state?
27. If an 8086 running at 10 MHz performs a bus cycle with two wait states, what is the duration of the bus cycle?

Section 6.7

28. What is the function of the stack?
29. If the current values in the stack segment register and stack pointer are $C000_{16}$ and $FF00_{16}$, respectively, what is the address of the top of the stack?
30. For the base and offset address in problem 29, how many words of data are currently held in the stack? Assume that SP was initialized to $FFFF_{16}$.
31. Show how the value $EE11_{16}$ from register AX would be pushed onto the top of the stack as it exists in problem 29.

Section 6.8

32. List the signals of the 8086's multiplexed local bus. The signals of the demultiplexed system bus.
33. In Fig. 6.19, which type of devices are used to latch the local address? Control the direction of data transfer over the data bus?

34. Explain the operation of the circuit in Fig. 6.19 as a word-wide read takes place from address $A0000_{16}$.

Section 6.9

35. What is meant by the term "nonvolatile memory"?

36. What does PROM stand for? EPROM stand for?

37. What must an EPROM be exposed to in order to erase its stored data?

38. If the block diagram of Fig. 6.21 has address lines A_0 through A_{16} and data lines D_0 through D_7, what are its bit density and byte capacity?

39. Summarize the read cycle of an EPROM. Assume that both $\overline{CE}$ and $\overline{OE}$ are active before the address is applied.

40. Which standard EPROM stores 64K 8-bit words?

41. What is the difference between a 2764A and a 2764A-1?

42. What are the values of V_{CC} and V_{PP} for the Intelligent Programming algorithm?

43. What is the duration of the programming pulses used for the Intelligent Programming algorithm?

Section 6.10

44. What do SRAM and DRAM stand for?

45. Are RAM ICs examples of nonvolatile or volatile memory devices?

46. What must be done to maintain the data in a DRAM valid?

47. Find the total storage capacity of the circuit in Fig. 6.28 if the devices are 43256As?

48. List the minimum values of each of the write cycle parameters that follow for the 4364-10 SRAM: t_{WC}, t_{CW1}, t_{CW2}, t_{WP}, t_{DW}, and t_{WR}.

49. Give two benefits of DRAMs over SRAMs.

50. Name the two parts of a DRAM address.

51. Show how the circuit in Fig. 6.37 can be expanded to 128K $\times$ 16 bits.

52. Give a disadvantage of the use of DRAMs in an application that does not require a large amount of memory.

Section 6.11

53. Make a diagram showing how four 2764 EPROMs are connected to form a 16K-word program storage memory subsystem.

54. If we assume that the high-order address bits in the circuit formed in problem 53 are all logic 0, what is the address range of the program memory subsystem?

55. How many 2142 static RAMs would be needed in the memory array of the circuit in Fig. 6.37 if the capacity of data storage memory is to be expanded to 64K bytes?

56. How many 2716 EPROMs would be needed in the program memory array in the circuit of Fig. 6.38 to expand its capacity to 96K bits?

Chapter 7

Input/Output Interface of the 8086 Microprocessor

7.1 INTRODUCTION

In Chapter 6 we studied the memory interface of the 8086. Here we will study another important interface of the 8086 microcomputer system, the I/O interface. These are the topics in the order in which they are covered.

1. The I/O interface
2. I/O address space and data transfers
3. I/O instructions
4. The I/O bus cycles
5. Eight byte-wide output ports
6. 8255A programmable peripheral interface
7. 8255A implementation of parallel I/O ports
8. Memory-mapped I/O
9. Serial communications interface
10. The 8251A programmable communications interface
11. The 8253 programmable interval timer
12. The 8237A programmable direct memory access controller
13. Special-purpose interface controllers

The *input/output (I/O) interface* of the 8086 microcomputer permits it to communicate with the outside world. The way in which the 8086 deals with I/O circuitry is similar to the way in which it interfaces with memory circuitry. That is, I/O data transfers also take place over the multiplexed address/data bus. This parallel bus permits easy interface to LSI peripherals such as parallel I/O expanders and communication controllers. Through these I/O interfaces, the 8086 can input or output data in bit, byte, or word formats.

Minimum-Mode Interface

Let us begin by looking at the I/O interface for a minimum-mode 8086 system. Figure 7.1 shows the minimum-mode interface. Here we find the 8086, interface circuitry, and I/O ports for devices 0 through N. The circuits in this interface section must perform functions such as select the I/O port, latch output data, sample input data, synchronize data transfers, and translate between TTL voltage levels and those required to operate the I/O devices.

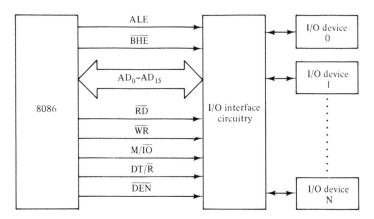

Figure 7.1 Minimum-mode 8086 system I/O interface.

The data path between the 8086 and I/O interface circuits is the multiplexed address/data bus. Unlike the memory interface, this time just the 16 least significant lines of the bus, AD_0 through AD_{15}, are in use. This interface also involves the control signals that we discussed as part of the memory interface. They are: ALE, $\overline{BHE}$, $\overline{RD}$, $\overline{WR}$, $M/\overline{IO}$, $DT/\overline{R}$, and $\overline{DEN}$.

Maximum-Mode Interface

When the 8086 system is strapped to operate in the maximum mode, the interface to the I/O circuitry changes. Figure 7.2 illustrates this configuration.

As in the maximum-mode memory interface, the 8288 bus controller produces the

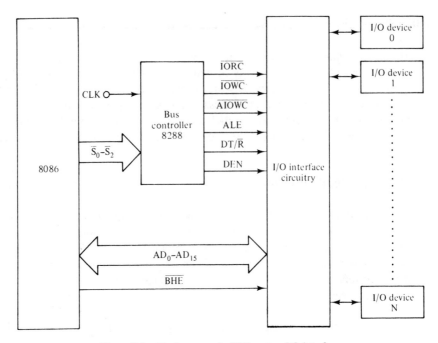

Figure 7.2 Maximum-mode 8086 system I/O interface.

control signals for the I/O subsystem. The 8288 decodes bus command status codes output by the 8086 at $\overline{S_2}\overline{S_2}\overline{S_0}$. These codes tell which type of bus cycle is in progress. If the code corresponds to an I/O read bus cycle, the 8288 generates the I/O *read command output* $\overline{IORC}$ and for an I/O write cycle it generates I/O *write command outputs* $\overline{IOWC}$ and $\overline{AIOWC}$. The 8288 also produces control signals ALE, DT/$\overline{R}$, and DEN. Moreover, the address and data transfer path between 8086 and maximum-mode I/O interface remains address/data bus lines AD_0 through AD_{15}. In this configuration the control signal $\overline{BHE}$ is still produced by the 8086 microprocessor.

The table in Fig. 7.3 shows the bus command status codes together with the

Status inputs			CPU cycle	8288 command
$\overline{S_2}$	$\overline{S_1}$	$\overline{S_0}$		
0	0	0	Interrupt acknowledge	$\overline{INTA}$
0	0	1	Read I/O port	$\overline{IORC}$
0	1	0	Write I/O port	$\overline{IOWC}$, $\overline{AIOWC}$
0	1	1	Halt	None
1	0	0	Instruction fetch	$\overline{MRDC}$
1	0	1	Read memory	$\overline{MRDC}$
1	1	0	Write memory	$\overline{MWTC}$, $\overline{AMWC}$
1	1	1	Passive	None

Figure 7.3 I/O bus cycle status codes (Courtesy of Intel Corp.).

command signals that they produce. Those for I/O bus cycles have been highlighted. The 8086 indicates that data are to be input (Read I/O port) by code $\overline{S_2}S_1\overline{S_0}$ = 001. This input causes the bus controller to produce control output I/O read command (IORC). There is one other code that represents an output bus cycle. This is the Write I/O port code $\overline{S_2}S_1S_0$ = 010. It produces two output command signals I/O write cycle (IOWC) and advanced I/O write cycle (AIOWC). These command signals are used to enable data from the I/O circuitry onto the system bus and control the direction in which data are transferred.

7.3 I/O ADDRESS SPACE AND DATA TRANSFERS

Earlier we indicated that I/O ports in the 8086 microcomputer can be either byte-wide or word-wide. The port that is accessed for input or output of data is selected by an *I/O address*. This address is specified as part of the instruction that performs the I/O operation.

I/O addresses are 16 bits in length and are output by the 8086 to the I/O interface over bus lines AD_0 through AD_{15}. As for memory addresses, AD_0 represents the LSB and AD_{15} the MSB. The most significant bits, A_{16} through A_{19}, of the memory address are held at the 0 logic level during the address period (T_1) of all I/O bus cycles.

The 8086 signals to external circuitry that the address on the bus is for an I/O port instead of a memory location by switching the M/$\overline{IO}$ control line to the 0 logic level. This signal is held at the 0 level during the complete input or output bus cycle. For this reason, it can be used to enable the address latch or address decoder in external I/O circuitry.

Figure 7.4 shows a map of the *I/O address space* of the 8086 system. This is an independent 64K-byte address space that is dedicated for I/O devices. Notice that its address range is from 0000_{16} through $FFFF_{16}$. The part of the map from address 0000_{16} through $00FF_{16}$ is referred to as page 0. Certain I/O instructions can only perform operations to ports in this part of the address space. Other I/O instructions can input or output data for ports anywhere in the I/O address space.

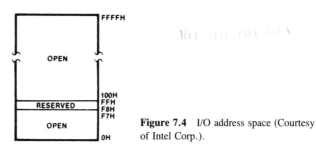

Figure 7.4 I/O address space (Courtesy of Intel Corp.).

Moreover, notice that the eight ports located from address $00F8_{16}$ through $00FF_{16}$ are specified as reserved. These port addresses are reserved by Intel Corporation for use in their future hardware and software products.

Data transfers between the MPU and I/O devices are performed over the data bus. Word transfers take place over the complete data bus, D_0 through D_{15}, and can require either one or two bus cycles. To assure that just one bus cycle is required for the word data transfer, word-wide I/O ports should be aligned at even address boundaries.

On the other hand, data transfers to byte-wide I/O ports always require one bus cycle. Therefore, they can be located at either an even or odd address. Byte data transfers to a port at an even address are performed over bus lines D_0 through D_7 and those to an odd-addressed port are performed over D_8 through D_{15}.

To input or output consecutive bytes of data to an LSI peripheral device, it should be connected such that all registers reside at either even or odd addresses. In this way, all data transfers take place over the same part of the bus. For this reason, A_0 cannot be used as a register select bit when addressing peripheral devices.

7.4 I/O INSTRUCTIONS

I/O operations are performed by the 8086 using its *in* (IN) and *out* (OUT) instructions together with the I/O port addressing mode. There are two types of IN and OUT instructions: the *direct I/O instructions* and *variable I/O instructions*. These instructions are listed in the table of Fig. 7.5. Their mnemonics and names are provided together with a brief description of their operations.

Either of these two types of instructions can be used to transfer a byte or word of data. In the case of byte transfers, data can be input or output over the upper or lower part of the bus. This is achieved by specifying an even or odd address, for the I/O port.

All data transfers take place between I/O devices and the 8086's AL or AX register. For this reason, this method of performing I/O is known as *accumulator I/O*. Byte transfers involve the AL register and word transfers the AX register. In fact, specifying AL as the source or destination register in an I/O instruction indicates that it corresponds to a byte transfer instead of a word transfer.

In a direct I/O instruction, the address of the I/O port is specified as part of the instruction. Eight bits are provided for this direct address. For this reason, its value is limited to the address range from $0_{10} = 0000_{16}$ to $255_{10} = 00FF_{16}$. This range corresponds to page 0 in the I/O address space of Fig. 7.4. An example is the instruction

IN   AL,FE

Execution of this instruction causes the contents of the byte-wide I/O port at address FE_{16} of the I/O address space to be input to the AL register.

Mnemonic	Meaning	Format	Operation	
IN	Input direct	IN Acc,Port	(Acc) ← (Port)	Acc = AL or AX
	Input indirect (variable)	IN Acc,DX	(Acc) ← ((DX))	
OUT	Output direct	OUT Port,Acc	(Port) ← (Acc)	
	Output indirect (variable)	OUT DX,Acc	((DX)) ← (Acc)	

Figure 7.5 I/O instructions.

EXAMPLE 7.1

Write a sequence of instructions that will output FF_{16} to a byte-wide output port at address AB_{16} of the I/O address space.

SOLUTION First the AL register is loaded with FF_{16} as an immediate operand in the instruction

```
MOV  AL, FF
```

Now the data in AL can be output to the byte-wide output port with the instruction

```
OUT  AB, AL
```

The difference between the direct and variable I/O instructions lies in the way in which the address of the I/O port is specified. We just saw that for direct I/O instructions an 8-bit address is specified as part of the instruction. On the other hand, the variable I/O instructions use a 16-bit address that resides in the DX register within the 8086. The value in DX is not an offset. It is the actual address that is to be output on AD_0 through AD_{15} during the I/O bus cycle. Since this address is a full 16 bits in length, variable I/O instructions can access ports located anywhere in the 64K-byte I/O address space.

When using either type of I/O instruction, the data must be loaded into or removed from the AL or AX register before another input or output operation can be performed. Moreover, in the case of the variable I/O instructions, the DX register must be loaded with an address. This requires execution of additional instructions.

For instance, the instruction sequence

```
MOV  DX, A000

IN   AL, DX
```

inputs the contents of the byte-wide input port at $A000_{16}$ of the I/O address space.

EXAMPLE 7.2

Write a series of instructions that will output FF_{16} to an output port located at address $B000_{16}$ of the I/O address space.

SOLUTION The DX register must first be loaded with the address of the output port. This is done with the instruction

```
MOV  DX, B000
```

Next the data that is to be output must be loaded into AL.

```
MOV  AL, FF
```

Finally, the data are output with the instruction

```
OUT   DX, AL
```

EXAMPLE 7.3

Data are to be read in from two byte-wide input ports at addresses AA_{16} and $A9_{16}$, respectively, and then output as a word to a word-wide output port at address $B000_{16}$. Write a sequence of instructions to perform this I/O operation.

SOLUTION   We can first read in the byte from the port at address AA_{16} into AL and move it to AH. This is done with the instructions

```
IN    AL, AA

MOV   AH, AL
```

Now the other byte can be read into AL by the instruction.

```
IN   AL, A9
```

To write out the word of data in AX, we can load DX with the address $B000_{16}$ and use a variable output instruction. This leads to the following

```
MOV  DX, B000

OUT  DX, AX
```

7.5 I/O BUS CYCLES

In Section 7.2 we found that the I/O interface signals for the minimum-mode 8086 system are essentially the same as those involved in the memory interface. In fact, the function, logic levels, and timing of all signals other than M/IO are identical to those already described for the memory interface in Chapter 6.

Waveforms for the *I/O input (I/O read) bus cycle* and *I/O output (I/O write) bus cycle* are shown in Figs. 7.6 and 7.7, respectively. Looking at the input and output bus cycle waveforms, we see that the timing of M/IO does not change. The 8086 switches it to logic 0 to indicate that an I/O bus cycle is in progress. It is maintained at the 0 logic level for the duration of the I/O bus cycle. As in memory cycles, the address (ADDRESS OUT) is output together with ALE during clock period T_1. For the input bus cycle, DEN is switched to logic 0 to signal the I/O interface circuitry when to put the data onto the bus and the 8086 reads data off the bus during period T_3.

On the other hand, for the output bus cycle in Fig. 7.7, the 8086 puts write data (DATA OUT) on the bus late in T_2 and maintains it during the rest of the bus cycle. This time WR switches to logic 0 to signal the I/O section that valid data are on the bus.

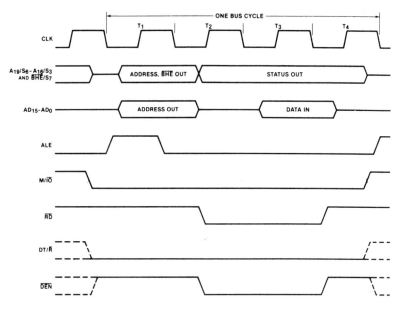

Figure 7.6 Input bus cycle (Courtesy of Intel Corp.).

The same bus cycle requirements exist for data transfers for I/O ports as were found for memory. That is, all byte transfers and word transfers to even-addressed ports require just one bus cycle. However, two bus cycles are required to perform data transfers for odd-addressed word-wide ports. Eight bits are transferred during each of these two bus cycles.

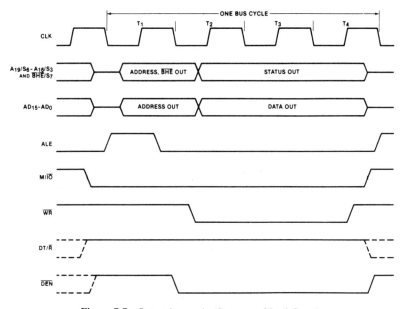

Figure 7.7 Output bus cycle (Courtesy of Intel Corp.).

Up to this point in the chapter, we have introduced the I/O interface of the 8086-based microcomputer, the I/O address space, the I/O instructions, and I/O bus cycles. Now we will show a circuit that can be used to implement parallel output ports in an 8086 system. Figure 7.8 is such a circuit. It provides eight byte-wide output ports that are implemented with 8282 octal latches. In this circuit, the ports are labeled PORT 0 through PORT 7. These eight ports give a total of 64 parallel output lines which are labeled O_0 through O_{63}.

Looking at the circuit, we see that the 8086's address/data bus is demultiplexed just as was done for the memory interface. Notice that two 8282 octal latches are used to form a 16-bit address latch. These devices latch the address A_0 through A_{15} synchronously with the ALE pulse. The latched address outputs are labeled A_{0L} through A_{15L}. Remember that address lines A_{16} through A_{19} are not involved in the I/O interface. For this reason they are not shown in the circuit diagram.

Actually, this circuit is designed such that the I/O ports reside at even byte addresses. This is the reason that only data bus lines AD_0 through AD_7 are shown connecting to the output latches. It is over these lines that the 8086 writes data into the output ports.

Address lines A_{0L} and A_{15L} provide two of the three enable inputs of the 8205 output address decoder. These signals are applied to enable inputs $\overline{E}_1$ and E_3, respectively. The decoder requires one more enable signal at its $\overline{E}_2$ input. It is supplied by M/$\overline{\text{IO}}$. These enable inputs must be $\overline{E}_1\overline{E}_2E_3$ equal to 001 to enable the decoder for operation. The condition $\overline{E}_1$ equal 0 corresponds to an even address and $\overline{E}_2$ equal 0 represents the fact that an I/O bus cycle is in progress. The third condition, E_3 equal 1, is an additional requirement that A_{15L} be at logic 1 during all data transfers for this section of parallel output ports.

Notice that the 3-bit code $A_{3L}A_{2L}A_{1L}$ is applied to select inputs ABC of the 8205 1-of-8 decoder. When the decoder is enabled, the P output corresponding to this select code switches to logic 0. Notice that logic 0 at this output enables the $\overline{\text{WR}}$ signal to the strobe (STB) input of the corresponding output latch. In this way, just one of the eight ports is selected for operation.

When valid output data are on D_0 through D_7, the 8086 switches $\overline{\text{WR}}$ to logic 0. This change in logic level causes the selected 8282 device to latch in the data from the bus. The outputs of the latches are permanently enabled by the 0 logic level at their $\overline{\text{OE}}$ inputs. Therefore, the data appear at the appropriate port outputs.

The 8286 in the circuit allows data to move from 8086 to the output ports. This is accomplished by enabling the 8286's T and $\overline{\text{OE}}$ pins with the DT/$\overline{\text{R}}$ and $\overline{\text{DEN}}$ signals which are at logic 1 and 0, respectively.

EXAMPLE 7.4

To which output port in Fig. 7.8 are data written when the address put on the bus during an output bus cycle is 8002_{16}?

SOLUTION Expressing the address in binary form, we get

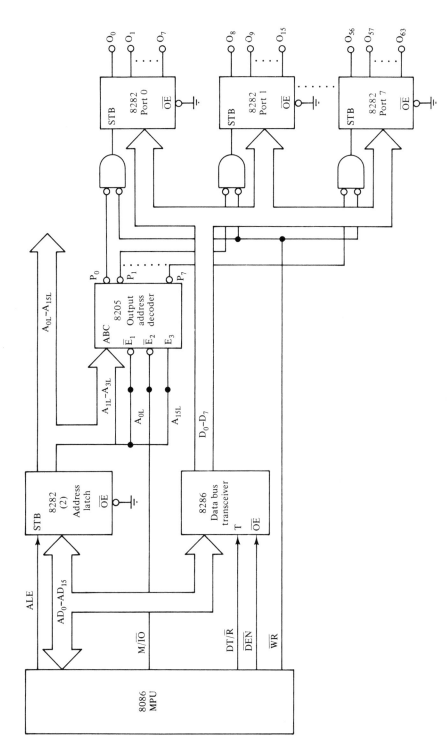

Figure 7.8 Sixty-four output lines circuit.

$$A_{15} \cdots A_0 = A_{15L} \cdots A_{0L} = 1000000000000010_{16}$$

The important address bits are

$$A_{15L} = 1$$

$$A_{0L} = 0$$

and

$$A_{3L}A_{2L}A_{1L} = 001$$

Moreover, whenever an output bus cycle is in progress $M/\overline{IO}$ is logic 0. Therefore, the enable inputs of the 8205 decoder are

$$\overline{E}_1 = A_{0L} = 0$$

$$\overline{E}_2 = M/\overline{IO} = 0$$

$$E_3 = A_{15L} = 1$$

These inputs enable the decoder for operation. At the same time, its select inputs are supplied with the code 001. This input causes output P_1 to switch to logic 0.

$$P_1 = 0$$

The gate at the strobe input of port 1 has its inputs P_1 and $\overline{WR}$. When valid data are on the bus, $\overline{WR}$ switches to logic 0. Since P_1 is also 0, the STB input of the 8282 for port 1 switches to logic 1. This causes the data on D_0 through D_7 to be latched at output lines O_8 through O_{15} of port 1.

EXAMPLE 7.5

Write a series of instructions that will output the byte contents of the memory location called DATA to output port 0 in the circuit of Fig. 7.8

SOLUTION   To write a byte to output port 0, the address which must be output on the 8086's address bus must be

$$A_{15}A_{14} \ldots \ldots A_0 = 1XXXXXXXXXXX0000_2$$

Assuming that the don't care bits are all made logic 0, we get

$$A_{15}A_{14} \ldots \ldots A_0 = 1000000000000000_2$$

$$= 8000_{16}$$

Then the instruction sequence needed to output the contents of memory location DATA is

```
MOV    DX, 8000

MOV    AL, DATA

OUT    DX, AL
```

The *8255A* is an LSI peripheral designed to permit easy implementation of *parallel I/O* in the 8086 microcomputer. It provides a flexible parallel interface which includes features such as: single-bit, 4-bit, and byte-wide input and output ports; level-sensitive inputs; latched outputs; strobed inputs or outputs; and strobed bidirectional inputs or outputs. These features are selected under software control.

A block diagram of the 8255A is shown in Fig. 7.9(a) and its pin layout in Fig. 7.9(b). The left side of the block represents the *microprocessor interface*. It includes an *8-bit bidirectional data bus* D_0 through D_7. Over these lines, commands, status information, and data are transferred between the 8086 and 8255A. These data are transferred whenever the 8086 performs an input or output bus cycle to an address of a register within the device. Timing of the data transfers to the 8255A is controlled by the *read/write* ($\overline{RD}$ and $\overline{WR}$) *control* signals.

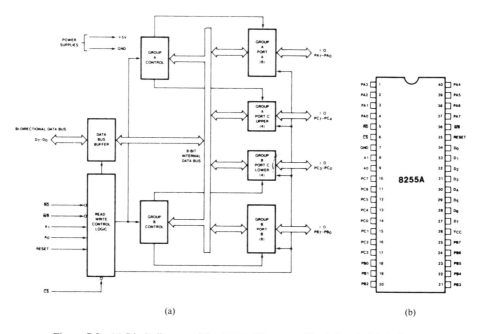

Figure 7.9 (a) Block diagram of the 8255A (Courtesy of Intel Corp.); (b) pin layout (Courtesy of Intel Corp.).

The source or destination register within the 8255A is selected by a 2-bit *register select code*. The 8086 must apply this code to the *register select inputs*, A_0 and A_1 of the 8255A. The *PORT A, PORT B*, and *PORT C registers* correspond to codes $A_1A_0 = 00$, $A_1A_0 = 01$, and $A_1A_0 = 10$, respectively.

Two other signals are shown on the microprocessor interface side of the block diagram. They are the *reset* (RESET) and *chip select* ($\overline{CS}$) inputs. $\overline{CS}$ must be logic 0 during all read or write operations to the 8255A. It enables the microprocessor interface circuitry for an input or output operation.

On the other hand, RESET is used to initialize the device. Switching it to logic 0 at power-up causes the internal registers of the 8255A to be cleared. *Initialization* configures all I/O ports for input mode of operation.

The other side of the block corresponds to three *byte-wide I/O ports*. They are called PORT A, PORT B, and PORT C and represent *I/O lines* PA_0 through PA_7, PB_0 through PB_7, and PC_0 through PC_7, respectively. These ports can be configured for input or output operation. This gives a total of 24 I/O lines.

We already mentioned that the operating characteristics of the 8255A can be configured under software control. It contains an 8-bit internal control register for this purpose. This register is represented by the *group A* and *group B control blocks* in Fig. 7.9(a). Logic 0 or 1 can be written to the bit positions in this register to configure the individual ports for input or output operation and to enable one of its three modes of operation. The control register is write only and its contents are modified under software control by initiating a write bus cycle to the 8255A with register select code $A_1A_0 = 11$.

The bits of the control register and their control functions are shown in Fig. 7.10.

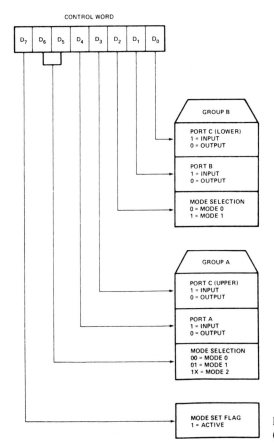

Figure 7.10 Control-word bit functions (Courtesy of Intel Corp.).

Here we see that bits D_0 through D_2 correspond to the group B control block in the diagram of Fig. 7.9(a). Bit D_0 configures the lower four lines of PORT C for input or output operation. Notice that logic 1 at D_0 selects input operation and logic 0 selects output operation. The next bit, D_1, configures Port B as an 8-bit-wide input or output port. Again, logic 1 selects input operation and logic 0 selects output operation.

The D_2 bit is the mode select bit for PORT B and the lower four bits of PORT C. It permits selection of one of two different modes of operation called *MODE 0* and *MODE 1*. Logic 0 in bit D_2 selects MODE 0, while logic 1 selects MODE 1. These modes will be discussed in detail shortly.

In Fig. 7.9(a) the next four bits in the control register, D_3 through D_6, correspond to the group A control block. Bits D_3 and D_4 of the control register are used to configure the operation of the upper half of PORT C and all of PORT A, respectively. These bits work in the same way as D_0 and D_1 configure the lower half of PORT C and PORT B. However, there are now two mode-select bits D_5 and D_6 instead of just one. They are used to select between three modes of operation known as *MODE 0, MODE 1,* and *MODE 2*.

The last control register bit, D_7, is the *mode set flag*. It must be at logic 1 (active) whenever the mode of operation is to be changed.

MODE 0 selects what is called *simple I/O operation*. By simple I/O, we mean that the lines of the port can be configured as level-sensitive inputs or latched outputs. To set all ports for this mode of operation, load bit D_7 of the control register with logic 1, bits $D_6 D_5 = 00$, and $D_2 = 0$. Logic 1 at D_7 represents an active mode set flag. Now PORT A and PORT B can be configured as 8-bit input or output ports and PORT C can be configured for operation as two independent 4-bit input or output ports. This is done by setting or resetting bits D_4, D_3, D_1, and D_0.

For example, if $80_{16} = 10000000_2$ is written to the control register, the 1 in D_7 activates the mode set flag. MODE 0 operation is selected for all three ports because bits D_6, D_5, and D_2 are logic 0. At the same time, the 0's in D_4, D_3, D_1, and D_0 set up all port lines to work as outputs. This configuration is illustrated in Fig. 7.11(a). (See page 246.)

By writing different binary combinations into bit locations D_4, D_3, D_1, and D_0, any one of 16 different MODE 0 I/O configurations can be obtained. The control word and I/O setup for these combinations are shown in Fig. 7.11(b) through (p).

EXAMPLE 7.6

What is the mode and I/O configuration for ports A, B, and C of an 8255A after its control register is loaded with 82_{16}?

SOLUTION Expressing the control register contents in binary form, we get

$$D_7 D_6 D_5 D_4 D_3 D_2 D_1 D_0 = 10000010_2$$

Since D_7 is 1, the modes of operation of the ports are selected by the control word. The three least significant bits of the word configure PORT B and the lower 4 bits of PORT C. They give

$D_0 = 0$ Lower 4 bits of PORT C are outputs

$D_1 = 1$ PORT B are inputs

$D_2 = 0$ MODE 0 operation for both PORT B and the lower 4 bits of PORT C

The next four bits configure the upper part of PORT C and PORT A.

$D_3 = 0$ Upper 4 bits of PORT C are outputs

$D_4 = 0$ PORT A are outputs

$D_6 D_5 = 00$ MODE 0 operation for both PORT A and the upper part of PORT C

This MODE 0 I/O configuration is shown in Fig. 7.11(c).

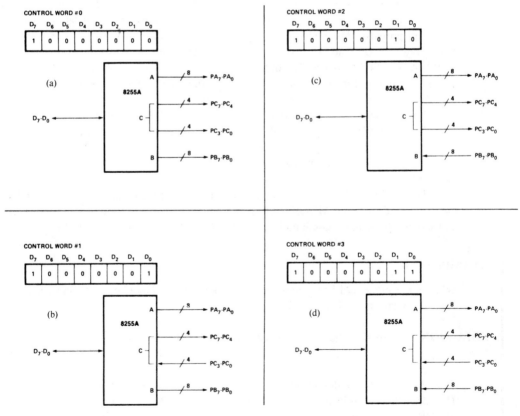

Figure 7.11 Mode 0 control words and corresponding I/O configuration (Courtesy of Intel Corp.).

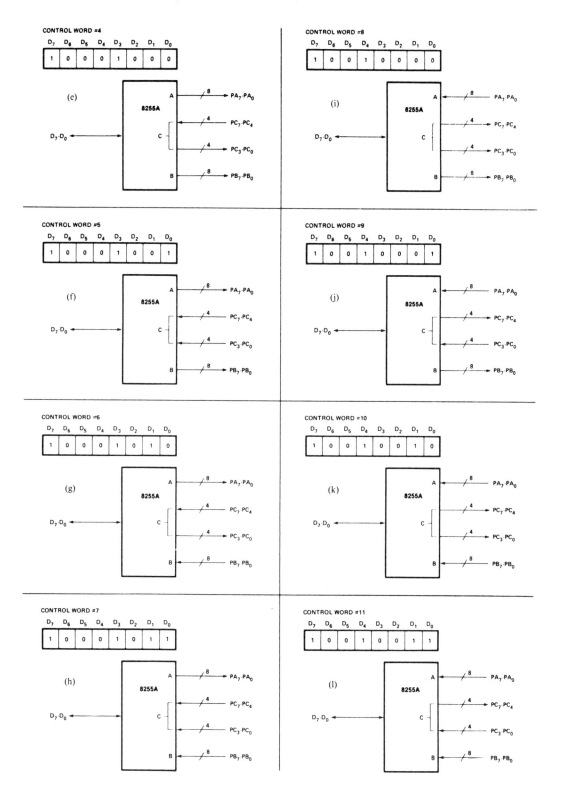

Figure 7.11 *(continued)*

247

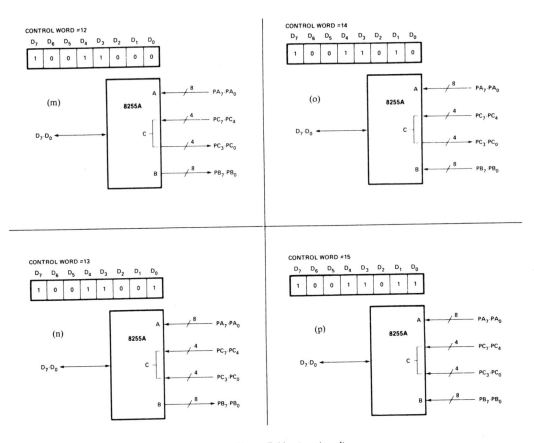

Figure 7.11 *(continued)*

MODE 1 operation represents what is known as *strobed I/O*. The ports of the 8255A are put into this mode of operation by setting $D_7 = 1$ to activate the mode set flag and setting $D_6 D_5 = 01$ and $D_2 = 1$.

In this way, the A and B ports are configured as two independent *byte-wide I/O ports* each of which has a *4-bit control/data port* associated with it. The control/data ports are formed from the lower and upper nibbles of PORT C, respectively.

When configured in this way, data applied to an input port must be strobed in with a signal produced in external hardware. Moreover, an output port is provided with handshake signals that indicate when new data are available at its outputs and when an external device has read these values.

As an example, let us assume for the moment that the control register of an 8255A is loaded with $D_7 D_6 D_5 D_4 D_3 D_2 D_1 D_0 = 10111XXX$. This configures PORT A as a MODE 1 input port. Figure 7.12(a) shows the function of the signal lines for this example. Notice that PA_7 through PA_0 from an 8-bit input port. On the other hand, the function of the upper PORT C leads are reconfigured to provide the PORT A control/data lines. The PC_4 line becomes $\overline{STB}_A$ *(strobe input),* which is used to strobe data at PA_7 through PA_0 into the input latch. Moreover, PC_5 becomes IBF_A *(input buffer full).*

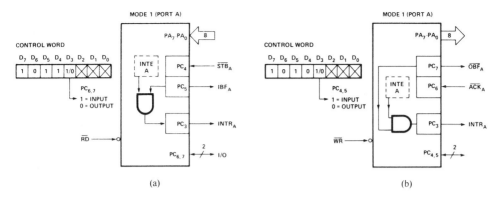

Figure 7.12 (a) Mode 1 port A input configuration (Courtesy of Intel Corp.); (b) mode 1 port A output configuration (Courtesy of Intel Corp.).

Logic 1 at this output indicates to external circuitry that a word has already been strobed into the latch.

The third control signal is at PC_3 and is labeled $INTR_A$ *(interrupt request)*. It switches to logic 1 as long as $\overline{STB}_A = 1$, $IBF_A = 1$, and an internal signal $INTE_A$ *(interrupt enable)* equals 1. $INTE_A$ is set to logic 0 or 1 under software control by writing to PC_4 using the bit set/reset feature of the 8255A. Looking at Fig. 7.12(a) we see that logic 1 in $INTE_A$ enables the logic level of IBF_A to the $INTR_A$ output. This signal can be applied to an interrupt input of the 8086 microcomputer to signal it that new data are available at the input port. The corresponding interrupt service routine can read the data and clear the interrupt request.

As another example, let us assume that the contents of the control register are changed to $D_7D_6D_5D_4D_3D_2D_1D_0 = 1010XXX$. This I/O configuration is shown in Fig. 7.12(b). Notice that PORT A is now configured for output operation instead of input operation. PA_7 through PA_0 are now an 8-bit output port. The control line at PC_7 is $\overline{OBF}_A$ *(output buffer full)*. When data have been written into the output port, $\overline{OBF}_A$ switches to the 0 logic level. In this way, it signals external circuitry that new data are available at the port outputs.

Signal line PC_6 becomes $\overline{ACK}_A$ *(acknowledge)*, which is an input. An external device can signal the 8255A that it has accepted the data provided at the output port by switching this input to logic 0. The last signal at the control port is output $INTR_A$ *(interrupt request)*, which is produced at the PC_3 lead. This output is switched to logic 1 when the $\overline{ACK}_A$ input is active. It is used to signal the 8086 with an interrupt that indicates that an external device has accepted the data from the outputs. $INTR_A$ switches to the 1 level when $\overline{OBF}_A = 1$, $\overline{ACK}_A = 0$, and $INTE_A = 1$. Again the interrupt enable $INTE_A$ bit (PC_6) must be set to 1 under software control.

EXAMPLE 7.7

Figure 7.13(a) and (b) show how PORT B can be configured for MODE 1 operation. Describe what happens in Fig. 7.13(a) when the $\overline{STB}_B$ input is pulsed to logic 0. Assume that $INTE_B$ is already set to 1.

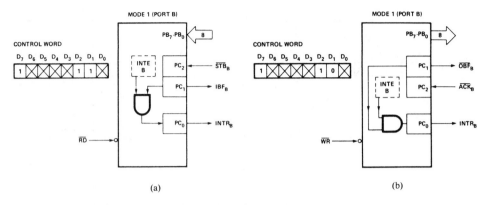

Figure 7.13 (a) Mode 1 port B input configuration (Courtesy of Intel Corp.); (b) mode 1 port B output configuration (Courtesy of Intel Corp.).

SOLUTION   As $\overline{STB}_B$ is pulsed, the byte of data at PB_7 through PB_0 are latched into the PORT B register. This causes the IBF_B output to switch to 1. Since $INTE_B$ is 1, $INTR_B$ also switches to logic 1.

The last mode of operation, MODE 2, represents what is known as *strobed bidirectional I/O*. The key difference is that now the port works as either inputs or outputs and control signals are provided for both functions. Only PORT A can be configured to work in this way.

In order to set up this mode, the control register is set to $D_7D_6D_5D_4D_3D_2D_1D_0 = 11XXXXXX$. The I/O configuration that results is shown in Fig. 7.14. Here we find that PA_7 through PA_0 operate as an *8-bit bidirectional port* instead of a unidirectional port. Its control signals are: $\overline{OBF}_A$ at PC_7, $\overline{ACK}_A$ at PC_6, $\overline{STB}_A$ at PC_4, IBF_A at PC_5, and $INTR_A$ at PC_3. Their functions are similar to those already discussed for MODE 1.

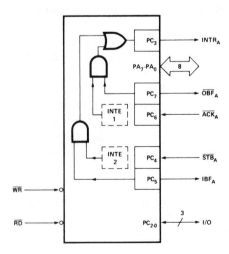

Figure 7.14 Mode 2 I/O configuration (Courtesy of Intel Corp.).

One difference is that $\overline{INTR_A}$ is produced by either gating $\overline{OBF_A}$ with $INTE_1$ or IBF_A with $INTE_2$.

In our discussion of MODE 1, we mentioned that the *bit set/rest* feature could be used to set the INTE bit to logic 0 or 1. This feature also allows the individual bits of PORT C to be set or reset. To do this, we write logic 0 to bit D_7 of the control register. This resets the bit set/reset flag. The logic level that is to be latched at a PORT C line is included as bit D_0 of the control word. This value is latched at the I/O line of PORT C, which corresponds to the 3-bit code at $D_3D_2D_1$.

The relationship between the set/reset control word and input/output lines is illustrated in Fig. 7.15. For instance, writing $D_7D_6D_5D_4D_3D_2D_1D_0 = 00001111_2$ into the control register of the 8255A selects bit 7 and sets it to 1. Therefore, output PC_7 at PORT C is switched to the 1 logic level.

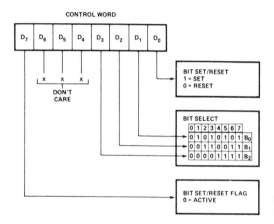

Figure 7.15 Bit set/reset format (Courtesy of Intel Corp.).

EXAMPLE 7.8

The interrupt control flag $INTE_A$ is controlled by bit set/reset of PC_6. What command code must be written to the control register of the 8255A to set its value to logic 1?

SOLUTION To use the set/reset feature, D_7 must be logic 0. Moreover, $INTE_A$ is to be set to logic 1; therefore, D_0 must be logic 1. Finally, to select PC_6, the code at bits $D_3D_2D_1$ must be 110. The rest of the bits are don't-care states. This gives the control word

$$D_7D_6D_5D_4D_3D_2D_1D_0 = 0XXX1101_2$$

Replacing the don't-care states with the 0 logic level, we get

$$D_7D_6D_5D_4D_3D_2D_1D_0 = 00001101_2 = 0D_{16}$$

We have just described and given examples of each of the modes of operation that can be assigned to the ports of the 8255A. In practice, the A and B ports are frequently configured with different modes. For example, Fig. 7.16(a) shows the control word and port configuration of an 8255A set up for bidirectional MODE 2 operation of PORT A and input MODE 0 operation of PORT B.

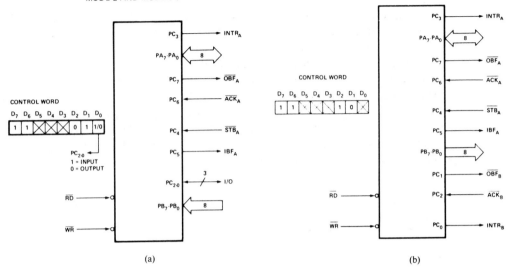

Figure 7.16 (a) Combined mode 2 mode 0 (input) control word and I/O configuration (Courtesy of Intel Corp.); (b) combined mode 2 and mode 1 (output) control word and I/O configuration (Courtesy of Intel Corp.).

EXAMPLE 7.9

What control word must be written into the the control register of the 8255A such that PORT A is configured for bidirectional operation and PORT B is set up with MODE 1 outputs?

SOLUTION To configure the mode of operation of the ports of the 8255A, D_7 must be 1.

$$D_7 = 1$$

PORT A is set up for bidirectional operation by making D_6 logic 1. In this case, D_5 through D_3 are don't-care states.

$$D_6 = 1$$

$$D_5 D_4 D_3 = XXX$$

MODE 1 is selected for PORT B by logic 1 in bit D_2 and output operation by logic 0 in D_1. Since MODE 1 operation has been selected, D_0 is a don't-care state.

$$D_2 = 1$$

$$D_1 = 0$$

$$D_0 = X$$

This gives the control word

$$D_7D_6D_5D_4D_3D_2D_1D_0 = 11XXX10X_2$$

Assuming logic 0 for the don't-care states, we get

$$D_7D_6D_5D_4D_3D_2D_1D_0 = 11000100_2 = C4_{16}$$

This configuration is shown in Fig. 7.16(b).

EXAMPLE 7.10

Write the sequence of instructions needed to load the control register of an 8255A with the control word formed in example 7.9. Assume that the 8255A resides at address $0F_{16}$ of the I/O address space.

SOLUTION   First we must load AL with $C4_{16}$. This is the value of the control word that is to be output to the control register at address $0F_{16}$. The move instruction used to load AL is

```
MOV  AL, C4
```

This data are output to the control register with the OUT instruction

```
OUT  OF, AL
```

7.8 8255A IMPLEMENTATION OF PARALLEL I/O PORTS

The circuit in Fig. 7.17 shows how PPI devices can be connected to the bus of the 8086 to implement parallel I/O ports. This circuit configuration is for a minimum-mode 8086 microcomputer. Here we find that two groups each of up to eight 8255A devices are connected to the data bus. Each group has its own 8205 address decoder. This decoder selects one of the devices at a time for input or output data transfers. The ports in the upper group are connected at odd-address boundaries and those in the lower group are at even-address boundaries. Each of these PPI devices provide up to three-byte-wide ports. In the circuit, they are labeled PORT A, PORT B, and PORT C. These ports can be individually configured as inputs or outputs through software. Therefore, each group is capable of implementing up to 192 I/O lines.

Let us look more closely at the connection of the upper port. Starting with the inputs of the 8205 address decoder, we see that its enable inputs are $\overline{E}_1 = \overline{BHE}$ and $E_2 = M/\overline{IO}$. $\overline{BHE}$ is logic 0 whenever the 8086 outputs an odd address on the bus. Moreover, $M/\overline{IO}$ is switched to logic 0 whenever an I/O bus cycle is in progress. For this reason, the upper decoder is enabled for I/O bus cycles to an odd address in its part of the I/O address range.

When the 8205 decoder is enabled, the code at its A_0 through A_2 inputs causes one of the eight 8255A PPIs to get enabled for operation. Bits A_5 through A_3 of the I/O address are applied to these inputs of the decoder. It responds by switching the output corresponding to this 3-bit code to the 0 logic level. Decoder outputs O_0 through

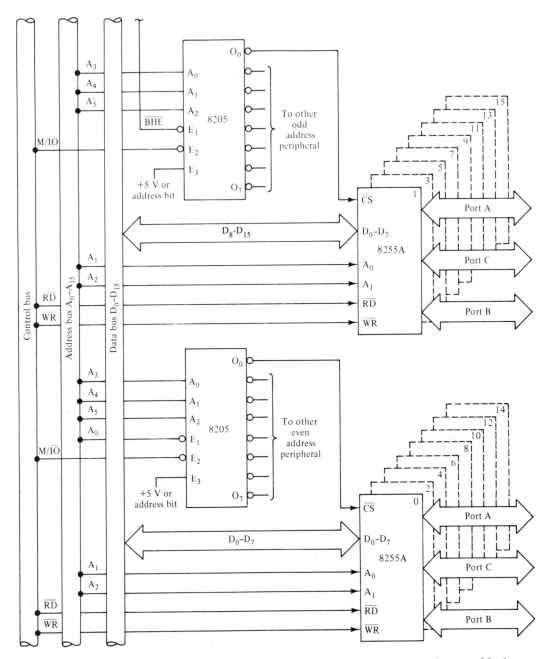

Figure 7.17 8255A parallel I/O ports at even- and odd-address boundaries (Courtesy of Intel Corp.).

O_7 are applied to the chip select ($\overline{CS}$) inputs of the odd-addressed PPIs. For instance, $A_5A_4A_3 = 000$ switches output O_0 to logic 0. This enables the first 8255A, which is numbered 1 in Fig. 7.17.

At the same time that the PPI chip is selected, the 2-bit code A_2A_1 at inputs A_1A_0 of the 8255A selects the port for which data are input or output. For example, A_2A_1 equal 00 indicates that PORT A is to be accessed.

Since the upper group is located at odd-address boundaries, I/O data transfers take place over data bus lines D_8 through D_{15}. The timing of these read/write transfers are controlled by signals $\overline{RD}$ and $\overline{WR}$.

EXAMPLE 7.11

What must be the address inputs of the even-addressed group of 8255As in Fig. 7.17 if PORT C of PPI 14 is to be accessed?

SOLUTION To enable PPI 14, the 8205 must be enabled for operation and its O_7 output switched to logic 0. This requires enable input $A_0 = 0$ and chip select code $A_5A_4A_3 = 111$.

$$A_0 = 0 \qquad \text{Enables 8205}$$

$$A_5A_4A_3 = 111 \qquad \text{Selects PPI 14}$$

PORT C of PPI 14 is selected with $A_1A_0 = 10$.

$$A_2A_1 = 10 \qquad \text{Accesses PORT C}$$

The rest of the address bits are don't-care states.

EXAMPLE 7.12

Assume that in Fig. 7.17 PPI 14 is configured such that port A is an output port and both port B and C are input ports and that all three ports are set up for MODE 0 operation. Write a program that will input the data at ports B and C, find the difference C-B, and output this difference to port A.

SOLUTION From the circuit diagram in Fig. 7.17, we find that the addresses of the three I/O ports on PPI 14 are

$$PORT\ A = 00111000_2 = 38_{16}$$

$$PORT\ B = 00111010_2 = 3A_{16}$$

$$PORT\ C = 00111100_2 = 3C_{16}$$

The data at ports B and C can be input with the instruction sequence

```
IN  AL, 3A   ; READ PORT B
MOV BL, AL   ; SAVE DATA FROM PORT B
IN  AL, 3C   ; READ PORT C
```

Now the data from port B is subtracted from the data at port C with the instruction

```
            SUB  AL,BL   ;  SUBTRACT  B  FROM  C
```

Finally, the difference is output to port A with the instruction

```
            OUT  38,AL   ;  WRITE  TO  PORT  A
```

7.9 MEMORY-MAPPED I/O

I/O devices such as the 8255A can be placed in the memory address space of the 8086 microcomputer as well as in an independent I/O address space. In this case the 8086 looks at an I/O port as though it were a memory location. For this reason, the method is known as *memory-mapped I/O*. In memory-mapped systems, some of the memory address space is dedicated to I/O ports. This permits talking to I/O ports using memory-oriented instructions such as MOV instead of the IN and OUT instructions.

The disadvantages of using this method are that part of the memory address space is lost and also the memory instructions tend to execute more slowly than those specifically designed for I/O. However, these disadvantages are frequently overcome by benefits such as that a larger number of instructions and addressing modes can be used to transfer data between the 8086 and its I/O ports. Another advantage is that data can now be located in registers other than just AL or AX.

The *memory-mapped I/O interface* of a minimum mode 8086 system is essentially the same as that employed in the accumulator I/O circuit of Fig. 7.17. Figure 7.18 (page 258) shows the equivalent memory-mapped circuit. Ports are still selected by an address on the address bus and byte or word data are transferred between the 8086 and I/O device over the data bus. One difference is that now the full 20-bit address is available for addressing I/O. Therefore, memory-mapped I/O devices can reside anywhere in the 1M address space of the 8086.

Another difference is that during I/O operations memory read and write bus cycles are initiated instead of I/O bus cycles. This is because we are using memory instructions, not input/output instructions, to perform the data transfers. Furthermore, $M/\overline{IO}$ stays at the 1 logic level throughout the bus cycle. This indicates that a memory operation is in progress instead of an I/O operation.

EXAMPLE 7.13

Which I/O port in Fig. 7.18 is selected for operation when the memory address output on the bus is 00402_{16}?

SOLUTION   We begin by converting the address to binary form. This gives

$$A_{19} \cdots A_1 A_0 = 00000000010000000010_2$$

In this address, bits $A_{10} = 1$, and $A_0 = 0$. Therefore, the lower 8205 address decoder is enabled.

$$A_{10} = 1 \quad \text{Enables lower 8205 decoder}$$

$$A_0 = 0$$

A memory-mapped I/O operation takes place to the port selected by $A_5A_4A_3 = 000$. This input code switches decoder output O_0 to logic 0 and chip slects PPI 0 for operation.

$$A_5A_4A_3 = 000 \quad \text{Selects PPI 0}$$

$$O_0 = 0$$

The address bits applied to the port select inputs of the PPI are $A_2A_1 = 01$. These inputs cause PORT B to be accessed.

$$A_2A_1 = 01 \quad \text{Port B accessed}$$

Thus the address 00402_{16} selects PORT B on PPI 0.

EXAMPLE 7.14

Write the sequence of instructions needed to initialize the control register of PPI 0 in the circuit of Fig. 7.18 such that port A is an output port, ports B and C are input ports, and all three ports are configured for mode 0 operation.

SOLUTION Referring to Fig. 7.10, we find that the control byte required to provide this configuration is

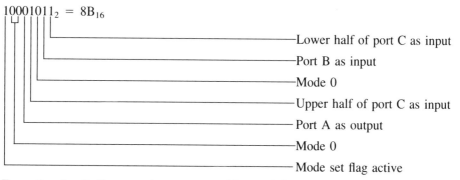

$10001011_2 = 8B_{16}$

— Lower half of port C as input
— Port B as input
— Mode 0
— Upper half of port C as input
— Port A as output
— Mode 0
— Mode set flag active

From the circuit diagram, the memory address of the control register for PPI 0 is found to be

$$\text{CONTROL REGISTER} = 0000000010000000110_2 = 00406_{16}$$

Since PPI 0 is memory-mapped, move instructions can be used to initialize the control register.

```
MOV   AX, 0        ; CREATE DATA SEGMENT AT 00000₁₆

MOV   DS, AX

MOV   AL, 8B       ; LOAD AL WITH CONTROL BYTE

MOV   [406], AL    ; WRITE CONTROL BYTE TO PPI 0
```

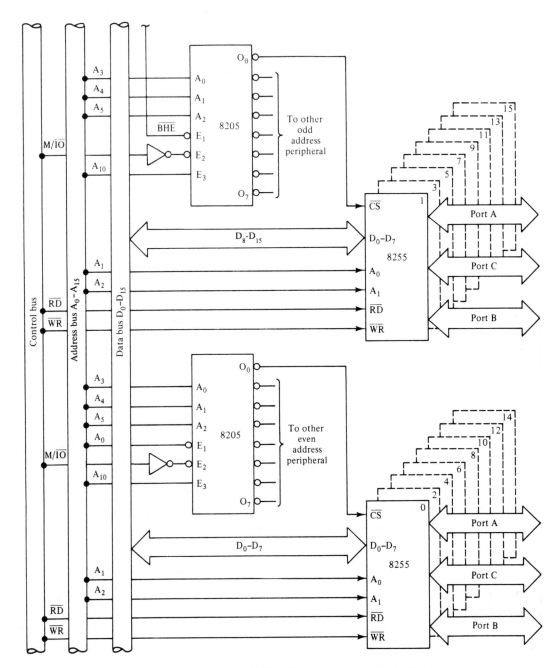

Figure 7.18 Memory-mapped 8255A I/O ports (Courtesy of Intel Corp.).

EXAMPLE 7.15

Assume that PPI 0 in Fig. 7.18 is configured as described in example 7.14. Write a program that will input the contents of ports B and C, AND them together, and output the results to port A.

SOLUTION From the circuit diagram, we find that the addresses of the three I/O ports on PPI 0 are

$$PORT\ A\ =\ 00400_{16}$$

$$PORT\ B\ =\ 00402_{16}$$

$$PORT\ C\ =\ 00404_{16}$$

Now we set up a data segment at 00000_{16} and input the data from ports B and C.

```
MOV   AX, 0        ; CREATE DATA SEGMENT AT 00000₁₆

MOV   DS, AX

MOV   BL, [402]    ; READ PORT B

MOV   AL, [404]    ; READ PORT C
```

Next the contents of AL and BL must be ANDed and the result output to port A.

```
AND   AL, BL       ; AND DATA AT PORTS B AND C

MOV   [400], AL    ; WRITE TO PORT A
```

7.10 SERIAL COMMUNICATIONS INTERFACE

Another type of I/O interface that is widely used in microcomputer systems is known as a *serial communications port*. This is the type of interface that is used to connect peripheral units, such as CRT terminals, modems, and printers, to a microcomputer. It permits data to be transferred between the various units of the system. For instance, data input at the keyboard of a terminal are passed to the MPU part of the microcomputer through this type of interface. Let us now look into the different types of serial interfaces that are implemented in microcomputer systems.

Synchronous and Asynchronous Data Communications

Two types of *serial data communications* are widely used in microcomputer systems. They are called *asynchronous communications* and *synchronous communications*. By synchronous, we mean that the receiver and transmitter sections of the two pieces of equipment that are communicating with each other must run synchronously. For this reason, as shown in Fig. 7.19(a), the interface includes a CLOCK line as well as

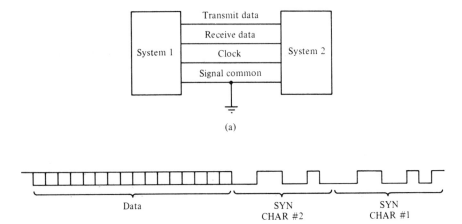

Figure 7.19 (a) Synchronous communications interface; (b) synchronous data transmission format.

TRANSMIT DATA, RECEIVE DATA, and SIGNAL COMMON lines. It is the clock signal that synchronizes both the transmission and reception of data.

The format used for synchronous communication of data is shown in Fig. 7.19(b). To initiate synchronous transmission, the transmitter first sends out synchronization characters to the receiver. The receiver reads the synchronization bit pattern and compares it to a known sync pattern. Once they are identified as being the same, the receiver begins to read character data off the communications line. Transfer of data continues until the complete block of data is received or synchronization is lost between the receiver and transmitter. If large blocks of data are being sent, the synchronization characters may be periodically resent to assure that synchronization is maintained. The synchronous type of communications is typically used in applications where high-speed data transfer is required.

The asynchronous method of communications eliminates the need for the CLOCK signal. As shown in Fig. 7.20(a), the simplest form of an asynchronous communication interface could consist of a RECEIVE DATA, TRANSMIT DATA, and SIGNAL COMMON communication lines. In this case, the data to be transmitted are sent out one character at a time and at the receiver end of the communication line synchronization is performed by examining synchronization bits that are included at the beginning and end of each character.

The format of a typical asynchronous character is shown in Fig. 7.20(b). Here we see that the synchronization bit at the beginning of the character is called the *START bit* and that at the end of the character the *STOP bit*. Depending on the communications scheme, 1, $1\frac{1}{2}$, or 2 STOP bits can be used. The bits of the character are embedded between the START and STOP bits. Notice that the START bit is either input or output first. It is followed in the serial bit stream by the LSB of the character, the other 6 bits of the character, a parity bit, and the STOP bits. For instance, 7-bit ASCII can be used and parity added as an eighth bit for higher reliability in transmission. The duration of each bit in the format is called a *bit time*.

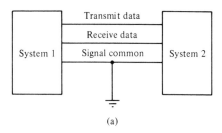

(a)

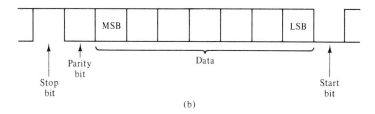

(b)

Figure 7.20 (a) Asynchronous communications interface; (b) asynchronous data transmission format.

The fact that a 0 or 1 logic level is being transferred over the communication line is identified by whether the voltage level on the line corresponds to that of a *MARK* or a *SPACE*. The START bit is always to the MARK level. It synchronizes the receiver to the transmitter and signals that the unit receiving data should start assembling the character. STOP bits are to the SPACE level. This assures that the receiving unit sees a transition of logic level at the START bit of the next character.

The USART and UART

Because serial communication interfaces are so widely used in modern electronic equipment, special LSI peripheral devices have been developed to permit easy implementation of these types of interfaces. Some of the names that these devices go by are *UART (universal asynchronous receiver/transmitter)* and *USART (universal synchronous/asynchronous receiver/transmitter)*.

Both UARTs and USARTs have the ability to perform the parellel-to-serial conversions needed in the transmission of data and the serial-to-parallel conversions needed in the reception of data. For data that are transmitted asynchronously, they also have the ability to frame the character automatically with a START bit, PARITY bit, and the appropriate STOP bits.

Moreover, for reception of data, UARTs and USARTs typically have the ability to check characters automatically as they arc received for correct parity, and for two other errors, known as *framing error* and *overrun error*. A framing error means that after the detection of the beginning of a character with a START bit the appropriate number of STOP bits were not detected. This means that the character that was transmitted was not received correctly and should be resent. An overrun error means that the prior character that was received was not read out of the USARTs receive data register by the microprocessor before another character was received. Therefore, the first character was lost and should be retransmitted.

A block diagram of a UART is shown in Fig. 7.21. Here we see that it has four key signal interfaces: the microprocessor interface, the transmitter interface, the receiver interface, and the handshake control interface. Let us now look at each of these interfaces in more detail.

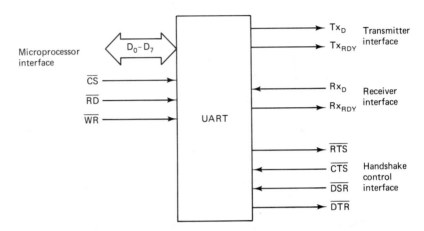

Figure 7.21 Block diagram of a UART.

LSI USARTs and UARTs cannot stand alone in a communication system. Their operation must be controlled by a general-purpose processor such as a microprocessor. The *microprocessor interface* is the interface that is used to connect the UART to an MPU. Looking at Fig. 7.21, we see that this interface consists of an 8-bit bidirectional data bus ($D_0 - D_7$) and three control lines, $\overline{CS}$, $\overline{RD}$, and $\overline{WR}$.

All data transfers between the UART and MPU take place over the 8-bit data bus. Two uses of this bus are for the input of character data from the receiver of the UART and for the output of character data to its transmitter. Other types of information are also passed between the MPU and UART. Examples are mode control instructions, operation command instructions, and status.

LSI UARTs, just like the 8255A LSI peripheral we discussed earlier in the chapter, can be configured for various modes of operation through software. Mode control instructions are what must be issued to a UART to initialize its control registers for the desired mode of operation. For example, the format of the data frame used for transmitted or received data can be configured through software. Typical options are character length equal to from 5 to 8 bits; even, odd, or no parity; and 1, $1\frac{1}{2}$, or 2 STOP bits.

Earlier we pointed out that a UART cannot perform the communication function on its own. Instead, the sequence of events that is needed to initiate transmission and reception is controlled by commands issued to the UART by the MPU. For instance, the MPU can initiate a request for transmission of data to another unit by writing a command to the UART that forces its $\overline{RTS}$ control output to its active 0 logic level. The logic 0 at $\overline{RTS}$ signals the system at the other end of the communication line to prepare to receive data. At the receiver end of the communication line, the MPU can acknowledge that it is ready to receive data by sending a command to its UART that forces the $\overline{DTR}$ control output to logic 0.

Most UARTs have a *status register* that contains information related to its current state. For example, it may contain flag bits that represent the current logic state of signal lines such as $\overline{RTS}$ and $\overline{DTR}$. This permits the MPU to examine the logic state of these lines through software.

Besides information about the logic level of control lines, the status register typically contains flag bits for error conditions such as parity error, overrun error, and framing error. After reception of a character, the MPU can first read these bits to assure that a valid character has been received, and if the bits are at their inactive levels, the character should be read from the receive data register within the UART.

At the other side of the block in Fig. 7.21, we find the *transmitter* and *receiver interfaces*. The transmitter interface has two signal lines: transmit data (Tx_D) and transmitter ready (Tx_{RDY}). Tx_D is the line over which the transmitter section of the UART outputs serial character data. As shown in Fig. 7.22, this output line is connected to the receive data (Rx_D) input of the receiver section in the system at the other end of the communication line.

Usually, the transmitter section of an LSI UART can hold only one character at a time. This character datum is held in the *transmit data register* within the UART. Since only one character can be held within the UART, it must signal the MPU when it has completed transmission of this character. The Tx_{RDY} line is provided for this purpose. As soon as transmission of the character is complete, the transmitter switches Tx_{RDY} to its active logic level. This signal should be returned to an interrupt input of the MPU. In this way, its occurrence can cause program control to be passed quickly to a service routine that will output another character to the transmitter data register and then reinitiate transmission.

The receiver section is similar to the transmitter we just described. However, here the receive data (Rx_D) line is the input that accepts bit-serial character data that are transmitted from the other system's transmitter. Notice in Fig. 7.22 that the receive data input connects to the transmit data (Tx_D) output of the transmitter section in the system at the other end of the communications line. Here the receiver ready (Rx_{RDY}) output is used as an interrupt to the MPU and it signals the MPU that a character has been received. The service routine that is initiated must first determine whether or not the character is valid, and if it is, it must read the character out of the UART's *receive data register*.

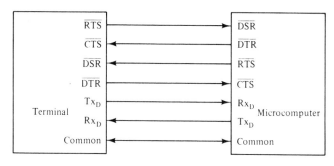

Figure 7.22 Simple asynchronous communications interface between a microcomputer and terminal.

Using the handshake control signals $\overline{\text{RTS}}$, $\overline{\text{DSR}}$, $\overline{\text{DTR}}$, and $\overline{\text{CTS}}$, different types of *asynchronous communication protocols* can be implemented through the serial I/O interface. By protocol we mean a handshake sequence by which two systems signal each other that they are ready to communicate.

A simple asynchronous communication interface that uses these control lines is shown in Fig. 7.22. In this example, a protocol can be set up such that when the terminal wants to send data to the microcomputer it will issue a request at its request to sent (RTS) output. To do this, the MPU of the terminal must issue a command to the UART that causes it to set the $\overline{\text{RTS}}$ line to its active 0 logic level. RTS of the terminal is applied to the data set ready ($\overline{\text{DSR}}$) input of the microcomputer. In this way, it tells the microcomputer that the terminal wants to transmit data to it.

When the microcomputer is ready to receive data, it acknowledges this fact to the terminal by activating the data terminal ready ($\overline{\text{DTR}}$) output of its UART. The MPU in the microcomputer does this by issuing a command to the UART that switches $\overline{\text{DTR}}$ to its active 0 logic level. This signal is returned to the clear to send ($\overline{\text{CTS}}$) input of the terminal's UART and tells the UART in the terminal to start outputting data on Tx_D. At the same time, the receiver section in the UART within the microcomputer begins to read data from its Rx_D input.

Baud Rate and the Baud Rate Generator

The rate at which data transfers take place over the receive and transmit lines is known as the *baud rate*. By baud rate we mean the number of bits of data that are transferred per second of time. For instance, some of the common data transfer rates are 300 baud, 1200 baud, and 9600 baud. They correspond to 300 bits/second (bps), 1200 bps, and 9600 bps, respectively.

The baud rate at which data are transferred determines the *bit time*. That is, the amount of time each bit of data is on the communication line. At 300 baud, the bit time is found to be

$$t_{\text{BT}} = 1/300 \text{ bps} = 3.33 \text{ ms}$$

Baud rate is set by a part of the serial communication interface called the *baud rate generator*. This part of the interface generates the clock signal that is used to drive the receiver and transmitter parts of the UART. Some LSI UARTs have a built-in baud rate generator; others need an external circuit to provide this function.

The RS-232C Interface

The *RS-232C interface* is a standard hardware interface for implementing asynchronous serial data communication ports on devices such as printers, CRT terminals, keyboards, and modems. The pin definitions and electrical characteristics of this interface are defined by the *Electronic Industries Association* (EIA). The aim behind publishing standards such as the RS-232C is to assure compatibility between equipment made by different manufacturers.

Peripherals that connect to a microcomputer can be located anywhere from several feet to many feet from the system. For instance, in large systems it is common to have the microcomputer part of the system in a separate room from the terminals and printers. This leads us to the main advantage of using a serial interface to connect peripherals to a microcomputer, which is that as few as three signal lines can be used to connect the peripheral to the MPU: a RECEIVE DATA line, a TRANSMIT DATA line, and SIGNAL COMMON. This results in a large savings in wiring costs and the small number of lines that need to be put in place also leads to higher reliability.

The RS-232C standard defines a 25-pin interface. Figure 7.23 lists each pin and its function. Note that the three signals that we mentioned earlier, TRANSMIT DATA, RECEIVE DATA, and SIGNAL GROUND, are located at pins 2, 3, and 7, respectively. Pins are also provided for additional control functions. For instance, pins 4 and 5 are the REQUEST TO SEND and CLEAR TO SEND control signals. These two signals are also frequently used when implementing an asynchronous communication interface.

The RS-232C interface is specified to operate correctly over a maximum distance of 100 feet. To satisfy this distance specification, a bus driver is used to buffer the transmit line to provide the appropriate drive current and a bus receiver is used at the receive line. RS-232C drivers and receivers are available as standard ICs. These buffers

Pin	Signal
1	Protective Ground
2	Transmitted Data
3	Received Data
4	Request to Send
5	Clear to Send
6	Data Set Ready
7	Signal Ground (Common Return)
8	Received Line Signal Detector
9	Reserved for Data Set Testing
10	Reserved for Data Set Testing
11	Unassigned
12	Secondary Received Line Signal Detector
13	Secondary Clear to Send
14	Secondary Transmitted Data
15	Transmission Signal Element Timing
16	Secondary Received Data
17	Receiver Signal Element Timing
18	Unassigned
19	Secondary Request to Send
20	Data Terminal Ready
21	Signal Quality Detector
22	Ring Indicator
23	Data Signal Rate Selector
24	Transmit Signal Element Timing
25	Unassigned

Figure 7.23 RS-232C interface pins and functions.

do both the voltage-level translation needed to convert the TTL-compatible outputs of the UART to the MARK and SPACE voltage levels defined for the RS-232C interface. The voltage levels that are normally transmitted for a MARK and a SPACE are $+12$ V dc and -12 V dc, respectively. For the RS-232C interface, all voltages below -3 V dc are equal to a MARK and all voltages above $+3$ V dc are considered a SPACE.

The RS-232C interface is specified to support baud rates of up to 20,000 bps. In general, the receive and transmit baud rates do not have to be the same; however, in most simpler systems they are set to the same value. For instance, a baud rate that is widely used in communication between an MPU and a printer is 1200 bps. This corresponds to a bit time equal to .833 ms.

Simplex, Half-Duplex, and Full-Duplex Communication Links

Applications require different types of asynchronous links to be implemented. For instance, the *communication link* needed to connect a printer to a microcomputer just needs to support communications in one direction. That is, the printer is an output-only device; therefore, the MPU only needs to transmit data to the printer. Data are not transmitted back. In this case, as shown in Fig. 7.24(a), a single unidirectional communication line can be used to connect the printer and microcomputer together. This type of connection is known as a *simplex communication link*.

Other devices, such as the CRT terminal with keyboard shown in Fig. 7.24(b), need to both transmit data to and receive data from the MPU. That is, they must both

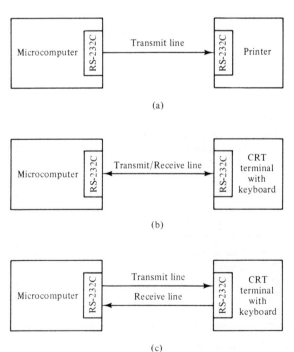

Figure 7.24 (a) Simplex communications link; (b) half-duplex communications link; (c) full-duplex communications link.

input and output data. This requirement can also be satisfied with a single communication line by setting up a *half-duplex communication link*. In a half-duplex link, data are transmitted and received over the same line; therefore, transmission and reception of data cannot take place at the same time.

If higher-performance communication is required, separate transmit and receive lines can be used to connect the peripheral and microcomputer. When this is done, data can be transferred in both directions at the same time. This type of link is illustrated in Fig. 7.24(c). It is called a *full-duplex communication link*.

7.11 THE 8251A PROGRAMMABLE COMMUNICATION INTERFACE

The *8251A programmable communication interface* is another important LSI peripheral for the 8086 microcomputer system. It permits simple implementation of a serial data communications interface. For instance, it can be used to implement an RS-232C port. This is the type of interface that is used to connect a CRT terminal or printer to a microcomputer. To support connection of these two peripheral devices, the microcomputer would need two independent RS-232C I/O ports. The 8251A is one of the most widely used USART ICs. As its name implies, the 8251A is capable of implementing either an asynchronous or synchronous communication interface. Here we will concentrate on its use as an asynchronous communication controller.

The programmability of the 8251A provides for a very flexible asynchronous communication interface. It contains a full-duplex receiver and transmitter, which can be configured through software for communication of data using formats with character lengths between five and eight characters, with even or odd parity, and with 1, $1\frac{1}{2}$, or 2 STOP bits. Moreover, it has the ability to detect automatically the occurrence of parity, framing, and overrun errors during data reception.

Internal Architecture of the 8251A

A block diagram showing the internal architecture of the 8251A is shown in Fig. 7.25(a) and its pin layout in Fig. 7.25(b). From this diagram we find that it includes four key sections: the *bus interface section,* which consists of the data bus buffer and read/write control logic blocks; the *transmit section,* which consists of the transmit buffer and transmit control blocks; the *receive section,* which consists of the receive buffer and receive control blocks; and the *modem control section.* Let us now look at each of these sections in more detail.

The bus interface section is used to connect the 8251A to a microprocessor such as the 8086. Notice that the interface includes an 8-bit bidirectional data bus D_0 through D_7 that is driven by the data bus buffer. It is over these lines that the microprocessor transfers commands to the 8251A, reads its status register, and inputs or outputs character data.

Data transfers over the bus are controlled by the signals C/$\overline{\text{D}}$ (control/data), $\overline{\text{RD}}$ (read), $\overline{\text{WR}}$ (write), and $\overline{\text{CS}}$ (chip select), which are all inputs to the read/write control logic section. Typically, the 8251A is located at a specific address in the microcompu-

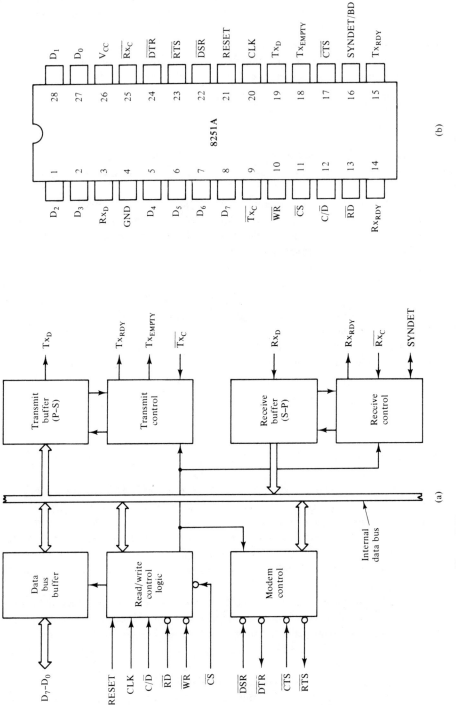

Figure 7.25 (a) Block diagram of the 8251 (Courtesy of Intel Corp.); (b) pin layout (Courtesy of Intel Corp.).

ter's I/O or memory address space. When the microprocessor is to access registers within the 8251A, it puts this address on the address bus. The address is decoded by external circuitry and must produce logic 0 at the $\overline{CS}$ input. This input must be logic 0 for a read or write bus cycle to take place to the 8251A.

The other three control signals, C/$\overline{D}$, $\overline{RD}$, and $\overline{WR}$, tell the 8251A what type of data transfer is to take place over the bus. Figure 7.26 shows the various types of read/write operations that can occur. For example, the first state in the table, C/$\overline{D}$ = 0, $\overline{RD}$ = 0, and $\overline{WR}$ = 1, corresponds to a character data transfer from the 8251A to the microprocessor. Notice that in general, $\overline{RD}$ = 0 signals that the microprocessor is reading data from the 8251A, $\overline{WR}$ = 0 indicates that data are being written into the 8251A, and the logic level of C/$\overline{D}$ indicates whether character data, control information, or status information is on the data bus.

EXAMPLE 7.16

What type of data transfer is taking place over the bus if the control signals are at $\overline{CS}$ = 0, C/$\overline{D}$ = 1, $\overline{RD}$ = 0, and $\overline{WR}$ = 1?

SOLUTION Looking at the table in Fig. 7.26, we see that $\overline{CS}$ = 0 means that the 8251A's data bus has been enabled for operation. Since C/$\overline{D}$ is 1 and $\overline{RD}$ is 0, status information is read from within the 8251A.

The receiver section is responsible for reading the serial bit stream of data at the Rx_D (receive data) input and converting it to parallel form. When a MARK voltage level is detected on this line, the receiver enables a counter. As the counter increments to a value equal to one-half a bit time, the logic level at the Rx_D line is sampled again. If it is still at the MARK level, a valid START pulse has been detected. Then Rx_D is examined every time the counter increments through another bit time. This continues until a complete character is assembled and the STOP bit is read. After this, the complete character is transferred into the receive data register.

During reception of a character, the receiver automatically checks the character data for parity, framing, or overrun errors. If one of these conditions occurs, it is flagged by setting a bit in the status register. Then the Rx_{RDY} (receiver ready) output is switched to the 1 logic level. This signal is sent to the microprocessor to tell it that a character is available and should be read from the receive data register. Rx_{RDY} is automatically reset to logic 0 when the MPU reads the contents of the receive data register.

The 8251A does not have a built-in baud rate generator. For this reason, the clock signal that is used to set the baud rate must be externally generated and applied to the

C/$\overline{D}$	$\overline{RD}$	$\overline{WR}$	$\overline{CS}$	Operation
0	0	1	0	8251A Data → Data bus
0	1	0	0	Data bus → 8251A Data
1	0	1	0	Status → Data bus
1	1	0	0	Data bus → Control
X	1	1	0	Data bus → 3-State
X	X	X	1	Data bus → 3-State

Figure 7.26 Read/write operations (Courtesy of Intel Corp.).

Rx_C input of the receiver. Through software the 8251A can be set up to internally divide the clock signal input at Rx_C by 1, 16, or 64.

The transmitter does the opposite of the receiver section. It receives parallel character data from the MPU over the data bus. The character is then automatically framed with the START bit, appropriate parity bit, and the correct number of STOP bits and put into the transmit data buffer register. Finally, it is shifted out of this register to produce a bit-serial output on the Tx_D line. When the transmit data buffer register is empty, the Tx_{RDY} output switches to logic 1. This signal is to be returned to the MPU to tell it that another character should be output to the transmitter section. When the MPU writes another character out to the transmitter buffer register, the Tx_{RDY} output resets.

Data are output on the transmit line at the baud rate set by the external transmitter clock signal that is input at Tx_C. In most applications, the transmitter and receiver operate at the same baud rate. Therefore, both Rx_C and Tx_C are supplied by the same baud rate generator. The circuit in Fig. 7.27 shows this type of system configuration.

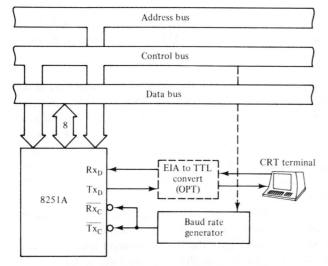

Figure 7.27 Receiver and transmitter driven at the same baud rate (Courtesy of Intel Corp.).

The operation of the 8251A is controlled through the setting of bits in three internal control registers: the *mode control register, command register,* and the *status register.* For instance, the way in which the 8251A's receiver and transmitter operate is determined by the contents of the mode control register. Figure 7.28 shows the organization of the mode control register and the function of each of its bits. Note that the two least significant bits B_1 and B_2 determine whether the device operates as an asynchronous or synchronous communication controller and how the external baud rate input is divided within the 8251A. For example, if these two bits are 11, it is set for asynchronous operation with divide by 64 for the baud rate input. The two bits that follow these, L_1 and L_2, set the length of the character. For instance, when information is being transmitted and received as 7-bit ASCII characters, these bits should be loaded with 10.

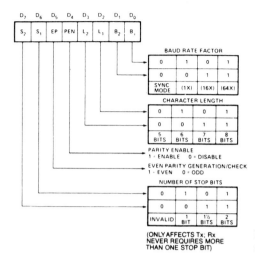

BAUD RATE FACTOR			
0	1	0	1
0	0	1	1
SYNC MODE	(1X)	(16X)	(64X)

CHARACTER LENGTH			
0	1	0	1
0	0	1	1
5 BITS	6 BITS	7 BITS	8 BITS

PARITY ENABLE
1 = ENABLE   0 = DISABLE

EVEN PARITY GENERATION/CHECK
1 = EVEN   0 = ODD

NUMBER OF STOP BITS			
0	1	0	1
0	0	1	1
INVALID	1 BIT	1½ BITS	2 BITS

(ONLY AFFECTS Tx; Rx
NEVER REQUIRES MORE
THAN ONE STOP BIT)

Figure 7.28 Mode instruction format (Courtesy of Intel Corp.).

The next two bits, PEN and EP, determine whether parity is in use and if so, whether it is even parity or odd parity. Looking at Fig. 7.28, we see that PEN enables or disables parity. To enable parity, it is set to 1. Furthermore, when parity is enabled, logic 0 in EP selects odd parity or logic 1 in this position selects even parity. To disable parity, all we need to do is reset PEN.

We will assume that the 8251A is working in the asynchronous mode; therefore, bits S_1 and S_2 determine the number of STOP bits. Note that if 11 is loaded into these bit positions, the character is transmitted with 2 STOP bits.

EXAMPLE 7.17

What value is to be written into the mode control register in order to configure the 8251A such that it works as an asynchronous communications controller with the baud rate internally divided by 16? Character size is to be 8 bits for EBCDIC, and odd parity and one STOP bit are also to be selected.

SOLUTION   From Fig. 7.28, we find that B_2B_1 must be set to 10 in order to select asynchronous operation with divide by 16 for the external baud rate input.

$$B_2B_1 = 10$$

To select a character length of 8 bits, the next two bits are both made logic 1. This gives

$$L_2L_1 = 11$$

To set up odd parity, EP and PEN must be made equal to 0 and 1, respectively.

$$EP\ PEN = 01$$

Finally, S_2S_1 are set to 01 for one STOP bit.

$$S_2S_1 = 01$$

Therefore, the complete control word is

$$D_7 D_6 \ldots\ldots D_0 = 01011110_2$$

$$= 5E_{16}$$

Once the configuration for asynchronous communications has been set up in the mode control register, the operation of the serial interface can be controlled by the microprocessor by issuing commands to the command register within the 8251A. The format of the *command instruction byte* and the function of each of its bits is shown in Fig. 7.29. Let us look at the function of just a few of its bits.

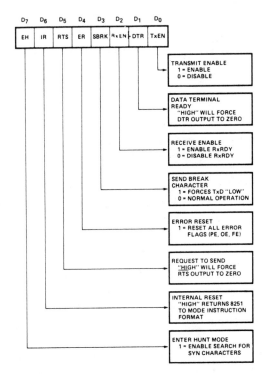

Figure 7.29 Command instruction format (Courtesy of Intel Corp.).

Tx_{EN} and Rx_{EN} are enable bits for the transmitter and receiver. Since both the receiver and transmitter can operate simultaneously, these two bits can both be set. Rx_{EN} is actually an enable signal to the Rx_{RDY} signal. It does not turn the receiver section on and off. The receiver runs at all times, but if Rx_{EN} is set to 0, the 8251A does not signal the MPU that a character has been received by switching Rx_{RDY} to logic 1. The same is true for Tx_{EN}. It enables the Tx_{RDY} signal.

The ER bit of the command register can be used to reset the error bits of the status register. The status register of the 8251A is shown in Fig. 7.30. Notice that bits PE, OE, and FE are error flags for the receiver. If the incoming character is found to have a parity error, the PE (parity error) bit gets set. On the other hand, if an overrun or framing error condition occurs, the OE (overrun error) or FE (framing error) flag is set,

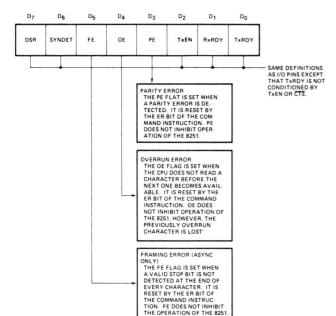

D7	D6	D5	D4	D3	D2	D1	D0
DSR	SYNDET	FE	OE	PE	TxEN	RxRDY	TxRDY

SAME DEFINITIONS
AS I/O PINS EXCEPT
THAT TxRDY IS NOT
CONDITIONED BY
TxEN OR C̅T̅S̅.

PARITY ERROR
THE PE FLAT IS SET WHEN
A PARITY ERROR IS DE-
TECTED. IT IS RESET BY
THE ER BIT OF THE COM-
MAND INSTRUCTION. PE
DOES NOT INHIBIT OPER-
ATION OF THE 8251.

OVERRUN ERROR
THE OE FLAG IS SET WHEN
THE CPU DOES NOT READ A
CHARACTER BEFORE THE
NEXT ONE BECOMES AVAIL-
ABLE. IT IS RESET BY THE
ER BIT OF THE COMMAND
INSTRUCTION. OE DOES
NOT INHIBIT OPERATION OF
THE 8251; HOWEVER, THE
PREVIOUSLY OVERRUN
CHARACTER IS LOST'

FRAMING ERROR (ASYNC
ONLY)
THE FE FLAG IS SET WHEN
A VALID STOP BIT IS NOT
DETECTED AT THE END OF
EVERY CHARACTER. IT IS
RESET BY THE ER BIT OF
THE COMMAND INSTRUC-
TION. FE DOES NOT INHIBIT
THE OPERATION OF THE 8251.

Figure 7.30 Status register (Courtesy of Intel Corp.).

respectively. The MPU should always examine these error bits before reading a character from the receive data register. If an error has occurred, a command should be issued to the command register to write a 1 into the ER bit. This causes all three of the error flags in the status register to be reset. Then a software routine can be initiated to cause the character to be retransmitted.

Let us look at just one more bit of the command register. The IR bit, which stands for *internal reset,* allows the 8251A to be initialized under software control. To initialize the device, the MPU simply writes a 1 into the IR bit.

EXAMPLE 7.18

What are the meanings of the Tx_{RDY}, Rx_{RDY}, and Tx_{EN} bits of the status register?

SOLUTION Looking at Fig. 7.30, we find that these three bits of the status register always reflect the logic levels of the Tx_{RDY}, Rx_{RDY}, and Tx_{EN} signal lines. Reading of the status register permits the MPU to determine the logic level of these signals through software.

Initializing the 8251A

Before the 8251A can be used to receive or transmit characters, its mode control and command registers must be initialized. The flowchart in Fig. 7.31 shows the sequence that must be followed when initializing the device. Let us just briefly trace through the sequence of events needed to set up the controller for asynchronous operation.

As the microcomputer powers up, it should issue a hardware reset to the 8251A. This is done by switching its RESET input to logic 1. After this, a load mode instruction

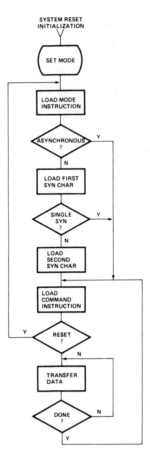

Figure 7.31 8251A initialization flow-chart (Courtesy of Intel Corp.).

must be issued to write the new configuration byte into the mode control register. Assuming that the 8251A is in the I/O address space of the 8086, the command byte formed in Example 7.16 can be written to the command register with the instruction sequence

```
MOV   DX, MODE

MOV   AL, 5E

OUT   DX, AL
```

where MODE is a variable assigned to the address of the mode register of the 8251A.

Since bits B_2B_1 of this register are not 00, asynchronous mode of operation is selected. Therefore, we go down the branch in the flowchart to the load command instruction. Execution of another OUT instruction can load the command register with its initial value. For instance, this command could enable the transmitter and receiver by setting the Tx_{EN} and Rx_{EN} bits, respectively. During its operation the status register can be read by the microprocessor to determine if the device has received the next byte, if it is ready to send the next byte, or if any problem occurred in the transmission such as a parity error.

7.12 THE 8253 PROGRAMMABLE INTERVAL TIMER

The 8253 is an LSI peripheral designed to permit easy implementation of timer and counter functions in a microcomputer system. It contains three independent 16-bit counters that can be programmed to operate in a variety of ways to implement timing functions. For instance, they can be set up to work as a one-shot pulse generator, square-wave generator, or rate generator.

Block Diagram of the 8253

Let us begin our study of the 8253 by looking at the signal interfaces shown in its block diagram of Fig. 7.32(a). The actual pin location for each of these signals is given in Fig. 7.32(b). In an 8086-based microcomputer system, the 8253 is treated as a peripheral device. Moreover, it can be memory mapped into the 8086's memory address space or I/O mapped into the I/O address space. The microprocessor interface of the 8253 allows the 8086 to read from or write to its internal register. In this way, it can configure the mode of operation for the timers, load initial values into the counters, or read the current value from a counter.

Now we will look at the signals of the microprocessor interface. The microprocessor interface includes an 8-bit bidirectional data bus, D_0 through D_7. It is over these lines that data are transferred between the 8086 and 8253. Register address inputs A_0 and A_1 are used to select the register to be accessed, and control signals read ($\overline{RD}$) and write ($\overline{WR}$) indicate whether it is to be read from or written into, respectively. A chip select ($\overline{CS}$) input is also provided to enable the 8253's microprocessor interface. This input allows the designer to locate the device at a specific memory or I/O address.

At the other side of the block in Fig. 7.32(a), we find three signals for each counter. For instance, counter 0 has two inputs that are labeled CLK_0 and $GATE_0$. Pulses applied to the clock input are used to decrement counter 0. The gate input is used to enable or disable the counter. $GATE_0$ must be switched to logic 1 to enable counter 0 for operation. For example, in the square-wave mode of operation, the counter is to run continuously; therefore, $GATE_0$ is fixed at the 1 logic level and a continuous clock signal is applied to CLK_0. The 8253 is rated for a maximum clock frequency of 3 MHz. Counter 0 also has an output line that is labeled OUT_0. The counter produces either a clock or a pulse at OUT_0, depending on the mode of operation selected. For instance, when configured for the squarewave mode of operation, this output is a clock.

Architecture of the 8253

The internal architecture of the 8253 is shown in Fig. 7.33. Here we find the *data bus buffer, read/write logic, control word register,* and three *counters.* The data bus buffer and read/write control logic represent the microprocessor interface we just described.

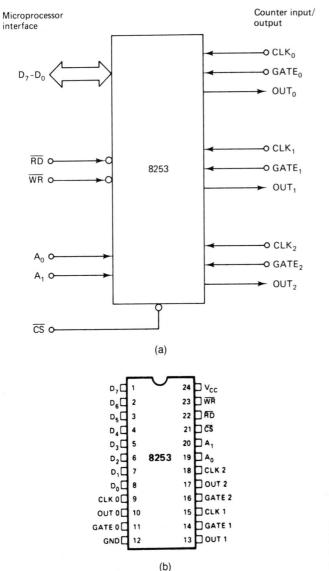

Microprocessor
interface

Counter input/
output

$D_7 - D_0$

$\overline{RD}$

$\overline{WR}$

8253

A_0

A_1

$\overline{CS}$

CLK$_0$
GATE$_0$
OUT$_0$

CLK$_1$
GATE$_1$
OUT$_1$

CLK$_2$
GATE$_2$
OUT$_2$

(a)

D_7	1	24	V_{CC}
D_6	2	23	$\overline{WR}$
D_5	3	22	$\overline{RD}$
D_4	4	21	$\overline{CS}$
D_3	5	20	A_1
D_2	6	19	A_0
D_1	7	18	CLK 2
D_0	8	17	OUT 2
CLK 0	9	16	GATE 2
OUT 0	10	15	CLK 1
GATE 0	11	14	GATE 1
GND	12	13	OUT 1

8253

(b)

Figure 7.32 (a) Block diagram of the 8253 interval timer (Courtesy of Intel Corp.); (b) pin layout (Courtesy of Intel Corp.).

The *control-word register* section actually contains three 8-bit registers that are used to configure the operation of counters 0, 1, and 2. The format of a *control word* is shown in Fig. 7.34. Here we find that the two most significant bits are a code that assigns the control word to a counter. For instance, making these bits 01 selects counter 1. Bits D_1 through D_3 are a 3-bit mode select code, $M_2M_1M_0$, that selects one of six modes of counter operation. The least significant bit D_0 is labeled BCD and selects either binary or BCD mode of counting. For instance, if this bit is set to logic 1, the counter acts as a 16-bit binary counter. Finally, the 2-bit code RL_1RL_0 is used to set the sequence in which bytes are read from or loaded into the 16-bit count registers.

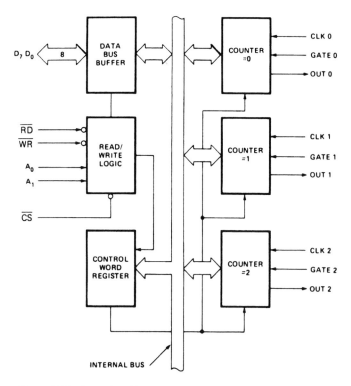

Figure 7.33 Internal architecture of the 8253 (Courtesy of Intel Corp.).

EXAMPLE 7.19

An 8253 receives the control word 10010000_2 over the bus. What configuration is set up for the counter?

SOLUTION   Since the SC bits are 10, the rest of the bits are for setting up the configuration of counter 2. Following the format in Fig. 7.34, we find that 01 in the RL bits sets counter 2 for the read/load sequence identified as the least significant byte only. This means that the next write operation performed to counter 2 will load the data into the least significant byte of its count register. Next the mode code is 000 and this selects mode 0 operation for this counter. The last bit, BCD, is also set to 0 and selects binary counting.

The three counters shown in the Fig. 7.33 are each 16 bits in length and operate as *down counters*. That is, when enabled by an active gate input, the clock decrements the count downward. Each counter contains a 16-bit *count register* that must be loaded as part of the initialization cycle. The value held in the count register can be read at any time through software.

To read from or write to the counters of the 8253 or load its control word register,

Control Word Format

D_7	D_6	D_5	D_4	D_3	D_2	D_1	D_0
SC1	SC0	RL1	RL0	M2	M1	M0	BCD

Definition Of Control

SC—SELECT COUNTER:

SC1	SC0	
0	0	Select Counter 0
0	1	Select Counter 1
1	0	Select Counter 2
1	1	Illegal

RL—READ/LOAD:

RL1	RL0	
0	0	Counter Latching operation (see READ/WRITE Procedure Section).
1	0	Read/Load most significant byte only.
0	1	Read/Load least significant byte only.
1	1	Read/Load least significant byte first, then most significant byte.

M—MODE:

M2	M1	M0	
0	0	0	Mode 0
0	0	1	Mode 1
X	1	0	Mode 2
X	1	1	Mode 3
1	0	0	Mode 4
1	0	1	Mode 5

BCD:

0	Binary Counter 16-Bits
1	Binary Coded Decimal (BCD) Counter (4 Decades)

Figure 7.34 Control-word format (Courtesy of Intel Corp.).

the microprocessor needs to execute instructions. Figure 7.35 shows the bus control information needed to access each register. For example, to write to the control register, the register address lines must be $A_1 A_0 = 11$ and the control lines $\overline{WR} = 0$, $\overline{RD} = 1$, and $\overline{CS} = 0$.

Input/Output Interface of the 8086 Microprocessor   Chap. 7

CS	RD	WR	A₁	A₀	
0	1	0	0	0	Load Counter No. 0
0	1	0	0	1	Load Counter No. 1
0	1	0	1	0	Load Counter No. 2
0	1	0	1	1	Write Mode Word
0	0	1	0	0	Read Counter No. 0
0	0	1	0	1	Read Counter No. 1
0	0	1	1	0	Read Counter No. 2
0	0	1	1	1	No-Operation 3-State
1	X	X	X	X	Disable 3-State
0	1	1	X	X	No-Operation 3-State

Figure 7.35 Accessing the registers of the 8253 (Courtesy of Intel Corp.).

EXAMPLE 7.20

Write an instruction sequence to set up the three counters of an 8253 located at I/O address 40H as follows:

Counter 0: Binary counter operating in mode 0 with an initial value of 1234H.

Counter 1: BCD counter operating in mode 2 with an initial value of 100H.

Counter 2: Binary counter operating in mode 4 with initial value of 1FFFH.

SOLUTION Since the base address of the 8253 is 40H, the mode register is at address 43H. The three counters 0, 1, and 2 are at addresses 40H, 41H, and 42H, respectively. Let us first determine the mode words for the three counters. Following the bit definitions in Fig. 7.34, we get

$$\text{Mode word for counter } 0 = 00110000_2 = 30_{16}$$

$$\text{Mode word for counter } 1 = 01010101_2 = 55_{16}$$

$$\text{Mode word for counter } 2 = 10111000_2 = B8_{16}$$

The following instruction sequence can be used to set up the 8253 with the modes and counts.

```
MOV  AL,30    ; Set up counter 0 mode

MOV  43,AL

MOV  AL,55    ; Set up counter 1 mode

OUT  43,AL

MOV  AL,B8    ; Set up counter 2 mode

OUT  43,AL

MOV  AL,34    ; Load counter 0

OUT  40,AL

MOV  AL,12
```

```
              OUT    40, AL

              MOV    AL, 01      ; Load counter 1

              OUT    41, AL

              MOV    AL, 00

              OUT    41, AL

              MOV    AL, FF      ; Load counter 2

              OUT    42, AL

              MOV    AL, 1F

              OUT    42, AL
```

Earlier we pointed out that the contents of a count register can be read at any time. Let us now look at how this is done in software. One approach is to simply read the contents of the corresponding register with an input instruction. In Fig. 7.35 we see that to read the contents of count register 0 the control inputs must be $\overline{CS} = 0$, $\overline{RD} = 0$, and $\overline{WR} = 1$, and the register address code must be $A_1A_0 = 00$. To assure that a valid count is read out of count register 0, the counter must be inhibited before the read operation takes place. The easiest way to do this is to switch the $GATE_0$ input to logic 0 before performing the input operation. The count is read as two separate bytes, low byte first followed by the high byte.

The contents of the count registers can also be read without first inhibiting the counter. That is, the count can be read on the fly. To do this in software, a command must first be issued to the mode register to capture the current value of the counter into a temporary storage register. In Fig. 7.34, we find that setting bits D_5 and D_4 of the mode byte to 00 specifies the latch mode of operation. Once this mode byte has been written to the 8253, the contents of the temporary storage register for the counter can be read just as before.

EXAMPLE 7.21

Write an instruction sequence to read the contents of counter 2 on the fly. The count is to be loaded into the AX register. Assume that the 8253 is located at I/O address 40H.

SOLUTION   First, we will latch the contents of counter 2 and then this value is read from the temporary storage register. This is done with the following sequence of instructions.

```
              MOV AL, 10000000B   ; Latch counter 2

              OUT 43, AL

              IN AL, 42           ; Read the low byte

              MOV BL, AL
```

Operating Modes of 8253 Counters

As indicated earlier, each of the 8253's counters can be configured to operate in one of six modes. Figure 7.36 shows waveforms that summarize operation for each mode. Notice that mode 0 operation is known as interrupt on terminal count and mode 1 is called programmable one-shot. The GATE input of a counter takes on different func-

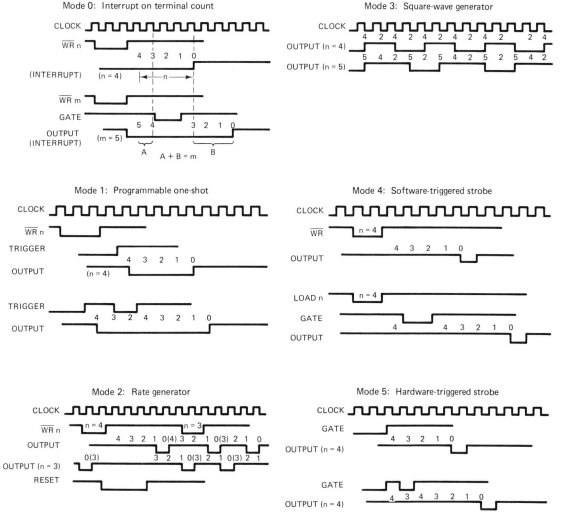

Figure 7.36 Operating modes of the 8253 (Courtesy of Intel Corp.).

tions, depending on which mode of operation is selected. The effect of the gate input is summarized in Fig. 7.37. For instance, in mode 0, GATE disables counting when set to logic 0 and enables counting when set to 1. Let us now discuss each of these modes of operation in more detail.

Signal Status Modes	Low Or Going Low	Rising	High
0	Disables counting	—	Enables counting
1	—	1) Initiates counting 2) Resets output after next clock	—
2	1) Disables counting 2) Sets output immediately high	1) Reloads counter 2) Initiates counting	Enables counting
3	1) Disables counting 2) Sets output immediately high	1) Reloads counter 2) Initiates counting	Enables counting
4	Disables counting	—	Enables counting
5	—	Initiates counting	—

Figure 7.37 Effect of the GATE input for each mode (Courtesy of Intel Corp.).

The *interrupt on terminal count* mode of operation is used to generate an interrupt to the microprocessor after a certain interval of time has elapsed. As shown in the waveforms for mode 0 operation in Fig. 7.36, a count of 4 is written into the count register synchronously with the pulse at WR. After the write operation is complete, the count is decremented by 1 for each clock pulse. When the count reaches 0, the terminal count, a 0-to-1 transition occurs at OUTPUT. This signal is used as the interrupt input to the microprocessor.

Earlier we found in Fig. 7.37 that GATE must be at logic 1 to enable the counter for interrupt on terminal count mode of operation. Figure 7.36 also shows waveforms for the case in which GATE is switched to logic 0. Here we see that the counter does not decrement below the value 4 until GATE returns to 1.

EXAMPLE 7.22

The counter of Fig. 7.38 is programmed to operate in mode 0. Assuming that the value 100_{16} is written into the counter, compute the time delay (TD) that occurs until the positive transition takes place at the counter 0 output.

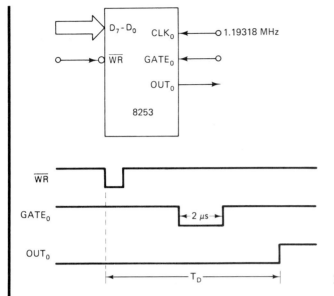

Figure 7.38 Mode 0 configuration.

SOLUTION Once loaded, counter 0 needs to decrement down for 100 pulses at the clock input. During this period, the counter is disabled by logic 0 at the GATE input for 2 μs. Therefore, the time delay is calculated as

$$TD = 2 \ \mu s \ + \ 100(T_{CLK0})$$

$$= 2 \ \mu s \ + \ 100(1/1.19318)\mu s$$

$$= 85.8 \ \mu s$$

Mode 1 operation implements what is known as a *programmable one-shot*. As shown in Fig. 7.36, when set for this mode of operation, the counter produces a single pulse at its output. The waveforms show that an initial count, which in this example is the number 4, is written into the counter synchronous with a pulse at $\overline{WR}$. When GATE, called TRIGGER in the waveshapes, switches from logic 0 to 1, OUTPUT switches to logic 0 on the next pulse at CLOCK and the count begins to decrement with each successive clock pulse. The pulse is completed as OUTPUT returns to logic 1 when the terminal count, which is 0, is reached. In this way, we see that the duration of the pulse is determined by the value loaded into the counter.

The pulse generator produced with an 8253 counter is what is called a *retriggerable one-shot*. By *retriggerable* we mean that, if after an output pulse has been started another rising edge is experienced at TRIGGER, the count is reloaded and the pulse width is extended by the full pulse duration. The lower one-shot waveform in Fig. 7.36 shows this type of operation. Notice that after the count is decremented to 2, a second rising edge occurs at TRIGGER. This edge reloads the value 4 into the counter to extend the pulse width to 7 clock cycles.

EXAMPLE 7.23

Counter 1 of an 8253 is programmed to operate in mode 1 and is loaded with the value 10. The gate and clock inputs are as shown in Fig. 7.39. How long is the output pulse?

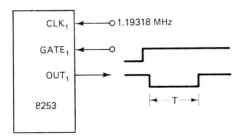

Figure 7.39 Mode 1 configuration.

SOLUTION The GATE input in Fig. 7.39 shows that the counter is operated as a non-retriggerable one-shot. Therefore, the pulse width is given by

$$T = (\text{counter contents}) \times (\text{clock period})$$

$$= 10 \times 1/1.19318 \text{ MHz}$$

$$= 8.38 \text{ } \mu s$$

When set for mode 2, *rate generator* operation, the counter within the 8253 is set to operate as a divide-by-N counter. Here N stands for the value of the count loaded into the counter. Figure 7.40 shows counter 1 of an 8253 set up in this way. Notice that the gate input is fixed at the 1 logic level. As shown in the table of Fig. 7.37, this enables counting operation. Looking at the waveforms for mode 2 operation in Fig. 7.36, we see that OUTPUT is at logic 1 until the count decrements to zero. Then the output switches to the active 0 logic level for just one clock pulse width. In this way, we see that there is one clock pulse at the output for every N clock pulses at the input. This is why it is called a divide-by-N counter.

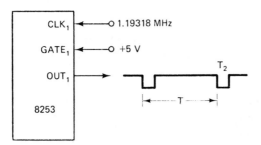

Figure 7.40 Mode 2 configuration.

EXAMPLE 7.24

Counter 1 of the 8253, as shown in Fig. 7.40, is programmed to operate in mode 2 and is loaded with the number 18. Describe the signal produced at OUT_1.

SOLUTION In mode 2 the output goes low for one period of the input clock after the counter contents decrement to 0. Therefore,

$$T_2 = 1/1.19318 \text{ MHz} = 838 \text{ ns}$$

and

$$T = 18 \times T_2 = 15.094 \text{ } \mu s$$

Mode 3 sets the counter of the 8253 to operate as a *square-wave rate generator*. In this mode, the output of the counter is a square wave with 50% duty cycle whenever the counter is loaded with an even number. That is, the output is at the 1 logic level for exactly the same amount of time that it is at the 0 logic level. As shown in Fig. 7.34, all transitions of the output take place with respect to the negative edge of the input clock. The period of the symmetrical square wave at the output equals the number loaded into the counter multiplied by the period of the input clock.

If an odd number (N) is loaded into the counter instead of an even number, the time for which the output is high is given by $(N + 1)/2$, and the time for which the output is low is given by $(N - 1)/2$.

EXAMPLE 7.25

The counter in Fig. 7.41 is programmed to operate in mode 3 and is loaded with the value 15. Determine the characteristics of the square wave at OUT_1.

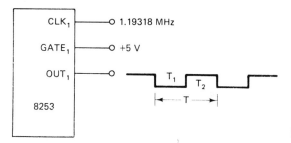

Figure 7.41 Mode 3 configuration.

SOLUTION

$$T_{CLK1} = 1/1.19318 \text{ MHz} = 838 \text{ ns}$$

$$T_1 = T_{CLK1}(N + 1)/2 = 838 \text{ ns} \times [(15 + 1)/2]$$

$$= 6.704 \text{ } \mu s$$

$$T_2 = T_{CLK1} (N - 1)/2 = 838 \text{ ns} \times [(15 - 1)/2]$$

$$= 5.866 \text{ } \mu s$$

$$T = T_1 + T_2 = 6.704 \ \mu s + 5.866 \ \mu s$$

$$= 12.57 \ \mu s$$

Selecting mode 4 operation for a counter configures the counter to work as a *software triggered strobed counter*. When in this mode, the counter automatically begins to decrement immediately upon loading with its initial value through software. Again, it decrements at a rate set by the clock input signal. At the moment the terminal count is reached, the counter generates a single strobe pulse with duration equal to one clock pulse at its output. This pulse can be used to perform a timed operation. Figure 7.36 shows waveforms illustrating this mode of operation initiated by writing the value 4 into a counter. Moreover, in the table of Fig. 7.37, we find that the gate intput needs to be at logic 1 for the counter to operate.

This mode of operation can be used to implement a long-duration interval timer or a free-running timer. In either application, the strobe at the output can be used as an interrupt input to a microprocessor. In response to this pulse, an interrupt service routine can be used to reload the timer and restart the timing cycle. Frequently, the service routine also counts the strobes as they come in by decrementing the contents of a register. Software can test the value in this register to determine if the timer has timed out a certain number of times, for instance, to determine if the contents of the register have decremented to 0. When it reaches 0, a specific operation, such as a jump or call, can be initiated. In this way, we see that software has been used to extend the interval of time at which a function occurs beyond the maximum duration of the 16-bit counter within the 8253.

EXAMPLE 7.26

Counter 1 of Fig. 7.42 is programmed to operate in mode 4. What value must be loaded into the counter to produce a strobe signal 10 μs after the counter is loaded?

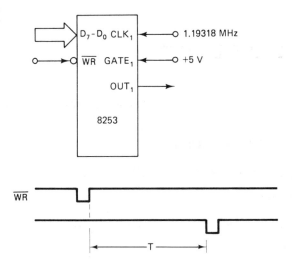

Figure 7.42 Mode 4 configuration.

SOLUTION   The strobe pulse occurs after counting down the counter to zero. The number of input clock periods required for a period of 10 μs is given by

$$N = T/T_{CLK}$$

$$= 10 \ \mu s/(1/1.19318 \ MHz)$$

$$= 12$$

Thus the counter should be loaded with the number 12 to produce a strobe pulse 10 μs after loading.

The last mode of 8253 counter operation, mode 5, is called the *hardware triggered strobe*. This mode is similar to mode 4 except that now counting is initiated by a signal at the gate input. That is, it is hardware triggered instead of software triggered. As shown in the waveforms of Fig. 7.36 and table of Fig. 7.37, a rising edge at GATE starts the countdown process. Just as for software triggered strobed operation, the strobe pulse is output after the count decrements to 0.

7.13 THE 8237A PROGRAMMABLE DIRECT MEMORY ACCESS CONTROLLER

The 8327A is the LSI controller IC that is most widely used to implement the *direct memory access* (DMA) function in 8086-based microcomputer systems. DMA capability permits devices, such as peripherals, to perform high-speed data transfers between either two sections of memory or between memory and an I/O device. In a microcomputer system, the memory or I/O bus cycles initiated as part of a DMA transfer are not performed by the MPU; instead, they are performed by a device known as a *DMA controller,* such as the 8237A. DMA mode of operation is most frequently used when blocks or packets of data are to be transferred. For instance, disk controllers, local area network controllers, and communication controllers are devices that normally process data as blocks or packets. A single 8237A supports up to four peripheral devices for DMA operation.

Microprocessor Interface of the 8237A

A block diagram that shows the interface signals of the 8237A DMA controller is given in Fig. 7.43(a). The pin layout in Fig. 7.43(b) identifies the pins at which these signals are available. Let us now look briefly at the operation of the microprocessor interface of the 8237A.

In a microcomputer system, the 8237A acts as a peripheral device and its operation must be initialized through software. This is done by reading from or writing to the bits of its internal registers. These data transfers take place through its microprocessor interface. Figure 7.44 shows how the 8086 connects to the 8237A's microprocessor interface.

Whenever the 8237A is not in use by a peripheral device for DMA operation, it

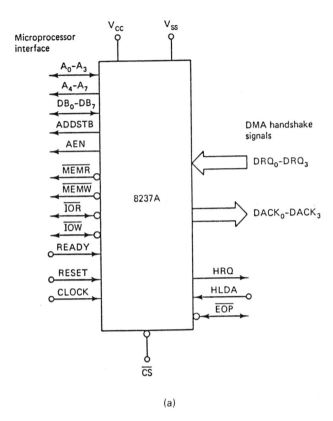

Microprocessor
interface

V_{CC} V_{SS}

A_0-A_3
A_4-A_7
DB_0-DB_7
ADDSTB
AEN
$\overline{MEMR}$
$\overline{MEMW}$
$\overline{IOR}$
$\overline{IOW}$
READY
RESET
CLOCK

8237A

DMA handshake
signals

DRQ_0-DRQ_3

$DACK_0$-$DACK_3$

HRQ
HLDA
$\overline{EOP}$

$\overline{CS}$

(a)

Figure 7.43 (a) Block diagram of the 8237A DMA controller; (b) pin layout (Courtesy of Intel Corp.).

is in a state known as the *idle state*. When in this state, the microprocessor can issue commands to the DMA controller and read from or write to its internal registers. Data bus lines DB_0 through DB_7 are the path over which these data transfers take place. Which register is accessed is determined by a 4-bit register address that is applied to address inputs A_0 through A_3. As shown in Fig. 7.44, these inputs are directly supplied by address bits A_0 through A_3 of the microprocessor.

During the data transfer bus cycle, other bits of the address are decoded in external circuitry to produce a chip select ($\overline{CS}$) input for the 8237A. When in the idle state, the 8237A continuously samples this input, waiting for it to become active. Logic 0 at this input enables the microprocessor interface. The microprocessor tells the 8237A whether an input or output bus cycle is in progress with the signal $\overline{IOR}$ or $\overline{IOW}$, respectively. In this way, we see that the 8237A is intended to be mapped into the I/O address space of the 8086 microcomputer.

DMA Interface of the 8237A

Now that we have described how a microprocessor talks to the registers of the 8237A, let us continue by looking at how peripheral devices initiate DMA service. The 8237A contains four independent DMA channels, channels 0 through 3. Typically, each of these channels is dedicated to a specific device, such as a peripheral. In Fig. 7.45, we

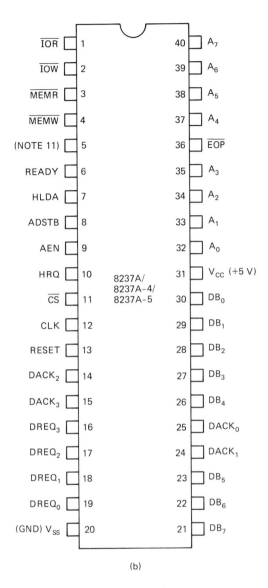

$\overline{IOR}$	1	40	A_7
$\overline{IOW}$	2	39	A_6
$\overline{MEMR}$	3	38	A_5
$\overline{MEMW}$	4	37	A_4
(NOTE 11)	5	36	$\overline{EOP}$
READY	6	35	A_3
HLDA	7	34	A_2
ADSTB	8	33	A_1
AEN	9	32	A_0
HRQ	10	31	V_{CC} (+5 V)
$\overline{CS}$	11	30	DB_0
CLK	12	29	DB_1
RESET	13	28	DB_2
$DACK_2$	14	27	DB_3
$DACK_3$	15	26	DB_4
$DREQ_3$	16	25	$DACK_0$
$DREQ_2$	17	24	$DACK_1$
$DREQ_1$	18	23	DB_5
$DREQ_0$	19	22	DB_6
(GND) V_{SS}	20	21	DB_7

8237A/ 8237A-4/ 8237A-5

(b)

Figure 7.43 *(continued)*

see that the device has four DMA request inputs, denoted as DRQ_0 through DRQ_3. These DRQ inputs correspond to channels 0 through 3, respectively. In the idle state, the 8237A continuously tests these inputs to see if one is active. When a peripheral device wants to perform DMA operations, it makes a request for service at its DRQ input by switching it to active logic.

In response to the DMA request, the DMA controller switches the hold request (HRQ) output to logic 1. Normally, this output is supplied to the HOLD input of the 8086 and signals the microprocessor that the DMA controller needs to take control of the system bus. When the 8086 is ready to give up control of the bus, it puts its bus signals into the high-impedance state and signals this fact to the 8237A by switching

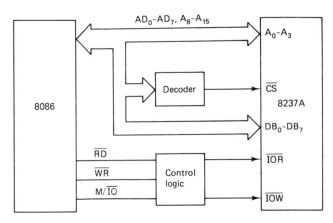

AD$_0$-AD$_7$, A$_8$-A$_{15}$

A$_0$-A$_3$

8086

Decoder

$\overline{\text{CS}}$

8237A

DB$_0$-DB$_7$

$\overline{\text{RD}}$

$\overline{\text{WR}}$

Control logic

M/$\overline{\text{IO}}$

$\overline{\text{IOR}}$

$\overline{\text{IOW}}$

Figure 7.44 Microprocessor interface.

the HLDA (hold acknowledge) output to logic 1. HLDA of the 8086 is applied to the HLDA input of the 8237A and signals that the system bus is now available for use by the DMA controller.

The 8237A tells the requesting peripheral device that it is ready by outputting a DMA acknowledge (DACK) signal. Notice in Fig. 7.45 that each of the four DMA request inputs DRQ$_0$ through DRQ$_3$, has a corresponding DMA acknowledge output, DACK$_0$ through DACK$_3$. Once this DMA request/acknowledge handshake sequence is complete, the peripheral device gets direct access to the system bus and memory under control of the 8237A.

During DMA bus cycles, the system bus is driven by the DMA controller, not the MPU. The 8237A generates the address and all control signals needed to perform the memory or I/O data transfers. At the beginning of all DMA bus cycles, a 16-bit address is output on lines A$_0$ through A$_7$ and DB$_0$ through DB$_7$. The upper 8 bits of the address, which are available on the data bus lines, appear at the same time that address strobe (ADDSTB) becomes active. Thus ADDSTB is intended to be used to strobe the most significant byte of the address into an external address latch. This 16-bit address gives the 8237A the ability to directly address up to 64K bytes of storage locations. The address enable (AEN) output signal is active during the complete DMA bus cycle and can be used to both enable the address latch and disable other devices connected to the bus.

Let us assume for now that an I/O peripheral device is to transfer data to memory. That is, the I/O device wants to write data to memory. In this case, the 8237A uses the $\overline{\text{IOR}}$ output to signal the I/O device to put the data onto data bus lines DB$_0$ through DB$_7$. At the same time, it asserts $\overline{\text{MEMW}}$ to signal that the data available on the bus are to be written into memory. In this case, the data are transferred directly from the I/O device to memory and do not go through the 8237A.

In a similar way, DMA transfers of data can take place from memory to an I/O device. Now the I/O device reads data from memory. For this data transfer, the 8237A activates the $\overline{\text{MEMR}}$ and $\overline{\text{IOW}}$ control signals.

The 8237A performs both the memory-to-I/O and I/O-to-memory DMA bus cycles in just four clock periods. The duration of these clock periods is determined by the frequency of the clock signal applied to the CLOCK input. For instance, at 5MHz the clock period is 200 ns and the bus cycle takes 800 ns.

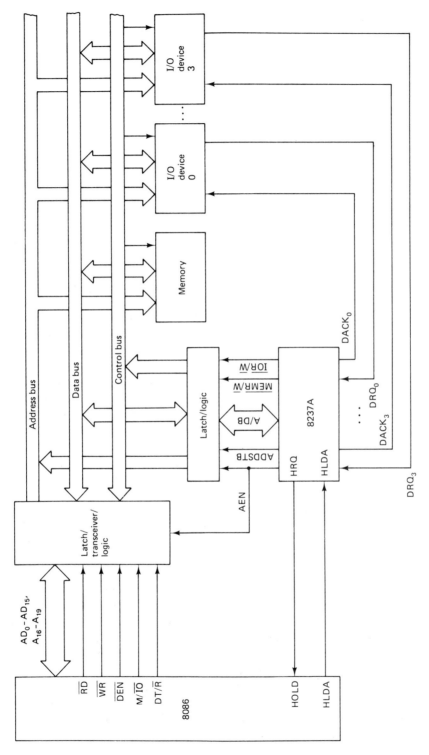

Figure 7.45 DMA interface.

291

The 8237A is also capable of performing memory-to-memory DMA transfers. In such a data transfer, both the MEMR and MEMW signals are utilized. Unlike the I/O-to-memory operation, this memory-to-memory data transfer takes eight clock cycles. This is because it is actually performed as a separate four-clock read bus cycle from the source memory location to a temporary register within the 8237A and then another four-clock write bus cycle from the temporary register to the destination memory location. At 5 MHz, a memory-to-memory DMA cycle takes 1.6 μs.

The READY input is used to accommodate for the slow memory of I/O devices. READY must go active, logic 1, before the 8237A will complete a memory or I/O bus cycle. As long as READY is at logic 0, wait states are inserted to extend the duration of the current bus cycle.

Internal Architecture of the 8237A

Figure 7.46 is a block diagram of the internal architecture of the 8237A DMA controller. Here we find the following functional blocks: the timing and control, the priority encoder and rotating priority logic, the command control, and 12 different types of registers. Let us now look briefly at the functions performed by each of these sections of circuitry and registers.

The timing and control part of the 8237A generates the timing and control signals needed by the external bus interface. For instance, it accepts as inputs the READY and CS signals and produces as outputs signals such as ADDSTB and AEN. These signals are synchronized to the clock signal that is input to the controller. The highest-speed version of the 8237A available today operates at a maximum clock rate of 5 MHz.

If multiple requests for DMA service are received by the 8237A, they are accepted on a priority basis. One of two priority schemes can be selected for the 8237A under software control. They are called *fixed priority* and *rotating priority*. The fixed priority mode assigns priority to the channels in descending numeric order. That is, channel 0 has the highest priority and channel 3 the lowest priority. Rotating priority starts with the priority levels initially the same way as in fixed priority. However, after a DMA request for a specific level gets serviced, priority is rotated such that the previously active channel is reassigned to the lowest priority level. For instance, assuming that channel 1, which was initially at priority level 1, was just serviced, then DRQ_2 is now at the highest priority level and DRQ_1 rotates to the lowest level. The priority logic circuitry shown in Fig. 7.46 resolves priority for simultaneous DMA requests from peripheral devices based on the enabled priority scheme.

The command control circuit decodes the register commands applied to the 8237A through the microprocessor interface. In this way it determines which register is to be accessed and what type of operation is to be performed. Moreover, it is used to decode the programmed operating modes of the device during DMA operation.

Looking at the block diagram in Fig. 7.46, we find that the 8237A has 12 different types of internal registers. Some examples are the current address register, current count register, command register, mask register, and status register. The names for all the internal registers are listed in Fig. 7.47, along with their size and how many are provided in the 8237A. Note that there are actually four current address registers and they are all 16 bits long. That is, there is one current address register for each of the four

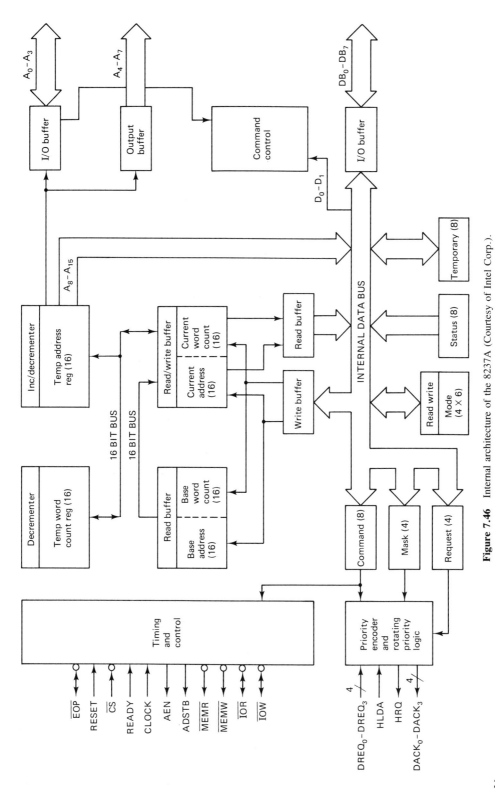

Figure 7.46 Internal architecture of the 8237A (Courtesy of Intel Corp.).

293

Name	Size	Number
Base Address Registers	16 bits	4
Base Word Count Registers	16 bits	4
Current Address Registers	16 bits	4
Current Word Count Registers	16 bits	4
Temporary Address Register	16 bits	1
Temporary Word Count Register	16 bits	1
Status Register	8 bits	1
Command Register	8 bits	1
Temporary Register	8 bits	1
Mode Registers	6 bits	4
Mask Register	4 bits	1
Request Register	4 bits	1

Figure 7.47 Internal registers of the 8237A (Courtesy of Intel Corp.).

DMA channels. We will now describe the function served by each of these registers in terms of overall operation of the 8237A DMA controller. Addressing information for the internal registers is summarized in Fig. 7.48.

Each DMA channel has two address registers. They are called the *base address register* and the *current address register*. The base address register holds the starting address for the DMA operation, and the current address register contains the address of the next storage location to be accessed. Writing a value to the base address register automatically loads the same value into the current address register. In this way, we see that initially the current address register points to the starting I/O or memory address.

These registers must be loaded with appropriate values prior to initiating a DMA cycle. To load a new 16-bit address into the base register, we must write two separate bytes, one after the other, to the address of the register. The 8237A has an internal flip-flop called the *first/last flip-flop*. This flip-flop identifies which byte of the address is being written into the register. As shown in the table of Fig. 7.48, if the beginning state of the internal flip-flop (FF) is logic 0, then software must write the low byte of the address word to the register. On the other hand, if it is logic 1, the high byte must be written to the register. For example, to write the address 1234_{16} into the base address register and the current address register for channel 0 of a DMA controller located at I/O address 'DMA', $(\leq F0_{16})$ the following instructions may be executed.

```
MOV    AL, 34      ; write low byte

OUT    DMA + 0, AL

MOV    AL, 12      ; write high byte

OUT    DMA + 0, AL
```

This routine assumes that the internal flip-flop was initially set to 0. Looking at the Fig. 7.48, we find that a command can be issued to the 8237A to clear the internal flip-flop. This is done by initiating an output bus cycle to address DMA + C_{16}.

If we read the contents of register address C_{16}, the value obtained is the contents of the current address register. Once loaded, the value in the base address register cannot be read out of the device.

The 8237A also has two word count registers for each of its DMA channels. They are called the *base count register* and the *current count register*. In Fig. 7.47, we find that these registers are also 16 bits in length, and Fig. 7.48 identifies their addresses.

Channel(s)	Register	Operation	I/O address	Internal FF	Data bus
0	Base and current address	Write	0_{16}	0 1	Low High
	Current address	Read	0_{16}	0 1	Low High
	Base and current count	Write	1_{16}	0 1	Low High
	Current count	Read	1_{16}	0 1	Low High
1	Base and current address	Write	2_{16}	0 1	Low High
	Current address	Read	2_{16}	0 1	Low High
	Base and current count	Write	3_{16}	0 1	Low High
	Current count	Read	3_{16}	0 1	Low High
2	Base and current address	Write	4_{16}	0 1	Low High
	Current address	Read	4_{16}	0 1	Low High
	Base and current count	Write	5_{16}	0 1	Low High
	Current count	Read	5_{16}	0 1	Low High
3	Base and current address	Write	6_{16}	0 1	Low High
	Current address	Read	6_{16}	0 1	Low High
	Base and current count	Write	7_{16}	0 1	Low High
	Current count	Read	7_{16}	0 1	Low High
All	Command register	Write	8_{16}	X	Low
All	Status register	Read	8_{16}	X	Low
All	Request register	Write	9_{16}	X	Low
All	Mask register	Write	A_{16}	X	Low
All	Mode register	Write	B_{16}	X	Low
All	Temporary register	Read	B_{16}	X	Low
All	Clear internal FF	Write	C_{16}	X	Low
All	Master clear	Write	D_{16}	X	Low
All	Clear mask register	Write	E_{16}	X	Low
All	Mask register	Write	F_{16}	X	Low

Figure 7.48 Accessing the registers of the 8237A.

The number of bytes of data that are to be transferred during a DMA operation is specified by the value in the base word count register. Actually, the number of bytes transferred is always one more than the value programmed into this register. This is because the end of a DMA cycle is detected by the rollover of the current word count from 0000_{16} to $FFFF_{16}$. At any time during the DMA cycle, the value in the current word count register tells how many bytes remain to be transferred.

The count registers are programmed in the same way as was just described for the address registers. For instance, to program a count of $0FFF_{16}$ into the base and current count registers for channel 1 of a DMA controller located at address 'DMA' ($< F0_{16}$), the instructions that follow can be executed.

```
MOV  AL, FF      ; write low byte

OUT  DMA + 3, AL

MOV  AL, 0F      ; write high byte

OUT  DMA + 3, AL
```

Again we have assumed that the internal flip-flop was initially cleared.

In Fig. 7.47, we find that the 8237A has a single 8-bit command register. The bits in this register are used to control operating modes that apply to all channels of the DMA controller. Figure 7.49 identifies the function of each of its control bits. Notice that the settings of the bits are used to select or deselect operating features such as memory-to-memory DMA transfer and the priority scheme. For instance, when bit 0 is set to logic 1, the memory-to-memory mode of DMA transfer is enabled, and when it is logic 0, DMA transfers take place between I/O and memory. Moreover, setting bit 4 to logic 0 selects the fixed priority scheme for all four channels or logic 1 in this location selects rotating priority. Looking at Fig. 7.48, we see that the command register is loaded by outputting the command code to register address 8_{16}.

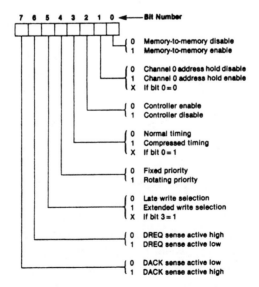

Figure 7.49 Command register format (Courtesy of Intel Corp.).

EXAMPLE 7.27

If the command register of an 8237A is loaded with 00_{16}, how does the controller operate?

SOLUTION Representing the command word as a binary number, we get

$$00_{16} = 00000000_2$$

Referring to 7.49, we find that the DMA operation can be described as follows:

Bit 0 = 0 = Memory-to-memory transfers are enabled

Bit 1 = 0 = Channel 0 address increments/decrements normally

Bit 2 = 0 = 8237A is enabled

Bit 3 = 0 = 8237A operates with normal timing

Bit 4 = 0 = Channels have fixed priority, channel 0 having the highest priority and channel 3 the lowest priority

Bit 5 = 0 = Write operation occurs late in the DMA bus cycle

Bit 6 = 0 = DREQ is an active high (logic 1) signal

Bit 7 = 0 = DACK is an active low (logic 0) signal

The *mode registers* are also used to configure operational features of the 8237A. In Fig. 7.47, we find that there is a separate mode register for each of the four DMA channels and that they are each 6 bits in length. Their bits are used to select various operational features for the individual DMA channels. A typical mode register command is shown in Fig. 7.50. As shown in the diagram, the two least significant bits are a 2-bit code that identifies the channel to which the mode command byte applies. For instance, in a mode register command written for channel 1, these bits must be made 01. Bits 2 and 3 specify whether the channel is to perform data write or data read or verify

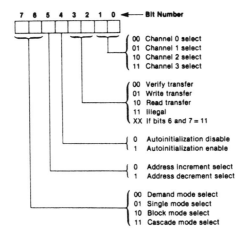

Figure 7.50 Mode register format (Courtesy of Intel Corp.).

bus cycles. For example, if these bits are set to 01, the channel will only perform write data transfers (DMA data transfers from an I/O device to memory).

The next 2 bits of the mode register affect how the values in the current address and current count registers are updated at the end of a DMA cycle and DMA data transfer, respectively. Bit 4 enables or disables the autoinitialization function. When autoinitialization is enabled, the current address and current count registers are automatically reloaded from the base address and base count registers, respectively, at the end of a DMA cycle. In this way, the channel is prepared for the next cycle to begin. The setting of bit 5 determines whether the value in the current address register is automatically incremented or decremented at completion of each DMA data transfer.

The two most significant bits of the mode register select one of four possible modes of DMA operation for the channel. The four modes are called *demand mode, single mode, block mode,* and *cascade mode.* These modes allow for either 1 byte of data to be transferred at a time or a block of bytes. For example, when in the demand transfer mode, once the DMA cycle is initiated, bytes are continuously transferred as long as the DRQ signal remains active and the terminal count (TC) is not reached. By reaching the terminal count, we mean that the value in the current word count register, which automatically decrements after each data transfer, rolls over from 0000_{16} to $FFFF_{16}$.

Block transfer mode is similar to demand transfer mode in that, once the DMA cycle is initiated, data are continuously transferred until the terminal count is reached. However, they differ in that, when in the demand mode, the return of DRQ to its inactive state halts the data transfer sequence. But, when in block transfer mode, DRQ can be released at any time after the DMA cycle begins, and the block transfer will still run to completion.

In the single transfer mode, the channel is set up such that it performs just one data transfer at a time. At the completion of the transfer, the current word count is decremented and the current address either incremented or decremented (based on an option setting). Moreover, an autoinitialize, if enabled, will not occur unless the terminal count has been reached at the completion of the current data transfer. If the DRQ input becomes inactive before the completion of the current data transfer, another data transfer will not take place until DRQ once more becomes active. On the other hand, if DRQ remains active during the complete data transfer cycle, the HRQ output of the 8237A is switched to its inactive 0 logic level to allow the microprocessor to gain control of the system bus for one bus cycle before another single transfer takes place. This mode of operation is typically used when it is necessary to not lock the microprocessor off the bus for the complete duration of the DMA cycle.

EXAMPLE 7.28

Specify the mode byte for DMA channel 2 if it is to transfer data from an input peripheral device to a memory buffer starting at address $A000_{16}$ and ending at $AFFF_{16}$. Ensure that the microprocessor is not completely locked off the bus during the DMA cycle. Moreover, at the end of each DMA cycle, the channel is to be reinitialized so that the same buffer is to be filled when the next DMA operation is initiated.

SOLUTION   For DMA channel 2, bit 1 and bit 0 must be loaded with 10_2.

$$B_1B_0 = 10$$

Transfer of data from an I/O device to memory represents a write bus cycle. Therefore, bit 3 and bit 2 must be set to 01.

$$B_3B_2 = 01$$

Selecting autoinitialization will set up the channel to automatically reset so that it points to the beginning of the memory buffer at completion of the current DMA cycle. This feature is enabled by making bit 4 equal to 1.

$$B_4 = 1$$

The address that points to the memory buffer must increment after each data transfer. Therefore, bit 5 must be set to 0.

$$B_5 = 0$$

Finally, to assume that the 8086 is not locked off the bus during the complete DMA cycle, we will select the single transfer mode of operation. This is done by making bits B_7 and B_6 equal to 01.

$$B_7B_6 = 01$$

Thus the mode register byte is $01010110_2 = 56_{16}$.

Up to now, we have discussed how DMA cycles can be initiated by a hardware request at a DRQ input. However, the 8237A is also able to respond to software-initiated requests for DMA service. The *request register* has been provided for this purpose. Figure 7.47 shows that the request register has just 4 bits, one for each of the DMA channels. When the request bit for a channel is set, DMA operation is started, and when reset, the DMA cycle is stopped. Any channel used for software-initiated DMA must be programmed for block transfer mode of operation.

The bits in the request register can be set or reset by issuing software commands to the 8237A. The format of a request register command is shown in Fig. 7.51. For instance, if a command is issued to the address of the request register with bits 0 and 1 equal to 01 and with bit 3 at logic 1, a block mode DMA cycle is initiated for channel 1. In Fig. 7.48, we find that the request register is located at register address 9_{16}.

A 4-bit *mask register* is also provided within the 8237A. One bit is provided in this register for each of the DMA channels. When a mask bit is set, the DRQ input for the corresponding channel is disabled. That is, hardware requests to the channel are

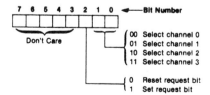

Figure 7.51   Request register format (Courtesy of Intel Corp.).

ignored and the channel is masked out. On the other hand, if the mask bit is cleared, the DRQ input is enabled and its channel can be activated by an external device.

The format of a software command that can be used to set or reset a single bit in the mask register is shown in Fig. 7.52(a). For example, to enable the DRQ input for channel 2, the command is issued with bits 0 and 1 set to 10 to select channel 2 and with bit 3 equal to 0 to clear the mask bit. For this example, the software command byte could be 03_{16}. The table in Fig. 7.48 shows that this command byte must be issued to the 8237A with register address A_{16}.

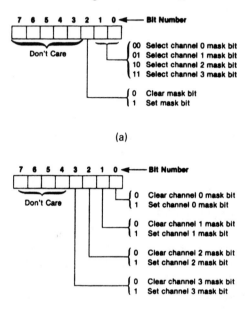

(a)

(b)

Figure 7.52 (a) Single-channel mask register command format (Courtesy of Intel Corp.); (b) four-channel mask register command format (Courtesy of Intel Corp.).

A second mask register command is shown in Fig. 7.52(b). This command can be used to load all 4 bits of the register at once. In Fig. 7.48, we find that this command is issued to register address F_{16} instead of A_{16}. For instance, to mask out channel 2 while enabling channels 0, 1, and 3, the command code 04_{16} is output to F_{16}. Either of these two methods can be used to mask or enable the DRQ input for a channel.

At system initialization, it is a common practice to clear the mask register. Looking at Fig. 7.48, we see that a special command is provided to perform this operation. Notice that the mask register can be cleared by executing an output cycle to register address E_{16}.

The 8237A has a *status register* that contains information about the operating state of its four DMA channels. Figure 7.53 shows the bits of the status register and defines their functions. Here we find that the four least significant bits identify whether or not channels 0 through 3 have reached their terminal count. When the DMA cycle for a channel reaches the terminal count, this fact is recorded by setting the corresponding TC bit to the 1 logic level. The four most significant bits of the register tell if a request is pending for the corresponding channel. For instance, if a DMA request has been issued for channel 0 either through hardware or software, bit 4 is set to 1. The 8086

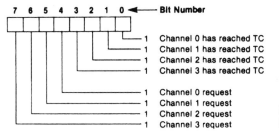

7 6 5 4 3 2 1 0 ◄──── Bit Number

1 Channel 0 has reached TC
1 Channel 1 has reached TC
1 Channel 2 has reached TC
1 Channel 3 has reached TC

1 Channel 0 request
1 Channel 1 request
1 Channel 2 request
1 Channel 3 request

Figure 7.53 Status register (Courtesy of Intel Corp.).

can read the contents of the status register through software. This is done by initiating an input bus cycle for register address 8_{16}.

Earlier we pointed out that during memory-to-memory DMA transfers, the data read from the source address are held in a register known as the *temporary register,* and then a write cycle is initiated to write the data to the destination address. At the completion of the DMA cycle, this register contains the last byte that was transferred. The value in this register can be read by the microprocessor.

EXAMPLE 7.29

Write an instruction sequence to issue a master clear to the 8237A and then enable all its DMA channels. Assume that the device is located at I/O address 'DMA' ($\le$ F0H).

SOLUTION In Fig. 7.48, we find that a special software command is provided to perform a master reset of the 8237A's registers. Since the contents of the data bus are a don't-care state when executing the master clear command, it is performed by simply writing to register address D_{16}. For instance, the instruction

OUT DMA + 0D, AL

can be used. To enable the DMA request inputs, all 4 bits of the mask register must be cleared. The clear mask register command is issued by performing a write to register address E_{16}. Again, the data put on the bus during the write cycle are a don't-care state. Therefore, the command can be performed with the instruction

OUT DMA + 0E, AL

DMA Interface for the 8086-Based Microcomputer Using the 8237A

Figure 7.54 shows how the 8237A is connected to the 8086 microprocessor to form a simplified DMA interface. Here we see that both the 8086 MPU and the 8237A DMA controller drive the three system buses, address bus, data bus, and control bus. Let us now look at how each of these devices attaches to the system bus. The 8086's multiplexed address/data bus is demultiplexed using three 8282 latches to form independent system address and data buses. The address bus is 20 bits in length and these lines are identified as A_0 through A_{19}. On the other hand, the data bus is word wide, with lines

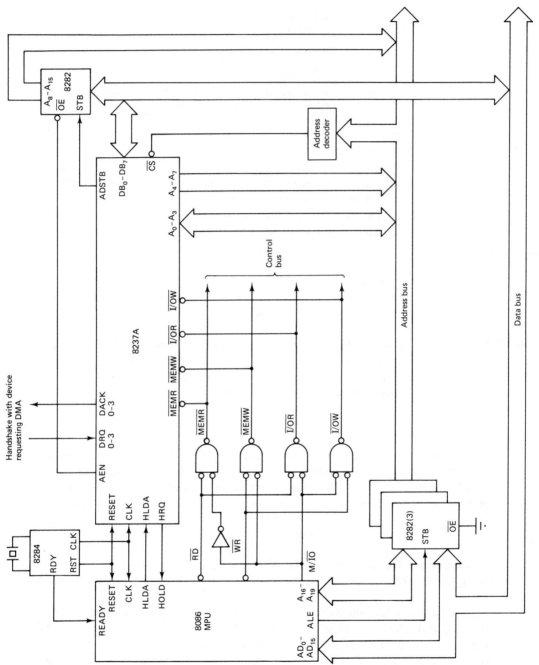

Figure 7.54 8086-based microcomputer with 8237A DMA interface.

302

D_0 through D_{15}. Notice that the ALE output of the 8086 is used as the strobe (STB) input to the latches.

Looking at the 8237A, we find that the lower byte of its address, which is identified by A_0 through A_3 and A_4 through A_7, is supplied directly to the system address bus. On the other hand, the most significant byte of its address, A_8 through A_{15}, is demultiplexed from data bus lines DB_0 through DB_7 by another 8282 latch. This latch is enabled by the AEN output of the DMA controller, and the address is loaded into the latch with the signal ADDSTB. DB_0 through DB_7 are also directly attached to the system data bus.

Finally, let us look at how the system control bus signals are derived. The $M/\overline{IO}$, $\overline{RD}$, and $\overline{WR}$ control outputs of the microprocessor are gated together to produce the signals $\overline{MEMR}$, $\overline{MEMW}$, $\overline{IOR}$, and $\overline{IOW}$. These signals are combined to form the system control bus. Notice that these same four signals are generated as outputs of the 8237A and are also supplied to the control bus.

Now that we have shown how the independent address, data, and control signals of the 8086 and 8237A are combined to form the system address, data, and control buses, let us continue by looking at how the DMA request/acknowledge interface is implemented. I/O devices request DMA service by activating one of the 8237A's DMA request inputs, DRQ_0 through DRQ_3. When the 8237A receives a valid DMA request on one of these lines, it sends a hold request to the HOLD input of the 8086. It does this by setting the HRQ output to logic 1. After the 8086 gives up control of the system buses, it acknowledges this fact to the 8237A by switching its HLDA output to the 1 logic level. This signal is received by the DMA controller at its HLDA input and tells it that the system buses are available. The 8237A is now ready to take over control of the system buses, and it signals this fact to the device that is requesting service by activating its DMA acknowledge (DACK) line.

7.14 SPECIAL-PURPOSE INTERFACE CONTROLLERS

Up to this point, we have introduced LSI controllers for some of the most widely used I/O interfaces. A large number of other LSI devices are available to simplify the implementation of other complex I/O interfaces. Some examples are keyboard/display controllers, CRT controllers, floppy disk controllers, Winchester disk controllers, and IEEE-488 bus controllers. Here we will introduce just one of these devices, the *8279 programmable keyboard/display interface*. However, before starting the 8279, let us briefly examine how the keyboard and display are typically serviced in a microcomputer system.

The Keyboard and Display Interfaces

A keyboard and display are important input and output devices in many digital electronic systems. For instance, all calculators and hand-held computers have both a keyboard and display.

The circuit diagram in Fig. 7.55 shows how a keyboard is most frequently interfaced to a microcomputer. Note that the switches in the keyboard are arranged in

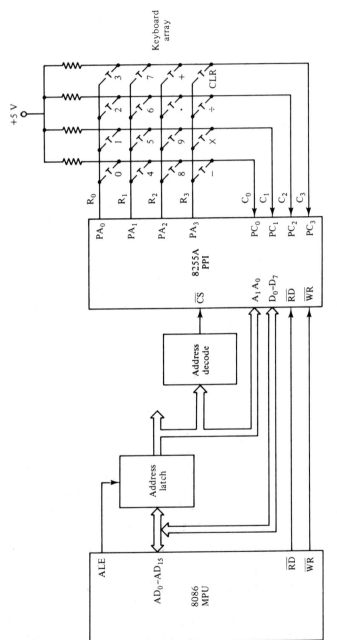

Figure 7.55 Keyboard interfaced to a microcomputer.

an *array*. The size of the array is described in terms of the number of rows and the number of columns. In our example, the keyboard array has four rows, which are labeled R_0 through R_3, and four columns, which are labeled C_0 through C_3. The location of the switch for any key in the array is uniquely defined by a row and a column. For instance, the 0 key is located at the junction of R_0 and C_0, while the 1 key is located at R_0 and C_1.

Now that we know how the keys of the keyboard are arranged, let us look at how the microcomputer services them. In most applications, the microcomputer scans the keyboard array. That is, it strobes one row of the keyboard after the other by sending out a short-duration pulse, to the 0 logic level, on the row line. During each row strobe, all column lines are examined by reading them in parallel. Typically, the column lines are pulled up to the 1 logic level; therefore, if a switch is closed, a logic 0 will be read on the corresponding column line. If no switches are closed, all 1s will be read when the column lines are examined.

For instance, if the 2 key is depressed when the microcomputer is scanning R_0, the column code read back will be $C_3C_2C_1C_0 = 1011$. Since the microcomputer knows which row it is scanning (R_0) and which column the strobe was returned on (C_2), it can determine that the number 2 key was depressed. The microcomputer does not necessarily store the row and column codes in the form that we have shown. It is more common to just maintain the binary equivalent of the row or column. In our example, the microcomputer would internally store the row number as $R_0 = 00_2$ and the column number as $C_2 = 10_2$. This is a more compact representation of the row and column information.

Several other issues arise when designing keyboards for microcomputer systems. One is that when a key in the keyboard is depressed, its contacts bounce for a short period of time. Depending on the keyboard sampling method, this could result in incorrect reading of the keyboard input. This problem is overcome by a technique known as *keyboard debouncing*. Debouncing is achieved by resampling the column lines a second time, about 10 ms later, to assure that the same column line is at the 0 logic level. If so, it is then accepted as a valid input. This technique can be implemented either in hardware or software.

Another problem occurs in keyboard sampling when more than one key is depressed at a time. In this case, the column code read by the microcomputer would have more than 1 bit that is logic 0. For instance, if the 0 and 2 keys were depressed, the column code read back during the scan of R_0 would be $C_3C_2C_1C_0 = 1010$. Typically, two keys are not actually depressed at the same time. It is more common that the second key is depressed while the first one is still being held down and that the column code showing two key closures would show up in the second test which is made for debouncing.

Several different techniques are used to overcome this problem. One is called *two-key lockout*. With this method, the occurrence of a second key during the debounce scan causes both keys to be locked out and neither is accepted by the microcomputer. If the second key that was depressed is released before the first key is released, the first key entry is accepted and the second key is ignored. On the other hand, if the first key is released before the second key, only the second key is accepted.

A second method of solving this problem is that known as *N-key rollover*. In this case, more than one key can be depressed at a time and get accepted by the microcom-

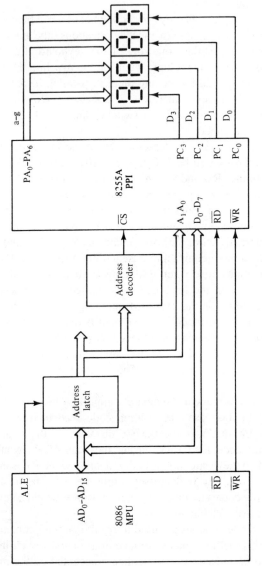

Figure 7.56 Display interfaced to a microcomputer.

puter. The microcomputer keeps track of the order in which they are depressed and as long as the switch closures are still present at another keyboard scan 10 ms later, they are accepted. That is, in the case of multiple key depressions, the key entries are accepted in the order in which their switches are closed.

The display interface used in most microcomputer systems is shown in Fig. 7.56. Here we are using a four-digit seven-segment numeric display. Notice that segment lines a through g of all digits of the display are driven in parallel by outputs of the microcomputer. It is over these lines that the microcomputer outputs signals to tell the display which segments are to be lighted to form the numbers in its digits. The way in which the segments of a seven-segment display digit are labeled is shown in Fig. 7.57. For instance, to form the number 1, a code is output to light just segments b and c.

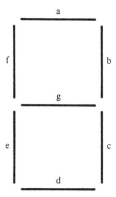

Figure 7.57 Seven-segment display labeling.

The other set of lines in the display interface correspond to the digits of the display. These lines, which are labeled D_0 through D_3, correspond to digits 0, 1, 2, and 3, respectively. It is with these signals that the microcomputer indicates to the display which digit the number corresponding to the code on lines a through g should be displayed.

The way in which the display is driven by the microcomputer is said to be *multiplexed*. That is, data are not permanently displayed; instead, they are output to one digit after the other in time. This scanning sequence is repeated frequently such that the fact that the display is not permanently lighted cannot be recognized by the user.

The scanning of the digits of the display is similar to the scanning we have just described for the rows of the keyboard. A digit drive signal is output to one digit of the display after the other in time and during each digit drive pulse the seven-segment code for the number that is to be displayed in that digit is output on segment lines a through g. In fact, in most systems the digit drive signals for the display and row drive signals of the keyboard are supplied by the same set of outputs.

The 8279 Programmable Keyboard/Display Controller

The 8279 is an LSI device that is designed to make implementation of a keyboard/display interface similar to that which we have just described quite simple. This device can drive an 8 × 8 keyboard switch array and a 16-digit eight-segment display. Moreover, it can be configured through software to support key debouncing, two-key lockout, or N-key rollover modes of operation, and either left or right data entry to the display.

A block diagram of the device is shown in Fig. 7.58(a) and its pin layout in Fig. 7.58(b). From this diagram we see that there are four signal sections: The *MPU interface,* the *key data inputs,* the *display data outputs,* and the *scan lines* that

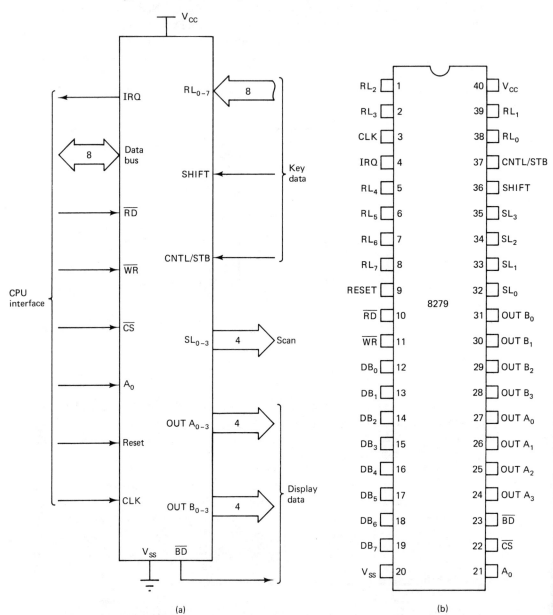

(a) (b)

Figure 7.58 (a) Block diagram of the 8279 (Courtesy of Intel Corp.); (b) pin layout (Courtesy of Intel Corp.)

are used by both the keyboard and display. Let us first look at the function of each of these interfaces.

The bus interface of the 8279 is similar to that found on the other peripherals that we have considered up to this point. It consists of the eight data bus lines DB_0 through DB_7. These are the lines over which the MPU outputs data to the display, inputs key codes, issues commands to the controller, and reads status information from the controller. Other signals found at the interface are the read ($\overline{RD}$), write ($\overline{WR}$), chip select ($\overline{CS}$), and address buffer (A_0) control signals. They are the signals that control the data bus transfers that take place between the microprocessor and 8279.

A new signal introduced with this interface is *interrupt request (IRQ)*. This is an output that gets returned to an interrupt input of the 8086 microcomputer. This signal is provided so that the 8279 can tell the MPU that it contains key codes that should be read.

The scan lines are used as row drive signals for the keyboard and digit drive signals for the display. There are just four of these lines, SL_0 through SL_3. However, they can be configured for two different modes of operation through software. In applications that require a small keyboard and display (four or less rows and digits), they can be used in what is known as the *decoded mode*. Scan output waveforms for this mode of operation are shown in Fig. 7.59(a). Notice that a pulse to the 0 logic level is produced at one output after the other in time.

The second mode of operation, which is called *encoded mode*, allows use of a keyboard matrix with up to eight rows and a display with up to 16 digits. When this mode of operation is enabled through software, the binary-coded waveforms shown in Fig. 7.59(b) are output on the SL lines. These signals must be decoded with an external decoder circuit to produce the digit and column drive signals.

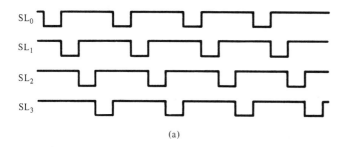

(a)

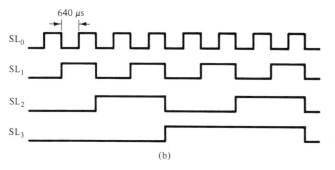

(b)

Figure 7.59 (a) Decoded-mode scan line signals (Courtesy of Intel Corp.); (b) encoded-mode scan line signals (Courtesy of Intel Corp.).

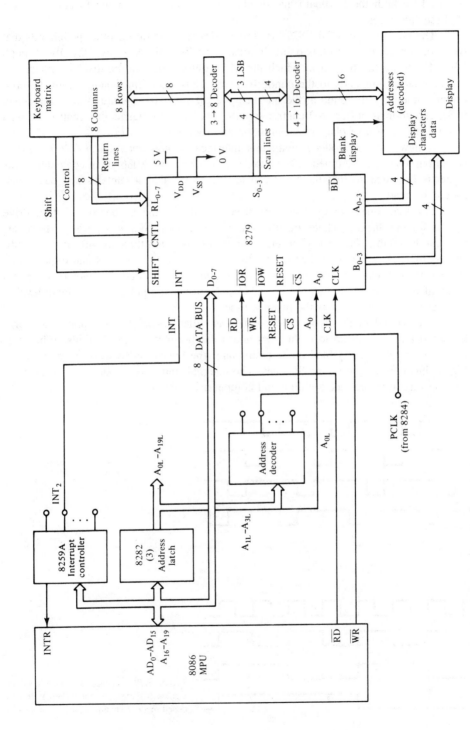

Figure 7.60 System configuration using the 8086 and 8279 (Courtesy of Intel Corp.).

Even though 16-digit drive signals are produced, only eight row drive signals can be used for the keyboard. This is because the key code that is stored when a key depression has been sensed has just 3 bits allocated to identify the row. Figure 7.60 shows this kind of circuit configuration.

The key data lines include the eight return lines RL_0 through RL_7. These lines receive inputs from the column outputs of the keyboard array. They are not tested all at once as we described earlier. Looking at the waveforms in Fig. 7.61, we see that the RL lines are examined one after the other during each 640-μs row pulse.

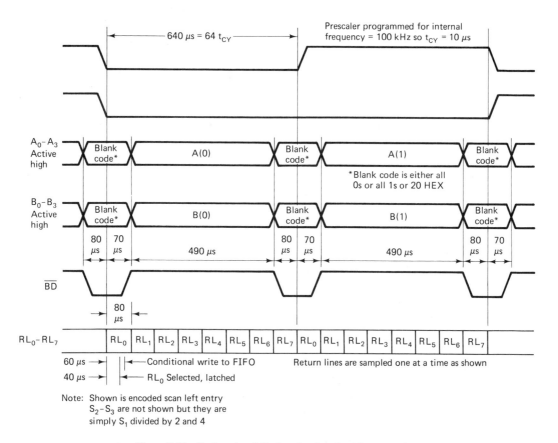

Figure 7.61 Keyboard and display signal timing (Courtesy of Intel Corp.).

If logic 0 is detected at a return line, the number of the column is coded as a 3-bit binary number and combined with the 3-bit row number to make a 6-bit key code. This key code input is first debounced and then loaded into an 8 × 8 key code FIFO within the 8279. Once the FIFO contains a key code, the IRQ output is set to logic 1. This signal can be used to tell the MPU that a keyboard input should be read from the 8279. There are two other signal inputs in this section. They are shift (SHIFT) and control/strobed (CNTL/STB). The logic levels at these two inputs are also stored as part

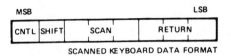

SCANNED KEYBOARD DATA FORMAT

Figure 7.62 Keycode byte format (Courtesy of Intel Corp.).

of the key code when a switch closure is detected. The format of the complete key code byte that is stored in the FIFO is shown in Fig. 7.62.

A status register is provided within the 8279 that contains flags that indicate the status of the *key code FIFO*. The bits of the status register and their meanings are shown in Fig. 7.63. Notice that the three least significant bits, which are labeled NNN, identify the number of key codes that are currently held in the FIFO. The next bit, F, indicates whether or not the FIFO is full. The two bits that follow it, U and O, represent two FIFO error conditions. O, which stands for overrun, indicates that an attempt was made to enter another key code into the FIFO when it was already full. This condition could occur if the microprocessor does not respond quick enough to the IRQ signal by reading key codes out of the FIFO. The other error condition, underrun (U), means that the microprocessor attempted to read the contents of the FIFO when it was empty. The microprocessor can read the contents of this register under software control.

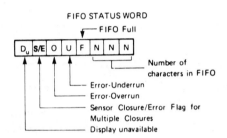

Figure 7.63 Status register (Courtesy oɪ Intel Corp.).

The display data lines include two 4-bit output ports, OUT A_0 through OUT A_3 and OUT B_0 through OUT B_3, that are used as display segment drive lines. Segment data that are output on these lines are held in a dedicated display RAM area within the 8279. This RAM is organized 16×8 and must be loaded with segment data by the microprocessor. In Fig. 7.61 we see that during each 640-ns scan time the segment data for one of the digits are output at the OUT A and OUT B ports.

The operation of the 8279 must be configured through software. Eight command words are provided for this purpose. These control words are loaded into the device by performing write (output) operations to the device with buffer address bit A_0 set to logic 1. Let us now look briefly at the function of each of these control words.

The first command *(command word 0)* is used to set the mode of operation for the keyboard and display. The general format of this word is shown in Fig. 7.64(a). Here we see that the three most significant bits are always reset. These three bits are a code by which the 8279 identifies which command is being issued by the microprocessor. The next two bits, which are labeled DD, are used to set the mode of operation for the display. The table in Fig. 7.64(b) shows the options that are available. After power-up reset, these bits are set to 01. From the table we see that this configures the display for 16 digits with left entry. By left entry we mean that characters are entered into the display starting from the left.

MSB   LSB

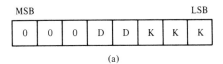

| 0 | 0 | 0 | D | D | K | K | K |

(a)

D	D	Display operation
0	0	8 8-bit character display — Left entry
0	1	16 8-bit character display — Left entry
1	0	8 8-bit character display — Right entry
1	1	16 8-bit character display — Right entry

(b)

K	K	K	Keyboard operation
0	0	0	Encoded Scan Keyboard — 2-Key Lockout
0	0	1	Decoded Scan Keyboard — 2-Key Lockout
0	1	0	Encoded Scan Keyboard — N-Key Rollover
0	1	1	Decoded Scan Keyboard — N-Key Rollover
1	0	0	Encoded Scan Sensor Matrix
1	0	1	Decoded Scan Sensor Matrix
1	1	0	Strobed Input, Encoded Display Scan
1	1	1	Strobed Input, Decoded Display Scan

(c)

Figure 7.64 (a) Command word 0 format (Courtesy of Intel Corp.); (b) display mode select codes (Courtesy of Intel Corp.); (c) keyboard select codes (Courtesy of Intel Corp.).

The three least significant bits of the command word (KKK) set the mode of operation of the display. They are used to configure the operation of the keyboard according to the table in Fig. 7.64(c). The default code at power up is 000 and selects encoded scan operation with two-key lockout.

EXAMPLE 7.30

What should be the value of command word 0 if the display is to be set for eight eight-segment digits with right entry and the keyboard for decoded scan with N-key rollover?

SOLUTION The three MSBs of the command word are always 0. The next two bits, DD, must be set to 10 for eight eight-segment digits with right entry. Finally, the three LSBs are set to 011 for decoded keyboard scan with N-key rollover. This gives

$$\text{COMMAND WORD 0} = 000DDKKK = 00010011_2$$

$$= 13_{16}$$

Command word 1 is used to set the frequency of operation of the 8279. It is designed to run at 100 kHz; however, in most applications a much higher frequency signal is available to supply its CLK input. For this reason, a *5-bit programmable prescaler* is provided within the 8279 to divide down the input frequency. The format of this command word is shown in Fig. 7.65.

Figure 7.65 Command word 1 format (Courtesy of Intel Corp.).

For instance, in a 5-MHz 8086-based microcomputer system, the PCLK output of the 8284 clock driver IC can be used for the 8279's clock input. PCLK is one-half the frequency of the oscillator or 2.5 MHz. In this case the divider P must be

$$P = 2.5 \text{ MHz}/100 \text{ kHz} = 25$$

Twenty-five expressed as a 5-bit binary number is

$$P = 11001_2$$

Therefore, the value of command word 1 written to the 8279 is

$$\text{COMMAND WORD 1} = 001PPPPP = 00111001_2$$

$$= 39_{16}$$

Let us skip now to *command word 6* because it is also used for initialization of the 8279. It can be used to initialize the complete display memory, the FIFO status,

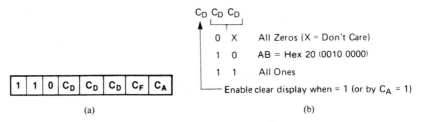

C_D C_D C_D

0	X	All Zeros (X = Don't Care)
1	0	AB = Hex 20 (0010 0000)
1	1	All Ones

Enable clear display when = 1 (or by C_A = 1)

| 1 | 1 | 0 | C_D | C_D | C_D | C_F | C_A |

(a)   (b)

Figure 7.66   (a) Command word 6 format (Courtesy of Intel Corp.); (b) C_D coding (Courtesy of Intel Corp.).

and the interrupt request output line. The format of this word is given in Fig. 7.66(a). The three C_D bits are used to control initialization of the display RAM. Figure 7.66(b) shows what values can be used in these locations. The C_F bit is provided for clearing the FIFO status and resetting the IRQ line. To perform the reset operation, a 1 must be written to C_F. The last bit, clear all (C_A), can be used to initiate both the C_D and C_F functions.

EXAMPLE 7.31

What clear operations are performed if the value of command word 6 written to the 8279 is $D2_{16}$?

SOLUTION   First we need to express the command word in binary form. This gives

$$\text{COMMAND WORD 6} = D2_{16} = 11010010_2$$

Note that the most significant C_D bit is set and the C_D bit that follows it is reset. This combination causes display memory to be cleared with all 0s. The C_F bit is also set and this causes the FIFO status and IRQ output to be reset.

As shown in Fig. 7.67, only one bit of *command word 7* is functional. This bit is labeled E and is an enable signal for what is called the special error mode. When this mode is enabled and the keyboard has N-key rollover selected, a multiple-key depression causes the S/E flag of the FIFO status register to be set. This flag can be read by the microprocessor through software.

| 1 | 1 | 1 | E | X | X | X | X | X = Don't care.

Figure 7.67   Command word 7 format (Courtesy of Intel Corp.).

The rest of the command codes are related to accessing the key code FIFO and display RAM. The key code FIFO is read only. However, before the microprocessor can access it, a read FIFO command must be issued to the 8279. This is *command word 2* and has the format shown in Fig. 7.68. When the 8279 is set up for keyboard scanning, the AI and AAA bits are don't-care states. Then all that needs to be done is issue the command $01000000_2 = 40_{16}$ to the 8279 and initiate read (input) cycles to the address of the 8279. For each read bus cycle, the key code at the top of the FIFO is read into the MPU.

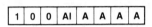 X = Don't Care

Figure 7.68 Command word 2 format (Courtesy of Intel Corp.).

The display RAM can be both read from or written into by the MPU. Just like for the FIFO, a command must be sent to the 8279 before reading or writing can be initiated. For instance, when the microprocessor wants to send new data to the display, it must first issue *command word 4*. This command has the format shown in Fig. 7.69. Here the AAAA in the four least significant bit locations is the address of the first location to be accessed. For instance, if 0000_2 is put into these bits of the command, the first write operation will be to the first location in display RAM. Moreover, if the AI bit is set in the command, autoincrement addressing is enabled. In this way, the display RAM address pointer is automatically incremented after the write operation is complete and a write cycle can be initiated to address 0001_2 of display RAM without first issuing another write command.

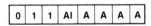

Figure 7.69 Command word 4 format (Courtesy of Intel Corp.).

The MPU can also read the contents of the display RAM in a similar way. This requires that *command word 3* be issued to the 8279. Figure 7.70 shows the format of this read display RAM command.

| 0 | 1 | 1 | AI | A | A | A | A |

Figure 7.70 Command word 3 format (Courtesy of Intel Corp.).

ASSIGNMENT

Section 7.2

1. What are the functions of the 8086's address and data bus lines relative to I/O operation?
2. Which signal indicates to the bus controller and external circuitry that the current bus cycle is for the I/O interface and not the memory interface?
3. In a maximum-mode system, which device produces the input (read), output (write), and bus control signals for the I/O interface?
4. Briefly describe the function of each block in the I/O interface circuit in Fig. 7.2.

Section 7.3

5. How large is the 8086's I/O address space?
6. What is the address range of page 0?
7. Which I/O addresses should not be assigned to external I/O ports?

Section 7.4

8. Describe the operation performed by the instruction IN AX,1A.

9. Write an instruction sequence to perform the same operation as that of the instruction in problem 8, but this time use register DX to address the I/O port.

10. Describe the operation performed by the instruction OUT 2A,AL.

11. Write an instruction sequence that will output the byte of data $0F_{16}$ to an output port at address 1000_{16}.

Section 7.5

12. If an 8086 running at 10 MHz inserts two wait states into all I/O bus cycles, what is the duration of a bus cycle in which a byte of data is being output?

13. If the 8086 in problem 12 was outputting a word of data to a word-wide port at I/O address $1A1_{16}$, what would be the duration of the bus cycle?

Section 7.6

14. Write a sequence of instructions to output the word contents of the memory location called DATA to output ports 0 and 1 in the circuit of Fig. 7.8.

Section 7.7

15. Describe the MODE 0, MODE 1, and MODE 2 I/O operations of the 8255A PPI.

16. What should be the control word if ports A, B, and C are to be configured for MODE 0 operation? Moreover, ports A and B are to be used as inputs and C as an output.

17. Assume that the control register of an 8255A resides at memory address 00100_{16}. Write an instruction sequence to load it with the control word formed in problem 16.

Section 7.8

18. What are the addresses of the A, B, and C ports of PPI 2 in the circuit of Fig. 7.17?

19. Assume that PPI 2 in Fig. 7.17 is configured as defined in problem 16. Write a program that will input the data at ports A and B, add these values together, and output the sum to port C.

Section 7.9

20. Distinguish between memory-mapped I/O and accumulator I/O.

21. Repeat problem 19 for the circuit in Fig. 7.18.

Section 7.10

22. Name a signal line that distinguishes an asynchronous communication interface from that of a synchronous communication interface.

23. Describe the sequence of signals that become active in Fig. 7.22 when the microcomputer transfers a character to the terminal.

24. Define a simplex, a half-duplex, and a full-duplex communication link.

Section 7.11

25. To write a byte of data to the 8251A, what logic levels must the microprocessor apply to control inputs C/$\overline{D}$, $\overline{RD}$, $\overline{WR}$, and $\overline{CS}$ of the 8251A?

26. The mode control register of an 8251A contains 11111111_2. What are the asynchronous character length, type of parity, and the number of STOP bits?

27. Write an instruction sequence to write the control word given in problem 26 to a memory-mapped 8251A that is located at address MODE.

28. Describe the difference between a mode instruction and a command instruction used in 8251A initialization.

Section 7.12

29. What are the inputs and outputs of counter 2 of an 8253?

30. Write a control word for counter 1 that selects the following options: load least significant byte only, mode 5 of operation, and binary counting.

31. What are the logic levels of inputs $\overline{CS}$, $\overline{RD}$, $\overline{WR}$, A_1, and A_0 when the byte in problem 30 is written to an 8253?

32. Write an instruction sequence that will load the control word in problem 30 into an 8253 that is located starting at address 01000_{16} of the memory address space.

33. Write an instruction sequence that will write the value 12_{16} into the least significant byte of the count register for counter 2 of an 8253 located starting at memory address 01000_{16}.

34. Repeat example 7.21 for the 8253 located at memory address 01000_{16}, but this time just read the least significant byte of the counter.

35. What is the maximum time delay that can be generated with the timer in Fig. 7.38? What will be the maximum time delay if the clock frequency is increased to 2 MHz?

36. What is the resolution of pulses generated with the 8253 in Fig. 7.38? What will be the resolution if the clock frequency is increased to 2 MHz?

37. Find the pulse width of the one-shot in Fig. 7.39 if the counter is loaded with the value 1000_{16}.

38. What count must be loaded into the square-wave generator of Fig. 7.41 to produce a 25-KHz output?

39. If the counter in Fig. 7.42 is loaded with the value 120_{16}, how long of a delay occurs before the strobe pulse is output?

Section 7.13

40. Are signal lines $\overline{MEMR}$ and $\overline{MEMW}$ of the 8237A used in the microprocessor interface?

41. Summarize the 8237A's DMA request/acknowledge handshake sequence.

42. What is the total number of user accessible registers in the 8237A?

43. Write an instruction sequence that will read the value of the address from the current address register into the AX register.

44. Assuming that an 8237A is located at I/O address DMA, what is the address of the command register?

45. Write an instruction sequence that will write the command word 00_{16} into the command register of an 8237A that is located at address DMA in the I/O address space.

46. Write an instruction sequence that will load the mode register for channel 2 with the mode byte obtained in example 7.28. Assume that the 8237A is located at I/O address DMA.

47. What must be output to the mask register in order to disable all the DRQ inputs?

48. Write an instruction that will read the contents of the status register into the AL register. Assume that the 8237A is located at address DMA.

Section 7.14

49. Referring to Fig. 7.55 what is the maximum number of keys that can be supported using all 24 I/O lines of an appropriately configured 8255A?

50. Specify the mode of operation for the keyboard and display when an 8279 is configured with command word 0 equal to $3F_{16}$.

51. Determine the clock frequency applied to the input of an 8279 if it needs command word 1 equal $1E_{16}$ to operate.

52. Summarize the function of each command word of the 8279.

Chapter 8

Interrupt Interface of the 8086 Microprocessor

8.1 INTRODUCTION

In Chapter 7 we covered the I/O interface of the 8086 microcomputer system. Here we continue with a special input interface, the *interrupt interface*. The following topics are presented in this chapter.

1. Types of interrupts
2. Interrupt address pointer table
3. Interrupt instructions
4. Masking of interrupts
5. External hardware interrupt interface
6. External hardware interrupt sequence
7. The 8259A programmable interrupt controller
8. Minimum-mode-system interrupt interface and maximum-mode-system interrupt interface
9. Software interrupts
10. Nonmaskable interrupt
11. Reset
12. Internal interrupt functions

Interrupts provide a mechanism for changing program environment. Transfer of program control is initiated by either the occurrence of an event internal to the 8086 microprocessor or an event in its external hardware. For instance, when an interrupt signal occurs indicating that an external device, such as a printer, requires service, the 8086 must suspend what it is doing in the main part of the program and pass control to a special routine that performs the function required by the device.

The section of program to which control is passed is called the *interrupt service routine*. When the 8086 terminates execution in the main program, it remembers the location where it left off and then picks up execution with the first instruction in the service routine. After this routine has run to completion, program control is returned to the point where the 8086 originally left the main body of the program.

The 8086 microcomputer is capable of implementing any combination of up to 256 interrupts. They are divided into five groups: *external hardware interrupts, software interrupts, internal interrupts*, the *nonmaskable interrupt*, and the *reset*. The function of the external hardware, software, and nonmaskable interrupts can be defined by the user. On the other hand, the internal interrupts and reset have dedicated system functions.

Hardware, software, and internal interrupts are serviced on a *priority* basis. Priority is achieved in two ways. First the interrupt processing sequence implemented in the 8086 tests for the occurrence of the various groups based on the hierarchy that follows: internal interrupt, nonmaskable interrupt, software interrupt, and external hardware interrupt. Thus we see that internal interrupts are the *highest-priority group* and the external hardware interrupts are the *lowest-priority group*. Second, the various interrupts are given different priority levels within a group by assigning to each a *type number*. *Type 0* identifies the highest-priority interrupt and *type 255* identifies the lowest-priority interrupt. A few of the type numbers are not available for use with software or hardware interrupts. This is because they are reserved for special interrupt functions of the 8086 such as internal interrupts. For instance, within the internal interrupt group, an interrupt known as divide error is assigned to type 0. Therefore, it has the highest priority of the internal interrupts. Another internal interrupt is called overflow and is assigned the type 4. Overflow is the lowest-priority internal interrupt.

The importance of priority lies in the fact that if an interrupt service routine has been initiated to perform a function at a specific priority level, only devices with higher priority can interrupt the active service routine. Lower-priority devices will have to wait until the routine is completed before their request for service can be acknowledged. For this reason, the user normally assigns tasks that must not be interrupted frequently to higher-priority levels and those that can be interrupted to lower-priority levels. An example of a high-priority service routine that should not be interrupted is that for a power failure.

We just pointed out that once an interrupt service routine is initiated, it can be interrupted only by a function that corresponds to a higher-priority level. For example, if a type 50 external hardware interrupt is in progress, it can be interrupted by any software interrupt, the nonmaskable interrupt, all internal interrupts, or any external interrupt with type number less than 50. That is, external hardware interrupts with priority levels equal to 50 or greater are *masked out*.

8.3 INTERRUPT ADDRESS POINTER TABLE

An *address pointer table* is used to link the interrupt type numbers to the locations of their service routines in the program storage memory. Figure 8.1 shows a map of the pointer table in the memory of the 8086 microcomputer system. Looking at this table, we see that it contains 256 *address pointers (vectors)*. One pointer corresponds to each of the interrupt types 0 through 255. These address pointers identify the starting locations of their service routines in program memory.

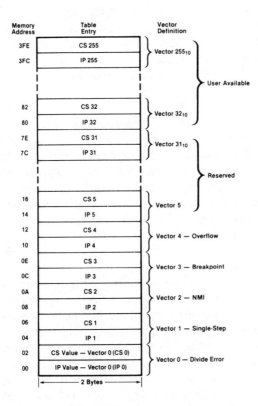

Figure 8.1 Interrupt vector table (Courtesy of Intel Corp.).

Notice that the pointer table is located at the low-address end of the memory address space. It starts at address 00000_{16} and ends at $003FE_{16}$. This represents the first 1K bytes of memory.

Each of the 256 pointers requires two words (4 bytes) of memory. These words are stored at even-address boundaries. The higher-addressed word of the two-word vector is called the *base address*. It identifies the program memory segment in which the service routine resides. For this reason, it is loaded into the code segment (CS) register within the 8086. The lower-addressed word of the vector is the *offset* of the first instruction of the service routine from the beginning of the code segment defined by the base address loaded into CS. This offset is loaded into the instruction pointer (IP) register. For example, the vector for type number 255, IP_{255} and CS_{255}, is stored at addresses $003FC_{16}$ and $003FE_{16}$.

Looking more closely at the table in Fig. 8.1, we find that the first five pointers have *dedicated functions*. Pointers 0, 1, 3, and 4 are required for the 8086's internal interrupts: *divide error, single step, breakpoint,* and *overflow*. Pointer 2 is used to identify the starting location of the nonmaskable interrupt's service routine. The next 27 pointers, 5 through 31, represent a *reserved portion* of the pointer table for the use of system operations. The rest of the table, the 224 pointers in the address range 00080_{16} through $003FF_{16}$, are available to the user for storage of interrupt vectors. These pointers correspond to type numbers 32 through 255 and can be employed by hardware or software interrupts. In the case of external hardware interrupts, the type number (priority level) is associated with an interrupt input level.

EXAMPLE 8.1

At what address should vector, CS_{50} and IP_{50} be stored in memory?

SOLUTION   Each vector requires four consecutive bytes of memory for storage. Therefore, its address can be found by multiplying the type number by 4. Since CS_{50} and IP_{50} represent the words of the type 50 interrupt pointer, we get

$$\text{Address} = 4 \times 50 = 200$$

Converting to binary form gives

$$\text{Address} = 11001000_2$$

and expressing it as a hexadecimal number results in

$$\text{Address} = C8_{16}$$

Therefore, IP_{50} is stored starting at $000C8_{16}$ and CS_{50} starting at $000CA_{16}$.

8.4 INTERRUPT INSTRUCTIONS

A number of instructions are provided in the instruction set of the 8086 for use with interrupt processing. These instructions are listed with a brief description of their functions in Fig. 8.2.

For instance, the first two instructions, which are STI and CLI, permit manipulation of the 8086's interrupt flag through software. STI stands for *set interrupt enable flag*. Execution of this instruction enables the external interrupt input (INTR) for operation. That is, it sets interrupt flag (IF). On the other hand, execution of CLI *(clear interrupt enable flag)* disables the external interrupt input. It does this by resetting IF.

The next instruction listed in Fig. 8.2 is the *software interrupt* instruction INT n. It is used to initiate a software vector call of a subroutine. Executing the instruction causes transfer of program control to the subroutine pointed to by the vector for type number n specified in the instruction.

Mnemonic	Meaning	Format	Operation	Flags Affected
CLI	Clear interrupt flag	CLI	$0 \rightarrow (IF)$	IF
STI	Set interrupt flag	STI	$1 \rightarrow (IF)$	IF
INT n	Type n software interrupt	INT n	$(Flags) \rightarrow ((SP) - 2)$ $0 \rightarrow TF,IF$ $(CS) \rightarrow ((SP) - 4)$ $(2 + 4 \cdot n) \rightarrow (CS)$ $(IP) \rightarrow ((SP) - 6)$ $(4 \cdot n) \rightarrow (IP)$	TF, IF
IRET	Interrupt return	IRET	$((SP)) \rightarrow (IP)$ $((SP) + 2) \rightarrow (CS)$ $((SP) + 4) \rightarrow (Flags)$ $(SP) + 6 \rightarrow (SP)$	All
INTO	Interrupt on overflow	INTO	INT 4 steps	TF, IF
HLT	Halt	HLT	Wait for an external interrupt or reset to occur	None
WAIT	Wait	WAIT	Wait for $\overline{TEST}$ input to go active	None

Figure 8.2 Interrupt instructions.

For example, execution of the instruction INT 50 initiates execution of a subroutine whose starting point is identified by vector 50 in the pointer table. That is, the 8086 reads IP_{50} and CS_{50} from addresses $000C8_{16}$ and $000CA_{16}$, respectively, in memory, loads these values into IP and CS, calculates a physical address, and starts to fetch instructions from this new location in program memory.

An *interrupt return* (IRET) instruction must be included at the end of each interrupt service routine. It is required to pass control back to the point in the program where execution was terminated due to the occurrence of the interrupt. When executed, IRET causes the three words IP, CS, and flags to be popped from the stack back into the internal registers of the 8086. This restores the original program environment.

INTO is the *interrupt on overflow* instruction. This instruction must be included after arithmetic instructions that can generate an overflow condition, such as add. It tests the overflow flag and if the flag is found to be set, a type 4 internal interrupt is initiated. This causes program control to be passed to an overflow service routine that is located at the starting address identified by the vector IP_4 at 00010_{16} and CS_4 at 00012_{16} of the pointer table.

The last two instructions associated with the interrupt interface are *halt* (HLT) and *wait* (WAIT). They produce similar responses by the 8086 and permit the operation of the 8086 to be synchronized to an event in external hardware. For instance, when HLT is executed, the 8086 suspends operation and enters the idle state. It no longer executes instructions; instead, it remains idle waiting for the occurrence of an external hardware interrupt or reset interrupt. With the occurrence of either of these two events, the 8086 resumes execution with the corresponding service routine.

If the WAIT instruction is used instead of the HLT instruction, the 8086 checks the logic level of the $\overline{TEST}$ input prior to going into the idle state. Only if $\overline{TEST}$ is at logic 1, will the MPU go into the idle state. While in the idle state, the 8086 continues to check the logic level at TEST looking for its transition to the 0 logic level. As TEST switches back to 0, execution resumes with the next sequential instruction in the program.

8.5 MASKING OF INTERRUPTS

An interrupt enable flag bit is provided within the 8086. Earlier we found that it is identified as IF. It affects only the external hardware interrupt interface, not the software or internal interrupts. The ability to initiate an external hardware interrupt at the INTR input is enabled by setting IF or masked out by resetting it. Through software, this can be done by executing the STI instruction or the CLI instruction, respectively.

During the initiation sequence of an interrupt service routine, the 8086 automatically clears IF. This masks out the occurrence of any additional external hardware interrupt. If necessary, the interrupt flag bit can be set with an STI instruction at the beginning of the service routine to reenable the INTR input. Otherwise, it is set at the end of the service routine.

8.6 EXTERNAL HARDWARE INTERRUPT INTERFACE

Up to this point in the chapter, we have introduced the interrupts of the 8086, its pointer table, interrupt instructions, and masking of interrupts. Let us now look at the *external hardware interrupt interface* of the 8086.

Minimum-System Interrupt Interface

We will begin with an 8086 microcomputer configured for the minimum-system mode. The interrupt interface for this system is illustrated in Fig. 8.3. Here we see that it includes the multiplexed address/data bus and dedicated interrupt signal lines INTR and INTA. Moreover, external circuitry is required to interface the interrupt inputs, INT_{32}

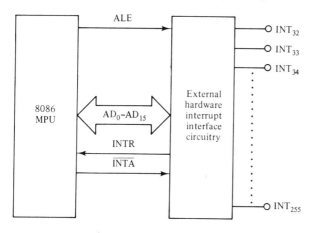

Figure 8.3 Minimum-mode 8086 system external hardware interrupt interface.

through INT_{255}, to the 8086's interrupt interface. This interface circuitry must identify which of the pending active interrupts has the highest priority and then pass its type number to the 8086.

In this circuit we see that the key interrupt interface signals are *interrupt request* (INTR) and *interrupt acknowledge* (INTA). The logic level input at the INTR line signals the 8086 that an external device is requesting service. The 8086 samples this input during the last clock period of each instruction execution cycle. Logic 1 represents an active interrupt request. INTR is *level triggered;* therefore, its active 1 level must be maintained until tested by the 8086. If it is not maintained, the request for service may not be recognized. Moreover, the 1 at INTR must be removed before the service routine runs to completion; otherwise, the same interrupt may be acknowledged a second time.

When an interrupt request has been recognized by the 8086, it signals this fact to external circuitry. It does this with pulses to logic 0 at its $\overline{INTA}$ output. Actually, there are just two pulses produced at $\overline{INTA}$ during the *interrupt acknowledge bus cycle.* The first pulse signals external circuitry that the interrupt request has been acknowledged and to prepare to send its type number to the 8086. The second pulse tells the external circuitry to put the type number on the data bus.

Notice that the lower 16 lines of the address/data bus, AD_0 through AD_{15}, are also part of the interrupt interface. During the second cycle in the interrupt acknowledge bus cycle, external circuitry must put an 8-bit type number on bus lines AD_0 through AD_7. The 8086 reads this number off the bus to identify which external device is requesting service. It uses the type number to generate the address of the interrupt's vector in the pointer table and to read the new values of CS and IP into the corresponding internal registers. CS and IP are transferred over the full 16-bit data bus. The old values

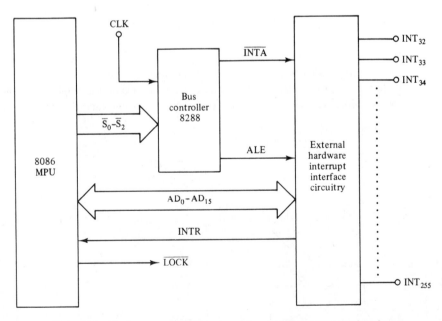

Figure 8.4 Maximum-mode 8086 system external hardware interrupt interface.

of CS, IP, and the internal flags are automatically pushed to the stack part of memory. These word-wide transfers take place over the complete data bus.

Maximum-Mode Interrupt Interface

The maximum-mode interrupt interface of the 8086 microcomputer is shown in Fig. 8.4. The primary difference between this interrupt interface and that shown for the minimum mode in Fig. 8.3 is that the 8288 bus controller has been added. In the maximum-mode system, the bus controller produces the $\overline{INTA}$ and ALE signals. Whenever the 8086 outputs an interrupt acknowledge bus status code, the 8288 generates pulses at its $\overline{INTA}$ output to signal external circuitry that the 8086 has acknowledged an interrupt request. This interrupt acknowledge bus status code, $\overline{S}_2\overline{S}_1\overline{S}_0 = 000$, is highlighted in Fig. 8.5.

Status inputs			CPU cycle	8288 command
$\overline{S}_2$	$\overline{S}_1$	$\overline{S}_0$		
0	0	0	Interrupt acknowledge	$\overline{INTA}$
0	0	1	Read I/O port	$\overline{IORC}$
0	1	0	Write I/O port	$\overline{IOWC}$, $\overline{AIOWC}$
0	1	1	Halt	None
1	0	0	Instruction fetch	$\overline{MRDC}$
1	0	1	Read memory	$\overline{MRDC}$
1	1	0	Write memory	$\overline{MWTC}$, $\overline{AMWC}$
1	1	1	Passive	None

Figure 8.5 Interrupt bus status code (Courtesy of Intel Corp.).

A second change in Fig. 8.4 is that the 8086 provides a new signal for the interrupt interface. This output, which is labeled $\overline{LOCK}$, is called the *bus priority lock* signal. $\overline{LOCK}$ is applied as an input to the *bus arbiter circuit*. In response to this signal, the arbitration logic assures that no other device can take over control of the system bus until the interrupt acknowledge bus cycle is completed.

8.7 EXTERNAL HARDWARE INTERRUPT SEQUENCE

In the preceding section we showed the interrupt interfaces for the external hardware interrupts in minimum-mode and maximum-mode 8086 systems. Now we will continue by describing in detail the events that take place during the interrupt request, interrupt acknowledge bus cycle, and device service routine.

The interrupt sequence begins when an external device requests service by activating one of the interrupt inputs, INT_{32} through INT_{255} of the external interrupt interface circuit in Fig. 8.3 or Fig. 8.4. For example, the INT_{50} input could be switched to the 1 logic level. This signals that the device associated with priority level 50 wants to be serviced.

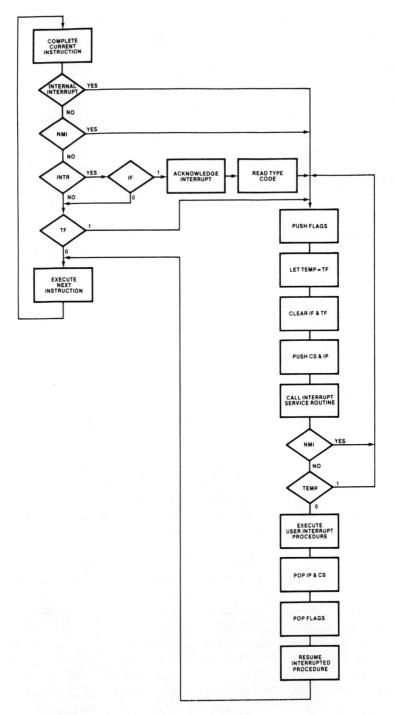

Figure 8.6 Interrupt processing sequence of the 8086 microprocessor (Courtesy of Intel Corp.).

The external circuitry evaluates the priority of this input. If there is no interrupt already in progress and this interrupt is of higher priority than any other interrupt that is simultaneously active, the external circuitry must issue a request for service to the 8086.

Let us assume that INT_{50} is the only active interrupt input. In this case, the external circuitry switches INTR to logic 1. This tells the 8086 that an interrupt is pending for service. To assure that it is recognized, the external circuitry must maintain INTR active until an interrupt acknowledge pulse is issued by the 8086.

Figure 8.6 is a flow diagram that outlines the events that take place when the 8086 processes an interrupt. The 8086 tests for an active interrupt during the last clock state of the current instruction. Notice that it tests first for the occurrence of an internal interrupt, then for the occurrence of the nonmaskable interrupt, and finally it checks the logic level of INTR to determine if an external hardware interrupt has occurred.

If INTR is logic 1, a request for service is recognized. Before the 8086 initiates the interrupt acknowledge sequence, it checks the setting of IF *(interrupt flag)*. If it is logic 0, external interrupts are masked out and the request is ignored. In this case, the next sequential instruction is executed. On the other hand, if IF is at logic 1, external hardware interrupts are enabled and the service routine is to be initiated.

Let us assume that IF is set to permit interrupts to occur when INTR is tested as 1. The 8086 responds by initiating the interrupt acknowledge bus cycles. This bus cycle is illustrated in Fig. 8.7. During T_1 of the first bus cycle, we see that a pulse is output on ALE but at the same time the address/data bus is put in the high-Z state. It stays in this state for the rest of the bus cycle. During periods T_2 and T_3, INTA is switched to logic 0. This signals external circuitry that the request for service has been granted. In response to this pulse, the logic 1 at INTR can be removed.

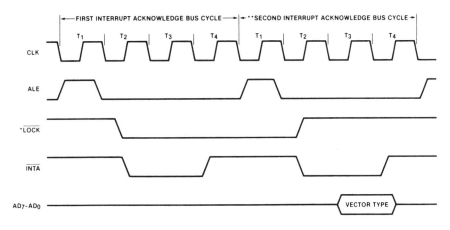

Figure 8.7 Interrupt acknowledge bus cycle (Courtesy of Intel Corp.).

The signal identified as $\overline{LOCK}$ is produced only in maximum-mode systems. Notice that $\overline{LOCK}$ is switched to logic 0 during T_2 of the first INTA bus cycle and is maintained at this level until T_2 of the second INTA bus cycle. During this time, the 8086 is prevented from accepting a HOLD request. Moreover, the $\overline{LOCK}$ output is used in external logic to lock other devices off the system bus, thereby assuring that the interrupt acknowledge sequence continues through to completion without interruption.

During the second interrupt acknowledge bus cycle, a similar signal sequence occurs. However, this interrupt acknowledge pulse tells the external circuitry to put the type number of the active interrupt on the data bus. External circuitry gates one of the interrupt codes $32 = 20_{16}$ through $255 = FF_{16}$, onto data bus lines AD_0 through AD_7. This code must be valid during periods T_3 and T_4 of the second interrupt acknowledge bus cycle.

The 8086 sets up its bus control signals for an input data transfer to read the type number off the data bus. $DT/\overline{R}$ and $\overline{DEN}$ are set to logic 0 to enable the external data bus circuitry and set it for input of data. Also, $M/\overline{IO}$ is set to 0, indicating that data are to be input from the interrupt interface. During this input operation, the byte interrupt code is read off the data bus. For the case of INT_{50}, this code would be $00110010_2 = 32_{16}$. This completes the interrupt acknowledge part of the interrupt sequence.

Looking at Fig. 8.6 we see that the 8086 first saves the contents of the flag register by pushing it to the stack. This requires one write cycle and 2 bytes of stack. Then it clears IF. This disables further external interrupts from requesting service. Actually, the TF flag is also cleared. This disables the single-step mode of operation if it happens to be active. Next, the 8086 automatically pushes the contents of CS and IP onto the stack. This requires two write cycles to take place over the system bus. The current value of the stack pointer is decremented by 2 as each of these values is put onto the top of the stack.

Now the 8086 knows the type number associated with the external device that is requesting service. It must next call the service routine by fetching the vector that defines its starting point from memory. The type number is internally multiplied by 4, and this result is used as the address of the first word of the interrupt vector in the pointer table. Two-word read operations (two bus cycles) are performed to read the two-word vector from memory. The first word, which is the lower-addressed word, is loaded into IP. The second, higher-addressed word, is loaded into CS. For instance, the vector for INT_{50} would be read from addresses $000C8_{16}$ and $000CA_{16}$.

The service routine is now initiated. That is, execution resumes with the first instruction of the service routine. It is located at the address generated from the new value in CS and IP. Figure 8.8 shows the structure of a typical interrupt service routine. The service routine must include PUSH instructions to save the contents of those inter-

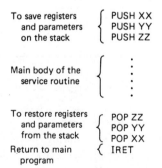

Figure 8.8 Structure of an interrupt service routine.

nal registers that it will use. In this way, their original contents are saved in the stack during execution of the routine.

At the end of the service routine, the original program environment must be restored. This is done by first popping the contents of the appropriate registers from the stack by executing POP instructions. Then an IRET instruction must be executed as the last instruction of the service routine. This instruction causes the old contents of the flags, CS, and IP to be popped from the stack back into the internal registers of the 8086. The original program environment has now been completely restored and execution resumes at the point in the program where it was interrupted.

8.8 THE 8259A PROGRAMMABLE INTERRUPT CONTROLLER

The 8259A is an LSI peripheral IC that is designed to simplify the implementation of the interrupt interface in an 8086 system. This device is known as a *programmable interrupt controller* or *PIC*. It is manufactured using the NMOS technology.

The operation of the PIC is programmable under software control and it can be configured for a wide variety of applications. Some of its programmable features are the ability to accept level-sensitive or edge-triggered inputs, the ability to be easily cascaded to expand from 8 to 64 interrupt inputs, and its ability to be configured to implement a wide variety of priority schemes.

Block Diagram of the 8259A

Let us begin our study of the PIC with its block diagram in Fig. 8.9(a). We just mentioned that the 8259A is treated as a peripheral in the 8086 microcomputer. Therefore, its operation must be initialized by the 8086 processor. The *host processor interface* is provided for this purpose. This interface consists of eight *data bus* lines D_0 through D_7 and control signals *read* ($\overline{RD}$), *write* ($\overline{WR}$), and *chip select* ($\overline{CS}$). The data bus is the path over which data are transferred between the 8086 and 8259A. These data can be command words, status information, or interrupt type numbers. Control input $\overline{CS}$ must be at logic 0 to enable the host processor interface. Moreover, $\overline{WR}$ and $\overline{RD}$ signal the 8259A whether data are to be written into or read from its internal registers. They also control the timing of these data transfers.

Two other signals are identified as part of the host processor interface. They are INT and $\overline{INTA}$. Together, these two signals provide the handshake mechanism by which the 8259A can signal the 8086 of a request for service and receive an acknowledgment that the request has been accepted. INT is the interrupt request output of the 8259A. It is applied directly to the INTR input of the 8086. Logic 1 is produced at this output whenever the 8259A receives a valid interrupt request.

On the other hand, $\overline{INTA}$ is an input of the 8259A. It is connected to the $\overline{INTA}$ output of the 8086. The 8086 pulses this input of the 8259A to logic 0 twice during the interrupt acknowledge bus cycle. Thereby, signaling the 8259A that the interrupt request has been acknowledged and that it should output the type number of the highest-priority active interrupt on data bus lines D_0 through D_7 such that it can be read by the 8086.

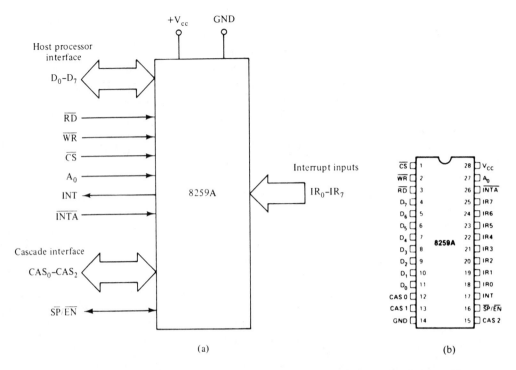

Figure 8.9 (a) Block diagram of the 8259A (Courtesy of Intel Corp.); (b) pin layout (Courtesy of Intel Corp.).

The last signal line involved in the host processor interface is the A_0 input. This input is supplied by an address line of the 8086 such as A_0. The logic level at this input is involved in the selection of the internal registers that are accessed during read and write operations.

At the other side of the block in Fig. 8.9(a), we find the eight *interrupt inputs* of the PIC. They are labeled IR_0 through IR_7. It is through these inputs that external devices issue a request for service. One of the software options of the 8259A permits these inputs to be configured for *level-sensitive* or *edge-triggered operation*. When configured for level-sensitive operation, logic 1 is the active level of the IR inputs. In this case, the request for service must be removed before the service routine runs to completion. Otherwise, the interrupt will be requested a second time and the service routine initiated again. Moreover, if the input returns to logic 0 before it is acknowledged by the 8086, the request for service will be missed.

Some external devices produce a short-duration pulse instead of a fixed logic level for use as an interrupt request signal. If the 8086 is busy servicing a higher priority interrupt when the pulse is produced, the request for service could be completely missed. To overcome this problem, the edge-triggered mode of operation is used.

Inputs of the 8259A that are set up for edge-triggered operation become active on the transition from the inactive 0 logic level to the active 1 logic level. This represents what is known as a *positive edge-triggered input*. The fact that this transition has occurred at an IR line is latched internal to the 8259A. If the IR input remains at the 1 logic level even after the service routine is completed, the interrupt is not reinitiated. Instead, it is locked out. To be recognized a second time, the input must first return to the 0 logic level and then be switched back to 1. The advantage of edge-triggered operation is that if the request at the IR input is removed before the 8086 acknowledges service of the interrupt, its request is maintained latched internal to the 8259A until it can be serviced.

The last group of signals on the PIC implement what is known as the *cascade interface*. As shown in Fig. 8.9(a), it includes bidirectional *cascading bus lines* CAS_0 through CAS_2 and a multifunction control line labeled $\overline{SP}/\overline{EN}$. The primary use of these signals is in cascaded systems where a number of 8259A ICs are interconnected in a master/slave configuration to expand the number of IR inputs from 8 to as high as 64.

In a cascaded system, the CAS lines of all 8259As are connected to provide a private bus between the master and slave devices. In response to the first $\overline{INTA}$ pulse during the interrupt acknowledge bus cycle, the master PIC outputs a 3-bit code on the CAS lines. This code identifies the highest-priority slave that is to be serviced. It is this device that is to be acknowledged for service. All slaves read this code off the *private cascading bus* and compare it to their internal ID code. A match condition at one slave tells that PIC that it has the highest-priority input. In response, it must put the type number of its highest-priority active input on the data bus during the second interrupt acknowledge bus cycle.

When the PIC is configured through software for the cascaded mode, the $\overline{SP}/\overline{EN}$ line is used as an input. This corresponds to its $\overline{SP}$ *(slave program)* function. The logic level applied at $\overline{SP}$ tells the device whether it is to operate as a master or slave. Logic 1 at this input designates master mode and logic 0 designates slave mode.

If the PIC is configured for single mode instead of cascade mode, $\overline{SP}/\overline{EN}$ takes on another function. In this case, it becomes an enable output which can be used to control the direction of data transfer through the bus transceiver that buffers the data bus.

A pin layout of the 8259A is given in Fig. 8.9(b).

Internal Architecture of the 8259A

Now that we have introduced the input/output signals of the 8259A, let us look at its internal architecture. Figure 8.10 is a block diagram of the PIC's internal circuitry. Here we find eight functional parts: the *data bus buffer, read/write logic, control logic, in-service register, interrupt request register, priority resolver, interrupt mask register,* and *cascade buffer/comparator.*

We will begin with the function of the data bus buffer and read/write logic sections. It is these parts of the 8259A that let the 8086 have access to the internal registers. Moreover, it provides the path over which interrupt type numbers are passed to the 8086. The data bus buffer is an 8-bit bidirectional three-state buffer that interfaces the internal circuitry of the 8259A to the data bus of the 8086. The direction, timing, and source or destination for data transfers through the buffer are under control of the outputs of the read/write logic block. These outputs are generated in response to control inputs $\overline{RD}$, $\overline{WR}$, A_0, and $\overline{CS}$.

The interrupt request register, in-service register, priority resolver, and interrupt mask register are the key internal blocks of the 8259A. The interrupt mask register

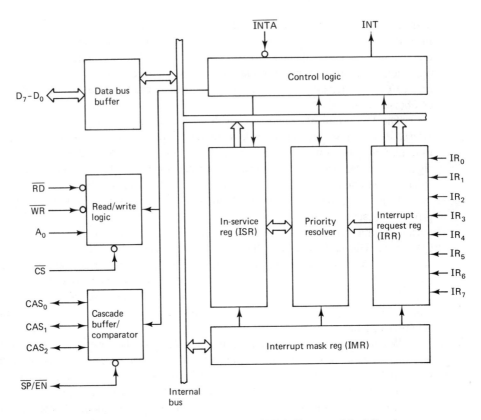

Figure 8.10 Internal architecture of the 8259A (Courtesy of Intel Corp.).

(IMR) can be used to enable or mask out individually the interrupt request inputs. It contains 8 bits identified by M_0 through M_7. These bits correspond to interrupt inputs IR_0 through IR_7, respectively. Logic 0 in a mask register bit position enables the corresponding interrupt input and logic 1 masks it out. This register can be read from or written into under software control.

On the other hand, the interrupt request register (IRR) stores the current status of the interrupt request inputs. It also contains one bit position for each of the IR inputs. The values in these bit positions reflect whether the interrupt inputs are active or inactive.

Which of the active interrupt inputs is identified as having the highest priority is determined by the priority resolver. This section can be configured to work using a number of different priority schemes through software. Following this scheme, it identifies the highest priority of the active interrupt inputs and signals the control logic that an interrupt is active. In response, the control logic causes the INT signal to be issued to the 8086.

The in-service register differs in that it stores the interrupt level that is presently being serviced. During the first $\overline{INTA}$ pulse in an interrupt acknowledge bus cycle, the level of the highest active interrupt is strobed into ISR. Loading of ISR occurs in response to output signals of the control logic section. This register cannot be written into by the microprocessor; however, its contents may be read as status.

The cascade buffer/comparator section provides the interface between master and slave 8259As. As we mentioned earlier, it is this interface that permits easy expansion of the interrupt interface using a master/slave configuration. Each slave has an *ID code* that is stored in this section.

Programming the 8259A

The way in which the 8259A operates is determined by how the device is programmed. Two types of command words are provided for this purpose. They are the *initialization command words* (ICW) and the *operational command words* (OCW). ICW commands are used to load the internal control registers of the 8259A. There are four such command words and they are identified as ICW_1, ICW_2, ICW_3, and ICW_4. On the other hand, the three OCW commands permit the 8086 to initiate variations in the basic operating modes defined by the ICW commands. These three commands are called OCW_1, OCW_2, and OCW_3.

Depending upon whether the 8259A is I/O mapped or memory mapped, the 8086 issues commands to the 8259A by initiating output or write cycles. This can be done by executing either the OUT or MOV instruction, respectively. The address put on the system bus during the output bus cycle must be decoded with external circuitry to chip select the peripheral. When an address assigned to the 8259A is on the bus, the output of the decoder must produce logic 0 at the $\overline{CS}$ input. This signal enables the read/write logic within the PIC and data applied at D_0 through D_7 are written into the command register within the control logic section synchronously with a write strobe at $\overline{WR}$.

The interrupt request input (INTR) of the 8086 must be disabled whenever commands are being issued to the 8259A. This can be done by clearing the interrupt enable flag by executing the CLI (clear interrupt enable flag) instruction. After completion of the command sequence, the interrupt input must be reenabled. To do this, the 8086 must execute the STI (set interrupt enable flag) instruction.

The flow diagram in Fig. 8.11 shows the sequence of events that the 8086 must perform to initialize the 8259A with ICW commands. The cycle begins with the 8086 outputting initialization command word ICW_1 to the address of the 8259A.

The moment that ICW_1 is written into the control logic section of the 8259A certain internal setup conditions automatically occur. First the internal sequence logic is set up such that the 8259A will accept the remaining ICWs as designated by ICW_1. It turns out that if the least significant bit of ICW_1 is logic 1, command word ICW_4 is required in the initialization sequence. Moreover, if the next least significant bit of ICW_1 is logic 0, the command word ICW_3 is also required.

In addition to this, writing ICW_1 to the 8259A clears ISR and IMR. Also three operation command word bits, *special mask mode* (SMM) in OCW_3, *interrupt request register* (IRR) in OCW_3, and *end of interrupt* (EOI) in OCW_2, are cleared to logic 0. Furthermore, the *fully masked mode* of interrupt operation is entered with an initial priority assignment such that IR_0 is the highest-priority input and IR_7 the lowest-priority input. Finally, the edge-sensitive latches associated with the IR inputs are all cleared.

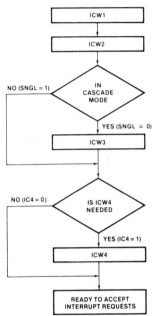

Figure 8.11 Initialization sequence of the 8259A (Courtesy of Intel Corp.).

If the LSB of ICW_1 was initialized to logic 0, one additional event occurs. This is that all bits of the control register associated with ICW_4 are cleared.

In Fig. 8.11 we see that once the 8086 starts initialization of the 8259A by writing ICW_1 into the control register, it must continue the sequence by writing ICW_2 and then optionally ICW_3 and ICW_4 in that order. Notice that it is not possible to modify just one of the initialization command registers. Instead, all words that are required to define the device's operating mode must be output once again.

We found that all four words need not always be used to initialize the 8259A. However, for its use in the 8086 system, words ICW_1, ICW_2, and ICW_4 are always required. ICW_3 is optional and is needed only if the 8259A is to function in the cascade mode.

Initialization Command Words

Now that we have introduced the initialization sequence of the 8259A, let us look more closely at the functions controlled by each of the initialization command words. We will begin with ICW_1. Its format and bit functions are identified in Fig. 8.12(a). Notice that address bit A_0 is included as a ninth bit and it must be logic 0. This corresponds to an even address boundary.

Here we find that the logic level of the LSB D_0 of the initialization word indicates to the 8259A whether or not ICW_4 will be included in the programming sequence. As we mentioned earlier, logic 1 at D_0 (IC_4) specifies that it is needed. The next bit, D_1 (SNGL), selects between *single device* or *multidevice cascaded mode* of operation. When D_1 is set to logic 0, the internal circuitry of the 8259A is configured for cascaded mode. Selecting this state also sets up the initialization sequence such that ICW_3 must

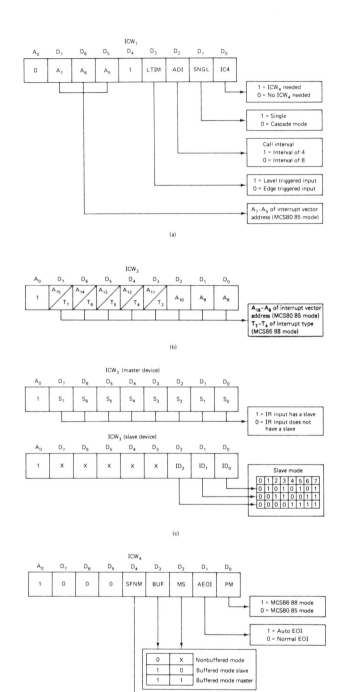

Figure 8.12 (a) ICW₁ format (Courtesy of Intel Corp.); (b) ICW₂ format (Courtesy of Intel Corp.); (c) ICW₃ format (Courtesy of Intel Corp.); (d) ICW₄ format (Courtesy of Intel Corp.).

be issued as part of the initialization cycle. Bit D_2 has functions specified for it in Fig. 8.12(a). However, it can be ignored when the 8259A is being connected to the 8086 and is a don't-care state. D_3, which is labeled LTIM, defines whether the eight IR inputs operate in the level-sensitive or edge-triggered mode. Logic 1 in D_3 selects level-triggered operation and logic 0 selects edge-triggered operation. Finally, bit D_4 is fixed at the 1 logic level and the three MSBs D_5 through D_7 are not required in 8086-based microcomputer systems.

EXAMPLE 8.2

What value should be written into ICW_1 in order to configure the 8259A such that ICW_4 is needed in the initialization sequence, the system is going to use multiple 8259As, and its inputs are to be level sensitive? Assume that all unused bits are to be logic 0. Give the result in both binary and hexadecimal form.

SOLUTION   Since ICW_4 is to be initialized, D_0 must be logic 1.

$$D_0 = 1$$

For cascaded mode of operation, D_1 must be 0.

$$D_1 = 0$$

and for level-sensitive inputs D_3 must be 1.

$$D_3 = 1$$

Bits D_2 and D_5 through D_7 are don't-care states and are all made logic 0.

$$D_2 = D_5 = D_6 = D_7 = 0$$

Moreover, D_4 must be fixed at the 1 logic level.

$$D_4 = 1$$

This gives the complete command word

$$D_7D_6D_5D_4D_3D_2D_1D_0 = 00011001_2 = 19_{16}$$

The second initialization word, ICW_2, has a single function in the 8086 microcomputer. As shown in Fig. 8.12(b), its five most significant bits D_7 through D_3 define a fixed binary code T_7 through T_3 that is used as the most significant bits of its type number. Whenever the 8259A puts the 3-bit interrupt type number corresponding to its active input onto the bus, it is automatically combined with the value T_7 through T_3 to form an 8-bit type number. The three least significant bits of ICW_2 are not used. Notice that logic 1 must be output on A_0 when this command word is put on the bus.

EXAMPLE 8.3

What should be programmed into register ICW_2 if the type numbers output on the bus by the device are to range from $F0_{16}$ through $F7_{16}$?

SOLUTION To set the 8259A up such that type numbers are in the range $F0_{16}$ through $F7_{16}$, its device code bits must be

$$D_7D_6D_5D_4D_3 = 11110_2$$

The lower three bits are don't-care states and all can be 0s. This gives the command word

$$D_7D_6D_5D_4D_3D_2D_1D_0 = 11110000_2 = F0_{16}$$

The information of initialization word ICW_3 is required by only those 8259As that are configured for the cascaded mode of operation. Figure 8.12(c) shows its bits. Notice that ICW_3 is used for different functions depending on whether the device is a master or slave. In the case of a master, bits D_0 through D_7 of the word are labeled S_0 through S_7. These bits correspond to IR inputs IR_0 through IR_7, respectively. They identify whether or not the corresponding IR input is supplied by either the INT output of a slave or directly by an external device. Logic 1 loaded in an S position indicates that the corresponding IR input is supplied by a slave.

On the other hand, ICW_3 for a slave is used to load the device with a 3-bit identification code $ID_2ID_1ID_0$. This number must correspond to the IR input of the master to which the slave's INT output is wired. The ID code is required within the slave so that it can be compared to the cascading code output by the master on CAS_0 through CAS_2.

EXAMPLE 8.4

Assume that a master PIC is to be configured such that its IR_0 through IR_3 inputs are to accept inputs directly from external devices but IR_4 through IR_7 are to be supplied by the INT outputs of slaves. What code should be used for the initialization command word ICW_3?

SOLUTION For IR_0 through IR_3 to be configured to allow direct inputs from external devices, bits D_0 through D_3 of ICW_3 must be logic 0.

$$D_3D_2D_1D_0 = 0000_2$$

The other IR inputs of the master are to be supplied by INT outputs of slaves. Therefore, their control bits must be all 1.

$$D_7D_6D_5D_4 = 1111_2$$

This gives the complete command word

$$D_7D_6D_5D_4D_3D_2D_1D_0 = 11110000_2 = F0_{16}$$

The fourth control word, ICW_4, which is shown in Fig. 8.12(d), is used to configure the device for use with the 8086 and selects various features that are available in its operation. The LSB D_0, which is called microprocessor mode (μPM), must be set to logic 1 whenever the device used is connected to the 8086. The next bit, D_1, is labeled

AEOI for *automatic end of interrupt*. If this mode is enabled by writing logic 1 into the bit location, the EOI *(end of interrupt)* command does not have to be issued as part of the service routine.

Of the next two bits in ICW$_4$, BUF is used to specify whether or not the 8259A is to be used in a system where the data bus is buffered with a bidirectional bus transceiver. When buffered mode is selected, the $\overline{SP}/\overline{EN}$ line is configured as $\overline{EN}$. As indicated earlier, $\overline{EN}$ is a control output that can be used to control the direction of data transfer through the bus transceiver. It switches to logic 0 whenever data are transferred from the 8259A to the 8086.

If buffered mode is not selected, the $\overline{SP}/\overline{EN}$ line is configured to work as the master/slave mode select input. In this case, logic 1 at the $\overline{SP}$ input selects master mode operation and logic 0 selects slave mode.

Assume that the buffered mode was selected; then the $\overline{SP}$ input is no longer available to select between the master and slave modes of operation. Instead, the MS bit of ICW$_4$ defines whether the 8259A is a master or slave device.

Bit D_4 is used to enable or disable another operational option of the 8259A. This option is known as the *special fully nested mode*. This function is only used in conjunction with the cascaded mode. Moreover, it is enabled only for the master 8259A, not for the slaves. This is done by setting the SFNM bit to logic 1.

The 8259A is put into the fully nested mode of operation as command word ICW$_4$ is loaded. When an interrupt is initiated in a cascaded system that is configured in this way, the occurrence of another interrupt at the slave corresponding to the original interrupt is masked out even if it is of higher priority. This is because the bit in ISR of the master 8259A that corresponds to the slave is already set; therefore, the master 8259A ignores all interrupts of equal or lower priority.

This problem is overcome by enabling special fully nested mode of operation at the master. In this mode, the master will respond to those interrupts that are at lower or higher priority than the active level.

The last 3 bits of ICW$_4$, D_5 through D_7, must always be logic 0 and the word must be written to an odd-address boundary.

Operational Command Words

Once the appropriate ICW commands have been issued to the 8259A, it is ready to operate in the fully nested mode. Three operational command words are also provided for controlling the operation of the 8259A. These commands permit further modifications to be made to the operation of the interrupt interface after it has been initialized. Unlike the initialization sequence, which requires that the ICWs be output in a special sequence after power-up, the OCWs can be issued under program control whenever needed and in any order.

The first operational command word, OCW$_1$, is used to access the contents of the interrupt mask register (IMR). A read operation can be performed to the register to determine its present status. Moreover, write operations can be performed to set or reset its bits. This permits selective masking of the interrupt inputs. Notice in Fig. 8.13(a) that bits D_0 through D_7 of command word OCW$_1$ are identified as mask bits M_0 through M_7, respectively. In hardware, these bits correspond to interrupt inputs IR_0 through IR_7,

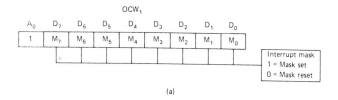

(a)

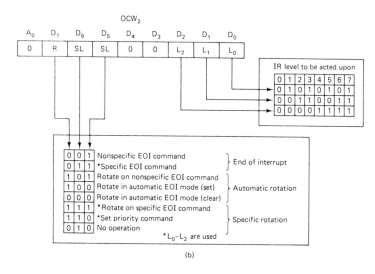

(b)

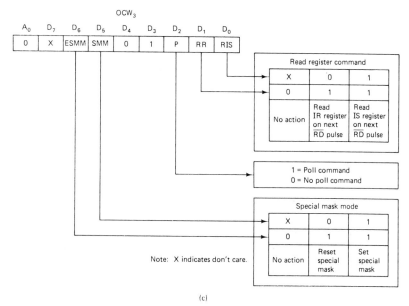

Figure 8.13 (a) OCW_1 format (Courtesy of Intel Corp.); (b) OCW_2 format (Courtesy of Intel Corp.); (c) OCW_3 format (Courtesy of Intel Corp.).

respectively. Setting a bit to logic 1 masks out the associated interrupt input. On the other hand, clearing it to logic 0 enables the interrupt input.

For instance, writing $F0_{16} = 11110000_2$ into the register causes inputs IR_0 through IR_3 to be enabled and IR_4 through IR_7 to be disabled. Input A_0 must be logic 1 whenever the OCW_1 command is issued.

EXAMPLE 8.5

What should be the OCW_1 code if interrupt inputs IR_0 through IR_3 are to be disabled and IR_4 through IR_7 enabled?

SOLUTION For IR_0 through IR_3 to be disabled, their corresponding bits in the mask register must be made logic 1.

$$D_3D_2D_1D_0 = 1111_2$$

On the other hand, for IR_4 through IR_7 to be enabled D_4 through D_7 must be logic 0.

$$D_7D_6D_5D_4 = 0000_2$$

Therefore, the complete word for OCW_1 is

$$D_7D_6D_5D_4D_3D_2D_1D_0 = 00001111_2 = 0F_{16}$$

The second operational command word OCW_2 selects the appropriate priority scheme and assigns an IR level for those schemes that require a specific interrupt level. The format of OCW_2 is given in Fig. 8.13(b). Here we see that the three LSBs define the interrupt level. For example, using $L_2L_1L_0 = 000_2$ in these locations specifies interrupt level 0, which corresponds to input IR_0.

The other three active bits of the word D_7, D_6, and D_5 are called *rotation* (R), *specific level* (SL), and *end of interrupt* (EOI), respectively. They are used to select a priority scheme according to the table in Fig. 8.13(b). For instance, if these bits are all logic 1, the priority scheme known as *rotate on specific EOI command* is enabled. Since this scheme requires a specific interrupt, its value must be included in $L_2L_1L_0$. A_0 must be logic 0 whenever this command is issued to the 8259A.

EXAMPLE 8.6

What OCW_2 must be issued to the 8259A if the priority scheme rotate on nonspecific EOI command is to be selected?

SOLUTION To enable the rotate on a nonspecific EOI command priority scheme, bits D_7 through D_5 must be set to 101. Since a specific level does not have to be specified, the rest of the bits in the command word can be 0. This gives OCW_2 as

$$D_7D_6D_5D_4D_3D_2D_1D_0 = 10100000_2 = A0_{16}$$

The last control word OCW_3, which is shown in Fig. 8.13(c), permits reading of the contents of the ISR or IRR registers through software, issue of the poll command, and enable/disable of the special mask mode. Bit D_1, which is called *read register* (RR), is set to 1 to initiate reading of either the in-service register (ISR) or interrupt request register (IRR). At the same time, bit D_0, which is labeled RIS, selects between ISR and IRR. Logic 0 in RIS selects IRR and logic 1 selects ISR. In response to this command, the 8259A puts the contents of the selected register on the bus, where it can be read by the 8086.

If the next bit, D_2, in OCW_3 is logic 1, a *poll command* is issued to the 8259A. The result of issuing a poll command is that the next $\overline{RD}$ pulse to the 8259A is interpreted as an interrupt acknowledge. In turn, the 8259A causes the ISR register to be loaded with the value of the highest-priority active interrupt. After this, a *poll word* is automatically put on the data bus. The 8086 must read it off the bus.

Figure 8.14 illustrates the format of the poll word. Looking at this word, we see that the MSB is labeled I for interrupt. The logic level of this bit indicates to the 8086 whether or not an interrupt input was active. Logic 1 indicates that an interrupt is active. The three LSBs $W_2W_1W_0$ identify the priority level of the highest-priority active interrupt input. This poll word can be decoded through software and when an interrupt is found to be active a branch is initiated to the starting point of its service routine. The poll command represents a software method of identifying whether or not an interrupt has occurred; therefore, the INTR input of the 8086 should be disabled.

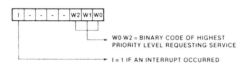

W0-W2 = BINARY CODE OF HIGHEST PRIORITY LEVEL REQUESTING SERVICE

I = 1 IF AN INTERRUPT OCCURRED

Figure 8.14 Poll word format (Courtesy of Intel Corp.).

D_5 and D_6 are the remaining bits of OCW_3 for which functions are defined. They are used to enable or disable the special mask mode. ESMM *(enable special mask mode)* must be logic 1 to permit changing of the status of the special mask mode with the SMM *(special mask mode)* bit. Logic 1 at SMM enables the special mask mode of operation. If the 8259A is initially configured for the fully nested mode of operation, only interrupts of higher priority are allowed to interrupt an active service routine. However, by enabling the special mask mode, interrupts of higher or lower priority are enabled, but those of equal priority remain masked out.

EXAMPLE 8.7

Write a program that will initialize an 8259A with the initialization command words ICW_1, ICW_2, and ICW_3 derived in examples 8.2, 8.3, and 8.4, respectively. Moreover, ICW_4 is to be equal to $1F_{16}$. Assume that the 8259A resides at address $0A000_{16}$ in the memory address space.

SOLUTION Since the 8259A resides in the memory address space, we can use a series of move instructions to write the initialization command words into its registers. However, before doing this, we must first disable interrupts. This is done with the instruction

```
          CLI                         ; DISABLE INTERRUPTS
```

Next we will set up a data segment starting at address 00000_{16}.

```
MOV   AX, 0
                        ; CREATE A DATA SEGMENT AT 00000₁₆
MOV   DS, AX
```

Now we are ready to write the command words to the 8259A.

```
MOV   AL, 19       ; LOAD ICW 1

MOV   [A000], AL   ; WRITE ICW 1 TO 8259A

MOV   AL, F0       ; LOAD ICW 2

MOV   [A001], AL   ; WRITE ICW 2 to 8259A

MOV   AL, F0       ; LOAD ICW 3

MOV   [A001], AL   ; WRITE ICW 3 to 8259A

MOV   AL, 1F       ; LOAD ICW 4

MOV   [A001], AL   ; WRITE ICW 4 to 8259A
```

Initialization is now complete and the interrupts can be enabled.

```
STI                      ; ENABLE INTERRUPTS
```

8.9 MINIMUM-MODE-SYSTEM AND MAXIMUM-MODE-SYSTEM INTERRUPT INTERFACES USING THE 8259A

Now that we have introduced the 8259A programmable interrupt controller, let us look at how it is used to implement the interrupt interface in the 8086 microcomputer system. The circuit in Fig. 8.15 shows three 8259A devices connected in a *master/slave config-uration* to construct an interrupt interface for a minimum-mode 8086 microcomputer system.

Let us begin by tracing the path taken from the interrupt request inputs of the slaves to the interrupt request input of the 8086. A request for interrupt service is initi-ated at an IR input of a slave. This causes the INT output of the corresponding slave to switch to logic 1. Looking at the circuit, we see that the INT output of the slave PICs are applied to separate interrupt inputs on the master PIC. Then the INT output of the master is supplied directly to the interrupt request input of the 8086.

Notice that the demultiplexed address bus and data bus lines connect to all three 8259As in parallel. It is over these lines that the 8086 initializes the internal registers of the 8259As, reads the contents of these registers, and reads the type number of the active interrupt during the interrupt acknowledge bus cycle. Each 8259A should reside at a unique address. In this way, during read or write cycles to the interrupt interface,

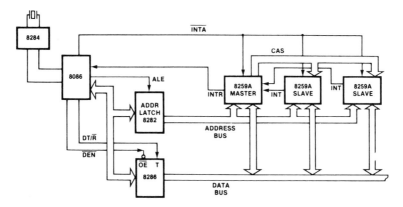

Figure 8.15 Minimum-mode interrupt interface using the 8259A (Courtesy of Intel Corp.).

the address output on the bus can be decoded to produce an enable signal to chip-select the appropriate device.

The last group of signals in the interrupt interface are the CAS bus. Notice that these lines on all three PICs are connected in parallel. It is over these lines that the master signals the slaves whether or not the interrupt request has been acknowledged. The master/slave connection is shown in more detail in Fig. 8.16.

Whenever an interrupt input is active at the master or at a slave and the priority is higher than that of an already active interrupt, the master controller switches INTR to logic 1. This signals the 8086 that an external device needs to be serviced. As long

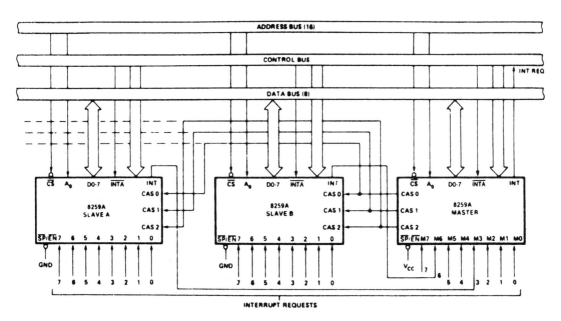

Figure 8.16 Master/slave connection.

as the interrupt flag within the 8086 is set to 1, the interrupt interface is enabled and the interrupt request will be accepted. Therefore, the interrupt acknowledge bus cycle is initiated. As the first pulse is output at interrupt acknowledge (INTA), the master PIC is signaled to output the 3-bit cascade code of the device whose interrupt request is being acknowledged on the CAS bus. The slaves read this code and compare it to their internal code. In this way, the slave corresponding to the code is signaled to output the type number of its highest-priority active interrupt onto the data bus during the second interrupt acknowledge bus cycle. The 8086 reads this number off the bus and then initiates a vectored transfer of control to the starting point of the corresponding service routine in program memory.

Figure 8.17 illustrates a similar interrupt interface implemented in a maximum-mode 8086 microcomputer system.

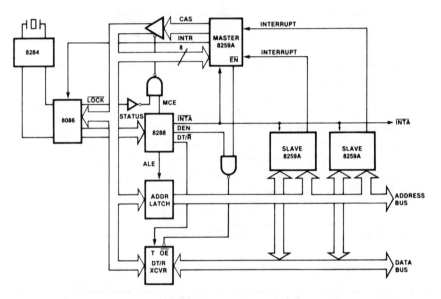

Figure 8.17 Maximum-mode interrupt interface using the 8259A (Courtesy of Intel Corp.).

8.10 SOFTWARE INTERRUPTS

The 8086 system is capable of implementing up to 256 software interrupts. They differ from the external hardware interrupts in that their service routines are initiated in response to the execution of a software interrupt instruction, not an event in external hardware.

The INT n instruction is used to initiate a software interrupt. Earlier in this chapter we indicated that ''n'' represents the type number associated with the service routine. The software interrupt service routines are vectored to, using pointers from the same memory locations as the corresponding external hardware interrupts. These locations are shown in the pointer table of Fig. 8.1. Our earlier example was INT 50. It has a type number of 50 and causes a vector in program control to the service routine whose starting address is defined by the values of IP and CS stored at addresses $00C8_{16}$ through $00CB_{16}$, respectively.

The mechanism by which a software interrupt is initiated is similar to that described for the external hardware interrupts. However, no external interrupt acknowledge bus cycles are initiated. Instead, control is passed to the start of the service routine immediately upon completion of execution of the interrupt instruction. As usual, the old flags, old CS, and old IP are automatically saved on the stack and then IF and TF are cleared.

If necessary, the contents of other internal registers can be saved on the stack by including the appropriate PUSH instructions at the beginning of the service routine. Toward the end of the service routine, POP instructions must be included to restore these registers. Finally, IRET instruction is included to reenable interrupts and restore the original program environment.

Software interrupts are of higher priority than the external interrupts and are not masked out by IF. The software interrupts are actually *vectored subroutine calls*. A common use of these software routines is as *emulation routines* for more complex functions. For instance, INT_{50} could define a *floating-point addition instruction* and INT_{51} a *floating-point subtraction instruction*. These emulation routines are written using assembly language instructions, are assembled into machine code, and then are stored in the main memory of the 8086 microcomputer system. Other examples of their use are for *supervisor calls* from an operating system and for *testing* of external hardware interrupt service routines.

8.11 NONMASKABLE INTERRUPT

The nonmaskable interrupt (NMI) is another interrupt that is initiated from external hardware. However, it differs from the other external hardware interrupts in several ways. First, it cannot be masked out with the IF flag. Second, requests for service by this interrupt are signaled to the 8086 with the 1 logic level at its NMI input, not the INTR input. Third, the NMI input is positive edge triggered. Therefore, a request for service is latched internal to the 8086.

If the contents of the NMI latch is sampled as being active for two consecutive clock cycles, it is recognized and the nonmaskable interrupt sequence initiated. Initiation of NMI causes the current flags, current CS, and current IP to be pushed onto the stack. Moreover, the interrupt enable flag is cleared to disable all external hardware interrupts and the trap flag is cleared to disable the single-step mode of operation.

As shown in Fig. 8.1, NMI has a dedicated type number. It automatically vectors from the type 2 vector location in the pointer table. This vector is stored in memory at word addresses 0008_{16} and $000A_{16}$.

Typically, the NMI is assigned to hardware events that must be responded to immediately. Two examples are the detection of a power failure and detection of a memory read error.

The RESET input of the 8086 provides hardware with the means for initializing the microcomputer. This is typically done at power-up to provide an orderly startup of the system.

Figure 8.18(a) shows that the reset interface of the 8086 includes part of the 8284 clock generator device. The 8284 contains circuitry that makes it easy to implement the hardware reset function. Notice that the $\overline{RES}$ input (pin 11) of the clock generator is attached to an *RC* circuit. The signal at $\overline{RES}$ is applied to the input of a Schmitt trigger circuit. If the voltage across the capacitor is below the 1-logic-level threshold of the Schmitt trigger, the RESET output (pin 10) stays at logic 1. This output is supplied to the RESET input at pin 21 of the 8086. It can also be applied in parallel to reset inputs on LSI peripheral devices such that they are also initialized at power-on.

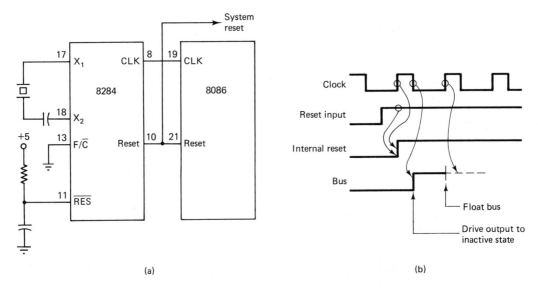

(a)   (b)

Figure 8.18 (a) Reset interface of the 8086 (Courtesy of Intel Corp.); (b) reset timing sequence (Courtesy of Intel Corp.).

At power-on, $\overline{RES}$ of the 8284 is shorted to ground through the capacitor. This represents logic 0 at the input of the Schmitt trigger and RESET switches to logic 1. At the RESET input of the 8086, this signal is synchronized to the 0-to-1 edge of CLK. This is shown in the waveforms of Fig. 8.18(b). RESET must be held at logic 1 for a minimum of four clock cycles; otherwise, it will not be recognized.

The 8086 terminates operation on the 0 to 1 edge of the internal reset signal. Its bus is put in the high-Z state and the control signals are switched to their inactive states. These signal states are summarized in Fig. 8.19. Here we see that in a minimum-mode system signals AD_0 through AD_{15}, A_{16}/S_3 through A_{19}/S_6, and $\overline{BHE}/S_7$ are immediately put in the high-Z state. On the other hand, signal lines M/$\overline{IO}$, DT/$\overline{R}$, $\overline{DEN}$, $\overline{WR}$, $\overline{RD}$, and $\overline{INTA}$ are first forced to logic 1 for one clock interval and then they are put in the

Signals	Condition
AD_{15-0}	Three-state
A_{19-16}/S_{6-3}	Three-state
BHE/S_7	Three-state
$\overline{S_2}/(M/\overline{IO})$	Driven to "1" then three-state
$\overline{S_1}/(DT/\overline{R})$	Driven to "1" then three-state
$\overline{S_0}/\overline{DEN}$	Driven to "1" then three-state
$\overline{LOCK}/\overline{WR}$	Driven to "1" then three-state
$\overline{RD}$	Driven to "1" then three-state
$\overline{INTA}$	Driven to "1" then three-state
ALE	0
HLDA	0
$\overline{RQ}/\overline{GT}_0$	1
$\overline{RQ}/\overline{GT}_1$	1
QS_0	0
QS_1	0

Figure 8.19 Bus and control signal status during system reset (Courtesy of Intel Corp.).

high-Z state synchronously with the positive edge of the next clock pulse. Moreover, signal lines ALE and HLDA are forced to their inactive 0 logic level. The 8086 remains in this state until the RESET input is returned to logic 0.

In the maximum-mode system, the 8086 responds in a similar way. However, this time the $\overline{S_2}\overline{S_1}\overline{S_0}$ outputs, which are inputs to the 8288 bus controller, are also forced to 1 logic and then put into the high-Z state. These inputs of the 8288 have internal pull-up resistors. Therefore, with the signal lines in the high-Z state, the input to the bus controller is $\overline{S_2}\overline{S_1}\overline{S_0} = 111$. In response, its control outputs are set to ALE = 0, DEN = 0, DT/$\overline{R}$ = 1, MCE/$\overline{PDEN}$ = 0/1, and all of its command outputs are switched to the 1 logic level. Moreover, outputs QS_0 and QS_1 of the 8086 are both held at logic 0 and the $\overline{RQ}/\overline{GT}_0$ and $\overline{RQ}/\overline{GT}_1$ lines are held at logic 1.

When RESET returns to logic 0, the 8086 initiates its internal initialization routine. The flags are all cleared; the instruction pointer is set to 0000_{16}; the CS register is set to $FFFF_{16}$; the DS register is set to 0000_{16}; the SS register is set to 0000_{16}; the ES register is set to 0000_{16}; and the instruction queue is emptied. The table in Fig. 8.20 summarizes this state.

CPU COMPONENT	CONTENT
Flags	Clear
Instruction Pointer	0000H
CS Register	FFFFH
DS Register	0000H
SS Register	0000H
ES Register	0000H
Queue	Empty

Figure 8.20 Internal state of the 8086 after initialization (Courtesy of Intel Corp.).

Since the flags were all cleared as part of initialization, the external hardware interrupts are disabled. Moreover, the code segment register contains $FFFF_{16}$ and the instruction pointer contains 0000_{16}. Therefore, execution after reset begins at $FFFF0_{16}$. This location can contain an instruction that will cause a jump to the start up program that is used to initialize the rest of the system's resources, such as I/O ports, the interrupt flag, and data memory. After system-level initialization is complete, another jump can be performed to the starting point of the microcomputer's application program.

8.13 INTERNAL INTERRUPT FUNCTIONS

Earlier we indicated that the first 32 of the 256 interrupts of the 8086 are reserved. Four of them are dedicated to the 8086's internal functions: divide error, overflow error, single step, and breakpoint. They are assigned unique type numbers, as shown in Fig. 8.21. Notice that they are the highest-priority type numbers. Moreover, in Fig. 8.6 we find that they are not masked out with the interrupt enable flag.

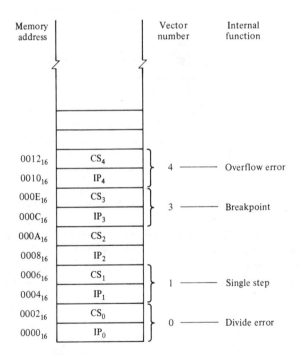

Figure 8.21 Internal interrupt vector locations.

The occurrence of any one of these internal conditions is automatically detected by the 8086, and causes an interrupt of program execution and a vectored transfer of control to a corresponding service routine. During the control transfer sequence, no external bus cycles are produced. Let us now look at each of these internal functions in more detail.

Divide Error

The *divide error* function represents an error condition that can occur in the execution of the division instructions. If the quotient that results from a DIV (divide) instruction or an IDIV (integer divide) instruction is larger than the specified destination, a divide error has occurred. This condition causes automatic initiation of a type 0 interrupt and passes control to a service routine whose starting point is defined by the values of IP_0 and CS_0 at addresses 0000_{16} and 0002_{16}, respectively, in the pointer table.

Overflow Error

The *overflow error* is an error condition similar to that of divide error. However, it can result from the execution of any arithmetic instruction. Whenever an overflow occurs, the overflow flag gets set. In this case, the transfer of program control to a service routine is not automatic at occurrence of the overflow condition. Instead, the INTO (interrupt on overflow) instruction must be executed to test the overflow flag and determine if the overflow service routine should be initiated. If the overflow flag is found to be set, a type 4 interrupt service routine is initiated. Its vector consists of IP_4 and CS_4 which are stored at 0010_{16} and 0012_{16}, respectively, in memory. The routine pointed to by this vector can be written to service the overflow condition. For instance, it could cause a message to be displayed to identify that an overflow has occurred.

Single Step

The *single-step* function relates to an operating option of the 8086. If the trap flag (TF) bit is set, the single-step mode of operation is enabled. This flag bit can be set or reset under software control.

When TF is set, the 8086 initiates a type 1 interrupt to the service routine defined by IP_1 and CS_1 at 0004_{16} and 0006_{16}, respectively, at the completion of execution of every instruction. This permits implementation of the single-step mode of operation such that the program can be executed one instruction at a time. For instance, the service routine could include a WAIT instruction. In this way, a transition to logic 0 at the TEST input of the 8086 could be used as the mechanism for stepping through a program one instruction at a time. This single-step operation can be used as a valuable software debugging tool.

Breakpoint Interrupt

The *breakpoint* function can also be used to implement a software diagnostic tool. A breakpoint interrupt is initiated by execution of the breakpoint instruction *(one-byte instruction)*. This instruction can be inserted at strategic points in a program that is being debugged to cause execution to be stopped. This option can be used in a way similar to that of the single-step option. The service routine could again be put in the wait state, and resumption of execution down to the next breakpoint can be initiated by applying logic 0 to the TEST input.

Section 8.2

1. What are the five groups of interrupts supported on the 8086 MPU?
2. What name is given to the special software routine to which control is passed when an interrupt occurs?
3. List in order the interrupt groups; start with the lowest priority and end with the highest priority.
4. What is the range of type numbers assigned to the interrupts in the 8086 microcomputer system?
5. Is the interrupt assigned to type 21 at a higher or lower priority than the interrupt assigned to type 35?

Section 8.3

6. Where are the interrupt pointers held?
7. How many bytes of memory does an interrupt vector take up?
8. What two elements make up an interrupt vector?
9. Which interrupt function's service routine is specified by $CS_4:IP_4$?
10. The breakpoint routine in an 8086 microcomputer system starts at address $AA000_{16}$ in the code segment located at address $A0000_{16}$. Specify how the breakpoint vector will be stored in the interrupt vector table.
11. At what addresses is the interrupt vector for type 40 stored in memory?

Section 8.4

12. What does STI stand for?
13. Which type of instruction does INTO normally follow? Which flag does it test?
14. What happens when the instruction HLT is executed?

Section 8.5

15. Explain how the CLI and STI instructions can be used to mask out external hardware interrupts during the execution of an uninterruptible subroutine.
16. How can the interrupt interface be reenabled during the execution of an interrupt service routine?

Section 8.6

17. Explain the function of the INTR and $\overline{INTA}$ signals in the circuit diagram of Fig. 8.4.
18. Which device produces $\overline{INTA}$ in a minimum-mode system? In a maximum-mode system?

19. Over which data bus lines does external circuitry send the type number of the active interrupt to the 8086?

20. What bus status code is assigned to interrupt acknowledge?

Section 8.7

21. Give an overview of the events in the order they take place during the interrupt request, interrupt acknowledge, and interrupt vector-fetch cycles of an 8086 microcomputer system.

22. If an 8086-based microcomputer is running 10 MHz with two wait states, how long does it take to perform the interrupt-acknowledged bus cycle sequence?

23. How long does it take the 8086 in problem 22 to push the values of the flags CS and IP to the stack? How much stack space do these values use?

24. How long does it take the 8086 in problem 22 to fetch its vector from memory?

Section 8.8

25. Specify the value of ICW_1 needed to configure an 8259A as follows: ICW_4 not needed, single-device interface, and edge-triggered inputs.

26. Specify the value of ICW_2 if the type numbers produced by the 8259A are to be in the range 70_{16} through 77_{16}.

27. Specify the value of ICW_4 such that the 8259A is configured for use in an 8086 system, with normal EOI, buffered-mode master, and special fully nested mode disabled.

28. Write a program that will initialize an 8259A with the initialization command words derived in problems 25, 26, and 27. Assume that the 8259A resides at address $0A000_{16}$ in the memory address space.

29. Write an instruction that when executed will read the contents of OCW_1 and place it in the AL register. Assume that the 8259A has been configured by the software of problem 28.

30. What priority scheme is enabled if OCW_2 equals 67_{16}?

31. Write an instruction sequence that when executed will toggle the state of the read register bit in OCW_3. Assume that the 8259A is located at memory address $0A000_{16}$.

Section 8.9

32. How many interrupt inputs can be directly accepted by the circuit in Fig. 8.15?

33. How many interrupt inputs can be directly accepted by the circuit in Fig. 8.17?

34. Summarize the interrupt request/acknowledge handshake sequence for an interrupt initiated at an input to slave B in the circuit of Fig. 8.17.

Section 8.10

35. Give another name for a software interrupt.

36. If the instruction INT 80 is to pass control to a subroutine at address $A0100_{16}$ in the code segment starting at address $A0000_{16}$, what vector should be loaded into the interrupt vector table?

37. At what address would the vector for the instruction INT 80 be stored in memory?

Section 8.11

38. What type number and interrupt vector table addresses are assigned to NMI?

39. What are the key differences between NMI and the other external-hardware-initiated interrupts?

40. Give a very common use of the NMI input.

Section 8.12

41. What device is normally used to generate the signal for the RESET input of the 8086?

42. List the states of the address/data bus lines and control signals BHE, ALE, DEN, DT/R, RD, and WR, in a minimum-mode system when reset is at its active level.

43. To what address does a reset operation pass control?

44. Write a reset subroutine that initializes the block of memory locations from address $0A000_{16}$ to $0A100_{16}$ to zero. The initialization routine is at address 01000_{16}.

Section 8.13

45. List the internal interrupts serviced by the 8086.

46. Which vector numbers are reserved for internal interrupts?

Chapter 9 _____

The Hardware of the SDK-86 Microcomputer _____

9.1 INTRODUCTION _____

In the preceding three chapters, we presented in detail the memory, I/O, and interrupt interfaces of the 8086 microprocessor and its microcomputer system. In this chapter we examine how these interfaces are implemented in a simple microcomputer system. The microcomputer used for this purpose is that employed in Intel's 8086 microcomputer system design kit (SDK-86). The topics presented in the chapter are

1. The microcomputer of the SDK-86
2. Clock generator and wait-state generator circuitry
3. Program storage memory
4. Data storage memory
5. Parallel I/O and interrupts
6. Serial I/O
7. The keypad and display

9.2 THE MICROCOMPUTER OF THE SDK-86 _____

The circuitry of the SDK-86 represents the implementation of a simple 8086-based microcomputer system. A block diagram of this microcomputer system is shown in Fig. 9.1. The heart of the microcomputer, the MPU, is an 8086 microprocessor. It is this

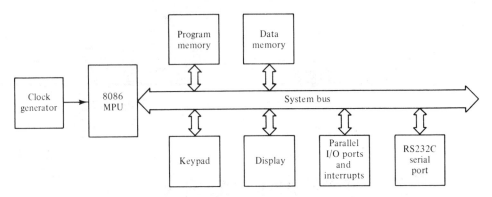

Figure 9.1 SDK-86 microcomputer block diagram.

device that performs the arithmetic, logic, and control operations defined by the keypad monitor program.

The operations of the microprocessor and other devices in the microcomputer system are synchronized by the clock signals produced by the *clock generator section*. The 8086 in this microcomputer is set up to operate at a frequency of 4.9 MHz.

The *program memory section* stores the instructions of the monitor program. The 8086 fetches these instructions over the system's bus as it executes the program. Program memory is implemented with EPROMs and has a total storage capacity of 8K bytes. Use of EPROM makes the program storage nonvolatile. That is, the monitor program is maintained within the EPROMs even when power is removed from the system.

Data that are being processed by the microcomputer are stored in the *data memory section*. During the execution of an instruction, source or destination operands that reside in data memory are accessed over the system's bus by the 8086 microprocessor. This section of memory is implemented with 2142 static RAMs and can be as large as 4K bytes. This part of the memory subsystem is actually volatile; therefore, any information stored in it is lost when power is turned off.

When using the SDK-86 microcomputer to enter, execute, and debug 8086 machine code programs, the instructions of the program are stored and executed from data memory and not from the program memory. This permits the program to be loaded and modified by the user from the keypad. Only the monitor program resides in program storage memory.

The microcomputer in the SDK-86 also has a number of *I/O resources*. Looking at the block diagram in Fig. 9.1, we see that there is a *keypad, display, parallel I/O section*, and an *RS-232C serial communication port*. The keypad allows the user to input information to the microcomputer. For example, in Chapter 5 we showed that monitor commands such as EW or ER are issued from the keypad. Commands like these allow the programmer to enter machine code programs by modifying the contents of data memory, single-step execute, and examine commands implementing program debug operations by giving the ability to examine register contents or memory contents.

The display unit is an output device and it provides the user with data related to the monitor commands that are entered through the keypad. For instance, as the EB command is used to enter a byte of a program, the current contents of a memory location are first displayed and then the new value is displayed digit by digit as it is entered from the keypad. Similarly, when a command is issued to examine the contents of a register such as AX, a register descriptor and the register contents are displayed.

The keypad and display interfaces of the SDK-86 microcomputer are implemented with the 8279 LSI peripheral device. This device takes data entered at the keypad, displays the data on the display unit, and passes it to the 8086 over the system bus.

The parallel I/O section of the microcomputer provides 48 individual I/O lines. This part of the I/O interface is implemented with 8255A parallel peripheral interface devices and can be configured under software control to work as inputs or outputs and with a variety of different modes of operation.

The last I/O interface is a serial communications port that permits a terminal or a CRT to be connected to the microcomputer. When this is done, the user I/O is through the terminal instead of through the keypad and display. This serial port is implemented with an 8251A universal asynchronous receiver/transmitter (UART) IC.

Figure 9.2 is a schematic diagram that details the circuits used to implement each of the functional blocks of the microcomputer in the SDK-86.

9.3 CLOCK GENERATOR AND WAIT-STATE GENERATOR CIRCUITRY

Now that we have introduced the architecture and functions of the fundamental blocks of the SDK-86 microcomputer, let us continue by examining the circuitry used to implement these blocks. We will begin with the *clock generator* and *wait-state circuits*. Figure 9.3 shows this segment of circuitry.

Looking at the circuit in Fig. 9.3, we find that the 8284 clock generator/driver IC is used to produce the system clock. The 14.7456-MHz crystal connected between the X_1 and X_2 pins of the 8284 sets up the operating frequency. Remember that this crystal frequency is divided by 3 within the 8284 to produce the 4.9-MHz output clock at the CLK pin. Notice that this clock output is applied in parallel to both the CLK input of the 8086 and the CLK input of the 74LS164 wait-state generator circuit.

A second clock signal produced by the 8284 is peripheral clock (PCLK). PCLK is 2.45 MHz, which is one-half the frequency of CLK. From the system schematic diagram of Fig. 9.2, we find that it is supplied to the CLK inputs of the 8251A UART and 8279 keypad/display controller. In this way, their operation is synchronized to that of the MPU.

Another function supported by the 8284 is to provide the reset logic for initialization of the microcomputer system. In Fig. 9.3 we see that the SYSTM RESET key on the microcomputer's keypad connects to the $\overline{\text{RES}}$ input of the clock generator/driver. When this key is not depressed, the capacitor between $\overline{\text{RES}}$ and ground is charged to $+ V_{CC}$ through the resistor. Therefore, the $\overline{\text{RES}}$ input of the 8086 is at the 1 logic level.

On the other hand, pressing the SYSTM RESET key causes $\overline{\text{RES}}$ to be short-circuited to ground. This applies logic 0 to $\overline{\text{RES}}$ and discharges the capacitor. As the key is released, the direct short to ground is broken; however, $\overline{\text{RES}}$ remains effectively

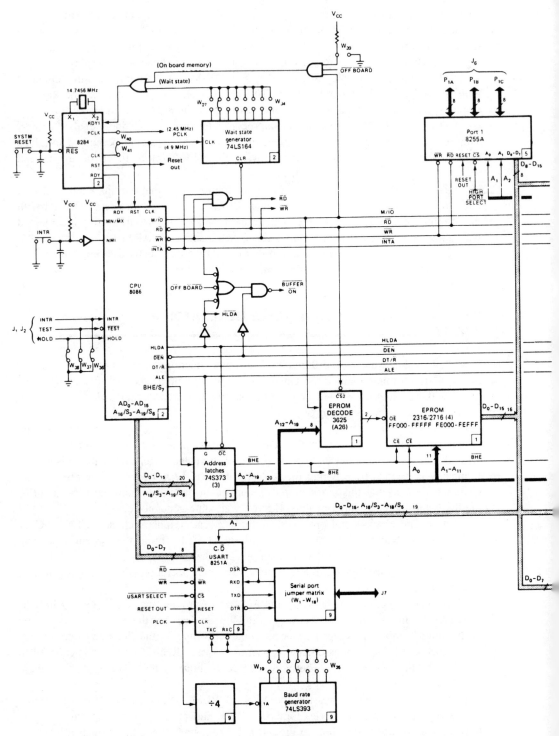

Figure 9.2 Schematic diagram of the SDK-86 microcomputer system (Courtesy of Intel Corp.).

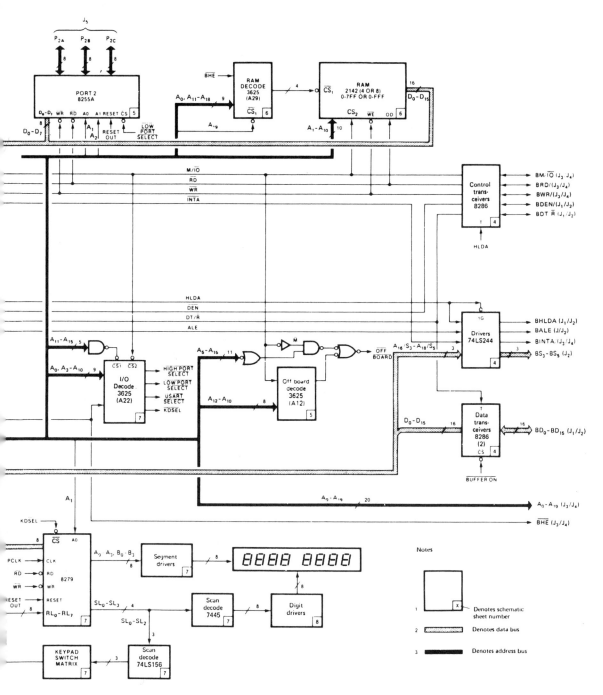

Figure 9.2 *(continued)*

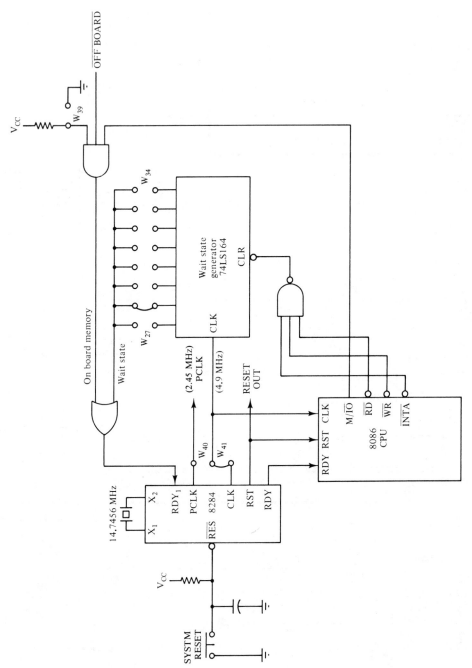

Figure 9.3 Clock generator and wait-state generator circuit.

short-circuited to ground through the discharged capacitor. The capacitor now begins to recharge with time toward the $+V_{CC}$ voltage level.

Remember that $\overline{RES}$ of the 8284 is a Schmitt trigger input. Therefore, as the voltage across the capacitor increases with time it remains detected as a 0 logic level as long as its value is below the logic 1 level threshold of the Schmitt trigger. Thus we assure that $\overline{RES}$ is maintained at logic 0 for at least four clock cycles so that the reset will be detected correctly by the MPU.

Whenever $\overline{RES}$ is at the 0 logic level, the RST output of the 8284 is switched to the 1 logic level. Notice in Fig. 9.3 that this output is supplied to the RST input of the 8086, where it initiates a hardware reset of the microcomputer. The clock generator's RST output is also used to produce a peripheral reset signal called RESET OUT.

The last function performed by the circuit in Fig. 9.3 is wait-stage generation. This function is implemented using several devices: the ready logic of the 8284, the 74LS164 wait-state generator, and a wait-state selection jumper. When the 8086 is running off a 4.9-MHz clock, bus cycles to memory or I/O devices take four states, or 800 ns. If slow memories or LSI peripherals are in use, wait states may have to be inserted into the bus cycle to lengthen its duration.

The circuitry in Fig. 9.3 allows for insertion of from 0 to seven wait states by simply installing a jumper in positions W_{27} through W_{34}, respectively. For instance, the jumper connection, which is shown at W_{28}, causes one wait state to be inserted into the bus cycle. Therefore, it is extended from 800 ns to 1 μs.

Now that we have introduced the function of the wait-state generator circuitry, let us look at its operation in more detail. The 74LS164 is an 8-bit serial-in, parallel-out shift register. Its serial data input, which is not shown in Fig. 9.3, is fixed at the 1 logic level. The outputs are supplied through the series of jumpers to the WAIT STATE input of the OR gate. At the same time, the other input of this OR gate is supplied by a signal called ON BOARD MEMORY. This signal is generated by a three-input AND gate as follows:

$$\text{ON BOARD MEMORY} = \text{M}/\overline{\text{IO}} \bullet \overline{\text{OFF BOARD}} \bullet 1$$

When accessing either on-board memory or on-board I/O (i.e., devices directly mounted on the SDK-86 microcomputer board), OFF BOARD is always 1. Therefore, ON BOARD MEMORY will always equal M/IO and will be logic 1 during all on-board memory bus cycles. This makes the output of the OR gate, which is applied to the RDY_1 input of the 8284, immediately become logic 1 during all on-board memory bus cycles.

The logic 1 at RDY_1 causes the RDY output of the 8284 to switch to the 1 logic level. This signal is applied to the RDY input of the MPU and signals that the current bus cycle should be completed without inserting wait states.

On the other hand, for all bus cycles to on-board I/O devices, the signal ON BOARD MEMORY is logic 0. In this case the output of the OR gate switches to logic 1 only when the output of the shift register corresponding to the inserted wait-state jumper switches to logic 1. This causes the appropriate number of wait states to be inserted into the I/O bus cycle.

Even though the output of the wait-state generator is used only for input or output bus cycles, it is operating during all bus cycles. Therefore, let us now look at the general operation of this part of the circuit. Notice that control signals $\overline{RD}$, $\overline{WR}$, and INTA are gated together to drive the clear (CLR) input of the shift register. The clear signal is produced as follows:

$$CLR = \overline{\overline{RD} \bullet \overline{WR} \bullet \overline{INTA}}$$

If all of these signals are at their inactive 1 logic level, CLR is logic 0 and the shift register is held with all of its outputs at the 0 logic level. However, when any one of the signals becomes active (logic 0), CLR switches to 1 and the shift register is released for operation. This will happen whenever a bus cycle is initiated for a read of memory or I/O, write to memory or I/O, or an interrupt acknowledge.

Earlier we pointed out that the serial input of the shift register is fixed at the 1 logic level. If CLR becomes 1, at the next pulse at CLK a 1 is loaded into the first stage of the shift register. This corresponds to the W_{27} jumper output. On the next pulse, another 1 is loaded and the first 1 is shifted from the first stage of the shift register into its second stage. Now the outputs corresponding to the W_{27} and W_{28} jumpers are both logic 1. The W_{28} output is supplied to the WAIT STATE input of the OR gate and in the case of an I/O bus cycle it signals the 8284 that the bus cycle can be completed. In this way, we see that one wait state, which is equal to one CLK period (200 ns), has been inserted into the bus I/O cycle.

EXAMPLE 9.1

What would be the duration of an external memory bus cycle if the jumper was connected in the W_{34} position?

SOLUTION With the jumper installed at W_{34}, every bus cycle to off-board memory would be performed with seven wait states. Therefore, the duration of a typical bus cycle is given in general as

$$
\begin{aligned}
t_D &= 800 \text{ ns} + 200 \text{ ns (number of WAIT STATES)} \\
&= 800 \text{ ns} + (200 \text{ ns})(7) \\
&= 800 \text{ ns} + 1400 \text{ ns} \\
&= 2200 \text{ ns} \\
&= 2.2 \text{ } \mu\text{s}
\end{aligned}
$$

EXAMPLE 9.2

Assuming that the SDK-86 microcomputer system does not power-up correctly when the SYSTM RESET key is depressed, outline a procedure that could be followed to check whether the reset, clock, and wait-state circuits are operating correctly.

SOLUTION First, the signal at the CLK input of the 8086 can be observed to assure that the 8284 is producing the clock signal needed to drive the MPU. Next, the RST input of the 8086 should be checked while the SYSTM RESET switch is depressed. This will assure that a hardware reset is initiated at the MPU. Resetting the MPU causes it to execute the startup program from EPROM. Bus cycles to this part of memory are performed without wait states. Therefore, a last test could be to observe the RDY input of the 8086 to assure that it is logic 1. If these signals are all correct, the cause of the problem probably does not reside in the clock or reset section of circuitry.

9.4 PROGRAM AND DATA STORAGE MEMORY

In Section 9.3 we covered the clock generator and wait-state generator circuitry. At that time, we found that for on-board memory the 8086 executes bus cycles without wait states. Let us now look into the circuits used to implement the program storage and data storage parts of the memory subsystem.

Program Storage Memory

Figure 9.4 shows the 8086 MPU and the program storage part of the memory subsystem in the SDK-86 microcomputer. Notice that it involves three key elements: the *74S373 address latches*, the *3625 PROM address decoder*, and the *2716 EPROMs*. The storage array is formed from four 2716 EPROMs. These devices are organized as $2K \times 8$ bits and are connected to give two $2K \times 16$ banks of memory, for a total of 4K words of program memory. It is in this section of memory that the instructions of the monitor program are stored.

The three 74S373 address latches are common to all memory and I/O sections. They are used to latch the address in order to demultiplex the 8086's address/data bus. Notice in Fig. 9.4 that the inputs of these latches are AD_0 through AD_{15}, A_{16}/S_3 through A_{19}/S_6, and $\overline{BHE}/S_7$. Moreover, control signals HLDA and ALE are applied in parallel to the G and OC inputs, respectively, of all three 74S373s. Since the HOLD input of the 8086 is not in use, the HLDA output is always at logic 0 and the $\overline{OC}$ enable input on all three devices is at its active 0 logic level. Thus, as the 8086 puts an address on its bus and outputs a pulse at ALE, the G input becomes active and the address A_0 through A_{19} and $\overline{BHE}$ are latched and become available at the outputs. From the circuit diagram in Fig. 9.4, we see that $\overline{BHE}$ and A_0 are directly applied to $\overline{CE}$ inputs in the banks of EPROM memories. These signals are used to enable EPROMs in the high part of the bank and the low part of the bank, respectively. Furthermore, bits A_1 through A_{11} of the address are applied directly to the address inputs of all four EPROMs in parallel. Here they are used to select the storage location that is to be accessed in the enabled EPROMs.

The seven most significant bits of the address, A_{12} through A_{19}, are supplied as inputs to a local address decoder. Here these bits are decoded to select between the two $2K \times 16$-bit banks of memory. Notice that two memory control signals are used to enable the decoder. They are $M/\overline{IO}$, which is logic 1 during all memory bus cycles, and $\overline{RD}$, which is logic 0 whenever an instruction is being fetched from program memory.

Let us now look more closely at the address decoding that takes place for the

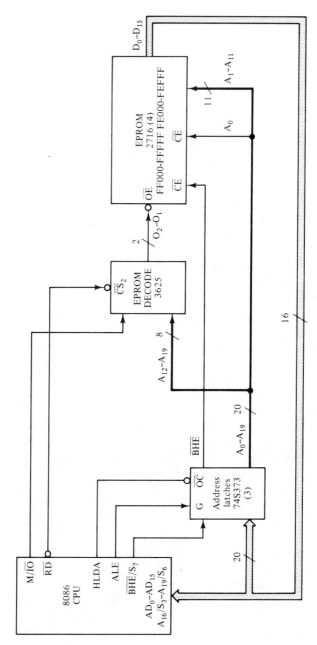

Figure 9.4 Program memory circuit diagram

decoder to produce the $\overline{\text{OE}}$ signal for the EPROMs. For the higher-addressed bank to be selected, all inputs of the local address decoder must be logic 1. That is,

$$A_{19}A_{18} \ldots \ldots A_{12} = 11111111_2$$

$$= FF_{16}$$

As shown in the address decoding table of Fig. 9.5, this input makes output O_1 of the decoder, which is applied to the $\overline{\text{OE}}$ input of the EPROM, switch to logic 0. The rest of the address bits can range from 000_{16} to FFF_{16}; therefore, one range of addresses that correspond to program memory is

$$A_{19}A_{18} \ldots \ldots A_0 = FF000_{16}$$

through

$$A_{19}A_{18} \ldots \ldots A_0 = FFFFF_{16}$$

This range is also shown in Fig. 9.5.

PROM Inputs				PROM Outputs				EPROM Address Block Selected
M/$\overline{\text{IO}}$	A_{14}–A_{19}	A_{13}	A_{12}	O_4	O_3	O_2	O_1	
1	1	1	1	1	1	1	0	FF000H-FFFFFH
1	1	1	0	1	1	0	1	FE000H-FEFFFH
1	1	0	1	1	0	1	1	FD000H-FDFFFH ($\overline{\text{CSX}}$)
1	1	0	0	0	1	1	1	FC000H-FCFFFH ($\overline{\text{CSY}}$)
All other states				1	1	1	1	None

Figure 9.5 Program memory address decoding (Courtesy of Intel Corp.).

The second address combination that decodes to an $\overline{\text{OE}}$ signal for the bank of EPROMs is

$$A_{19}A_{18} \ldots \ldots A_{12} = 11111110_2$$

$$= FE_{16}$$

Figure 9.5 shows that this input address causes decoder output O_2 to become active. Again the lower part of the address can have any value from 000_{16} to FFF_{16}. This gives a second range for program memory as

$$A_{19}A_{18} \ldots \ldots A_0 = FE000_{16}$$

through

$$A_{19}A_{18} \ldots \ldots A_0 = FEFFF_{16}$$

Similarly, we can determine the address locations occupied by the other two EPROMs. These are also shown in Fig. 9.5. In this way, we see that EPROMs reside at the high end of the microcomputer's address space. Data read out of the EPROMs are carried to the MPU over the complete data bus D_0 through D_{15}.

EXAMPLE 9.3

The address latched into the outputs of the address latches during an instruction acquisition bus cycle is $FE330_{16}$. $\overline{BHE}$ is also latched and is at logic 0. What is the output of the EPROM address decoder, and which storage location in EPROM is accessed?

SOLUTION   Since an instruction acquisition bus cycle is taking place,

$$M/\overline{IO} = 1$$

and

$$\overline{RD} = 0$$

These signals enable the EPROM address decoder. The high-order address bits, which are used as inputs to the address decoder, are

$$A_{19}A_{18} \ldots \ldots \ldots A_{14} = 111111_2$$
$$A_{13} = 1$$
$$A_{12} = 0$$

Looking at the table in Fig. 9.5, we see that output O_2 of the address decoder is switched to logic 0. This provides an output enable (OE) signal in the bank of EPROMs at address $FE000_{16}$ through $FEFFF_{16}$. The $\overline{CE}$ inputs on these EPROMs are $\overline{BHE}$ and A_0, which are also both at their active 0 logic levels. Therefore, the word at location

$$A_{11}A_{10} \ldots \ldots \ldots A_1 = 330_{16}$$

is read out.

Data Storage Memory

The data storage memory interface of the SDK-86 microcomputer is similar to that just described for program storage memory. Looking at Fig. 9.6, we see that it again includes the *74S373 address latches*, the *3625 RAM address decoder*, and an *array of 2142 static RAMs*. The 2142 is organized 1K × 4 bits and the data RAM area can be filled with either four or eight of them to give either 1K words or 2K words, respectively. It is this part of the memory subsystem that is used to store data and programs that are keyed in for execution and debugging.

The same 74S373 address latches that we discussed relative to program storage memory are shown demultiplexing the 8086's address/data bus to give address lines A_0 through A_{19} and $\overline{BHE}$. Another 3625 PROM is used as a local address decoder to produce chip select signals for the banks of RAMs. This 3625 device is referred to as the RAM decoder. Comparing the local PROM decoder in Fig. 9.4 with the local RAM decoder in Fig. 9.6, we find that their address inputs and chip select signals are different. First we see that the address inputs of the RAM address decoder are A_0, A_{11}

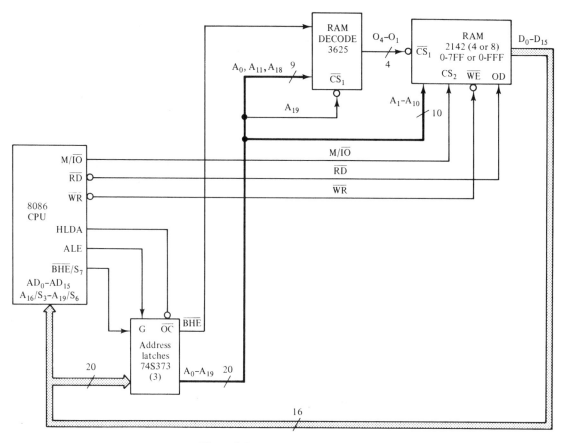

Figure 9.6 Data memory circuit diagram.

through A_{18}, and $\overline{BHE}$. Moreover, its chip enable input is A_{19} and this input must be logic 0 to enable the decoder for operation.

Figure 9.7 shows the relationship between input address and chip select outputs

PROM Inputs				PROM Outputs				RAM address block selected
A_{12}-A_{18}	A_{11}	$\overline{BHE}$	A_0	O_4	O_3	O_2	O_1	
0	0	0	0	1	1	0	0	Both Bytes (0H-007FFH)
0	0	0	1	1	1	0	1	High Byte (0H-007FFH)
0	0	1	0	1	1	1	0	Low Byte (0H-007FFH)
0	1	0	0	0	0	1	1	Both Bytes (00800H-00FFFH)
0	1	0	1	0	1	1	1	High Byte (00800H-00FFFH)
0	1	1	0	1	0	1	1	Low Byte (00800H-00FFFH)
All other states				1	1	1	1	None

Figure 9.7 Data memory address decoding (Courtesy of Intel Corp.).

O_4, O_3, O_2, and O_1. Here we see that address bits A_{12} through A_{18} must all be logic 0. Moreover, address bit A_{11} is used to select between the two 1K word banks of RAM. When A_{11} is logic 0, data stored in the lower-addressed bank are accessed and when it is 1, data in the high-addressed bank are accessed. The next two signals, $\overline{BHE}$ and A_0, are the 8086's byte select signals. From Fig. 9.7, we see that a word access takes place from the selected banks of RAMs when both of these signals are at logic 0, a high byte access occurs when $\overline{BHE}$ = 0 and A_0 = 1, and a low byte access occurs when $\overline{BHE}$ = 1 and A_0 = 0.

The storage location that is to be accessed is selected by the part of the address that is on lines A_1 through A_{10}. It is directly applied in parallel to the address inputs of all RAMs. Since the upper 8 bits of the address are always all logic 0, RAM resides in the lower 4K of the address space, that is, the address range

$$A_{19}A_{18} \ldots \ldots \ldots A_0 = 00000_{16}$$

through

$$A_{19}A_{18} \ldots \ldots \ldots A_0 = 00FFF_{16}$$

In Fig. 9.7 we see that the lower 1K word bank is located at 00000_{16} through $007FF_{16}$ and the upper 1K word bank is located at 00700_{16} through $00FFF_{16}$.

The M/IO, $\overline{RD}$, and $\overline{WR}$ memory control lines are applied directly to all RAMs in parallel. From Fig. 9.6, we see that M/$\overline{IO}$ goes to the CS_2 input. During all memory bus cycles, it is at logic 1 and enables the RAMs. $\overline{RD}$ is connected to output disable (OD) of the RAMs. During bus cycles when data are read from memory, $\overline{RD}$ is switched to logic 0. This enables the output buffers of the 2142 memories to put the data stored at the addressed location onto the bus. Finally, during write cycles from MPU to RAM, $\overline{WR}$ is switched to logic 0. This signal is supplied to $\overline{WE}$, where it enables the data inputs of the RAMs to accept write data from the bus.

EXAMPLE 9.4

Write a program that could be used to clear (write 0s) lower 2K-byte storage locations of data memory in the SDK-86 microcomputer system.

SOLUTION The 2K bytes of RAM reside in the address range 00000_{16} to $007FF_{16}$. To clear this segment of memory, we must first load the data segment register with 0000_{16} and initialize the destination index register to 0000_{16}. This is done with the instructions

```
MOV   AX, 0
MOV   DS,
MOV   DI, 0
```

Now a count equal to 800_{16} is loaded into the CX register.

```
MOV   CX, 800
```

To clear the bank of memory, we need to form a loop that writes 0 to the byte address formed from DS and DI, then increment the pointer in DI and decrement the counter in CX, and finally test the value of the count for 0. If the count is equal to 0 the memory clear routine is complete and the program halts; otherwise, control is returned to the beginning of the loop. This loop is implemented with the following sequence of instructions.

```
NXT:    MOV BYTE PTR [DI],0
        INC DI
        DCR CX
        JNZ NXT
```

This program is repeated in Fig. 9.8.

```
        MOV    AX,0                ; LOAD DATA SEGMENT REGISTER
        MOV    DS,AX
        MOV    DI,0                ; LOAD DESTINATION INDEX REGISTER
        MOV    CX,800              ; LOAD COUNT REGISTER
NXT:    MOV    BYTE PTR [DI],0     ; CLEAR MEMORY LOCATION
        INC    DI                  ; INCREMENT DESTINATION POINTER
        DCR    CX                  ; DECREMENT COUNTER
        JNZ    NXT                 ; CHECK FOR BANK DONE
        HLT                        ; MEMORY INITIALIZATION COMPLETE
```

Figure 9.8 Memory bank initialization routine.

9.5 I/O INTERFACES OF THE SDK-86 MICROCOMPUTER

There are four I/O interfaces provided in the SDK-86 microcomputer. Looking at the block diagram in Fig. 9.1, we find that they are the *keypad*, the *display*, the *parallel I/O ports*, and the *RS-232C serial port*. Let us now look at how each of these interfaces implemented in the microcomputer system.

Parallel I/O Ports

The *parallel I/O circuitry* of the SDK-86 microcomputer is shown in Fig. 9.9. Here we see that two 8255A programmable peripheral interface (PPI) ICs have been used to implement two independent I/O ports called PORT 1 and PORT 2. Each of these ports has three byte-wide groups of lines. For instance, at PORT 1 they are labeled P_{1A}, P_{1B}, and P_{1C}, respectively. This gives a total of 48 I/O lines for the two ports.

Input or output data transfers between the 8086 and the A, B, and C ports are performed by reading from or writing to a corresponding data register within the 8255A. Figure 9.9(a) lists the addresses of these registers in the SDK-86 microcomputer's I/O address space. For example, the P_{1A} I/O lines at PORT 1 are accessed through the data register at address $FFF9_{16}$.

Remember that the I/O lines on an 8255A can be configured for several different modes of operation. In general, they can be set up to work as level-sensitive inputs,

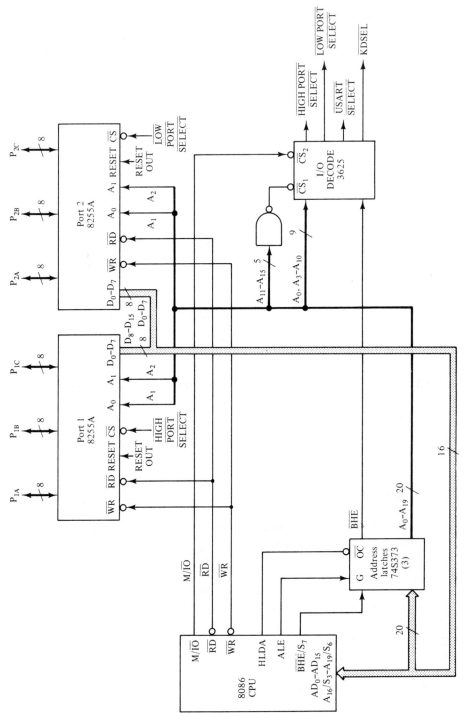

Figure 9.9 Parallel I/O interface circuit.

latched outputs, or strobed inputs or outputs. In Chapter 7 we found that the control register is loaded with an appropriate byte to configure the I/O lines of the A, B, and C ports as inputs or outputs and select between MODE 0, MODE 1, or MODE 2 operations. From Fig. 9.10, we see that the control register of the PORT 1 PPI is at I/O address FFFF$_{16}$.

Port	Address
P_{1A}	FFF9
P_{1B}	FFFB
P_{1C}	FFFD
$P_{1 \text{ Control}}$	FFFF

(a)

Port	Address
P_{2A}	FFF8
P_{2B}	FFFA
P_{2C}	FFFC
$P_{2 \text{ Control}}$	FFFE

(b)

Figure 9.10 (a) Register addresses for PORT 1 (Courtesy of Intel Corp.); (b) register addresses for PORT 2 (Courtesy of Intel Corp.).

Now that we have introduced the parallel I/O interface, let us trace through the operation of the circuitry in Fig. 9.9 as the 8086 writes a byte to the control register of the PORT 1 PPI. Since the 8255As are located in the I/O address space, this represents an output bus cycle and would be initiated by executing an OUT instruction.

As the output bus cycle begins, M/$\overline{\text{IO}}$ is switched to the 0 logic level. M/$\overline{\text{IO}}$ is applied to the $\overline{\text{CS}}_2$ input of the I/O address decoder and signals that an I/O bus cycle instead of a memory bus cycle is in progress. At the same time, the control register address, which is FFFF$_{16}$, is output on AD$_0$ through AD$_{15}$ and latched along with $\overline{\text{BHE}}$ into the 74S373 address latches on the trailing edge of the ALE pulse. Expressing this address in binary form, we get

$$A_{15}A_{14} \ldots \ldots \ldots A_0 = 1111111111111111_2$$

Looking at the circuit in Fig. 9.9, we see that bits A$_{11}$ through A$_{15}$ of the address are decoded with a NAND gate to produce the second chip select input ($\overline{\text{CS}}_1$) for the I/O address decoder. These address bits, which are all logic 1 in the address FFFF$_{16}$, cause $\overline{\text{CS}}_1$ to switch to logic 0.

With both $\overline{\text{CS}}_1$ and $\overline{\text{CS}}_2$ logic 0, the 3625 PROM is enabled for operation. Therefore, the rest of its inputs A$_0$, A$_3$, through A$_{10}$, and $\overline{\text{BHE}}$ are decoded to produce one of the four I/O select outputs: HIGH PORT SELECT, LOW PORT SELECT, USART SELECT, or KDSEL. Looking at the PORT 1 8255A in Fig. 9.9, we see that its $\overline{\text{CS}}$ input is supplied by the HIGH PORT SELECT output of the *I/O address decoder*. The decoding performed by the I/O address decoder is illustrated in Fig. 9.11. Here we see that to produce an active HIGH PORT SELECT, signal bits A$_3$ through A$_{10}$ of the address must all be logic 1, $\overline{\text{BHE}}$ must be logic 0, and A$_0$ can be either 0 or 1. The address bits are all at the 1 logic level in the address FFFF$_{16}$ and $\overline{\text{BHE}}$ is 0; thus the PORT 1 PPI is enabled for operation.

The last two address bits, A$_1$ and A$_2$, are applied to the A$_0$ and A$_1$ inputs, respectively, of the 8255As in parallel. It is the code on these lines that selects the internal register of the PPI that will be accessed. These bits must both be logic 1 to select the control register. In our example, they are both 1; however, just the PORT 1 PPI is enabled. Therefore, its control register is to be accessed. That is, a byte-wide output operation is to be performed over the bus to the PORT 1 PPI's control register.

PROM Inputs					PROM Outputs			
A_5-A_{10}	A_4	A_3	$\overline{BHE}$	A_0	O_4 $\overline{\text{HIGH PORT SELECT}}$	O_3 $\overline{\text{LOW PORT SELECT}}$	O_2 $\overline{\text{USART SELECT}}$	O_1 $\overline{\text{KDSEL}}$
1	0	1	0	0	1	1	1	0
1	0	1	1	0	1	1	1	0
1	1	0	0	0	1	1	0	1
1	1	0	1	0	1	1	0	1
1	1	1	0	0	0	0	1	1
1	1	1	0	1	0	1	1	1
1	1	1	1	0	1	0	1	1
All other states					1	1	1	1

Figure 9.11 I/O device address decoding (Courtesy of Intel Corp.).

Later in the bus cycle, the 8086 outputs the byte of data on data bus lines D_8 through D_{15} and then switches $\overline{WR}$ to logic 0. The 0 level on $\overline{WR}$ signals the PORT 1 8255A to read the data off of the bus and put the data into the control register.

EXAMPLE 9.5

What is the difference between the two I/O address decoder output states during which $\overline{\text{HIGH PORT SELECT}}$ is active 0?

SOLUTION From the table of Fig. 9.11, we see that for the first state when $\overline{\text{HIGH PORT SELECT}}$ is active.

$$A_{10}A_9 \ldots \ldots \ldots A_3 = 11111111_2$$

$$\overline{BHE} = 0$$

$$A_0 = 0$$

Notice that both $\overline{\text{HIGH PORT SELECT}}$ and $\overline{\text{LOW PORT SELECT}}$ are at their active 0 logic level

$$\overline{\text{HIGH PORT SELECT}} = 0$$

$$\overline{\text{LOW PORT SELECT}} = 0$$

and both the PORT 1 and PORT 2 PPIs are enabled for operation. This state corresponds to a word I/O bus cycle during which registers from both PORT 1 and PORT 2 are accessed at the same time.

The second state where $\overline{\text{HIGH PORT SELECT}}$ is active is for

$$A_{10}A_9 \ldots \ldots \ldots A_3 = 11111111_2$$

$$\overline{BHE} = 0$$

$$A_0 = 1$$

This state produces just

$$\overline{\text{HIGH PORT SELECT}} = 0$$

Now the PORT 1 PPI is enabled but PORT 2 remains disabled. It corresponds to an I/O bus cycle where a byte operation is performed to a register in the PORT 1 device.

EXAMPLE 9.6

Write a program that will initialize PORT 2 such that it is configured with P_{2A} set for MODE 0 input operation, P_{2B} set for MODE 0 input operation, and P_{2C} for MODE 0 output operation. Then write a sequence of instructions that will input the contents at P_{2A} and P_{2B} and output their sum to P_{2C}.

SOLUTION In Chapter 7 we discussed how to configure the ports of the 8255A by forming control bytes and loading them into the control registers. For this example, the control byte needed to configure P2's ports is shown in Fig. 9.12(a). Its value is

$$10010010_2 = 92_{16}$$

D_7	D_6	D_5	D_4	D_3	D_2	D_1	D_0
1	0	0	1	0	0	1	0

(a)

```
MOV   AL,92      ; LOAD AL WITH CONTROL BYTE
MOV   DX,FFFE    ; LOAD I/O POINTER
OUT   DX,AL      ; LOAD PORT 2 CONTROL REGISTER
MOV   DX,FFF8    ; LOAD I/O POINTER
IN    AL,DX      ; READ PORT P2A
MOV   BL,AL      ; SAVE FIRST BYTE
MOV   DX,FFFA    ; LOAD I/O POINTER
IN    AL,DX      ; READ PORT P2B
ADD   AL,BL      ; ADD INPUT DATA
MOV   DX,FFFC    ; LOAD I/O POINTER
OUT   DX,AL      ; WRITE TO PORT P2C
```

(b)

Figure 9.12 (a) PORT 2 control word; (b) I/O program.

This byte must be written to the control register at address $FFFE_{16}$ of the I/O address space. To do this, we must first load the accumulator with 92_{16} and then output it to the control register. This is done with the instructions

```
MOV   AL, 92
MOV   DX, FFFE
OUT   DX, AL
```

Now we can read the first byte of data from the input port at address FFF8$_{16}$ and save it in BL. This is done with the instruction sequence

```
MOV  DX, FFF8

IN   AL, DX

MOV  BL, AL
```

The byte from the input port at FFFA$_{16}$ is next read into the accumulator with the instruction

```
MOV  DX, FFFA

IN   AL, DX
```

The two values of input data are now added

```
ADD  AL, BL
```

and their sum is output to the port at address FFFC$_{16}$.

```
MOV  DX, FFFC

OUT  DX, AL
```

The complete program is repeated in Fig. 9.12(b).

RS-232C Communications Port

Another important I/O interface in the SDK-86 microcomputer is the *RS-232C serial I/O port*. This port permits a CRT terminal to be connected to the microcomputer. In this way, information can be input from the keyboard of the terminal instead of from the build-in keypad.

The serial port circuitry is shown in Fig. 9.13. Note that the 8251A USART is the communications controller used. In Chapter 7 we introduced this device. Here it is configured by the monitor software to operate in the asynchronous mode. At power-up, the monitor configures the 8251A for 8-bit character length, no parity, and two STOP bits. Moreover, it sets up the internal clock divider circuitry such that the externally generated baud clock input signal is divided by 64 within the device.

The 8251A is located in the I/O address space of the SDK-86 microcomputer. Figure 9.14 shows the logic states of the control signals and corresponding addresses needed to access each of its registers. For instance, execution of an IN instruction to address FFF2$_{16}$ lets the 8086 read the contents of the 8251A's status register. On the other hand, executing an OUT instruction to the same address causes the mode control register to be loaded.

Looking at Fig. 9.13, we find that the chip select input of the 8251A is driven by

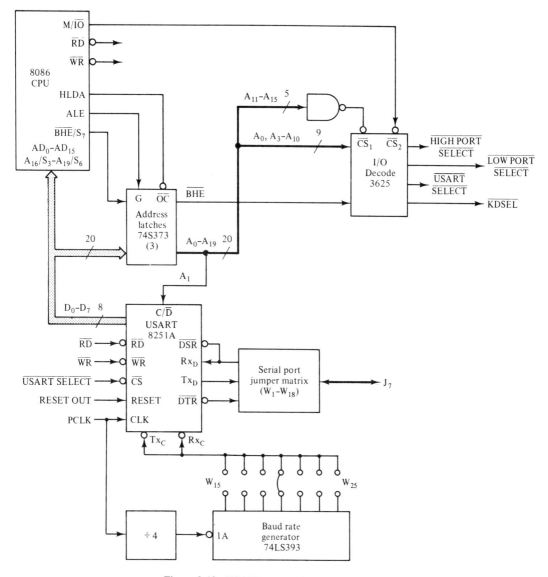

Figure 9.13 USART communications interface.

USART Input			Port Addresses	Port Function
A_1	$\overline{RD}$	$\overline{WR}$		
0	0	1	FFF0H	Read USART Data
0	1	0	FFF0H	Write USART Data
1	0	1	FFF2H	Read USART Status
1	1	0	FFF2H	Write USART Control

Figure 9.14 USART register selection (Courtesy of Intel Corp.).

the USART SELECT output of the I/O decode circuit. Earlier we found that bits A_{11} through A_{15} of the address must all be logic 1 to enable the I/O address decoder for operation. From Fig. 9.11 we find that to produce the $\overline{\text{USART SELECT}}$ output, bits A_4 through A_{10} must all be logic 1 while A_0 and A_3 must be logic 0. Therefore, to input data from or output data to the registers of the 8251A, the address on the bus must be

$$A_{15}A_{14} \ldots \ldots A_0 = 1111111111100X0_2$$

For $X = 0$ this gives

$$A_{15}A_{14} \ldots \ldots A_0 = 1111111111110000_2$$

$$= \text{FFF0}_{16}$$

and for $X = 1$

$$A_{15}A_{14} \ldots \ldots A_0 = 1111111111110010_2$$

$$= \text{FFF2}_{16}$$

Note that an X is in bit A_1 of the address and this signal is applied to the $C/\overline{D}$ input of the 8251A. As shown in Fig. 9.14, the logic level of this bit is used to select between the data registers and status/control registers. Moreover, the fact that data are input or output depends on whether $\overline{\text{RD}}$ or $\overline{\text{WR}}$ is at logic 0.

Now that we have examined the microprocessor interface of the 8251A let us continue by looking at how the clock signal that sets the baud rate of the receiver and transmitter sections is generated. In Fig. 9.13 we see that the *baud rate generator* is formed by a 74LS393 dual 4-bit binary counter. The PCLK signal produced by the clock generator section of the microcomputer is first divided by 4 and then applied to the 1A input of the baud rate generator circuit. The two counters within the 73LS393 are set up for cascaded operation and seven of its parallel outputs are available for use as the receiver and transmitter clock signals.

In the circuit, both the receiver and transmitter are to run at the same baud rate; therefore, the Tx_C and Rx_C inputs are connected together. Any one of the clock outputs of the baud rate generator can be connected into the clock input by simply installing a jumper in the appropriate location. The baud rate jumpers are labeled W_{19} through W_{25}.

Figure 9.15 shows the relationship between jumper setting, baud rate generator output frequency, and baud rate of the USART. Remember that the baud rate clock

Baud rate	Shorting plug position	Output frequency
4800	W_{25}	307.2 kHz
2400	W_{24}	153.6 kHz
1200	W_{23}	76.8 kHz
600	W_{22}	38.4 kHz
300	W_{21}	19.2 kHz
150	W_{20}	9.6 kHz
75	W_{19}	4.8 kHz
110	W_{20}, W_{26}	6.98 kHz

Figure 9.15 Baud rate selection (Courtesy of Intel Corp.).

input is divided by 64 within the 8251A. This is the reason that the output frequencies and corresponding baud rates are different.

EXAMPLE 9.7

If the jumper is installed in the W_{21} position, what is the output frequency of the baud rate generator and baud rate of the USART? Show how the value of the baud rate is derived from the clock frequency.

SOLUTION   Looking at Fig. 9.15, we see that when the jumper is installed at W_{21} the 19.2-kHz clock has been selected and that this results in a baud rate of 300 baud (307.2 baud). The input clock frequency is divided by 64 to give the baud rate

$$\text{Baud rate} = f_{BRG}/64 = 19.2 \text{ kHz}/64$$

$$= 300 \text{ baud}$$

The last part of the serial I/O interface in Fig. 9.13 is the RS-232C port. Here we see that this part of the circuit includes the receive data (Rx_D) and transmit data (Tx_D) lines of the 8251A, a serial port jumper matrix, and the connector J_7. The connector is a DB-25S 25-pin female EIA connector. This is the type of connector used at RS-232C ports. The pin assignments of signals at this connector can be changed by jumpers W_1 through W_{18} to support interface to a wide variety of equipment. For instance, to configure it for connection to a stand-alone CRT terminal a jumper should be installed between the W_1 and W_5 positions. This simply connects the receive data line to pin 2 of J_1, the transmit data line to pin 3, and supplies a common signal ground at pin 7. These signal locations are consistent with those identified for the RS-232C interface in Fig. 7.23.

Keypad and Display Interface

The last I/O device that we will consider is the 8279. This device provides the interface to the keypad and display in the SDK-86 microcomputer system. The 8279 keyboard/display control IC was described in detail in Chapter 7. At power-up, the monitor program configures the 8279 at power-up for encoded keyboard scanning with two-key lockout, eight-digit eight-segment display with left entry, and a prescaler of 25.

The circuitry involved in the scanning of the keypad and display is shown in Fig. 9.16. Let us begin by examining the microprocessor interface. Just like the other I/O devices we have considered up to this point, the 8279 is located in the SDK-86 microcomputer's I/O address space. Figure 9.16 shows the control signals and addresses for each type of bus access that can be performed by the 8086. For instance, to read data from the display RAM, an IN instruction can be executed to the address $FFE8_{16}$, or to write data into this RAM, an OUT instruction can be executed to the same address. Remember that a read or write display memory command must be issued to the 8279 before executing the IN or OUT instruction, respectively.

Looking at Fig. 9.16, we see that the $\overline{CS}$ input of the 8279 is connected to the $\overline{KDSEL}$ output of the I/O address decoder. Earlier we found that the decoder was chip

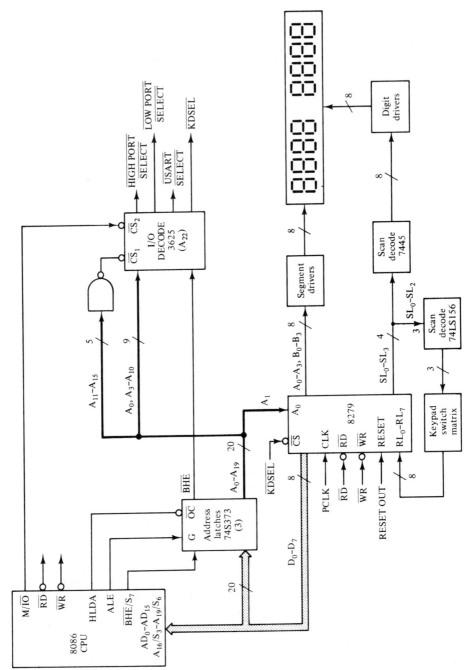

Figure 9.16 Keypad/display interface.

selected when bits A_{11} through A_{15} of the address are all logic 1 and $M/\overline{IO}$ is logic 0. Figure 9.10 shows that bits A_5 through A_{10} and A_3 must also be all logic 1, while A_4 and A_0 must be logic 0 in order to produce an active $\overline{KDSEL}$ output. Therefore, the address used in an IN or OUT instruction that is used to access the 8279 is

$$A_{15}A_{14} \ldots \ldots \ldots A_0 = 1111111111010X0_2$$

For $X = 0$ this gives

$$A_{15}A_{14} \ldots \ldots \ldots A_0 = 1111111111101000_2$$

$$= \text{FFE8}_{16}$$

and for $X = 1$, we get

$$A_{15}A_{14} \ldots \ldots \ldots A_0 = 1111111111101010_2$$

$$= \text{FFEA}_{16}$$

From Fig. 9.17, we find that bit A_1 of the address determines whether the bus operation to the 8279 is a memory access or status/command operation. When A_1 is logic 0, the on-chip display RAM or keyboard FIFO is being accessed. On the other hand, logic 1 in this bit position corresponds to reading of the 8279's status register or writing of a command to the command register.

8279 Input			Port Address	Port Function
A1	$\overline{RD}$	$\overline{WR}$		
0	0	1	FFE8H	Read Display RAM or Keyboard FIFO
0	1	0	FFE8H	Write Display RAM
1	0	1	FFEAH	Read Status
1	1	0	FFEAH	Write Command

Figure 9.17 Keypad/display controller register selection (Courtesy of Intel Corp.).

Scan outputs, SL_0 through SL_3, of the 8279 are decoded separately in the display and keypad sections. In the display section, a 7445 4-line to 10-line decoder IC is used as the scan decoder. Here we see that just eight of its outputs are used as digit select signals for the display. These signals are buffered by the *digit driver circuit*. Eight bits of segment data are output to the display at ports A and B. They are buffered by the segment driver circuit and then applied to the segment inputs of the display.

The *keypad scan decoder* is a 74LS156 three to eight-line decoder. Just three of its outputs are used as row inputs to the keypad switch matrix. The eight outputs of the switch matrix are applied to return line inputs, RL_0 through RL_7 of the 8279.

EXAMPLE 9.8

All of the keys that attach to one row of the keypad matrix do not work. What signal should be tested first to determine the cause of the malfunction? Assume that all digits of the display work correctly.

SOLUTION Since the display works correctly, it can be assumed that the scan line outputs of the 8279 are functioning correctly. Moreover, if the problem was at the return line inputs of the 8279, we would expect to find that all keys attached to a column of the keypad matrix do not work instead of all keys in a row. Therefore, the source of the problem would be expected to be in the keypad scan decoder section, and the first signal to be examined should be the row output that connects to the malfunctioning row of keys.

ASSIGNMENT

Section 9.2

1. What is the size of the program storage memory in the SDK-86 microcomputer system?
2. How much RAM is supplied in the data storage part of memory?
3. What happens to the contents of program storage memory when power is turned off? What would happen to the contents of the data storage memory?
4. Where are programs that are keyed in at the keypad stored?
5. What I/O resources are supplied on the SDK-86 microcomputer?
6. What LSI device is used to interface the keypad and display to the 8086 microprocessor?
7. What do the 8255A devices implement in the SDK-86 microcomputer?
8. In Fig. 9.2, what is the logic level of the $\overline{\text{MN/MX}}$ pin? What mode of operation does this select?
9. In Fig. 9.2, what is the significance of the jumper connections (W_{36}, W_{37}, and W_{38}) made for the INTR, TEST, and HOLD inputs of the 8086?

Section 9.3

10. If a 12-MHz crystal is used in the SDK-86 microcomputer instead of the 14.7456-MHz crystal, at what frequency will the microcomputer run?
11. What is the frequency of PCLK if the 8084 has a 12-MHz crystal, as indicated in problem 10?
12. Summarize what happens when the SYSTM RESET key is depressed.
13. Which devices in the microcomputer system are initialized with the RESET OUT signal?
14. What is the duration of an I/O bus cycle if the wait state jumper is inserted at the W_{30} position?
15. Assuming that all bus cycles are to on-board memory and I/O, what affect on wait-state operation would be found if jumper W_{39} were installed? Explain your answer.
16. Assume that in Example 9.2 the RDY input was found to be fixed at the 0 logic level. Which signal should be examined next?
17. Measurements are taken to determine the duration of the on-board memory and I/O bus cycle to assure that on-board memory accesses are performed without wait states and I/O accesses are performed with one wait state. However, it was found that both bus cycles are always being performed with one wait state. Jumper W_{39} was then checked and found to be removed. Finally, the signals M/IO, ON BOARD MEMORY, and $\overline{\text{OFF BOARD}}$ were examined. M/IO and OFF BOARD were found to work correctly, but the ON BOARD MEMORY output was found to be always logic 0. Which of the following could be the cause?

(a) Jumper W_{39} was not installed.

(b) The AND gate that produces ON BOARD MEMORY is burned out.

(c) The jumper at W_{28} should be moved to W_{27}.

(d) None of the above.

Section 9.4

18. Assume that the address latched at the output of the 74S373 in the circuit of Fig. 9.4 during a memory read cycle is $FF400_{16}$ and BHE = 0. What is the output of the EPROM address decoder, and which EPROM storage location is accessed?

19. What would be the output of the EPROM address decoder in the circuit of Fig. 9.4 if a bus cycle is initiated to read a word of data out of storage location $000FE_{16}$? Assume that $\overline{BHE}$ is at logic 0.

20. Assume that in Example 9.2 the cause of the malfunction was not found in the reset, clock, or ready logic circuits and the testing of circuitry was continued into the program storage memory section. Additional measurements were taken and it was observed that when an address was latched at the outputs of the 74S373, M/IO was at the 1 logic level, CS_2 was at logic 0, BHE was at logic 0, and A_0 was also at logic 0. However, all outputs of the EPROM address decoder remained at the 1 logic level. What should be done next?

(a) Replace the address decoder IC.

(b) Replace all four EPROMs.

(c) Verify that the address is in the program memory address range $FE000_{16}$ through $FFFFF_{16}$.

(d) None of the above.

21. During the bus cycle initiated by the instruction MOV AH,3F, what will become the logic levels of the signals M/IO, $\overline{WE}$, and CS_1 on the RAM address decoder, and at outputs O_4 through O_1 of the RAM address decoder?

22. Draw a memory map for the SDK-86 microcomputer.

23. Write a simple program that could be used to verify that all RAM in the SDK-86 microcomputer is operating correctly.

Section 9.5

24. What address must be output on the bus in order to write a byte of data into the control register of the PORT 2 8255A?

25. What are the logic levels of $\overline{CS_1}$ on the I/O address decoder, $\overline{CS}$ on the PORT 1 8255A, and $\overline{CS}$ on the PORT 2 8255A when the address found in problem 24 is output on the bus?

26. Assume that I/O PORT 2 is already configured as described in Example 9.6. Write a program that will input the contents of P_{2A}, mask off the four MSBs, and output the result to the four MSBs of P_{2C}.

27. Assume that I/O PORT 2 is already configured as described in Example 9.6. Write a diagnostic program that will test output operation at P_{2C} by producing symmetrical square waves at each of its eight output lines.

28. What address must be output on the address bus for the 8086 to read the contents of the receive data register of the 8251A?

29. Write an instruction sequence that will load the transmitter data register of the 8251A with the ASCII character A.

30. What baud rate is produced when the baud rate selection jumper is in the W_{23} position?

31. If the internal baud rate divider of the 8251A was set to 4 instead of 64, what clock frequency would need to be input to result in a baud rate of 110 baud?

32. If the serial port does not work, what should be checked first?

33. If a measurement is taken to observe the clock signal at Rx_C and it is found that the signal is missing, what other signals should be checked to identify the source of the problem?

34. What address and data must be output over the bus to the 8279 in order to set the keyboard/display mode to encoded scan keypad with two-key lockout and eight-digit eight-segment display with left entry?

35. What address and data must be output on the bus to the 8279 to set the clock divider for divide by 25?

36. Write the instruction sequence needed to perform the two programming operations described in problems 34 and 35.

37. Write the instruction sequence needed to read a key code off the top of the key code FIFO.

38. If one segment in one digit of the display never lights, what would you expect to be the cause of the problem?
    (a) Bad display unit.
    (b) Bad segment driver.
    (c) Bad display scan decoder.
    (d) None of the above.

39. If all segments in one of the digits of the display never light, which signal (signals) should you check first?
    (a) A and B port segment outputs.
    (b) Segment driver outputs.
    (c) Display scan decoder output for the digit.
    (d) Digit driver output for the digit.

40. Draw a map of the SDK-86's I/O address space.

Chapter 10

Software Architecture of the 80286 Microprocessor

10.1 INTRODUCTION

In this chapter, we study the software architecture of the 80286 microprocessor and its assembly language instruction set. The 80286 can operate in either of two modes, the *real-address mode* (real mode) or the *protected-address mode* (protected mode). Here we will first examine the real-address mode software architecture and its extended instruction set. This material is followed by a detailed study of the 80286's protected-address mode of operation and system control instructions. The following topics are covered in the chapter:

1. Real-mode software model
2. Real-mode extended instruction set
3. Protected-mode software architecture
4. Descriptors
5. Protected-mode system control instruction set
6. Multitasking and protection

10.2 REAL-ADDRESS MODE SOFTWARE MODEL

We will begin our study of the 80286 microprocessor by exploring its real-address mode software model and operation. Whenever the 80286 is powered on or reset, it comes up in the real mode. The 80286 will remain in the real mode unless it is switched to protected mode under software control. In fact, in many applications the 80286 is simply used in real mode.

In real mode, the 80286 operates like a high-performance 8086. Figure 10.1 compares the performance of the 80286 with the 8086. For example, the standard 8 MHz 80286 provides more than five times higher performance than the standard 5 MHz 8086. Furthermore, the 10 MHz 80286 out performs the same 8086 by a factor of 7.

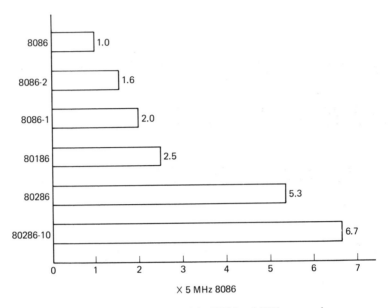

Figure 10.1 Performance of the 80286 and 8086 compared.

When in the real mode, the 80286 can be used to execute the base instruction set of the 8086/8088 architectures. Object code for the base instructions of the 80286 is identical to that of the 8086/8088. This means that operating systems and programs written for the 8086 and 8088 can be run directly on the 80286 without modification. For this reason, we can say that the 80286 is *object code compatible* with the 8086 and 8088 microprocessors.

A number of new instructions have been added in the instruction set of the 80286 to enhance performance and functionality. For example, instructions have been added to push or pop the complete register set, perform string I/O, and check the boundaries of data array accesses. We also say that object code is *upward compatible* within the 8086 architecture. By this, we mean that 8086/8088 object code will run on the 80286, but the reverse is not true if any of the new instructions are in use.

The real-mode software model of the 80286 is shown in Fig. 10.2. Here we see that it has 15 internal registers. Fourteen of them, the instruction pointer (IP), data registers (AX, BX, CX, and DX), pointer registers (BP and SP), index registers (SI and DI), segment registers (CS, DS, SS, and ES), and the flag register (F) are identical to the corresponding registers in the 8086's software model, and they serve the same functions. For instance, CS:IP points to the next instruction that is to be fetched.

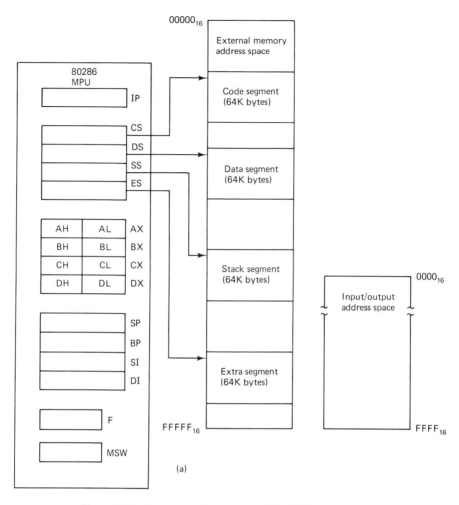

Figure 10.2 Real-mode software model of the 80286 microprocessor.

A new register called the *machine status word register* (MSW) is added in the 80286 model. The only bit in MSW that is active in the real mode is the *protected-mode enable* (PE) bit. This is the bit that is used to switch the 80286 from real to protected mode.

Looking at Fig. 10.2, we find that the 80286 microcomputer's real-mode address space is also identical to that of the 8086 microcomputer. It is partitioned into a 1M-byte memory address space and a separate 64K-byte input/output address space. The memory address space resides in the range from address 00000 to FFFFF$_{16}$. I/O addresses span 64K bytes of the range 0000$_{16}$ to FFFF$_{16}$. Moreover, in the memory address space, just four 64K-byte segments are active at a time for a total of 256K bytes of active memory. Again, 64K bytes of the active memory are allocated for code storage, 64K bytes for stack, and 128K bytes for data storage.

Figures 10.3 (a) and (b) show that the real-mode 80286 memory and I/O address

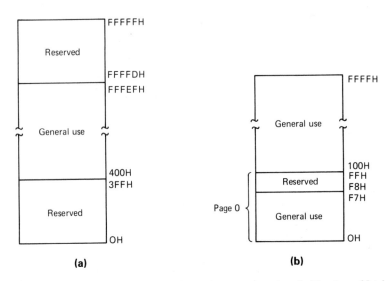

Figure 10.3 (a) Dedicated and general use of memory in real-mode (Courtesy of Intel Corp.); (b) I/O address space (Courtesy of Intel Corp.).

spaces are partitioned into general-use and reserved areas in the same way as for the 8086. For instance, in Fig. 10.3(a) we find that the first 1K bytes of the memory address space, addresses 0_{16} through $3FF_{16}$, are reserved and are used for storage of the interrupt vector table. Moreover, Fig. 10.3(b) shows that the first 256-byte I/O addresses are identified as page 0. They can be directly addressed by an IN or OUT instruction.

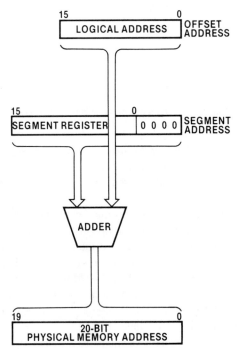

Figure 10.4 Real-address mode physical address generation (Courtesy of Intel Corp.).

Finally, the real-mode 80286 generates physical addresses in the same manner as the 8086. This address generation is illustrated in Fig. 10.4. Notice that the 16-bit contents of a segment register, such as CS, are shifted left by four bit positions, the four least-significant bits are filled with 0s, and the result is added to a 16-bit logical address, such as the value in IP, to form the 20-bit physical memory address CS:IP.

10.3 REAL-MODE EXTENDED INSTRUCTION SET

Figure 10.5 shows the evolution of the instruction set for the 8086 architecture. The instruction set of the 8086, 8088, 80186 and 80188 microprocessors, which is called the *base instruction set,* was enhanced in the 80286 microprocessor to implement what is called the *extended instruction set.* This extended instruction set includes several new instructions and implements additional addressing modes for a few of the instructions already available in the basic instruction set. For example, two instructions added as extensions to the basic instruction set are *push all* (PUSHA) and *pop all* (POPA). In Fig. 10.6, we see that the PUSH and IMUL instructions have been enhanced to permit the use of immediate operand addressing. In this way, we see that the 80286's real-mode instruction set is a superset of the basic instruction set. These instructions are all executable by the 80286 in the real mode. Let us now look at the new instructions in more detail.

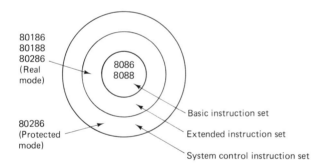

80186
80188
80286
(Real mode)

8086
8088

80286
(Protected mode)

Basic instruction set

Extended instruction set

System control instruction set

Figure 10.5 Evolution of the instruction set for the 8086 microprocessor family (Courtesy of Intel Corp.).

Push-All and Pop-All Instructions—PUSHA and POPA

When writing the compiler for a high-level language such as C, it is very common to push the contents of all of the general registers of the 80286 to the stack before calling a subroutine. If we use the PUSH instruction to perform this operation, many instructions need to be coded. To simplify this operation, special instructions are provided in the instructon set of the 80286. They are called *push all* (PUSHA) and *pop all* (POPA).

Looking at Fig. 10.6 we see that execution of PUSHA causes the values in AX, CX, DX, BX, SP, BP, SI, and DI to be pushed, in that order, onto the top of the stack. Figure 10.7 shows the state of the stack before and after execution of the instruction. As shown in Fig. 10.8, executing a POPA instruction at the end of the subroutine restores the old state of the 80286.

Mnemonic	Meaning	Format	Operation
PUSH	Push	PUSH dw/db	Push the specified data word (dw) or sign extended data byte (db) onto the stack.
PUSHA	Push all	PUSHA	Push the contents of registers AX, CX, DX, BX, original SP, BP, SI, and DI onto the stack.
POPA	Pop all	POPA	Pop the stack contents into the registers DI, SI, BP, SP, BX, DX, CX, and AX.
IMUL	Integer multiply	IMUL rw, ew, dw/db	Perform the signed multiplication as follows: rw = ew*dw/db where rw is the word size register, ew is the effective word size operand, and the third operand is the immediate data word (dw) or a byte (db).
Logic instructions		Instruction db	Perform the logic instruction using the specified byte (db) as the count.
INS	Input string	INSB, INSW	Input the byte or the word size element of the string from the port specified by DX to the location ES: [DI].
OUTS	Output string	OUTSB, OUTSW	Output the byte or the word size element of the string from ES: [SI] to port specified by DX.
ENTER	Enter procedure	ENTER dw, 0/1/db	Make stack frame for procedure parameters.
LEAVE	Leave procedure	LEAVE	Release the stack space used by the procedure.
BOUND	Check array index against bounds	BOUND rw, md	Interrupt 5 occurs if the register word (rw) is not greater than or equal to the memory word at md and not less than or equal to the second memory word at md + 1.

Figure 10.6 Extended instruction set.

Stack Frame Instructions—ENTER and LEAVE

Before the main program calls a subroutine, quite often it is necessary for the calling program to pass the values of some *variables (parameters)* to the subroutine. It is a common practice to push these variables onto the stack before calling the routine. Then during the execution of the subroutine, they are accessed by reading them from the stack and used in computations. Two instructions are provided in the extended instruction set of the 80286 to allocate and de-allocate a data area called a *stack frame*. This data area, which is located in the stack part of memory, is used for local storage of parameters and other data.

Normally, high-level languages allocate a stack frame for each procedure in a program. The stack frame provides a dynamically allocated local storage space for the procedure and contains data such as variables, pointers to the stack frames of the previous procedures from which the current procedure was called, and a return address for

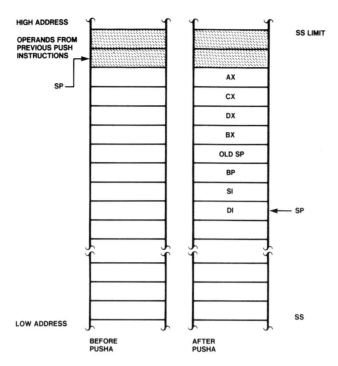

HIGH ADDRESS

OPERANDS FROM
PREVIOUS PUSH
INSTRUCTIONS

SP

SS LIMIT

AX
CX
DX
BX
OLD SP
BP
SI
DI

SP

LOW ADDRESS

SS

BEFORE
PUSHA

AFTER
PUSHA

Figure 10.7 State of the stack before and after executing PUSHA (Courtesy of Intel Corp.).

linkage to the stack frame of the calling procedure. This mechanism also permits access to the data in stack frames of the calling procedures.

The instructions used for allocation and de-allocation of stack frames are given in Fig. 10.6 as *enter* (ENTER) and *leave* (LEAVE). Execution of an ENTER instruction allocates a stack frame; it is de-allocated by executing LEAVE. For this reason, as shown in Fig. 10.9, the ENTER instruction is used at the beginning of a subroutine, and LEAVE at the end, just before the return instruction.

Looking at Fig. 10.6, we find that the ENTER instruction has two operands. The first operand, identified as Imm16, is a word-size immediate operand. This operand specifies the number of bytes to be allocated on the stack for local data storage of the procedure. The second operand, Imm8, which is a byte-size immediate operand, specifies what is called the *lexical nesting level* of the routine. This lexical level defines how many pointers to previous stack frames can be stored in the current stack frame. This list of previous stack frame pointers is called a *display*. The value of the lexical level byte must be limited to a maximum of 32 in 80286 programs.

An example of an ENTER instruction is

$$\text{ENTER} \quad 12, \ 2$$

Execution of this instruction allocates 12 bytes of local storage on the stack for use as

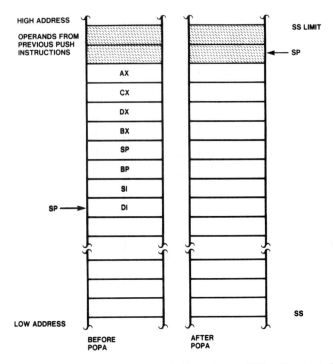

Figure 10.8 State of the stack before and after executing POPA (Courtesy of Intel Corp.).

a stack frame. It does this by decrementing SP by 12. This defines a new top of stack at address SS:SP-12. Also the *base pointer* (BP) that identifies the beginning of the previous stack frame is copied into the stack frame created by the ENTER instruction. This value is called the *dynamic link* and is held in the first storage location of the stack frame. The number of stack frame pointers that can be saved in a stack frame is equal

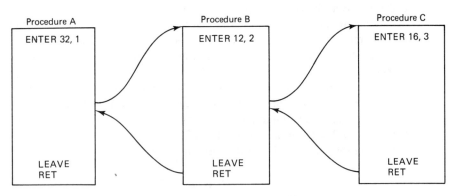

Figure 10.9 Enter/leave example.

to the value of the byte that specifies the lexical level of the procedure. Therefore, in our example, just two levels of nesting is permitted.

The BP register is used as a pointer into the stack segment of memory. When a procedure is called, the value in BP points to the stack frame location that contains the previous stack frame pointer (dynamic link). Therefore, based indexed addressing can be used to access variables in the stack frame by referencing the BP register.

The LEAVE instruction reverses the process of an ENTER instruction; that is, its execution de-allocates the stack frame. This is done by first automatically loading SP from the BP register. This returns the storage locations of the current stack frame to the stack. Now SP points to the location where the dynamic link (pointer to the previous stack frame) is stored. Next popping the contents of the stack into BP returns the pointer to the stack frame of the previous procedure.

To illustrate the operation of the stack frame instructions, let us consider the example of Fig. 10.9. Here we find three procedures. Procedure A is used to call procedure B, which in turn calls procedure C. It is assumed that the lexical levels for these procedures are 1, 2, and 3, respectively. The ENTER, LEAVE, and RET instructions for each procedure are shown in the diagram. Notice that the ENTER instructions specify the lexical levels for the procedures.

The stack frames created by executing the ENTER instructions in the three procedures are shown in Fig. 10.10. As the ENTER instruction in procedure A is executed, the old BP from the procedure that called procedure A is pushed onto the stack. BP is loaded from SP to point to the location of the old BP. Since the second operand is 1, only the current BP that is the BP for procedure A is pushed onto the stack. Finally, to allocate 32 bytes for the stack frame, 32 is subtracted from the current value in SP.

After entering procedure B, a second ENTER instruction is encountered. This time the lexical level is 2. Therefore, the instruction first pushes the old BP that is the BP for procedure A onto the stack, then pushes the BP previously stored on the stack frame for A to the stack, and last it pushes the current BP for procedure B to the stack. This mechanism provides access by procedure B to the stack frame for procedure A. 202 Next, 12 bytes as specified by the instruction are allocated for local storage.

The ENTER instruction in procedure C is next executed. This instruction has the lexical level of 3; therefore it pushes the BPs for the two previous procedures, that is, B and A, to the stack.

Input String and Output String Instructions—
INS and OUTS

In Fig. 10.6 we find that there are also input and output string instructions in the extended instruction set of the 80286. Using these string instructions, a programmer can either input data from an input port to a storage location directly in memory or output data from a memory location to an output port.

The first instruction, called *input string,* can be denoted either of two ways, INSB or INSW. INSB stands for *input string byte* and INSW means *input string word.* Let us now look at the operation performed by the INSB instruction. INSB assumes that the address of the input port that is to be accessed is in the DX register. This value must

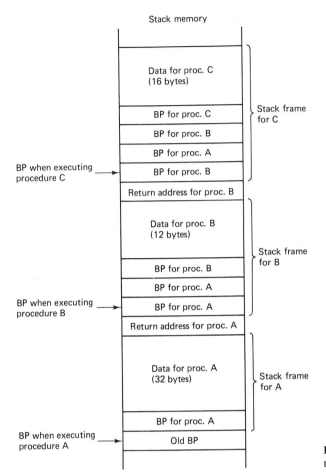

Stack memory

Data for proc. C
(16 bytes)

BP for proc. C

BP for proc. B

BP for proc. A

BP when executing
procedure C → BP for proc. B

Stack frame
for C

Return address for proc. B

Data for proc. B
(12 bytes)

BP for proc. B

BP for proc. A

BP when executing
procedure B → BP for proc. A

Stack frame
for B

Return address for proc. A

Data for proc. A
(32 bytes)

Stack frame
for A

BP for proc. A

BP when executing
procedure A → Old BP

Figure 10.10 Stack after execution of enter instructions for procedures A, B, and C.

be loaded prior to executing the string instruction. Moreover, the address of the memory storage location into which the bytes of data are input is identified by the current values in ES and DI; that is, when executed, the input operation performed is

$$(ES:DI) \longleftarrow ((DX))$$

Just as for the other byte string instructions, the value in DI is either incremented or decremented by 1 after the data transfer takes place.

$$DI \longleftarrow DI \pm 1$$

In this way, it points to the next byte-wide storage location in memory to be accessed. Whether the value in DI is incremented or decremented depends on the setting of the DF flag. Notice in Fig. 10.6 that INSW performs the same data transfer operation except that since the word contents of the I/O port are stored in memory, the value in DI is incremented or decremented by 2.

The INSB instruction performs the operation we just described on one data element not on an array of elements. However, this basic operation can be repeated to handle a block input operation. Block operations are done by inserting a repeat (REP) prefix in front of the string instruction. For example, the instruction

REPINSW

will cause the contents of the word-wide port pointed to by the I/O address in DX to be input and saved in the memory location at address ES:DI. Then the value in DX is incremented by 2 (assuming that DF equals 0), the count in CX is decremented by 1, and the value in CX is tested to determine if it is 0. As long as the value in CX is not 0, the input operation is repeated. When CX equals 0, all elements of the array have been input, and the input string operation is complete. Remember that the count representing the number of times the string operation is to be repeated must be loaded into the CX register prior to executing the repeat input string instruction.

In Fig. 10.6 we also see that OUTSB and OUTSW are the two forms of the *output string* instruction. These instructions operate in a way similar to the input string instructions; however, they perform an output operation. For instance, executing OUTSW causes the operation that follows.

$$(ES:SI) \longrightarrow ((DX))$$

$$SI \pm 2 \longrightarrow SI$$

That is, the word of data held at the memory location pointed to by address ES:SI is output to the word-wide port pointed to by the I/O address in DX. After the output data transfer is complete, the value in SI is either incremented or decremented by 2.

An example of an output string instruction that can be used to output an array of data is

REPOUTSB

When executed this instruction causes the data elements of the array of byte-wide data pointed to by ES:SI to be output one after the other to the output port located at the I/O address in DX. Again, the count in CX defines the size of the array.

Check Array Index Against Bounds Instruction—BOUND

The *check array index against bounds* (BOUND) instruction, as its name implies, can determine if the contents of a register, known as the *array index,* lies within a set of minimum/maximum values, called the *upper and lower bounds*. This type of operation is important when accessing elements of an array of data in memory.

The format of the BOUND instruction is given in Fig. 10.6. An example is the instruction

BOUND   SI,LIMITS

Notice that the instruction contains two operands. The first operand represents the register whose word contents are to be tested to verify whether or not it lies within the boundaries. In our example, this is the source index register (SI). The second operand is the effective relative address of the first of two word-storage locations in memory that contain the values of the lower and upper boundaries. In the example, the word of data starting at address LIMITS is the value of the lower boundary and that stored at address LIMITS + 2 is the value of the upper boundary.

When this BOUND instruction is executed, the contents of SI are compared with both the value of the lower bound at LIMITS and the upper bound at LIMITS + 2. If it is found to be either less than the lower bound or more than the upper bound, an exception occurs and control is passed to a service routine through the vector for type 5. Otherwise, the next sequential instruction is performed.

10.4 PROTECTED-ADDRESS MODE SOFTWARE ARCHITECTURE OF THE 80286

Having completed our study of the real-mode operation of the 80286 microprocessor and its extended instruction set, we are now ready to turn our attention to its protected mode of operation. Earlier we indicated that whenever the 80286 microprocessor is reset, it comes up in real mode. Moreover, we indicated that the PE bit of the machine status word can be used to switch the 80286 to the protected mode under software control. When configured for protected mode, the 80286 provides an advanced software architecture that supports memory management and virtual addressing, protection, and multitasking. In this section we will examine the 80286's protected-mode register model, virtual memory address space, and memory management.

Protected-Mode Register Model

The protected-mode register set of the 80286 microprocessor is illustrated in Fig. 10.11. Looking at this diagram, we see that it is a superset of the real-mode register set shown in Fig. 10.2. Comparing these two diagrams, we find five new registers in the protected-mode model: the *global descriptor table register* (GDTR), *interrupt descriptor table register* (IDTR), *machine status word* (MSW), *task register* (TR), and *local descriptor table register* (LDTR). Let us next discuss the purpose of each of the new registers and how they are used to implement the protected-mode operation for the microprocessor.

Global descriptor table register. As shown in Fig. 10.12, the contents of the *global descriptor table register* defines a table in the 80286's physical memory address space called the *global descriptor table* (GDT). The global descriptor table is an important element of the 80286's memory management system.

GDTR is a 40-bit register that is located inside the 80286. The lower two bytes of this register, which are identified as LIMIT in Fig. 10.12, specify the size in bytes of the GDT. The decimal value of LIMIT is one less than the actual size of the table. For instance, if LIMIT equals $00FF_{16}$ the table is 256 bytes in length. Since LIMIT has 16 bits, the GDT can be up to 65,536 bytes long. The upper three bytes of the GDTR,

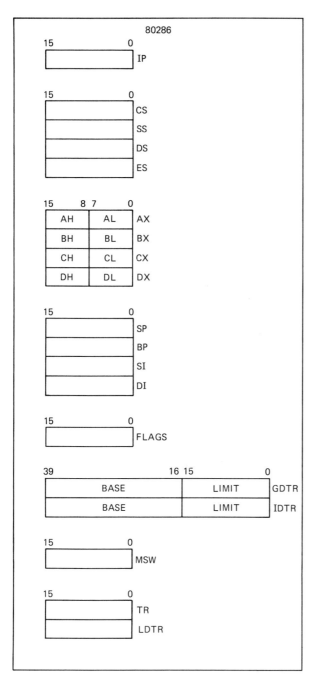

Figure 10.11 Protected-mode register model.

which are labeled BASE in Fig. 10.12, locate the beginning of the GDT in memory. This 24-bit base address allows the table to be positioned anywhere in the 80286's 16M-byte protected-mode address space.

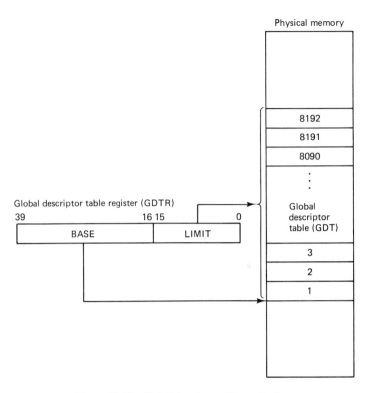

Figure 10.12 Global descriptor table mechanism.

If the limit and base in the global descriptor table register are $0FFF_{16}$ and 100000_{16}, respectively, what is the beginning address of the descriptor table, the ending address of the table, and the size of the table in bytes?

SOLUTION The starting address of the global descriptor table in physical memory is given by the base. Therefore,

$$GDT_{START} = 100000_{16}$$

The limit is the offset to the end of the table. This gives

$$GDT_{END} = 100000_{16} + 0FFF_{16} = 100FFF_{16}$$

Finally, the size of the table is equal to the decimal value of the limit plus 1.

$$GDT_{SIZE} = FFF_{16} + 1 = 4096 \text{ bytes}$$

The GDT provide a mechanism for defining the characteristics of the 80286's *global memory* address space. Global memory is a general system resource that is shared by all software tasks; that is, storage locations in global memory are accessible by any task that runs on the microprocessor. This table contains what are called *system segment descriptors*. Descriptors are what identify the characteristics of the segments of global memory. For instance, a segment descriptor provides information about the size, starting point, and access rights of a global memory segment. Each descriptor is 8 bytes long, thus our earlier example of a 256-byte table provides enough storage space for just 32 descriptors. Remember that the size of the global descriptor table can be expanded by simply changing the value of LIMIT in the GDTR under software control. If the table is increased to its maximum size of 65,536 bytes, it can hold up to 8192 descriptors.

EXAMPLE 10.2

How many descriptors can be stored in the global descriptor table defined in example 10.1?

SOLUTION   Each descriptor takes up 8 bytes; therefore, a 4096-byte table can hold

$$\text{DESCRIPTORS} = 4096/8 = 512$$

The values of the BASE and LIMIT must be loaded into the GDTR before the 80286 is switched from real mode of operation to the protected mode. Special instructions are provided for this purpose in the instruction set of the 80286. These instructions will be introduced later in this chapter. Once the 80286 is in protected mode, the location of the table is typically not changed.

Interrupt descriptor table register.   Just like the global descriptor table register, the *interrupt descriptor table register* (IDTR) defines a table in physical memory; however, this table contains what are called *interrupt descriptors* not system segment descriptor. For this reason, it is known as the *interrupt descriptor table* (IDT). This register and table of descriptors provide the mechanism by which the microprocessor passes program control to interrupt and exception service routines.

As shown in Fig. 10.13, the IDTR is also a 40-bit register. Again, the lower two bytes of the register (LIMIT) define the table size; that is, the size of the table equals LIMIT + 1 bytes. Since two bytes define the size, the IDT can also be up to 65,536 bytes long. But the 80286 supports only up to 256 interrupts and exceptions; therefore, its size should not be set to allow more than 256 interrupts. The upper three bytes of IDTR (BASE) identify the starting address of the IDT in memory.

The interrupt descriptors normally used in the IDT are called *interrupt gates*. These gates provide a means for passing program control to the beginning of an interrupt service routine. Each gate is 8 bytes long and contains both attributes and a starting address for the service routine.

EXAMPLE 10.3

What is the maximum value that should be assigned to the LIMIT in the IDTR?

SOLUTION   The maximum number of interrupt descriptors that can be used in the 80286 microcomputer system is 256. Therefore, the maximum table size in bytes is

$$\text{IDT}_{\text{SIZE}} = 8 \times 256 = 4096 = 1000_{16}$$

$$\text{LIMIT} = 1000_{16} - 1 = 0\text{FFF}_{16}$$

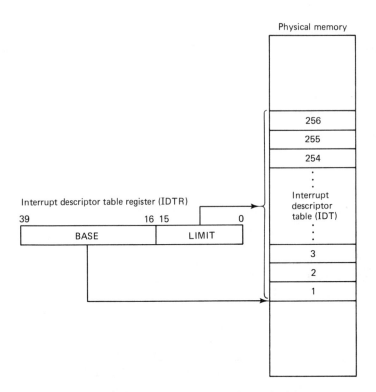

Figure 10.13 Interrupt descriptor table mechanism.

This table can also be located anywhere in the physical address space addressable with the 80286's 24-bit address. Just like the GDTR, the IDTR is to be loaded before switching the 80286 from the real mode to protected mode. Special instructions are provided for loading and saving the contents of the IDTR. Once the location of the table is set, it is not typically changed after entering protected mode.

EXAMPLE 10.4

What is the address range of the last descriptor in the interrupt descriptor table defined by base address 011000_{16} and limit $01FF_{16}$?

SOLUTION From the values of the base and limit, we find that the table is located in the address range

$$IDT_{START} = 011000_{16}$$

$$IDT_{END} = 0111FF_{16}$$

The last descriptor in this table takes up the 8 bytes of memory from address $0111F8_{16}$ through $0111FF_{16}$.

Machine status word. The *machine status word* (MSW) is a 16-bit register that contains information about the 80286's protected-mode configuration and status. The four implemented bits are identified in Fig. 10.14. Notice that the three lower bits are labeled PE, MP, and EM. They are control bits that define the protected-mode configuration. The fourth bit, TS, is a status bit. Each of these bits can be modified through software.

TS EM MP PE   **Figure 10.14** Machine status word.

The *protected-mode enable* (PE) bit determines if the 80286 is in the real or protected mode. At reset, the MSW is cleared. This makes PE logic 0 and enables real mode of operation. To enter protected mode, we simply switch PE to 1 through software. Once in protected mode, the 80286 cannot be switched back to real mode under software control. The only way to return to real mode is by initiating a hardware reset.

The *monitor processor extension* (MP) bit is set to 1 to indicate that an 80287 numerics coprocessor is present in the 80286 microcomputer system. On the other hand, if the system is to be configured so that a software emulator instead of a coprocessor is used to perform 80287 operations, the *emulate processor extension* (EM) bit is set to 1. Only one of these two bits can be set at a time.

The last bit in the MSW, *task switched* (TS), automatically gets set whenever the 80286 switches from one task to another. It can be cleared under software control.

Task register. The *task register* (TR) is one of the key elements in the protected-mode task-switching mechanism of the 80286 microprocessor. This register holds a 16-bit index value called a *selector*. The initial selector must be loaded into TR under software control. This starts the initial task. After this is done, the selector is automatically changed whenever the 80286 executes an instruction that performs a task switch.

As shown in Fig. 10.15, the selector in the TR is used to locate a descriptor in the global descriptor table. Notice that when a selector is loaded into the TR, the corresponding *task state segment (TSS) descriptor* automatically gets read from memory and loaded into the on-chip *task descriptor cache*. This descriptor defines a block of memory called the *task state segment*. It does this by providing the starting address (BASE) and the size (LIMIT) of the segment. Every task has its own TSS. The TSS holds the information needed to initiate the task, such as initial values for the user-accessible registers.

Local descriptor table register. The *local descriptor table register* (LDTR) is also part of the 80286's memory management support mechanism. As shown in Fig. 10.16(a), each task can have access to its own private descriptor table in addition to the global descriptor table. This private table is called the *local descriptor table* (LDT) and defines a *local memory* address space for use by the task. The LDT holds segment descriptors that provide access to code and data in segments of memory that are reserved for the current task. Since each task can have its own segment of local memory, the

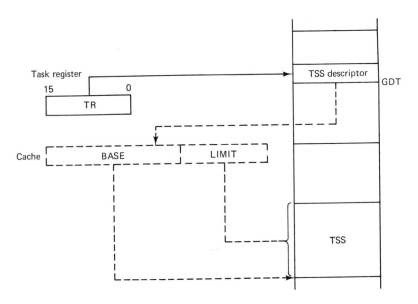

Figure 10.15 Task register and task switching mechanism.

protected-mode software system may contain many local descriptor tables. For this reason, we have identified LDT_1, through LDT_m in Fig. 10.16(a).

Figure 10.16(b) shows that the 16-bit LDTR does not directly define the local descriptor table. Instead, it holds a selector that points to a *LDT descriptor* in the GDT. Whenever a selector is loaded into the LDTR, the corresponding 40-bit descriptor is transparently read from the GDT and loaded into the *local descriptor table cache* within the 80286. It is this descriptor that defines the local descriptor table. As shown, the 24-bit base value identifies the starting point of the table in physical memory and the 16-bit limit determines the size of the table. The loading of this descriptor creates the LDT for the current task. Every time a selector is loaded into the LDTR, a local descriptor table descriptor is cached and a new LDT is activated.

Registers with changed functionality. The function of a few of the registers that are common to both the real-mode and protected-mode register models change as the 80286 is switched into the protected mode of operation. For instance, the segment registers are now called the *segment selector registers,* and instead of holding a base address, they are loaded with what is known as a *selector*.

The format of a selector is shown in Fig. 10.17. Here we see that the two least significant bits are labeled RPL, which stands for *requested privilege level*. These bits contain either 0, 1, 2, or 3 and assign a request protection level to the selector. The next bit, which is identified as *task indicator* (TI) in Fig. 10.17, selects the table to be used when accessing a segment descriptor. Earlier we identified the two descriptor tables that exist in the protected mode, the global descriptor table and the local descriptor table. For example, looking at Fig. 10.17, we see that if TI is 0 the selector corresponds to a descriptor in the global descriptor table. Finally, the 13 most significant bits

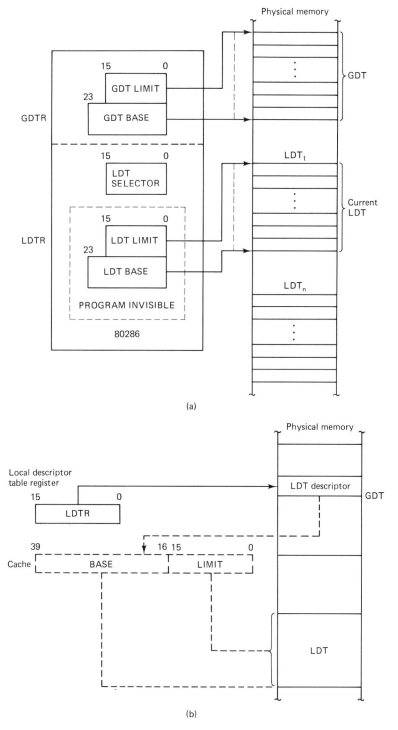

Figure 10.16 (a) Task with global and local descriptor table; (b) loading the local descriptor table register to define a local descriptor table.

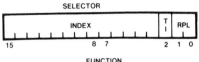

BITS	NAME	FUNCTION
1-0	REQUESTED PRIVILEGE LEVEL (RPL)	INDICATES SELECTOR PRIVILEGE LEVEL DESIRED
2	TABLE INDICATOR (TI)	TI = 0 USE GLOBAL DESCRIPTOR TABLE (GDT) TI = 1 USE LOCAL DESCRIPTOR TABLE (LDT)
15-3	INDEX	SELECT DESCRIPTOR ENTRY IN TABLE

Figure 10.17 Selector format (Courtesy of Intel Corp.).

contain an *index* that is used as a pointer to pick a specific descriptor in the table selected by TI.

EXAMPLE 10.5

Assume that the base address of the LDT is 00120000_{16} and the GDT base address is 00100000_{16}. If the value of the selector loaded into the CS register is 1007_{16}, what is the request privilege level? Is the segment descriptor in the GDT or LDT? What is the address of the segment descriptor?

SOLUTION   Expressing the selector in binary form, we get

$$CS = 0001000000000111_2$$

Since the two least significant bits are both 1,

$$RPL = 3$$

The next bit, bit 2, is also 1. This means that the segment descriptor is in the LDT. Finally, the value in the 13 most significant bits (INDEX) must be scaled by 8 to give the offset of the descriptor from the base address of the table. Therefore,

$$OFFSET = 0001000000000_2 \times 8 = 512 \times 8 = 4096$$

$$= 1000_{16}$$

and the address of the segment descriptor is

$$DESCRIPTOR_{ADDRESS} = 0010000 + 1000_{16}$$

$$= 0011000_{16}$$

Another register whose function changes in protected mode is the flag register. The protected-mode flag register of the 80286 is given in Fig. 10.18. Comparing this illustration with the 80286 real-mode (8086) flag register in Fig. 2.15, we see that three additional bits are identified as special fields. These bits are active only when the 80286 is in protected mode. They are the two-bit *input/output privilege level* (IOPL) code and the *nested task* (NT) flag. The IOPL bits are used to assign a maximum privilege level

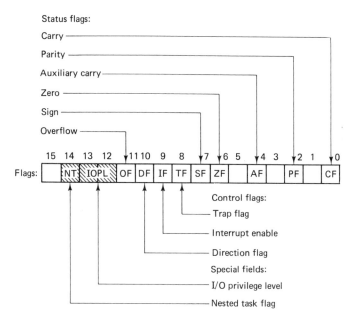

Status flags:

Carry

Parity

Auxiliary carry

Zero

Sign

Overflow

Flags:

| 15 | 14 | 13 12 | | 11 | 10 | 9 | 8 | 7 | 6 | 5 | 4 | 3 | 2 | 1 | 0 |

NT IOPL OF DF IF TF SF ZF AF PF CF

Control flags:
- Trap flag
- Interrupt enable
- Direction flag

Special fields:
- I/O privilege level
- Nested task flag

Figure 10.18 Protected-mode flag register.

to input/output. For instance, if 00 is loaded into IOPL, I/O can be performed only when the 80286 is in the highest privilege level, which is called *level 0*. On the other hand, if IOPL is 11, I/O is assigned to the lowest privilege level, level 3.

NT identifies whether or not the current task is a nested task; that is, if it was called from another task. This bit is automatically set when a nested task is initiated and can be reset only through software.

Protected-Mode Memory Management and Address Translation

Up to this point in the section, we have introduced the register set of the protected-mode software model for the 80286 microprocessor; however, the software model of a microprocessor also includes its memory structure. Because of the memory management capability of the 80286, the organization of protected-mode memory appears quite complex. Here we will examine how the *memory management unit* of the 80286 implements the address space and how it translates virtual addresses to physical addresses.

The virtual address and virtual address space. The protected-mode memory management unit employs memory pointers that are 32 bits in length and consist of two parts, the *selector* and the *offset*. This 32-bit memory pointer is called a *virtual address* and is used by the program to specify the memory location of instructions or data. As shown in Fig. 10.19, both the selector and offset are 16 bits in length. Earlier we pointed out that one source of selectors is the segment selector registers within the 80286. For instance, if code is being accessed in memory, the active segment

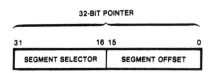

32-BIT POINTER

31   16 15   0

| SEGMENT SELECTOR | SEGMENT OFFSET |

Figure 10.19 Protected-mode memory pointer (Courtesy of Intel Corp.).

selector will be that held in CS. This part of the pointer selects a unique segment of the 80286's *virtual address space.*

The offset is held in one of the 80286's other user-accessible registers. For our example of a code access, the offset would be in the IP register. This part of the pointer is the displacement of the memory location that is to be accessed within the selected segment of memory. In our example, it points to the first byte of the instruction that is to be fetched for execution. Since the offset is 16 bits in length, segment size can be as large as 64K bytes. We say as large as 64K bytes because segment size is actually variable and can be defined to be as small as 1 byte to as large as 64K bytes.

Figure 10.20 shows that the 16-bit segment selector breaks down into a *13-bit index, table select bit,* and two bits used for a *request privilege level.* The two RPL bits are not used in the selection of the memory segment. That is, just 14 of its 16 bits are employed in addressing memory. Therefore, the virtual address space can consist of 2^{14} (16,384) unique segments of memory, each of which has a maximum size of 64K bytes. These segments are the basic elements into which the memory management unit of the 80286 organizes the virtual address space.

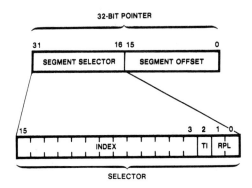

Figure 10.20 Segment selector format (Courtesy of Intel Corp.).

Another way of looking at the size of the virtual address space is that by combining the 14-bit segment selector with the 16-bit offset, we get a 30-bit virtual address. Therefore, the 80286's virtual address space can contain 2^{30} = 1G byte (Gigabyte) unique byte addresses.

Partitioning the virtual address space. The 1G-byte virtual address space of the 80286 is actually partitioned by the memory management unit into a 1/2G-byte *global memory address space* and a 1/2G-byte *local memory address space.* This partitioning is illustrated in Fig. 10.21. The TI bit of the segment selector in Fig. 6.10 is used to select the global or local descriptor tables that define the virtual address space.

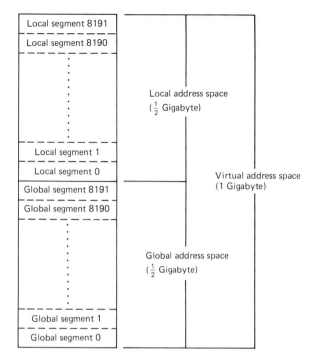

Local segment 8191		
Local segment 8190		
⋮	Local address space ($\frac{1}{2}$ Gigabyte)	
Local segment 1		
Local segment 0		Virtual address space (1 Gigabyte)
Global segment 8191		
Global segment 8190		
⋮	Global address space ($\frac{1}{2}$ Gigabyte)	
Global segment 1		
Global segment 0		

Figure 10.21 Partitioning the virtual address space.

Within each of these address spaces, as many as 8192 segments may exist. This assumes that every descriptor in both the global descriptor table and local descriptor table is in use. These descriptors define the attributes of the corresponding segment; however, in practical system applications not all descriptors are normally in use. Let us now briefly look at how global and local segments of memory are used by software.

In the multiprocessing software environment of the 80286, an application is expressed as a collection of tasks. By *task* we mean a group of program routines that together perform a specific function. When the 80286 initiates a task, it can have both global and local segments of memory active. This idea is illustrated in Fig. 10.22. Notice that tasks 1, 2, and 3 each have a reserved segment of the local address space. This part of memory stores data or code that can be accessed only by the corresponding task. That is, task 2 cannot access any of the information in the local address space of task 1. On the other hand, all the tasks are shown to share the same segment of the global address space. This segment typically contains operating system resources and data that are to be shared by all or many tasks.

Physical address space and virtual-to-physical address translation. We just found that the virtual address space available to the programmer is 1G byte in length. However, the 24-bit protected-mode address bus of the 80286 supports just a 16M-byte *physical address space*. For this reason, systems that employ a virtual address space that is larger than the implemented physical memory are equipped with a secondary storage device such as a hard disk. In this way, segments that are not currently in use are stored on disk.

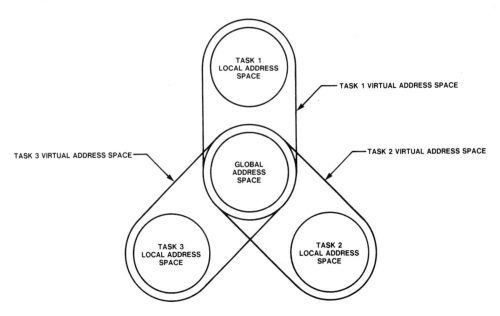

Figure 10.22 Global and local memory for a task (Courtesy of Intel Corp.).

The memory management unit (MMU) of the 80286 provides the mechanism by which 32 bit virtual addresses are mapped into the 24-bit physical addresses needed by hardware. This address translation is illustrated in Fig. 10.23. The memory manager identifies whether or not the corresponding segment of the virtual address space currently exists in internal storage memory. If not, it signals this condition to the operating system as an error. By receiving the error signal, the operating system can initiate loading of the segment from the external storage device to internal memory. This operation is called a *swap*. That is, an old segment gets transferred to disk to make room in physical memory, then the new segment is moved into this freed space. Even though a swap has taken place, it appears to the program that all segments are available in physical memory. We will now look closer at the address translation process.

Earlier we found that the 80286's segment registers, CS, DS, ES, and SS, provide the segment selectors that are used to index into either the global descriptor table or the local descriptor table. Whenever a selector value is loaded into a segment register, the descriptor pointed to by the index in the table selected by the TI bit is automatically fetched from memory and loaded into the corresponding *segment descriptor cache register*.

Notice in Fig. 10.24 that the 80286 has one 48-bit internal segment descriptor cache register for each of the segment selector registers. These cache registers are not accessible by the programmer. Instead, they are transparently loaded with a complete descriptor whenever an instruction is executed that loads a new selector into a segment register. For instance, if an operand is to be accessed from a new data segment, a local memory data segment selector would be first loaded into DS with the instruction

MOV DS, AX

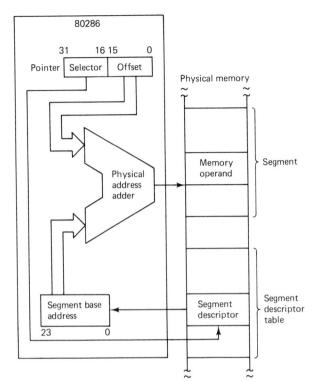

Figure 10.23 Translating a virtual address into a physical address (Courtesy of Intel Corp.).

As this instruction is executed, the selector in AX is loaded into DS and then the corresponding descriptor in the local descriptor table is read from memory and loaded into the data segment descriptor cache register.

In this way, we see that the segment descriptors held in the caches dynamically change as a task is performed. At any one time, the memory management unit permits just four segments of memory to be active. These segments correspond to the four segment registers, CS, DS, ES, and SS, and can reside in either local or global memory. Once the descriptors are cached, subsequent references to them are performed without any overhead for loading of the descriptors.

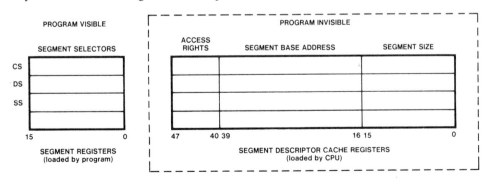

Figure 10.24 Segment registers and the segment descriptor cache registers (Courtesy of Intel Corp.).

In Fig. 10.24 we find that this data segment descriptor has three parts, an *access rights byte,* a *24-bit segment base address,* and a *segment-size word.* The value of the 24-bit segment base address identifies the beginning of the data segment that is to be accessed in physical memory. The loading of the data segment descriptor cache completes the table lookup that maps the 16-bit selector to its equivalent 24-bit data segment base address.

The location of the operand in this data segment is determined by the offset part of the virtual address. For example, let us assume that the next instruction to be executed needs to access an operand in this data segment and that the instruction uses based addressing mode to specify the operand. Then the BX register holds the offset of the operand from the base address of the data segment. Figure 10.23 shows that the base address is directly added to the offset to produce the 24-bit physical address of the operand. This addition completes the translation of the 32-bit virtual address into the 24-bit physical address needed to access data memory.

EXAMPLE 10.6

Assume that in Fig. 10.23, the virtual address is made up of a segment selector equal to 0100_{16} and offset equal to 2000_{16}. If the segment base address read in from the descriptor is 020000_{16}, what is the physical address of the operand?

SOLUTION   The virtual address is

$$\text{VIRTUAL ADDRESS} = 01002000_{16}$$

This virtual address translates to the physical address

$$\text{PHYSICAL ADDRESS} = \text{BASE ADDRESS} + \text{OFFSET}$$

$$= 020000_{16} + 2000_{16}$$

$$= 022000_{16}$$

10.5 DESCRIPTORS

In the previous section of this chapter we frequently used the term *descriptor.* We talked about the descriptor as an element of the global descriptor, local descriptor, and interrupt descriptor tables. Actually, there are several kinds of descriptors supported by the 80286, and they all serve different functions relative to overall system operation. Some examples are the *segment descriptor, system segment descriptor, local descriptor table descriptor, call gate descriptor, task state segment descriptor,* and *task gate descriptor.*

Descriptors are the elements by which the on-chip memory manager manages the 80286's 1G-byte virtual memory address space. One descriptor exists for each segment of memory in the virtual address space. Descriptors are assigned to the local descriptor table, global descriptor table, task state segment, call gate, task gate, and interrupts. The contents of a descriptor provide mapping from virtual addresses to physical addresses for code, data, stack, and the task state segments and assigns attributes to the segment.

Each descriptor is 8 bytes long and contains three kinds of information. Earlier we identified the 16-bit *LIMIT* field and showed that its value defines the size of the segment or the table. Moreover, we found that the 24-bit *BASE* value provides the beginning physical address for the segment or the table. The third element of a descriptor, which is called the *access rights byte,* is different for each type of descriptor. Let us now look at the format of just two types of descriptors, the segment descriptor and system segment descriptor.

The segment descriptor is the type of descriptor that is used to describe the code, data, and stack segments. Figure 10.25(a) shows the general structure of a segment

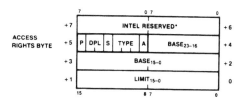

*Must be set to 0 for compatibility with 80386.

(a)

	Bit Position	Name		Function	
	7	Present (P)	P = 1	Segment is mapped into physical memory.	
			P = 0	No mapping to physical memory exits, base and limit are not used.	
	6–5	Descriptor Privilege Level (DPL)		Segment privilege attribute used in privilege tests.	
	4	Segment Descriptor (S)	S = 1	Code or Data (includes stacks) segment descriptor	
			S = 0	System Segment Descriptor or Gate Descriptor	
Type Field Definition	3	Executable (E)	E = 0	Data segment descriptor type is:	If Data Segment (S = 1, E = 0)
	2	Expansion Direction (ED)	ED = 0	Expand up segment, offsets must be $\leq$ limit.	
			ED = 1	Expand down segment, offsets must be > limit.	
	1	Writeable (W)	W = 0	Data segment may not be written into.	
			W = 1	Data segment may be written into.	
	3	Executable (E)	E = 1	Code Segment Descriptor type is:	If Code Segment (S = 1, E = 1)
	2	Conforming (C)	C = 1	Code segment may only be executed when CPL $\geq$ DPL and CPL remains unchanged.	
	1	Readable (R)	R = 0	Code segment may not be read	
			R = 1	Code segment may be read.	
	0	Accessed (A)	A = 0	Segment has not been accessed.	
			A = 1	Segment selector has been loaded into segment register or used by selector test instructions.	

(b)

Figure 10.25 (a) Segment descriptor format (Courtesy of Intel Corp.); (b) access byte bit definitions (Courtesy of Intel Corp.).

descriptor. Here we see that the two lowest addressed bytes hold the limit; the next three bytes hold the base, and the sixth byte is the access rights byte. The last two bytes are reserved by Intel for use with the 80386 microprocessor. Segment descriptors are found in the local and global descriptor tables.

Figure 10.26 shows how the loading of a descriptor from the local descriptor table

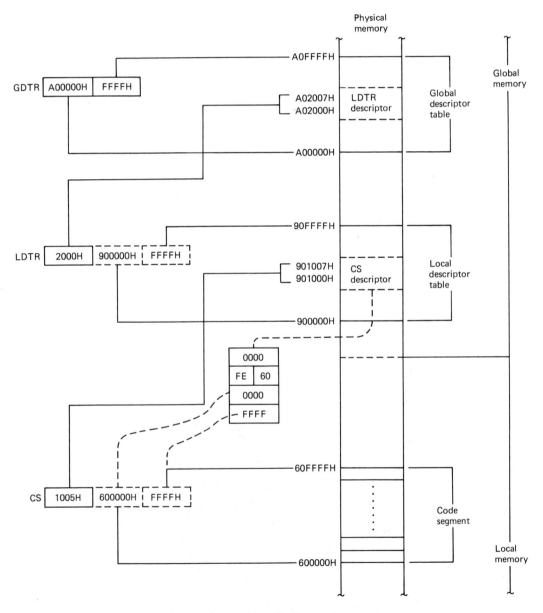

Figure 10.26 Creating a code segment.

in global memory defines a code segment in local memory for use in program execution. Notice that the LDTR descriptor defines a local descriptor table at address 900000_{16}. The value 1005_{16}, which is held in the code segment selector register, causes the descriptor at offset 1000_{16} in the local descriptor table to be cached into the code segment descriptor cache. In this way, a 64K-byte code segment is activated starting at address 600000_{16} in local memory.

The access rights byte includes such information about a segment as whether the descriptor has been accessed, whether it is a code or data segment descriptor, its privilege level, whether it is readable or writeable, and whether it is currently in physical memory. The function of each bit in the access rights byte is listed in Fig. 10.25(b). Notice that if bit 0 is logic 1 the descriptor has been accessed. A descriptor is marked this way to indicate to the operating system that its value has been cached on the 80286. Bit 4 identifies whether the descriptor represents a code/data segment or is a control descriptor. Let us assume that this bit is 1 to identify a segment descriptor. Then, the type bits, bits 1 through 3, determine whether the descriptor describes a code segment or a data segment. The DPL bits, bits 5 and 6, assign a privilege level to the segment. Finally, the present bit indicates whether or not the segment is currently mapped into physical memory. This bit can be tested by the operating system software to determine if the segment should be loaded from a secondary storage device such as a hard disk. For example if the access rights byte has logic 1 in bit 7, the data segment is already available in internal memory and does not have to be loaded from an external device. Figure 10.27(a) shows the general form of a code segment descriptor and Fig. 10.27(b) a general data/stack segment descriptor.

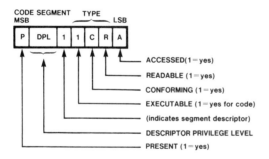

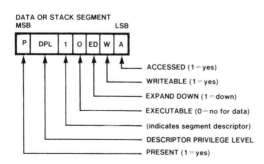

Figure 10.27 (a) Code segment descriptor access byte configuration (Courtesy of Intel Corp.); (b) data or stack segment access byte configuration (Courtesy of Intel Corp.).

EXAMPLE 10.7

The access rights byte of a segment descriptor contains FE_{16}. What type of segment descriptor does it describe and what are its characteristics?

SOLUTION   Expressing the byte in binary form, we get

$$FE_{16} = 11111110_2$$

Since bit 4 is 1, the access rights byte is for a code/data segment descriptor. This segment has the characteristics that follow.

$$P = 1 = \text{Segment is mapped into physical memory}$$

$$DPL = 11 = \text{Privilege level 3}$$

$$E = 1 = \text{Executable code segment}$$

$$C = 1 = \text{Conforming code segment}$$

$$R = 1 = \text{Readable code segment}$$

$$A = 0 = \text{Segment has not been accessed}$$

An example of a system segment descriptor is the descriptor used to define the local descriptor table. This descriptor is located in the GDT. Looking at Fig. 10.28, we find that the format of a system segment descriptor is similar to the segment descriptor just discussed; however, the type field of the access rights byte takes on new functions.

EXAMPLE 10.8

If a system segment descriptor has an access rights byte equal to 82_{16}, what type of descriptor does it represent? What is its privilege level? Is the descriptor present in physical memory?

SOLUTION   First, we will express the access rights byte in binary form. This gives

$$82_{16} = 10000010_2$$

Now we see that the type of the descriptor is

$$TYPE = 0010 = \text{Local descriptor table descriptor}$$

The privilege level is

$$DPL = 00 = \text{Privilege level 0}$$

and since

$$P = 1$$

the descriptor is present in physical memory.

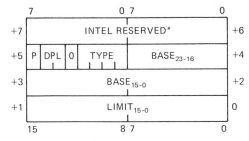

*Must be set to 0 for compatability with 80386.

(a)

Name	Value	Description
Type	0	Invalid descriptor
	1	Available task state segment
	2	LDT descriptor
	3	Busy task state segment
	4-7	Control descriptor
	8	Invalid descriptor (reserved by Intel)
	9-F	Reserved by Intel
P	0	Descriptor contents are not valid
	1	Descriptor contents are valid
DPL	0-3	Descriptor Privilege Level
BASE	24-bit number	Base Address of special system data segment in real memory
LIMIT	16-bit number	Offset of last byte in segment

(b)

Figure 10.28 System segment descriptor format and field definitions (Courtesy of Intel Corp.).

10.6 PROTECTED-MODE SYSTEM CONTROL INSTRUCTION SET

In chapters 4 and 5, we studied the instruction set of the 8086 microprocessor. The part of the instruction set introduced in these chapters represents the basic instruction set of the 8086 architecture. In section 10.3, we introduced a number of new instructions that are available in the real-mode instruction set of the 80286. They are called the extended instruction set. In protected mode, the 80286 executes all the instructions that are available in the real mode. Moreover, it is enhanced with a number of additional instructions that either apply only to protected-mode operation or are used in the real mode to prepare the 80286 for entry into the protected mode. As shown in Fig. 10.29, these instructions are known as the *system control instruction set*.

The instructions of the system control instruction set are listed in Fig. 10.30. Here we find the format of each instruction along with a description of its operation. More-

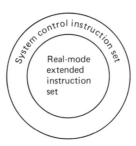

Figure 10.29 Protected-mode instruction set.

over, the mode or modes in which the instruction is available are identified. Let us now look at the operation of some of these instructions in detail.

Looking at Fig. 10.30, we see that the first six instructions can be executed in either the real mode or the protected mode. They provide the ability to load (L) or store (S) the contents of the global descriptor table (GDT) register, interrupt descriptor table (IDT) register, and machine status word (MSW) register. Notice that the instruction *LGDT (load global descriptor table register)* is used to load the GDTR from memory. Operand S specifies the location of the six bytes of memory that hold the limit and base that specify the size and beginning address of the GDT. The first word of memory contains the limit, the next three bytes contain the base, and the last byte is ignored. For instance, executing the instruction

LGDT   [INIT_GDTR]

loads the GDTR with the base and limit pointed to by address INIT_GDTR to create a global descriptor table in memory. This instruction is meant to be used during system initialization and before switching the 80286 to the protected mode.

Once loaded, the current contents of the GDTR can be saved in memory by executing the *SGDT (store global descriptor table)* instruction. An example is the instruction

SGDT   [SAVE_GDTR]

The instructions LIDT and SIDT perform similar operations for the IDTR. The IDTR is also set up during initialization.

The contents of the machine status word (MSW) register are loaded and stored by the instructions *LMSW (load machine status word)* and *SMSW (store machine status word)*, respectively. These instructions are used to switch the 80286 from real to protected mode. To do this, we must set the least significant bit in the MSW to 1. This can be done by first reading the contents of the machine status word register, setting the LSB, and then writing the modified value back into the register. The instruction sequence that follows will switch an 80286 operating in real mode to the protected mode.

```
SMSW    AX              ; read from the MSW register
OR      AX, 1           ; set the PE bit
LMSW    AX              ; write to the MSW register
```

Instruction	Description	Mode
LGDT S	Load the global descriptor table register. S specifies the memory location that contains the first byte of the 6 bytes to be loaded into the GDTR.	Both
SGDT D	Store the global descriptor table register. D specifies the memory location that gets the first byte of the 6 bytes to be stored from the GDTR.	Both
LIDT S	Load the interrupt descriptor table register. S specifies the memory location that contains the first byte of the 6 bytes to be loaded into the IDTR.	Both
SIDT D	Store the interrupt descriptor table register. D specifies the memory location that gets the first byte of the 6 bytes to be stored from the IDTR.	Both
LMSW S	Load the machine status word. S is an operand to specify the word to be loaded into the MSW.	Both
SMSW D	Store the machine status word. D is an operand to specify the word location or register where the MSW is to be stored.	Both
LLDT S	Load the local descriptor table register. S specifies the operand to specify a word to be loaded into the LDTR.	Protected
SLDT D	Store the local descriptor table register. D is an operand to specify the word location where the LDTR is to be saved.	Protected
LTR S	Load the task register. S is an operand to specify a word to be loaded into the TR.	Protected
STR D	Store the task register. D is an operand to specify the word location where the TR is to be stored.	Protected
LAR D, S	Load access rights byte. S specifies the selector for the descriptor whose access byte is loaded into the upper byte of the D operand. The low byte specified by D is cleared. The zero flag is set if the loading completes successfully; otherwise it is cleared.	Protected
LSL R16, S	Load segment limit. S specifies the selector for the descriptor whose limit word is loaded into the word register operand R16. The zero flag is set if the loading completes successfully; otherwise it is cleared.	Protected
ARPL D, R16	Adjust RPL field of the selector. D specifies the selector whose RPL field is increased to match the PRL field in the register. The zero flag is set if successful; otherwise it is cleared.	Protected
VERR S	Verify read access. S specifies the selector for the segment to be verified for read operation. If successful the zero flag is set; otherwise it is reset.	Protected
VERW S	Verify write access. S specifies the selector for the segment to be verified for write operation. If successful the zero flag is set; otherwise it is reset.	Protected
CLTS	Clear task switched flag.	Protected

Figure 10.30 Protected mode system control instruction set.

The next four instructions in Fig. 10.30 are also used to initialize or save the contents of protected-mode registers; however, they can be used only when the 80286 is in the protected mode. The contents of the LDTR are loaded and saved by the instructions LLDT and SLDT, respectively. Moreover, for loading and saving the contents of the TR, the equivalent instructions are LTR and STR.

The rest of the instructions in Fig. 10.30 are for accessing the contents of descriptors. For instance, to read a descriptor's access rights byte, the *LAR (load access rights byte)* instruction is executed. An example is the instruction

LAR   AX, LDIS_1

Execution of this instruction causes the access rights byte of local descriptor 1 to be loaded into AH. To read the segment limit of a descriptor, we use the *LSL (load segment limit)* instruction. For instance, to copy the segment limit for local descriptor 1 into register BX, the instruction

LSL   BX, LDIS_1

is executed. In both cases, ZF is set to 1 if the operation is performed correctly.

The instruction *ARPL (adjust RPL field of selector)* can be used to increase the RPL field of a selector in memory or a register (D) to match the protection level of the selector in a register (S). If a change in RPL level takes place, ZF is set to 1. Finally, the instructions VERR and VERW are provided to test the accessibility of a segment for a read or write operation, respectively. If the descriptor does permit the type of access tested for by executing the instruction, the zero flag is set to 1.

10.7 MULTITASKING AND PROTECTION

We say that the 80286 microprocessor implements a *multitasking* software architecture. By this we mean that it contains on-chip hardware that permits multiple tasks to exist in a software system and allows them to be scheduled for execution in a time-shared manner; that is, program control is switched from one task to another after a fixed interval of time elapses. For instance, the tasks can be executed in a round-robin fashion. This means that the most recently executed task is returned to the end of the list of tasks being executed.

Earlier we defined a task as a collection of program routines that performs a specific function. This function is also called a *process*. Software systems typically need to perform many processes. In the protected-mode 80286-based microcomputer, each process is identified as an independent task. The 80286 provides an efficient mechanism called the *task switching mechanism* for switching between tasks. For instance, an 80286 running at 10 MHz can perform a task-switch operation in just 18 μs.

We also indicated earlier that when a task is called into operation, it can have both global and local memory resources. The local memory address space is divided among tasks. This means that each task normally has its own private segments of local memory. The segments of global memory can be accessed by any task. Therefore, a task can have access to any of the segments in this shared memory. As shown in Fig. 10.31, task A has both a private address space and a global address space available for its use.

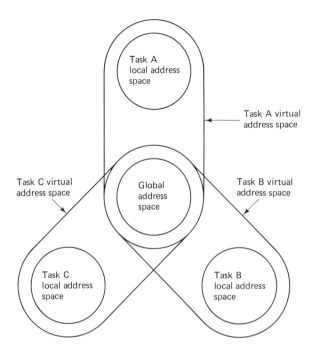

Figure 10.31 Virtual address space of a task (Courtesy of Intel Corp.).

Protection and the Protection Model

There are safeguards that can be built into the protected-mode software system to deny unauthorized or incorrect accesses of a task's memory resources. The concept of safeguarding memory is known as *protection*. The 80286 includes on-chip hardware that implements a *protection mechanism*. This mechanism is designed to put restrictions on the access of local and system resources by a task and to isolate tasks from each other in a multitasking environment.

Segmentation of memory and the descriptors are the key elements of the 80286's protection mechanism. We already identified the segment as the smallest element of the virtual memory address space that has unique protection attributes. These attributes are defined by the access rights byte and limit fields in the segment's descriptor. As shown in Fig. 10.32, the on-chip protection hardware performs a number of checks during all memory. For example, when a storage location in data memory is written into, the type field of the access rights byte in the descriptor is tested to assure that the type attributes are consistent with the register cache being loaded. Moreover, the limit field of the descriptor is checked to verify that the offset is within the limit of the segment.

Let us just summarize the attributes that can be assigned to a segment with the access rights byte in its descriptor. Remember that bits are available in the access rights byte to define whether or not a segment of memory is present in physical memory. If a segment is present, in the physical memory, additional bits in the access rights byte make it either a code segment or a data segment. Moreover, attributes such as readable, writeable, conforming, and expand up or down can be assigned to a segment. Finally,

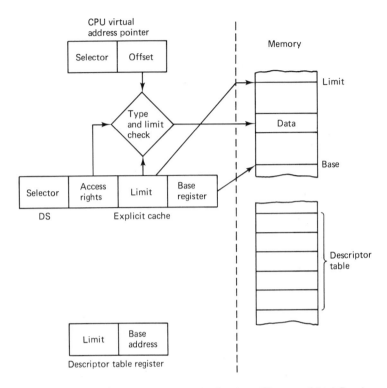

Figure 10.32 Testing the access rights of a descriptor (Courtesy of Intel Corp.).

Earlier we showed that whenever a segment is accessed, the base address and limit are cached inside the 80286. In Fig. 10.32, we find that the access rights byte is also loaded into the cache register; however, before loading the descriptor, the MMU verifies that the selected segment is currently present in physical memory and is at a privilege level that is accessible from the privilege level of the current program and that the type is consistent with the target segment selector register (CS = code segment, DS, SS, or ES = data segment). Moreover, each reference to a segment is checked to assure that it does not exceed the address limit of the segment. If a violation is detected, an error condition is signaled.

Let us now look at some examples of memory accesses that result in protection violations. For example, if the selector loaded into the CS register points to a descriptor that defines a data segment, the type check leads to a protection violation. Another example of an invalid memory access is an attempt to read an operand from a code segment that is not marked as readable. Finally, any attempt to access a byte of data at an offset greater than LIMIT or a word at an offset equal to or greater than LIMIT extends beyond the end of the data segment and results in a protection violation.

The 80286's protection model provides four possible privilege levels for each task. They are called *levels 0, 1, 2, and 3* and can be illustrated by concentric circles as shown in Fig. 10.33. Here level 0 is the highest privilege level (most privileged) and level 3 is the lowest (least privileged).

System and application software are typically partitioned in the manner as shown in Fig. 10.33. The kernal represents application-independent software that provides system oriented functions such as I/O control, task sequencing, and memory management. For this reason, it is kept at the most privileged level, level 0. Level 1 contains processes that provide system services such as file accessing. Level 2 is used to implement custom routines to support special purpose system operations. Finally, the least privileged level, level 3, is the level at which user applications are run. This example also demonstrates how privilege levels are used to isolate system-level software (operating system software in levels 0 through 2) from the user's application software (level 3). Tasks at a level can use programs from the more privileged levels but cannot modify the contents of these routines in any way. In this way, applications are permitted to use system software routines from the three higher privilege levels without affecting their integrity.

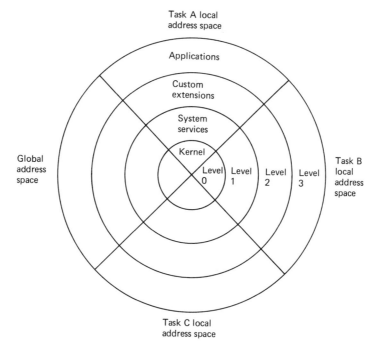

Figure 10.33 Protection model.

Earlier we pointed out that each task is assigned its own local descriptor table. Therefore, as long as none of the descriptors in a task's local descriptor table reference code or data available to another task, it is isolated from all other tasks. For instance, in Fig. 10.33 multiple applications running at level 3 are isolated from one another by assigning them different local resources. This shows that segments, privilege levels, and the local descriptor table provide protection for both code and data within a task. This type of protection results in improved software reliability because errors in one application will not affect the operating system or other applications.

Let us now look more closely at how the privilege level is assigned to a code or data segment. Remember that when a task is running it has access to both local and global code segments, local and global data segments, and stack segments. A privilege level is assigned to each of these segments through the access rights byte in its descriptor. A segment may be assigned to any privilege level simply by entering the number for the level into the DPL bits.

To provide more flexibility I/O has two types of privilege. First, the I/O drivers, which are normally system resources, are assigned to a privilege level. For the software system of Fig. 10.33, we indicated that the I/O control routines were part of the kernel and are at level 0.

The IN, INS, OUT, OUTS, CLI, and STI instructions are what are called *trusted instructions*. This means that additional restrictions are put on their use by the protected mode of the 80286. They can be executed only at a privilege level that is equal to or more privileged than the *input-output privilege level* (IOPL) code. IOPL supplies the second level of I/O privilege. Remember that the IOPL bits exist in the protected-mode flag register. These bits must be loaded with the value of the privilege level that is to be assigned to I/O instructions through software. The value of IOPL may change from task to task. Assigning the I/O instructions to a level higher than 3 restricts applications from directly performing I/O. Instead, to perform I/O, the application must request service by an I/O driver through the operating system.

Accessing Code and Data through the Protection Model

During the running of a task, the 80286 may need either to pass control to program routines at another privilege level or to access data in a segment that is at a different privilege level. Accesses to code or data in segments at a different privilege level are governed by strict rules. These rules are designed to protect the code or data at the more-privileged level from contamination by a less-privileged routine.

Before looking at how accesses are made for routines or data at the same or different privilege levels, let us first look at some terminology defined for identifying privilege levels. We have already been using the terms "descriptor privilege level" (DPL) and "I/O privilege level" (IOPL); however, when discussing the protection mechanisms by which processes access data or code, two new terms come into play. They are *current privilege level* (CPL) and *requested privilege level* (RPL). CPL is defined as the privilege level of the code or data segment that is currently being accessed by a task; that is, the CPL of an executing task is the DPL of the access rights byte held in the descriptor cache for the CS register. This value normally equals the DPL of the code segment. RPL is the privilege level of the new selector loaded into a segment register. For instance, in the case of code, it is the privilege level of the code segment that contains the routine that is being called; that is, RPL is the DPL of the code segment to which control is to be passed.

As a task executes, it may require access to other code routines that reside in segments at any of the four privilege levels. Therefore, the current privilege level of the task changes dynamically with the programs it executes. This is because the CPL of a task always equals the DPL of the code segment currently being executed.

The protection rules of the 80286 determine what code or data can be accessed by a program. Before looking at how control is passed to code at different protection levels, let us first look at how data segments are accessed by code at the CPL. The general rule is that code can access only data that is at the same or a less privileged level. For instance, if the current privilege level of a task is 1, it can access operands that are in data segments with DPL equal to 1, 2, or 3. Whenever a new selector is loaded into the DS or ES register, the DPL bits of the target data segment are checked to make sure that they are equal to or less than the higher privilege level of CPL or RPL. As long as DPL satisfies this condition, the descriptor is cached inside the 80286 and the data access takes place.

One exception to this rule is when the SS register is loaded. In this case, the DPL must always equal the CPL; that is, the active stack (one is required for each privilege level) is always at the CPL.

Different rules apply to how control is passed between code at the same privilege level and between code at different privilege levels. To transfer program control to another instruction in the same code segment, one can simply use a near jump or a call instruction. In these cases, just a limit check is made to assure that the destination does not exceed the limit of the current code segment. To pass control to code in another segment that is at the same or different privilege level a far jump or call instruction is used. For this transfer of program control, both type and limit checks are performed and privilege rules are applied. There are two conditions under which the program control transfer will take place. First, if CPL equals the DPL the two segments are at the same protection level and the transfer occurs. Second, if the CPL represents a more privileged level then DPL, but the conforming code (C) bit in the type field of the new segment is set, the routine is executed at the CPL.

The general rule that applies when control is passed to code in a segment that is at a different privilege level is that the new code segment must be at a more privileged level. A special kind of descriptor called a *gate descriptor* comes into play to implement the change in privilege level. An attempt to transfer control to a routine in a code segment at a different privilege level is initiated with either a far jump or a far call instruction that references a gate descriptor. In this case the 80286 goes through a more complex transfer mechanism.

The structure of a gate descriptor is shown in Fig. 10.34. Notice that there are four types of gate descriptors: the *call gate*, the *task gate*, the *interrupt gate*, and the *trap gate*. The call gate implements an indirect transfer of control within a task from code at the CPL to code at a higher privilege level. It does this by defining a valid entry point into the more privileged segment. The contents of a call gate are the virtual address of the entry point: the *destination selector* and the *destination offset*. In Fig. 10.34 we see that the destination selector identifies the code segment that contains the program to which control is to be redirected. The destination offset points to the instruction in this segment where execution is to resume. Call gates can reside in either the GDT or a LDT.

The operation of the call gate mechanism is illustrated in Fig. 10.35. Here we see

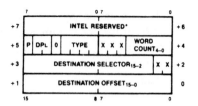

*Must be set to 0 for compatibility with 80386 (X is don't care)

Gate Descriptor Fields

Name	Value	Description
TYPE	4 5 6 7	–Call Gate –Task Gate –Interrupt Gate –Trap Gate
P	0 1	–Descriptor Contents are not valid –Descriptor Contents are valid
DPL	0–3	Descriptor Privilege Level
WORD COUNT	0–31	Number of words to copy from callers stack to called procedures stack. Only used with call gate.
DESTINATION SELECTOR	16-bit selector	Selector to the target code segment (Call, Interrupt or Trap Gate) Selector to the target task state segment (Task Gate)
DESTINATION OFFSET	16-bit offset	Entry point within the target code segment

Figure 10.34 Gate descriptor format (Courtesy of Intel Corp.).

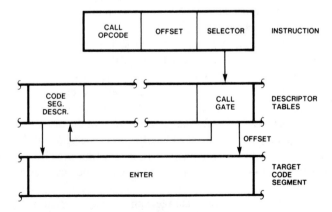

Figure 10.35 Call gate operation (Courtesy of Intel Corp.).

that the call instruction includes an offset and a selector. When the instruction is executed, the selector is loaded into CS and points to the call gate. In turn, the call gate causes its destination selector to be loaded into CS. This leads to the caching of the descriptor for the called code segment. The called code segment descriptor provides the base address, which when combined with the offset from the call gate descriptor locates the entry point of the procedure. Whenever the task's current privilege level changes, a new stack is activated. The old SP and SS are saved on the new stack along with any parameters and the old IP and CS. This information is needed to preserve linkage for return to the old program environment.

Now the procedure at the higher privilege level begins to execute. At the end of the routine, a RET instruction must be included to return program control back to the calling program. Execution of RET causes the old values of IP, CS, the parameters, SP, and SS to be popped from the stack. This restores the original program environment. Now program execution resumes with the instruction following the call instruction in the lower-privileged code segment. For the call to be successful the DPL of the gate must be the same as the CPL, and the RPL of the called code must be higher than the CPL.

Task Switching and the Task State Segment Table

Earlier we identified the task as the key program element of the 80286's multitasking software architecture and explained that another important feature of this architecture is the high-performance task-switching mechanism. A task can be either directly or indirectly invoked. This is done by executing either the intersegment jump or the intersegment call instruction. When a jump instruction is used to initiate a task switch, no return linkage to the prior task is supported. On the other hand, if a call is used instead of a jump, back linkage information is automatically saved. This information permits a return to be performed to the instruction following the call instruction in the old task at completion of the new task.

Each task that is to be performed by the 80286 is assigned a unique selector called a *task state selector*. This selector is an index to a corresponding *task state segment descriptor* in the global descriptor table. The format of a task state segment descriptor is given in Fig. 10.36.

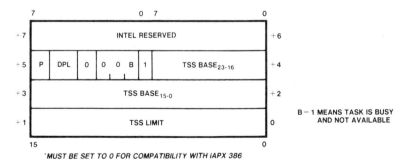

Figure 10.36 TSS descriptor format (Courtesy of Intel Corp.).

If a jump or call instruction has a task state selector as its operand, a direct entry is performed to the task. As shown in Fig. 10.37, when a call instruction is executed the selector is loaded into the 80286's task register (TR). Then, the corresponding task state segment descriptor is read from the GDT and loaded into the task register cache. Of course this happens only if the criteria specified in the access rights byte of the descriptor are satisfied. This is, the descriptor is present (P = 1); the task is not busy (B = 0); and protection is not violated (CPL must be equal to DPL). Looking at Fig. 10.37, we see that once loaded the base address and limit specified in the descriptor define the starting point and size of the task's *task state segment* (TSS). This TSS contains all the information that is needed either to start or to stop a task.

Before explaining the rest of the task switch sequence, let us look more closely at what is contained in the task state segment. A typical TSS is shown in Fig. 10.37. Its

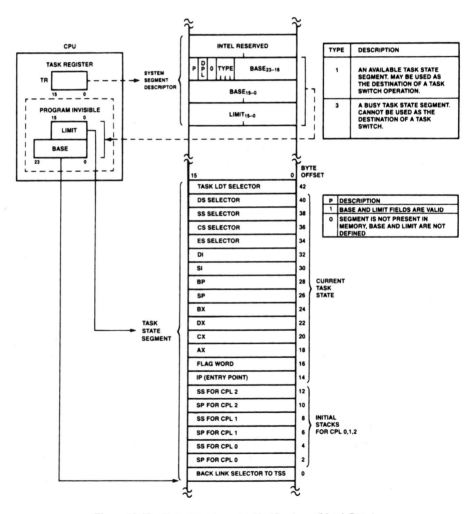

Figure 10.37 Task state segment table (Courtesy of Intel Corp.).

minimum size is 44 bytes. For this reason, the minimum limit that can be specified in a TSS descriptor is $002B_{16}$. Notice that the segment contains information such as the state of the microprocessor (general registers, segment selectors, instruction pointer, and flag word) needed to initiate the task, a back-link selector to the TSS of the task that was active when this task was called, the local descriptor table register selector, and a stack selector and pointer for privilege levels 0, 1, and 2.

Now we will continue with the procedure by which a task is invoked. Let us assume that a task was already active when a new task was called. The new task is what is called a *nested task* and causes the NT bit of the flag word to be set to 1. In this case, the current task is first suspended and then the state of the 80286's user-accessible registers is saved in the old TSS. Next, the B bit in the new task's descriptor is marked busy (B = 1); the TS bit in the machine status word is set to indicate that a task is active; the state information from the new task's TSS is loaded into the MPU; and the selector for the old TSS is saved as the back-link selector in the new task state segment. The task switch operation is now complete and execution resumes with the instruction identified by the new contents of the code segment selector (CS) and instruction pointer (IP).

The old program context is preserved by saving the selector for the old TSS as the back-link selector in the new TSS. By executing a return instruction at the end of the new task, the back-link selector for the old TSS is automatically reloaded into TR. This activates the old TSS and restores the prior program environment. Now program execution resumes at the point where it left off in the old task.

The indirect method of invoking a task is by jumping to or calling a *task gate*. This is the method used to transfer control to a task at an RPL that is higher than the CPL. Figure 10.38 shows the format of a task gate. This time the instruction includes

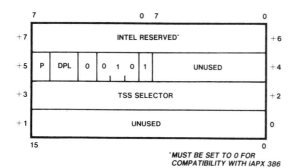

MUST BE SET TO 0 FOR COMPATIBILITY WITH iAPX 386

Figure 10.38 Task gate descriptor format (Courtesy of Intel Corp.).

a selector that points to the task gate, which is in either the LDT or GDT, instead of a task state selector. The TSS selector held in this gate is loaded into TR to select the TSS and initiate the task. Figure 10.39 illustrates a task initiated through a task gate.

Let us consider an example to illustrate the principle of task switching. In Fig. 10.40, we have a table that contains TSS descriptors SELECT0 through SELECT3 that contain access rights and selectors for tasks 0 through 3, respectively. To invoke the task corresponding to selector SELECT2 in the data segment where these selectors are stored, we can use the following procedure. First, the data segment register is loaded

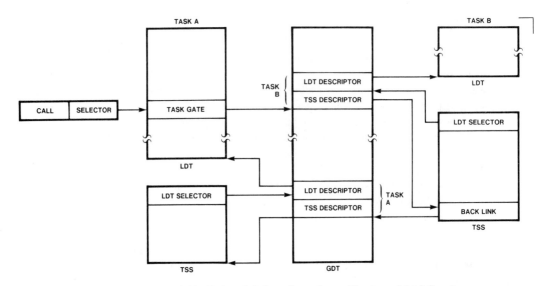

Figure 10.39 Task switch through a task gate (Courtesy of Intel Corp.).

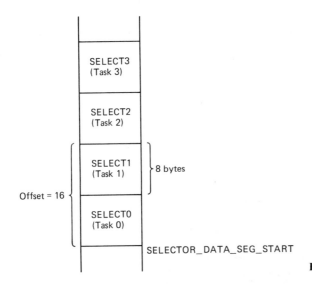

Figure 10.40 Task gate selectors.

with the address SELECTOR_DATA_SEG_START to point to the segment that contains the selectors. This is done with the instructions

```
MOV     AX, SELECTOR_DATA_SEG_START

MOV     DS, AX
```

Since each selector is 8 bytes long, SELECT2 is offset from the beginning of the segment by 16 bytes. Let us load this offset into register BX.

MOV BX,10

At this point we can use SELECT2 to implement an intersegment jump with the instruction

JMP   DWORD PTR [BX]

Execution of this instruction switches program control to the task specified by the selector in descriptor SELECT2. In this case, no program linkage is preserved. On the other hand, by calling the task with the instruction

CALL   DWORD PTR [BX]

linkage is maintained.

ASSIGNMENT

Section 10.2

1. How does the performance of an 8-MHz 80286 compare to that of a 5-MHz 8086?
2. What is meant when we say that the 80286 is object code compatible with the 8086?
3. What register has been added in the 80286's real-mode software model?

Section 10.3

4. Describe the operation performed by the instruction PUSHA.
5. Which registers and in what order does the instruction POPA pop from the stack?
6. What is a stack frame?
7. How much stack does the instruction ENTER 1F,4 allocate for the stack frame? What is the lexical level?
8. If DS = ES = 1075_{16}, DI = 100_{16}, DF = 0, and DX = 1000_{16}, what happens when the instruction INSW is executed?
9. If DS = ES = 1075_{16}, SI = 100_{16}, DF = 1, CF = F, and DX = 2000_{16}, what happens when the instruction REPOUTSB is executed?
10. Explain the function of the bound instruction in the sequence

```
SCAN:     DEC    DI
          BOUND  DI,LIMITS
          .
          .
          JNZ    SCAN
```

Assume that address LIMITS contains the value 0000_{16} and LIMITS + 2 holds the value $00FF_{16}$.

Section 10.4

11. List the protected-mode registers that are not part of the real-mode model.

12. What are the two parts of the GDTR called?

13. What is the function of the GDTR?

14. If the contents of the GDTR are $21000001FF_{16}$, what are the starting and ending addresses of the table? How large is the table? How many descriptors can be stored in the table?

15. What is stored in the GDT?

16. What do IDTR and IDT stand for?

17. What is the maximum limit that should be used in the IDTR?

18. What is stored in the IDT?

19. What MSW bit settings identify that floating point operations are to be performed by an 80287 coprocessor?

20. Which bit is used to switch the 80286 from real-address mode to protected-address mode?

21. What does TS stand for?

22. What gets loaded into TR? What is its function?

23. What is the function of the task descriptor cache?

24. What determines the location and size of a task state segment?

25. What descriptor table defines the local memory address space?

26. What gets loaded into the LDTR? What happens when it gets loaded?

27. What is the name of the CS register in the protected mode? The DS register?

28. What are the names and sizes of the three fields in a selector?

29. What does TI equal to 1 mean?

30. If the GDT register contains $13000000FF_{16}$ and the selector loaded into the LDTR is 0040_{16}, what is the starting address of the LDT descriptor that is to be loaded into the cache?

31. What does NT stand for?

32. If the IOPL bits of the flag register contain 10, what is the privilege level of the I/O instructions?

33. How large is the 80286's virtual address?

34. What are the two parts of a virtual address called?

35. How large can a data segment be? How small?

36. How large is the 80286's virtual address space? What is the maximum number of segments that can exist in the virtual address space?

37. How large is the global memory address space? How many segments can it contain?

38. In Fig. 10.22 which segments of memory does task 3 have access to? Which segments does it not have access to?

39. What part of the 80286 is used to translate virtual addresses to physical addresses?

40. What happens when the instruction sequence that follows is executed?

```
MOV AX, [SI]

MOV CS, AX
```

41. If the descriptor accessed in problem 40 has the value $200000FFFF_{16}$ and IP contains 0100_{16}, what is the physical address of the next instruction to be fetched?

Section 10.5

42. How many bytes are in a descriptor? Name each of its fields and give its size.

43. Which registers are segment descriptors associated with? System segment descriptors?

44. The selector 0224_{16} is loaded into the data segment register. This value points to a segment descriptor starting at address 100220_{16} in the local descriptor table. If the contents of the descriptor are

$$
\begin{aligned}
100220H &= 0110H \\
100222H &= 0000H \\
100224H &= 1A20H \\
100226H &= 0000H
\end{aligned}
$$

what are the LIMIT and BASE?

45. Is the segment of memory identified by the descriptor in problem 44 already loaded into physical memory? Is it a code segment or a data segment?

46. If the current value of IP is 0226_{16}, what is the physical address of the next instruction to be fetched from the code segment of problem 44?

Section 10.6

47. If the instruction LGDT[INIT_GDTR] is to load the limit $FFFF_{16}$ and base 300000_{16}, show how the descriptor must be stored in memory.

48. Write an instruction sequence that can be used to clear the task-switched bit of the MSW.

49. Write an instruction sequence that will load the local descriptor table register with the selector $02F0_{16}$ from register BX.

Section 10.7

50. Define the term ''multitasking.''

51. What is a task?

52. What two safeguards are implemented by the 80286's protection mechanism?

53. What happens if either the segment limit check or the segment attributes check fails?

54. What is the highest privilege level of the 80286 protection model called? What is the lowest level called?

55. At what protection level are applications run?

56. What is the protection mechanism used to isolate local and global resources?

57. What protection mechanism is used to isolate tasks?

58. What is the privilege level of the segment defined by the descriptor in problem 44?

59. What does CPL stand for? RPL?

60. Summarize the data access protection rule.

61. Which privilege level data segments can be accessed by an application running at level 3?

62. Summarize the code access protection rules.

63. If an application is running at privilege level 3, what privilege level operating system software is available to it?

64. What purpose does a call gate serve?

65. Explain what happens when the instruction CALL[NEW_ROUTINE] is executed within a task. Assume the NEW_ROUTINE is at a privilege level that is higher than the CPL.

66. What is the purpose of the task state descriptor?

67. What is the function of a task state segment?

68. Where is the state of the prior task saved? Where is the linkage to the prior task saved?

69. Into which register is the TSS selector loaded to initiate a task?

70. Summarize the task switch sequence illustrated in Fig. 10.39.

Chapter 11

Hardware Architecture of the 80286 Microprocessor

11.1 INTRODUCTION

In chapter 10 we studied the software architecture of the 80286 microprocessor. We covered its real- and protected-mode software architectures, extended instruction set, and system control instruction set. Now we will turn our interest to the hardware architecture of the 80286-based microcomputer system. In this chapter, we examine the signal interfaces of the 80286, its memory interface, I/O interface, and interrupts and exception processing. For this purpose, we have included the following topics in the chapter.

1. The 80286 microprocessor
2. Internal architecture
3. Interfaces of the 80286
4. The 82288 bus controller
5. System clock
6. The bus cycle and bus states
7. Memory interface
8. Program and data storage memory circuits
9. I/O interface
10. Interrupt and exception processing

The 80286, first announced in 1982, was the fifth member of Intel Corporation's 8086 microprocessor family. We have already learned that from the software point of view the 80286 offers two modes of operation: real mode for compatibility with the existing 8086/8088 software base and protected mode, which offers enhanced system-level features such as memory management, multitasking, and protection. A number of changes have been made to the hardware architecture of the 80286 primarily to improve its performance. For example, additional pipelining is provided within the 80286 to provide higher performance, the address and data buses are demultiplexed to simplify memory subsystem design, and the bus is designed to support interleaved memory subsystems.

The 80286 is manufactured using the high-performance metal-oxide-semiconductor III (HMOSIII) process, and its circuitry is equivalent to approximately 125,000 transistors. It is available in *plastic leaded chip carrier* (PLCC), *ceramic leadless chip carrier* (LCC), and *pin grid array* (PGA) packages. An 80286 in the LCC package is shown in Fig. 11.1. The PLCC is the lowest-cost package type and is the most widely used in commercial applications such as personal computers. The LCC and PGA are more rugged and are typically used in applications that require higher reliability.

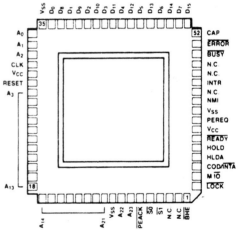

Figure 11.1 80286 IC (Courtesy of Intel Corp.).

Figure 11.2 Pin layout of the 80286 (Courtesy of Intel Corp.).

Each of these packages has 68 leads. The signal pinned out to each lead is shown in Fig. 11.2. Notice that unlike in the earlier 8086 and 8088 devices none of the signal lines of the 80286 are multiplexed with another signal at a single pin. This is intended to simplify the microcomputer circuit design.

11.3 INTERNAL ARCHITECTURE

The internal architecture of the 80286 microprocessor is shown in Fig. 11.3. The 8086 and 8088 had just two processing units, the *bus interface unit* (BIU) and *execution unit* (EU). In Fig. 11.3 we find that the 80286 is internally partitioned into four independent processing units: the *bus unit* (BU), the *instruction unit* (IU), the *execution unit* (EU), and the *address unit* (AU). This additional parallel processing provides an important contribution to the higher level of performance achieved with the 80286 architecture.

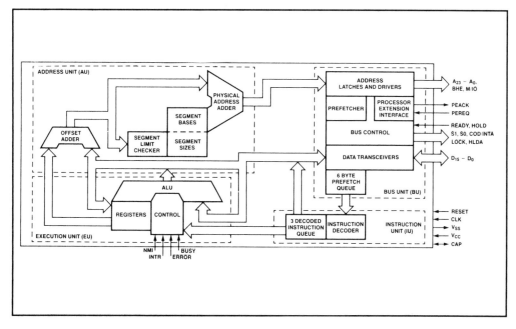

Figure 11.3 Internal architecture of the 80286 (Courtesy of Intel Corp.).

The bus unit is the 80286's interface with the outside world. It provides a 16-bit data bus, 24-bit address bus, and the signals needed to control bus transfers. These buses are demultiplexed instead of multiplexed as in the 8086/8088 hardware architecture; that is, the 80286 has separate pins for its address and data lines. Demultiplexing of these buses further improves the performance of the 80286's hardware architecture.

The bus unit is responsible for performing all external bus operations. In Fig. 11.3 we see that this processing unit contains the latches and drivers for the address bus, transceivers for the data bus, and control logic for generating the control signals needed to perform memory and I/O bus cycles.

Notice in Fig. 11.3 that the bus unit also contains elements called the *prefetcher* and *prefetch queue*. Together these elements implement a mechanism known as an *in-*

struction stream queue. This queue permits the 80286 to prefetch up to six bytes of instruction code. Whenever the queue is not full, that is, whenever it has room for at least two more bytes and, at the same time, the execution unit is not asking it to read or write operands from memory, the bus unit is free to look ahead in the program by fetching the next sequential instructions. These prefetched instructions are held in a first-in, first-out (FIFO) queue. With its 16-bit data bus, the 80286 fetches two instruction bytes in a single memory cycle. When a byte is loaded at the input end of the queue, all other bytes shift up through the FIFO to the empty locations nearer the output. In this way, the fetch time for most instructions is hidden.

The prefetcher that is provided in the 80286's bus unit has more intelligence than that implemented in the 8086/8088 architecture. It has the ability to determine that an instruction that has been prefetched will cause a transfer in program control; for instance, a jump. When this type of instruction is detected, the queue is flushed and prefetch resumes at the point to which control is to be passed. The reset of the queue happens prior to the actual execution of the instruction. This feature results in an additional performance improvement for the 80286.

The address unit provides the memory management and protection services for the 80286. It off-loads the responsibility for address generation, translations, and checking from the bus unit and thereby further boosts the performance of the MPU; that is, it contains dedicated hardware for performing high-speed address calculations, virtual-to-physical address translations, and limit and access rights attribute checks. For instance, in the real mode, the address unit calculates the address of the next instruction to be fetched. This is done by shifting the current contents of the code segment (CS) register left by 4-bit positions, filling the least significant bits with 0s, and adding the value in the instruction pointer (IP) register. This gives the 20-bit physical address that is to be output on the address bus.

For protected mode, the address unit performs more functions. It contains the *4-word X 48-bit cache* that is used to hold the current segment descriptors within the 80286. Moreover, it performs the various address translations and protection checks needed when performing bus cycles. For example, if an instruction loads a selector into CS, the address unit first checks the index in the selector to be sure that it does not exceed the limit of the referenced descriptor table (GDT or LDT). Then the type of the descriptor is checked to assure that it is consistent with the CS register. The access rights byte of the descriptor is tested to verify that the descriptor is located in physical memory. If the descriptor is in physical memory, its privilege level is next tested for a protection violation. If *all* these tests are passed, the descriptor is cached on chip.

Looking at Fig. 11.3 we see that the instruction unit accesses the output end of the prefetch queue. It reads one instruction byte after the other from the output of the queue and decodes them into the 69-bit instruction format used by the 80286's execution unit; that is, it off-loads the responsibility for instruction decoding from the execution unit. The instruction queue within the instruction unit permits three fully decoded instructions to be held waiting for the execution unit. Once again the result is improved performance for the MPU.

Notice in Fig. 11.3 that the execution unit includes the *arithmetic logic unit* (ALU), the 80286's registers, and a control ROM. The block labeled registers represent all the user-accessible registers, such as the general-purpose registers and segment registers. The control ROM contains the microcode sequences that define the operation performed by each of the 80286's instructions. The execution unit reads decoded instructions from the instruction queue and performs the operations that they specify. If necessary during the execution of an instruction, it requests that the address unit generate operand addresses and that the bus unit perform read or write bus cycles to access data in memory or at I/O devices.

11.4 INTERFACES OF THE 80286

Earlier we found that the 80286 microprocessor can be configured to work in either of two modes. These modes are known as the *real-address mode* and the *protected address mode*. Let us now look at the signals produced at each of the 80286's interfaces when in these modes.

A block diagram of the 80286 microprocessor is shown in Fig. 11.4. Here we have grouped its signal lines into four interfaces: the *memory/IO interface, interrupt*

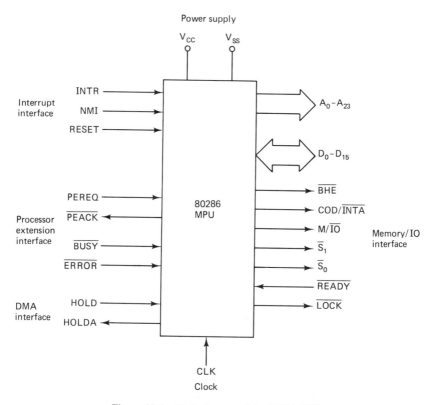

Figure 11.4 Block diagram of the 80286 MPU.

interface, DMA interface, and *processor extension interface.* Figure 11.5 lists each of the signals at the 80286's interfaces. Included in this table are a mnemonic, function, and type for each signal. For instance, the memory/IO control signal with the mnemonic M/IO stands for memory/IO select. This signal is an output produced by the 80286 that is used to signal external circuitry whether the current address available on the address bus is for memory or an I/O device. On the other hand, the signal INTR at the interrupt interface is the interrupt request input of the 80286. External devices can signal the 80286 that they need to be serviced with this input.

Name	Function	Type
CLK	System clock	I
$D_{15}-D_0$	Data bus	I/O
$A_{23}-A_0$	Address bus	O
$\overline{BHE}$	Bus high enable	O
$\overline{S}_1, \overline{S}_0$	Bus cycle status	O
M/$\overline{IO}$	Memory I/O select	O
COD/$\overline{INTA}$	Code/interrupt acknowledge	O
$\overline{LOCK}$	Bus lock	O
$\overline{READY}$	Bus ready	I
HOLD	Bus hold	I
HLDA	Hold acknowledge	O
INTR	Interrupt request	I
NMI	Nonmaskable interrupt request	I
PEREQ	Processor extension request	I
$\overline{PEACK}$	Processor extension acknowledge	O
$\overline{BUSY}$	Processor extension busy	I
$\overline{ERROR}$	Processor extension error	I
RESET	System reset	I
V_{SS}	System ground	I
V_{CC}	System power	I

Figure 11.5 Signal mnemonics, functions, and types.

Memory/IO Interface

In a microcomputer system the address bus and data bus signal lines form the path over which the MPU talks with its memory and I/O subsystems. Unlike the older 8086 and 8088 microprocessors, the 80286 has a demultiplexed address/data bus. Notice in Fig. 11.2 that the address bus and data bus lines are located at different pins of the IC.

From an external hardware point of view, there is only one difference between an 80286 configured for the real-address mode or protected-address mode. This difference is the size of the address bus. When in real mode, just the lower 20 address lines, A_0 through A_{19}, are active; in the protected mode all 24 lines, A_0 through A_{23}, are functional. Of these, A_{23} is the most-significant address bit and A_0 the least-significant bit. As shown in Fig. 11.5 the address lines are outputs. They are used to carry address information from the 80286 to memory and I/O ports. In real-address mode, the 20-bit address gives the 80286 the ability to address a 1M-byte physical memory address space. On the other hand, in protected mode the extended 24-bit address results in a 16M-byte physical memory address space; however, in protected mode, virtual addressing is provided through software, and this results in a 1G-byte virtual memory address space.

In both the real and protected mode, the 80286 microcomputer has an independent I/O address space which is 64K bytes in length. Therefore, just address lines A_0 through A_{15} are used when addressing I/O devices.

Since the 80286 is a 16-bit microprocessor, its data bus is formed from the 16 data lines D_0 through D_{15}. D_{15} is the MSB and D_0 the least significant bit. These lines are identified as bidirectional in Fig. 11.5. This is because they have the ability to carry data either in or out of the MPU. The kinds of data transferred over these lines are read/write data for memory, I/O data for I/O devices, and interrupt-type codes from an interrupt controller.

Control signals are required to support data transfers over the 80286's address/data bus. They are needed to signal when a valid address is on the address bus, in which direction data are to be transferred over the data bus, when valid write data are on the data bus, and when an external device can put read data on the data bus. The 80286 does not produce these signals directly. Instead, just like the 8086 in maximum mode, it outputs a 4-bit *bus status code* prior to the initiation of each bus cycle. This code identifies which type of bus cycle is to follow and must be decoded in external circuitry to produce the needed memory and I/O control signals.

In Fig. 11.6 we see that the bus status code is output on four of the 80286's signal lines: COD/INTA, M/IO, $\overline{S}_1$, and $\overline{S}_0$. The logic level of *code/interrupt acknowledge* (COD/INTA) identifies whether the current bus cycle is for an instruction fetch or interrupt-acknowledge operation. From the table we find that COD/INTA is logic 1 whenever an instruction-fetch is taking place and logic 0 when an interrupt is being acknowledged. The next signal, *memory/IO select* (M/IO), tells whether a memory or I/O cycle is to take place over the bus. Logic 1 at this output signals a memory operation, and logic 0 signals an I/O operation. Looking at the table in Fig. 11.6 more closely, we find

COD/INTA	M/IO	S1	S0	Bus Cycle Initiated
0 (LOW)	0	0	0	Interrupt acknowledge
0	0	0	1	Will not occur
0	0	1	0	Will not occur
0	0	1	1	None; not a status cycle
0	1	0	0	IF A1 = 1 then halt; else shutdown
0	1	0	1	Memory data read
0	1	1	0	Memory data write
0	1	1	1	None; not a status cycle
1 (HIGH)	0	0	0	Will not occur
1	0	0	1	I/O read
1	0	1	0	I/O write
1	0	1	1	None; not a status cycle
1	1	0	0	Will not occur
1	1	0	1	Memory instruction read
1	1	1	0	Will not occur
1	1	1	1	None; not a status cycle

Figure 11.6 Bus status codes (Courtesy of Intel Corp.).

that if the code on these two lines is 00 an interrupt is to be acknowledged, if it is 01 a data memory read or write is taking place, if it is 10 an I/O operation is in progress, and, finally, if it is 11 instruction code is being fetched.

The last two signals in Fig. 11.6 are called *status lines* and they identify the specific type of memory or I/O operation that will occur during a bus cycle. For example, when COD/INTA M/IO is 01, a status code of 01 indicates that data are to be read from memory. On the other hand, 10 at $S_1 S_0$ says that data are to be written into memory. As another example, we find that COD/INTA M/IO equals 11 and $S_1 S_0$ equals 01 whenever the 80286 is reading instruction code from memory.

EXAMPLE 11.1

What type of bus cycle is taking place if the bus status code $\overline{\text{COD}/\text{INTA}}$ $\overline{\text{M}/\text{IO}}$ $\overline{S}_1$ $\overline{S}_0$ is 1001?

SOLUTION Looking at the table in Fig. 11.6 we see that the status code 1001 identifies an I/O read (input) bus cycle.

Two bus control signals are directly produced by the 80286. These signals are *bus high enable* ($\overline{\text{BHE}}$) and *bus ready* ($\overline{\text{READY}}$). The logic level of $\overline{\text{BHE}}$ along with that of address bit A_0 identify whether a word or byte of data will be transferred during the current bus cycle. Moreover, if a byte transfer is to take place, the 2-bit code output at $\overline{\text{BHE}}$ and A_0 tells whether the byte will be transferred over the upper or lower eight lines of the data bus. Figure 11.7 summarizes the state of these two signals for each type of data transfer. Notice that whenever a word of data is transferred over the bus both $\overline{\text{BHE}}$ and A_0 are made logic 0.

$\overline{\text{BHE}}$	A0	Function
0	0	Word transfer
0	1	Byte transfer on upper half of data bus ($D_{15} - D_8$)
1	0	Byte transfer on lower half of data bus (D_{7-0})
1	1	Will never occur

Figure 11.7 $\overline{\text{BHE}}$ and A_0 encoding (Courtesy of Intel Corp.).

EXAMPLE 11.2

If a byte of data is being written to memory over data bus lines D_0 through D_7, what code is output at $\overline{\text{BHE}}$ and A_0?

SOLUTION In Fig. 11.7, we find that all transfers of byte data over the lower part of the address bus are accompanied by the code

$$\overline{\text{BHE}} \; A_0 = 10$$

$\overline{\text{READY}}$ can be used to insert wait states into the current bus cycle such that it is extended by a number of clock periods. This signal is an input to the 80286. Normally it is produced by the microcomputer's memory or I/O subsystem and supplied to the 80286 by way of the clock generator device. By signaling READY, slow memory or I/O devices can tell the 80286 when they are ready to permit a data transfer to be completed.

One other control signal is supplied by the 80286 to support multiple-processor architectures. This signal is the *bus lock* (LOCK) output. In multi-processor systems that employ shared resources, such as global memory, this signal can be employed to assure that the 80286 can have uninterrupted control of the system bus and the shared resource if needed; that is, by switching its LOCK output to logic 0, an MPU can lock up the shared resource for exclusive use.

Interrupt Interface

Looking at Fig. 11.4, we find that the key interrupt interface signals are *interrupt request* (INTR), *nonmaskable interrupt* (NMI), and *system reset* (RESET). INTR is an input to the 80286 that can be used by external devices to signal that they need to be serviced. This input is sampled at the beginning of each processor cycle. Logic 1 on INTR represents an active interrupt request. After an interrupt request has been recognized by the 80286, it initiates interrupt acknowledge bus cycles. In Fig. 11.6, we see that the occurrence of an interrupt acknowledge bus cycle is signaled to external circuitry with the bus status code COD/INTA M/IO $\overline{S}_1\overline{S}_0$ equal to 0000. This status code is decoded in external circuitry to produce an interrupt acknowledge signal.

The INTR input is maskable; that is, its operation can be enabled or disabled with the interrupt enable flag (IF) within the 80286's flag register. On the other hand, the NMI input, as its name implies, is a nonmaskable interrupt input. On the 0-to-1 transition of NMI, a request for service is latched within the 80286. Independent of the setting of the IF flag, control is now passed to the beginning of the nonmaskable interrupt service routine at completion of execution of the current instruction.

Finally, the RESET input is used to provide a hardware reset to the 80286 microprocessor. Switching RESET to logic 1 initializes the internal registers of the 80286. When it is returned to logic 0, program control is automatically passed to a reset service routine.

DMA Interface

Now that we have examined the signals of the 80286's interrupt interface, let us turn to the *direct memory access* (DMA) interface. From Fig. 11.4 we find that the DMA interface is implemented with just two signals: *bus hold request* (HOLD) and *hold acknowledge* (HLDA). When an external device, such as a *DMA controller,* wants to take control of the address/data bus, it signals this fact to the 80286 by switching the HOLD input to logic 1. At completion of the current bus cycle, the 80286 enters the hold state. When in this state, the local bus signals are in the high-Z state. The 80286 signals external devices that it has given up control of the bus by switching its HLDA output to the 1 logic level. This completes the hold/hold acknowledge handshake.

Processor Extension Interface

A processor extension interface is provided on the 80286 microprocessor to permit it to easily interface with the *80287 numeric coprocessor*. Whenever the 80287 needs the 80286 to read or write operands from memory, it signals this fact to the 80286. The 80287 does this by switching the *processor extension operand request* (PEREQ) input of the 80286 to logic 1. The processor extension handshake is completed when the 80286 signals the 80287 that it can have access to the bus. It signals this to the 80287 by switching the *processor extension acknowledge* (PEACK) output to logic 0.

The other two signals included in the external coprocessor interface are $\overline{BUSY}$ and $\overline{ERROR}$. *Processor extension busy* ($\overline{BUSY}$) is an input to the 80286. Whenever the 80287 is executing a numeric instruction, it signals this fact to the 80286 by switching the $\overline{BUSY}$ input to logic 0. In this way, the 80286 knows not to request that the numerics coprocessor perform another calculation until $\overline{BUSY}$ returns to 1. Moreover, if an error occurs in a calculation performed by the numerics coprocessor, it signals this condition to the 80286 by switching the *bus extension error* ($\overline{ERROR}$) input to the 0 logic level.

11.5 THE 82288 BUS CONTROLLER—GENERATION OF THE MEMORY/IO CONTROL SIGNALS

In the previous section we pointed out that the 80286 does not directly produce all the signals that are required to control the memory, I/O, and interrupt interfaces. Instead, it outputs a status code prior to the initiation of each bus cycle that identifies which type of bus cycle is to follow. In an 80286-based microcomputer, three of these status lines, $M/\overline{IO}, \overline{S}_1$, and $\overline{S}_0$, are supplied as inputs to an external *bus controller* device, the 82288. Just as in a maximum-mode 8086 system, the bus controller decodes them to identify the type of MPU bus cycle and then generates appropriately timed command and control signals at its outputs.

Let us now look at how the 82288 interfaces with the 80286 MPU. A block diagram for the 82288 IC is shown in Fig. 11.8 (a), and its pin layout is given in Fig. 11.8 (b). Here we can find each of the signals that it accepts as inputs and produces as outputs. For instance, status inputs $M/\overline{IO}$, $\overline{S}_1$, and $\overline{S}_0$ are located at pins 18, 3, and 19, respectively.

The 82288 connects to the 80286 as shown in Fig. 11.9. Notice that the status outputs of the 80286 are simply connected directly to the corresponding input of the 82288. Moreover, the clock (CLK) and ready (READY) inputs of the 82288 are wired to the respective inputs of the 80286 and both are driven by outputs of the 82C284 clock generator.

At the other side of the bus controller, we find the bus command and control signal outputs. The command outputs are: *memory read command* ($\overline{MRDC}$), *memory write command* ($\overline{MWTC}$), *I/O read command* ($\overline{IORC}$), *I/O write command* ($\overline{IOWC}$),

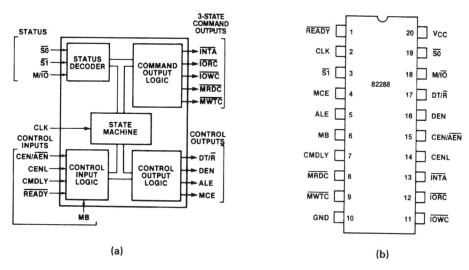

(a)   (b)

Figure 11.8 (a) Block diagram of the 82288 (Courtesy of Intel Corp.); (b) pin layout of the 82288 (Courtesy of Intel Corp.).

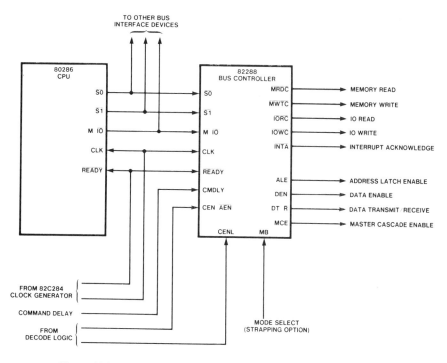

Figure 11.9 Decoding bus status with the 82288 (Courtesy of Intel Corp.).

and *interrupt acknowledge command* ($\overline{\text{INTA}}$). In Fig. 11.10 we see that just one of these command outputs becomes active for each of the bus status codes. For instance, when the 80286 outputs the code $\text{M}/\overline{\text{IO}}\ \overline{S_1}\ \overline{S_0}$ equal to 001, it indicates that an I/O read cycle is to be performed. In turn, the 82288 makes its $\overline{\text{IORC}}$ output switch to logic 0. On the other hand, if the code 111 is output by the 80286, it is signaling the bus controller that no bus activity is to take place.

Type of Bus Cycle	$\text{M}/\overline{\text{IO}}$	$\overline{S1}$	$\overline{S0}$	Command Activated	DT/$\overline{\text{R}}$ State	ALE, DEN Issued?	MCE Issued?
Interrupt Acknowledge	0	0	0	$\overline{\text{INTA}}$	LOW	YES	YES
I/O Read	0	0	1	$\overline{\text{IORC}}$	LOW	YES	NO
I/O Write	0	1	0	$\overline{\text{IOWC}}$	HIGH	YES	NO
None; Idle	0	1	1	None	HIGH	NO	NO
Halt/Shutdown	1	0	0	None	HIGH	NO	NO
Memory Read	1	0	1	$\overline{\text{MRDC}}$	LOW	YES	NO
Memory Write	1	1	0	$\overline{\text{MWTC}}$	HIGH	YES	NO
None; Idle	1	1	1	None	HIGH	NO	NO

Figure 11.10   Control signals for each bus cycle (Courtesy of Intel Corp.).

EXAMPLE 11.3

If the $\overline{\text{MRDC}}$ output of the 82288 has just switched to logic 0, what bus status code was output by the 80286?

SOLUTION   Looking at Fig. 11.10 we find that the status code input to the 82288 that makes $\overline{\text{MRDC}}$ active is

$$\text{M}/\overline{\text{IO}}\ \overline{S_1}\ \overline{S_0} = 101$$

The 82288 also produces the control signals *data transmit/receive* (DT/$\overline{\text{R}}$), *address latch enable* (ALE), *data enable* (DEN), and *master cascade enable* (MCE). Figure 11.10 shows the states of the control signals during each bus cycle. For example, during an I/O read cycle DT/$\overline{\text{R}}$ is set to logic 0, and both ALE and DEN are issued.

These command and control signals are needed to support memory and I/O data transfers over the address/data bus. Earlier we pointed out that they need to identify when the bus is carrying a valid address, in which direction data are to be transferred over the bus, when valid write data are on the bus, and when to put read data on the bus. For example, the ALE line signals external circuitry when a valid address word is on the bus. This address can be latched in external circuitry on the 0-to-1 edge of the pulse at ALE.

The direction in which data are to be transferred over the bus are signaled to external circuitry with the DT/$\overline{\text{R}}$ output. When this line is logic 1 during the data transfer part of a bus cycle, the bus is in the transmit mode. Therefore, data are either written into memory or output to an I/O device. On the other hand, logic 0 at DT/$\overline{\text{R}}$ signals that the bus is in the receive mode. This corresponds to reading data from memory or input of data from an input device.

The signals $\overline{MRDC}$ and $\overline{MWTC}$, respectively, indicate that a memory read bus cycle or a memory write bus cycle is in progress. The 82288 switches $\overline{MWTC}$ to logic 0 to signal external devices that valid write data are on the bus. On the other hand, $\overline{MRDC}$ indicates that the 80286 is performing a read of data off the bus. During read operations, one other control signal is supplied. This is DEN, and it is an output that signals external devices when they should put data onto the microprocessor's bus. Input and output bus cycles are performed in the same way; however, in this case $\overline{IORC}$ and $\overline{IOWC}$ are produced by the 82288 instead of $\overline{MRDC}$ and $\overline{MWTC}$.

The 82288 also has several control inputs. In Fig. 11.9 we find a *Multibus*™ *mode select* (MB) input. When the system is not using *Multibus* as the system bus, this input is connected to ground. Figure 11.8 includes three other signal lines that were not shown in the 80286/82288 interface circuit of Fig. 11.9. For instance, the *command enable/ address enable* (CEN/AEN) input can be used to enable or disable the command and DEN outputs of the 82288. To enable the 82288 for operation, this input must be at the 1 logic level. Designs which either use multiple 82288s or require the command output signals to be delayed are implemented by the last two inputs, CENL and CMDLY, respectively.

11.6 SYSTEM CLOCK

The time base for synchronization of the internal and external operations of the 80286 micropocessor is provided by the *clock* (CLK) input signal. At present, the 80286 is available with three different clock speeds. The standard 80286 MPU operates at 8 MHz and its two faster versions, the 80286-10 and 80286-12, operate at 10 MHz and 12.5 MHz, respectively. CLK is generated externally by the 82C284 clock generator/driver IC. Figure 11.11(a) is a block diagram of this device, and Fig. 11.11(b) shows its pin layout.

The normal way in which the clock chip is used is to connect a crystal with twice the microprocessor clock frequency between the X_1 and X_2 inputs. This circuit connection is shown in Fig. 11.12. For instance, to run the 80286 at 8 MHz, a 16-MHz crystal is needed. Notice that loading capacitors C_1 and C_2 are required from X_1 and X_2, respectively, to ground. Typical values (device value plus stray capacitance) for these capacitances are 25 pF and 15 pF, respectively. The fundamental crystal frequency produced by the oscillator within the 82C284 is divided by 2 to give the 8-MHz, 10-MHz, or 12.5-MHz CLK output. As shown in Fig. 11.12, CLK is applied directly to the CLK input of the 80286.

The waveform of the CLK input of the 80286 is given in Fig. 11.13. Here we see that the signal is specified at MOS-compatible voltage levels and not TTL levels. Its mimimum and maximum low logic levels are $V_{Lmin} = -0.5$ V and $V_{Lmax} = 0.6$ V, respectively. Moreover, the minimum and maximum high logic levels are $V_{Hmin} = 3.8$ V and $V_{Hmax} = +5.5$ V, respectively. The period of the 8-MHz signal is a minimum of 62.5 ns, and the maximum rise and fall times of its edges are equal to 10 ns.

In Fig. 11.11(a) we see that there is another clock output on the 82C284. This is

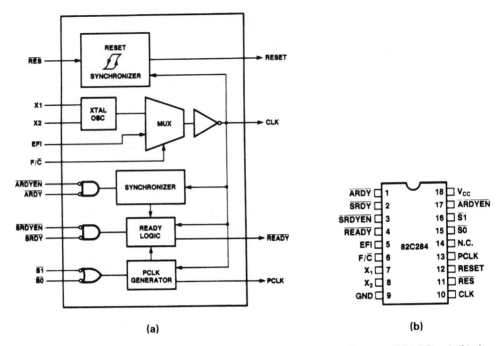

Figure 11.11 (a) Block diagram of the 82C284 clock generator (Courtesy of Intel Corp.); (b) pin layout (Courtesy of Intel Corp.).

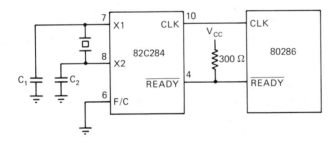

Figure 11.12 Connecting the 82C284 to the 80286 (Courtesy of Intel Corp.).

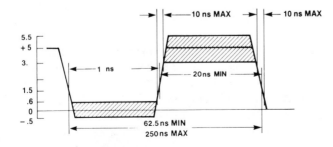

Figure 11.13 CLK voltage and timing characteristics (Courtesy of Intel Corp.).

the *processor clock* (PCLK) signal, which is provided to drive peripheral ICs. The clock produced at PCLK is always half the frequency of CLK; that is, if the 80286 is to operate at 8 MHz, PCLK will be 4 MHz. This relationship is illustrated in Fig. 11.14. Also, it is at TTL-compatible voltage levels rather than at CMOS levels.

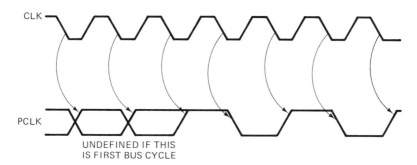

Figure 11.14 Timing relationship between CLK and PCLK (Courtesy of Intel Corp.).

The 82C284 can also be driven from an external clock source. In this case, the external clock signal is applied to the *external frequency input* (EFI). Input F/C *(frequency/crystal select)* is provided for clock source selection. When it is strapped to the 0 logic level, as in Fig. 11.12, the crystal between X_1 and X_2 is used. On the other hand, applying logic 1 to F/C selects EFI as the source of the clock.

11.7 THE BUS CYCLE AND BUS STATES

A bus cycle is the activity performed whenever a microprocessor accesses information in program memory, data memory, or an I/O device. Figure 11.15 shows a traditional microprocessor bus cycle. It represents a sequence of events that starts with an address, denoted as n, being output on the address bus in clock state T_1. Later in the bus cycle, while the address is still available on the address bus, a read or write data transfer takes

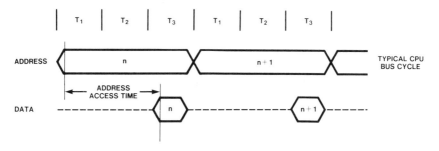

Figure 11.15 Traditional bus cycle (Courtesy of Intel Corp.).

place over the data bus. Notice that the data transfer for address n is shown to occur in clock state T_3. The interval denoted as *address access time* in Fig. 11.15 represents the amount of time that the address is stable prior to the read or write of data actually taking place. During the bus cycle, a series of control signals is also produced by the MPU to control the direction and timing of the bus operation.

Before looking at the bus cycle of the 80286, let us examine the relationship between the timing of the 80286's CLK input and bus cycle states. In the last section we pointed out that the processor clock (PCLK) signal was at half the frequency of CLK. Therefore, as shown in Fig. 11.16, one processor clock cycle corresponds to two CLK cycles. These CLK cycles are labeled *phase 1* (ϕ_1) and *phase 2* (ϕ_2). In an 8-MHz 80286 microcomputer system, each system clock cycle has a duration of 125 ns. Therefore, a processor clock cycle is 250 ns long.

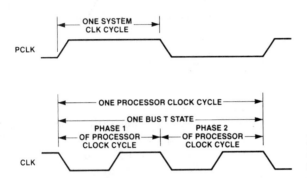

Figure 11.16 Send-status and perform-command bus states (Courtesy of Intel Corp.).

In Fig. 11.16 we see that the two phases ($\phi_1 + \phi_2$) of a processor cycle are identified as one bus *T state*. Figure 11.17 (a) shows a typical 80286 bus cycle. Notice that here the clock T states are labeled T_s and T_c. T_s stands for the *send-status state*. During this part of the bus cycle, the 80286 outputs a bus status code to the 82288 bus controller, and in the case of a write cycle, write data are also output on the data bus. The second state, T_c, is called the *perform-command state*. It is during this part of the bus cycle that external devices are to accept write data from the bus, or in the case of a read cycle, put data on the bus. Also the address for the next bus cycle is output on the address bus during T_c. Since each bus cycle has a minimum of two T states, the minimum bus cycle duration in an 8-MHz system is 250 ns.

The bus cycle of the 80286 employs a technique known as *pipelining*. By pipelining we mean that addressing for the next bus cycle is overlapped with the data transfer of the prior bus cycle. In Figure 11.17(a) we see that address n becomes valid in the T_c state of the prior bus cycle and then the data transfer for address n takes place in the next T_c state. Moreover, notice that at the same time that data transfer n occurs address n + 1 is output on the address bus. In this way, we see that the 80286 begins addressing the next storage location that is to be accessed while it is still performing the read or write of data for the previously addressed storage location. Because of the address/data pipelining, the memory or I/O subsystem actually has five CLK periods to complete the data transfer even though the effective duration of every bus cycle is just four CLK periods.

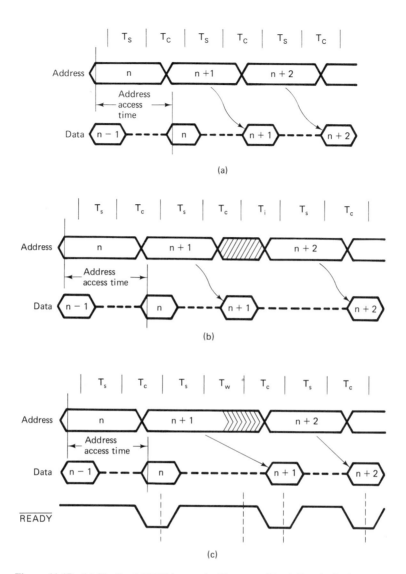

Figure 11.17 (a) Pipelined 80286 bus cycle (Courtesy of Intel Corp.); (b) bus cycle with idle states (Courtesy of Intel Corp.); (c) bus cycle with wait states (Courtesy of Intel Corp.).

Figure 11.17(a) shows that the effective address access time equals the duration of a complete bus cycle. This leads us to the benefit of the pipelined bus operation of the 80286 not found in the traditional bus operation shown in Fig. 11.15. This benefit is that for a fixed address access time (equal-speed memory design), the 80286 will have a shorter duration bus cycle than a processor that uses a nonpipelined bus cycle. This results in improved bus performance for the 80286.

Another way of looking at this is to say that when using equal-speed memory designs, a pipelined microprocessor can be operated at a higher clock rate than a processor that executes a nonpipelined bus cycle. Once again the result is higher system performance. A pipelined memory subsystem design is much more complex and requires more hardware than that of a nonpipelined memory subsystem.

In Fig. 11.17(a) we see that at completion of the bus cycle for address n another bus cycle is initiated immediately for address n + 1. Sometimes another bus cycle will not be initiated immediately. For instance, if the 80286's prefetch queue is already full and the instruction that is currently being executed does not need to access operands in memory, no bus activity will take place. In this case, the bus goes into a mode of operation known as an *idle state* and no bus activity occurs. Figure 11.17(b) shows a sequence of bus activity in which several idle states exist between the bus cycles for addresses n and n + 1. The duration of a single idle state is equal to one processor cycle (two clock cycles).

Wait states can also be inserted into the 80286's bus cycle. This is done in response to a request by an event in external hardware instead of an internal event such as a full queue. In fact the $\overline{READY}$ input of the 80286 is provided specifically for this purpose. This input is sampled in the later part of the T_c state of every bus cycle to determine if the data transfer should be completed. Figure 11.17(c) shows that logic 1 at this input indicates that the current bus cycle should not be completed. As long as $\overline{READY}$ is held at the 1 level, the read or write data transfer does not take place and the current T_s state becomes a wait state (T_w) to extend the bus cycle. The bus cycle is not completed until external hardware returns $\overline{READY}$ back to logic 0. This ability to extend the duration of a bus cycle permits the use of slower memory or I/O devices in the microcomputer system.

11.8 MEMORY INTERFACE

In the preceding sections we studied the 80286 microprocessor, its internal architecture, the 82288 bus controller, the 82C284 clock generator, and read/write bus cycles. Here we will continue by introducing its memory interface, hardware organization of the address space, data transfers through the memory interface, and the read and write bus cycles.

Memory Interface Circuit

A memory interface circuit diagram for a real-mode 80286-based microcomputer system is shown in Fig. 11.18. Here we find that the interface includes the 82288 bus controller, an address decoder and address latches, data bus transceiver/buffers, and bank select logic. Status signals, M/$\overline{IO}$, $\overline{S_1}$, and $\overline{S_0}$, which are output by the 80286, are supplied directly to the 82288 bus controller. Here they are decoded to produce the command and control signals needed to control data transfers over the bus. In Fig. 11.19, the two status codes that relate to the memory interface are highlighted. The code M/$\overline{IO}$ $\overline{S_1}$ $\overline{S_0}$ = 101 indicates that a memory read bus cycle is in progress. This code makes the $\overline{MRDC}$ output switch to logic 0. Notice in Fig. 11.18 that $\overline{MRDC}$ is applied to the output enable ($\overline{OE}$) input of the memory subsystem.

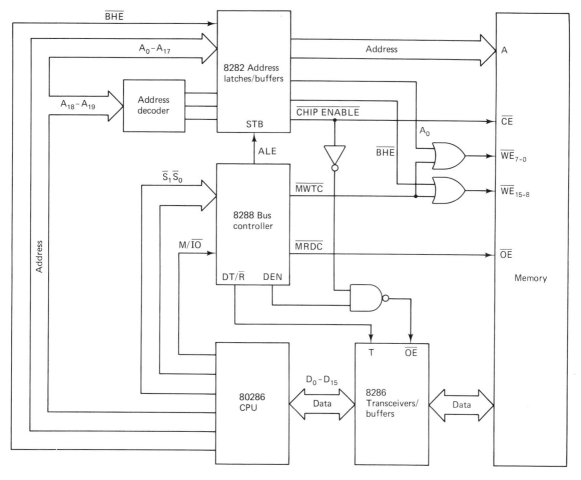

Figure 11.18 80286 system memory interface.

Next let us look at how the address bus is decoded, latched, and buffered. Address lines A_0 through A_{17} and $\overline{BHE}$ are sent directly to inputs of the 8282 address latches. On the other hand, bits A_{18} and A_{19} are first decoded and then passed on to the latch. Finally, the pulse at ALE is used to strobe address bits A_0 through A_{17}, $\overline{BHE}$, and the

M/$\overline{IO}$	$\overline{S}_1$	$\overline{S}_0$	Type of bus cycle
0	0	0	Interrupt acknowledge
0	0	1	I/O Read
0	1	0	I/O Write
0	1	1	None; idle
1	0	0	Halt or shutdown
1	0	1	Memory read
1	1	0	Memory write
1	1	1	None; idle

Figure 11.19 Memory bus status codes (Courtesy of Intel Corp.).

output of the decoder, which is chip enable ($\overline{\text{CE}}$), into the latches. The address latches also buffer the address lines and control signals before passing them on to the memory subsystem.

This part of the memory interface demonstrates one of the benefits of the 80286's pipelined bus. Remember that the 80286 actually outputs the address in the T_c state of the prior bus cycle. Therefore, by putting the address decoder before the address latches instead of after, the code at address lines A_{18} and A_{19} can be fully decoded and stable prior to the occurrence of ALE in the T_s state of the current bus cycle; that is, since the address can be decoded prior to ALE, the decode propagation delay is transparent and does not decrease the overall access time of the memory subsystem.

During read bus cycles, the $\overline{\text{MRDC}}$ output of the bus controller enables the data at the outputs of the memory subsystem onto data bus lines D_0 through D_{15}. On the other hand, during write operations to memory, control logic must determine whether data are written into the lower memory bank, the upper memory bank, or both banks. This depends on whether an even byte, odd byte, or word data transfer is taking place over the bus. The bank-select logic performs this function. Notice in Fig. 11.18 that $\overline{\text{MWTC}}$ is gated with address bit A_0 to produce write enable $\overline{\text{WE}}_{7-0}$ for the low memory bank. For $\overline{\text{WE}}_{7-0}$ to be at its active logic 0 level, both A_0 and $\overline{\text{MWTC}}$ must be logic 0. This happens only when either an even addressed byte of data or a word of data is written to memory. Moreover, $\overline{\text{MWTC}}$ is gated with $\overline{\text{BHE}}$ to produce the high memory bank write enable signal $\overline{\text{WE}}$. For this signal to switch to its active 0 logic level, $\overline{\text{BHE}}$ and $\overline{\text{MWTC}}$ must both be logic 0. This occurs when either an odd addressed byte of data or a word of data is written to memory.

The bus transceiver/buffers control the direction of data transfers between the MPU and memory subsystem. Notice that the transceivers get enabled by switching their output enable ($\overline{\text{OE}}$) inputs to logic 0. Signals data bus enable (DEN) and chip enable ($\overline{\text{CE}}$) are combined with an inverter and NAND gate to produce $\overline{\text{OE}}$. When DEN is logic 1 and $\overline{\text{CE}}$ is logic 0, the output of the NAND gate switches to logic 0 and the transceivers are enabled. This happens during all read and write bus cycles to memory.

The direction in which data are passed through the transceiver/buffers is controlled by the bus controller. The bus controller sets its data transmit/receive (DT/$\overline{\text{R}}$) output to logic 0 during all read cycles and logic 1 during all write cycles. This signal is applied to the T input of the transceiver to select the direction in which data are transferred.

Hardware Organization of the Memory Address Space

From a hardware point of view, the memory address space of the 80286 is implemented exactly the same as that of the 8086; that is, it is organized as two independent banks called the *low (even) bank* and the *high (odd) bank*. Data bytes associated with an even address (000000_{16}, 000002_{16}, etc.) reside in the low bank, and those with odd addresses (000001_{16}, 000003_{16}, etc.) reside in the high bank.

Looking at Fig. 11.20, we find that the 80286's real-mode physical address space is partitioned into a 512K-byte low bank and a 512K-byte high bank. When in the protected mode, the banks can each be as large as 8M bytes. In the real mode, address bits A_1 through A_{19} select the storage location that is to be accessed. Therefore, they are applied to both banks in parallel. Just as for the 8086, A_0 and bank high enable

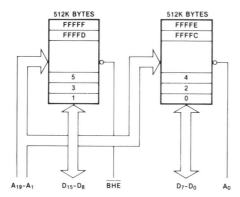

Figure 11.20 High and low memory banks (Courtesy of Intel Corp.).

$(\overline{BHE})$ are used as bank-select signals. Logic 0 and A_0 identifies an even-addressed byte of data and causes the low bank of memory to be enabled. On the other hand, $\overline{BHE}$ equal to 0 enables the high bank for access of an odd-addressed byte of data. Each of the memory banks supplies half the 80286's 16-bit data bus. Notice that the lower bank transfers bytes of data over data lines D_0 through D_7; data transfers for the high bank use D_8 through D_{15}. Figures 11.21(a) through (d) show how an even-addressed byte of

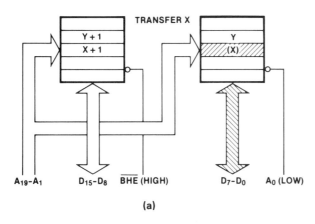

(a)

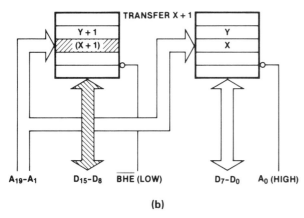

(b)

Figure 11.21 (a) Even-addressed byte transfer (Courtesy of Intel Corp.); (b) odd-addressed byte transfer (Courtesy of Intel Corp.); (c) even-addressed word transfer (Courtesy of Intel Corp.); (d) odd-addressed word transfer (Courtesy of Intel Corp.).

Sec. 11.8   Memory Interface

451

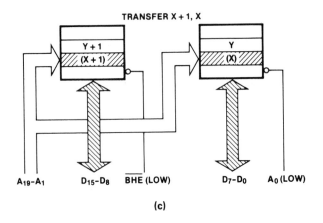

TRANSFER X + 1, X

(c)

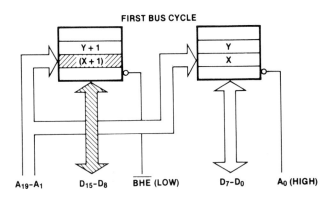

FIRST BUS CYCLE

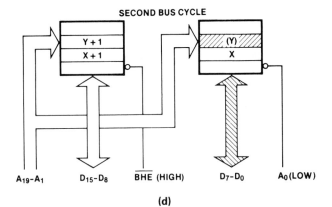

SECOND BUS CYCLE

(d)

Figure 11.21 *(continued)*

data, odd-addressed byte of data, even-addressed word of data, and odd-addressed word of data, respectively, are accessed.

Read Cycle Timing

The memory interface signals that occur when the 80286 reads data from memory are shown in Fig. 11.22. Since the pipelined bus of the 80286 overlaps bus cycles, we have shown parts of three cycles in the timing diagram: the previous cycle, the current read cycle, and the next cycle. Let us now trace through the events that take place as data or instructions are read from memory.

The occurrence of all signals in the read bus cycle timing diagram are illustrated relative to the two timing states, T_s (send-status state) and T_c (perform-command state), of the 80286's bus cycle. The read cycle begins at phase 2 (ϕ_2) in the T_c state of the previous bus cycle. During this period, the 80286 outputs the 24-bit address of the memory location to be accessed on address bus lines A_0 through A_{23}. Also we see in Fig. 11.22 that at the start of ϕ_2, signal $M/\overline{IO}$ is set to logic 1 to indicate to the circuitry

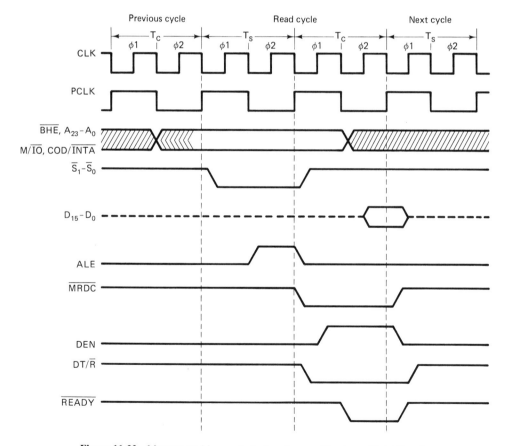

Figure 11.22 Memory read bus cycle timing diagram (Courtesy of Intel Corp.).

Sec. 11.8   Memory Interface

in the memory interface that a memory bus cycle is in progress, and COD/$\overline{\text{INTA}}$ is set to logic 1 if the bus cycle is being performed to fetch code data. In our description of the memory interface circuit of Fig. 11.18, we pointed out that these signals are stable during the T_c state of the previous bus cycle; therefore, the address decode logic circuitry should begin to decode them immediately. This will assure that a maximum amount of time will be left to access the memory subsystem. Notice that the status signals, M/$\overline{\text{IO}}$, and COD/$\overline{\text{INTA}}$ are maintained valid through ϕ_1 of state T_c of the read cycle. In ϕ_2 of T_c they are replaced with new values in preparation for the next bus cycle.

At the beginning of ϕ_1 of the read cycle, the 80286 outputs status code $\overline{S_1}\overline{S_0}$ equal 01 on the status bus. Remember that this code identifies that a read bus transfer is to take place. This status information is maintained through the T_s state. At the falling edge of CLK in the middle of T_s, the status lines are sampled by the 82288 bus controller and the read cycle bus control sequence is started. At the same time that the status information is output, $\overline{\text{BHE}}$ is also switched to logic 0 or 1, depending on whether or not the high memory bank is to be enabled during the read cycle.

With ϕ_2 of T_s, the bus controller takes over the timing control for the bus. It begins by producing a pulse to logic 1 at ALE during ϕ_2. The leading edge of this pulse should be used to latch the address and $\overline{\text{BHE}}$ into external circuitry.

At the start of the T_c state of the read cycle, the bus controller switches both DT/$\overline{\text{R}}$ and $\overline{\text{MRDC}}$ to logic 0. Logic 0 at DT/$\overline{\text{R}}$ is used to set the direction of the data bus transceivers so that they will pass data from the memory subsystem to the 80286. On the other hand, the logic 0 at $\overline{\text{MRDC}}$ enables the output buffers of the memory subsystem so that they output data to the inputs of the data bus transceivers. Later in ϕ_1, DEN is set to 1. This active logic level enables the data bus transceivers and lets the data available at its inputs pass through to the outputs, which are attached to the data bus of the 80286.

The 80286 and 82288 sample the logic level of their $\overline{\text{READY}}$, inputs at the end of ϕ_2 in the T_c state of the read cycle. Assuming that $\overline{\text{READY}}$ is at its active 0 logic level, the MPU reads the data off the bus. The read cycle is now completed as the bus controller returns $\overline{\text{MRDC}}$, DEN, and DT/$\overline{\text{R}}$ to their inactive logic levels.

Write Cycle Timing

The write bus cycle timing diagram, shown in Fig. 11.23, is similar to that given for a read cycle in Fig. 11.22. Looking at the write cycle waveforms, we find that the address, M/$\overline{\text{IO}}$, and COD/$\overline{\text{INTA}}$ signals are output at the beginning of ϕ_2 of the T_c state in the previous bus cycle. All these signals are to be latched in external circuitry with the ALE pulse during ϕ_2 of the T_s state in the write cycle. Up to this point, the bus cycle is identical to that for the read cycle.

The $\overline{\text{BHE}}$ signal and status code $\overline{S_1}\overline{S_0}$ are output at the beginning of the T_s state of the write cycle. This also happened in the read cycle, but this time the status code is 10 instead of 01. This code is sampled by the 82288 later in the T_s state and is determined to be that for the memory write cycle.

Let us now look at the control signal sequence produced by the bus controller for the write bus cycle. Notice that the 80286 outputs the data that is to be written to

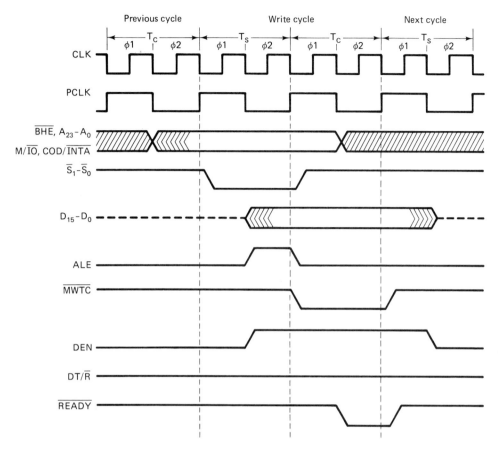

Figure 11.23 Memory write bus cycle timing diagram (Courtesy of Intel Corp.).

n mory on the data bus at the beginning of ϕ_2 in the T_s state. After identifying the status code as that for a write cycle, the 82288 switches DT/$\overline{R}$ (DT/$\overline{R}$ is normally in the 1 state) and DEN to logic 1. This sets the data bus transceivers to pass data from the MPU to the memory subsystem and enables it for operation. Finally, the memory write ($\overline{\text{MWTC}}$) output is switched to logic 0 at the beginning of the T_c state of the write cycle. MWTC signals the memory subsystem that valid write data are on the bus. Finally, late in the T_c state, the 80286 and 82288 test the logic level of $\overline{\text{READY}}$. If READY is logic 0, the write cycle is completed and the buses and control signals are prepared for the next read or write cycle.

Wait States in the Memory Bus Cycle

Wait states can be inserted to lengthen the memory bus cycle of the 80286. This is done with the $\overline{\text{READY}}$ input signal. Upon request from an event in external hardware, for instance, slow memory, the $\overline{\text{READY}}$ input is switched to logic 0. This signals the 80286 and the 82288 that the current bus cycle should not be completed. Instead, it is extended by repeating the T_c state. Therefore, the duration of one wait state (T_w) equals 125 ns for 8-MHZ clock operation. Figure 11.24 shows a read cycle extended by one wait state. Notice that the control signals DT/R, DEN, and MRDC are maintained throughout the wait-state period. In this way, the read cycle is not completed until READY is switched to logic 0 in the T_c state that follows.

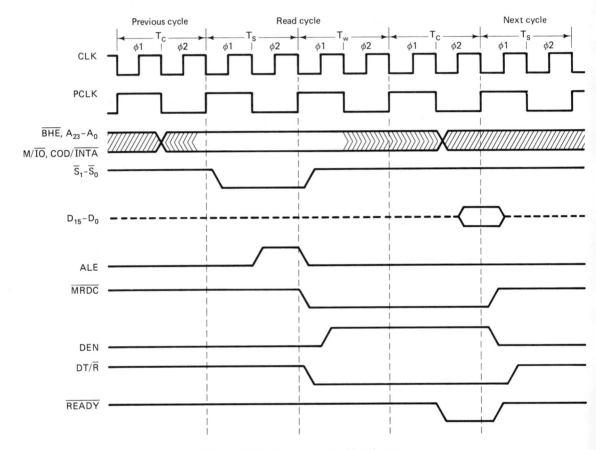

Figure 11.24 Read bus cycle with wait state.

11.9 PROGRAM AND DATA STORAGE MEMORY CIRCUITS

In the last section, we showed how the memory of an 80286-based microcomputer is organized from a hardware point of view and how a memory subsystem can be interfaced with the 80286. Here we will look at how *EPROM, static RAMs,* and *dynamic RAMs (DRAMs)* are connected to the system bus to implement *program and data storage memory subsystems.*

Program Storage Memory

The program storage memory part of a microcomputer is used to store fixed information such as instructions of the program or tables of data. Typically it is read-only and for this reason is implemented with ROM, PROM, or EPROM devices. EPROM devices, such as the 2764, 27128, and 27256, are organized with a byte-wide output; therefore, two devices are required to supply the 16-bit data bus of the 80286.

Figure 11.25 shows how two 2764 EPROMs are connected to the system bus of the 80286 to provide an 8K-word (16K-byte) program storage memory. Each of the 2764s supplies 8K, 8-bit storage locations. The upper of the two devices represents the high memory bank, and the lower device represents the low memory bank. Notice that both EPROM devices are addressed in parallel over the bus. To select one of the 8K storage locations, we need a 13-bit address. In the circuit diagram, this corresponds to address bits A_1 through A_{13}.

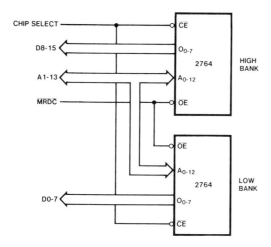

Figure 11.25 16K-byte program storage memory (Courtesy of Intel Corp.).

The additional high-order lines of the 80286's address bus, which are not shown in Fig. 11.25, must be decoded to produce the CHIP SELECT signal. Notice that the $\overline{CE}$ (chip enable) inputs of the two 2764s are connected in parallel and supplied by CHIP SELECT. Whenever the address on the system bus corresponds to program storage memory, the output of the address decoder must switch this line to logic 0 to enable the EPROMs for operation. If we assume that the high-order address bits are all at logic 0 to select program storage memory, its word storage locations correspond to the address range

$$A_{13}A_{12}\ldots\ldots\ldots A_0 = 0000000000000_2 = 00000_{16}$$

through

$$A_{13}A_{12}\ldots\ldots\ldots A_0 = 1111111111110_2 = 03FFE_{16}$$

In Fig. 11.25 we also find that data output lines O_0 through O_7 of the high bank EPROM are connected to 80286 data bus lines D_8 through D_{15}. Furthermore, the O_0

through O_7 outputs of the low bank EPROM supply D_0 through D_7 of the data bus. Data held at the addressed storage location are enabled onto the data bus by the control signal $\overline{\text{MRDC}}$, which is applied to the $\overline{\text{OE}}$ (output enable) input of both EPROMs, in parallel. In this way, we see that data held in program storage memory are always accessed as words.

Data Storage Memory

Information that frequently changes is stored in the data storage part of the microcomputer's memory subsystem. Examples of information typically stored in this part of memory are application programs and data bases. The data storage part of the memory subsystem is normally implemented with random access read/write memory (RAM). If the amount of memory required in the microcomputer is small, for instance, less than 64K bytes, the memory subsystem will usually be designed with static RAMs. On the other hand, systems that require a larger amount of data storage memory normally use DRAMs. This is because standard DRAMs are organized 64K × 1-bit, 256K × 1-bit, or 1M × 1-bit. Moreover, DRAMs require refresh support circuits. This additional circuitry is not warranted if storage requirements are small.

A 4K-word random access read/write memory can be implemented for an 80286-based microcomputer with the circuit shown in Fig. 11.26. This part of the memory subsystem is constructed with sixteen 2147 static RAM ICs. Each 2147 contains 4K, 1-bit storage locations; therefore, they each store just 1 bit of the word. Notice that the

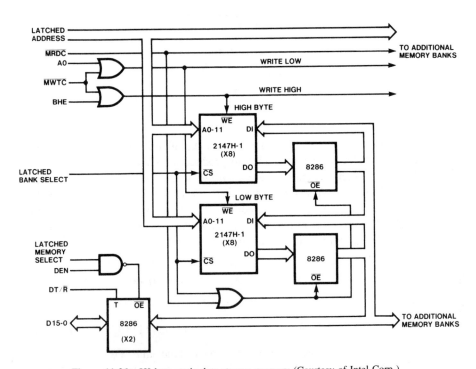

Figure 11.26 8K-byte static data storage memory (Courtesy of Intel Corp.).

bank-select signal (LATCHED BANK SELECT), which is formed by decoding the higher-order address bits, is applied to the $\overline{CS}$ input of all 16 RAM devices. Logic 0 at this input enables them for operation. The storage location to be accessed is selected by the 12-bit address A_1 through A_{12}, which is applied to the A_0 through A_{11} inputs of all RAMs in parallel.

Now that we know how the storage location to be accessed is selected, let us look at how data are transferred between the 80286 and memory. Data are read from or written in the selected storage location over data bus lines D_0 through D_{15}. Remember that through software the 80286 can read or write data from memory either as bytes or words. Because of the design of this memory circuit, data reads are always performed as words. This can be done because even though a word of data is available on the bus during a read cycle, the microprocessor will read the appropriate byte of data only off the bus. Therefore, words of data, whether they are read from or written to memory, are transferred across the complete data bus. On the other hand, byte-wide data writes are performed only to the appropriate bank of RAMs; that is, odd-addressed bytes of data are always written to the high-byte RAMs. This data transfer takes place across bus lines D_0 through D_7. Moreover, all even-addressed bytes of data are located in the low-byte RAMs and are transferred over bus lines D_8 through D_{15}.

When data are being read from memory, the byte of data held at the addressed storage location in the high and low banks are output at the data out (DO) leads of the RAMs. In Fig. 11.26 we see that these outputs are isolated from the data bus by 8286 transceivers. When the word of data is to be put on the data bus, the 82288 bus controller switches its $\overline{MRDC}$ output to logic 0. This signal is gated with LATCHED BANK SELECT to produce the $\overline{OE}$ input for the two data-out transceivers. When a read cycle is in progress from data memory, both LATCHED BANK SELECT and $\overline{MRDC}$ are logic 0. Therefore, the $\overline{OE}$ inputs of the 8286's are also logic 0 and the word of data is passed to the data bus.

During write operations, $\overline{MWTC}$ signals the memory circuit when the data are to be written to the RAMs. Notice that this signal is gated with $\overline{BHE}$ to produce $\overline{WE}$ for the high bank and with A_0 to give $\overline{WE}$ for the lower bank. If a word of data is being written to an even address, both A_0 and $\overline{BHE}$ are logic 0. Therefore, when $\overline{MWTC}$ switches to logic 0, the $\overline{WE}$ input of both banks of RAMs is active, and the bytes of data applied to the data inputs (DI) of the two banks are stored as a word in memory. If, however, an odd-addressed byte of data is to be written to memory, A_0 is at logic 1, and $\overline{BHE}$ at logic 0. In this case, $\overline{WE}$ is active just for the high bank of RAMs. Therefore, only the byte of data from D_8 through D_{15} is written to memory.

Figure 11.27(a) shows a memory subsystem for the 80286 microprocessor implemented with DRAMs. Here we find that the 82288 bus controller is used only to produce the signals that control the data bus—that is, DEN and DT/$\overline{R}$. An *8207 refresh controller* is used to multiplex the address into a row and column address, generate row and column address strobes, produce the write enable signal, and refresh the DRAMs.

Another 8207-based memory subsystem is shown in Fig. 11.27(b). This circuit is identical to the design shown in Fig. 11.27(a); however, this diagram does not show the processor complex (80286, 82284, and 82288) but does show the memory array and address signals in more detail. Notice that the memory array contains four banks of DRAMs. Each bank is formed from sixteen 16K × 1-bit DRAMs and provides 16K

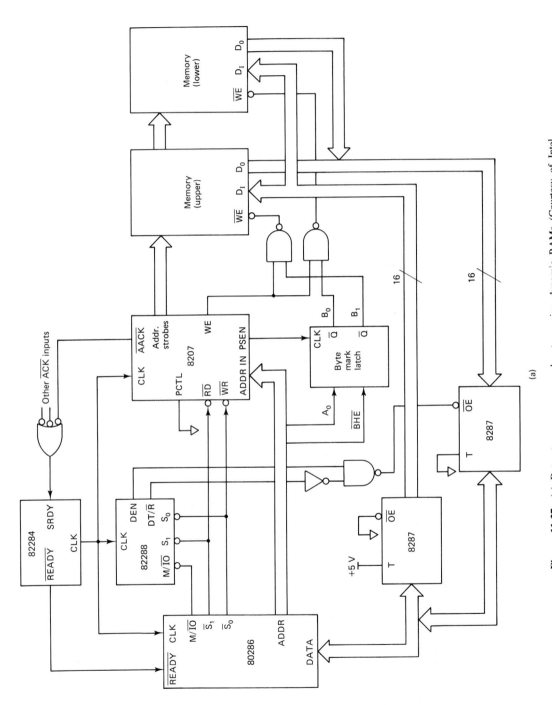

Figure 11.27 (a) Data storage memory subsystem using dynamic RAMs (Courtesy of Intel Corp.); (b) DRAM control circuitry and memory array (Courtesy of Intel Corp.).

(a)

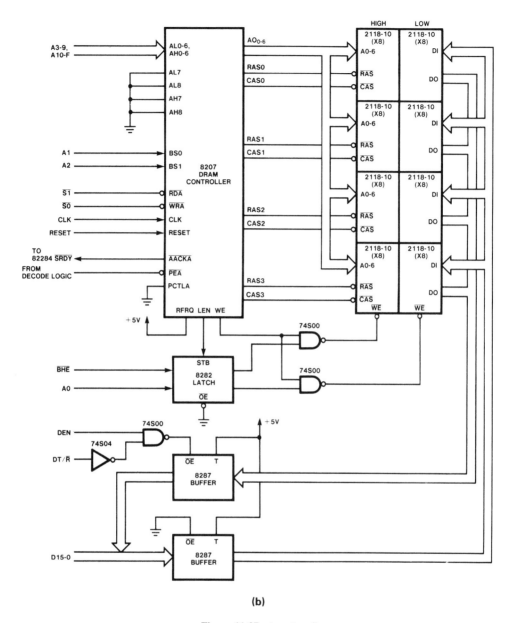

Figure 11.27 *(continued)*

words of storage. This gives the memory subsystem a total storage capacity of 64K words. Again the banks are partitioned into a high-byte section and a low-byte section.

Let us now look at how the 8207 handles addressing of the memory array. From Fig. 11.27(b) we see that address lines A_3 through A_9 of the 80286 are applied to *address low inputs* AL_0 through AL_6 of the 8207. Moreover, address bits A_{10} through A_{16} are supplied to *address high inputs* AH_0 through AH_6. Notice that two more address bits, A_1 and A_2, are inputs to the 8207. They are applied to *bank select inputs* BS_0 and BS_1, respectively.

At the output side of the 8207, these address inputs are multiplexed as a row address at *address outputs* AO_0 through AO_6 followed by a column address later. The AH inputs correspond to the bits of the row address, and the AL inputs make up the column address. These address outputs are applied to all DRAMs in parallel; however, a *row address strobe* (RAS) and *column address strobe* (CAS) are produced for just one bank of memories. This is the bank selected by the code at the bank select inputs. For instance, if BS_0BS_1 equals 00, RAS_0 and CAS_0 are produced and the row and column addresses are strobed into the upper most bank of DRAMs.

The 8207 can also perform the *refresh* function needed by DRAMs. In fact, in Fig. 11.27(b) we find that the *refresh request* (RFRQ) input of the 8207 is fixed at the 1 logic level. This selects internal automatic refresh mode of operation for the memory subsystem.

11.10 I/O INTERFACE

In sections 11.8 and 11.9, we studied the memory interface of the 80286 microprocessor. Here we will examine another important interface of the 80286-based microcomputer system, the I/O interface.

The I/O Interface

The I/O interface of the 80286 microcomputer permits it to communicate with the outside world. The way in which the 80286 deals with I/O circuitry is similar to the way in which it interfaces with memory circuitry; that is, the transfer of I/O data also takes place over the data bus. This parallel bus permits easy interface to LSI peripheral devices such as parallel I/O expanders, interval timers, and serial communication controllers. Let us continue by looking at how the 80286 interfaces to its I/O subsystem.

Figure 11.28(a) shows a typical I/O interface. Here we see that the way in which the 80286 interfaces with I/O devices is identical to that of the maximum-mode 8086 microcomputer system. Notice that the interface includes the 82288 bus controller, an address decoder, address latches/buffers, data bus transceiver/buffers, and I/O devices. An example of an I/O device is a programmable peripheral interface IC, such as the 8255A, that is used to implement parallel I/O ports. The circuit in Fig. 11.28(b) demonstrates how 8255As are used to implement a parallel I/O interface for the 80286 microcomputer.

The I/O device that is accessed for input or output of data is selected by an *I/O address*. This address is specified as part of the instruction that performs the I/O operation. Just as for the 8086 architecture, the 80286's I/O address is 16 bits in length. As shown in Fig. 11.28(a), they are output to the I/O interface over address bus lines A_0 through A_{15}. The more significant address bits, A_{16} through A_{23}, are held at the 0 logic level during the address period of all I/O bus cycles.

In the circuit of Fig. 11.28(a), addresses output on address lines A_0 through A_{15} of the 80286 are decoded by the address decoder and then latched into the 8282 address

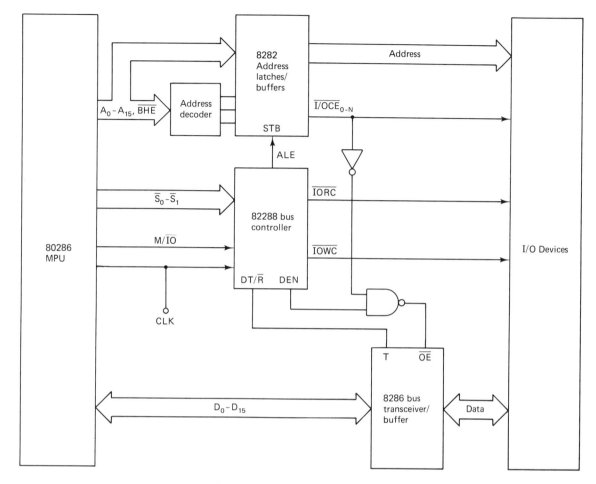

Figure 11.28(a) I/O interface circuit.

latches. Latching of the address is achieved with the pulse output on the ALE line of the 82288. Notice that some of the address bits are decoded to produce I/O chip enable signals, $\overline{I/O\ CE_0}$ through $\overline{I/O\ CE_N}$, for the I/O devices. For instance, with three address bits, we can produce enough chip enable outputs to select up to eight I/O devices. Other address bits are sent directly to the I/O devices. Typically these signals are used to select the register within the peripheral device that is to be accessed. For example, with four address lines, we can select one of 16 registers.

During I/O bus cycles, data are passed between the 80286 and the selected register within the enabled I/O device over data bus lines D_0 through D_{15}. The 80286 can input or output data in either byte-wide or word-wide format; however, most LSI peripherals used as I/O controllers in the 80286 microcomputer system are designed to interface with an 8-bit bus and are attached to either the upper or lower part of the bus. For this reason, I/O operations usually involve byte-wide data transfers, not word transfers.

Just as for the memory interface, the signals A_0 and $\overline{BHE}$ are used to signal

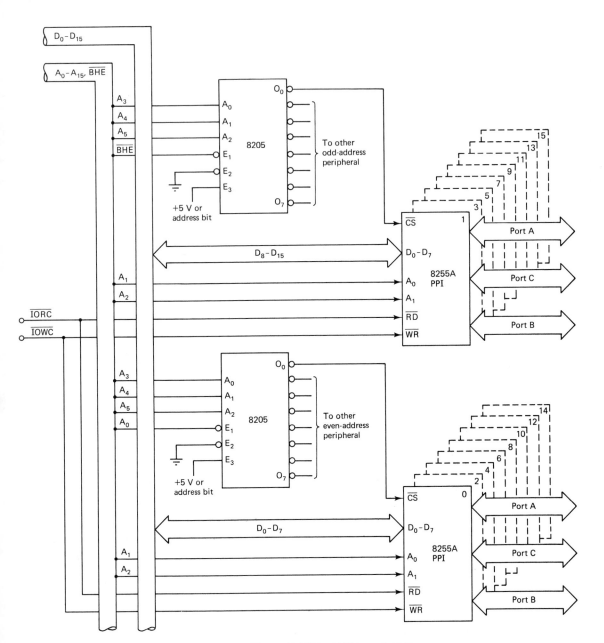

Figure 11.28(b) 8255A parallel I/O ports.

whether an even- or odd-addressed byte of data is being transferred over the bus. Again logic 0 at A_0 and $\overline{BHE}$ equal to 1 identifies an even byte, and the byte of data is input or output over data bus lines D_0 through D_7. Moreover, logic 1 at A_0 and logic 0 at $\overline{BHE}$ identifies an odd byte, and the data transfer occurs over bus lines D_8 through D_{15}.

As in the memory interface, the 82288 bus controller produces the control signals for the I/O interface in Fig. 11.28(a). The 82288 decodes bus cycle status codes that are output by the 80286 on M/IO, S_1, and S_0. The table in Fig. 11.29 shows the bus command status codes together with the type of bus cycle they produce. Those for I/O bus cycles have been highlighted. If the code corresponds to an I/O read bus cycle (M/IO S_1 S_0 = 001), the 82288 generates the *I/O read command output* ($\overline{IORC}$), and for I/O write bus cycles (M/IO S_1 S_0 = 010), it generates the *I/O write command output* ($\overline{IOWC}$). Looking at Fig. 11.28(b), we see that $\overline{IORC}$ and $\overline{IOWC}$ are applied directly to the I/O devices and tell them whether data are to be input from or output to the enabled I/O device.

M/$\overline{IO}$	$\overline{S}_1$	$\overline{S}_0$	Type of bus cycle
0	0	0	Interrupt acknowledge
0	0	1	I/O Read
0	1	0	I/O Write
0	1	1	None; idle
1	0	0	Halt or shutdown
1	0	1	Memory read
1	1	0	Memory write
1	1	1	None; idle

Figure 11.29 I/O bus cycle status codes (Courtesy of Intel Corp.).

Notice in Fig. 11.28(a) that the 82288 also produces control signals ALE, DT/$\overline{R}$, and DEN. These signals are used to set up the I/O interface circuitry for the input or output data transfer. The 8286 bus transceiver/buffers control the direction of data transfers between the 80286 and I/O devices. The 8286s get enabled for operation whenever their output enable ($\overline{OE}$) inputs are switched to logic 0. Notice that the signals data bus enable DEN and I/O CE are combined with an inverter and NAND gate to produce $\overline{OE}$. To enable the transceiver, $\overline{DEN}$ must be at logic 1 and $\overline{I/O\ CE}$ at logic 0. These conditions occur during all I/O bus cycles.

The direction in which data are passed through the transceivers is determined by the logic level of the T input of the 8286s. This input is supplied by the DT/$\overline{R}$ output of the 82288. During all input cycles, DT/$\overline{R}$ is logic 0, and the transceivers are set to pass data from the selected I/O device to the 80286. On the other hand, during output cycles, DT/$\overline{R}$ is switched to logic 1, and data passes from the 80286 to the I/O device.

Input and Output Bus Cycle Timing

We just found that the I/O interface signals of the 80286 microcomputer are essentially the same as those involved in the memory interface. In fact, the function, logic levels, and timing of all signals other than the M/$\overline{IO}$ are identical to those already described for the memory interface in section 11.8.

Timing diagrams for the 80286's *input bus cycle* and *output bus cycle* are shown in Figs. 11.30 and 11.31, respectively. Looking at the input bus cycle waveforms, we see that address A_0 through A_{15} along with $\overline{BHE}$ and M/$\overline{IO}$ are output during the T_c state of the previous bus cycle. This time the 80286 switches M/$\overline{IO}$ to logic 0 to signal

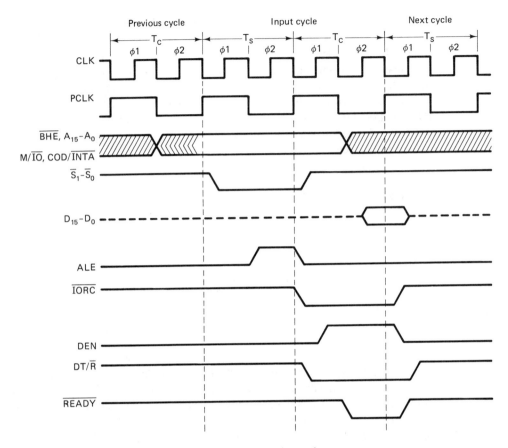

Figure 11.30 Input bus cycle.

that an I/O bus cycle is to take place. At the beginning of T_s of the input cycle, $\overline{S}_1 S_0$ is set to 01_2 to signal that an input operation is in progress. This status information is input to the 82288 and initiates an I/O read bus control sequence. Let us continue with the sequence of events that takes place in external circuitry during the I/O bus cycle.

First the 82288 outputs a pulse to the 1 logic level on ALE. As shown in the circuit of Fig. 11.28(a), this pulse is used to latch the address information into the external address latch devices. At the beginning of T_c, $\overline{IORC}$ is switched to logic 0 to signal the enabled I/O device that data are to be input to the MPU, and DT/$\overline{R}$ is switched to logic 0 to set the data bus transceivers to the input direction. A short time later, the transceivers are enabled as DEN switches to logic 1, and the data from the I/O device are passed onto the 80286's data bus. As shown in Fig. 8.5 $\overline{READY}$ is at its active 0 logic level when sampled at the end of the T_c state; therefore, the data are read by the 80286. Finally, the 82288 returns $\overline{IORC}$, DEN, and DT/$\overline{R}$ to their inactive logic level, and the input cycle is complete.

Looking at the output bus cycle timing diagram in Fig. 11.31, we see that the 80286 puts the data that is to be output onto the data bus at the beginning of ϕ_2 in the

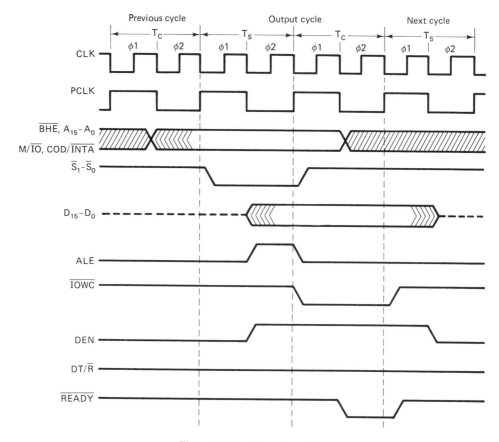

Figure 11.31 Output bus cycle.

T_s state of the output cycle. At this same time, the 82288 switches DEN to logic 1 and DT/$\overline{R}$ is maintained at the 1 level for transmit mode. From Fig. 11.28(a) we find that since DEN is logic 1, as soon as I/O CE switches to logic 0, the 8286 transceivers are enabled and set up to pass data from the 80286 to the I/O devices. Therefore, the data output on the bus is available on the data inputs of the enabled I/O device. Finally, the signal $\overline{IOWC}$ switches to logic 0 during the T_c state and tells the I/O device that valid output data are on the bus. Now the I/O device must read the data off the bus before the bus controller terminates the bus cycle. If the device cannot read data at this rate, it can hold $\overline{READY}$ at the 1 logic level to extend the bus cycle.

Protected-Mode I/O

When the 80286 is in the protected-address mode, the I/O instructions are what are called *trusted instructions*. They can be executed only if the current privilege level is greater than or equal to the I/O privilege level. That is, CPL is numerically equal to or less than the value in IOPL. Remember that IOPL is defined by the code in bits 12 and

13 of the flag register. If the current privilege level is less that IOPL, the instruction is not executed; instead, a general protection fault occurs. The general protection fault is an example of an 80286 exception and will be examined in detail in the next section.

11.11 INTERRUPT AND EXCEPTION PROCESSING ————————————————

In our study of the 8086 microprocessor, we found that interrupts provide a mechanism for quickly changing program environments. Moreover, we found that the transfer of program control to the interrupt service routine can be initiated by either an event internal to the microprocessor or an event in its external hardware.

Just as for the 8086-based microcomputer, the 80286 is capable of implementing up to 256 prioritized interrupts. They are divided into five groups: *external hardware interrupts, software interrupts, internal interrupts and exceptions, the nonmaskable interrupt,* and *reset.* The functions of the external hardware, software, and nonmaskable interrupts are identical to those in the 8086 microcomputer and are again defined by the user. On the other hand, the internal interrupt and exception processing capability of the 80286 has been greatly enhanced. These internal interrupts and exceptions and reset perform dedicated system functions. The priority scheme by which the 80286 services interrupts and exceptions is identical to that described for the 8086.

Interrupt Vector and Interrupt Descriptor Tables

An address pointer table is used to link the interrupt type numbers to the locations of their service routines in program storage memory. In a real-mode 80286-based microcomputer system, this table is called the *interrupt vector table.* On the other hand, in a protected-mode system, the table is referred to as the *interrupt descriptor table.* Figure 11.32 shows a map of the interrupt vector table in the memory of a real-mode 80286 microcomputer. Looking at the table, we see that it is identical to the interrupt vector table of the 8086 microcomputer. It contains 256 address pointers (vectors), one for each interrupt type number, 0 through 255. These address pointers identify the starting locations of their service routines in program memory. The content of this table is either held as firmware in EPROMs or loaded into RAM as part of the system initialization procedure.

Notice that in Fig. 11.32 the interrupt vector table is again located at the low-address end of the memory address space. It starts at address 00000_{16} and ends at word address $003FE_{16}$. Each of the 256 vectors requires two words (base address and offset) and is stored at an even-address boundary. Unlike for the 8086, the interrupt vector table or interrupt descriptor table in an 80286-based microcomputer can be located anywhere in the memory address space. Its starting location and size are actually identified by the contents of a register within the 80286 called the *interrupt descriptor table register* (IDTR). When the 80286 is initialized at power-on, it comes up in the real mode with the bits of the base address in IDTR all equal to zero and the limit set to $03FF_{16}$. This positions the interrupt vector table as shown in Fig. 11.32. Moreover, in the real mode, the value in IDTR is normally left at this initial value to maintain compatibility with 8086/8088-based microcomputer software.

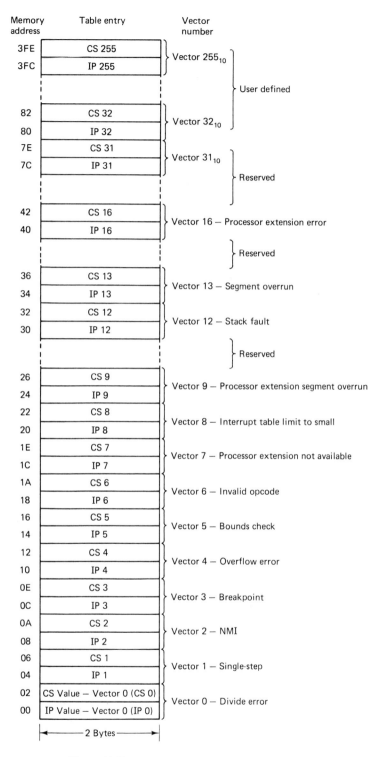

Figure 11.32 Real-mode interrupt vector table.

469

The protected-mode interrupt descriptor table can reside anywhere in the 80286's physical address space. The location and size of this table is again defined by the contents of the *interrupt descriptor table register* IDTR. Figure 11.33 shows that the IDTR contains a 24-bit *base address* and a 16-bit *limit*. The base address identifies the starting point of the table in memory; the limit determines the number of bytes in the table.

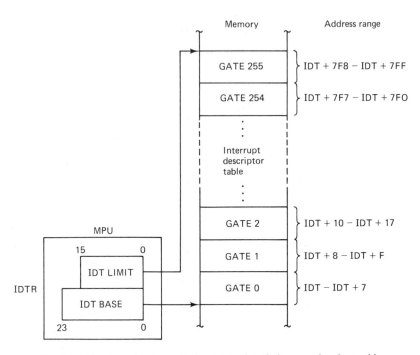

Figure 11.33 Accessing a gate in the protected-mode interrupt descriptor table.

The interrupt descriptor table contains gate descriptors not vectors. In Fig. 11.33 we find that the table contains a maximum of 256 gate descriptors. These descriptors are identified as GATE 0 through GATE 255. Each gate descriptor can be defined as a *task gate, interrupt gate,* or *trap gate.* Interrupt and trap gates permit control to be passed to a service routine that is located within the current task. The task gate permits program control to be passed to a different task.

Just like in real-mode a gate acts as a pointer that is used to redirect program execution to the starting point of a service routine; however, unlike an interrupt vector, a gate descriptor takes up four words of memory. For instance in Fig. 11.33 we see that GATE 0 is located at addresses IDT+0 through IDT+7, and GATE 255 at addresses IDT+7F8 through IDT+7FF. If all 256 gates are not needed for an application, limit can be set to a value lower than $0FFF_{16}$ to minimize the amount of memory reserved for the table.

Figure 11.34 illustrates the format of a typical interrupt or trap gate descriptor. Here we see that the two lower-addressed words are the interrupt's *code offset* and *code segment selector*. These two words identify the starting point of the service routine. The

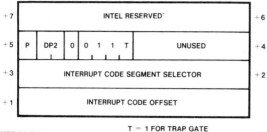

+7	INTEL RESERVED'						+6
+5	P	DP2	0	0	1	1	T	UNUSED	+4
+3	INTERRUPT CODE SEGMENT SELECTOR							+2
+1	INTERRUPT CODE OFFSET							

'MUST BE SET TO 0 FOR
COMPATIBILITY WITH THE 80386

T = 1 FOR TRAP GATE
T = 0 FOR INTERRUPT GATE

Figure 11.34 Format of a trap or inter-rupt gate descriptor (Courtesy of Intel Corp.).

upper byte of the third word is called the *access rights byte*. The settings of the bits in this byte identify whether or not this gate descriptor is valid, the privilege level of the service routine, and type of gate. For example, the *present bit* (P) needs to be set to logic 1 if the gate descriptor is to be active. The next two bits, identified as DPL in Fig. 11.34, are used to assign a privilege level to the service routine. If these bits are made 00, level 0, which is the most privileged level, is assigned to the gate. Finally, the setting of the *type bit* (T) determines whether the descriptor works as a trap gate or an interrupt gate. T equal to 0 selects interrupt gate mode of operation. The only differ-ence between the operation of these two types of gates is that when a trap gate context switch is performed, IF is not cleared to disable external hardware interrupts.

Normally, external hardware interrupts are configured with interrupt gate descrip-tors. Once an interrupt request has been acknowledged for service, the external hard-ware interrupt interface is disabled with IF. In this way, additional external interrupts cannot be accepted unless the interface is reenabled under software control. Internal interrupts, such as software interrupts, usually use trap gate descriptors. In this case, the hardware interrupt interface in not affected when the service routine for the software interrupt is initiated. Sometimes low-priority hardware interrupts are assigned trap gates instead of an interrupt gate. This will permit higher-priority external events to interrupt their service routine easily.

External Hardware Interrupt Interface

Up to this point in the section, we have introduced the types of interrupts supported by the 80286, its interrupt descriptor table, and interrupt descriptor format. Let us now look at the external hardware interrupt interface of the 80286 microcomputer.

A general interrupt interface for an 80286-based microcomputer system is illus-trated in Fig. 11.35(a). Looking at this diagram, we see that it is similar to the interrupt interface of a maximum-mode 8086 microcomputer system. Notice that it includes the address and data buses, status signals $\overline{S}_0$, $\overline{S}_1$, and M/$\overline{IO}$, and dedicated interrupt signals INTR and $\overline{INTA}$. Moreover, external circuitry is required to interface interrupt inputs, INT_{32} through INT_{255}, to the 80286's interrupt interface. Just as in an 8086 system, this interface circuitry must identify which of the pending active interrupts has the highest priority, perform an interrupt request/acknowledge handshake, then pass a type number to the 80286.

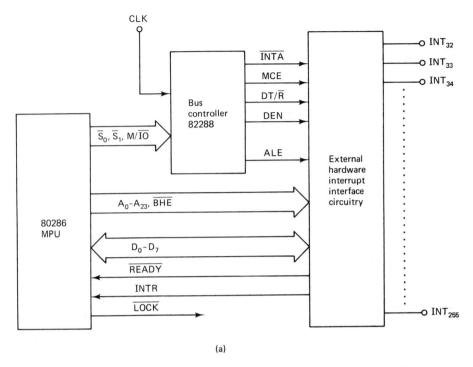

CLK

$\overline{S}_0, \overline{S}_1, M/\overline{IO}$

Bus
controller
82288

$\overline{INTA}$

MCE

$DT/\overline{R}$

DEN

ALE

80286
MPU

A_0–A_{23}, $\overline{BHE}$

D_0–D_7

$\overline{READY}$

INTR

$\overline{LOCK}$

External
hardware
interrupt
interface
circuitry

INT_{32}

INT_{33}

INT_{34}

INT_{255}

(a)

Figure 11.35(a)   80286 microcomputer system external hardware interrupt interface.

In this circuit we see that the key interrupt interface signals are *interrupt request* (INTR) and *interrupt acknowledge* ($\overline{INTA}$). The logic level input at the INTR line signals the 80286 that an external device is requesting service. The 80286 samples this input during the last clock period of each instruction execution cycle—that is, at instruction boundaries. Logic 1 at INTR represents an active interrupt request. INTR is *level triggered;* therefore, its active level must be maintained until tested by the 80286. If it is not maintained, the request for service may not be recognized. For this reason, inputs INT_{32} through INT_{255} are normally latched. Moreover, the 1 at INTR must be removed before the service routine runs to completion; otherwise, the same interrupt may be acknowledged a second time.

When an interrupt request has been recognized by the 80286, it signals this to external circuitry by outputting the interrupt acknowledge bus cycle status code on $M/\overline{IO}$ $\overline{S}_1$ $\overline{S}_0$. This code, which equals 000_2, is highlighted in Fig. 11.36. Notice in Fig. 11.35(a) that this code is input to the 82288 bus controller where it is decoded to produce a pulse to logic 0 at the $\overline{INTA}$ output. Actually, there are two pulses produced at $\overline{INTA}$ during the *interrupt acknowledge bus cycle*. The first pulse signals external circuitry that the interrupt request has been acknowledged and to prepare to send its type number to the 80286. The second pulse tells the external circuitry to put the interrupt type number on the data bus.

Notice that only the lower eight lines of the data bus, D_0 through D_7, are part of the interrupt interface. During the second cycle in the interrupt acknowledge bus se-

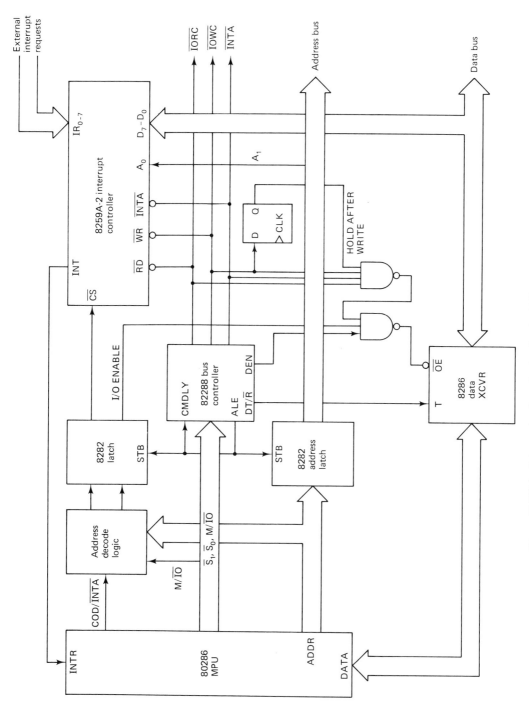

Figure 11.35(b) Interrupt interface circuit using the 8259A (Courtesy of Intel Corp.).

473

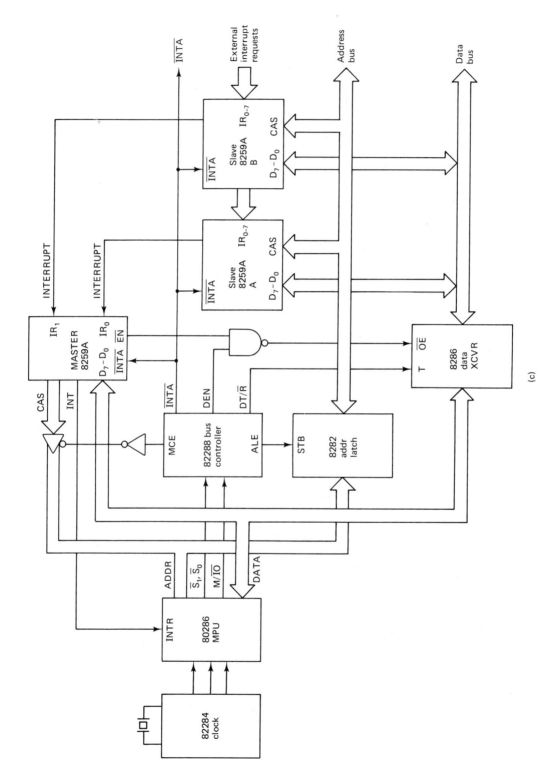

Figure 11.35(c) Interrupt interface circuit with master-slave controller configuration (Courtesy of Intel Corp.).

M/$\overline{\text{IO}}$	$\overline{S}_1$	$\overline{S}_0$	Type of bus cycle
0	0	0	Interrupt acknowledge
0	0	1	I/O Read
0	1	0	I/O Write
0	1	1	None; idle
1	0	0	Halt or shutdown
1	0	1	Memory read
1	1	0	Memory write
1	1	1	None; idle

Figure 11.36 Interrupt bus status code (Courtesy of Intel Corp.).

quence, external circuitry must put an 8-bit type number of the highest priority active interrupt request onto this part of the data bus. The 80286 reads this number off the bus to identify which external device is requesting service. Then, it uses the type number to generate the address of the interrupt's vector or gate in the interrupt vector or interrupt descriptor table, respectively.

Address lines A_0 through A_{23} are also shown in the interrupt interface circuit of Fig. 11.35(a). This is because LSI interrupt controller devices are typically used to implement most of the external circuitry. When a read or write bus cycle is performed to the controller, for example, to initialize its internal registers after system reset, some of the address bits are decoded to produce a chip select to enable the controller device, and other address bits are used to select the internal register that is to be accessed. Of course, the interrupt controller could be I/O mapped instead of memory mapped; in this case just address lines A_0 through A_{15} are used in the interface.

Figure 11.35(b) shows an interrupt interface circuit that uses a single 8259A programmable interrupt controller. This circuit implements eight interrupt request inputs. For applications that require more than eight interrupt request inputs, 8259A devices are cascaded into a master/slave configuration. Figure 11.35(c) shows such a circuit.

External Hardware Interrupt Processing Sequence

In the real mode, the 80286 processes interrupts in exactly the same way as the 8086; that is, the same events that we described in Chapter 8 take place during the interrupt request, interrupt acknowledge bus cycle, and device service routine. In protected mode a more complex processing sequence is performed. When the 80286-based microcomputer is configured for protected-mode operation, the interrupt request/acknowledge handshake sequence appears to take place exactly the same way in the external hardware; however, a number of changes do occur in the internal processing sequence of the 80286. Let us now look at how the protected-mode 80286 reacts to an interrupt request.

When processing interrupts in protected mode, the general protection mechanism of the 80286 comes into play. The general protection rules dictate that program control can be passed only to a service routine that is in a code segment with an equal or higher privilege level. Any attempt to transfer program control to a segment with lower privilege level results in an exception unless the transition is made through a gate.

Typically interrupt drivers are in code segments at a high privilege level, possibly level 0. Moreover, interrupts occur randomly; therefore, there is a good chance that the microprocessor will be executing user code that is at a low privilege level. In the case of interrupts, the current privilege level (CPL) is the privilege level assigned by the descriptor of the software that was executing when the interrupt occured. This can be any of the 80286's valid privilege levels. The descriptor privilege level (DPL) of the service routine is that defined in the interrupt or trap gate descriptor for the type number.

When a service routine is initiated, the current privilege level may change. This depends on whether the software that was interrupted was in a code segment that was configured as *conforming* or *noncomforming*. If the interrupted code is in a conforming code segment, CPL does not change when the service routine is initiated. In this case, the contents of the stack after the context switch is as illustrated in Fig. 11.37(a). Since the privilege level does not change, the current stack (OLD SS:OLD SP) is used. Notice that as part of the interrupt initiation sequence the old flags, old CS, and old IP are automatically saved on the stack. Actually, the *requested privilege level* (RPL) code is also saved on the stack. This is because it is part of CS. RPL identifies the protection level of the interrupting routine. If, however, the segment is nonconforming, the value

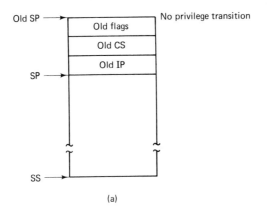

(a)

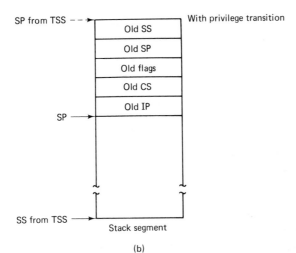

Stack segment

(b)

Figure 11.37 (a) Stack after context switch with no privilege level transition (Courtesy of Intel Corp.); (b) stack after context switch with a privilege level transition (Courtesy of Intel Corp.).

of the DPL is assigned to the CPL as long as the service routine is active. As shown in Fig. 11.37(b), this time the stack is changed to that for the new privilege level. The MPU is loaded with a new SS and SP from TSS and then the old stack pointer, SS, and SP, are saved on the stack followed by the old flags, old CS, and old IP. Remember that for an interrupt gate, IF is cleared after the context switch, but for a trap gate IF remains unchanged. In both cases, the NT flag is reset after the contents of the flag register are pushed to the stack.

Figure 11.38 summarizes all the checks that are made before an interrupt service routine is initiated in the protected mode. For example, the offset produced from the type number is tested to assure that it corresponds to an address within the limit of the interrupt descriptor table; the access rights byte of the descriptor is tested to assure that it identifies either a trap, interrupt, or task gate; the P bit is tested to assure that the gate is assigned the present status; and, finally, a number of checks are made on the DPL and CPL—that is, tests are made that compare the CPL and DPL to determine if the rules of protection will be violated if a privilege level transition is made by initiating

Check	Exception*	Error Code
Interrupt vector is in IDT limit	GP	IDT entry × 8 + 2 + EXT
Trap, Interrupt, or Task Gate in IDT Entry	GP	IDT entry × 8 + 2 + EXT
If INT instruction, gate DPL ≥ CPL	GP	IDT entry × 8 + 2 + EXT
P bit of gate is set	NP	IDT entry × 8 + 2 + EXT
Code segment selector is in descriptor table limit	GP	CS selector × 8 + EXT
CS selector refers to a code segment	GP	CS selector × 8 + EXT
If code segment is non-conforming, Code Segment DPL ≤ CPL	GP	CS selector × 8 + EXT
If code segment is non-conforming, and DPL < CPL and if SS selector in TSS is in descriptor table limit	TS	SS selector × 8 + EXT
If code segment is non-conforming, and DPL < CPL and if SS is a writable data segment	TS	SS selector × 8 + EXT
If code segment is non-conforming, and DPL < CPL and code segment DPL = stack segment DPL	TS	Stack segment selector + EXT
If code segment is non-conforming, and DPL < CPL and if SS is present	SF	Stack segment selector + EXT
If code segment is non-conforming, and DPL < CPL and if there is enough space for 5 words on the stack (or 6 if error code is required)	SF	SS selector + EXT
If code segment is conforming, then DPL ≤CPL	GP	Code segment selector + EXT
If code segment is not present	NP	Code segment selector + EXT
If IP is not within the limit of code segment	GP	0 + EXT

* GP = General Protection Exception
NP = Not Present Exception
SF = Stack Fault

Figure 11.38 Checks made during context switch for a trap or interrupt gate (Courtesy of Intel Corp.).

the service routine. For example for a nonconforming code segment, we see that if the numerical value of the DPL is less than or equal to the CPL, a valid transition is in progress. Therefore, the CPL is set equal to the DPL and the service routine is initiated. If, however, the value of the DPL is greater than that of the CPL, the service routine is not initiated; instead, a general protection exception (GP) occurs.

We just saw that if any one of the tests in Fig. 11.38 fails, the interrupt service routine is not processed; instead, an exception is initiated. Looking at the table we see that one of three types of exceptions can occur: the *general protection exception* (GP), *not present exception* (NP), and *stack fault* (SF). Whenever one of these conditions occurs, an error code is also pushed onto the stack. Figure 11.39 shows the stack as it exists after an attempt to initiate an interrupt service routine in which the privilege level transition had failed. Notice that the context switch to the exception service routine causes the *error code* to be pushed onto the stack following the values of the old flags, CS and IP.

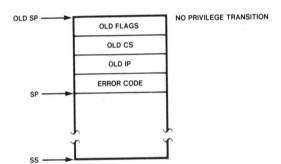

Figure 11.39 Stack contents after interrupt with an exception (Courtesy of Intel Corp.).

The format of the error code is given in Fig. 11.40. Here we see that the least significant bit, which is labeled EXT, indicates whether the error was for an externally or internally initiated interrupt. For external interrupts, such as the hardware interrupts, the EXT bit is always set to logic 1. The next two bits are set to 1 and 0, respectively, if the error is produced as the result of an interrupt. The next eight bits contain the type number of the interrupt that was attempted. With this information available on the stack, the exception service routine can determine which interrupt attempt failed and whether it was internally or externally initiated.

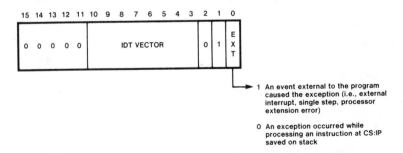

Figure 11.40 IDT selector error code format (Courtesy of Intel Corp.).

In Fig. 11.38 equations are listed for calculating each of the error codes. For instance the error code produced for a general protection fault that results from the P bit not being set is calculated as

$$\text{IDT entry} \times 8 + 2 + \text{EXT}$$

Let us assume that this type of error occurred when an attempt was made to initiate an external hardware interrupt for type 50. This results in the error code

$$50 \times 8 + 2 + 1 = 403_{10}$$

Converting to a hexadecimal number, we get

$$403_{10} = 193_{16}$$

and to a binary number gives

$$193_{16} = 0000000110010011_2$$

Finally comparing this binary error code to the format in Fig. 11.40, we see that

$$\text{Bit } 0 = 1 \longrightarrow \text{External interrupt}$$

$$\text{Bits 2-1} = 01 \longrightarrow \text{IDT associated cause}$$

$$\text{Bits 11-4} = 00110010 \longrightarrow \text{Type 50}$$

Just as in real mode, the IRET instruction is used to return from a protected-mode interrupt service routine. For service routines using an interrupt gate or trap gate, IRET is restricted to the return from a higher privilege level to a lower privilege level, for instance, from level 1 to level 3. Once the flags, OLD CS, and OLD IP are returned to the 80286, the RPL bits of OLD CS are tested to see if they equal CPL. If RPL = CPL, an intralevel return is in progress. In this case the return is complete, and program execution resumes at the point in the interrupted routine where execution had stopped.

If RPL is numerically greater than CPL, an interlevel return is taking place not an intralevel return. During an interlevel return the checks shown in Fig. 11.41 are per-

Type of Check	Exception*	Error Code
SP is not within Segment Limit	SF	0
SP + N + 7 is not in Segment Limit	SF	0
RPL of Return CS is Greater than CPL	GP	Return CS id
Return CS Selector is not null	GP	Return CS id
Return CS segment is within Descriptor Table Limit	GP	Return CS id
Return CS Descriptor is a Code Segment	GP	Return CS id
Return CS Segment is Present	NP	Return CS id
DPL of Return Non-Conforming Code Segment = RPL of CS	GP	Return CS id
SS Selector at SP + N + 6 is not Null	SF	Return SS id
SS Selector at SP + N + 6 is within Descriptor Table Limit	SF	Return SS id
SS Descriptor is Writable Data Segment	SF	Return SS id
SS Segment is Present	SF	Return SS id
SS Segment DPL = RPL of CS	SF	Return SS id

*SF = Stack Fault, GP = General Protection Exception, NP = Not-Present Exception

Figure 11.41 Inter-level return checks (Courtesy of Intel Corp.).

formed to determine if a protection violation will occur because of the protection level transition. Assuming that no violation will occur, the OLD SS and OLD SP are popped from the stack into the MPU and program execution resumes.

Internal Interrupt and Exception Functions

Earlier we indicated that some of the 256 interrupt vectors of the 80286 are dedicated to internal interrupt and exception functions. Internal interrupts and exceptions differ from external hardware interrupts in that they result from the execution of an instruction not an event that takes place in external hardware; that is, an internal interrupt or exception is initiated because a fault condition was detected either during or after execution of an instruction. In this case, a routine must be initiated to service the internal condition before resuming with execution of the next instruction of the program.

Figure 11.42 identifies the internal interrupts and exceptions that are active in real mode. Here we find internal interrupts such as single step and breakpoint and exception functions such as divide error and overflow error that were also detected by the 8086; however, the 80286 also implements several new real-mode exceptions. For example, invalid opcode, bounds check, and processor extension error are all new with the 80286. Let us now look at these new real-mode internal functions in more detail.

Bounds check exception. Earlier we pointed out that the BOUND (check array index against bounds) instruction can be used to test an operand, which is used as the index into an array, to verify that it is within a predefined range. If the index is less than the lower bound (minimum value) or greater than the upper bound (maximum value), a *bounds check exception* has occurred and control is passed to the exception handler pointed to by $CS_5:IP_5$.

Invalid opcode exception. The exception processing capability of the 80286 permits detection of undefined opcodes. This feature of the 80286 allows it to detect automatically whether or not the opcode to be executed as an instruction corresponds to one of the instructions in the instruction set. If it does not, execution is not attempted; instead, the opcode is identified as being undefined and the *invalid opcode exception* is initiated. In turn, control is passed to the exception handler identified by IP_6 and CS_6. This *undefined opcode detection mechanism* permits the 80286 to detect errors in its instruction stream.

Processor extension not available exception. When the 80286 comes up in the real mode both the EM (emulate) and MP (math present) bits of its machine status word are reset. This mode of operation corresponds to that of the 8088 or 8086 microprocessors. When set in this way, the *processor extension not available exception* cannot occur; however, if the EM bit has been set to 1 under software control (no math coprocessor is present) and the 80286 executes an ESC (escape) instruction for the 80287 math coprocessor, a processor extension not present exception is initiated through the vector at $CS_7:IP_7$. This service routine could pass control to a software emulation routine for the floating-point arithmetic operation. Moreover, if the MP (math present) bit and TS bit are both set (meaning that a math coprocessor is available in the system

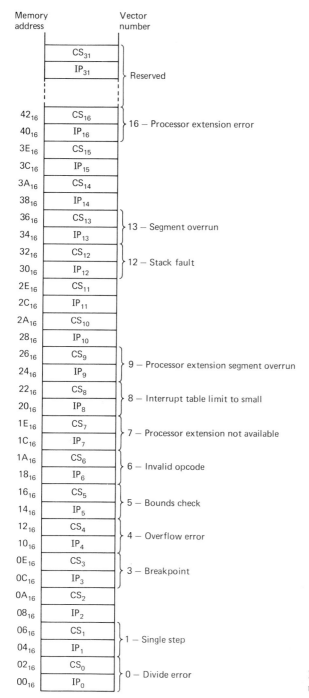

Figure 11.42 Real-mode internal exception vector locations.

and a task is in progress) when the ESC or wait instruction is executed, an exception also takes place.

Interrupt table limit too small exception. Earlier we pointed out that the LIDT instruction can be used to relocate the interrupt vector table in memory. If the location of the real-mode table has been changed such that the table extends beyond

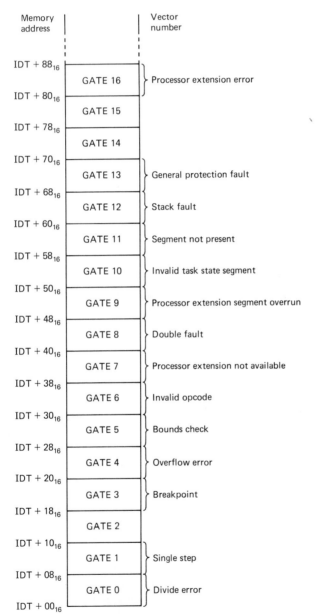

Figure 11.43 Protected-mode internal exception gate locations.

address $003FF_{16}$ and an interrupt is invoked that attempts to access a vector stored at an address higher than the limit, the *interrupt table limit too small exception* occurs. In this case, control is passed to the service routine by the vector $CS_8:IP_8$.

Processor extension segment overrun exception. The *processor extension segment overrun exception* signals that the 80287 numerics coprocessor has overrun the limit of a segment while attempting to read or write its operand. This event is detected by the processor extension data channel within the 80286 and passes control to the service routine through interrupt vector 9. This exception handler can clear the exception, reset the 80287, determine the cause of the exception by examining the registers within the 80287, and then initiate a corrective action.

Stack fault exception. In the real-mode, if the address of an operand access for the stack segment crosses the boundaries of the stack, a *stack fault exception* is produced. This causes control to be transferred to the service routine defined by CS_{12} and IP_{12}.

Segment overrun exception. This exception occurs in the real mode if an instruction attempts to access an operand that extends beyond the end of a segment. For instance, if a word access is made to the address CS:FFFF, DS:FFFF, or ES:FFFF, a *segment overrun exception* occurs.

Processor extension exception. As part of the handshake sequence between the 80286 microprocessor and 80287 math coprocessor, the 80286 checks the status of its ERROR input. If the 80287 encounters a problem performing a numerics operation, it signals this to the 80286 by switching its ERROR output to logic 0. This signal is normally applied directly to the ERROR input of the 80286. Logic 0 at this input signals that an error condition has occurred and causes a *processor extension exception* through vector 16.

Protected-mode internal interrupts and exceptions. In protected mode, more internal conditions can initiate an internal interrupt or exception. Figure 11.43 identifies each of these functions and its corresponding type number.

ASSIGNMENT

Section 11.2

1. Name the technology used to fabricate the 80286 microprocessor.
2. What is the transistor count of the 80286?
3. In what three packages is the 80286 manufactured?

Section 11.3

4. Name the four internal processing units of the 80286.
5. What are the word lengths of the 80286's address bus and data bus?
6. Does the 80286 have a multiplexed address/data bus or independent address and data buses?
7. How large is the 80286's instruction queue?
8. List three functions performed by the address unit.
9. What is the function of the instruction queue?

Section 11.4

10. How large is the real-address mode address bus and physical address space? How large is the protected-address mode address bus and physical address space? How large is the protected-mode virtual address space?
11. What type of bus cycle is in progress when the bus status code $\overline{COD/INTA}$ $M/\overline{IO}$ $\overline{S_1}$ $\overline{S_0}$ equals 1010?
12. If the code output as $\overline{BHE}$ A_0 equals 01, what type data transfer is taking place over the bus?
13. Is the logic level output on $COD/\overline{INTA}$ intended to be directly used as the interrupt acknowledge signal to the external hardware interrupt interface circuitry?
14. Which signals implement the DMA interface?
15. What processor extension is most frequently attached to the processor extension interface?

Section 11.5

16. Which of the 80286's status outputs are input to the 82288?
17. If the input status code to the 82288 is 010, what command output is active?
18. What bus control signals are produced by the 82288?
19. To what logic level must $CEN/\overline{AEN}$ be set to enable the command outputs of the 82288?

Section 11.6

20. What speed 80286 ICs are available from Intel Corporation? How are these speeds denoted in the part number?
21. What frequency crystal must be connected between the X_1 and X_2 inputs of the 80C284-12 to run the device at full speed?
22. What clock outputs are produced by the 82C284? What would be their frequencies if a 20 MHz crystal is used?

Section 11.7

23. How many clock states are in an 80286 bus cycle that has no wait states? What would be the duration of this bus cycle if the 80286 is operating at 10 MHz?
24. What does T_s stand for? What happens in this part of the processor cycle?
25. What does T_c stand for? What happens in this part of the processor cycle?
26. Explain what is meant by pipelining of the 80286's bus.

27. What is an idle state?

28. What is a wait state? If an 80286 running at 10 MHz performs a bus cycle with two wait states, what is the duration of the bus cycle?

Section 11.8

29. Summarize the function of each of the blocks in the memory interface diagram of Fig. 11.18.

30. When the instruction PUSH AX is executed, what bus status code is output by the 80286 and what read/write control signal is produced by the 82288?

31. What are the four types of data transfers that can take place over the data bus? How many bus cycles are required for each type of data transfer?

32. If an 80286 is running at 10 MHz and all memory accesses involve one wait state, how long will it take to fetch the word of data starting at address $0FF1A_{16}$? At address $0FF1D_{16}$?

33. During a bus cycle that involves an odd-addressed word transfer, which byte of data is transferred over the bus during the first bus cycle?

34. Describe the bus activity that takes place as the 80286 writes a byte of data into memory address $B0010_{16}$.

35. If the write cycle in Fig. 11.23 is for an 80286 running at 12.5 MHz, what is the duration of the bus cycle?

36. If the read cycle in Fig. 11.24 is for an 80286 running at 12.5 MHz, what is the duration of the bus cycle?

Section 11.9

37. Make a diagram showing how four 2764 EPROMs are connected to form a 16K-word program storage memory subsystem.

38. If we assume that the high-order address bits in the circuit formed in problem 37 are all logic 0, what is the address range of the memory subsystem?

39. How many 2147 static RAMs would be needed in the memory array of the circuit in Fig. 11.26 if the capacity is to be expanded to 64K bytes?

40. What functions are performed by the 8207 refresh controller in the circuit of Fig. 11.27?

Section 11.10

41. Which signal indicates to the bus controller and external circuitry that the current bus cycle is for the I/O interface and not for the memory interface?

42. Which device produces the input (read), output (write), and bus control signals for the I/O interface?

43. Briefly describe the function of each block in the I/O interface circuit in Fig. 11.28(a).

44. If an 80286 running at 10 MHz inserts two wait states into all I/O bus cycles, what is the duration of a bus cycle in which a byte of data is being output?

45. If the 80286 in problem 44 was outputting a word of data to a word-wide port at I/O address $1A1_{16}$, what would be the duration of the bus cycle?

46. Summarize the sequence of events that take place at the I/O interface in Fig. 11.28(a) as a word of I/O data is output over data bus lines D_0 through D_{15} to a port at an even address.

Section 11.11

47. What are the five groups of interrupts supported on the 80286 MPU?

48. What is the range of type numbers assigned to the interrupts in the 80286 microcomputer system?

49. What is the real-mode interrupt address pointer table called? The protected-mode address pointer table?

50. What is the size of a real-mode interrupt vector? A protected-mode gate?

51. The contents of which register determines the location of the interrupt address pointer table? To what value is this register initialized at reset?

52. The breakpoint routine in a real-mode 80286 microcomputer system starts at address $AA000_{16}$ in the code segment located at address $A0000_{16}$. Specify how the breakpoint vector will be stored in the interrupt vector table.

53. At what addresses is the protected-mode gate for type 20 stored in memory?

54. Assume that gate 3 consists of the four words that follow

$$IDT + 8 = 1000H$$
$$IDT + A = B000H$$
$$IDT + C = A600H$$
$$IDT + E = 0000H$$

    a. Is the gate descriptor active?
    b. What is the privilege level?
    c. Is the gate a trap gate or an interrupt gate?
    d. What is the starting address of the service routine?

55. Explain the function of the INTR and INTA signals in the circuit diagram of Fig. 11.35(a).

56. How many interrupt inputs can be directly accepted by the circuit in Fig. 11.35(b)?

57. How many interrupt inputs can be directly accepted by the circuit in Fig. 11.35(c)?

58. Summarize the interrupt request/acknowledge handshake sequence for an interrupt initiated at an input to slave B in the circuit of Fig. 11.35(b).

59. What is the key difference between the real-mode and protected-mode interrupt request/acknowledge handshake sequence?

60. What are the three exceptions that may occur during an attempt to service an interrupt in a protected-mode 80286 microcomputer system?

61. If the error code 0103H is pushed to the stack when an exception occurs as a result of an attempt to initiate an interrupt in a protected-mode 80286 microcomputer, which interrupt was requesting service when the error occurred and was it an internal or external event that caused the error?

62. List the real-mode internal interrupts serviced by the 80286.

63. Which real-mode vector numbers are reserved for internal interrupts and exceptions?

64. Which exceptions take on a new meaning or are active only in the protected mode?

Suggested Laboratory Assignments ———————

LABORATORY 1: EXPLORING THE SOFTWARE ARCHITECTURE OF THE 8086 MICROPROCESSOR ———————

Objective

Learn how to

1. Use the SDK-86 monitor commands.
2. Examine and modify the contents of the 8086's internal registers.
3. Examine and modify the contents of the 8086's code, data, and stack segments of memory.
4. Calculate the physical addresses of storage locations in the memory address space.
5. Examine the contents of the dedicated parts of the 8086's memory address space.

Part 1: Using the SDK-86 Monitor Commands

Here we will learn how to bring up the monitor program of the SDK-86 from its keyboard. *Check off each step as it is completed.*

Check	Step	Procedure
_____	1	Turn on the SDK-86.
_____	2	Press the SYSTM RESET key on its keyboard. What is displayed on the seven segment displays? Ans. _____

The SDK-86 is now ready to be used.

Part 2: Examining and Modifying the Contents of the 8086's Internal Registers

Now we will use the Examine Register (ER) command to first examine the contents of the 8086's internal registers and then modify the values in the registers and state of its flags. *Check off each step as it is completed.*

Check	Step	Procedure
_____	1	Use the ER command to display the current contents of all the 8086's internal registers. List the initial values held in CS, DS, SS, IP, and SP. Ans. _____ Calculate the physical address of the next instruction to be executed. Ans. _____ Calculate the physical address of the current top of the stack. Ans. _____
_____	2	Use ER commands to examine the contents of register AX, modify this value to 1234, and verify the new contents.
_____	3	Use the ER command to display the current contents of the flag register and then change the state of the parity flag to represent even parity.
_____	4	Redisplay the contents of all the 8086's internal registers. Compare the displayed register contents with those found in step 1. Make a list of these registers whose contents have changed. Ans. _____

Part 3: Examining and Modifying the Contents of Memory

Next we will explore the memory subsystem of the SDK-86 and the operation of the examine/modify memory (EB, EW, and MV) commands of the SDK-86's monitor. *Check off each step as it is completed.*

Check	Step	Procedure
_____	1	Use the information from step 1 of part 2 to draw a diagram that shows how the active memory segments are initially mapped. In the diagram identify the lowest and highest physical address of each segment.

Memory

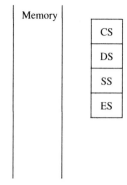

_____ 2 Use the EB command to display the first four bytes of the current code segment?
List these values.

Ans. *CS:0* =

CS:1 =

CS:2 =

CS:3 =

_____ 3 Use the EW command to modify the first word location in the current data
segment to contain the number 1234. Verify that the value has changed.

_____ 4 Display the contents of location FF00:0. Ans. _____
Change it to 55. What happens and why? Ans. _____

_____ 5 With an MV command, copy the contents of the 16 storage locations starting at
DS:00 to the 16 storage locations starting at DS:20. Verify that the block of data
has been copied.

Part 4: Exploring the Dedicated Part of the 8086's Memory Address Space

Certain parts of the 8086's memory address space have dedicated functions. Here we
will determine the contents of some of these dedicated addresses. *Check off each step
as it is completed.*

Check	Step	Procedure
_____	1	Change the contents of the DS register to 0000.
_____	2	Display the bytes stored at addresses 00000 through 00003 of the interrupt vector table.
_____	3	Dedicated addresses 00000 through 00003 store a pointer that is the starting address of an interrupt service routine. Use the values displayed in step 2 to calculate the physical address corresponding to this pointer. Ans. _____

	4	The address pointer that identifies the starting location of the nonmaskable interrupt (NMI) service routine is held in storage locations 00008 through 0000B. Use the EW command to determine the address represented by this pointer.
_____		Ans. _____

LABORATORY 2: LOADING, EXECUTING, AND DEBUGGING PROGRAMS

Objective

Learn how to

1. Enter a program into the memory of the SDK-86 microcomputer and verify its loading.
2. Run a program and verify its operation from the results that it produces.
3. Debug a program with an error.

Part 1: Encoding, Loading, and Executing a Program

In this part of the laboratory, we will learn how to encode and enter a program into the SDK-86's memory and then execute it to verify that it performs the operation for which it was written. *Check off each step as it is completed.*

Check	Step	Procedure
_____	1	Read the following program and describe the function that it performs.

```
MOV   AX, 0
MOV   DS, AX
MOV   AL, [200]
NOT   AL
MOV   [201], AL
INT   3
```

Ans. _____

| _____ | 2 | Using the instruction encoding information covered in Chapter 5, encode each instruction of the program in step 1. |

Instruction   Code

_____   _____
_____   _____
_____   _____
_____   _____
_____   _____
_____   _____

	3	Using the EB command, load the machine code program into the SDK-86's memory starting at address 100.
_____	4	Verify the loading of the program by examining it with the EB command. How many bytes of memory does the program take up? Ans. _____ At what address is the INT 3 instruction stored? Ans. _____
_____	5	Initialize the data as follows: (a) Use an EB command to clear the storage location at 0:0201. (b) Use the EB command to fill the storage location at 0:0200 with the value 55.
_____	6	Run the complete program by issuing a single GO command. What is the starting address in the GO command? Ans. _____
_____	7	Examine the memory location 0:201. What is stored in it? Ans. _____ Give an overview of the operation performed by the program. Ans. _____ _____

PART 2: DEBUGGING A PROGRAM

The SDK-86's monitor includes commands to support debugging of programs. These commands provide the programmer with the ability to execute a single instruction or a group of instructions and to examine the contents of the 8086's internal registers and storage locations in external memory. In this way, the operations performed by the instructions can be verified. Here we will reexecute the program entered in Part 1. This time observe its operation step by step using the debugging commands. *Check off each step as it is completed.*

Check	Step	Procedure
_____	1	Using the EB command initialize memory locations 0:200 to 55 and 0:201 to 0.
_____	2	Use a GO command to execute the program up to the instruction MOV AL, [200]. Use an ER command to verify that the DS register is loaded with 0.
_____	3	Use an ST command to execute the next instruction. Then, use an ER command to verify that register AL contains 55.
_____	4	Use a step (ST) command to execute the next instruction. Verify that the AL register now contains AA by using the ER command.
_____	5	Execute the next instruction using the ST command. Verify that memory location 201 contains AA with an EB command.
_____	6	Use the GO command to execute the program to completion. Describe the difference in using the debug commands instead of a single GO command to execute the program. Ans. _____ _____ _____

LABORATORY 3: WORKING WITH THE DATA TRANSFER, ARITHMETIC, LOGIC, SHIFT, AND ROTATE INSTRUCTIONS

Objective

Learn how to

1. Verify the operation of data transfer instructions.
2. Verify the operation of arithmetic instructions.
3. Verify the operation of logic instructions.
4. Verify the operation of shift and rotate instructions.

PART 1: DATA TRANSFER INSTRUCTIONS

Here we will use SDK-86 monitor commands to execute some 8086 instructions from the data transfer group to observe the operation they perform. *Check off each step as it is completed.*

Check	Step	Procedure
_____	1	Encode the instructions of the program shown in Fig. L3.1(a). Let MEM1 = 200 and TABL1 = 400. Verify that the machine code is as given in Fig. L3.1(b). Enter the program into memory starting at location 100.

```
; LAB 3, Part 1

; This program translates a given byte to another byte using
; the given translation table.


; Data Segment

; Byte to be translated is at offset MEM1.
; Translation table start offset is TABL1.
; The translation table bytes are as follows:
; FF, FE, FD, FC, FB, FA, F9, F8


; Code Segment

        MOV     AL, MEM1            ;Get the given byte
        MOV     BX, OFFSET TABL1    ;Form translation table address
        XLAT                       ;Translate
        MOV     MEM1, AL            ;Save the translated byte
```

Figure L3.1(a)

```
0000:0100   A10002      MOV    AX,[0200]
0000:0103   8B1E0004    MOV    BX,[0400]
0000:0107   D7          XLAT
0000:0108   A20002      MOV    [0200],AL      Figure L3.1(b)
```

_____	2	Initialize the data segment as per the description in Fig. L3.1(a). Let the byte to be translated be equal to number 5.
_____	3	Execute the first instruction. What number is placed in register AL? Ans. _____
_____	4	Execute the second instruction. What number is placed in register BX? Ans. _____
_____	5	Execute the third instruction. What number is placed in register AL? Ans. _____
_____	6	Execute the fourth instruction. What are the contents of the memory location designated as MEM1? Ans. _____
_____	7	Explain the operation implemented by the instruction sequence in Fig. L3.1(a). Ans. _____ _____

Part 2: Arithmetic Instructions

We continue here by using SDK-86 commands to execute some instructions from the arithmetic group to observe the operation that they perform. *Check off each step as it is completed.*

Check	Step	Procedure
_____	1	Encode the instructions of the program shown in Fig. L3.2(a) into machine code. Let NUM1, NUM2, and NUM3 be memory locations 200, 201, and 202, respectively. Verify that the machine code is the same as given in Fig. L3.2(b). Enter the program into memory starting at location 100.

```
; LAB 3, Part 2

; This program subtracts two BCD numbers in two memory locations
; and places the result in a third memory location.

; Data Segment

; The two numbers to be subtracted are at NUM1 and NUM2 respectively.
; The result after subtraction is to be stored at NUM3 location.

; Code Segment
        MOV     AL, NUM2            ;Get the 2nd number
        SUB     AL, NUM1            ;Subtract the first
        DAS                         ;Apply decimal adjustment
        MOV     NUM3, AL            ;Save the result
```

Figure L3.2(a)

```
0000:0100   A00102      MOV     AL,[0201]
0000:0103   2A060002    SUB     AL,[0200]
0000:0107   2F          DAS
0000:0108   A20202      MOV     [0202],AL    Figure L3.2(b)
```

Laboratory 3   493

Part 3: Logic Instructions

Now we will execute some of the instructions from the logic group to examine the operation they perform. *Check off each step as it is completed.*

Check	Step	Procedure
_____	1	Encode the instructions of the program shown in Fig. L3.3(a). Let MEM1 = [200] and MEM2 = [202]. Verify that the resulting machine code is the same as that given in Fig. L3.3(b). Enter the program starting at location 100.

```
; LAB 3, Part 3

; This program is for the demonstration of logic instructions.

; Data Segment

; There are two memory locations MEM1 and MEM2 that are used in
; the instructions.

; Code Segment
            MOV     AX, 5555              ;Load AX with 5555
            MOV     WORD PTR MEM1, 5555   ;Load MEM1 with 5555
            NOT     AX                    ;Complement AX
            XOR     AX, MEM1              ;XOR AX with MEM1
            MOV     MEM2, AX              ;Save the result in AX
            NOT     AX                    ;Complement AX
            ADD     AX, 1                 ;Add 1 to AX
```

Figure L3.3(a)

```
0000:0100    B85555          MOV     AX,5555
0000:0103    C70600025555    MOV     WORD PTR [0200],5555
0000:0109    F7D0            NOT     AX
0000:010B    33060002        XOR     AX,[0200]
0000:010F    A30202          MOV     [0202],AX
0000:0112    F7D0            NOT     AX
0000:0114    050100          ADD     AX,0001
```

Figure L3.3(b)

_____ 2 Execute the instructions by using the ST command of the SDK-86 monitor. Record the contents of register AX, memory location MEM1, and the memory location MEM2 as each instruction is executed.

Instruction	(AX)	(MEM1)	(MEM2)
_____	_____	_____	_____
_____	_____	_____	_____
_____	_____	_____	_____
_____	_____	_____	_____
_____	_____	_____	_____
_____	_____	_____	_____

_____ 3 What is the relation of the number held in AX before and after executing the last two instructions in Fig. L3.3(a).
Ans. _____

Part 4: Shift and Rotate Instructions

Let us now execute some instructions from the 8086's shift and rotate instruction groups to observe their operation. _Check off each step as it is completed._

Check	Step	Procedure
_____	1	Encode the instructions in the program shown in Fig. L3.4(a). Verify that the machine code is as given in Fig. L3.4(b). Enter the program into memory starting at location 100.

```
; LAB 3, Part 4

; This program is for the demonstration of the shift and rotate
; instructions

; Code Segment

        CLC                             ;Reset carry flag
        MOV     BX, AA55                ;Load BX with AA55
        MOV     CL, 5                   ;Load CL with 5
        SHR     BX, CL                  ;Shift BX right using CL
        INT     3                       ;Return to the monitor
```

Figure L3.4(a)

```
0000:0100    F8          CLC
0000:0101    BB55AA      MOV     BX,AA55
0000:0104    B105        MOV     CL,05
0000:0106    D3EB        SHR     BX,CL
0000:0108    CC          INT     3
```

Figure L3.4(b)

_____ 2 Execute the program to completion. What number results in register BX?
          Ans. _____

_____ 3 Change the first instruction to STC and repeat step 2. What number results in
          register BX? Ans. _____

_____ 4 Change the SHR instruction to SHL and repeat step 2. What number results in
          register BX? Ans. _____

_____ 5 Change the SHL instruction to ROR and repeat step 2. What number results in
          register BX? Ans. _____

_____ 6 Change the ROR instruction to ROL and repeat step 2. What number results in
          register BX? Ans. _____

LABORATORY 4: WORKING WITH THE FLAG-CONTROL, COMPARE, JUMP, SUBROUTINE, LOOP, AND STRING INSTRUCTIONS

Objective

Learn how to

1. Verify the operation of the flag-control instructions.
2. Verify the operation of the compare instruction.
3. Verify the operation of the jump instructions.
4. Verify the operation of the subroutine-handling instructions.
5. Verify the operation of the loop-handling instructions.
6. Verify the operation of the string-handling instructions.

Part 1: Flag-Control Instructions

In this part of the lab we will execute a program sequence that includes instructions from the flag-control group to observe the operation they perform. *Check off each step as it is completed.*

Check	Step	Procedure
_____	1	Encode the instruction sequence

> LAHF
> MOV   BH, AH
> AND   BH, 1F
> AND   AH, EO
> MOV   [200] , BH
> SAHF

Enter the machine code instructions into memory starting at address CS:100. Verify loading of the instructions. How many bytes of memory do the instructions take up?

Ans. _____

_____	2	Initialize the byte of memory at DS:200 with the value 0 and then verify that the contents of memory have been updated.
_____	3	Clear registers AX and BX and verify by examining their contents.
_____	4	Display the current state of the flags.
_____	5	Execute the instructions one at a time with ST commands. Describe the operation performed by each instruction.

INSTRUCTION 1 _____

INSTRUCTION 2 _____

INSTRUCTION 3 _____

INSTRUCTION 4 _____

INSTRUCTION 5 _____

INSTRUCTION 6 _____

Briefly describe the overall operation performed by the instruction sequence.

Ans. _____

Part 2: Compare Instruction

Here we will use SDK-86 monitor commands to execute an instruction sequence that involves the compare instruction to observe the operations they perform. *Check off each step as it is completed.*

Check	Step	Procedure
_____	1	Encode the instruction sequence

> MOV   BX, 1111
> MOV   AX, BBBB
> CMP   BX, AX

Enter the machine code instructions into memory starting at address CS:100 and then verify loading of the instructions. How many bytes of memory these instructions take up?

Ans. _____

_____ 2 Clear registers AX and BX and verify by redisplaying their contents.

_____ 3 Display the current state of the flags.

_____ 4 Execute the instructions one at a time with ST commands. Describe the operation performed by each instruction.

INSTRUCTION 1 _____

INSTRUCTION 2 _____

INSTRUCTION 3 _____

Briefly describe the overall operation performed by the instruction sequence.

Ans. _____

_____

_____

Part 3: Jump Instructions

Now we will use SDK-86 commands to execute and observe the operation of a factorial calculation program that performs both unconditional and conditional jumps. *Check off each step as it is completed.*

Check	Step	Procedure
_____	1	Encode the program in Fig. L4.3(a) assuming that it is to be stored starting at address 100. Let the variable location FACT be equal to 200. The encoded program is given in Fig. L4.3(b). Load the program into the memory of the microcomputer.

```
; LAB 4, Part 3


; This program calculates factorial of a number in register DL


; Data Segment:
; Program uses a byte of data at offset FACT to save the result.


; Code Segment:
        MOV     AX, 0                   ;Establish data segment
        MOV     DS, AX
        MOV     AL, 1
        MOV     CL, 0
NXT:    CMP     CL, DL                  ;All numbers multiplied ?
        JE      DONE                    ;If done, exit
        INC     CL                      ;If not, do next
        MUL     CL
        JMP     NXT
DONE:   MOV     FACT, AL                ;Save the result
        INT     3                       ;Return to the monitor
```

Figure L4.3(a)

```
0000:0100    B80000    MOV    AX,0000
0000:0103    8ED8      MOV    DS,AX
0000:0105    B001      MOV    AL,01
0000:0107    B100      MOV    CL,00
0000:0109    38D1      CMP    CL,DL
0000:010B    7406      JE     0113
0000:010D    FEC1      INC    CL
0000:010F    F6E1      MUL    CL
0000:0111    EBF6      JMP    0109
0000:0113    A20002    MOV    [0200],AL
0000:0116    CC        INT    3          Figure L4.3(b)
```

_____ 2 Verify loading of the program by examining the contents of memory starting at address 0:100.

_____ 3 Execute the program according to the instructions that follow.

    (a) GO from address CS:100 to CS:105.

    (b) Load the number whose factorial is to be calculated (N = 5) into register DX.

    (c) Clear the storage location for the value of the factorial (FACT), which is register CX.

    (d) GO from address CS:105 to CS:10B. What is the state of the zero flag?
Ans. _____

    (e) Execute the JE instruction with an ST command. Was the jump taken?
Ans. _____

    (f) GO from address CS:10D to CS:111.

    (g) Execute the JMP instruction with an ST command. Was the jump taken?
Ans. _____ What is the address of the next instruction to be executed?
Ans. _____

    (h) GO from address CS:109 to CS:10B. What is the state of the zero flag?
Ans. _____

    (i) Execute the JE instruction with an ST command. Was the jump taken?
Ans. _____

    (j) GO from address CS:10D to CS:111. What is the current value in AL?
Ans. _____

    (k) Execute the JMP instruction with an ST command. Was the jump taken?
Ans. _____

    (l) GO from address CS:109 to CS:10B. What is the state of the zero flag?
Ans. _____

    (m) Execute the JE instruction with an ST command. Was the jump taken?
Ans. _____

    (n) GO from address CS:10D to CS:111. What is the current value in AL?
Ans. _____

    (o) Execute the JMP instruction with an ST command. Was the jump taken?
Ans. _____

    (p) GO from address CS:109 to CS:10B. What is the state of the zero flag?
Ans. _____

    (q) Execute the JE instruction with an ST command. Was the jump taken?
Ans. _____

    (r) GO from address CS:10D to CS:111. What is the current value in AL?
Ans. _____

    (s) Execute the JMP instruction with an ST command. Was the jump taken?
Ans. _____

    (t) GO from address CS:109 to CS:10B. What is the state of the zero flag?
Ans. _____

    (u) Execute the JE instruction with an ST command. Was the jump taken?
Ans. _____

Laboratory 4

(v) GO from address CS:10D to CS:111. What is the current value in AL? Ans. _____

(w) Execute the JMP instruction with an ST command. Was the jump taken? Ans. _____

(x) GO from address CS:109 to CS:10B. What is the state of the zero flag? Ans. _____

(y) Execute the JE instruction with an ST command. Was the jump taken? Ans. _____ What instruction is to be executed next? Ans. _____

(z) Execute the program to completion. What is the final value in AL? Ans. _____ At what address is the value in AL stored in memory as FACT? Ans. _____

(aa) Display the value stored for FACT in memory. If the program is correct and you were trying to find the factorial of 5, then the FACT location should contain 78 (or 120 decimal).

Part 4: Subroutine-Handling Instructions

Next we will use SDK-86 commands to execute and observe the operation of a program that employs a subroutine. *Check off each step as it is completed.*

Check	Step	Procedure
_____	1	Encode the program in Fig. L4.4(a) assuming that the calling program is to be stored starting at address 0:100. Let the subroutine be stored starting at address 0:150. The encoded program is given in Fig. L4.4(b). Load the complete program into memory.

```
; LAB 4, Part 4

; This program calls the subroutine 'SUM' to add the contents of
; registers AX, BX, and CX and place the result in register SI.


; Calling Program
        MOV     AX, 0           ;Establish the stack
        MOV     SS, AX
        MOV     SP, 100
        CALL    SUM             ;Call the subroutine
        INT     3               ;Return to the monitor


; Subroutine
; Name:         SUM
; Input:        Contents of AX, BX, CX
; Output:       (SI) = (AX) + (BX) + (CX)
; Note:         Register DX used for computations

SUM     PROC    NEAR
        PUSH    DX              ; Save the register to be used
        MOV     DX, AX
        ADD     DX, BX
        ADD     DX, CX          ; (DX) = (AX) + (BX) + (CX)
        MOV     SI, DX          ; Save the sum in SI
        POP     DX              ; Restore the used register
        RET                     ; Return to the caller
SUM     ENDP
```

Figure L4.4(a)

0000:0100	B80000	MOV	AX,0000
0000:0103	8ED0	MOV	SS,AX
0000:0105	BC0001	MOV	SP,0100
0000:0108	E84500	CALL	0150
0000:010B	CC	INT	3
0000:0150	52	PUSH	DX
0000:0151	89C2	MOV	DX,AX
0000:0153	01DA	ADD	DX,BX
0000:0155	01CA	ADD	DX,CX
0000:0157	89D6	MOV	SI,DX
0000:0159	5A	POP	DX
0000:015A	C3	RET	

Figure L4.4(b)

Check	Step	
_____	2	Verify loading of the program by examining the memory contents starting at address 0:100 and address 0:150.
_____	3	Execute the program according to the instructions that follow:

(a) Go from address CS: 100 to CS:108. What instruction is to be executed next? Ans. _____

(b) Load the registers as follows:

$$(AX) = -32_{10} = FFE0$$
$$(BX) = 27_{10} = 001B$$
$$(CX) = 10_{10} = 0012$$
$$(DC) = 0_{10} = 0000$$

(c) Execute the call instruction with an ST command. What instruction is to be executed next? Ans. _____

(d) GO to address CS:155. What is the sum in DX? Ans. _____

(e) Check the value of the last word pushed to the stack.

(f) Run the program to completion with a GO command. What is the final value in DX? Ans. _____

Part 5: Loop-Handling Instructions

Here we will use SDK-86 commands to execute and observe the operation of a block search program written using a loop. *Check off each step as it is completed.*

Check	Step	Procedure
_____	1	Encode the program in Fig. L4.5(a) assuming that the calling program is to be stored starting at address 0:100. The encoded program is given in Fig. L4.5(b). Load the program into the SDK-86's memory.
_____	2	Verify loading of the program by examining the memory contents starting at address 0:100.
_____	3	Execute the program according to the instructions that follow.

(a) GO from address CS:100 to CS:10D.

(b) Clear all storage locations in the range DS:200 through DS:20F.

(c) Initialize the byte storage location DS:203 with the value AB_{16}.

```
; LAB 4, Part 5

; This program searches a data block looking for a specific
; number AB.


; Data Segment
; A data block of 16 elements starting at address 200.

; Code Segment
                MOV     DL, AB
                MOV     AX, 0
                MOV     DS, AX
                MOV     SI, 200
                MOV     CX, F
AGAIN:          INC     SI
                CMP     [SI], DL
                LOOPNE  AGAIN
                INT     3
```

Figure L4.5(a)

0000:0100	B2AB	MOV	DL,AB
0000:0102	B80000	MOV	AX,0000
0000:0105	8ED8	MOV	DS,AX
0000:0107	BE0002	MOV	SI,0200
0000:010A	B90F00	MOV	CX,000F
0000:010D	46	INC	SI
0000:010E	3814	CMP	[SI],DL
0000:0110	E0FB	LOOPNZ	010D
0000:0112	CC	INT	3

Figure L4.5(b)

(d) Display the contents of all storage locations in the range DS:200 through DS:20F.

(e) GO to address CS:110. What is the value in SI? Ans. _____ What is the state of CF? Ans. _____

(f) Execute the LOOPNZ instruction with an ST command. Was the loop taken? Ans. _____

(g) GO to address CS:110. What is the value in SI? Ans. _____ What is the state of CF? Ans. _____

(h) Execute the LOOPNZ instruction with a trace command. Was the loop taken? Ans. _____

(i) GO to address CS:110. What is the value in SI? Ans. _____ What is the state of CF? Ans. _____

(j) Execute the LOOPNZ instruction with an ST command. Was the loop taken? Ans. _____ What is the next instruction to be executed? Ans. _____ Why? Ans. _____
_____

(k) Run the program to completion with a GO command. Summarize the operation performed by the program. Ans. _____
_____

502   Suggested Laboratory Assignments

Part 6: String-Handling Instructions

In this part of the laboratory, we will use monitor commands to execute and observe the operation of an array comparison program that employs a string instruction. *Check off each step as it is completed.*

Check	Step	Procedure
———	1	Encode the program in Fig. L4.6(a) assuming that the program is to be stored starting at address 0:100. The encoded program is given in Fig. L4.6(b). Load the program into the microcomputer's memory.

```
; LAB 4, Part 6

; This program compares a string with a master string
; till unequal elements are found.


; Data Segment
; There are two strings each 16 elements long. The master string
; starts at address 200 and the string to be compared starts at
; address 210


; Code Segment
        MOV     AX, 0           ;Set up the segments
        MOV     DS, AX
        MOV     ES, AX
        CLD                     ;Autoincrement mode
        MOV     CX, 10          ;CX = String size
        MOV     SI, 200         ;Source string start offset
        MOV     DI, 210         ;Destination string start offset
        REPNE   CMPSB           ;Compare the two strings till
                                ;unequal elements
        INT     3               ;Return to the monitor
```

Figure L4.6(a)

```
0000:0100   B80000      MOV     AX,0000
0000:0103   8ED8        MOV     DS,AX
0000:0105   8EC0        MOV     ES,AX
0000:0107   FC          CLD
0000:0108   B91000      MOV     CX,0010
0000:010B   BE0002      MOV     SI,0200
0000:010E   BF1002      MOV     DI,0210
0000:0111   F2          REPNZ
0000:0112   A6          CMPSB
0000:0113   CC          INT     3       Figure L4.6(b)
```

Check	Step	Procedure
———	2	Verify loading of the program by examining the memory contents starting at address 0:100.
———	3	Execute the program according to the instructions that follow. (a) GO from address CS:100 to CS:111. What is the state of the direction flag? Ans. ————— Does this mean that autoincrement or autodecrement addressing will be performed? Ans. ————— What is the state of ZF?

Ans. _____ What are the values in the DS, SI, and DI registers?

Ans. _____, _____, _____ What is the count in CX.

Ans. _____ What is the next instruction to be executed?

Ans. _____

(b) Clear all storage locations in the range DS:200 through DS:20F.

(c) Fill all storage locations in the range DS:210 through DS:21F with FF.

(d) Initialize the word storage location starting at DS:204 with the value FFFF.

(e) Examine the contents of all storage locations in the range DS:200 through DS:21F.

(f) Run the program to completion with a GO command and then display the registers. What is the state of ZF? Ans. _____ What are the values in the DS, SI, and DI registers? Ans. _____, _____, _____ What is the count in CX? Ans. _____ Summarize the operation performed by the program. Ans. _____

LABORATORY 5: WRITING A PROGRAM TO CALCULATE THE AVERAGE OF A SERIES OF NUMBERS

Objective

Learn how to

1. Describe a function that is to be performed with a program.
2. Write a program to implement the function.
3. Run the program to verify that it performs the function for which it was written.

Part 1: Description of the Problem

It is required to determine the average of a set of data points stored in a buffer. The number of points in the buffer, the offset address of the beginning of the buffer, and the data segment address are stored in a table called a *parameter table*. Figure L5.1(a) shows an example of the parameters needed for the average program. Notice that the beginning address of this table is 400_{16}. This first address holds the number that indi-

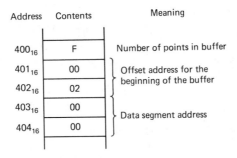

Figure L5.1(a)

cates how many data points are in the buffer. Since a byte is used to specify the number of data points, the size of the buffer is limited to 255 bytes. The offset address of the beginning of the buffer is stored at table locations 401_{16} and 402_{16}. This buffer table offset address is taken with respect to the data segment defined by the address in locations 403_{16} and 404_{16}. Assuming that the data points are signed 8-bit binary numbers, write a program to find their average. Further assume that the number of points are greater than zero.

Part 2: Writing the Program

The average can be found by adding all the signed numbers and then dividing their sum by the number of points that were added. Even though 8-bit data points are being added, the sum that results can be more than 8 bits. Therefore, we will consider a 16-bit result for the sum, and it will be held in register DX. The average that is obtained must turn out to be just 8 bits long. It will be available in AL at the completion of the program.

Our plan for the program that will solve this problem is shown in Fig. L5.1(b). This flowchart can be divided into six basic operations: initialization, preparing the next point for addition, performing the addition, updating the counter and pointer, testing for the end of the summation, and computing the average.

Initialization involves establishing the data segment and data buffer addresses and loading the data point counter. This is achieved by loading the appropriate registers within the 8086 with parameters from the parameter table. The instructions that perform this initialization are

```
MOV   AX, 0
MOV   DS, AX
MOV   CL, [400]
MOV   BL, CL
LDS   SI, [401]
```

The first two instructions define the data segment in which the parameter table resides. This is achieved by first loading AX with the immediate operand 00_{16} of a MOV instruction and then copying it into DS. The instruction that follows this loads CL from the first address in the parameter table. This address is 400_{16} and contains the number of points to be used in forming the average. Looking at Fig. L5.1(a), we see that this value is $0F_{16}$. The next instruction copies the number in CL into BL for later use. The LDS instruction is used to define the buffer together with the data segment in which it resides. This instruction first loads SI with the offset address of the beginning of the buffer from table locations 401_{16} and 402_{16} and then DS with the address of the data segment in which the data table lies from table locations 403_{16} and 404_{16}. The sum must start with zero; therefore, register DX, which is to hold the sum, is loaded with zeros by the instruction

```
MOV   DX, 0
```

The next operation involves obtaining a byte of data from the buffer, making it

Laboratory 5

505

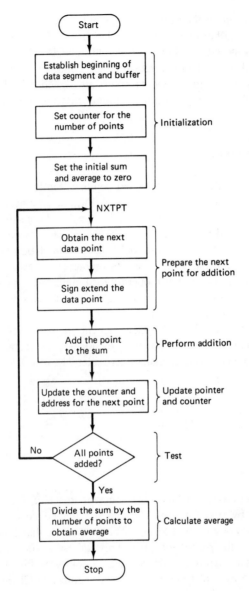

Start

Establish beginning of
data segment and buffer

Set counter for the
number of points

Set the initial sum
and average to zero

Initialization

NXTPT

Obtain the next
data point

Sign extend the
data point

Prepare the next
point for addition

Add the point
to the sum

Perform addition

Update the counter and
address for the next point

Update pointer
and counter

No

All points
added?

Test

Yes

Divide the sum by the
number of points to
obtain average

Calculate average

Stop

Figure L5.1(b)

into a 16-bit number by sign extension, and adding it to the contents of the DX register. This is accomplished by the following sequence of instructions.

```
NXTPT: MOV   AL, [SI]
       CBW
       ADD   DX, AX
```

The first instruction loads AL with the element in the buffer that is pointed to by the address in SI. The CBW instruction converts the signed byte in AL to a signed word in AX by extending its sign. Next the 16-bit signed number in AX is added to the sum in DX. Notice that the label NXTPT (next point) has been used on the first instruction.

To prepare for the next addition, we must increment the value in SI such that it points to the next element in the buffer and decrement the count in CL. To do this, we use the following instructions.

```
INC  SI
DEC  CL
```

If the contents of CL at this point are nonzero, we should go back to obtain and add the next element from the buffer; otherwise, we just proceed with the next instruction in the program. To do this, we execute the following instruction.

```
JNZ  NXTPT
```

Execution of this instruction tests the value in ZF that results from the DEC CL instruction. If this flag is not set to 1, a jump is initiated to the instruction corresponding to the label NXTPT. Remember that NXTPT is placed at the instruction used to move a byte into AL for addition to the sum. In this way we see that this part of the program will be repeated until all data points have been added. After this is complete, the sum resides in DX.

The average is obtained by dividing the accumulated sum in DX by the number of data points. The count of data points was saved earlier in BL. However, the content of DX cannot be divided directly. It must first be moved into AX. Once there, the signed divide instruction can be used to do the division. This gives the following instructions.

```
MOV   AX,DX
IDIV  BL
```

The result of the division, which is the average, is now in AL The entire average calculation program is shown in Fig. L5.1(c).

```
                MOV    AX,0
                MOV    DS,AX
                MOV    CL,[400]
                MOV    BL,CL
                LDS    SI,[401]
                MOV    DX,0
        NXTPT:  MOV    AL,[SI]
                CBW
                ADD    DX,AX
                INC    SI
                DEC    CL
                JNZ    NXTPT
                MOV    AX,DX
                IDIV   BL
                HLT
```

Figure L5.1(c)

Part 3: Running the Program

The source program in Fig. L5.1(c) implements the average calculation. In this section we will encode the program and run it to verify or debug its operation. *Check off each step as it is completed.*

Check	Step	Procedure
_____	1	Encode the program in Fig. L5.1(c). Enter it into the SDK-86 microcomputer starting at memory location 100.
_____	2	Enter the parameter table as shown in Fig. L5.1(a) starting at location 400.
_____	3	Enter 16 data points starting at location 200. Let these data points be 4,5,6,4,5,6,FF,FE,FF,1,2,0,1,5,5,5.
_____	4	Run the program up to the instruction at the address corresponding to label NXTPT. What are the contents of the following registers? DS = _____ CL = _____ SI = _____ What has been accomplished to this point? Ans. _____
_____	5	Next run the program to instruction JNZ NXTPT. What are the contents of the following registers? DX = _____ CL = _____ SI = _____ What has been accomplished to this point? Ans. _____
_____	6	Next run the program to instruction IDIV BL. What are the contents of the following registers? AX = _____ CL = _____ SI = _____ What has been accomplished to this point? Ans. _____
_____	7	Next run the program to completion. What are the contents of register AL? Ans. _____ Verify the result by calculating the average of the data values in step 3.

LABORATORY 6: WRITING A PROGRAM TO GENERATE ELEMENTS FOR A MATHEMATICAL SERIES

Objective

Learn how to

1. Describe a function that is to be performed with a program.
2. Write a program to implement the function.
3. Run the program to verify that it performs the function for which it was written.

Part 1: Description of the Problem

Write a program to generate the first ten elements of a Fibonacci series. In this series, the first and second elements are 0 and 1, respectively. Each element that follows is obtained by adding the previous two elements. Use a subroutine to generate the next element from the previous two elements. Store the elements of the series starting at address FIBSER.

Part 2: Writing the Program

Our plan for the solution of this problem is shown in Fig. L6.1(a). This flowchart shows the use of a subroutine to generate an element of the series, store it in memory, and prepare for generation of the next element.

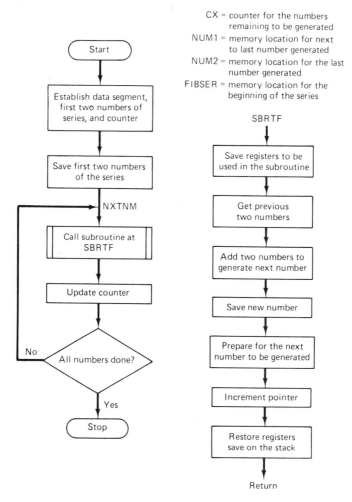

Figure L6.1(a)

The first step in the solution is initialization. It involves setting up a data segment, generating the first two numbers of the series, and storing them at memory locations with offset addresses FIBSER and FIBSER + 1. Then a pointer must be established to address the locations for other terms of the series. This address will be held in the DI register. Finally, a counter with initial value equal to 8 can be set up in CX to keep track of how many numbers remain to be generated. The instructions needed for initialization are

```
MOV   AX, DATASEGSTART
MOV   DS, AX
MOV   NUM1, 0
MOV   NUM2, 1
MOV   FIBSER, 0
MOV   FIBSER + 1, 1
LEA   DI, FIBSER + 2
MOV   CX, 8
```

Notice that the data segment address defined by variable DATASEGSTART is first moved into AX, and then DS is loaded from AX with another MOV operation. Next the memory locations assigned to NUM_1 and NUM_2 are loaded with immediate data 0000_{16} and 0001_{16}, respectively. These same values are then copied into the storage locations for the first two series elements, FIBSER and FIBSER + 1. Now DI is loaded with the address of FIBSER + 2, which is a pointer to the storage locations starting with the third element of the series. Finally, CX is loaded with 8 of the remaining elements of the series.

To generate the next term in the series, we call a subroutine. This subroutine generates and stores the elements. Before returning to the main program, it also updates memory locations NUM_1 and NUM_2 with the values of the immediate past two elements. After this, the counter in CX is decremented to record that an element of the series has been generated and stored. This process must be repeated until the counter becomes equal to 0. This leads to the following assembly language code.

```
NXTNM:   CALL  SBRTF
         DEC   CX
         JNZ   NXTNM
DONE:    INT   3
```

The call is to the subroutine labeled SBRTF. After the subroutine runs to completion, program control returns to the DEC CX statement. This statement causes the count in CX to be decremented by 1. Next, a conditional jump instruction tests the zero flag to determine if the result after decrementing CX is 0. If CX is not 0, control is returned to the CALL instruction at NXTNM. If it is 0, the program is complete and execution returns to the monitor.

The subroutine itself is given next.

```
SBRTF:   PUSH   AX
         PUSH   BX
         MOV    AL, NUM1
         MOV    BL, NUM2
         ADD    AL, BL
         MOV    [DI] , AL
         MOV    NUM1, BL
         MOV    NUM2, AL
         INC    DI
         POP    BX
         POP    AX
         RET
```

First, we save the contents of AX and BX on the stack. Then NUM$_1$ and NUM$_2$ are copied into AL and BL, respectively. They are then added together to form the next element. The resulting sum is produced in AL. Now the new element is stored in memory indirectly through DI. Remember that DI holds a pointer to the storage location of the next element of the series in memory. Then the second element, which is held in BL, becomes the new first element by copying it into NUM$_1$. The sum, which is in AL, becomes the new second term by copying it into NUM$_2$. Finally, DI is incremented by one such that it points to the next element of the series. The registers saved on the stack are restored and we return back to the main program.

Notice that both the subroutine call and its return have Near-proc operands. The entire program is presented in Fig. L6.1(b).

```
                 MOV    AX,DATASEGSTART
                 MOV    DS,AX
                 MOV    NUM1,0
                 MOV    NUM2,1
                 MOV    FIBSER,0
                 MOV    FIBSER+1,1
                 LEA    DI,FIBSER+2
                 MOV    CX,8
NXTNM:           CALL   SBRTF
                 DEC    CX
                 JNZ    NXTNM
DONE:            INT    3
SBRTF:           PUSH   AX
                 PUSH   BX
                 MOV    AL,NUM1
                 MOV    BL,NUM2
                 ADD    AL,BL
                 MOV    [DI],AL
                 MOV    NUM1,BL
                 MOV    NUM2,AL
                 INC    DI
                 POP    BX
                 POP    AX
                 RET                     Figure L6.1(b)
```

Part 3: Running the Program

The source program in Fig. L6.1(b) implements the generation of the elements of Fibonacci series. In this section we will encode the program and run it to verify or debug its operation. *Check off each step as it is completed.*

Check	Step	Procedure
_____	1	Encode the program in Fig. L6.1(c). Use the memory locations starting at 200 for the variables in the program. Let NUM1 = [200], NUM2 = [201], FIBSER = [202], FIBSER + 1 = [203], etc. Enter it into the SDK-86 microcomputer starting at memory location 100.
_____	2	Run the program up to the instruction at label NXTNM. What are the contents of the following registers and memory locations? (DS) = _____ (200) = _____ (201) = _____ (203) = _____ (204) = _____ (DI) = _____ (CX) = _____ What has been accomplished to this point? Ans. _____
_____	3	Run the program up to the instruction JNZ NXTNM. What are the contents of the following memory locations and registers? (203) = _____ (204) = _____ (205) = _____ (DI) = _____ (CX) = _____ What has been accomplished to this point? Ans. _____
_____	4	Run the program to its completion. What are the contents of the memory locations from 203 to 20B? Ans. _____ What has been accomplished by the program? Ans. _____

LABORATORY 7: WRITING A PROGRAM TO SORT DATA IN A TABLE

Objective

Learn how to

1. Describe a function that is to be performed with a program.
2. Write a program to implement the function.
3. Run the program to verify that it performs the function for which it was written.

Part 1: Description of the Problem

It is required to sort an array of 16-bit signed binary numbers such that they are arranged in ascending order. For instance, if the original array is

$$5, 1, 29, 15, 38, 3, -8, -32$$

after sorting, the array that results would be

$$-32, -8, 1, 3, 5, 15, 29, 38$$

Assume that the array of numbers is stored at consecutive memory locations from addresses 400_{16} through $41E_{16}$ in memory. Write a sort program.

Part 2: Writing the Program

First, we will develop an algorithm that can be used to sort an array of elements $A(0)$, $A(1)$, $A(2)$, through $A(N)$ into ascending order. One way of doing this is to take the first number in the array, which is $A(0)$, and compare it with the second number, $A(1)$. If $A(0)$ is greater than $A(1)$, the two numbers are swapped; otherwise, they are left alone. Next $A(0)$ is compared with $A(2)$ and, on the basis of the result of this comparison, they are either swapped or left alone. This sequence is repeated until $A(0)$ has been compared with all numbers up through $A(N)$. When this is complete, the smallest number will be in the $A(0)$ position.

Now $A(1)$ must be compared with $A(2)$ through $A(N)$ in the same way. After this is done, the second-smallest number is in the $A(1)$ position. Up to this point, just two of the N numbers have been put in ascending order. Therefore, the procedure must be continued for $A(2)$ through $A(N - 1)$ to complete the sort.

Figure L7.1(a) illustrates the use of this algorithm for an array with just four numbers. The numbers are $A(0) = 5$, $A(1) = 1$, $A(2) = 29$, and $A(3) = -8$. During the sort sequence, $A(0) = 5$ is first compared with $A(1) = 1$. Since 5 is greater than 1, $A(0)$ and $A(1)$ are swapped. Now $A(0) = 1$ is compared with $A(2) = 29$. This time

I	0	1	2	3	Status
A(I)	5	1	29	-8	Original array
A(I)	1	5	29	-8	Array after comparing A(0) and A(1)
A(I)	1	5	29	-8	Array after comparing A(0) and A(2)
A(I)	-8	5	29	1	Array after comparing A(0) and A(3)
A(I)	-8	5	29	1	Array after comparing A(1) and A(2)
A(I)	-8	1	29	5	Array after comparing A(1) and A(3)
A(I)	-8	1	5	29	Array after comparing A(2) and A(3)

Figure L7.1(a)

1 is less than 29; therefore, the numbers are not swapped and A(0) remains equal to 1. Next A(0) = 1 is compared with A(3) = −8. A(0) is greater than A(3). Thus A(0) and A(3) are swapped and A(0) becomes equal to −8. Notice in Fig. L7.1(a) that the lowest of the four numbers now resides in A(0).

The sort sequence in Fig. L7.1(a) continues with A(1) = 5 being compared first

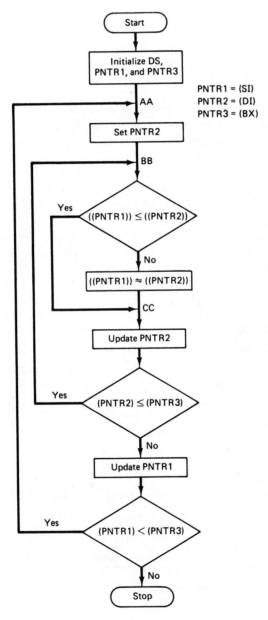

PNTR1 = (SI)
PNTR2 = (DI)
PNTR3 = (BX)

Figure L7.1(b)

with $A(2) = 29$ and then to $A(3) = 1$. In the first comparison, $A(1)$ is less than $A(2)$. For this reason, their values are not swapped. But in the second comparison, $A(1)$ is greater than $A(3)$; therefore, the two values are swapped. In this way, the second-lowest number, which is 1, is sorted into $A(1)$.

It just remains to sort $A(2)$ and $A(3)$. Comparing these two values, we see that 29 is greater than 5. This causes the two values to be swapped such that $A(2) = 5$ and $A(3) = 29$. As shown in Fig. L7.1(a), the sorting of the array is now complete.

Now we will implement the algorithm on the 8086 microprocessor. The flowchart for its implementation is shown in Fig. L7.1(b).

The first block in the flowchart represents the initialization of data segment register DS and pointers $PNTR_1$ and $PNTR_3$. The DS register is initialized with 0 to define a data segment starting from memory address 0. $PNTR_1$ points to the first element in the array. It will be register SI and will be initialized to 0400_{16}. Therefore, the first element of the array is at address 400_{16}. For pointer $PNTR_3$, we will use register BX and will initialize it to $41E_{16}$. It points to the last element in the array, which is at address $41E_{16}$. Next, $PNTR_2$, the moving pointer, is initialized so that it points to the second element in the array. Register DI will be used for this pointer. This leads to the following instruction sequence for initialization.

```
        MOV   AX, 0
        MOV   DS, AX
        MOV   SI, 0400
        MOV   BX, 041E
AA:     MOV   DI, SI
        ADD   DI, 02
```

Notice that DS was loaded via AX with the immediate data 0 to define a data segment starting at 0. SI and BX, which are $PNTR_1$ and $PNTR_3$, respectively, are loaded with immediate operands 0400_{16} and $041E_{16}$. In this way they point to the first and last elements of the array, respectively. Finally, register DI, which is $PNTR_2$, is loaded with 0400_{16} from SI and then incremented by 2 with an ADD instruction such that it points to the second element in the array. This completes the initialization process.

Next, the array element pointed to by $PNTR_1$ is to be compared to the element pointed to by $PNTR_2$. If the element corresponding to $PNTR_1$ is arithmetically less than the element corresponding to pointer $PNTR_2$, the two elements are already in ascending order. But if this is not the case, the two elements must be interchanged. Both of these elements are in memory. However, the 8086 cannot directly compare two values in memory. For this reason, one of the two elements must be moved to a register within the 8086. We will use AX for this purpose. The resulting code is as follows:

```
BB:     MOV   AX, [SI]
        CMP   AX, [DI]
        JLE   CC
        MOV   DX, [DI]
        MOV   [SI], DX
        MOV   [DI], AX
CC:
```

The first instruction moves the element pointed to by $PNTR_1$ into AX. The second instruction compares the value in AX with the element pointed to by $PNTR_2$. The result of this comparison is reflected in the status flags. The jump-on-less-than-or-equal-to instruction that follows checks if the first element is arithmetically less than or equal to the second element. If the result of this check is yes, control is transferred to CC. CC is a label to be used in the segment of program that will follow. If the check fails, the two elements must be interchanged. In this case, the instructions executed next move the element pointed to by $PNTR_2$ into the location pointed to by $PNTR_1$. Then the copy of the original value pointed to by $PNTR_1$ which is saved in AX, is moved to the location pointed to by $PNTR_2$.

To continue sorting through the rest of the elements in the array, we update $PNTR_2$ such that it points to the next element in the array. This comparison should be repeated until the first element has been compared to each of the other elements in the array. This condition is satisfied when $PNTR_2$ points to the last element in the array. That is, $PNTR_2$ equals $PNTR_3$. This part of the program can be done with the code that follows.

```
CC:    INC   DI
       INC   DI
       CMP   DI,BX
       JBE   BB
```

The first two instructions update $PNTR_2$ such that it points to the next element. The third instruction compares $PNTR_2$ to $PNTR_3$ to determine whether or not they are equal. If they are equal to each other, the first element has been compared with the last element and we are ready to continue with the second element; otherwise, we must repeat from the label BB. This test is done with the jump-on-below-or-equal-to instruction. Notice that label BB corresponds to the beginning of the part of the program that compares the elements of the array. Once we fall through the JBE instruction, we have placed the smallest number in the array into the position pointed to by $PNTR_1$. To process the rest of the elements in the array in a similar way, $PNTR_1$ must be moved over the entire range of elements and the foregoing procedure repeated. This can be done by implementing the code that follows.

```
       INC   SI
       INC   SI
       CMP   SI,BX
       JB    AA
       INT   3
```

The first two instructions increment pointer $PNTR_1$ such that it points to the next element in the array. The third instruction checks if all the elements have been sorted. The fourth instruction passes control back to the sorting sequence of instructions if $PNTR_1$ does not point to the last element. However, if all elements of the array have been sorted, we come to the end of the program. The entire program appears in Fig. L7.1(c).

```
                MOV   AX,0
                MOV   DS,AX
                MOV   SI,0400
                MOV   BX,041E
    AA:         MOV   DI,SI
                ADD   DI,2
    BB:         MOV   AX,[SI]
                CMP   AX,[DI]
                JLE   CC
                MOV   DX,[DI]
                MOV   [SI],DX
                MOV   [DI],AX
    CC:         INC   DI
                INC   DI
                CMP   DI,BX
                JBE   BB
                INC   SI
                INC   SI
                CMP   SI,BX
                JB    AA
                INT   3            Figure L7.1(c)
```

Part 3: Running the Program

The source program in Fig. L7.1(c) implements the sort algorithm. In this section we will encode the program and run it to verify or debug its operation. *Check off each step as it is completed.*

Check	Step	Procedure
_____	1	Encode the program in Fig. L7.1(c). Enter it into the SDK-86 microcomputer starting at memory location 100.
_____	2	Enter the following 16 decimal values as 16-bit numbers starting at address 400. 5,0,−3,1,12,−20,77,2,9,−2,53,−5,1,28,15,19
_____	3	Run the program up to the instruction at label BB. What are the contents of registers DS, SI, BX, and DI? Ans. _____ What has been accomplished to this point? Ans. _____
_____	4	Run the program up to the instruction CMP SI,BX. What are the contents of registers SI and DI and memory locations 400 and 402? Ans. _____ What has been accomplished to this point? Ans. _____

_____ 5
Run the program to its completion.
What are the contents of registers SI and DI and memory locations 400 to 41E?
Ans. _____
What has been accomplished by the program?
Ans. _____
_____

LABORATORY 8: WRITING AN INTERRUPT SERVICE ROUTINE ──────────

Objective

Learn how to

1. Set up an interrupt table vector.
2. Write an interruptible program
3. Write an interrupt service routine.
4. Run and debug an interrupt service routine.

Part 1: Description of the Interrupt Service Routine

We wish to write an interrupt service routine that when invoked doubles the value of the current number on the top of the stack. We will set up the mechanism to initiate the interrupt service routine whenever the INTR button on the SDK-86 keyboard is pressed. The INTR button is connected to the nonmaskable interrupt (NMI) input of the 8086 microprocessor.

Part 2: Writing an Interruptible Program

A program is interruptible if the interrupt vector table has been set up to provide addresses for the service routines, the stack pointer is set to point to the stack area, and the interrupt flag is set to accept interrupts. The following sequence of instructions may be used to achieve this objective.

```
MOV    AX, 0
MOV    [4] , AX
MOV    AX, 200
MOV    [6] , AX
MOV    SP, 100
MOV    AX, 5
PUSH   AX
STI
```

In writing these instructions we have assumed that the various segment registers are already set appropriately. Since we will be running the program on the SDK-86, these registers are initialized as follows when the SYSTM RESET key is depressed.

$$(CS) = (DS) = (ES) = (SS) = 0$$

If the SDK-86 monitor had not set these registers or a different setup is needed, we would have needed additional instructions in the program to load them appropriately.

The first four instructions in the sequence above load the interrupt vector. The vector loaded is at address 0:4 and corresponds to the vector for the NMI. This vector specifies the service routine address as 0:200. Therefore, we will be writing an interrupt service routine that will reside in the SDK-86's memory starting at address 0:200. The next instruction sets up the stack pointer to the memory location 0:100. The next two instructions place a word-size number 5 on the top of the stack. The last instruction enables the interrupt flag. At this point the processor has been enabled to accept interrupts.

A jump-to-itself instruction can be used to put the processor in an infinite loop where it will receive the interrupt. Finally the usual INT 3 instruction is added to support debugging. This gives the following instruction sequence.

```
HERE:   JMP     HERE
        INT     3
```

Part 3: Writing an Interrupt Service Routine

Just before entering the interrupt service routine the number to be doubled is on the top of the stack. While entering the subroutine three words, the contents of the flags, code segment register, and instruction pointer register, are placed on the stack. Thus the top of the stack contains the return IP. To access a number on the stack that is to be doubled, we can use the BP. The following instruction sequence can be used to read the number, double it and put it back on the stack.

```
PUSH    BP
MOV     BP, SP
PUSH    BX
MOV     BX, [BP + 8]
ADD     BX, BX
MOV     [BP + 8], BX
POP     BX
POP     BP
IRET
```

The first two instructions save the current contents of BP and reload BP with a value that points to the top of the stack. The next instruction saves the value in BX on the stack. Note that the BP still points to the last top of the stack; that is, to the location where the old BP was pushed. The next three instructions copy the number, double it, and save it back on the stack. The rest of the instructions restore the BX and BP and initiate a return from the interrupt service routine.

Part 4: Executing the Interrupt Service Routine

Now we will run the program and the service routine developed in the last two sections. *Check off each step as it is completed.*

Check	Step	Procedure
_____	1	Convert the program and the interrupt service routine to binary codes. Enter the program starting at 0:100 of the SDK-86 memory, and the interrupt service routine starting at 0:200.
_____	2	Execute the program up to the instruction MOV AX,5. Verify that the interrupt vector table is set up so that the vector corresponding to the NMI is pointing to the service routine at 0:200. What pointers are stored for type 1, type 2, and type 3 interrupts? Type 1 _____ Type 2 _____ Type 3 _____
_____	3	Execute the next two instructions and verify the contents of the stack. What is stored on the top of the stack? Ans. _____
_____	4	Now issue a GO command to execute the rest of the program. Press the INTR key. What is now on the top of the stack? Ans. _____

If the number on the top of the stack is not doubled, then it may be the time to debug the interrupt service routine.

Part 5: Debugging an Interrupt Service Routine

One cannot use ST commands to single step an interrupt service routine in conjunction with the program in which it is invoked. This is because when the processor enters the interrupt service routine, the trace flag is reset to disable the single-step operation. Therefore, to debug an interrupt service routine one can consider it an independent program and debug it using single-step capability. *Check off each step as it is completed.*

Check	Step	Procedure
_____	1	Set up the stack corresponding to the state it should be in at the time of executing the first instruction in the interrupt service routine.
_____	2	Verify that the stack location 0:FE contains the number that is to be doubled.
_____	3	Execute the instructions using the ST command to verify that the number is read, doubled, and saved back on the stack.

LABORATORY 9: PROGRAMMABLE I/O USING THE SDK-86 MICROCOMPUTER

Objective

Learn how to

1. Configure parallel I/O ports on the SDK-86.

2. Use SDK-86 I/O ports.

Part 1: SDK-86 I/O Map

The SDK-86 has two 8255 devices to implement its parallel I/O system. These devices provide programmable byte, word, and bit I/O capability for the microcomputer. To access and configure these ports, the keyboard monitor includes four I/O commands: input byte (IB), input word (IW), output byte (OB), and output word (OW). The I/O circuitry and the monitor commands were discussed in a previous chapter. Review the circuitry and the monitor commands to answer the following questions. *Check off each step as it is completed.*

Check	Step	Procedure
_____	1.	Make a list of the I/O addresses for the SDK-86 ports.
		Byte-size ports:
		P_{1A} _____
		P_{1B} _____
		P_{1C} _____
		P_{2A} _____
		P_{2B} _____
		P_{2C} _____
		Word-size ports:
		$P_{1A}P_{2A}$ _____
		$P_{1B}P_{2B}$ _____
		$P_{1C}P_{2C}$ _____
_____	2.	Determine the control byte needed to configure the ports as follows: P_{1A} as input and P_{1B} as output in MODE 0. Ans. _____
_____	3.	Configure the ports by writing the control byte determined in step 2 to the PORT 1 PPI. What is the address used to write the control byte? Ans. _____
_____	4.	Supply the logic 1 voltage level to even input bits of input port P_{1A} and the logic 0 voltage level to the odd inputs bits. What is the byte of data that is to be input? Ans. _____
_____	5.	Use the SDK-86's I/O commands to read the data at the input port. What value is found? Ans. _____
		Write the byte of data just read in to output port P_{1B}. Measure the voltage levels produced on the individual outputs. What is the byte of data at the output? Ans. _____

Is the output byte the same as the input byte? If not then explain the difference and the reason for it.

Ans. _____

_____

Part 2: Controlling Individual Outputs of Port C

The 8255 provides a bit set/reset function to control the logic state of the individual bits of port C. Review this capability in section 7.7 to answer the following questions. *Check off each step as it is completed.*

Check	Step	Procedure
_____	1.	Determine the control bytes needed to configure port C so that the even outputs are at logic 0 and the odd outputs are at logic 1.
_____	2.	Issue a command that will write the control bytes determined in 1 to the PORT 1 PPI.
_____	3.	Measure the voltages at the individual outputs of port C. What is the byte of data at the output? Ans. _____

Answers to Selected Problems _____

_____

CHAPTER 1

Section 1.2

1. Instructions.
3. Very large scale ICs.

Section 1.3

5. The microcomputer is similar to the minicomputer in that it is designed to perform general-purpose data processing; however, it is smaller, has reduced capabilities, and costs less than a minicomputer.
7. A computer that has been tailored to meet the needs of a specific application.

Section 1.4

9. Input unit, output unit, central processing unit, and memory unit.
11. Input information and commands to the CPU for processing.
13. Store programs, data, and other information.
15. Read-only memory.

Section 1.5

17. Microprocessing unit.

19. Program storage memory and data storage memory.

21. Nonvolatile.

23. A multichip microcomputer is constructed from an MPU, an external memory, and I/O ICs. A single-chip microcomputer has the MPU, memory, and I/O functions integrated into a single IC.

Section 1.6

25. 4004, 8008, 8086.

27. 30,000, 140,000.

29. Event controller and data controller.

31. Real mode and protected mode.

33. Memory management, protection, and multitasking.

CHAPTER 2

Section 2.2

1. HMOS.

3. 17.

5. IM byte.

Section 2.3

7. The logic level of input $\overline{\text{MN/MX}}$.

9. $\overline{\text{WR}}$, $\overline{\text{LOCK}}$.

Section 2.4

11. 20-bit, 16-bit.

13. A_0, D_{15}.

15. $\overline{\text{BHE}}$.

17. $\overline{\text{WR}}$.

19. HOLD, HLDA.

Section 2.5

21. $\underline{\text{HOLD}}$, $\underline{\text{HLDA}}$, $\overline{\text{WR}}$, $\text{M}/\overline{\text{IO}}$, $\text{DT}/\overline{\text{R}}$, $\overline{\text{DEN}}$, ALE, and $\overline{\text{INTA}}$, in minimum mode are $\overline{\text{RQ/GT}}_{1,0}$, $\overline{\text{LOCK}}$, $\overline{S}_2 - \overline{S}_0$, QS_1, and QS_0, respectively, in the maximum mode.

23. $\overline{\text{MRDC}}$, $\overline{\text{MWTC}}$, $\overline{\text{AMWC}}$, $\overline{\text{IORC}}$, $\overline{\text{IOWC}}$, $\overline{\text{AIOWC}}$, $\overline{\text{INTA}}$, and $\overline{\text{MCE/PDEN}}$.

25. 101_2.

27. 10_2.

Section 2.6

29. $+4.5$ V to $+5.5$ V.

31. $+2.0$ V.

Section 2.7

33. 6 bytes.

35. The execution unit extracts instructions from the queue, decodes them, and performs the operation defined by the instruction.

Section 2.8

37. AX   Word multiply, word divide, word I/O
       BX   Translate
       CX   Strings, loops
       DX   Word multiply, word divide, indirect I/O

43. IF $= 1$.

Section 2.9

45. 24 MHz.

Section 2.10

48. 4; T_1, T_2, T_3, and T_4.

49. 400 ns.

51. An extension of the current bus cycle by a period equal to one or more T states because the READY input is tested and found to be logic 0.

CHAPTER 3

Section 3.2

1. Aid to the assembly language programmer for understanding the 8086's software operation.

3. Code segment (CS) register, stack segment (SS) register, data segment (DS) register, and extra segment (ES) register.

5. With a postfix X (e.g. BX, DX).

7. Offset addresses of memory locations relative to segment addresses.

9. Data segment (DS) register.

11.

Flag	Type
CF	Status
PF	Status
AF	Status
ZF	Status
SF	Status
OF	Status
TF	Control
IF	Control
DF	Control

13. Instructions are provided that can load the complete register or modify specific flag bits.

14. Unsigned integer, signed integer, unpacked BCD, packed BCD, ASCII.

16. (0A000) = F4
(0A001) = 01

18. **(a)** 00000010,00001001; 00101001.
(b) 00001000, 00001000; 10001000.

20. NEXT I.

Section 3.3

23. Instructions encoded in machine language are coded in 0s and 1s; assembly language instructions are written in alphanumeric symbols such as MOV, ADD, or SUB.

25. The data that are to be processed during execution of an instruction; source operand and destination operand.

27. An assembler is a program that is used to convert an assembly language source program to its equivalent program in machine code. A compiler is a program that converts a program written in a high-level language to equivalent machine code.

29. It takes up less memory and executes faster.

Section 3.4

31.

Instruction	Source	Destination
(a)	Register	Register
(b)	Register	Immediate
(c)	Register indirect	Register
(d)	Register indirect	Register
(e)	Register	Based
(f)	Register	Indexed
(g)	Register	Based-indexed

Section 3.5

33. Data transfer instructions, arithmetic instructions, logic instructions, shift instructions, and rotate instructions.

Section 3.6

35. (a) Value 0110H is moved into AX.
   (b) 0110H is copied into DI.
   (c) 10H is copied into BL.
   (d) 0110H is copied into memory address DS:0100H.
   (e) 0110H is copied into memory address DS:0120H.
   (f) 0110H is copied into memory address DS:0114H.
   (g) 0110H is copied into memory address DS:0124H.

37. MOV [1010],ES

39. (a) Contents of AX and BX are swapped.
   (b) Contents of BX and DI are swapped.
   (c) Contents of memory location DATA and register AX are swapped.
   (d) Contents of the memory location pointed to by BX + DI are swapped with that of register AX.

41. AL is loaded from address $10000_{16} + 0100_{16} + 0010_{16} = 10110_{16}$.

43.

```
NAME:   PUSH AX              ; Save flags and registers in stack
        PUSH DS
        PUSH BX
        PUSHF
        MOV  AX, DATA_SEG    ; Establish the data segment
        MOV  DS, AX
        MOV  AL, MEM1        ; Get the given code at MEM1
        MOV  BX, OFFSET_TABL1
        XLAT                 ; Translate
        MOV  MEM1, AL        ; Save new code at MEM1
        MOV  AL, MEM2        ; Repeat for the second code at MEM2
        MOV  BX, OFFSET_TABL2
        XLAT
        MOV  MEM2, AL
        POPF                 ; Pop flags and registers from stack
        POP  BX
        POP  DS
        POP  AX
        RET                  ; subroutine ends
```

Section 3.7

45. (a) AX = 00FFH
   (b) SI = 0011H
   (c) DS:100 = 11H
   (d) DL = 20H
   (e) DL = 1FH
   (f) DS:220 = 2FH
   (g) DS:210 = C0H
   (h) AX = 039CH
       DX = 0000H
   (i) AL = F0H
       AH = 07H

(j) AL = 02H
     AH = 00H
(k) AL = 08H
     AH = 00H

47. SBB AX,[BX].

49. (AH) = remainder = 3_{16}, (AL) = quotient = 12_{16}, therefore, (AX) = 0312_{16}.

51. AAS.

53. AX = 7FFFH, DX = 0000H.

Section 3.8

55. (a) 0FH is ANDed with the contents of the memory address DS:300.
   (b) Contents of DX are ANDed with the contents of the storage location pointed to by SI.
   (c) Contents of AX is ORed with the contents of the memory location pointed to by BX + DI.
   (d) F0H is ORed with the contents of the memory location pointed to by BX + DI + 10H.
   (e) Contents of the memory location pointed to by SI + BX is exclusive-ORed with the contents of AX.
   (f) The bits of memory location DS:300 are inverted.
   (g) The bits of the word memory location pointed to by BX + DI are inverted.

57. AND DX,0080.

59. The new contents of AX are the 2's complement of the old contents.

Section 3.9

61. (a) Contents of DX are shifted left by a number of bit positions equal to the contents of CL. LSBs are filled with 0s, and CF equals the value of the last bit shifted out of the MSB position.
   (b) Contents of the byte-wide memory location DS:400 are shifted left by a number of bit positions equal to the contents of CL. LSBs are filled with 0s, and CF equals the value of the last bit shifted out of the MSB position.
   (c) Contents of the byte-wide memory location pointed to by DI are shifted right by one bit position. MSB is filled with 0, and CF equals the value shifted out of the LSB position.
   (d) Contents of the byte-wide memory location pointed to by DI + BX are shifted right by a number of bit positions equal to the contents of CL. MSBs are filled with 0s, and CF equals the value of the last bit shifted out of the LSB position.
   (e) Contents of the word-wide memory location pointed to by BX + DI are shifted right by one bit position. MSB is filled with the value of the original MSB, and CF equals the value shifted out of the LSB position.
   (f) Contents of the word-wide memory location pointed to by BX + DI + 10H are shifted right by a number of bit positions equal to the contents of CL. MSBs are filled with the value of the original MSB, and CF equals the value of the last bit shifted out of the LSB position.

63. SHL CX,1.

65. The original contents of AX must have the four most significant bits equal to 0.

Answers to Selected Problems

Section 3.10

67. **(a)** Contents of DX are rotated left by a number of bit positions equal to the contents of CL. As each bit is rotated out of the MSB position, the LSB position and CF are filled with this value.

(b) Contents of the byte-wide memory location DS:400 are rotated left by a number of bit positions equal to the contents of CL. As each bit is rotated out of the MSB position, it is loaded into CF, and the prior contents of CF are loaded into the LSB position.

(c) Contents of the byte-wide memory location pointed to by DI are rotated right by one bit position. As the bit is rotated out of the LSB position, the MSB position and CF are filled with this value.

(d) Contents of the byte-wide memory location pointed to by DI + BX are rotated right by a number of bit positions equal to the contents of CL. As each bit is rotated out of the LSB position, the MSB position and CF are filled with this value.

(e) Contents of the word-wide memory location pointed to by BX + DI are shifted right by one bit position. As the bit is rotated out the LSB location, it is loaded into CF, and the prior contents of CF are loaded into the MSB position.

(f) Contents of the word-wide memory location pointed to by BX + DI + 10H are rotated right by a number of bit positions equal to the contents of CL. As each bit is rotated out of the LSB position, it is loaded into CF, and the prior contents of CF are loaded into the MSB position.

69. RCL WORD PTR [BX],1.

CHAPTER 4

Section 4.2

1. Executing the first instruction causes the contents of the status register to be copied into AH. The second instruction causes the value of the flags to be saved in memory at the location pointed to by BX + DI.

3. STC, CLC.

5.
```
CLI
LAHF
MOV AX, 0
MOV DS, AX
MOV BX, A000
MOV [BX] , AH
CLC
```

Section 4.3

7. **(a)** The byte of data in AL is compared with the byte of data in memory at address DS:100 by subtraction, and the status flags are set or reset to reflect the results.

(b) The word contents of the data storage memory location pointed to by SI are compared with the contents of AX by subtraction, and the status flags are set or reset to reflect the results.

(c) The immediate data 1234H are compared with the word contents of the memory location pointed to by the value in DI by subtraction, and the status flags are set or reset to reflect the results.

9.

Instruction	ZF	CF
Initial state	0	0
MOV BX,1111	0	0
MOV AX,BBBB	0	0
CMP BX,AX	0	1

Section 4.4

11. IP, CS and IP.

13. Intersegment.

15. (a) 1075:310.
   (b) 1075:1000.
   (c) 1075:1000.

17. SF = 0.

19. (a) Intrasegment; Short-label; if the carry flag is set, a jump is performed by adding the value 10H to the current value in IP.
   (b) Intrasegment; Near-label; if PF is not set, a jump is performed by loading IP with the value assigned to PARITY_ERROR.
   (c) Intersegment; Memptr32; if the overflow flag is set, a jump is performed by loading the two words of the 32-bit pointer addressed by the value in BX into IP and CS, respectively.

21. (a) $1000_{16} = 2^{12} = 4096$ times.
   (b)
```
          MOV   CX, 11H
   DLY:   DEC   CX
          JNZ   DLY
   NXT:   ----
```

   (c)
```
          MOV   AX, 0FFFFH
   DLY1:  MOV   CX, 0
   DLY2:  DEC   CX
          JNZ   DLY2
          DEC   AX
          JNZ   DLY1
   NXT:   ----
```

23.
```
          MOV   AX, DATA_SEG   ; Establish data segment
          MOV   DS, AX
          MOV   CX, 64H        ; Set up array counter
          MOV   SI, 0A000H     ; Set up source array pointer
          MOV   DI, 0B000H     ; Set up destination array
                               ; pointer
   GO_ON: MOV   AX, [SI]
          CMP   AX, [DI]       ; Compare the next element
```

```
                        JNE   MIS_MATCH      ; Skip on a mismatch
                        ADD   SI, 2          ; Update pointers and counter
                        ADD   DI, 2
                        DEC   CX
                        JNZ   GO_ON          ; Repeat for the next element
                        MOV   FOUND, 0       ; If arrays are identical, save
                                             ; a zero
                        JMP   DONE
            MIS_MATCH:  MOV   FOUND, SI      ; Else, save the mismatch address
                        DONE: ——
```

25. ;For the given binary number B, the BCD number's digits are
    ;DO = R(B/10)
    ;D1 = R(Q(B/10)/10)
    ;D2 = R(Q(Q(B/10)/10)/10)
    ;D3 = R(Q(Q(Q(B/10)/10)/10)/10)
    ;where R and Q stand for the remainder and the quotient.

```
                    MOV   SI, 0          ; Result = 0
                    MOV   CH, 4          ; Counter
                    MOV   BX, 10         ; Divisor
                    MOV   AX, DX         ; Get the binary number
                    MOV   DX, 0          ; For division male (DX) = 0
    NEXTDIGIT:
                    DIV   BX             ; Compute the next BCD digit
                    CMP   DX, 9          ; Invalid if > 9
                    JG    INVALID
                    MOV   CL, 12         ; Position as most significant digit
                    SHL   DX, CL
                    OR    SI, DX
                    DEC   CH             ; Repeat for all four digits
                    JZ    DONE
                    MOV   CL, 4          ; Prepare for next digit
                    SHR   SI, CL
                    JMP   NEXTDIGIT
        INVALID:    MOV   DX, 0FFFFH     ; Invalid code
                    JMP   DONE1
          DONE:     MOV   DX, SI
          DONE1:    ——
```

Section 4.5

27. The call instruction saves the value in the instruction pointer (and maybe both segment registers) in addition to performing the jump operation.

29. IP; IP and CS.

31. (a) 1075:1000.
    (b) 1075:1000.
    (c) 1000:0100.

33. (a) The value in the DS register is pushed onto the top of the stack.

(b) The word of data in memory pointed to by SI is pushed onto the top of the stack.

(c) The word at the top of the stack is popped into the DI register.

(d) The word at the top of the stack is popped into the memory location pointed to by BX + DI.

(e) The word at the top of the stack is popped into the status register.

35.

```
;For the decimal number = D₃D₂D₁D₀.
;the binary number = 10(10(10(0+D₃)+D₂)+D₁)+D₀
```

the binary number $= 10(10(10(0+D_3)+D_2)+D_1)+D_0$

```
            MOV   BX,0           ;Result = 0
            MOV   SI,10          ;Multiplier = 10
            MOV   CH,4           ;Number of digits = 4
            MOV   CL,4           ;Rotate counter = 4
            MOV   DI,DX
NXTDIGIT:   MOV   AX,DI          ;Get the decimal number
            ROL   AX,CL          ;Rotate to extract the digit
            MOV   DI,AX          ;Save the rotated decimal number
            AND   AX,0FH         ;Extract the digit
            ADD   AX,BX          ;Add to the last result
            DEC   CH
            JZ    DONE           ;Skip if this is the last digit
            MUL   SI             ;Multiply by 10
            MOV   BX,AX          ;and save
            JMP   NXTDIGIT       ;Repeat for the next digit
DONE:       ——                   ;Result = (AX)
```

37.

```
;Assume that the offset of A[I] is AI1ADDR
;and the offset of B[I] is BI1ADDR
```

```
          MOV   AX,DATA_SEG   ;Initialize data segment
          MOV   DS,AX
          MOV   CX,98
          MOV   SI,AI1ADDR     ;Source array pointer
          MOV   DI,BI1ADDR     ;Destination array pointer
          MOV   AX,[SI]
          MOV   [DI],AX        ;B[1] = A[1]
MORE:     MOV   AX,[SI]        ;Store A[I] into AX
          ADD   SI,2           ;Increment pointer
          MOV   BX,[SI]        ;Store A[I+1] into BX
          ADD   SI,2
          MOV   CX,[SI]        ;Store A[I+2] into CX
          ADD   SI,2
          CALL  ARITH          ;Call arithmatic subroutine
          MOV   [DI],AX
          SUB   SI,4
          ADD   DI,2
          LOOP  MORE           ;Loop back for next element
          ADD   SI,4
DONE:     MOV   AX,[SI]        ;B[100] = A[100]
```

```
          MOV    [DI],AX
          HLT

    Subroutine for arithmatic
    ;(AX) ← ((AX) - 5(BX) + 9)CX))/4

    ARITH:    PUSHF            ;Save flags and registers in stack
              PUSH   BX
              PUSH   CX
              PUSH   DX
              PUSH   DI
              MOV    DX,CX
              MOV    DI,CX     ;Keep copy of A[I+2]
              MOV    CL,3
              SAL    DX,CL     ;8A[I+2]
              ADD    DX,DI     ;9A[I+2]
              MOV    CL,2
              MOV    DI,BX     ;Save copy of A[I+1]
              SAL    BX,CL     ;4A[I+1]
              ADD    BX,DI     ;5A[I+1]
              SUB    AX,BX     ;A[I] - 5A[I+1]
              ADD    AX,DX     ;A[I] - 5A[I+1] + 9A[I+2]
              SAR    AX,CL     ;Divide by 4
              POP    DI        ;Restore flags and registers
              POP    DX
              POP    CX
              POP    BX
              POPF
              RET              ;Return
```

Section 4.6

39. ZF.

41. 127 bytes.

43.
```
                 MOV    AL,1
                 MOV    CX,N
                 JCXZ   DONE      ;N = 0 CASE
                 LOOPZ  DONE      ;N = 1 CASE
                 INC    CX        ; Restore N
        AGAIN:   MUL    CL
                 LOOP   AGAIN
        DONE:    MOV    FACT,AL
```

Section 4.7

45. DF.

47. (a) CLD
         MOVSB

(b) CLD
LODS
(c) STD
CMPLS

49.
```
        MOV   SI,OFFSET DATASEG1_ASCII_CHAR; ASCII offset
        MOV   DI,OFFSET DATASEG2_EBCDIC_CHAR; EBCDIC offset
        MOV   BX,OFFSET DATASEG3_ASCII_TO_EBCDIC; Translation table offset
        CLD                    ; Select autoincrement mode
        MOV   CL,100          ; Byte count
        MOV   AX,DATASEG1     ; ASCII segment
        MOV   DS,AX
        MOV   AX,DATASEG2     ; EBCDIC segment
        MOV   ES,AX
NEXTBYTE:
        LODS  BYTE            ; Get the ASCII
        MOV   DX,DATASEG3     ; Translation table segment
        MOV   DS,DX
        XLAT                  ; Translate
        STOS  BYTE            ; Save EBCDIC
        MOV   DX,DATASEG1     ; ASCII segment for next ASCII
        MOV   DS,DX           ; element
        LOOP  NEXTBYTE
DONE:   ——
```

CHAPTER 5

Section 5.3

1. $0000001111000010_2 = 03C2H$; **3.** (a) $00011110_2 = 1EH$; (c) $10010001_2 = 91H$.

Section 5.4

5.

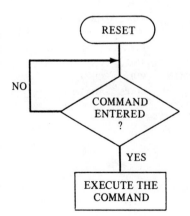

Section 5.5

7. ER CS 10
   ER DS 20
   ER ES 30
   ER SS 40

9. GO 50, FF. or EB CS 25 GO 0, AF.

Section 5.6

11. Program execution begins at address 260_{16} and ends at address $27A_{16}$.

CHAPTER 6

Section 6.2

1. 8086, 8288.
3. Bytes.
5. 0A001H = 78H
   0A002H = 56H
   0A003H = 34H
   0A004H = 12H
7. $A0000_{16}$ through $AFFFF_{16}$.
9. 192K bytes.
11. 0_{16} through 13_{16}.

Section 6.3

13. High bank, $\overline{BHE}$.
15. $\overline{BHE}$ = 0, A_0 = 0, $\overline{WR}$ = 0, M/$\overline{IO}$ = 1, DT/$\overline{R}$ = 1, DEN = 0.

Section 6.4

17. 01.

Section 6.5

19. $\overline{S_2}\overline{S_1}\overline{S_0}$ = 100, $\overline{MRDC}$.
21. $\overline{S_3}\overline{S_4}$ = 10; $\overline{S_2}\overline{S_1}\overline{S_0}$ = 110, $\overline{MWTC}$, $\overline{AMWC}$.

Section 6.6

23. T state 1; address is output on A_0 through A_{19}, $\overline{BHE}$, is output, M/$\overline{IO}$ and DT/$\overline{R}$ are set to the appropriate logic levels.

25. An idle state is a period of no bus activity that occurs because the prefetch queue is already full and the instruction currently being executed requires no bus activity.

27. 600 ns.

Section 6.7

29. CFF00$_{16}$.

31. Contents of address CFF00$_{16}$ equals 11EE$_{16}$.

Section 6.8

33. 8282 octal latches; 8286 or 8287 octal transceivers.

Section 6.9

35. When the power supply for the memory device is turned off, its data contents are not lost.

37. Ultraviolet light.

39. We are assuming that external decode logic has already produced active signals for $\overline{CE}$ and $\overline{OE}$. Next the address is applied to the A inputs of the EPROM and decoded within the device to select the storage location to be accessed. After a delay equal to t_{ACC}, the data at this storage location are available at the D outputs.

41. The access time of the 2764A is 250 ns and that of the 2764A-1 is 170 ns. That is, the 2764-1 is a faster device.

43. 1 ms.

Section 6.10

45. Volatile.

47. 64K × 16.

49. Higher density and lower power.

Section 6.11

55. 128.

CHAPTER 7

Section 7.2

1. Address lines A$_0$ through A$_{15}$ and $\overline{BHE}$ carry the address of the I/O port to be accessed; address lines A$_{16}$ through A$_{19}$ are held at the 0 logic level. Data bus lines D$_0$ through D$_{15}$ carry the data that are transferred between the MPU and I/O port.

3. 8288.

Section 7.3

5. 64K bytes.

7. $00F8_{16}$ through $00FF_{16}$.

Section 7.4

9.
```
          MOV   AX, 1A
          IN    DX, AX
```

11.
```
          MOV   AL, 0F
          MOV   DX, 1000
          OUT   DX, AL
```

Section 7.5

13. 1200 ns.

Section 7.7

15. MODE 0 selects simple I/O operation. This means that the lines of the port can be configured as level-sensitive inputs or latched outputs. Port A and port B can be configured as 8-bit input or output ports, and port C can be configured for operation as two independent 4-bit input or output ports.

MODE 1 operation represents what is known as strobed I/O. In this mode, ports A and B are configured as two independent byte-wide I/O ports, each of which has a 4-bit control/data port associated with it. The control/data ports are formed from port C's lower and upper nibbles, respectively. When configured in this way, data applied to an input port must be strobed in with a signal produced in external hardware. An output port is provided with handshake signals that indicate when new data are available at its outputs and when an external device has read these values.

MODE 2 represents strobed bidirectional I/O. The key difference is that now the port works as either input or output, and control signals are provided for both functions. Only port A can be configured to work in this way.

17.
```
          MOV   AX, 0
          MOV   DS, AX
          MOV   AL, 92
          MOV   BX, 0100
          MOV   [BX], AL
```

Section 7.8

19.
```
          IN    AL, 08      ; READ PORT A
          MOV   BL, AL      ; SAVE IN BL
          IN    AL, 0AH     ; READ PORT B
          ADD   AL, BL      ; ADD THE TWO NUMBERS
          OUT   0C, AL      ; OUTPUT TO PORT C
```

Section 7.9

21.
```
                              MOV   CX, 0408
                              MOV   AL, [CX]
                              MOV   BL, AL
                              MOV   AL, 040A
                              MOV   AL, [CX]
                              ADD   AL, BL
                              MOV   CX, 040C
                              MOV   [CX] , AL
```

Section 7.10

23. The microcomputer activates its $\overline{\text{RTS}}$ line, which is applied to $\overline{\text{DSR}}$ of the terminal; the terminal responds by activating its DTR line, which is returned to the CTS input of the microcomputer; then the microcomputer sends character bits along with the start bit and stop bits on the TX_D line. These bits are received by the terminal on its RX_D line.

Section 7.11

25. $\text{C}/\overline{\text{D}} = 0, \overline{\text{RD}} = 1, \overline{\text{WR}} = 0$, and $\overline{\text{CS}} = 0$.

27.
```
                              MOV   AL, FF
                              MOV   MODE, AL
```

Section 7.12

29. CLK_2, $\overline{\text{GATE}_2}$, and $\overline{\text{OUT}_2}$.

31. $\overline{\text{CS}} = 0$, $\overline{\text{RD}} = 1$, $\overline{\text{WR}} = 0$, $A_1 = 1$, and $A_0 = 1$.

33. MOV AL,12
MOV [1002],AL

35. 54.9 ms.

37. 3.43 ms.

39. 241.35 μs.

Section 7.13

41. When a peripheral device wants to perform DMA operations, it makes a request for service at one of the DRQ inputs of the 8237A. In response to this DMA request, the DMA controller (8237A) switches its hold request (HRQ) output to logic 1. This is applied to HOLD input of the 8086, and the 8086 puts the bus signal into high-impedence state and signals this to DMA controller by switching the hold acknowledge (HLDA) output to logic 1. This is applied to HLDA input of 8237A and signals that the system bus is now available for use by the DMA controller.

43. Assume that the DMA is located at an address less than F0_{16}. To read current address of DMA channel 0, the instructions are:

```
        MOV   AL, 0
        OUT   DMA + 0C, AL    ; Clear internal flip-flop to read
                              ; low byte first
        IN    AL, DMA
        MOV   BL, AL          ; Save low byte in BL
        IN    AL, DMA         ; High byte
        MOV   AH, AL
        MOV   AL, BL          ; AX now contains the contents of the
                              ; current address register
```

45. Assume that DMA is less than or equal to $F0_{16}$.

```
                    MOV   AL, 0
                    OUT   DMA + 8, AL
```

Section 7.14

49. 12 rows $\times$ 12 columns $= 144$ keys.
51. P $= 30$
   CLK $= (100 \text{ kHz}) (30) = 3 \text{ MHz}$

CHAPTER 8

Section 8.2

1. Hardware interrupts, software interrupts, internal interrupts, software interrupts, and reset.
3. Software interrupts, external hardware interrupts, nonmaskable interrupt, and internal interrupts.
5. Higher priority.

Section 8.3

7. 4 bytes.
9. Overflow.
11. $IP_{40} \rightarrow A0H$ and $CS_{40} \rightarrow A2H$.

Section 8.4

13. Aritmetic, overflow flag.

Section 8.5

15.   CLI   ; DISABLE INTERRUPTS AT ENTRY POINT OF
                          ; UNINTERRUPTIBLE SUBROUTINE

```
                    .
                    .
                    .
              ; BODY OF SUBROUTINE
                    .
                    .
                    .
      IRET    ; RETURN TO MAIN PROGRAM
```

Section 8.6

17. INTR is the interrupt request signal that must be applied to the 8086 MPU by external interrupt interface circuitry to request service for an interrupt-driven device. When this request is acknowledged by the MPU, it outputs an interrupt acknowledge bus status code on $\overline{S}_2\overline{S}_1\overline{S}_0$, and this code is decoded by the 8288 bus controller to produce the $\overline{\text{INTRA}}$ signal. $\overline{\text{INTRA}}$ is the signal that is used to signal the external device that its request for service has been granted.

19. D_0 through D_7.

Section 8.7

21. When the 8086 microprocessor recognizes an interrupt request, it checks whether the interrupts are enabled. It does this by checking the IR flag. If the IR flag is set, an interrupt acknowledge cycle is initiated. During this cycle $\overline{\text{INTA}}$ and $\overline{\text{LOCK}}$ signals are inserted. This tells the external interrupt hardware that the interrupt request has been accepted. Following the acknowledge bus cycle, the 8086 initiates a cycle to read interrupt vector type. During this cycle an $\overline{\text{INTA}}$ signal is again inserted to get the vector type presented by the external interrupt hardware. Finally, the interrupt vector words corresponding to the type number are fetched from memory and loaded into IP and CS.

23. 1.8 μs, 6 bytes.

Section 8.8

25. $D_0 = 0$ ICW$_4$ not needed
   $D_1 = 1$ Single-device
   $D_3 = 0$ Edge-triggered
   and assuming that all other bits are logic 0 gives ICW$_1 = 00000010_2 = 02_{16}$

27. $D_0 = 1$ Use with the 8086
   $D_1 = 0$ Normal end of interrupt
   $D_3D_2 = 11$ Buffered mode master
   $D_4 = 0$ Disable special fully nested mode and assuming that the rest of the bits are 0, we get ICW$_4 = 00001101_2 = 0D_{16}$

29.   MOV AL, [A001].

Section 8.9

33. 22.

Section 8.10

35. Vectored subroutine call.

37. $CS_{80} \rightarrow 142H$; $IP_{80} \rightarrow 140H$.

Section 8.11

39. NMI is different from the external hardware interrupts in three ways.
   a. NMI is not masked out by IF.
   b. NMI is initiated from the NMI input lead instead of from the INTR input.
   c. The NMI input is edge-triggered instead of level-sensitive like INTR. Therefore, its occurrence is latched inside the 8086 as it switches to its active 1 logic level.

Section 8.12

41. 8284.
43. FFFF0H.

Section 8.13

45. Divide error, single step, breakpoint, overflow error.

CHAPTER 9

Section 9.2

1. 8K.
3. Program storage memory contents remain intact when power is turned off; data storage memory is lost at power off.
5. Keypad, display, parallel I/O, and serial communications port.
7. Parallel I/O.

Section 9.3

11. 2 MHz.
13. Peripherals.
15. ON BOARD MEMORY will be logic 0. Thus, even if we access onboard memory, the wait states are inserted as per the jumper setting (W_{27} through W_{34}).
17. b.

Section 9.4

19. $O_4O_3O_2O_1 = 1111$.
21. $M/\overline{IO} = 1$, $\overline{WE} = 1$, $\overline{CS}_1 = 0$, and $O_4O_3O_2O_1 = 1101$.

Section 9.5

24. FFFE$_{16}$.

27.
```
          AGAIN:    MOV   AL, 0
                    OUT   FFC, AL       ; WRITE 0s
                    CALL  DELAY         ; WAIT A WHILE
                    MOV   AL, FF
                    OUT   FFFCH, AL     : WRITE 1s
                    CALL  DELAY         ; WAIT A WHILE
                    JMP   AGAIN
          DELAY:    MOV   CX, FFFF      ; START TIME DELAY
          NEXT:     DEC   CX
                    JNZ   NEXT
                    RET
```

29.
```
          MOV AL, 'A' ; LOAD AL WITH ASCII 'A'
          MOV DX, FFF0
          OUT DX, AL
```

31. 436.25 Hz.

33. PCLK and the output of the divide by 4 circuit.

39. c.

CHAPTER 10

Section 10.2

1. 5X.

3. MSW register.

Section 10.3

5. DI, SI, BP, SP, BX, DX, CX, and AX.

7. 1F = 32 bytes; 4.

9. The 16 bytes of data in the range 1075:100 through 1075:0F0 are output one after the other to the byte-wide output port at I/O address 2000H. Each time a byte is output, the count in the CX register and the pointer in SI are decremented by 1. The output sequence is repeated until the count in CX is 0.

Section 10.4

11. Global descriptor table register, interrupt descriptor table register, task register, and local descriptor table register.

13. Defines the location and size of the global descriptor table.

15. System segment descriptors.

17. 0FFFH.

19. MP = 1, EM = 0.

21. Task switched.

23. The selected task state segment descriptor is loaded into this register for on-chip access.

25. Local descriptor table.

27. Code segment selector register; data segment selector register.

29. Access the local descriptor table.

31. NT = nested task.

33. 32 bits.

35. 64K byte, 1 byte.

37. ½G byte, 8192.

39. Memory management unit.

41. 200100H.

Section 10.5

43. CS, DS, ES, or SS; GDTR or LDTR.

45. ACCESS RIGHTS BYTE = 1AH
$\quad$ P = 0 = Not in physical memory
$\quad$ E = 1, R = 1 = Readable code segment
$\quad$ A = 0 = Descriptor is not cached

Section 10.6

47. INIT_GDTR $\quad$ = FFFFH
$\quad$ INIT_GDTR + 2 = 0000H
$\quad$ INIT_GDTR + 4 = 0030H

49.
```
                    MOV   BX, 2F0
                    LLDT  BX
```

Section 10.7

51. A collection of program routines that perform a specific function.

53. The descriptor is not loaded; instead, an error condition is signaled.

55. Level 3.

57. Use of a separate LDT for each task.

59. Current privilege level, requested privilege level.

61. Level 3.

63. Level 0, level 1, and level 2.

65. Execution of this instruction initiates a call to a routine at a higher privilege level through the call gate pointed to by address NEW_ROUTINE.

67. Defines the state of the task that is to be initiated.

69. TR.

CHAPTER 11

Section 11.2

1. HMOSIII.

3. PLCC, LCC, and PGA.

Section 11.3

5. 24 bits, 16 bits.

7. 6 bytes.

9. The execution units reads decoded instructions from the instruction queue and performs the operations that they specify.

Section 11.4

11. I/O write (output) bus cycle.

13. No, it is a status line that must be decoded to produce an interrupt acknowledge signal.

15. 80287 numeric processor.

Section 11.5

17. $\overline{\text{IOWC}}$.

19. 1.

Section 11.6

21. 25 MHz.

Section 11.7

23. Two clocks; 200 ns.

25. Perform-command state; external devices accept write data from the bus or, in the case of a read cycle, put data on the bus.

Section 11.8

29. The bus controller produces appropriately timed command and control signals needed to control transfers over the data bus. The decoder decodes the higher-order address bits to produce chip enable signals. The address latch is used to latch and buffer the lower bits of the address and chip enable signals. The data bus buffer/transceiver controls the direction of data transfers between the MPU and memory subsystem.

31. Odd-addressed byte, even-addressed byte, even-addressed word, and odd-addressed word.

33. Odd-addressed byte.

35. 160 ns.

Section 11.9

39. 256.

Section 11.10

41. $M/\overline{IO}$.

43. The decoder is used to decode several of the upper I/O address bits to produce the I/O CE signals. The latch is used to latch lower-order address bits and I/O CE outputs of the decoder. The bus controller decodes I/O bus commands to produce the I/O and bus control signals for the I/O interface. The bus transceivers control the direction of data transfer over the bus.

45. 800 ns.

Section 11.11

49. Interrupt vector table; interrupt descriptor table.

51. Interrupt descriptor table register, 0.

53. B0H through B3H

55. INTR is the interrupt request signal that must be applied to the 80286 MPU by external interrupt interface circuitry to request service for an interrupt-driven device. When this request is acknowledged by the MPU, it outputs an interrupt acknowledge bus status code on $M/\overline{IO}$ $\overline{S_1}\overline{S_0}$, and this code is decoded by the 82288 bus controller to produce the $\overline{INTRA}$ signal. $\overline{INTRA}$ is the signal that is used to signal the external device that its request for service has been granted.

57. 22.

59. The 80286's protection mechanism comes into play and checks are made to confirm that the gate is present, the offset is within the limit of the interrupt descriptor table, the access byte of the descriptor for the type number is for either a trap, interrupt, or task gate, and to assure that a privilege level violation will not occur.

61. Type 32, external event.

63. Vectors 0 through 16.

Bibliography ───────────────

BRADLEY, DAVID J., *Assembly Language Programming for the IBM Personal Computer*. Englewood Cliffs, N.J.: Prentice-Hall, Inc. 1984.

INTEL CORPORATION, *Component Data Catalog*. Santa Clara, Calif.: Intel Corporation, 1980.

_____, *80286 Hardware Reference Manual*. Santa Clara, Calif.: Intel Corporation, 1987.

_____, *80286 Operating Systems Writer's Guide*. Santa Clara, Calif.: Intel Corporation, 1986.

_____, *80286 and 80287 Programmer's Reference Manual*. Santa Clara, Calif.: Intel Corporation, 1987.

_____, *iAPX86,88 User's Manual*. Santa Clara, Calif.: Intel Corporation, July 1981.

_____, *MCS-86™ User's Manual*. Santa Clara, Calif.: Intel Corporation, February 1979.

_____, *Microprocessor and Peripheral Handbook,* vols. 1 and 2. Santa Clara, Calif.: Intel Corporation, 1987.

_____, *Peripheral Design Handbook*. Santa Clara, Calif.: Intel Corporation, April 1978.

MORSE, STEPHEN P., *The 8086 Primer*. Rochelle Park, N.J.: Hayden Book Company, Inc., 1978.

RECTOR, RUSSELL, and GEORGE ALEXY, *The 8086 Book*. Berkeley, Calif. Osborne/McGraw-Hill, 1980.

SINGH, AVTAR, and WALTER TRIEBEL, *The 8088 Microprocessor: Programming, Interfacing, Software, Hardware, and Applications*. Englewood Cliffs, N.J.: Prentice Hall, 1989.

_____, *IBM PC/8088 Microprocessor Assembly Language Programming*. Englewood Cliffs, N.J.: Prentice Hall, 1985.

STRAUSS, ED, *Inside the 80286*. New York: Brady Books, 1986.

TRIEBEL, WALTER A., *Integrated Digital Electronics,* 2nd ed. Englewood Cliffs, N.J.: Prentice Hall, 1985.

TRIEBEL, WALTER A., and ALFRED E. CHU, *Handbook of Semiconductor and Bubble Memories*. Englewood Cliffs, N.J.: Prentice-Hall, Inc., 1982.

Index

M

System design kit (SDK-86), *(cont.)*
  loading a program, 178–79
  microcomputer of the, 355–57
  parallel I/O, 356, 357, 369–74
  program memory, 356, 363–66
  RS-232C port, 369, 374–77
  serial communication, 356, 357
  wait-state generation, 357, 361

T

Tag, 51
Task, 396, 399, 405, 416, 419, 420, 423–27, 470
  descriptor cache, 399, 424
  gate, 408, 425
  indicator (TI), 400, 402, 404, 406
  state segment, 399, 408, 424, 425, 477
  state selector, 423, 424
  switch, 399
  switching mechanism, 399, 416, 423–27
Time delay, 282, 283
Time state (T), 36, 202, 446
Trusted instructions, 420, 467
Two-key lockout, 305, 377
Type check, 421

U

UART *(see* Universal asynchronous receiver/transmitter)
UART signal interfaces, 262–64
  block diagram, 262
  handshake control interface, 262, 264

microprocessor interface, 262–63
  receiver interface, 262, 263
  transmitter interface, 262, 263
Undefined opcode, 480
Universal asynchronous receiver/transmitter (UART), 12, 261–64
Universal synchronous/asynchronous receiver/transmitter (USART), 261, 374
Upward compatible, 384
USART *(see* Universal synchronous/asynchronous receiver/transmitter)

V

Vectored subroutine call, 323, 347
Very large-scale integration (VLSI), 1, 3, 4, 13
Virtual address (addressing), 394, 403–8, 421, 437
Virtual memory address space, 394, 403–8, 417, 437
VLSI *(see* Very large-scale integration)
Volatile, 356

W

Wait states, 21, 36, 203–4, 351, 361, 438, 456
Word, 30, 45, 188, 191, 198, 233, 236, 322, 450, 453, 457–59, 463, 468
  even-address boundary, 190, 468
  odd-address boundary, 190
Word boundary, 190
Word length, 9